Knowledge Ecology in Global Business:
Managing Intellectual Capital

Miltiadis D. Lytras
University of Patras, Greece

Patricia Ordóñez de Pablos
The University of Oviedo, Spain

Information Science REFERENCE

INFORMATION SCIENCE REFERENCE
Hershey · New York

Director of Editorial Content: Kristin Klinger
Senior Managing Editor: Jamie Snavely
Manaing Editor: Jeff Ash
Assistant Managing Editor: Carole Coulson
Typesetter: Carole Coulson
Cover Design: Lisa Tosheff
Printed at: Yurchak Printing Inc.

Published in the United States of America by
Information Science Reference (an imprint of IGI Global)
701 E. Chocolate Avenue, Suite 200
Hershey PA 17033
Tel: 717-533-8845
Fax: 717-533-8661
E-mail: cust@igi-global.com
Web site: http://www.igi-global.com

and in the United Kingdom by
Information Science Reference (an imprint of IGI Global)
3 Henrietta Street
Covent Garden
London WC2E 8LU
Tel: 44 20 7240 0856
Fax: 44 20 7379 0609
Web site: http://www.eurospanbookstore.com

Library of Congress Cataloging-in-Publication Data

Knowledge ecology in global business : managing intellectual capital / Miltiadis D. Lytras and Patricia Ordonez de Pablos, editors.
p. cm. -- (Advances in emerging IT issues)
Summary: "This book explains the interrelationships among different intellectual capital elements and their value creation consequences through support from emerging technologies services, business processes and strategic decisions"--Provided by publisher.
Includes bibliographical references.
ISBN 978-1-60566-270-1 (hardcover) -- ISBN 978-1-60566-271-8 (ebook)
1. Intellectual capital. 2. Knowledge management. I. Lytras, Miltiadis D., 1973- II. Pablos, Patricia Ordonez de.
HD53.K5934 2009
658.4'038--dc22

2008020497

British Cataloguing in Publication Data
A Cataloguing in Publication record for this book is available from the British Library.

All work contributed to this book set is original material. The views expressed in this book are those of the authors, but not necessarily of the publisher.

Knowledge Ecology in Global Business: Managing Intellectual Capital is part of the IGI Global series named Advances in *Advances in Emerging Information Technology Issues (AEITI)* Series, ISBN: pending

Dedication

To the skater, rock-to-fakie
Patricia

Table of Contents

Detailed Table of Contents

occurs only when the majority of individuals change their behavior or attitudes (Whelan-Berry et al., 2003). In 2005, interviews were conducted with members of top management teams of 105 Estonian organizations about implementation of organizational changes after joining European Union. The results of these interviews are compared to the results of 137 interviews in 2001. The theories of learning from Dewey (1933), Mumford (1999), DiBella and Nevis (1998), and Probst and Büchel (1997) are applied for deeper analysis of elements of process of change. The chapter starts with a theoretical framework for studying organizational changes and learning, followed by an analysis of the interviews about changes in Estonian companies. The author then proposes the model connecting changes and learning in organizations during societal transience.

Traditionally companies have measured economic, financial, and operational performances, while they have disregarded the intangible and cognitive dimensions of their business. As a result, the value incorporated in a company, as well as the company's capability to create value, have been usually underestimated. However, the 21st –century organisations are realising that most of their capacity to create value does not reside in the traditional tangible and financial assets, but rather than on the ownership and development of key knowledge assets. Nowadays, successful companies are those that continuously innovate, take advantage of new technologies, and utilise the skills and know-how of their employees, rather than those that leverage their physical assets. In today's company, knowledge assets are recognised key value drivers to be assessed and managed. Therefore, the assessment of knowledge assets plays a fundamental role both to manage a company's value creation and to disclose and communicate the value of a company and of its components. In this chapter, the attention is focused on the strategies for assessing organisational knowledge assets. In particular, first the contents of the assessment process of knowledge assets are introduced and it is discussed the twofold nature of a knowledge asset assessment, distinguishing between stock and flow, which correspond to a static and dynamic perspective of the evaluation. Then on the base of the analysis of the managerial reasons at the basis of the assessment of knowledge assets, four main assessment strategies are introduced. Their definition is based on the distinction between the assessment approach and the assessment architecture. The assessment approach distinguishes between value management and value communication, while the assessment architecture identifies two measurement structures, the index-based approach and the scorecard-based approach. Finally, the relationships between the different knowledge-asset assessment strategies are discussed.

In order to capture market dividends and stay at par with the competition in the knowledge-based economy, firms must constantly develop their skill profile. There is considerable scope for learning through interfirm learning processes. However, the uncertain and costly nature of this process hampers

attributes. It is based on this backdrop that this chapter identifies three organizational phenomena (i.e., organizational learning, organizational creativity, and organizational justice) that confer a competitive edge on multicultural organizations in relation to specific sectors of today's global business environment. The chapter also presents the historical relevance of the multicultural organization to the academic field of organizational theory.

This chapter focuses on the challenges of developing a knowledge management platform to support organizational memory and knowledge transfer. The study is based on a qualitative study in the ICT sector. First, the chapter discusses the development of the KM platform. Second, the benefits and a competitive advantage of such a platform are discussed. Finally, the conclusions are made based on the case study.

This chapter reports the findings of an empirical study whose purpose is to identify the attributes of the organization infrastructure that support organizational learning in small manufacturing firms through the creation of routine knowledge. The research is based on the following assumptions: a) organizations are cognitive systems that process information and knowledge; b) knowledge is a by-product of technical problem solving; c) innovation occurs as a stream of random or planned problem solving; d) many attributes of the organization infrastructure that foster innovation also foster knowledge generation during technical problem solving. Findings show that three dimensions of the organization infrastructure have an influence on learning: openness, innovativeness, and leadership. These attributes identify two typologies of organization infrastructures that are more or less effective in supporting the generation of routine knowledge and learning. Implications for technical education are also discussed.

The present study explores the relationship between the knowledge-enabling environment and the demand of training in 18 small private companies providing educational and consultancy services in Sweden. In this way, the chapter is an exploration of the ways Swedish knowledge-intensive companies manage their knowledge. The 18 companies have participated in a European programme for employee's competence financed by the European Social Fund. As part of this European financed programme, companies have evaluated their business activity and determined their training needs in order to remain competitive. The 18 companies, thus, are in a position of providing information on the demand for learning that is rarely available. Knowledge is understood here both as the structure and the content of the mental schemas. It is embodied in individuals; it differs from information and data; and it can be tacit or explicit. Knowledge is a dynamic entity that is in a constant dialectic process with the reality it represents. It is through this dialectic process that people learn. This conceptualization of knowledge implies that when looking at organizational processes for managing knowledge, it is important not only to look at formal organized activities for learning, but also informal learning activities that constitute the main source for tacit knowledge as well as the conditions in place for knowledge creation; what is here called the knowledge enabling environment. It is argued that through knowledge management, companies are indeed implementing strategies for the promotion of lifelong learning. Lifelong learning has been used in policy arenas as a guiding principle for educational policies and reforms.

The increasing pressure of today's highly globalised markets has lead organisations to continuously compete for knowledge and innovation. Despite the fact that there is extensive analysis of the concepts of knowledge and innovation management as autonomous areas of research, there is limited investigation for identifying and managing an integrated knowledge innovation concept. Therefore, the aim of this chapter is to conceptualise an amalgamation between innovation and knowledge process management. This chapter is based on a single case, selected to provide description and generate theory around the introduced knowledge innovation lifecycle model. Skandia is an appropriate example, since it has significant reputation on knowledge and innovation management strategy. The proposed conceptual model of highly interlinked and recursive knowledge and innovation process flow is believed to offer enhanced utilisation of knowledge management in organisational settings.

During the last decade, many calls for improving disclosure practices in relation to intellectual capital and intangibles have been uttered in the standard-setting, academic, and business communities. There seem to be two types of solutions to this problem. One angle of attack is to seek to improve transparency through implementation of global accounting standards and moving from historic value to fair-value practices. Another way of dealing with the problem is to step outside the accounting paradigm to see if transparency and relevance problems can be solved by way of supplementary disclosures. For some this is a logical step. However, for many this represents shaky ground. It is ironic that while supplementary information has been shown to reduce investors' uncertainty, it is not being acknowledged as a key element in solving the existing problems by standard setters and academics. This chapter is a wake-up call to the drowsy constituents of academia and policy making, asking them to see beyond their normative accounting paradigm and in turn, showing them how far the strategy-oriented solutions they choose to

Preface

The determinants of growth and profitability of firms and organizations, as well as of national economies as a whole, is reliant upon their effectiveness and efficiency in gathering and utilising knowledge assets to solve current problems and exploit future opportunities (OECD, 1999). The strategic building material of the modern organization is the creation and use of knowledge-based resources. However, these intangible resources are invisible to many companies, making measurement and management difficult for most managers. If we understand the key elements of intellectual capital that do, in fact, drive value, we will be able to achieve a competitive advantage for the organization. Undoubtedly, these new strategic decisions will reflect new forms of working, new models of business, and new approaches to management thinking (Lytras & Ordóñez, 2007, 2009)

The concept of intellectual capital is still unknown to many because it is difficult to measure in explicit terms (Bontis, 1998; Lytras & Ordóñez, 2008; Seetharaman *et al.*, 2002). In this sense, Chaharbaghi and Cripps (2006, p. 30) state that "it is impossible and undesirable to reduce intellectual capital to a calculable number that establishes whether an organization's intellectual capital has increased or diminished." Furthermore, Marr (2005) believes that different people talk about intellectual capital from different perspectives, using the same language to describe different constructs (Ordóñez de Pablos, Edvinsson, & Lytras, 2008; Roos & Roos, 1997).

We can understand intellectual capital as the sum of all knowledge-based factors (i.e., resources, capabilities, and competences) that are critical to the creation of organizational value and a long–term, sustained, competitive advantage. This incremental value is a resultant of a set of activities described within the knowledge management literature (Bontis, 2002). The purpose of knowledge management is to build the intellectual capital of a firm. As such, the academic field benefits from a wide variety of perspectives such as accounting (Bontis, 1996; Bontis & Choo, 2001), library science (Lytras et al., 2005), information systems (Lytras & Pouloudi, 2006), project management (Lytras & Pouloudi, 2003), and strategic management (Choo & Bontis, 2002; Lytras & Ordóñez, 2007).

Knowledge-based resources, like human capital, relational capital, or structural capital, seldom have a direct impact on performance. Indirectly they work impact through complementary and nonlinear relationships of cause and effect (Kaplan & Norton, 2004; Ordóñez de Pablos, 2001). Research on the economics of knowledge-based resources shows that investments in knowledge-based resources do not always stimulate productivity and growth without a number of complementary developments. Recent studies have been placing more emphasis on the analysis of interactions and interdependencies of various intellectual capital components (Bontis, 2004; Ordóñez de Pablos, 2001; Tsan & Chang, 2005).

However, much more detailed and empirically grounded research involving the interrelationships between the different components of intellectual capital is needed to understand how these enable (or impinge upon) value creation. The purpose of this book is to exploit the interrelationships among different intellectual capital elements and their value creation consequences through well-justified support from emerging technologies services on the top of business processes and strategic decisions.

Literature Review

Intellectual capital literature covers diverse typologies of intellectual capital that have been developed until now. Most authors agree with the idea that intellectual capital is formed by three subconstructs: human capital, relational capital, and structural capital (Bontis, Crossan, & Hulland, 2002; Lytras & Ordóñez, 2007; Ordóñez et al., 2008; Roos & Roos, 1997.).

Human capital reflects the set of knowledge, abilities, skills, and experience of the employees of the company or the people of a region or country. It represents the accumulated value of investments in people training, competence, and the future. It also includes an even more intangible element: people motivation. Relational capital reflects the value of organizational relationships (customers, suppliers, shareholders, and the administrations) or the relations that a region or country has with other regions and/or countries. Finally, structural capital represents knowledge that has moved from individuals or from the relationships between individuals to be embedded in organizational structures (such as organizational culture, routines, policies, or procedures) or regional or national structures. Generally, this subconstruct is divided into technological capital and organizational capital (Bontis, Chong, & Richardson, 2000; Ordóñez de Pablos, 2007). Technological capital represents industrial and technical knowledge, such as results from R&D and process engineering. Organizational capital includes all aspects that are related with the organization of the company and its decision-making process, for example, organizational culture, organizational structure design, coordination mechanisms, organizational routines, planning, and control systems, among others, as well as the the knowledge embbedded in regional and national policies.

Summarizing, human capital, relational capital, and structural capital respectively represent strategic knowledge stocks that can contribute to the creation of a long-term competitive advantage.

Intellectual Capital and Value Creation in Organizations

Intellectual capital is seen as the main trigger of value creation and sustainable competitive advantage (Prahalad & Hamel, 1990). This suggests evidence of an empirical relationship between intellectual capital and organizational value creation. This link is embedded in a firm's ability to continually build its intellectual capital base by generating new knowledge. Knowledge generation is a process of creating value by recombining previous knowledge through Schumpeterian innovation for an overview. When this recombination builds on already existing intellectual capital, a transformative positive effect on performance is expected.

Researchers from a variety of disciplines have highligthed the close tie between a firm's orientation toward organizational learning and knowledge management and its stock of knowledge-based resources. In this book, we focus on one type of these resources: human capital. Human capital is the primary foundation for organizational learning (Bontis et al., 2002). Human resource management departments can contribute to the creation or acquisition of knowledge.

Thus, an internal human resource management system, or make system, contributes to the internal creation of human capital. On the other hand, an external human resource management system, or buy system, focuses on the acquisition of human capital with specific features. Each system has its own advantages and disadvantages. However, we must never forget that the organizational stock of knowledge-based resources is also formed by relational, organizational, and technological capital.

The architecture of human, relational, technological, and organizational capital plays unique roles in the process of acquiring and integrating new knowledge. As Crossan et al. (1999) state, organizational learning is a dynamic process of strategy renewal occurring across three levels of the organization: individual, group, and organizational.

These authors propose the "4I Framework of Organizational Learning" focused on the relationships between the three levels of learning and two learning flows. At an individual level, the intuiting process takes place. At a group level, the interpreting and integrating processes are developed. Finally, the institutionalizing process is the last stage in the organizational learning process. These modes of learning are linked both by social and psychological processes. This framework is operationalized as the strategic learning assessment map (SLAM), and analyzes, simultaneously, knowledge stocks and flows in the organization. In sum, the organizational learning proceeds through a continuous cycle of identifying and interpreting new knowledge at the individual level, integrating and institutionalizing individual knowledge at the collective level, and finally, enforcing existing organizational knowledge back on individuals and groups.

Taking all this into account, this book aims to contribute to our vision, and also fits excellently with the vision of IGI-Global to develop books that are valued by their targeted audiences for their practical implication and the communication of sound propositions. The scholarly value of this book is anchored in the following key pillars: 1) Exploiting state of the art and emerging trends in intellectual capital, knowledge management and organizational learning; 2) Providing students and academics, as well as to other target markets, an excellent match of theory and practice; 3) Giving an excellent opportunity for discussing some of the hot topics in intellectual capital management and providing fresh ideas on how real-world business challenges set new frontiers for IT and management

We also include further readings of a complimentary nature to the contents of the rest of our publication. As an added value to our readers, the further readings are to provide additional related data in support of the book's comprehensive concepts, principles, and results, as well as studies that build upon the appeal of this publication as a one-stop reference source

REFERENCES

Bontis, N. (1996). There's a price on your head: Managing intellectual capital strategically. *Business Quarterly*, Summer, 41-47.

Bontis, N. (1998). Intellectual capital: An exploratory study that develops measures and models. *Management Decision, 36*(2), 63-76.

Bontis, N., Chong, W., & Richardson, S. (2000). Intellectual capital and business performance in Malaysian industries. *Journal of Intellectual Capital, 1*(1), .85-100.

Bontis, N., & Choo, C. W. (2001). *Strategic management of intellectual capital and organizational knowledge.* Oxford: Oxford University Press.

Bontis, N., Crossan, M., & Hulland, J. (2002). Managing an organizational learning system by aligning stocks and flows. *Journal of Management Studies, 39*(4), 437-469.

Chaharbaghi, K., & Cripps, S. (2006). Intellectual capital: Direction not blind faith. *Journal of Intellectual Capital, 7*(1), 29-42.

Gibbert, M., Leibold, M., & Voelpel, S. (2001). Rejuvenating corporate intellectual capital by co-opting customer competence. *Journal of Intellectual Capital, 2*(2), 109–126.

Joia, L. (Ed.). (). Strategies for information technology and intellectual capital: Challenges and opportunities. Hershey, PA: IGI Global.

Kaplan, R. S., & Norton, D. P. (2004). Measuring the strategic readiness of intangible assets. *Harvard Business Review, 82*(1), 52–63.

Lytras M., Naeve A., & Pouloudi A (2005). Knowledge management as a reference theory for e-learning: A conceptual and technological perspective. *International Journal of Distance Education Technologies, 3*(2), 66-73.

Lytras M., Naeve A., & Pouloudi A. (2005). A knowledge management roadmap for e-learning: The way ahead. *International Journal of Distance Education Technologies, 3*(2), 1-11.

Lytras, M. D., & Ordóñez de Pablos, P. (2007). The building of the intellectual capital statement in multinationals: challenges for the future. In K. O'Sullivan, *Strategic knowledge management in multinational organizations* (pp. 195-206). Hershey, PA:IGI Global.

Lytras, M. D., & Ordóñez de Pablos, P. (2009). Managing, measuring and reporting knowledge-based resources in hospitals. *International Journal Technology Management*, forthcoming.

Lytras, M., & Pouloudi, A. (2003). Project management as a knowledge management primer: The learning infrastructure in knowledge-intensive organizations: Projects as knowledge transformations and beyond. *The Learning Organization, 10*(4), 237–250.

Lytras, M. D., & Pouloudi, N. (2006). Towards the development of a novel taxonomy of knowledge management systems from a learning perspective. *Journal of Knowledge Management, 10*(6), 64-80. Lytras, M., & Sicilia, M. (2005). Knowledge society a manifesto for knowledge and learning. *International Journal of Knowledge and Learning, 1*(1), 1-11.

Lytras M., Sicilia M., Davies J., & Kashyap V. (2005). Digital libraries in the knowledge era: Knowledge management and Semantic Web technologies. *Library Management Journal, 26*(4 & 5), 170-176.

Marr, B. (Ed.). (2005). *Perspectives on intellectual capital.* Boston: Elsevier Butterworth Heinemann.

Moran, P., & Ghoshal, S. (1996). Value creation by firms. In J. B. Keys & L. N. Dosler (Eds), *Academy of management best paper proceedings*. Statesbora, GA: Southern University. Nahapiet, J., & Ghoshal, S. (1998). Social capital, intellectual capital and the organizational advantage. A*cademy of Management Review, 23*, 242-266.

OCDE. (1999a). *The knowledge-based economy: A set of facts and figures.* París.

OCDE. (1999b). *Science, technology and industry.* Scoreboard 1999. Benchmarking knowledge-based economies, París.

Ordóñez de Pablos, P. (2001). *Intellectual capital, knowledge management and human resource management systems: Influence on organizational performance*. Doctoral thesis. University of Oviedo, Spain (in Spanish, Capital intelectual, gestión del conocimiento y sistemas de gestión de recursos humanos: Influencia sobre los resultados organizativos. Tesis Doctoral, Universidad de Oviedo)

Ordóñez de Pablos, P., Edvinsson, L., & Lytras, M. D. (2008). The intellectual capital statements: Evolution and how to get started. In M. Lytras, M. Russ, R. Maier, & A. Naeve, *Knowledge management strategies* (, pp. 64-91). Hershey, PA: IGI Global.

Prahalad, C. K. & Ramaswamy, V. (2000). Co-opting customer competence. *Harvard Business Review*, January–February, 79–87.

Roos, G., & Roos, J. (1997). Valuing intellectual capital: The next generation. *Financial Times, Mastering Management*, May.

Tsan, W-N., & Chang, C-C. (2005). Intellectual capital system interaction in Taiwan. *Journal of Intellectual Capital*, 6(2), 285–298.

Ulrich, D. (1997). *Human resource champions: The next agenda for adding value and delivering results*. Boston: Harvard Business School Press.

Ulrich, D. (1998). Intellectual capital = competence X commitment. *Sloan Management Review*, *39*(20), 15–26.

Chapter I
Knowledge Sharing and Sociality:
On the Linguistic Embeddedness of Knowledge Exchange in International Subsidiaries

Jakob Lauring
University of Aarhus, Denmark

Toke Bjerregaard
University of Aarhus, Denmark

ABSTRACT

This chapter deals with the role of language use and knowledge sharing in the context of international subsidiaries. The chapter analyzes the role of language use for the control and sharing of knowledge in a multicultural organizational setting using findings from an ethnographic field study in a subsidiary. Whilst previous research has addressed how objective, static cultural differences impede communication and knowledge sharing, the perspective of the chapter is on the actual use of language in knowledge sharing. The empirical study thus shows how language use shapes the flow of knowledge in an international subsidiary. The findings describe the use of language differences for controlling knowledge flows and highlight how this affects the execution of long-term corporate strategies of international development. The chapter argues that the management of language use should not be viewed as an outpost of cross-cultural management but as an integral element of the effective management of international operations. This perspective is supported by research in other disciplines covering the use of language and the social dimensions of knowledge communication such as social anthropology.

INTRODUCTION

Research has addressed how the management of communication and language has become increasingly crucial for the acquisition of competitive advantage with the intensified internationalization of business and the expanding knowledge-based economy (Dhir, 2005). Dhir and Goke-Pariola (2002) thus argue that multinational corporations need to acknowledge the fact that essential language skills form the basis of organizational human resources, and that business communication ensures the right information for the right people (Lagerström & Andersson, 2003). This is even more important in an international context where sharing of knowledge across national, cultural and linguistic boundaries may be crucial for the understanding of foreign markets (Hambrick, Davison, Snell, & Snow, 1998). In addition, language not only communicates information, but also facilitates the creation of value through the exchange of ideas, making it a vital resource in all developmental activities (Buckley, Carter, Clegg, & Tan, 2005).

One context in which language may constitute a particular important managerial challenge is international subsidiaries. Park and his associates (Park, Hwangt, & Harrison, 1996) thus argue that communication problems within subsidiaries located in countries that do not share the language of the headquarters, primarily stem from three different sources: an inequitable internal communication structure, different cultural backgrounds, and ethnocentrism. Language is associated with the communication and understanding of knowledge, which, in the context of international business, has long been identified as a key part of the firm's comparative advantages in doing business in foreign markets (Dunning, 1993). Knowledge sharing refers to the process through which knowledge is communicated from one individual to another or from a group to an entire organization, a process that may cross linguistic boundaries. Consequently, much work may have to be done in order to understand the shared knowledge. Knowledge sharing is thus dependent on the use of language and communication to enable knowledge absorption (Lagerström & Andersson, 2003).

So far, only limited research has investigated the practices of language use in international corporations (Janssens, Lambert, & Steyaert, 2004; Marschan, Welch, & Welch, 1997). Unfortunately, the role of language in multinational corporations has not always been properly recognized in the theory of international transfer and management (Dowling & Welch, 2004; Janssens et al., 2004; Marschan-Piekkaria, Welch, & Welch, 1999). In this regard, Marschan et al. (1997) note that language, for a while, had almost disappeared from the research agenda in the topic of cross-cultural management. A reason for this may be the tendency to associate the concept of language in an international context with cross-cultural communication, focusing solely on measurable parameters with regard to cultural distance, as for example, reflected in the work of Hofstede (1991) and others (e.g., Kim, 2005). This extensive work on cross-cultural communication (e.g., Beamer & Varner, 2001; Gudykunst, 2004), to a certain extent, has led researchers to neglect the studies of the dynamic role played by language use in cross-cultural communication and focus more on the apparently static cultural traits, such as Hofstede's (1991) description of national differences in norms and values (Welch, Welch, & Marschan-Piekkari, 2001).

Language differences are likely to play an important part in understanding the possible challenges in managing intellectual capital in a global knowledge ecology in which knowledge is embedded in an international work force. The theme of this chapter concerns this aspect of managing knowledge in a globalising business world. The present chapter thus addresses, on the basis of a literature review and an empirical study, the role of language use in knowledge sharing in international subsidiaries. More specifically, it analyzes the interrelation between language use and knowledge sharing amongst expatriates in a Danish subsidiary situated in Saudi Arabia. In this local unit, 14 different nationalities were represented and almost as many languages were being used. Through an ethnographic account of the control and coordination processes in the multinational subsidiary, the chapter thus describes the role of language as a negotiated source of power influencing the flow of knowledge. As indicated, the main focus of attention is on the dynamics of social interaction in communication processes shaping the sharing of knowledge. Since relatively little research on cross-cultural management has examined language use, the present research draws on insights from social anthropology. The view taken in this chapter is that the interrelation between language differences and knowledge sharing should be viewed as a two-way interplay that also shapes, and is shaped by, the social organization of the international workplace. Thereby, our argument may be illustrated by the Figure 1.

THE DYNAMICS OF LANGUAGE AND ETHNICITY IN SOCIAL INTERACTION

Since the beginning of the 20th century, the immersion of language in society and the social functions of language have been an important issue in social anthropology (Evans-Pritchard, 1951; Malinowski, 1922). While early anthropological studies did not focus so much on language use by itself, but tried to relate different social and cultural constructs to each other, social anthropologists and others have, in more recent years, developed an interest in linking the concept of language to the concept of ethnicity and culture (Keesing, 1972; SanAntonio, 1988; Smith, 1984). In social anthropological theory, ethnicity generally refers to relationships between groups whose members may consider themselves as different, and these groups may, in some situations, be ranked within a society, or an organization (e.g., Eriksen, 2002). In anthropological debates, it is often discussed whether more objectified features such as race, nationality, language group, or more subjective

Figure 1.

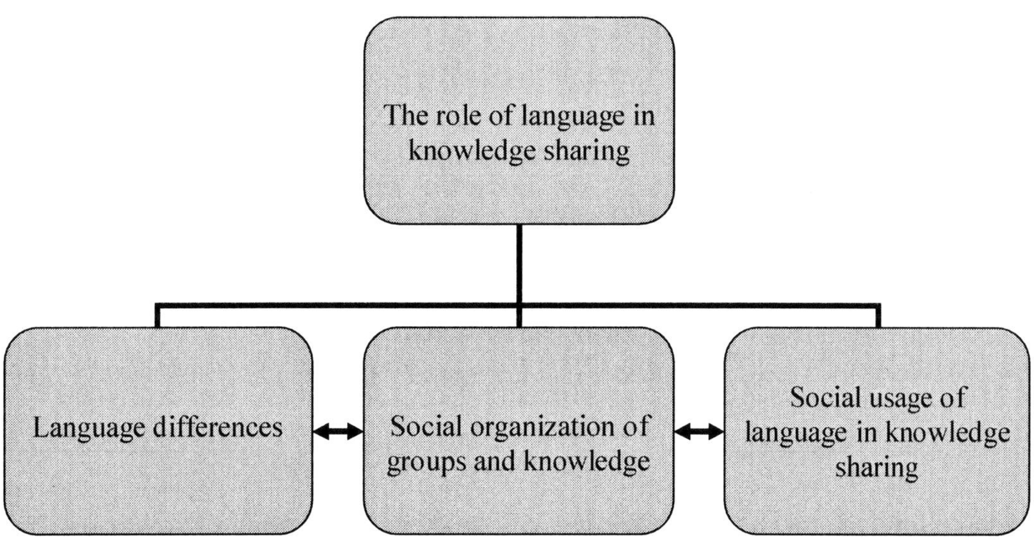

aspects such as individuals' conception of affinity to particular categories, determine the ethnicity of an individual (Comaroff, 1996). However, most scholars seem to agree that individuals use social categories to organize their social environment and to reduce the complexities of their surroundings (Gudykunst, 2004; Jenkins, 1996; 1997a).

The particular contribution of social anthropology to the understanding of ethnicity is the notion that the formation of cultural groups is based on a continual, internal and external social categorization of certain individuals forming a unit that is differentiated from other groups of individuals (e.g., Barth, 1971). This means that the construction of the group is generally built on a categorization distinguishing between "us and them" whereby, for example, individuals of other nationalities are described as different from the native group. As opposed to functionalist and primordial theories on culture, such as, for example, the ideas of Hofstede (1991), it is, in the social-constructivist-oriented anthropological tradition, argued that groups cannot exist without social categorization, neither ethnic, national, nor other groups (Brubaker, 2002; Jenkins, 1997a). This implies that the researcher should focus particularly on the processes involved in categorizing individuals and groups as different, as well as try to identify the motives, ideals, and strategies behind the categorization. Hence, the focus of anthropology lies on the creation and maintenance of social boundaries instead of the objectified categories to which the group is ascribed, such as nationality. Departing from this line of thought, Barth (1971) argues that researchers should direct their attention to boundary spanning and recruitment processes rather than the "cultural stuff," or what could be termed "the collective values and norms" maintained by the group. Following this, social and cultural boundaries are to be viewed as constituted by continuous social processes of inclusion and exclusion through socialization and categorization of differences. Rather than reflecting the objectified cultural differences, the relation between groups mirrors the social organization of those differences (Bourdieu, 2004; Roosens, 1989).

It is in the process of social organization of differences that language becomes an important factor in the categorization process (Giles & Johnson, 1981; Usunier, 1998). Differences in language have a tendency to be used as markers of social differences, and groups tend to cluster together according to the use of language (Erez & Earley, 1993; Tajfel, 1982; Wright, Kumagai, & Bonney, 2001). Hence, language use may have a great impact on the definition of boundaries, relationship building, and knowledge sharing between groups in international corporations.

The Social Dimensions of Knowledge Sharing

Over the past decade, knowledge has become an organizational asset of increasing importance (Drucker, 1993). In recent years, the sharing of knowledge within organizations has been described from a number of different perspectives. One line of research focuses on knowledge sharing in specific units of the organization. Postrel (2002), for example, has investigated knowledge sharing in teams, whereas Spencer (2003) has addressed knowledge sharing in relation to social networks. In the latter perspective, knowledge sharing is viewed differently according to the character of the unit sharing the knowledge. Researchers have also looked at effective knowledge sharing tools within the organization, such as intranet (Anand, Manz, & Glick, 1998; Newell, Scarborough, Swan, & Hislop, 2000), whilst other literature is mainly concerned with addressing social, managerial aspects of knowledge-sharing processes (Hansen, Nohria, & Tierney, 1999; Von Krogh, Ichijo, & Nonaka, 2000).

Kalling and Styhre (2003) have argued that for knowledge sharing to be effective, it has to be linked to general organizational targets and business advantages. However, for the single individual, knowledge sharing may be seen as being part of intraorganizational processes of social negotiation and power struggle. Others have argued that some individuals are motivated to share knowledge by the expectation of improved reputation within the organization (Wasko & Faray, 2000).

Organizational members may also be reluctant to share knowledge with each other, due to an insufficient understanding of the benefits of doing so. The individual may fail to see a personal benefit from sharing knowledge, or he or she may perceive insufficient support from the management of the organization to apply new ideas to their work (Cabrera & Cabrera, 2002). Accordingly, a number of social barriers may hinder individuals from communicating their knowledge. This has important implications for the outcome of individual interaction with regard to exchanges of ideas and information.

In this chapter, knowledge sharing refers to the general communication and application of information and data through interaction among organizational members (e.g., Boisot, 1998; Orlikowski, 2002). Consequently, interaction and communication are perceived as critical mediating factors of knowledge sharing (Brown & Duguid, 2001). Accordingly, it is not possible to fully separate the distribution and employment of knowledge from other social activities taking place. It is thus recognized that knowledge can be perceived as raw data and information that is not commonly debated, but that when used and shared, knowledge has to be treated as part of a larger social field (Brown & Duguid, 2001; Lave, 1993; Orlikowski, 2002). As Wittgenstein (1996) once argued, knowledge should always be understood in relation to the structures of local social practice surrounding us. To him, objectification of knowledge happens neither in the physical world nor in the mind alone (Wittgenstein, 1969). Interaction and knowledge sharing takes place in the social structures that are continuously negotiated through, what he terms, language games. It is the fact that knowledge is something that is used, rather than just contained and transmitted, that makes it a social concept (Wittgenstein, 1969).

This conception of the use and distribution of knowledge as social practice provides an interesting frame for understanding the processes leading to creation of knowledge resources in international environments. Knowledge, when being linked to social practice, cannot be distributed undisturbed between individuals, but is restrained in different ways of different reasons that can be difficult for management to predict and control without serious investigation of the local context. When knowledge sharing takes place in international settings, managers are faced with even larger challenges due to cultural and linguistic variation, divergent backgrounds, and values of the different groups and individuals (Kostova, 1999). Thus, one dimension, impinging on knowledge communication in global business, concerns language use and linguistic differences.

The Social Organization of Language Use and Knowledge Sharing

To outline the social and cultural barriers to knowledge communication, the theories of Pierre Bourdieu (1991) have proven informative. Bourdieu (1977) argues that cultural structures not only determine individuals' actions, but are also created by those actions. This viewpoint provides room for social dynamics and intentionality. Thus, Bourdieu (1991) presents a model of communication that takes the social context into account. In this way, language use is always linked to power by social strategies, applied in the negotiation of meaning (e.g., Robichaud, 2006). Furthermore, when cultural distance reduces understanding in the communicative encounter, the disturbance of communication may be more than just a matter of misunderstanding (Bourdieu, Passeron, & Martin, 1994). The speaker's competence not only refers to the capability to speak the legitimate language, but also to the ability to relate linguistic expression to a symbolic logic of distinction. To put it differently: On the one hand, language skills are resources that can be used in communication and, on the other hand, language skills can be applied by individuals or groups as a way to distinguish themselves in a particular setting. Subsequently, what counts as legitimate language use depends on the context. Hence, in understanding the relation between language and social organization, it can be useful to analyse the speech acts as a way in which individuals negotiate the production and reproduction of social structures and power relations (Cooren, 2006; Varey, 2006).

By dominating the production and reproduction of communication structures, it cannot be avoided that domination of the legitimized access to recognition and resources also occurs. Powerful groups, then, are in a position to decide whether certain statements and information should be viewed as relevant knowledge or as ignorance (Wenger, 1999). Altogether, the level of comprehension, as well as the intentions and positions of groups and individuals, affect the sharing of knowledge as well as the development of relationships that result potentially from communicative encounters. Hence, when understanding communication barriers, the objectified differences are not the only factors that should be investigated, but rather, the active use of these differences in social strategies should also be included. Consequently, understanding the relation between the use of language as a social process of exclusion and inclusion is of great importance in dealing with language issues and knowledge sharing in international management.

METHODOLOGY

The chapter draws on the results of an exploratory, ethnographic fieldwork in a Saudi Arabian subsidiary of a large Danish multinational corporation, here called Dan Firm. The objective of the study was to understand and analyse the social barriers hindering the cross-cultural interaction between the group of expatriates, local employees, and third-country nationals.

For many years, the subsidiary had been the most financially successful foreign subsidiary of the Dan Firm Corporation. It was mainly based on the sale of Danish products, though a local production was kept to satisfy the Saudi Arabian authorities. At the time of the fieldwork, the subsidiary employed 470 employees of 13 different nationalities. The employees could be divided into groups of 251 Indians, 80 Egyptians, 45 Saudi-Arabians, 37 Filipinos, 26 Pakistani, 16 Danes, and 1 Englishman. All employees were men, due to Saudi Arabian employment laws.

The Dan Firm Corporation was one of Denmark's largest companies, employing more than 20,000 people in more than 20 countries. As many other international corporations, it had a vision of developing an overall international corporate culture. The top corporate management had formulated a policy, describing the company's aim to utilize the potential in international transfer of valuable knowledge sharing and internationalization. In other words, the idea was for employees from Dan Firm to develop international competences through overseas stationing, and by "getting acquainted with people holding different cultural values and norms and a way of living differing from everyday Danish lifestyle" (personnel manual). Those competences should mainly be understood as improved language skills, local knowledge of markets and partners, and generally, a broader worldview. While the corporate strategy's intention was to use cultural diversity constructively, third-country nationals were being used mainly as cheap labor in the Saudi subsidiary. This recruitment strategy was a decision that was made locally, but it was approved by the corporate management. The top management in the Danish parent company, however, did not know details about the personnel policy of the Saudi subsidiary.

The advantage of an ethnographic fieldwork in the studies of ethnicity and language use is that it enables the researcher to investigate the more or less implicit ways in which ethnic relations are being defined and conceived by groups and individuals. Thus, it is possible to map how informants talk and think about their own group as well as other groups, and how their implicit understanding of the situation is being created, maintained or contested (Eriksen, 2002).

The use of participant observation in data collection was linked to the argument of this chapter that social structure should be experienced and mapped mainly through speech acts or events observed in the setting (Adler & Adler, 1994; Jorgensen, 1989). Through its use of longitudinal studies, the ethnographic fieldwork has the unique advantage that it generates data on social processes at the level of everyday interaction, which is where the communicative structures and boundaries of ethnic groups are created and recreated (Dewalt, Dewalt, & Wayland, 1998; Eriksen, 2002; Kunda, 1992).

To discuss and further document the observations done in the field, 29 semistructured interviews were conducted with Danish expatriates and employees of different other nationalities (See appendix 1). Generally, the interviews were kept as an open dialogue between the researcher and the informant. Apart from 16 interviews in Danish, all other interviews were conducted in English, all but one being with nonnative speakers. The use of an interpreter was deemed inappropriate and unnecessary, given the possibilities of interpreter distortion during the data collection process.

Observations and interview material were analysed by constructing taxonomies according to the guidelines of Spradley (1980). This implicates hand coding the collected data material-printed material as well as interview transcriptions and observation notes–and sorting it in different categories. From that, a taxonomy tree could be constructed consisting of categories, subcategories, and sub-subcategories. This process is subjective in the way that the placement of spoken statements or other bits of information is not always unequivocal. Nevertheless, it is on the basis of these formed categories that the writing process departed, creating narratives as sequences of events (e.g., Clifford & Marcus, 1986; Geertz, 1988).

EMPIRICAL FINDINGS: LANGUAGE USE AND KNOWLEDGE SHARING

Expatriating Danish employees in the Dan Foods Corporation had many different purposes, and not all of them were valued equally. The parent company had formally described how the firm, when sending expatriates to subsidiaries, aimed at utilizing the potential for knowledge sharing across cultural boundaries. The cross-cultural interaction was meant to develop international skills such as language competences and knowledge about the market and business situation. In spite of those general formulations, the Saudi-Arabian subsidiary was mainly perceived as a sales company. The Danish expatriate management was evaluated exclusively on the basis of sales targets and market shares. Those evaluation criteria had a great effect on the daily running of the subsidiary in regard to cross-cultural communication and learning.

All the Danes lived together in a large compound. This created a very interrelated and tight-knit group structure with a lot of socialisation of members and newcomers. The tight-knit group structure amongst the Danes had a great influence on the relation to the other nationalities at the workplace. It had been decided that the management should be kept purely Danish. In that way, the managers felt they could better understand each other and the communication and decision making went faster.

In this environment, it had been decided to maintain the traditional Saudi Arabian organizational form in the subsidiary. The subsidiary, subsequently, was organized in what could be called an ethnically segregated hierarchy; nationality defining all positions. Hence, one had to be European to be a manager and Egyptian to be a supervisor. The Philippine employees often had good technical skills, and they were, therefore, generally employed in technical positions or vehicle maintenance. The Indians were ranked lowest in the hierarchy and worked mainly in the production. As mentioned by one of the Danish managers, "To have an Indian boss for a Saudi worker, that is almost impossible. Same thing with an Egyptian worker and an Indian boss, that is difficult in many cases as well. There exists some sort of informal class division, which divides people hierarchically depending on where they come from."

The segregation could be said to somewhat ease the daily communication because the different national groups were able to use their own natural languages most of the time. In addition, it made the managerial process easier because managers did not have to confer or discuss business issues with subordinates. As it was explained, the managers needed only to tell subordinates in simple English terms what to do. This conception made members of the management team recommend the researcher to speak only in imperatives when addressing non-Danish employees, since they would not understand long sentences in English. The researcher's impression was, however, that a large share of the non-European employees, such as Indians and some Egyptians, spoke significantly better English compared to most of the Danes.

The negative evaluation of the language competences of the national groups could, to a high extent, be related to the separation of nationalities into speech communities. As the single English manager expressed it "we have very much a situation where the Danes are divorced from the rest like feudal landlords." Hence, it was very uncommon to see employees of different nationalities engaged in longer conversation, while the national groupings internally exercised an extensive informal socialization. However, not only did the management not involve other nationalities in the discussion of business issues, they went as far as to use the Danish language to protect the integrity and decision-making power of their own group. By using mostly Danish language in the daily interaction, information was kept strictly within the group of managers. As one of the Egyptian middle managers expressed it, "If you want to work in this company, you have to be like those monkeys that cover their mouth and eyes and ears. We have to be their monkeys.

Even the English manager was kept out of the conversation, and when attending social arrangements, he was totally excluded from the conversation. He did not understand the language and felt that the Danes were behaving so rudely that he did not want to participate in the "embarrassing scene." As he said, "Communication is only for the Danes. No question. Nothing has changed in that respect. As you have seen it here in formal or informal get-togethers inevitably the conversation moves to Danish."

Another example of the way the Danes excluded other nationalities from the communication channels and withheld information from the rest of the company was presented to the researcher by one of the Philippine employees. He once told the researcher that "big guests" would soon arrive, so we should dress suitably the next few days. The researcher asked him how he knew that and was told that he had just seen the carpets being cleaned, and he had noticed that this happened every time "big guests" arrived. At lunch with the Danes later that day, it was confirmed that there was to be a board meeting a few days later. Such an event was never publicly announced or mentioned in other ways. Only through the internal Danish conversation (or from observing the floor being cleaned) could the information be achieved. There was no formal information system in the company, but messages were passed on orally, both between the Danish families in the compound where they lived and between the non-Danish members of the organization. Even in eventful situations, such as lethal car accidents, there was no formal information, and employees outside the group of Danes had to rely on rumors and guesses.

The Danish management was aware that information was spread informally, and tried to prevent other nationalities from acquiring knowledge of the business. They deliberately spoke Danish when other nationalities were in the room, and the foreign secretaries were prohibited from reading incoming fax messages. This was done to stop information leaks, even though most of the information they tried to protect seemed quite harmless to share with the other employees, such as the knowledge of a coming board meeting. However, the Danes generally were annoyed with the curiosity of the subordinates, feeling more confident keeping information within the managerial group.

It was explained to the researcher by the general manager that it was a deliberate strategy to keep the management team all Danish to increase the decision-making speed, not having to deal with cultural or linguistic barriers. The ethnical segregation strategy was applied by organizing the remaining part of the subsidiary for the same reasons, to limit the conflicts and misunderstandings in communicating across linguistic and cultural boundaries. Hence, the use of language was strategically applied to fulfill the personal aim of the expatriate managers. Through intensive internal socialization and recruitment of like-minded individuals, the Danes reproduced the social structure of ethnical stratification along with cultural and linguistic exclusion. At least in their opinion, this was the most obvious way to run the subsidiary efficiently.

The maintained group structures between and within the nationalities created an environment where only very limited knowledge was shared across the cultural boundaries and no innovative interaction was initiated. Subsequently, the mutual suspicion implied that knowledge was contained within group boundaries. Furthermore, the Danish expatriates did not achieve the cultural learning they were formally sent out to experience. Instead, knowledge sharing and informal communication were very well developed within the group. The parent company, evaluating only on sales targets, did not intervene.

Even the marketing department only employed Danes, which gave them a quite limited knowledge of the needs of their customers and consumers. Instead, the marketing group would work deliberately from a trial and error principle. That approach, among other incidents, caused a large financial loss when a commercial movie, featuring a boy and a girl holding hands, did not fit the Arabian taste and was quickly withdrawn. As it was put, "What you learn is that if you do like this you get this reaction from the Arab, but you don't know what happens when the Arab does like this to another Arab. We assume it is the same but we know very little of what they do together. We have assumptions. We have seen them on the street and on film. But we are not integrated in the society - not at all" (manager, Denmark).

CONCLUSION

The usage of language has received little attention in the literature on international management (Janssens et al., 2004; Marschan et al., 1997). To contribute to this area, the present research has examined the implications of exclusive language use in the specific practices employed in a Danish subsidiary in Saudi Arabia. Though the field of language in multinational corporations has yet to be fully investigated, scholars seem to agree that language use is essential to the creation of networks and to the management of knowledge sharing as a valuable contribution to organizational and managerial development (e.g., Bonache & Brewster, 2001; Harris & Kumra, 2000). The present account makes it clear that the management of language use should not be viewed as an outpost of cross-cultural management, but as an integral element of the effective management of international operations (e.g., Marschan et al., 1997).

The field study, presented, describes the effects of language use in relation to the maintenance of a stratified social structure, and has highlighted how important this factor can be in the execution of long-term corporate strategies of international development. The Danish management team of the Saudi Arabian subsidiary strategically utilized their powerful position to reinforce a general practice of language use that excluded other nationalities from participating in the decision-making process. By this approach, the managers felt they had a better grasp of communication and could make fast responses to market changes, even though costly mistakes were made. Furthermore, through this practice, the position of the expatriates could not be challenged, and decision making was comfortably in the hands of the Danish managers. By using language to control access to information and participation, the Danes placed themselves in a totally dominating position.

This chapter has illustrated how the linguistic exchange that takes place depends on, as well as shapes, social structures of relations between organization members, and how the communicative actions are used in positioning actors within an organization. Thereby, language use becomes a specific expression of the power relations between the individuals and groups involved in communication. Hence, language should not be treated only as a neutral communication device by international corporations when formulating their communication policies (e.g., Erez & Earley, 1993; Tajfel, 1982; Wright et al., 2001). Rather, language is to be seen as linked to other social structures, facilitating the social categorization of groups and individuals (Bourdieu, 1991; 2004; Jenkins, 1997b). In other words, language can be used in processes of both exclusion and inclusion of individuals, and differences in language use might form distinctions by which individuals and groups can be restrained from influence (Bourdieu, 1991; Janssens et al., 2004). Language, to sum up, is thus not only used for communication and information transfer, since the speech act, in itself, also becomes a means in the ongoing negation of power, resources, recognition, and influence (Varey, 2006).

With this in mind, it can be recommended that the dynamic role of language in the creation and maintenance of social structures should be integrated in the theories of international management. If the aim is to achieve cross-cultural development, networking and knowledge sharing, subsidiary managers should, to a larger extent, be held accountable for the management of communication (Welch, Welch, & Piekkari, 2005). It is also suggested that a communication policy motivating expatriates to learn and use foreign languages, in order to facilitate cross-cultural communication, should be considered if the targets of the corporation depend on cross-cultural networks and knowledge sharing. First, such a policy could have a positive effect on the ongoing dialogue and relationship building between nationalities and hence, soften the hegemonic and impermeable position of the dominant expatriate group. Secondly, this could also invite language minorities to participate in knowledge sharing. Finally, it might even keep ethnocentrically oriented expatriates from accepting the important subsidiary positions (e.g., Janssens et al., 2004). As it has been indicated, policies of language use should thus be part of a broad organizational approach to international management, even in the selection, training, and positioning of personnel (Dowling & Welch, 2004).

Both researchers and managers could benefit from considering the role of the expatriate community in establishing knowledge-sharing behaviour. Even in well-trained groups of expatriates, mistrust and pursuit of personal interests may hinder knowledge sharing. Consequently, managers should be aware that communicative actions and language use may be related to the processes of maintaining or establishing social positions. Hence, apart from cross-cultural awareness training, other measures may be useful in facilitating interaction across cultural and linguistic boundaries.

To avoid the initiation of vicious circles of antagonistic categorization, cultural diversification of the expatriate group could be applied strategically. This may leave less incentive for exclusion of other nationalities. As such, a less ethnocentric approach to international staffing may resolve some intercultural knowledge-sharing problems. One concrete way to open the groups to intercultural communication could be to recruit some members of the managerial team from local personnel of different other subsidiaries. Thereby, the cultural and linguistic diversity in the management group would promote a more internationalized attitude toward interaction. Hence, managing communication by introducing ethnic diversity also in the management team may be a constructive tool in facilitating and dealing with cross-cultural encounters.

These suggestions have been made in the knowledge that there is a general need for more research on the management of language. The analytical framework of this chapter has suggested an interrelation between language use and social strategy. Scholars in the field of international management could use this notion as a point of departure in further studies on the influences of language on decision making and performance as well as networking and knowledge sharing. In the present chapter, an interdisciplinary approach combining anthropology, linguistics, and business studies has been applied to understand language and management in a social setting. However, other combinations of perspectives within the social sciences might provide additional or complementary information on the use of language in an international managerial setting.

REFERENCES

Adler, P. A., & Adler, P. (1994). Observational techniques. In N. Denzin & Y. Lincoln (Eds.), *Handbook of qualitative research* (pp. 377-392). London: Sage.

Anand, V., Manz, C. C., & Glick, W. H. (1998). An organization memory approach to information management. *Academy of Management Review, 23*(4), 796-809.

Barth, F. (1971). *Ethnic groups and boundaries: The social organization of cultural difference.* Bergen: Universitetsforlaget.

Beamer, L., & Varner, I. (2001). *Intercultural communication in the global workplace.* New York: McGraw-Hill Irvin.

Boisot, M. H. (1998). *Knowledge assets.* New York: Oxford University Press.

Bonache, J., & Brewster, C. (2001). Knowledge transfer and the management of expatriation. *Thunderbird International Business Review, 43*(1), 3-20.

Bourdieu, P. (1977). *Outline of a theory of practice.* Cambridge: Cambridge University Press.

Bourdieu, P. (1991). *Language and symbolic power.* Cambridge: Polity Press.

Bourdieu, P. (2004). *Distinction: A social critique of the judgement of taste.* London: Routledge.

Bourdieu, P., Passeron, J.-C., & Martin, M. (1994). *Academic discourse.* Cambridge: Polity.

Brown, J. S., & Duguid, P. (2001). Knowledge and organization. *Organization Science, 12*(2), 198-213.

Brubaker, R. (2002). Ethnicity without groups. *European Journal of Sociology, XLIII*(2), 163-189.

Buckley, P., Carter, J., Clegg, J., & Tan, H. (2005). Language and social knowledge in foreign-knowledge transfer to China. *International Studies of Management and Organization, 35*(1), 47-65.

Cabrera, Á., & Cabrera, E. F. (2002). Knowledge-sharing dilemmas. *Organisation Studies, 23*(5), 687-710.

Clifford, J., & Marcus, G. E. (1986). *Writing culture: The poetics and politics of ethnography.* Berkeley: University of California Press.

Comaroff, J. N. (1996). Ethnicity, nationalism, and the politics of difference in an age of revolution. In E. N. Wilmsen & P. McAllister (Eds.), *The politics of difference* (pp. 162-184). Chicago: The University of Chicago Press.

Cooren, F. (2006). The organizational world as a plenum of agencies. In F. Cooren, J. R. Taylor, & E. J. Van every (Eds.), *Communication as organizing* (pp. 81-101). London: LEA.

Dewalt, K. M., Dewalt, B. R., & Wayland, C. B. (1998). Participant observation. In H. R. Bernard (Ed.), *Handbook of methods in cultural anthropology* (pp. 259-300). Walnut Creek: AltaMira.

Dhir, K. S. (2005). The value of language: Concept, perspectives, and policies. *Corporate Communications: An International Journal, 10*(4), 358-382.

Dhir, K. S., & Góké Paríolá, A. (2002). The case for language policies in multinational corporations. *Corporate Communications: An International Journal, 7*(4), 241-251.

Dowling, P. J., & Welch, D. E. (2004). *International human resource management - Managing people in a multinational environment.* London: Thomson Learning.

Drucker, P. F. (1993). *Post-capitalist society.* New York: Harper Collins.

Dunning, J. H. (1993). *Multinational enterprises and the global economy.* New York: Addison-Wesley.

Erez, M., & Earley, P. C. (1993). *Culture, self-identity and work.* New York: Oxford University Press.

Eriksen, T. H. (2002). *Ethnicity and nationalism.* London: Pluto Press.

Evans-Pritchard, E. E. (1951). *Social anthropology.* London: Cohen and West.

Geertz, C. (1988). *Works and lives: The anthropologist as author.* Standford: Standford University Press.

Giles, H., & Johnson, P. (1981). The role of language in ethnic group relations. In J. C. Turner & H. Giles (Eds.), *Intergroup behavior* (pp. 199-243). Oxford: Blackwell.

Gudykunst, W. B. (2004). *Bridging differences: Effective intergroup communication.* London: Sage Publications.

Hambrick, D. C., Davison, S. C., Snell, S. A., & Snow, C. C. (1998). When groups consist of multiple nationalities. *Organization Studies, 19*(2), 181-206.

Hansen, M. T., Nohria, N., & Tierney, T. (1999). What is your strategy for managing knowledge? *Harvard Business Review, 77*(2), 106-107.

Harris, H., & Kumra, S. (2000). International manager development. *Journal of Management Development, 19*(7), 607-620.

Hofstede, G. (1991). *Cultures and organizations: Software of the mind.* London: MCGraw publications.

Janssens, M., Lambert, J., & Steyaert, C. (2004). Developing language strategies for international companies: The contribution of translation studies. *Journal of World Business, 39,* 414-430.

Jenkins, R. (1996). *Social identity.* New York: Routledge.

Jenkins, R. (1997a). *Categorization and power.* England: Sage Publication.

Jenkins, R. (1997b). *Rethinking ethnicity - Arguments and explorations.* London: Sage Publications.

Jorgensen, D. L. (1989). *Participant observation: A methodology for human studies.* London: Sage.

Kalling, T., & Styhre, A. (2003). *Knowledge sharing in organizations.* Copenhagen: Copenhagen Business School Press.

Keesing, R. (1972). Paradigm lost: The new ethnography and the new linguistics. *South-western Journal of Anthropology 28*(2), 299-332.

Kim, Y. Y. (2005). Inquiry in intercultural and development communication. *Journal of Communication, September,* 554-577.

Kostova, T. (1999). Transnational transfer of strategic organizational practices: A contextual perspective. *Academy of Management Review, 24,* 308-324.

Kunda, G. (1992). *Engineering culture.* Philadelphia: The University Press.

Lagerström, K., & Andersson, M. (2003). Creating and sharing knowledge within a transnational team: The development of a global business system. *Journal of World Business, 38,* 84-95.

Lave, J. (1993). The practice of learning. In S. Chaiklin & J. Lave (Eds.), *Understanding practice: Perspectives on activity and context* (pp. 3-32). Canada: Cambridge University Press.

Malinowski, B. (1922). *Argonauts of the western Pacific.* London: Routledge.

Marschan, R., Welch, D., & Welch, L. (1997). Language: The forgotten factor in multinational management? *European Management Journal, 15*(5), 591-598.

Marschan-Piekkaria, R., Welch, D., & Welch, L. (1999). In the shadow: The impact of language on structure, power and communication in the multinational. *International Business Review, 8,* 421–440.

Newell, S., Scarborough, H., Swan, J., & Hislop, D. (2000). Intranets and knowledge management: De-centred technologies and the limits of technological discourse. In C. Pritchard, R. Hull, M. Chumer, & H. Willmott (Eds.), *Managing knowledge: Critical investigations of work and learning* (pp. 88-106). London: MacMillan.

Orlikowski, W., J. (2002). Knowing in practice: Enacting a collective capability in distributed organizing. *Organization Science, 13*(3), 249-273.

Park, H., Hwangt, S. D., & Harrison, J. K. (1996). Sources and consequences of communication problems in foreign subsidiaries: The case of United States firms in South Korea. *International Business Review, 5*(1), 79-98.

Postrel, S. (2002). Islands of shared knowledge: Specialization and mutual understanding in problem-solving teams. Organization Science, 13(3), 303-320.

Robichaud, D. (2006). Steps toward a relational view of agency. In F. Cooren, J. R. Taylor, & E. J. Van every (Eds.), *Communication as organizing* (pp. 101-115). London: LEA.

Roosens, E. E. (1989). *Creating ethnicity.* London: Sage.

SanAntonio, P. M. (1988). Social mobility and language use in an American company in Japan. In W. B. Gudykunst (Ed.), *Language and ethnic identity* (pp. 35-45). Clevedon: Clevedon, Multilingual Matters Ltd.

Smith, S. J. (1984). Negotiating ethnicity in an uncertain environment. *Ethnic and Racial Studies, 7,* 360-372.

Spencer, J. W. (2003). Firms' knowledge-sharing strategies in the global innovation system: Empirical evidence from the flat panel display industry. *Strategic Management Journal, 24,* 217-233.

Spradley, J. P. (1980). *Participant observation.* New York: Holt Rinehart and Winston.

Tajfel, H. (1982). Social psychology of intergroup relations. *Annual Review of Psychology, 33,* 1-39.

Usunier, J. (1998). *International and cross-cultural management research.* London: Sage Publications.

Varey, R. J. (2006). Accounts in interactions: Implications of accounting practices for managing. In F. Cooren, J. R. Taylor, & E. J. Van every (Eds.), *Communication as organizing* (pp. 181-197).

Von Krogh, G., Ichijo, K., & Nonaka, I. (2000). *Enabling knowledge creation.* Oxford: Oxford University Press.

Wasko, M. M., & Faray, S. (2000). It is what one does: Why people participate and help others in electronic communities of practice. *Journal of Strategic Information Systems, 9*(1), 155-173.

Welch, D., Welch, L., & Marschan-Piekkari, R. (2001). The persistent impact of language on global operations. *Prometheus, 19*(3), 193-209.

Welch, D., Welch, L., & Piekkari, R. (2005). Speaking in tongues: The importance of language in international management processes. *International Studies of Management & Organization, 35*(1), 10-27.

Wenger, E. (1999). *Communities of practice. Learning, meaning, and identity.* Cambridge: Cambridge university Press.

Wittgenstein, L. (1969). *On certainty.* New York: Harper.

Wittgenstein, L. (1996). *Philosophical investigations.* Oxford: Basil Blackwell.

Wright, C., Kumagai, F., & Bonney, N. (2001). Language and power in a Japanese transplant in Scotland. *Sociological Review, 49*(2), 236-250.

APPENDIX 1

Data collection tools	
Participant observation	740 hours
Semistructured interviews	
Danes	16
Indians	6
Filipinos	3
Egyptians	3
British	1
Photos	43
Corporate documents	528 pages

Chapter II
Organizational Learning During Changes in Estonian Organization

Ruth Alas
Estonian Business School, Estonia

ABSTRACT

This chapter analyzes organizational changes and organizational learning in Estonian companies. During the last decades, Estonia has transformed from being an authoritarian, centralised, totalitarian, socialist state to a democratic country with a free market economy and different attitudes and values. Empirical study in Estonian organizations indicates connections between the institutionalization stage at the societal level and types of changes and organizational learning within organizations. The author proposes the model connecting changes and learning in organizations during societal transience, which could help managers of international companies to plan and implement changes in subsidiaries locating in countries in transition.

INTRODUCTION

The modern organisations operate using three types of capital: physical (plant and equipment), financial (cash and investment), and intellectual, with the latter continuing to grow rapidly in importance (Wall, 2005). One reason for this is a steady decline in the number of workers encaged in traditional industries and an increase in those working in service industries, such as banking and telecommunication. Therefore, the tangible assets, those that tend to appear on balance sheet, are now less important than employee and customer satisfaction, innovation, and corporate culture.

At the same time, increased globalization of business has resulted in increased global competition and much greater requirements placed upon employees today than decades ago (Quinn & Spreitzer, 1997). This pressure may seem especially high for employees from former Soviet countries, including Estonia, because these demands are fundamentally different to those made under the Soviet regime. Transformation from being an authoritarian, centralised, totalitarian, socialist state, to a democratic country with a free market economy is a process in which a complex set of normative and operating principles, embodied in historical structures, systems, and practices becomes replaced by another unknown set (Clark & Soulsby, 1999, p. 18).

Several Estonian companies have experienced several waves of changes. For example, Kalev is the biggest and the oldest sweet factory in Estonia. The birth of the Estonian confectionery industry dates back to 1806, when a pastry cook, Lorenz Caviezel, opened a confectionery business in Tallinn. Soviet occupation in 1940 was the time of nationalization. Throughout the Soviet period, Kalev produced sweets at full capacity for Estonia, as well as almost the whole of the former Soviet Union, also supplying the "uncrowned rulers" of the Kremlin. After gaining independence in 1991, the state enterprise of Kalev was founded on the basis of the Kalev confectionery factory. In 1995, the privatisation of the state enterprise became possible and a public limited company was founded. Since 1996, the shares of the public limited company Kalev (AS Kalev) have been listed on the Tallinn Stock Exchange.

During Soviet period, the Soviet state was responsible for guaranteeing work for everyone and so, enterprises were internally overstaffed, and passive and work places were over-secured (Liuhto, 1999, p. 16). Organizational change has been seen as an individual-level phenomenon because it occurs only when the majority of individuals change their behavior or attitudes (Whelan-Berry, Gordon, & Hinings, 2003). The challenge has been to internalise a new type of organisational behaviour in order to operate successfully under unfamiliar conditions. Learning, both collaborative and individual, and the ensuing corporate changes, are seen as a prerequisite for the success and survival of organisations.

According to Edwards and Lawrence (2000), the emergent change to processes in transforming countries can only be truly understood by examining the constitutive practices of individuals and groups at the local microlevels of the economic system. Research in countries going through transformation has shown that the transfer of knowledge from market-economy practices often fails because of institutional and cultural tensions and conflict (Clark & Geppert, 2002). The

Figure 1. The structure of the chapter

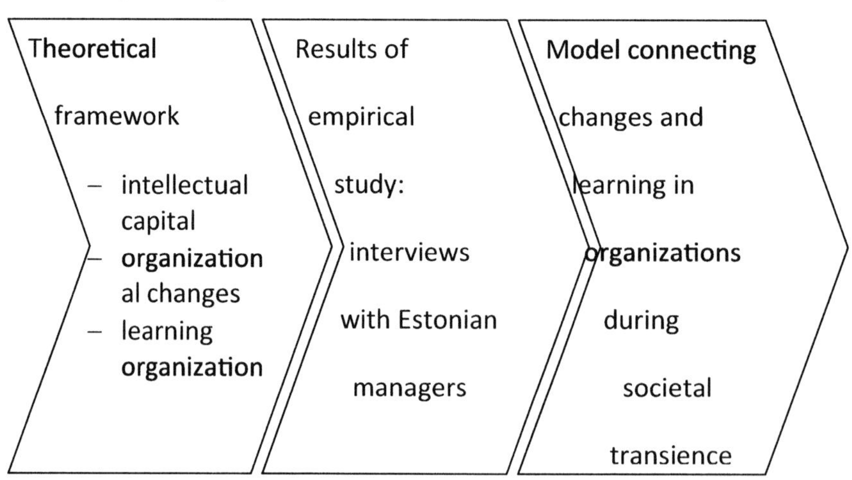

research question is which type of learning is needed in organizations during social transience in society. The object of the research is learning in Estonian organization during implementation of changes.

The structure of this chapter is shown in Figure 1. In this chapter, a theoretical framework for studying organizational changes and learning is followed by an analysis of the interviews about changes in Estonian companies. The author then proposes the model connecting changes and learning in organizations during societal transience.

THEORETICAL BACKGROUND

The Role of Intellectual Capital in the Organization

A true value of a company's performance lies in its ability to create sustainable value by pursuing a business vision and its resulting strategy. Success factors that should be maximized are focused onto four distinct areas (Edvinsson & Malone, 1997). The "financial focus" on the top of the house is the past of the firm. It includes, in addition to the balance sheet, also such new measures as ratios performance, speed, and quality. The walls of the house are the distinct type of intellectual capital "costumer focus," and "process focus" as a part of structural capital. The walls indicate the present situation.

The other part of structural capital, "renewal and development focus," forms the foundation of the house and indicates how company prepares itself for the future through employee training and new product development.

"Human focus"' has been considered as central part of intellectual capital, the heart, the intelligence, the soul of the organisation. It is the only active force in organisation, commonly shared fifth area. Human capital is the primary source for organisational innovation, and renewal (Agor, 1997) distinguishes an organisation from others and helps to build competitive advantage.

The precondition for renewal and development of organization is the ability to make changes and learn as the organization.

Implementation of Organisational Changes

An effective organisation meets the expectations of multiple stakeholders including shareholders, employees, suppliers, customers, and the society in which it is located. It also demands the loyalty and commitment of these stakeholders to the long-term survival of the organisation and of the social network in which it is embedded (Kochan & Useem, 1992).

Both the popular press and academic literature tend to consider organizational change as a step-by-step process leading to success. The basic model, developed by Lewin (1989), consists of three steps: unfreezing, moving, and refreezing. Tichy and Devanna (1986) got also three steps: (1) recognizing need for change, (2) creating vision, and (3) institutionalizing change.

Most theorists divide change into two groups according to scope: change taking place within the given system, and change aiming to change the system itself.

One of the most popular classifications divides changes as first-order change and second-order change. First-order change helps one to manage current strategy more effectively and efficiently (Bartunek, 1993). It provides a method for managing stability. This type of change proceeds via a sequential step-by-step assessment, guided by a specific objective, making systematic and rational evaluations of an organisation and its environment. A first-order change cannot produce transformation because it lacks the creativity to discover new strategic ideas (Hurst, 1986).

Second-order change is more difficult to carry out because information gathering in an organisation will tend to reify the rules, culture, strategy, and core processes that make up its current paradigm (Nutt & Backoff, 1997). Second-order change calls for innovation in order to lead the change. It searches for agreement about what the end result should be, and then considers how the organisation could be changed to meet these new expectations.

Transformation calls for a second-order change process (Watzawick, Weakland, & Fisch, 1974). First-order change stresses growth and single loop learning. Second-order change stresses development and double loop learning. In the second-order change process, change agents should gather information without value judgements. This enables new ideas to emerge (Pribram, 1983).

Ackerman (1986) describes three types of organisational change: (1) developmental change, (2) transitional change, and (3) transformational change. Developmental change improves what already exists through the improvement of skills, methods, or conditions. Transitional change replaces current ways of doing things with something new over a controlled period of time. Transformational change means the emergence of a new state, unknown until it takes shape, out of the remains of the chaotic death of the old state.

Burke and Litwin (1992) have developed a model for making a distinction between two types of deeper change. They argue that transformational change occurs as a response to the external environment and directly affects the organisational mission and strategy, the leadership, and the culture. Transitional change deals with psychological and organisational variables that predict and control the motivational and performance consequences of the work group climate (Burke & Litwin, 1992).

The author argues that in order to describe the changes that have taken place in Estonian companies over the last decades, we need more than two types, therefore, Ackerman's (1986) classification is applied in analysis.

The most difficult part of the whole change process is getting it started (Hendry, 1996). Past experiences and learning have a significant part here (Schein, 1992).

Capacity to Learn, Learning Organization, and Organisational Learning

The ability to learn, continually, means remaining open to experience, understanding instances when things do not work out as expected, spotting shifts in the environment, seeking new information, learning from customers and everyone else, challenging assumptions and beliefs, moving outside of comfort zone, and turning into inner creativity and wisdom in order to change behavior in response to external changes and to develop ever-greater capacity to achieve results (Jaffe, Scott, & Tobe, 1994, p. 221).

The organization's capacity to learn is critical resource. There are three key criteria that lead to success (Probst & Büchel, 1997): First responsiveness to the needs of the members of the organization who will be affected by change; second the learning capacity of the organization; and finally, organization's capacity for action.

The concept of learning organization presumes ability to adapt to change. Management must anticipate, or at a minimum, recognize problems and use learning skills to solve them (DiBella & Nevis, 1998). Accelerating change and continuing advances in network information technology have stimulated a growing interest in organization learning and knowledge management, the development of an organization's intellectual capital (Edvinsson & Malone, 1997).

An organization skilled at creating, acquiring, and transferring knowledge, and at modifing its behavior to reflect new knowledge and insights, is called learning organization (Garvin, 1993, p. 80). Learning organization facilitates the learning of all its members and continuously transforms itself (Pedler, Bourgoyne, & Boydell, 1991).

Organisational learning has been generally defined as a vital process by which organisations adapt to change in their social, political, or economic settings (Rosenstiel & Koch, 2001). Tsang (1997) defines organisational learning, in more detail, as the learning that occurs in an organisation that produces real or potential change after a shift in the relationship between thought, organisational action, and environmental response. Emphasis on the connection between organisational learning and the environment, in both definitions, indicates that certain types of change in an environment may require a particular type of learning.

One critical issue in the literature, dealing with the learning organisation, is the relationship between individual and organisational learning. According to Senge (1997), organisations learn only through learning individuals. Individual learning has been viewed by different theorists as a rational, information-based system or as a socially constructed process. Organisational learning emphasizes the social constructed process, which proceeds through sharing interpretations of events and through reflection on these interpretations (Mahler, 1997).

Without individual learning, organisational learning does not occur. However, individual learning does not guarantee organisational learning. As knowledge sharing is a human behavior that is influenced by both the environment and other employees in the environment (Small & Sage, 2005/2006), collaborative learning is needed.

There are different views about the process of organizational learning. According to Dewey (1933), organizational learning consists of four processes:

1. **Discovery.** By this process errors or gaps between desired and actual conditions are detected.
2. **Invention.** It involves diagnosing the causes of the gap and inventing appropriate solutions to reduce it.
3. **Production.** It includes implementing solutions.
4. **Generalization** means drawing conclusions about effects of the solutions and applying this new knowledge to other situations.

These processes are interrelated.

Mumford (1999) developed a learning cycle consisting of four actions: (1) having an experience, (2) reviewing, (3) concluding, and (4) planning. According to Probst and Büchel (1997), the process of organizational learning is characterized by: (1) change in organizational knowledge, (2) increase in the range of possible actions, and (3) change in subjective constructions of reality.

Organizations acquire new knowledge differently. DiBella and Nevis (1998) have identified four organizational learning styles. They define organizational learning style as a function of how organizations learn, and is determined by knowledge source and learning scope:

- **Correction:** Learning to adjust or correct what we already doing.
- **Innovation:** Learning from their own operations and use that knowledge transformativly, creating new products or process innovation.
- **Adaptation:** Making incremental changes or improvements to knowledge acquired externally.
- **Acquisition:** Acquiring what has been learned by others and then incorporating that learning into their own operations. It involves some amount of acquisition.

In order to answer the research question, which type of learning is needed in organizations during social transience in society, the empirical studies were conducted in Estonian organizations about implementation of organizational changes and organizational learning after joining European Union. The theories of learning from

Dewey (1933), Mumford (1999), DiBella and Nevis (1998), and Probst and Büchel (1997) are applied for deeper analysis of elements of process of change.

EMPIRICAL STUDY IN ESTONIAN ORGANIZATIONS

In 2001, structured interviews about the implementation of organizational changes and learning during this process were conducted (Alas & Sharifi, 2002). Interviews were conducted with members of top management teams from Estonian companies. These changes took place in the 1990s, during a period of social transience in Estonian society. In 2005, when economic situation had already stabilised, interviews were again conducted with members of top management teams, from 105 Estonian organizations, about changes implemented. The interview questions were similar during both interviews. In order to evaluate the dynamics, the results from both interviews are compared. Examples from the interview transcripts have been used to illustrate the statistics.

Results

According to types of changes during the first survey in 2001, 90% of the changes were transformational in terms of scope, involving changes in strategy, mission, leadership style, or culture. For year 2005, only 64% of changes were the deepest.

In change process, most of attention was turned to first step: unfreezing. Institutionalization took place around 20% of organizations only.

During changes in Estonian organizations, formal and nonformal learning took place. Managers learned that in order to achive employee involvement, *"it was necessary to work out a way to sell the new vision to our employees and then look further together about how to take it to the clients."* (interviewee 79) This was nonformal learning. The results were rather positive; there was no resistance to change in 44.6% of transformational changes and 48.4% of transactional changes.

In 38.7% of transactional changes and 53.6% of transformational changes, the reaction was negative. There were more neutral employees during transitional changes than during transformational. Usually, reactions were negative in the beginning, but in the process of implementing the changes, if people could already see the positive results and positive changes for themselves, the reaction changed to a positive one. *"Emotions were rather different within the company and the confused employees had to go through periods of hesitation, questions and fear. Having seen the positive direction of the changes, the feelings of the employees changed in the direction of satisfaction."* (interviewee 51)

The greatest difficulty was to change habits and the traditional ways of doing things: 41.9% for transactional and 48.2% for transformational changes. Also, the need for the changes was not always understood: around 25% for both types of changes. There were problems with providing training and mentoring, in both cases around 20%. Difficulties, stemming from organizational cultures, arose in 10.7% of transformational changes. This problem was less significant during transactional changes; only 3.2% reported this.

Managers tried to analyse the sources of resistance beforehand: "People were afraid of losing their jobs." (interviewee 5) "We understood that the success of the implementation process was mainly dependent on the middle managers and on how well they could explain the need for the changes to their employees." (interviewee 35)

The most common reasons for resistance in 2001, inertia of thinking and fear of the unknown, dominated also in 2005. Also, employees often found changes unclear and too quick.

The lessons learnt from the changes were similar according to both surveys. Managers realized the need to behave differently, recognized the need for more explanation and for more preparation during transformational changes. This was nonformal learning.

Communication was the most popular strategy for overcoming resistance, in 48% of both types of changes. *"It is necessary to talk about everything, and if there is nothing to be said, this has to be made clear as well."* (interviewee 17) or *"The chairman of the board started organising regular informative meetings that were meant for all the employees. At those meetings he explained the reasons for the change and the goals of the company. These meetings were also aimed at creating a feeling of working "side by side" i.e. the employees worked not only to achieve their personal goals but to achieve the company goals through their contribution."* (interviewee 67) Also, *"to make communication more efficient, several formal and informal channels of information were established. Among the formal channels were the Intranet i.e. the in-company home page, in-company newspaper, informative meetings to all the employees, a scheme of meetings, strategic seminars for the leaders of the major functional divisions, the division of managers' working time between different sub-institutions, regular meetings with trade union representatives."* (interviewee 31)

Special training sessions organized for employees could be considered as formal learning. *"When changes started appearing within the concern and in the surrounding environment, we started with training the managements of the companies. All the company managers passed a two stage training session at Company University "X in Change". The training session dealt with the whole process of change by beginning with supplying information to the employees and clients and finishing with the probable dangers and tackling them"* (interviewee 81)

In some companies, steering tactics was used: *"The implementation of changes was monitored via weekly meetings and informative briefings. The deadlines were generally met. In case any problems appeared with the deadlines, an immediate plan of action was made to resolve the situation."* (interviewee 11)

Managers organised *"preparation of interim reports in order to find out the problems, what disturbed people the most and what they were afraid of."* (interviewee 19) Informing employees helped to handle emotions: *"Before we informed the people there was a lot of electricity, ignorance and dread in the air. After being informed about the changes, people became scared, but this feeling passed rather quickly."* (interviewee 32) Handling emotions was necessary because, *"The organization went through several emotional stages — confusion and loss of understanding, fear about the future and finally enthusiasm about the challenges opening up with the new solutions."* (interviewee 13) Also, *"using an outplacement programme helped to avoid excessive emotions and prepared those people who were to be made redundant for competition in the labour market."* (interviewee 9)

Handling power issues helped to remove obstacles in the implementation process: *"the "old time" middle management were replaced."* (interviewee 29)

To summarize the lessons learnt from implementations of changes nonformally, the following points could be made:

- More people should be involved in the process of discussion at the beginning stage.
- The processes should be described and mapped immediately. This would make it possible to approach the changes in a rather more process centred than function centred manner.
- The relationship between core and support services should be described.
- The company should try to preserve a positive internal climate and create a belief in the employees as part of the results. It is essential that people learn and develop through the changes.

- Superiors should talk more to subordinates, ask for solutions to problems, and give them more freedom in their activities.
- It is necessary to talk to the employees more at different levels in order to avoid the spreading of news in the form of gossip and the probable resulting confusion.

CONCLUSION AND DISCUSSION

The management challenge for the 21st century, according to Drucker (1999), is the integration of what were once several procedures into a single analysis. This chapter is an attempt to combine change research with theories of learning. Empirical study was conducted in Estonian companies, and results indicate that the types of organizational changes and the need for organizational learning are connected to institutional environments. During this societal transience, transformational changes, deepest by scope, take place in most companies. During more stable institutional stages, organizations face a decreasing number of transformational changes. At the same time, transactional changes take place.

It was especially hard to get changes started in a stagnated society with overstaffed organizations, lacking any knowledge of a market economy. In this situation, correction from organizational learning styles, defined by DiBella and Nevis (1998), was not enough; innovation, adaptation, and acquisition were needed.

In 2005, when the transition to a free-market economy was completed, the main players have learnt from previous experiences with change. True involvement of employees (not only asking for opinions and forgetting about them) began to take place, even already in the earlier stages of the planning phase. Communication has changed from being speeches and information travelling in one direction to listening and two-sided conversations and discussions. Also, collaborative learning was encouraged more. It could be concluded that Estonian managers have started to turn more attention to human side of change: development of learning abilities of organization has helped to increase knowledge sharing, which is basis for intellectual capital.

As during implementation of organizational changes, most of attention was turned to first step; unfreezing and institutionalization took place only in one fifth of organizations, it could be concluded, that reflection, in most of cases, did not happen. Without reflection, which is prerequisite for increase in knowledge, learning process is unfinished and change in subjective constructions of reality does not take place. Therefore, it is crutial to take steps to continue changes until generalization could take place. For this purpose, the author developed a model of the interconnected processes of change and learning for transition countries. The proposed model could help managers of international companies to plan and implement changes in subsidiaries located in countries in transition (Figure 2).

The reason why changes are undertaken in the organization is need to make the organization more valuable. Therefore, author applies Porter's value chain model (Porter, 1985) as a basis in creating model for implementation changes in Estonia organizations.

The goal of organizational learning is to increase the range of possible behaviours for implementing the necessary changes. In order to do this, people should first realise that changes have taken place in the external environment of the organisation. These changes trigger the change process, which is accompanied by learning. During the unfreezing phase, people realize that a gap exists between the existing reality in the organization and the situation required by changes in the environment. This constitutes new knowledge for the organization, and it takes time before everyone accepts this difference and a change in the collective understanding takes place.

The next stage, moving, is full of experimenting with new behaviours. People experience new

Figure 2. Author's model of the interconnected processes of change and learning for transition countries

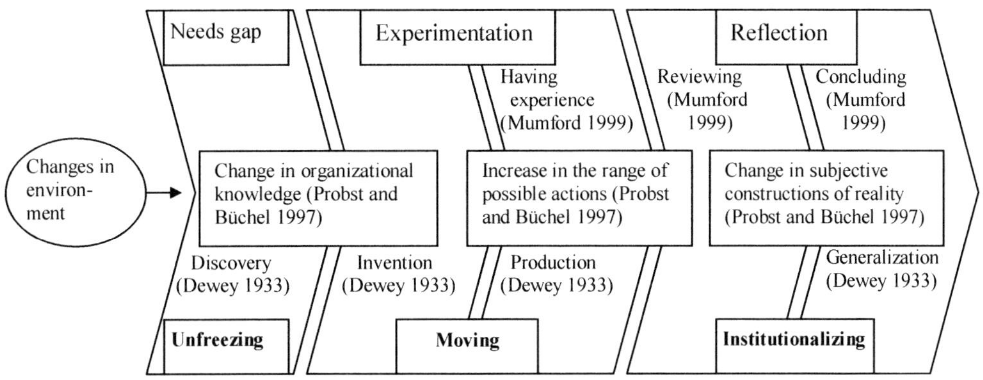

ways of doing things and the range of possible behaviours increases. In the institutionalizing stage, reflection takes place: participants review their positions, generalizations are made on the basis of experience, and conclusions are drawn for the future. A change in the subjective constructions of reality takes place.

Transformational changes in organizations, taking place during societal transition, require a higher level of learning from the participants. Changes in the organizational knowledge base are essential. In order to achieve this, individual learning should develop and become organizational learning and organizations should then become learning organizations. Only an increase in the learning ability of organizations can increase the intellectual capital of the organization and ensure the successful implementation of change and the future competitiveness of the organization. This is especially true in during economic and social transition in country.

ACKNOWLEDGMENT

Research was supported by ETF Grant 7537.

REFERENCES

Ackerman, L. S. (1986). Development, transition, or transformation: The question of change in organizations. *Organizational Development Practicioner*, December, 1-8.

Agor, W. H. (1997). The measurement, use, and development of intellectual capital to increase public sector productivity. *Public Personnel Management, 26*(2), 175-186.

Alas, R., & Sharifi, S. (2002). Organizational learning and resistance to change in Estonian companies. *Human Resource Development International, 5*(3), 313-331.

Bartunek, J. M. (1993). The multiple cognitions and conflicts associated with second-order organizational change. In J. K. Murnighan (Ed.), *Social psychology in organizations: Advances in theory and research* (pp. 322-349). NJ: Prentice Hall.

Burke, W., & Litwin, G. (1992). A casual model of organizational performance and change. *Journal of Management, 18*, 523-545.

Clark, E., & Geppert, M. (2002). Management learning and knowledge transfer in transforming societies: Approaches, issues, and future directions. *Human Resource Development International, 5*(3), 263-277.

Clark, E., & Soulsby, A. (1999). *Organisational change in post-communist Europe: Management and transformation in the Czech Republic.* Routledge.

Dewey, J. (1933). *How ee think.* Boston: D.C. Heath & Company.

DiBella, A. J., & Nevis, E. C. (1998). *How organizations learn. An integreted strategy for building learning capability.* Jossey-Bass Publishers.

Drucker, P. (1999). *Mangement challenge of the 21st century.* HarperCollins.

Edvinsson, L., & Malone, M. S. (1997). *Intellectual capital.* Piatcus.

Garvin, D. A. (1993). Building a learning organization. *Harvard Business Review*, July-August, 78-91.

Hendry, C. (1996). Understanding and creating whole organizational change through learning theory. *Human Relations, 49*, 621-641.

Hurst, D. K. (1986). Why strategic management is bankrupt. *Organizational Dynamics*, Spring, 5-27.

Jaffe, D. T., Scott, C. D., & Tobe, G. R. (1994). *Rekindling commitment: How to revitalize yourself, your work, and your organization.* San Francisco: Jossey-Bass Publishers.

Kochan, T. A., & Useem, M. (1992). *Transforming organizations.* Oxford University Press.

Lewin, K. (1989). Changing as three steps: Unfreezing, moving, and freezing of group standards. In W. L. French, C. H. Bell Jr., & R. A. Zawacki (Eds.), *Organizational development. theory, practice, and research* (3rd ed.) (p. 87). Irwin.

Liuhto, K. (1999). *The organisational and managerial transformation in turbulent business environments – Managers' views on the transition of their enterprise in some of the European former Soviet Republics in the 1990's.* Publications of the Turku School of Economics and Business Administration. Series A-9.

Mahler, J. (1997). Influences of organizational culture on learning in public agencies. *Journal of Public Administration Research & Theory, 7*(4), 519-541.

Mumford, A. (1999). Individual and organizational learning: The pursuit of change. In C. Mabey, & P. Iles (Eds.), *Managing learning* (pp. 77-86). International Thompson Business Press.

Nutt, P. C., & Backoff, R. W. (1997). Crafting vision, *Journal of Management Inquiry, 6*(4), 308-329.

Pedler, M., Bourgoyne, J., & Boydell (1991). *The learning company: A strategy of sustainable development.* London: McGraw-Hill.

Porter, M. E. (1985). *Competitive advantage.* New York: Free Press.

Pribram, K. I. (1983). The brain, cognitive commodities, and the enfolded order. In K. Boulding, & L. Senesch (Eds.), *The optimum utilization of knowledge.* Westview Press.

Quinn, R., & Spreitzer, G. (1997). The road to empowerment: Seven questions every leader should answer. *Organisational Dynamics, 26*(2), 37-50.

Rosenstiel, L., & Koch, S. (2001). Change in socioeconomic values as a trigger of organisational learning. In M. Dierkes, A.B. Antal, J. Child, & I. Nonaka (Eds.), *Organisational learning and knowledge* (pp. 198-220). Oxford University Press.

Schein, E. H. (1992). *Organizational culture and leadership.* Jossey Bass Publishers.

Senge, P. M., (1997). *The fifth discipline. The art and practice of the learning organization.* Century Business.

Senge, P. M. (1999). The leader's new work: Building learning organization. In C. Mabey, & P. Iles (Eds.), *Managing learning* (pp. 5-21). International Thompson Business Press.

Small, C. T., & Sage, A. P. (2005/2006). Knowledge management and knowledge sharing: A review. *Information Knowledge Systems Management, 5*, 153–169.

Tsang, E. W. K. (1997). Organisational learning and the learning organisation: A dichotomy between descriptive and prescreptive research, *Human Relations, 50*, 73-89.

Wall, A. (2005). The measurement and management of intellectual capital in public sector. *Public Management Review, 7*(2), 289-303.

Watzlawick, P., Weakland, J. H., & Fisch, R. (1974). *Change: Principles of problem formulation and resolution.* New York: Norton.

Whelan-Berry, K. S., Gordon, J. R., & Hinings, C. R. (2003). The relative effect of change drivers in large-scale organizational change: An empirical study. In R. W. Woodman, & W. A. Pasmore, W. A. (Eds.), *Research in organizational change and development* (vol. 14, pp. 99-146). Greenwich: JAI Press.

Chapter III
Strategies for Assessing Organisational Knowledge Assets

Giovanni Schiuma
Università degli Studi della Basilicata, Italy
Centre for Business Performance, Cranfield School of Management, UK

ABSTRACT

Today's global business is characterised by interconnectedness, interdependence, and an increasing level of complexity that force organisations to be flexible, proactive, and dynamic. In this emerging global scenario most of the traditional strategies, approaches, and policies no longer work the way they used to. The new challenge, particularly for companies coping with global business, is the ability to drive their transformation into intelligent organisations, that is, organisations that are able to leverage their intellectual capital to achieve their business objectives and envision new development paths. This chapter, assuming that the organisational intellectual capital corresponds to the knowledge assets attributed to a company, discusses the "What," "Why," and "How" of the knowledge asset assessment. First, the subprocesses of the assessment are discussed, highlighting the main features of the assessment of knowledge assets as well as the twofold nature of the knowledge asset assessment, distinguishing between stock and flow perspective of the evaluation. Second, the managerial reasons at the basis of the implementation of measurement systems for disclosing organisational knowledge resources are discussed. Finally, on the base of a distinction between the assessment approaches and the evaluation architectures, four main knowledge-asset assessment strategies are defined

INTRODUCTION

Why do companies need to formulate strategies for assessing organisational knowledge assets? And particularly, which is the role of these strategies for global business? These two questions are strictly interdependent and represent an issue for those organisations operating on global scale and aiming to improve their competitiveness. Starting from the recognition of the strategic relevance of assessing and managing intellectual capital in today's global business, the aim of this chapter is to delineate the possible strategies that organisations can put in place to assess the knowledge assets driving value-creation dynamics.

The relevance of assessing and managing intangible and knowledge assets is emerged as a key concern. Managers have recognised that the competitiveness of their organisations no longer resides in traditional financial and tangible resources. Although they can still represent relevant assets, they are not able to guarantee sustainable and differentiating competitive advantages. The 21st century organisations are realising that most of their capacity to create value does not reside into the traditional tangible and financial assets, but rather than on the ownership and development of organisational intellectual capital (Carlucci, Marr, & Schiuma, 2004; Carmeli & Tishler, 2004; Schiuma et al, 2007). Indeed, the concept of intellectual capital is risen as a key interpretation to denote the overall intangible and knowledge resources at the basis of company's competencies (Barney, 1991; Carlucci & Schiuma, 2007; Grant, 1991; Liebowitz, 1999; Rumelt, 1984; Wernerfelt, 1984).

Today's global business is characterised by interconnectedness, interdependence, and an increasing level of complexity that force organisations to be flexible, proactive, and dynamic. In today's global scenario most of the traditional strategies, approaches, and policies no longer work the way they used to. The new challenge, particularly for companies coping with global business, is the ability to drive their transformation into intelligent organisations, that is, organisations that are able to leverage their intellectual capital to achieve their business objectives and envision new development paths.

The intellectual capital assessment and management is at the cornerstone of the development of new business models that, through the valorisation of intangible and knowledge resources, are able to prompt creativity, imagination, energy, and passion within organisations. These represent the new competitive factors for creating value in the global business.

Traditionally companies have measured economic, financial, and operational performances, while they have disregarded the intangible and knowledge dimensions of their business. As result the value incorporated in a company, as well as the company's capability to create value, have been usually underestimated. Nowadays, successful companies are those that continuously innovate, take advantage of new technologies, and utilise the skills and know-how of their employees, rather than those companies that leverage their physical assets. In this context, knowledge assets represent the key value drivers in global business. They need to be assessed and managed. In particular, the assessment of knowledge assets plays a fundamental role in global business both to manage the value creation capabilities and to disclose and communicate the value of corporate components.

The chapter is structured, as depicted in Figure 1, and discusses the "What," "Why," and "How" of the knowledge asset assessment. The first section is concerned about the "What" of the knowledge asset assessment and is aimed to set some relevant conceptual issues related to the meaning and contents of the assessment of knowledge assets. In particular, the subprocesses of the assessment are discussed, highlighting the main features of the assessment of knowledge assets. Then the

Figure 1. The structure and contents of the chapter

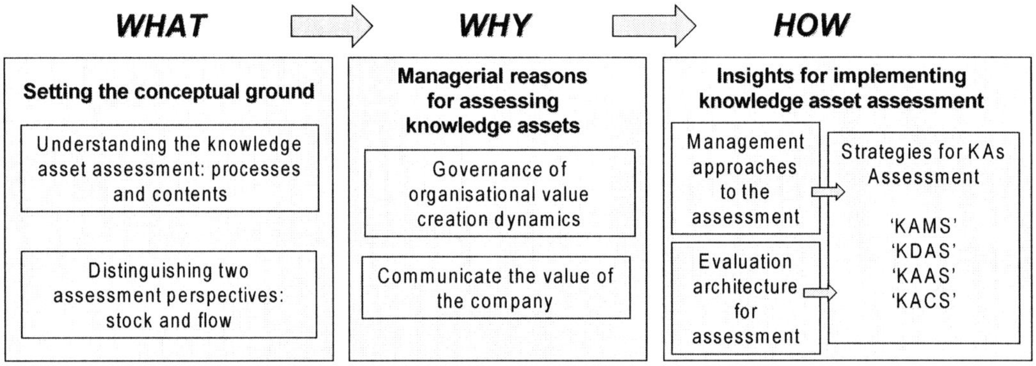

twofold nature of the knowledge-asset assessment is introduced, distinguishing between stock and flow, which correspond to a static and dynamic perspective of the evaluation. The second section focuses on the "Why" of the knowledge-asset assessment discussing the managerial reasons at the basis of the implementation of measurement systems for disclosing organisational knowledge resources. Two fundamental managerial purposes of the knowledge-asset assessment are identified: the governance of company's value creation dynamics and the communication of the value of a company. Finally, in the last section, the attention is paid on the "How" of the knowledge asset assessment. Four main assessment strategies are defined. Their definition is based on the distinction between the assessment approach and the evaluation architecture. The assessment approach distinguishes between value management and value communication, while the evaluation architecture identifies two measurement structures, the index-based approach and the scorecard-based approach.

ASSESSING KNOWLEDGE ASSETS: CONCEPTUAL NOTES

The Assessment Process of Knowledge Assets

Generally, in the intellectual capital-management literature, the concepts of measurement and assessment are used as interchangeable and as synonymous. However, they are conceptually different and in particular, the concept of measurement represents a subsystem of the assessment one. To pay attention on the clarification of the differences between these concepts it is useful not only from a theoretical point of view, but also from a practical standpoint. Indeed, the meaning that we attributed to management constructs affects our understanding of the phenomena. This involves that a different interpretation can drive a diverse quality and effectiveness of the management processes and actions. It is therefore not rhetoric and superfluous to clarify the meaning and the contents of an assessment process with specific attention to the object of our analysis, that is, the knowledge assets.

Figure 2. The process dimensions of the assessment of knowledge assets

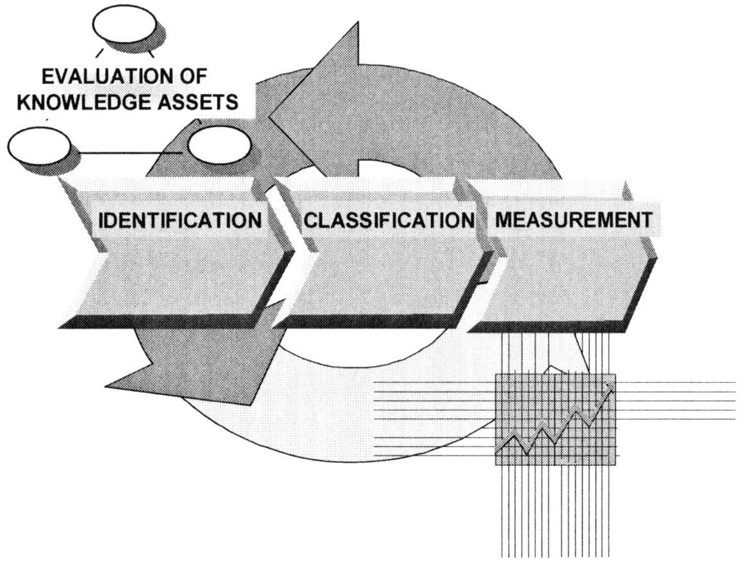

The assessment of knowledge assets can be interpreted as a process of collection, analysis, and communication of qualitative and quantitative information concerning an organisation's knowledge-assets endowment. It is based on three complementary processes, which are integrated and overlapped. As depicted in Figure 2, the subprocesses of an assessment are: the identification, the classification, and the measurement of a company's knowledge assets. Each process has specific characteristics and managerial aims. In the following, each process is described.

An assessment process starts with an identification of the objects to be evaluated. The identification process aims to recognise and discover the knowledge assets within an organisation. It plays a fundamental role because it affects the selection of the "object" to be evaluated.

Regarding, specifically, the assessment of knowledge assets, their identification within an organisation is not an effortless and straightforward task. This is due to the intangible nature of such assets, which generally entails some difficulties in providing a clear and unambiguous definition. This is also due to the difficulty to interpret and analyse organisational resources in accordance with a cognitive interpretation that recognises the knowledge contents of organisation's components.

Within an organisation, it is easier and intuitive to attribute importance to tangible resources because it is easier to understand the role and position they cover in the organisational working mechanisms. The human resources, for example, even if they represent the most important cognitive resources of an organisation, are often analysed and considered as tangible assets. Each individual is essentially considered as a person responsible for some working activities, rather then to be considered as a cognitive resource. Other organisational knowledge resources, such as relationships, sociocultural values, knowledge flows, routines and practices due to their intangibility are much more difficult to recognise and typify. This involves that usually within organisations there are difficulties to reveal, from both a conceptual and practical point of view, the knowledge assets. However, their identification is fundamental because first drives the recognition of their importance and second allows their measurement.

The identification process is at the basis of the classification process that allows one to label knowledge resources within an organisation. In particular, the classification process is aimed to define the categories to group the organisational knowledge assets. The different possible categories are defined on the base of the different criteria adopted for the classification, which in turn tend to reflect the managerial purposes of the classification process.

In the last decades, in the economic and management literature, several categorisations of the knowledge resources have been proposed. Many of them are based on dichotomy taxonomies distinguishing knowledge assets on the basis of two opposite dimensions. A first fundamental classification, which has affected the understanding of knowledge resources within organisations, is that one distinguishing between tangible and intangible resources. Indeed, at present there is a consistent orientation to consider knowledge resources as intangible, while there is the tendency to not recognise the cognitive nature of tangible resources. This is a significant limitation because tangible assets can represent important codified knowledge and as such, they need to be considered as knowledge resources within an organisation. Therefore, the tangibility of a resource does not exclude its cognitive nature. Other classifications of knowledge resources can be found in the management literature. They are mainly based on the use of the following criteria to categorise knowledge resources: level of codification, degree of control, transferability, and nature.

The use of criteria to classify knowledge resources not only allows the definition of clusters, but also supports their identification within an organisation. This means that the identification and the classification are strongly interrelated serving each other. The identification is aimed to screen an organisation in order to reveal its knowledge assets, while the classification is intended to discern the different typologies of knowledge assets. Both processes are fundamental for the assessment and represent a prerequisite for measuring knowledge assets within an organisation.

Neely (1998), taking into account the two main dimensions of performance, efficiency and effectiveness, defines performance measurement as the process of evaluating the efficiency and effectiveness of an organisation's actions. This process can be performed by putting in place performance measures that allow a quantitative and/or qualitative evaluation of the efficiency and effectiveness of a specific organisation's action. The definition of a set of metrics and indicators to monitor the efficiency and/or effectiveness of an organisation's management actions leads to setting up what is named a performance measurement system (Bourne, 2001).

On the basis of this interpretation of the performance measurement, it is possible to define the knowledge asset measurement as a process of collection of qualitative and quantitative information concerning a specific knowledge asset or a bundle of organisational knowledge resources. Its main purpose is to assign a value to a knowledge asset on the basis of a specific economic and/or managerial aim. From an operative point of view, the measurement can be carried out by the definition and implementation of a system of indicators and metrics.

Indicators and metrics can be defined adopting measurement units that can be of monetary or not monetary nature. In the first case, the indicators and metrics are aimed essentially to provide economic and financial information in order to support the negotiation, the transaction, and/or the transfer of knowledge assets in the market. While not monetary metrics allow to define and describe, both from a qualitative and a quantitative perspective, the properties and the specific features of organisational knowledge assets. Due to the difficulty to quantifying knowledge assets in economic and financial terms, not monetary indicators and metrics tend to be more frequently defined and adopted in managerial and operational practices.

An important aspect related to the assessment of knowledge assets is the time-based nature of the measures. In this regard, it is critical to stress that knowledge assets are dynamic in nature, and this aspect should be taken into account by the performance measurement systems. For this reason, two forms of assessment can be distinguished, a static assessment vs. a dynamic assessment. In the following paragraph, the two assessment perspectives are introduced.

A Stock vs. a Flow Assessment Perspective

Most of the groups of indicators and metrics adopted for the measurement of knowledge assets provide information about the stock level of the analysed organisational resources. Where the stock level is concerned about a qualitative and/or a quantitative information of some specific aspects and features of the assets.

Conceptually, the definition of a set of metrics corresponds to the construction of an "evaluation space" which dimensions stand for the specific measured aspects and features of the assets. This involves that once the categories of measures have been defined, the assessment process of a knowledge asset it is like, imaginary, to identify a position in the "evaluation space" in which it is possible to locate the measured knowledge asset. From conceptual point of view, this interpretation of the assessment process is particularly powerful to reflect on the time-based nature of the measures that we define within an organisation in order to evaluate organisational knowledge resources. Indeed, a set of measures provides the position of a knowledge asset in a specific time. However, due to their intrinsic dynamic nature, knowledge assets evolve over the time, changing their position in the imaginary evaluation space. Knowledge assets can evolve or can become obsolete and loose their importance. The changing forces can be represented by contingent factors and/or managerial actions as well as by the evolution of technology trajectories.

On the basis of these considerations, it is possible to highlight the issue that most of the assessment and measurement systems adopted to evaluate organisational resources tend to disregard; the dynamism of knowledge resources. They tend to provide snapshots that give a static understanding of organisational knowledge resources. For this reason, it is important to implement measurement systems that are able to integrate information about the knowledge asset stocks with information concerning the evolution of knowledge assets over the time. The integration of a stock assessment with a flow assessment offers information about the changes and the evolution of knowledge assets. Adopting the imaginary evaluation space, this equals to define indicators and measures that track the trajectories and the knowledge assets development. In Figure 3, it is depicted the conceptual evaluation space highlighting the differences between stock and flow evaluation.

In order to take into account the dynamic nature of organisational knowledge assets, it is possible to adopt two assessment approaches. On the one hand, measures should be defined with the aim to assess the "flow" characteristics of knowledge assets. In particular, this involves the definition of indicators capable of characterising the properties of the flow, and to disclose the forces driving the evolution and the development of knowledge resources. On the other hand, the evaluation of the flow can be performed by a systematic collection of static information that tracks the evolution trajectories. This equals to collect stock evaluations on the base of a defined frequency that allows one to build a sequence of pictures describing the development of the analysed knowledge assets.

Both the stock and flow assessment of knowledge assets allow to define the managerial priorities on which to focus the attention. They allow

Figure 3. A Stock and Flow perspective of knowledge asset assessment

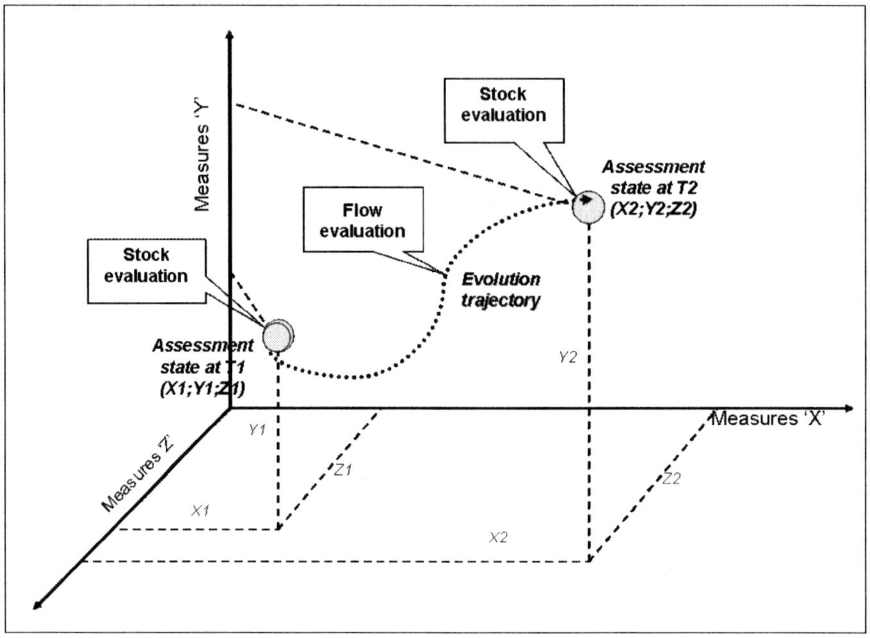

to drive organisational behaviour and to align organisation's energies and managerial efforts towards the achievement of targeted performance objectives.

MANAGERIAL PURPOSES FOR ASSESSING KNOWLEDGE ASSETS

The assessment of knowledge assets can have two main managerial purposes: the governance of company's value-creation dynamics, and the communication of the value generated and/or incorporated by a company. The governance is aimed to drive the company's strategy planning and to manage the organisational behaviour in order to achieve strategic objectives and to support value creation dynamics. While the communication is at the basis of the organisational reporting activities with the aim to disclose internally and/or externally relevant information about the value of a company's components.

Assessing Knowledge Assets to Govern Organisational Value Creation

The assessment of knowledge assets provides information to govern company's value creation dynamics. This is performed both by driving the organisational strategy planning and by influencing the organisational behaviour.

Regarding the strategy planning process, it is possible to distinguish three main stages: the design, the implementation, and the review or improvement of a strategy (Marr, Grey, & Schiuma, 2004; Marr & Schiuma, 2003). In each stage, the assessment of knowledge asset plays a relevant role. In particular, in the design of a strategy, the knowledge asset assessment allows to acknowledge the strategic position knowledge resources play in company's value creation dynamics.

In today's knowledge economy, the definition and formulation of a strategy, aimed to support and drive company's value creation in global business, have to consider the knowledge nature of the organisation and of its components, as well as of the business. This involves that the identification of the strategic organisational knowledge assets at the basis of company competitiveness needs to be taken into account both as intrinsic objects of a company's strategy and as instrumental lever to achieve strategic outcomes. In this regard, organisations can adopt two main approaches in designing a strategy: i) managers can explicitly and directly focus their attention on knowledge assets and include their development in the objectives of the company's strategy; and/or ii) managers can focus the strategy definition around business and performance objectives and afterwards, to identify the strategic organisational knowledge resources grounding the achievement of the targeted strategic objectives.

In the implementation stage of a company's strategy, the assessment of knowledge assets allows to align strategic objectives with knowledge-asset management initiatives. The alignment between knowledge-asset management initiatives aimed to develop the organisational knowledge domains with the strategic business and performance objectives is of fundamental importance to support the growth of organisation's competencies (Bierly & Chakrabarti, 1996; Hansen, Nohtria, & Tierney, 1999; Wiig, 1997; Zack, 1999). Moreover, the assessment of knowledge assets allows one to account the benefits produced by the implementation of knowledge-asset management initiatives, proving the links between knowledge assets and organisational performances as well as assessing their impacts.

Finally, in the review and improvement stage of a company's strategy, the knowledge-asset assessment contributes to shed more light on the reasons explaining the cause-and-effect relationships linking the development of organisational knowledge domains with the achievement of targeted strategic performance objectives. This contributes to identify and define the new objectives on which to focus the strategy planning attention in accordance with the changes occurred inside and outside the organisation.

The assessment of knowledge assets supports the governance of an organisation not only by improving the strategy planning, but most importantly, by affecting the organisational behaviour. Indeed, by means of measures, it is possible to highlight the role and the relevance of knowledge assets for company's success and the importance of taking care of organisational knowledge resources. For an organisation, defining a measure equals to state that the object of the assessment is important. Indeed, measuring corresponds to spotlight issues. In addition, the definition of measures for knowledge assets allows to describe the organisation position in terms of knowledge resources endowments, and to identify the knowledge-asset development priorities.

Assessing Knowledge Assets to Communicate the Value of an Organisation

Through the assessment of organisational knowledge resources, it is possible to make a company more transparent in terms of its own assets, competencies, and growing capabilities. The assessment represents a fundamental means for reporting relevant company's information to stakeholders both for internal and external purposes.

In the last years, there has been a great attention about the reporting of knowledge assets. Many scholars and international accounting associations are focusing their efforts on the definition of standards for accounting intangible and knowledge assets.

The reporting represents a further stage of an assessment process. It is aimed to collect, aggregate, and represent the data gathered through the measurement in order to disclose and communicate important information. In particular, it seems possible to distinguish internal reporting, which is mainly aimed to communicate information internally to an organisation, from external reporting ,which is directed to disclose information to the public domain.

The external reporting of organisational knowledge assets offers to the market a more comprehensive view of a company's value and of its capability of gaining a competitive advantage and increasing continuously its business performances. This can have different benefits for an organisation. For example, the reporting of knowledge assets can support a better estimation of a company during mergers and acquisitions. It can improve the market's understanding of the value of a company's assets as well as of a company's ability to leverage value from those assets (Sullivan & Sullivan, 2000). This can support investors' understanding of the risks related to investments in the company. Several studies have highlighted how evaluating knowledge assets can influence shares value and its volatility. For example, Baruch Lev and his colleagues (1999), investigating 126 FDA (Food and Drug Administration) approvals, have found that the average stock price reaction to FDA approvals, announced on the basis of traditional information, was 0.51%. When the approval announcement was accompanied by qualitative information (e.g., description of the properties of the drug), the average reaction was 1.13%, whereas when the drug developer disclosed quantitative information regarding intangibles, the average increase in stock price quadrupled to 2.01%. Other scholars have argued the existence of positive relationships between brand value and company's capitalisation (Barth, Clement, Foster, & Kasznik, 2003). In addition, it has been stressed that the investments in intangible assets represent a fundamental means to sustain the economic and financial value creation dynamics accounted both by the capitalisation and the returns on investments (Deng, Lev, & Narin, 2003; Hang, 2003). These studies show the relevance of making a company transparent in terms of its knowledge assets ownership. This issue is also addressed by the recent international agreement named as "Basilea 2," which has put new emphasis on the evaluation of company's intangible dimensions. It underlines the importance for a company to provide to banks and credit institutions with information related to organisational managerial capabilities, organisational structure, competitive capability, and other intangible and knowledge dimensions, in order to get access to credit.

The reporting of knowledge assets has positive effects also within an organisation. In fact, the assessment and reporting identifying and making transparent the knowledge dimensions of an organisation allows, on the one hand, to guide knowledge assets allocation and, on the other hand, to assess the benefits associated to investments on knowledge assets management initiatives. Moreover, the disclosure of information about knowledge assets drives organisational behaviour, contributing to delineate company's evolution trajectories, required changes, and progresses achieved.

Finally, the knowledge-assets reporting is at basis of company's internal and external benchmarking. Benchmarking is generally recognized as an approach that enables a company to understand its current performance levels and set future targets (Camp, 1989). Knowledge assets assessment and reporting improve an organisation's understanding of its competitive position and of growing challenges and opportunities.

STRATEGIES OF KNOWLEDGE ASSET ASSESSMENT

Management Aproaches to the Assessment of Knowledge Assets

The managerial purposes presented concur to delineate two main management approaches to the assessment of knowledge assets: the "value management" approach, mainly oriented to collect and communicate information about the knowledge assets endowment, acquisition, and development in order to support organisational value creation and performance improvements; and the "value communication" approach, oriented to communicate the value related to company's knowledge assets.

The "value management" approach especially focuses on the strategy planning and on the management of organisational behaviour, and tends to adopt measures for gathering qualitative and quantitative information about organisational knowledge resources and for analysing knowledge assets evolution trajectories. The adopted measures tend to be not monetary. However, also, some economic and financial measures linked to knowledge assets management can be considered, such as, for example, training expenses, socio-cultural events expenses, and costs sustained for acquiring and developing company's knowledge assets.

While the "value communication" approach is mainly oriented to communicate the value of organisational knowledge assets to company's stakeholders. For this reason, it prefers the use of economic and financial measures and/or of aggregated indices appraising the organisation's knowledge in accordance with a holistic view.

Knowledge-Asset Assessment Strategies

A knowledge-asset assessment strategy is interpreted as the set of economic and managerial decisions and purposes at the basis of the assessment of an organisation's knowledge assets. The definition of a knowledge-asset assessment strategy has to consider both the choice of the managerial approach to the assessment, "value management" vs. "value communication," and the most appropriate "evaluation architecture" to collect and communicate the information related to the measurement.

The "evaluation architecture" refers to the structure and to the operational methods by means which it is possible to collect assessment information. In particular, it is possible to define two main "evaluation architectures": the "scorecard-based" and "index-based" architecture. Both architectures share a holistic interpretation of a company. However, they are different in terms of methods used for analysing and assessing organisational knowledge assets.

The "scorecard–based" architecture is based on the identification of the main areas of assessment, and defines a set of key measures for each area. The measures are defined according to a "top-down" approach. In each assessment area, a panel of key indicators related to company's strategic objectives is defined. The indicators are implemented starting from the top of the organisation and then cascading down. This equals to translating the strategic objectives in activities and actions, and to associate to these activities/actions measures. This allows not only to translate company's strategic objects across functions and activities of each components of an organisational system, but also to collect, according to a bottom-up approach, information on the development of knowledge assets.

While the "index-based" architecture aims to define measures that provide aggregate information. This is particularly useful to provide a holistic representation of an organisation.

The assessment approach and the evaluation architecture represent the building blocks of a knowledge-asset assessment strategy. On the basis of their combination, it is possible to identify four main assessment strategies of knowledge assets. In Figure 4, the following four categories of knowledge-asset assessment strategies are represented:

- Knowledge asset measurement strategy (KAMS);
- Knowledge domain assessment strategy (KDAS);
- Knowledge asset accounting strategy (KAAS);
- and knowledge asset communication strategy (KACS).

Figure 4. Knowledge asset assessment strategies

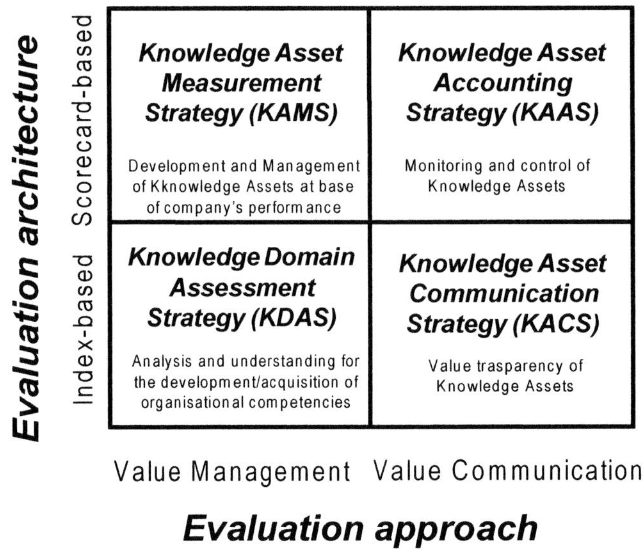

The "KAMS" is aimed to identify and measure the organisational knowledge assets with the main purpose of managing them in order to achieve defined targeted performance objectives. This strategy points mainly to guarantee an alignment between the company's knowledge assets endowment and the strategic performance objectives. It allows one to provide managers with tools for designing and implementing knowledge-assets management initiatives aimed to sustain company's value creation dynamics. The collection of information concerning knowledge assets allows one to understand their quality and quantity, and to analyse their role in company's processes and business performance. This kind of information provides a valuable base for designing managerial initiatives aimed to manage and renew those knowledge assets that are strategically relevant for the solution of specific organisational and operation problems or, more in general, to guarantee the achievement of company's performance objectives. So, a "KAMS" is aimed to support the management and the renewal of those knowledge assets that significantly influence company's performances.

The "KDAS" aims to define, according to a holistic view, the nature and the characteristics of company's knowledge domains grounding organisational competencies, and, in particular, the "core" competencies. It is based on the definition of aggregate indicators that allow to develop benchmarking analysis. It is based on the assumption that the knowledge assets, playing a strategic relevance within a company, build up the strategic knowledge domains, grounding the company's competencies (Von Krogh et al., 2001).

An organisation can identify and assess knowledge assets domains across its different units, can monitor and compare them, as well as can benchmark them with competitors' knowledge assets and with knowledge assets of successful companies operating in other industries.

This knowledge-asset assessment strategy provides the substratum for understanding the competitive position of a company and to identify those knowledge domains to be developed, acquired, and protected in order to achieve and maintain a competitive advantage. The adoption of this assessment strategy means to shift the attention from the management and development of a single knowledge asset or a group of knowledge assets related to the improvement of a specific performance, to the understanding of the knowledge foundations of a company's competencies. Consequently, the "KDAS" is aimed to analyse the knowledge foundations of a company's competencies, and to plan strategic management programs and initiatives to support the growth of key knowledge assets domains.

The "KAAS" allows to assess, according to an analytic approach, company's knowledge assets. Similarly to "cost accounting" process, this assessment aims to collect and to communicate information within an organisation system suitable to drive managers in monitoring knowledge assets. The choice of the measures to be adopted for measuring knowledge-assets value depends on the specific managerial needs. This kind of assessment strategy meets managers' needs to have an understanding about the endowment and the development of organisational knowledge assets. The information gathered through this assessment strategy can be used to communicate within an organisation the status and the evolution of the knowledge assets endowment. This is particularly significant in order to create an organisation's attention to the valorisation and management of knowledge assets. Then, a "KAAS" is aimed to define a monitoring and control system of the endowment and development of organisational knowledge assets.

Finally, the "KACS" is aimed essentially to communicate the value of a company's knowledge assets to the market and more generally, to a company's stakeholders. This assessment strategy allows to reveal, to the market and to the public domain, information suitable for a right evaluation of a company's value and of its capability to create value. The main idea at basis of the "KACS" is that company's value can be evaluated only by taking into account both tangible and intangible assets. In fact, assets, such as brand, people's know-how and competencies, company's culture, stakeholders relationships, market access capabilities, and many other intangible and knowledge assets traditionally disregarded or only partially evaluated by traditional performance measurement and reporting systems, are fundamental for revealing the true value of a company (Harvey & Lusch, 1999). In particular, this assessment strategy has a great relevance when most of a company's value is related to intangible components and, then, there is a high risk that the absence of a comprehensive evaluation of the value of a company's components does not allow, for example, to financial analysts and investors, to understand the realistic company's capability of creating value. Indeed, the assessment of knowledge assets reduces the risk associated to the investments in the company, as well as allows to better control the volatility of a company's capitalisation. In addition, the availability of information about organisational competencies and knowledge assets allows to better understand company's growing capability. Therefore a "KACS" is aimed to make more transparent a company's value, as well as to communicate externally the capacity of a company to create value.

The four described assessment strategies sustain company's value creation dynamics by providing important information both to reinforce and improve organisational knowledge assets, and to develop new organisational knowledge domains and competencies. In addition, they allow to define the company's comprehensive value by taking into account the knowledge assets.

Integrating Knowledge-Asset Assessment Strategies

The knowledge-asset assessment strategies are strictly interrelated, and synergically interact in the disclosure and valorisation of company's knowledge assets. They do not operate as silos, but they need to be integrated. For this reason, in Figure 5, the relationships between the different assessment strategies are depicted and in the following, they are described.

The "KAAS" provides an informative base for defining and implementing the "KAMS" (Relation A, Figure 5). In fact, the definition of a monitoring and control system of a company's knowledge assets allows to identify the overall knowledge resources that are strategic for achieving specific performance objectives. The "KAAS" provides a possible list of indicators that allows, once the performance objectives to be achieved have been defined, to select a set of key indicators in order to drive managers towards the choice of the most appropriate knowledge-management initiatives to be implemented to achieve the targeted performance objectives. On the other hand, the identification of the knowledge assets that play a critical role for company's performance improvement allows to up-date the "KAAS" highlighting those critical knowledge assets to be monitored and controlled.

The "KAMS," focusing on the key knowledge assets grounding the company's performance achievement, drives managers in the understanding of those knowledge domains that are strategic for company's competitiveness. Therefore, "KADS" can utilise information resulting from "KAMS" (Relation B, Figure 5). In particular, indicators and metrics defined in "KAMS" can be handled for obtaining aggregate indicators. Moreover, the analysis and understanding of a company's knowledge domains and competencies provide important information for identifying the key knowledge assets supporting the achievement of company's performances.

The aggregate assessment of company's knowledge domains and competencies can contribute to define the type and nature of the information to be provided to the market in "KACS" (Relation C, Figure 5). In addition, the information required from the market can be particularly useful for understanding the knowledge domains and competencies to be developed to sustain organisation growth and wealth creation.

Finally, the "KACS," facilitating the understanding of the type and nature of the information required from the market and from company's

Figure 5. Relationships among the knowledge asset assessment strategies

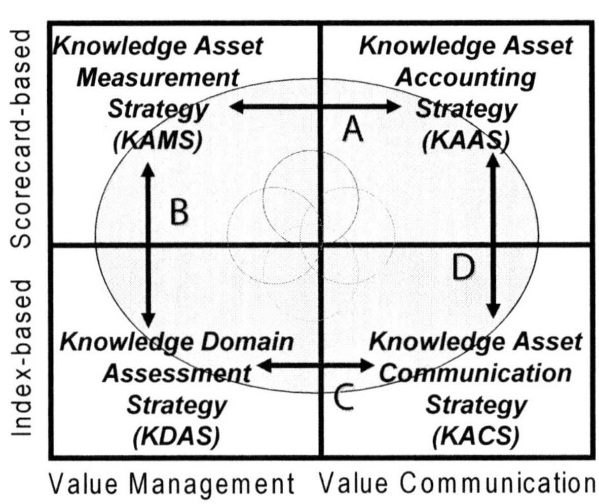

stakeholders, can drive the development of "KAAS" (Relazione D, Figure 5), as well as the "KAAS" define a framework for building aggregated indicators suitable for communicating company's knowledge assets endowment to the market.

CONCLUSION

The exploitation of knowledge resources, as strategic source for acquiring and maintaining company's competitive advantage requires, at organisational level, approaches and tools for its evaluation. In today's global business, organisations need to integrate the measurement and management of company's tangible assets with the assessment of knowledge assets. This involves, at organisational level, the need of approaches and tools to disclose, evaluate, manage, and monitor knowledge assets.

This chapter has analysed an issue not enough explored in the strategic and management literature, the meaning and contents of knowledge-asset assessment strategies. Indeed, even if in the last decade a number of models to assess intellectual capital have been proposed, they lack a clarification of their strategic focus. With the aim to fill this gap, four main knowledge-assets assessment strategies have proposed. They can be adopted by organisations to evaluate their knowledge resources. The identification of these strategies not only contribute to advance the theory of knowledge-asset assessment, but also provide insights to managers to better define and implement models and approaches for measuring organisational knowledge resources. Especially, they support managers in choosing and arranging critical information for defining the most suitable decisions and actions concerning the effective management and development of company's intellectual capital.

REFERENCES

Barney, J. B. (1991). Firm resources and sustained competitive advantage. *Journal of Management, 17*(1), 99-120.

Barth, M. E., Clement, M. B., Foster, G., & Kasznik, R. (2003). Brand values and capital market valuation. In J. Hand, & B. Lev (Eds.), *Intangible assets: Measures, values, rnd Risks.* NY: Oxford University Press.

Bierly, P., & Chakrabarti A. (1996). Generic knowledge strategies in the US pharmaceutical industry. *Strategic Management Journal, 17,* Winter Special, 123-135.

Bourne, M. (Ed.). (2001). *Handbook of performance measurement.* London: GEE Publishing Ltd.

Camp, R. S. (1989). *Benchmarking: The search for industry best practices that lead to superior performance.* Milwaukee, WI: ASQC Quality Press.

Carmeli, A., & Tishler, A. (2004). The relationships between intangible organizational elements and organizational performance. *Strategic Management Journal, 25,* 1257-1278.

Carlucci, D., Marr, B., & Schiuma, G. (2004). The knowledge value chain – How intellectual capital impacts business performance. *International Journal of Technology Management, 27*(6-7), 575-590.

Carlucci, D., & Schiuma, G. (2007). Exploring intellectual capital concept in strategic management research. In L. Joia (Ed.), *Strategies for Information Technology and Intellectual Capital: Challenges and Opportunities.* London: Idea Group Inc.

Deng, Z., Lev, B., & Narin, F. (2003). Science and technology as predictors of stock performance. In J. Hand& B. Lev (Eds.), *Intangible assets: Measures, values and risks.* NY: Oxford University Press.

Grant, R. M. (1991). The resource-based theory of competitive advantage: Implications for strategy formulation. *California Management Review, 33*(3), 14-35.

Hand, J. R. M. (2003). Profits, losses, and the nonlinear pricing of Internet stocks. In J. Hand, & B. Lev (Eds.), *Intangible assets: Measures, values and risks.* NY: Oxford University Press.

Hansen M. T., Nohtria N., & Tierney T. (1999). What's your strategy for managing knowledge? *Harvard Business Review*, March-April, 106-116.

Harvey M. G., & Lusch R. F. (1999). Balancing the intellectual capital books: Intangible liabilities. *European Management Journal, 17*(1), 85-92.

Lev B. (1999). Seeing is believing-A better approach to estimating knowledge capital. *CFO Magazine*, April.

Liebowitz, J. (1999). *Knowledge management handbook.* Boca Raton, FL: CRC Press.

Marr, B., Grey, D., & Schiuma, G. (2004). Measuring and valuing intangible assets – What, why, and how. In M. Bourne (Ed.), *Handbook of performance measurement.* London: Gee.

Marr, B., & Schiuma, G. (2003). Intangible assets – Defining key performance indicators for organisational knowledge assets. *Business Process Management Journal, 10*, 4.

Neely, A. (1998). *Performance measurement - Why, what, and how.* London: The Economist Books.

Roos G., Pike S., & Fernström L., (2005). Valuation and reporting of intangibles – State of the art in 2004. *International Journal of Learning and Intellectual Capital, 2*(1), 21-48.

Roos, G., & Roos, J. (1997). Measuring your company's intellectual performance. *Long Range Planning, 30*, 3.

Roos, J., Roos G., Dragonetti, N. C., & Edvinsson, L. (1997). *Intellectual capital: Navigating the new business landscape.* London: Macmillan.

Rumelt, R. P. (1984). Towards a strategic theory of the firm. In R. B. Lamp (Ed.) *Competitive strategic management.* NJ: Prentice Hall.

Sullivan, P. H., Jr., & Sullivan, P. H. S. (2000). Valuing intangible companies - An intellectual capital approach. *Journal of Intellectual Capital, 1*(4), 328-340.

Wernerfelt, B. (1984). A resource based view of the firm. *Strategic Management Journal, 5*(3), 171-180.

Wiig, K. M. (1997). Knowledge management: An introduction and perspective. *The Journal of Knowledge Management, 1*(1), 6-14.

Zack, M. (1999). Developing a knowledge strategy. *California Management Review, 41*(3), 125-145.

Chapter IV
Division of Interfirm Activities in the Knowledge-Based Economy:
The Crucial Role of Knowledge Processors

Poul Houman Andersen
University of Aarhus, Denmark

He who receives an idea from me receives instruction himself without lessening mine; as he who lights his taper at mine receives light without darkening me.

Thomas Jefferson, 1813

ABSTRACT

In order to capture market dividends and stay at par with the competition in the knowledge-based economy, firms must constantly develop their skill profile. There is considerable scope for learning through interfirm learning processes. However, the uncertain and costly nature of this process hampers exchange of knowledge in interfirm networks. This opens up for a new form of intermediary specialised in the absorption, generation, and dissemination of knowledge: the knowledge processor. This contribution addresses the core strategic issues faced by this type of firm, and illustrates the process through a case study of a knowledge processor.

INTRODUCTION

In the current debate, the role of learning and knowledge is repeatedly stressed as a distinguishing feature of the new economic realities. Several contributions point at the importance of knowledge and learning as the true generators of economic growth (Freeman & Soete, 1997; Romer, 1995). Knowledge has always been central to production activities, and it may therefore seem inaccurate to use this term to describe the present state of affairs in economic development as compared to the "old economy." However, a distinguishing mark today is that firms can no longer rely on a relatively stable set of skills and resources for capturing market dividends, but must constantly renew their knowledge for to stay at least at par with the competition (Lundvall & Foray, 1996).

The single most important distinguishing factor of the learning or knowledge-based economy[1] is the widespread utilisation information and communication technology networks, which has made possible an economy in which trade and specialisation are driven by the supply-side learning behaviour of specializers (Storper & Salais, 1997). Maintaining competitiveness is increasingly linked to the range and speed of innovation in the globalizing marketplace. The competitive stance of the single firm hinges upon its ability to outpace the imitation and catch-up attempts of competitors by constantly renewing and generating knowledge as well as capturing knowledge from intellectual property rights. Interfirm interaction plays a crucial role in such learning processes (Lundvall, 1993). In order to survive the race for innovation and technological flexibility, firms seek external partners to exchange and develop technological capabilities (Andersen & Christensen, 2000).

Behind the alleged growing importance of learning in the economy, a new rationale for explaining interfirm division of labour is arising. Whereas traditional theory explains segregation of firm activities from potential efficiency gains from deepened specialisation, recent thinking in knowledge-based economy may explain division of labour based on incentives to learn rather than achieving gains from specialisation. This chapter contributes to this discussion by conceptualising one particular role in this new scheme of coordination: the knowledge processor. The particular competence of this firm is in the area of identifying potential learning synergies between firms with complementary learning profiles. Taking on a case study of Cotas Computer Technology, a Danish developer and manufacturer of advanced electronic control systems within the machining industry, we follow an example on how this strategic role can evolve and become organised. We use this to address more fundamental issues in the knowledge-based economy pertaining to property rights and governance structures. An overview of the chapter is provided in Frame 1.

CONCEPTUALISING THE ROLE OF KNOWLEDGE PROCESSORS IN THE KNOWLEDGE-BASED ECONOMY

There are many viewpoints on how to conceptualise knowledge and how this concept relates to information and learning (Burton-Jones, 1999; Nonaka & Takeuchi, 1995; Weick, 1991). These concepts are often loosely defined and used interchangeably, which adds confusion rather than clarity to the issue. In this contribution, knowledge is defined as process of establishing and restructuring the logical structures held by a recipient or group of recipients. Rather than hoarding stocks of knowledge, as might be the case in stable environments, knowledge processing in the knowledge-based economy is an ongoing genesis of restructuring knowledge that both includes cumulating and discarding information (Hedberg, 1981). Central to this process is the human brain and its capacity to

Frame 1.

process information. Organisations may be seen as complementary memory bins that extend the individuals' information processing capabilities by storing, selecting, and directing information to recipients (Walsh & Ungson, 1991). Information, on the other hand, consists of sensory data that are intelligible to the recipient, whereas learning and unlearning concerns the process of acquiring and discarding information and skills.

Learning from other firms lies in the centre of what is discussed as the increasing returns to scope of network externalities. By interfirm learning, we here mean how an organization, though interacting with another firm, may develop resources and skills that make it possible to alter existing patterns of organizational practice. From the viewpoint of traditional economics, it could be argued that the immediate benefits of interfirm learning are positively related to exchanging proprietary knowledge. However, this type of knowledge should be protected from other companies, as openness may mean sacrificing the rationale of the company due to the public good nature of knowledge (Arrow, 1974). This notion hinges on an understanding of information and knowledge as interchangeable. In our view, knowledge and information represents different but strongly complementary concepts. Information differs from knowledge as information may represent different value, depending on the existing knowledge of the recipient. From the viewpoint of knowledge-based economies, the link between knowledge and value is transitory. There is a fundamental trade-off between the utility and the scarcity of knowledge, as existing technology-based advantages are constantly challenged. Hence, knowledge that is not constantly renewed through interaction with competent exchange partners will eventually lose value (Boisot, 1995; Nooteboom, 1999).

The linkage between learning and interfirm collaboration is well-known (Lundvall, 1985;

Maskell & Malmberg, 1997; Porter, 1998). Learning presupposes exposure to optimum learning possibilities that may be provided through problem solving in interfirm contexts. As firms collaborate, they join resources and provide access to their resources and activities to other organizations. Another and equally salient feature of the new economic realities is the association between intensified competition and interfirm collaboration. A survey of more than 1,860 Danish firms showed a significant linkage between firms experiencing strong competitive pressure and the propensity to collaborate with suppliers and customers (Lundvall, 1997).

Most discussions of the knowledge-based economics take place in a macroeconomic setting. Less discussed, however, are coordination processes at the microeconomic level by which knowledge is obtained, processed, and disseminated through interfirm interaction. Interfirm learning and knowledge acquisition possibilities seldom present themselves in the raw. Knowledge is often only represented in partly codified forms, which makes linking, and transmission of knowledge resource demanding (Von Hippel, 1994). Unbundling and rebundling of knowledge remains one of the most important features of the learning economy (Lundvall, 1995). Moreover, there are specific complications related to knowledge that are partly private and partly public as they represent a shared strategic asset that utilisation may lead to interfirm rivalry (Arrow, 1994; Chesbrough & Teece, 1996). For the individual firm, the contradicting interests of firms may hinder knowledge-sharing activities, as uncertainty avoidance may lead to safeguarding behaviour and ignorance of possibilities (Foxall, 1988). Markets have fundamental problems in carrying out the identification of potential partners (Andersen, 1999). Assortment and search costs are fundamental obstacles for the individual firm in the process. Moreover, institutionalising learning processes is a costly endeavour for the individual firm. Therefore, in the ongoing exchange of knowledge, interfirm learning may, in itself, be a target for specialisation and interfirm division of labour, as some actors take up the core responsibility for coordinating flows of knowledge exchange whereas others may contribute to the exchange as affiliated firms to this exchange process.

Possibilities for interfirm learning relate to interfirm cognitive distance (Nooteboom, 1999). The problem of matching competent partners is connected to the question of the limits on the knowledge of other market participants and the possible gains from collaboration. Hence, adjoining in interaction with the purpose of mutual learning gains necessitates a mediating institution (Andersen, 1999). Often (but not always) firms take on this role. This contribution seeks to clarify the role of this type of economic actor and the underlying merits of its strategic position. This role is described as one of knowledge processors. We define a knowledge processor as an economic actor who obtains knowledge from matching firm's complementary needs for learning and disperses their findings when fulfilling other firms' learning needs. Participating firms adhere to norms of reciprocity as they expect to obtain knowledge in exchange of offering their own know-how. Central in this process is the knowledge processor, which obtains, processes, and disseminates knowledge. Usually, the knowledge processor acts as a core, where information is obtained from one actor, codified, and further transmitted to the remaining actor in the "ring" of firms in an ongoing exchange of focused technological knowledge.

Knowledge Processors Compared to R&D Joint Ventures

In the so-called "old economy," the knowledge-sharing task was clarified either by emerging standards issued by firms controlling substantial market power to enact the dominant design, or by third-party industry associations issuing common standards, or through consortia of firms, working in R&D joint ventures. In the 1980s, as the attention towards technological interfirm cooperation started to stir interest among researchers, international joint ventures were seen as key form of collaborating on developing a specific set of capabilities. Joint ventures in R&D were seen as a short-time purposeful arrangement between two (often otherwise competing) firms aiming at achieving some common goal by each dedicating a significant set of resources (Hamel, 1991). The key motive behind such arrangements concerned the reduction, minimizing, and sharing of uncertainty related to inventing new technologies or even setting industrial standards. The strategic alliance between Sony and Phillips, when developing and introducing to the market the CompactDisc standard, may be seen as an archetype in this form of collaboration. However, as the economic demand shifts towards increasing needs for constant learning, the potential risk of lock-in with a specific partner in developing a specific technology may become too restrictive. A looser coupling of partners may be called for, allowing for a relatively easier entry and exit of partners into the ongoing "conversation" of knowledge development. Thus, although the role of the knowledge processor clearly fits into the type of technological cooperation aiming at improving the long-term competitiveness of the product-market combinations of the firms involved (Haagedoorn, 1993), it is distinguishable from the type of joint-venturing activities of an economy driven by economies of scale and scope rather than by economies of variety and learning. First, in a rapidly changing industrial setting, it is very difficult ex ante to access the possible costs and benefits of engaging in shared R&D activities as the potential outcome is hard to access. R&D ventures "lock-in" partners in a scheme of codependence that includes overspecialization, and may lead to limited learning possibilities (Miles & Snow, 1992). Knowledge processors aim at administering flows of knowledge rather than hoarding knowledge stocks for subsequent capitalization (Table 1). By constantly assessing new needs and developing new solutions for customers, clients of knowledge developers do not risk lock-in problems or problems of overspecialization to the same extent. Also, literature on traditional R&D ventures points to the dangers of competitive learning. In R&D joint ventures, participating firms seek to maximize their appropriation of shared outcomes while reducing their own costs, undermining the conditions for the generation of mutual gains in order to win the race of getting to the future first (Hamel, 1991). These problems are less salient in the scheme of the knowledge processor, as actors do not directly collaborate and are not joining in the same race and are not approaching the same future. Incentives for mutual learning are therefore more salient among complementary partners.

Moreover, there is a variation of the problem of revelation in R&D joint ventures, as issued by Arrow (1974): How do you judge whether coinvesting in a specific technology is worthwhile before you commit yourself? Knowledge processors at

Table 1. Knowledge processors and R&D Joint Ventures: A comparison of key issues

	R&D Joint Ventures	***Knowledge processors***
Knowledge development	Generating stocks of knowledge	Generating a nd a dministering k nowledge flows
Synergistic effects	Competitive learning	Complementary learning
Governance	Ensuring mutual safeguards	Developing partner confidence

the same time can as trusted consultants for the individual firm helping them overcoming their knowledge gap without revealing the information and, at the same time, bridge a generic gap over an array of industrial settings. For the knowledge processor, therefore, an important issue is to assess and develop the partners' confidence.

Strategic Challenges for the Knowledge Processor

There is clearly room for economic actors to take on the function of matching and adjoining diverse learning profiles of firms, which are dispersed in economic space, but which may have complementary needs for exchanging knowledge in the eyes of the actor. As described by Hayek (1945), economic actors possess knowledge of circumstances of the fleeting moment that may be translated into economic value by interlinking actors with complementary schemata of needs and wants. For the knowledge processor, at the core, the advantage of this arrangement clearly lies in its ability to both source and supply knowledge for the ring firms; the basic incentive lies in the ability to participate in a buyer-supplier relationship with a capable and innovative supplier. Two principal problems, however, are general to the role of the knowledge processor. First, there is the problem of identifying and gaining access to solve learning problems that are crucial and generic to a group of firms and second, the problem on how to coordinate the process of knowledge development.

Identifying Learning Problems and Gaining Access to Solve Them

Discovering opportunities for adjoining firms in learning processes can best be characterised as an entrepreneurial networking process. Such learning problems do not present themselves "in the raw." Their discovery depends on the intentionality and framing capability of specific actors, who may identify a possibility for effectuating problem solving across a range of industries. This form of enterprising behaviour clearly is linked to entrepreneurship. Kirzner (1973) describes the entrepreneur as a person who assiduously exploits opportunities by organising those in control of resources. From the perspective of entrepreneurial actors in the learning economy, the industrial context presents itself as a set of complex interdependencies that may be arranged according to their interpreting abilities. A learning-exchange opportunity arises when the entrepreneur invents and devises a pattern that is seen as exchange effective to other actors (Snehota, 1990). Successful actors possess unique capabilities in this respect and enact knowledge-matching opportunities rather than filling out learning-opportunity slots.

The nature of knowledge resources puts employer relationships at the centre stage in the company policy. Knowledge capital is essentially vested in the employed personnel. Knowledge capital concerns the training, experience, judgement, intelligence, relationships, and insights of employees (Barney, 1991). In the new realities of the knowledge-based economy, employment relationships change. Flexible arrangements, where knowledge-workers constantly develop their skills through a variety of temporary work arrangements, are increasingly becoming the rule in OECD countries (Standing, 1997). In order to manage their portfolio of career opportunities, workers are carefully considering their knowledge acquisition possibilities at specific employers and how they affect the future career options. For the firm in the knowledge-based economy, this development presents a serious challenge of attracting and maintaining relationships to knowledge workers important for maintaining the interpretative abilities of the organisation. Firms are therefore increasingly using employee leasing and outsourcing schemes to cope with the transitory nature of employment relationships.

Abilities to spot opportunities for matching knowledge often go hand in hand with their network positions as knowledge in a market economy is localised and situational (Hayek, 1945). Entrepreneurs, like everybody else, obtain information in a social context and make judgements based on their interaction with others. Hence, spotting opportunities and accessing actors often coexist. In itself, accessibility presents a unique problem for the knowledge processor. Even though firms may find it relevant to engage in interfirm learning, they may also be reluctant to this type of activity, as it presents a potential threat of being "outlearned" to them. As described by Hamel (1990), interfirm collaboration may be conceptualised as a competitive race of getting to the future first. Providing access to other firms may therefore entail problems of establishing safeguards. Therefore, the challenge for the knowledge processor is to achieve an interlocking on intentionality that is to convince potential partners that being involved in a learning collaboration is worth the effort and not associated with problems pertaining to the moral hazard of partners. Given that there is a temptation to defect because the advantage may outdo associated costs; a knowledge processor fulfils the role of establishing order through issuing trust to partners involved. Hence, all partners regarding both competence and intent must trust a third party. Trust between firms refers to the confidence that a partner will not exploit the vulnerabilities of the other (Barney & Hansen, 1994). The knowledge processor must hold a credible reputation of both competence and it must be clear for involved parties that acting as a partner for this particular firm is complementary to any other business activity taken on by the knowledge processor (Nooteboom, 1999). In this sense, the knowledge processor can remedy the problem of knowledge revelation, as pointed out by Arrow (1974). By being viewed as competent and trustworthy by all parties involved, it is able to assess both the value and relevance of knowledge exchange without actually revealing (and thereby supplying) this valuable knowledge.

Organizing Processes of Interfirm Knowledge Development

The second strategic challenge facing knowledge processors relates to the question of accessibility. Here, the social capital of the actors vested in their network of friends, colleagues, and general contacts are of great importance. The critical issue is to achieve organizing; that is, to align the interests, timing, and so forth, among actors involved in a complementary fashion, and to ensure and monitor the progress of knowledge development of these firms. The structure of the actors' network with other firms plays an important role for accessibility and combination of actors with complementary needs for knowledge development (Burt, 1992). Working with firms from different industries may enhance the knowledge processors' ability to develop novel innovations, as the scope for technological synergies are better achieved across complementary rather than identical knowledge sharing interfaces (Kotabe & Swan, 1995). According to this view on social networking, developing links between firms may be conceived as a process of accumulating social capital, which can be optimised by avoiding redundancy in network connections, as multiple links into the same knowledge area does not provide the focal actor with any novel information. On the other hand, such policies must be traded off by a policy maintaining coherence in a portfolio of learning relationships (Andersen, 1995).

Knowledge processors face a classical problem of organising stakeholders: They must develop an organisational form that both coordinates bilateral knowledge flows efficiently (that is avoiding problems of both shirking and opportunism) and at the same time provides the necessary incentives for participants to continue their collaboration. Social relations that provide participants the incentives to collaborate are of crucial importance in a specialised division of labour aiming at mutual gains of learning (Lazonick, 2000). Both problems relate to the selection of members. First, members must have complementary interests in a specific area (i.e., process technology). At the same time, they should not have conflicting interests, for instance, being rivals in specific technologies or markets. Secondly, knowledge processors must ensure that the learning contribution is fairly critical and relevant to all partners, and that learning can be transmitted between partners with little additional costs, meaning that each partners' devotion of resources into this area creates good administered by the knowledge processor. This raises the important problem of economising on the limited cognitive capabilities of attention and absorption decision-makers (Cohen & Levinthal, 1990). Therefore, buffering participants from superfluous information is a related and important task of intermediation for the knowledge processor.

THE WILLS AND WAYS OF A KNOWLEDGE PROCESSOR: COTAS COMPUTER TECHNOLOGY (CCT)

Methodology and Data

The methodology used is a detailed case study as described by Yin (1991). During the data collection process, multiple sources of evidence and chains of evidence were established. Data has been collected through interviews with personnel from Cotas as well as from its main customers, archival data, press releases, and observation. A semistructured interview guide has been used, and follow-up interviews have been made in order to clarify specific issues. All interviewed persons have received interview transcripts and have commented on these. Also, involving key interviewees to comment and review the case drafts helped to ensure the validity of the case.

Cotas: Background information

CCT is an advanced subcontracting firm within the electromechanical and apparatus industry, encompassing a wide range of industrial branches. In these branches of industry, it is increasingly often the case that the accelerating pace of technological change forces a wide range of producers to constantly renew their product lines.

The company was formed in 1979 by three engineers who decided to leave DTI, a consultancy firm, in order to start a development and manufacturing enterprise based on their current knowledge of the EC technology and the industry, including their existing customer relationships. Their business activities included (among other things) manufacturing and development of electronic control systems tailored to meet specific customers needs, which quickly grew into their major business area. Although still a small firm, it has experienced a rapid growth over the past 2 decades. In 1999, the turnover reached 103 million DKK, and they have more than 120 employed. More than 50% of operating costs stem from research and development activities. Recently, Vestas Wind Energy, the largest producer of wind turbines in the world and its most important customer, acquired CCT. However, the company continues to operate as an independent business unit, as recently pointed out by the chairman of Vestas Wind Energy[2]. Moreover, Cotas continues as an independent profit centre, with representatives from Vestas on the board.

If we are to continue as a valuable R&D partner for Vestas we must maintain a range of diverse development activities in order to attract skilled personnel and maintain the inflow of impulses from other branches of industry... Vestas are sure that we remain competitive if we are also competing on the open market (Ole R. Hansen, Cotas).

Spotting the Opportunity for Knowledge Transmission Through Interfirm Partnerships

Based on their consultant experience from serving customers in the machine industry, the founding engineers had realised that from a technical consulting point of view, customers in even diverse industrial settings were often facing similar problems. Clients faced a similar generic task of aligning sensor responses with machinery, which was solvable through electronic processor controls: The problem is well known from cybernetic theory: How to obtain signals from an external environment and transform this into information useful for some automated response. Whatever it concerned obtaining wind strength and relating this to the control of blade angels on wind turbines or measuring the temperatures on frozen food in order to reach the optimum "freeze-in" sequence in food processing, a fair number of the components in a solution would be the same. Moreover, whatever knowledge was obtained in one case may quickly be implemented in other solutions. Hence, by spotting and taking over this activity for clients, economies of scope would be reachable.

Our business philosophy is that we should concentrate on the development of PLCs and free resources internally for the firm to work on their core skills...because of our focus we cultivate technological disciplines that none of our customers would be able to take up and may not know about...this is our advantage. This idea has proven valid, especially in the latter years. The costs of software and hardware are so extensive that no single firm in Denmark can capitalise its investments in this equipment. (Ole Riis Hansen, Cotas)

However, there was a problem of gaining access. As process logic controls often was regarded as critical to the performance of the customers' product, it was often not possible to take over the design of these systems. Moreover, electronic control systems are often an integral part of the product design. Standard interfaces are therefore not obtainable as in modular designs. Experience from their work as consultants had taught the engineers that customers often called for consultants at a fairly late state of product design, meaning that optimal solutions were not always applicable. EC systems often tamper with the fundamental product architecture, which is partly frozen at the late stages of product development.

Cotas provides us with PLCs, which are tailored to our product assortment of industrial laundry machines. So far we the only producer of this type of machinery which have an interfaces completely adapted to our needs. Our competitors use standard interfaces. They (Cotas) typically join us in our product development activities as an active participant and perform cost-benefit analyses before they contribute to our activities...so far this has been a excellent partnership for both us and them (Carsten Thomsen, Jensen Group).

Therefore, in order to reach the full potential of the idea of knowledge sharing between customers, CCT would have to find a way to associate with the internal product design teams at a fairly early stage of the product. This was basically an incentive problem, which CCT solved by giving away, for free, its ideas on a "no cure no pay" basis. Customers allowing CCT in at the early project planning stage of a new product design would not have to pay for development costs, but was only to be charged from the subsequent buying of control devices from CCT. As expressed by CCT in their information material:

We develop the electronics and you only pay the development costs if the end result lives up to your specification of requirements. You can even spread the cost, so that you only pay us once we are busy manufacturing the electronic components

Figure 1. Activity portfolio for Cotas

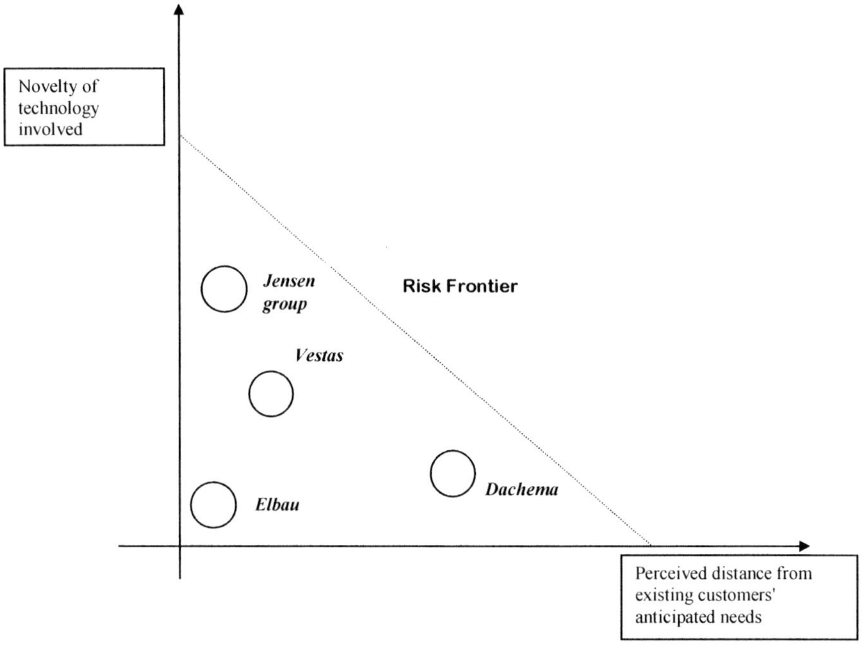

and your product is being sold on the market. We believe this is the best, most inexpensive and least risky alternative available to anyone wishing to integrate electronics into commercial products (Cotas Handout).

In this sense, CCT acts as a risk sharer, and has a direct interest in the commercial success of the product, which further convinced customers of the loyalty of CCT.

We start a new customer relationship by assessing whether this customer is interesting for us, as seen from our existing customer portfolio. Next, we conduct an analysis - which is free for the customer and present a sketch including a price estimate, presenting the novel possible features of the product. (Søren Jakobsen, Sales Engineer, Cotas).

This also means that Cotas takes an active role in assessing the commercial possibilities for taking up activities a client, and relating them to existing activities in order to assess coherence of development activities (see Figure 1).

The portfolio model presents a range of activities carried out by Cotas with respect to the novelty of technology and the ability to share the developed skills with other customers. Some projects hold only little merits for other customers (for instance a project for Dachema involving measurement of pressure in gas containers). Other projects hold strong sharing opportunities, but also entail great development efforts and demand investments in new hardware and training of personnel (as in the case of a project for Jensen Group). In some cases, truly generic projects are found that hold great potential benefits for all partners. For instance, Cotas has recently developed a system for integrating electronics and mechanics that substantially reduced the assembly costs, as cables and electronic can be mounted with little use of equipment. Finally, Cotas may also face development tasks that are beyond their risk frontier, that is, involve too high costs, are too distanced from existing activities, or both at the same time.

Figure 2. The generic steps of knowledge transmission

Coordinating Processes of Knowledge Transmission at CCT

Paraphrasing the literature on product development, three generic steps in the knowledge processing activities of a knowledge transmitter can be found (Von Hippel, 1994) These steps concern (i) absorbing ideas, (ii) integrating them into existing knowledge base (memorising), and (iii) further distribution into other relations (dissemination). These steps are visualised in Figure 2, and absorption, integration, and dissemination are further discussed in the subsequent sections.

Absorption

CCTs first customer on the "no-cure-no-pay" partnership basis was Vestas Wind Energy. Personal trust between engineers at Vestas and the founders of CCT undoubtedly played a role as lubricant for convincing partners to join this unusual set-up. However, references from solving control problems for Vestas worked as a pathbreaker for CCT in developing subsequent partnerships with other customers. Soon CCT realised that adjoining similar development needs in close collaboration with customers however, had to be carefully balanced against critical spillover of knowledge between competitors. Therefore, CCT developed a strategy of having only one partner in each industrial branch, carefully controlling for any possible clash of interests in the marketplace among its customers. Gradually, as CCT customer portfolio enlarged, CCT enforced its position as a central node in a knowledge-sharing network. It became a transmitter of knowledge on electronic control systems between firms with adjoining and complementary learning interests. Its customers account representatives from diverse industrial branches, such as packaging, wind turbine production, textile processing, and industrial cleaning machinery. Gradually, CCT has developed standard procedures on how to tackle their role in the product planning process, and has now routinized their procedures with respect to engagement in product development. For instance, CCT has built large meeting facilities in order to take over some of the product development meetings from their clients and have them in-house. CCT has found this to be an important signal when convincing partners on the partnership nature of the business arrangement and helping to blur the mental boundaries between CCT and its partners.

An important task is to spot new needs for electronic control systems and translating these into possible solutions for product development. The most important for Cotas, here, is their personnel of talented engineers. In a labour market characterized by scarcity of knowledge workers within this field, Cotas sees it as extremely important to develop an attractive work environment where not only firms benefit from talented engineers, but also that engineers constantly meet new challenges in a rewarding community of peers. Cotas, therefore, also has a project-based organisation, where the engineers team up for a given round and disband when the activity is carried out.

We have 60 engineers in our development facilities and more their budget is more than half of our total budget. .. Typically producers have room for no more than 2 or 3 persons developing plc-applications and this is not attractive for the type of engineers entering the labour market today. They will only go if the professional environment is rewarding, as they are able to obtain jobs in numerous places (Ole Riis Hansen, Cotas).

Integration

The founding engineers of CCT knew from their former employer that keeping up with all projects and sharing information between development teams was a hard task. Therefore, in order to cope with the growing array of technological knowledge and in order to make access to company knowledge easier, CCT very quickly introduced a policy of documentation on standard modules. Thus, for each new project, any new developments had to be documented and related to existing modules. For instance, program bits from systems for sensing possible wind turbine overload stemming from wind strength may be used to pick up environmental information on overload from sorting systems in the cold stores of retail chain warehouses. In this sense, by developing generic and reusable solutions, the component architecture gradually grows. Increasingly, the problems faced by firms can be solved using already existing components. Thus, developing a library and constantly adding to the stock of solutions, following simple formulas for documentation and possible applications, made this form of knowledge sharing much easier, and may be seen as a strategy of knowledge codification. Moreover, all client meetings are always handled by at least two engineers from CCT. This to make sure that some continuity and flexibility in terms of a collective organisational memory exist, should one specific engineer decide to leave CCT. Other organisational memory bins include written memos, customer files, and even videotaped meetings. Moreover, these memory bins are, in some cases, even shared with customers, using Web hotels and other devices for smooth knowledge sharing and virtual teamwork.

Dissemination

Utilising and sharing knowledge embodied in existing designs for solving new problems follows from the modularization and codification scheme addressed in the previous section. CCT has no patents or forms of legal protection around its developed components. CCT finds this unnecessary, as knowledge is constantly reformed and renewed through ongoing customer interaction.

In the EC industry, the average lifetime of a new technology is counted in months. We find the retentive approach of protecting knowledge more costly and less appealing than ensuring we are always at the forefront of the technological development (Ole Riis Hansen, Managing Director, CCT).

Thus, CCT sees their core capability in mastering this storage, and in- and outflow of knowledge through network relationships rather than protecting a core of knowledge through patent rights, and so forth. This also means that customers have access to most of the CCT component library through extranet.

As more customers adjoin with CCT on a partnership basis, the possibility for sharing development costs increases, thus decreasing the no-cure-no-pay risk for CCT and enhancing the overall value for other partners, as new clients also mean the possibility for having new ideas transferred by an increasingly competent supplier. Thus, when Vestas Wind Energy took over CCT, this had no effect on the existing relationships as this directly threatened no partner, and the interests of Vestas are only to continue the current set-up for knowledge sharing rather than restricting it.

In some cases, CCT acts not only as a translator of possible needs into technical wants, but may also use its current knowledge on control systems from complementary industries to develop ideas on control features that the customer has not thought of beforehand. Cotas clearly see it in their interest to constantly update their clients on new technologies, as this helps to justify their price policy and to raise capital for new equipment. Moreover, by constantly renewing the technology of their customers, they can focus on frequent adjustments rather than on issuing radical modifications of products.

When we develop for our customers our interests are not always matching our customers. Sometimes our customers find these development projects unnecessary and would rather prefer a general cut in our prices for providing our components. Our argument typically is, that we are paying for the development and they only pay by missing the opportunity to cut prices. On the other hand they will for the same costs receive an updated product which hopefully will contribute positively to their market position and turnover. (Ole Riis Hansen, Cotas).

INTERFIRM DIVISION OF LABOUR IN THE KNOWLEDGE-BASED ECONOMY: SOME CONCLUDING REMARKS ON CONSEQUENCES TO CONVENTIONAL THEORETICAL EXPLANATIONS ON INTERFIRM RELATIONSHIPS

Constructing new theoretical concepts in order to match the changing realities of the increasingly knowledge-based economy calls for many explorative endeavours. We have used a case study in order to provide food for thought in this process. The point made here is that the increasing importance of interactive learning in interfirm relationships calls for a new social division of economic roles, one which may be described in terms of knowledge processors and producers/users. However, the presented strategy followed by CCT may only be one of several possible solutions. There is no one optimum solution for managing knowledge flows between firms. Clearly, this is a situation of multiple equilibria, where some may be more successful than others, and some may be more enduring than others (Boisot, 1995; Nooteboom, 1999). The case presented here may be seen as an illustration fleshing out a potential game plan under the conventions of the new economy. Some important lessons can, however, be learned from CCTs example, which may help us further in developing new conceptual frames for understanding the role of property rights and the division of labour between firms in the knowledge-based economy.

If one accepts the notion that market positioning in more and more industries is fuelled by the ability to constantly renew market knowledge through interfirm learning relationships, managing knowledge flows and participating in knowledge exchange networks becomes more important than the hoarding and protection of knowledge stocks. As a consequence, property rights, with regards to protecting knowledge utilisation options are fading in importance. In the present case, this raises an important question in relation to the recent acquisition of CCT by its largest customer. The question is whether Vestas acquired this company because of its accumulated stock of knowledge, or whether Vestas simply added ownership to an existing relationship and has no intentions of changing CCTs' present role. The latter point might indicate that the true resource value lies in CCT's central position as knowledge processor within the network of complementary users and producers of knowledge, rather than within the company itself. In the first case, one may predict a scenario along the lines of conventional theorising, where Vestas integrate the company as a specialised R&D unit, given its importance for the functionality of its product. Vestas will start to erect barriers for unintended knowledge spillover to competitive producers of wind turbines. Hence, fewer resources are given to existing networking activities, which eventually are halted. In the latter case, the acquisition of Vestas have no consequences to the functioning of the network, as all interests are served most purposefully by maintaining this forum for exchanging and developing knowledge on EC controls. In the latter case, Vestas has simply added on ownership to its existing dense relations with CCT. So far, the second scenario has proven viable; CCT maintains its present customer base and as mentioned earlier, see footnote 2) the firm has signalled that it has no intentions of changing the present way of doing business.

A related point concerns the role of governance in the exchange of interfirm knowledge. The linking and coordination processes described in the case bear little resemblance with the traditional transaction cost economics view of governance with regards to activities surrounded by much asset specifity. Traditionally, such activities are ridden with information failure, as contracts concerning this exchange cannot be stipulated in advance and may involve prohibitive costs. Hence, such activities are best left to internal processes of coordination, allowing an entrepreneur the right to governance within certain limits (Coase, 1937). However, the possible advantages of exchanging knowledge between cognitive dispersed firms turn the equation of transaction and governance costs in favour of more distributed organisations. One explanation for this is that actors are involved in repeated interactions, and nonappliance to norms of reciprocity may exclude firms from future participation. Hence, reputational linking and credible commitments enter the interorganisational game as a norm-setting device (Dei Otatti, 1994; Kristensen, 1995).

In the set-up of CCT described here, reputational linking under the norms of reciprocity seems to play a central role (Andersen & Kristensen, 1999). We may define the existence of norms of reciprocity as the widespread acceptance of two related assumptions among actors: 1) that B reciprocates A's services and 2) that B's services to A are contingent on A's performance of positive functions for B (Gouldner, 1960). This contradicts the logic of transaction cost thinking, where one would expect CCT to charge lump-sum payments, given the potential risk of opportunism from its customers. In this case, the set-up described would resemble one of trilateral governance, where a third party is introduced to solve the problems of hold-up costs arising in the case of infrequent exchange of dedicated investments and significant advantages of externalisation (Nooteboom, 1999; Williamson, 1985).

Initial exchange is obtained through a combination of personal confidence, stemming from foregone business episodes, and the ability to return services in the form of knowledge access. Establishing the role of the knowledge processor is fuelled by only little more than reputational value. They draw mainly on external resources in their growth, and a central role is to keep the network in place and expanding it gradually (rather than abruptly). Later, as the network is established, CCT take on the role as a mechanism that compensates for or controls the tensions that arise in events of breakdown in reciprocity. The role of CCT is now one of ensuring and sustaining multilateral rather than bilateral norms of reciprocity. Under norms of multilateral reciprocity, A provides a service to (B,,,,n) under the assumption that an intermediary institution ensures the reciprocation of this service. Hence, norms of multilateral reciprocity are close to definition of market governance. Exactly by moving from one type of reciprocity to another enables CCT to perform the integration and balancing act as processor and transmitter of knowledge. Hence, their role is one of intermediating and balancing the interests of partners that, at times, may be conflicting.

REFERENCES

Andersen, M. M. (1999). Market institutions and interorganisational learning, In *Proceedings from Druid Winter Seminar.*

Andersen, P. H. (1995). Managing market resources. In L. Nørreklit, & H. M. Schoenfeld (Eds.), *Resources of the firm, creating, controlling, and cccounting.* DJØF Publishing Company.

Andersen, P. H., & Christensen, P. R. (2000). Interpartner learning in global supply chains: Lessons from NOVO nordisk. *European Journal of Purchasing and Supply Management, 6,* 105-116.

Andersen, P. H., & Kristensen P. H. (1999). The systemic qualities of Danish industrialism. In

P. Karnøe, P. H. Kristensen, & P. H,. Andersen (Eds.), *Mobilising resources and generating competencies.* Copenhagen Business School Press.

Arrow, K. (1974). *The limits of organisation.* New York: Norton & Company.

Arrow, K. (1994). Methodological Individualism and social knowledge, Richard T. Ely Lecture. In *AeA Papers and Proceedings, 84,* 2.

Barney, J. B., & Hansen, M. H. (1994). Trustworthiness as a form of competitive advantage. *Strategic Management Journal, 15,* 175–190.

Barney, J. G. (1991). Firms, resources, and sustained competitive advantage. *Journal of Management, 17*(1) 99-119.

Boisot, M. H. (1995). Is your company a creative destroyer? Competitive learning and knowledge flows in the technological strategies of firms. *Research Policy,* 485-506

Burt, R. S. (1992). The social structure of competition. In N. Nohria, & R. G. Eccles (Eds.), *Networks and organisation.* Boston: Harvard Business School Press.

Burton-Jones, A. (1999). *Knowledge capitalism.* London: Oxford University Press.

Chesbrough, H. W., & Teece, D. (1996). When is virtual virtuous? Organising for innovation. *Harvard Business Review, January-February,* 65-73.

Coase, R. H. (1937). The nature of the firm. *Economica, 4,* 386-405.

Cohen, W. M., & Levinthal, D. A. (1990). Absorptive capacity: A new perspective on learning and innovation. *Administrative Science Quarterly, 35,* 128-152.

Cotas Computer Technology. (2000). *There is only one thing we want to show you....*

Dei Otatti, G. (1994). Trust, interlinking transaction and credit in the industrial district. *Cambridge Journal of Economics, 18,* 529-546.

Foxall, G. R. (1988). The theory and practice of user-initiated innovation. *Journal of Marketing Management, 4*(2) 230-248.

Freeman, C., & Soete. L. (1997). *The economics of industrial innovation* (3rd ed.). Pinter Publishers.

Gouldner, A. W. (1960). The norm of reciprocity: A preliminary statement. *American Sociological Review, 25*(2) 161-178.

Hamel, G. (1990). Competition for competence and interpartner learning within international strategic alliances. *Strategic Management Journal, 12,* 83-103.

Hayek, A. (1945). The use of knowledge in society. *American Economic Review, 35,* 519-530.

Hedberg, B. (1981). How organizations learn and unlearn. In P. C. Nystrøm, & W. H. Starbuck (Eds.), *Handbook of organizational design*, volume I. Oxford University Press

Jefferson, T. (1813). *Thomas Jefferson to Isaac McPherson, 1813.* ME 13:333. Retrieved from http://etext.virginia.edu/jefferson/quotations/jeffcont.htm

Kotabe, M., & Swan, K. S. (1995). The role of strategic alliances in high-technology new product development. *Strategic Management Journal, 16*, 621-636.

Kristensen, P. H. (1995). On the constitution of economic actors in Denmark: Interacting skill containers and project organizers. In P. H. Hull, & R. W. Whitley (Eds.), *The changing European firm: Limits to convergence.* London: Routledge.

Krizner, I. M. (1973). *Competition and entrepreneurship.* University of Chicago Press

Lazonick, W. (2000). *The theory of innovative enterprise: Organization of innovation in the learning economy, DRUID 2000 Summer Conference paper.*

Lundvall, B-Å. (1985). *Product innovation and user-producer interaction.* Aalborg: Aalborg University Press.

Lundvall, B-Å. (1993). Explaining interfirm coorporation and innovation – limits of the transaction cost approach. In G. Graebher. (Ed.), *The embedded firm.* Routledge.

Lundvall, B-Å. (1995). *The learning economy – Challenges to economic theory and policy.* Working Paper no 9514, Bureau D'Economie Theorique et Appliquee, Universite Louis Pasteur, Strasbourg.

Lundvall, B-Å. (1997). Competition and industrial dynamics in a small, open economy. In *Proceedings from Druid Summer Seminar.*

Maskell, P., & Malmberg, A. (1997). Proximity, institutions, and learning Towards an explanation of industry agglomeration and regional specialization. In H. Eskelinen (Ed.), *Regional specialisation and local environment - Learning and competitiveness*, NordREFO Report 1997:3.

Miles, R. E., & Snow, C. S. (1992). Causes of failure in network organisations. *California Management Review, Summer*, 53-72.

Nonaka, I., & Takeuchi, H. (1995). The knowledge-creating company. London: Oxford University Press.

Nooteboom, B. (1999). Innovation and interfirm linkages: New implications for policy. *Research Policy, 28*, 793-805.

Porter, M. E. (1998). Clusters and the new economics of competition. *Harvard Business Review, November-December*, 77-90.

Romer, P. (1995). Beyond the knowledge worker. *World Link, January/February*, 56-60.

Snehota, I. (1990). *Notes on a theory of business enterprise.* Doctoral Dissertation, Uppsala University.

Standing, G. (1997). Globalisation, labour flexibility, and insecurity: The era of market regulation. *European Journal of Industrial Relations, 3*(1), 7-37.

Steinmueller, W. E. (2000). *Knowledge and learning in the information age.* DRUID conference paper, Rebild 2000.

Storper, M., & Salais, R. (1997). *Worlds of production.* Harvard University Press.

Valentin, F., Andersen, P. H., Dalum, B, Pedersen, T., & Villumsen, G. (1995). *Strategiske Virksomhedsrelationer (Strategic firm relationships)*, Velstand og Velfærd, bd. 5, Erhvervsministeriet.

Von Hippel, E. (1994). Sticky information and the locus of problem-solving. *Management Science, 4*, 429-439.

Walsh, J. P., & Ungson, G. D. (1991). Organizational memory. *Academy of Management Review, 18*(1), 57-91.

Weick, K. E. (1991). The nontraditional quality of organizational learning. *Organization Science, 2*(1), 116-123.

Williamson, O. E. (1985). *The economic institutions of capitalism.* Free Press

ENDNOTES

1 Whether to use the term learning economy or knowledge-based economy is the target of some dispute (Lundvall, 1995)

2 It was Vestas' intention that Cotas should continue to operate within the current business areas. "With Cotas' current strategy and with Vestas being Cotas' largest single customer, our need for deliveries from the company will be covered - and the versatility of the current business areas contributes keeping the very qualified staff and maintaining the research and development activities at a high level", informs Johannes Poulsen, Managing Director of Vestas. [Stock Exchange announcement, November 9, 1999]

Chapter V
The Conundrum of Valuing a Company's Intellectual Capital:
The Role of Taken-for-Granted Indicators

Luiz Antonio Joia
Brazilian School of Public Business Administration of Getulio Vargas Foundation, Brazil
Rio de Janeiro State University, Brazil

Paulo Sérgio da Silva Sanz
Brazilian School of Public Business Administration of Getulio Vargas Foundation, Brazil

ABSTRACT

Since the early 1990s, research has been conducted in an attempt to establish a viable and reliable manner of measuring the intangible assets, also referred to as the intellectual capital, of companies. Several models have been devised, most of them using indicators to evaluate the intangible assets of a given undertaking. In this chapter, exploratory field study methodology is used to analyse the behaviour of the "customer retention" indicator, which has been widely used to evaluate a company's relationship capital. Two of the largest Brazilian e-retailing groups are analysed in order to obtain an in-depth insight into the behaviour of their frequent customers via their digital channel. Conclusions are presented, indicating that the role of frequent customers in e-retailing companies can sometimes be widely divergent from that presented in existing academic literature. Finally, recommendations are made in order to reach a clearer understanding of the conundrum of valuing a company's intellectual capital via taken-for-granted indicators.

INTRODUCTION

The consolidation of intellectual capital as an actual knowledge field is still in progress. It should be remembered that years ago, some mavericks foresaw the importance of intangible assets for a company, laying down the initial foundations for this very recent discipline.

In 1945, Frederick Hayek presented research about the use of knowledge in society (Hayek, 1945). In a seminal work, Fritz Machlup from Princeton University produced an eight-volume work in 1962, under the general title: "Knowledge: Its creation, distribution, and economic significance" (Machlup cited in Stewart, 1997, p. 11). In this work, using data gathered in 1958, it was established that 34.5% of the gross national product of the United States could be ascribed to the information sector. In 1993, Peter Drucker analysed the new knowledge economy and its consequences (Drucker, 1993). Consequently, academics, researchers, and practitioners have increasingly highlighted the importance of the intangible assets of a corporation and even those of both countries and other organisations, including nonprofit entities.

A watershed was reached in July 1994, when a meeting took place in Mill Valley with a view to establishing how the knowledge of an organisation could be measured. Knowledge may be intangible, but that does not mean that it cannot be measured. Markets do precisely that when they value the stock of highly knowledge-intensive companies way above their book value.

In 1995, Skandia, the largest insurance and financial services company in Scandinavia, released its Intellectual Capital Annual Report, based on its Navigator framework (Edvinsson & Malone, 1997). Some other companies, like Dow Chemical, the Canadian Imperial Bank of Commerce, Posco, and so forth, to name but a few, also entered this new era.

Several research articles have been published, and timely *praxis* has been developed to measure the intellectual capital of an enterprise, such as Sveiby (1997); Roos *et al.* (Roos, Roos Dragonetti, & Edvinsson, 1997); Bontis *et al.* (Bontis, Keow, & Richardson, 2000); Guthrie and Petty (2000); Low (2000); Sánchez *et al.* (Sánchez, Chaminade, & Olea, 2000); Guthrie (2001); St Leon (2002); Rodov & Leliaert (2002); Hunt (2003), among others.

In order to understand the peculiarities associated with the measurement of intangible assets better, this chapter sets out to prove that some indicators used to measure the intellectual capital of a company cannot be taken for granted as effective measures for doing so, nor can they be adopted in these valuation models as a rule of thumb. This chapter posits that more rigour is required to verify whether or not these indicators are truly valid, that is, if they really contribute to explaining the final results of a company, namely its financial performance. The "customer retention" indicator, widely used in several methodologies to measure intellectual capital, is specifically analysed in this chapter in order to verify whether it can always be considered a valid measure for assessing intangible corporate assets.

The chapter is organised as follows: firstly, a bibliographical reference section is reviewed in order to elucidate the rationale used for this study; secondly, the research design, based on an exploratory field study, is described, as well as the hypothesis to be tested; thirdly, the data-set collected is presented and analysed, which leads to several findings. Lastly, conclusions are drawn and recommendations made in order to reach a clearer understanding of the conundrum of valuing a company's intellectual capital via indicators.

BIBLIOGRAPHICAL REFERENCES

Intellectual Capital Taxonomy

Based on research carried out by Edvinsson and Malone (1997), Roos *et al.* (1997), Sveiby (1997),

Stewart (1997) and Joia (2000), it is proposed that corporate capital taxonomy be used in this chapter.

The taxonomy adopted is based on the following equation:

MARKET VALUE = BOOK VALUE + INTELLECTUAL CAPITAL

This equation shows that stock value has a tangible portion (book value) in addition to an intangible component. Hence, assuming that the intellectual capital is greater than zero (IC>0), the market value/book value is greater than 1 (M/B>1); the more knowledge-intensive the company, the greater the M/B value.

The book value (also called financial capital) is then calculated using the following formula:

BOOK VALUE = MONETARY CAPITAL + PHYSICAL CAPITAL

and intellectual capital, formerly called goodwill by accountants, is calculated using the formula below:

INTELLECTUAL CAPITAL = HUMAN CAPITAL + STRUCTURAL CAPITAL

Human capital does not belong to the company, as it is a direct consequence of the sum of the expertise and skills of its employees. Structural capital belongs to the company, and can be traded (at least theoretically), as it is the actual environment built by the company to manage and generate its knowledge adequately. It is compounded by the internal structure or day-to-day operations of the company, encompassing its processes, databases, codes, culture, management style, and internal networks (such as intranets), namely its internal capital. Then, there is the external capital, which is concerned with the customers, suppliers, subcontractors, and other major players involved. Finally, there is the innovation capital, a direct consequence of the company's culture and its ability to create new knowledge from the existing base. Thus, the following formula summarises what has been said:

STRUCTURAL CAPITAL = INTERNAL CAPITAL + EXTERNAL CAPITAL + INNOVATION CAPITAL

Finally, the overall intellectual capital formula can be presented as:

INTELLECTUAL CAPITAL = HUMAN CAPITAL + INTERNAL CAPITAL + EXTERNAL CAPITAL + INNOVATION CAPITAL

It can be noticed that intellectual capital is compounded of four constructs, namely HC, IC, EC and IVC – that is, human, internal, external, and innovation capitals, respectively, each one of which interacts with the others (Hussi & Ahonen, 2002).

Some academics, including Alle (2000), have argued that a holistic rather than a cartesian approach is indicated for intellectual capital management. It would indeed seem to be the wisest option. However, the very reason for splitting the intellectual capital into different capitals lies in the need to measure the influence of each one of these capitals on the company's performance, so as to calculate an intellectual capital index (Joia, 2000; Roos *et al.*, 1997), which would be almost impossible to achieve using a holistic model. Furthermore, several authors, including Roos *et al.* (1997, p. 125), have argued that intellectual capital analysis must take the time factor into account as a very important variable, that is, that any intellectual capital analysis must be dynamic rather than static. Again, this is advisable, and the explanation for it lies in the difference between "stock" and "flow" of knowledge (Johnson, 1999). However, as stated and proven by Joia (2000, pp. 81-83), some phenomena, such as the "time-lag trap" (the asynchronous relationship between a company's strategy and its intellectual capital index) have prevented academics and practitioners from fully grasping the dynamics of intellectual capital.

Based on Edvinsson and Malone (1997); Roos *et al.* (1997); Joia (2000); Bontis *et al.* (2000), and McPherson and Pike (2001), it can be stated that the correct strategic management of intellectual capital leads to superior business performance, specifically, better financial results, as stated by

Peppard and Rylander (2001, p. 231). These financial results support the leverage of the company's intellectual capital, which again impacts positively on its financial results, and so on, in a sustainable loop. Hence, each construct of intellectual capital should have a causal effect on the financial results of a company with the passing of time, and as these capitals are evaluated through indicators, every indicator should be validated, in order to show its influence on the company's financial results.

Moreover, as Roos (Roos cited in Chatzkel, 2002, p. 106) argued, addressing a company's drivers of value:

> *... Why are drivers of value important? These are drivers of value in the minds of customers. These are the drivers of perceived value. They are important because they impact on two drivers of cash. The first driver of cash is margin and the other driver of cash is revenue. Revenue is driven by revenue drivers. These are, for example, the number of client relationships, how long they last, how much they buy every time, and how frequently they buy ... .*

Thus, it can be perceived from this statement that the mark-up of frequent customers, their average ticket, and their interest in purchasing more expensive products/services are important drivers of cash and, consequently, potential intangible corporate assets.

External Capital and its Indicators

According to Edvinsson and Malone (1997), the main focus of the external capital (referred to by them as customer capital) of a company is the customer. The authors argue (pp. 94-95) that: "... the indicators associated to this capital must capture the flow of relationship between a company and its current and potential customers... ." According to them (pp. 95-99), customer type, customer duration, customer role, customer support, and customer success are the main facets of this capital.

Roos *et al.* (1997) broadened this concept (referred to by them as customer and relationship capital), adding supplier relationships, alliances with partners and shareholders, and other stakeholder relationships (p. 43) to the former categories.

Sveiby (1997), for his part, calls this concept external structure, and in addition to the customer and supplier relationships, adds the company's brand equity as another component.

It is important to stress here the very fact that all these academics and practitioners understood, in different ways, that it was important for a company to strengthen its links with its customers or, in other words, to cultivate the customers by winning over their loyalty. Sveiby (1997) divides customers into three categories, in order to establish which are the most profitable (pp. 178-179). Even Kaplan and Norton (1996), when defining the balance scorecard concepts, stated the importance of customer retention, defined by them as " ... the rate at which a business unit retains or maintains ongoing relationships with its customers" (Kaplan & Norton, 1996, p. 68).

As respected authors in this very recent knowledge field, these academics and practitioners have paved the way for other researchers and practitioners to take it as an established fact that the customer retention indicator has a positive effect on valuing the external capital; every time, everywhere, and for every industry.

Consequently, the impressive number of important authors who quote this indicator in their research as a relevant parameter for measuring the external intangible dimension of a business, without feeling the need to prove its reliability and validity, is hardly surprising. Among these authors we find Alle (2000, pp. 20 and 25); Sullivan Jr. and Sullivan Sr. (2000, pp. 36 and 43); Liebowitz and Suen (2000, p. 57); Sánchez *et al.* (2000, p. 323); Guthrie and Petty (2001, pp 35-36);

Gibbert *et al.* (Gibbert, Leibold, & Voelpel, 2001, pp. 113-116), Lim and Dallimore (2002, p. 270), and Pablos (2002, p. 298), to name but a few.

The main issue is not just whether or not an indicator is reliable, but also whether it is valid, every time, for every industry, everywhere. Reliability and validity are very different things. A given measure can be reliable but not valid in a given situation, that is, to be reliable is a necessary condition, albeit not sufficient for a measure to be valid all the time (see, for instance, Churchill, 1979). Even though an indicator can have no significant relationship with the financial results of a company, it can be a reliable one, as can be calculated using the alpha of Cronbach (Nunnally, 1967, pp. 226-35), for instance. However, it can be lacking in validity and jeopardize the construct and the model as a whole.

The next section explains why this indicator needs to be better understood.

Customer Retention and Customer Profitability

In relationship marketing literature, several authors have stressed the beneficial impact of customer retention on a corporation. Kotler (1999) claims that the longer a customer remains with a supplier, the more profitable this customer becomes for this supplier. Day (1999) suggests that companies achieve higher profitability by building long-term relationships with their customers. Peppers and Rogers (1993) claim that there is only one way a business can guarantee its financial sustainability, namely by cultivating loyal and satisfied customers. These authors allege that the more purchases a customer makes, the higher the mark-up obtained by the company will be. McKenna (1993) stresses this concept, stating that the development of strong ties with the customer is an effective way of leveraging a company's competitive advantage. Seybold (1998) ratifies all these ideas, stating that when a company loses a customer, it loses not only the potential profits that would be derived from this customer, but also the profits from the chain of customers who hear the disgruntled customer's negative commentaries. Reichheld and Sasser (1990) declare that the loss of a customer can have a higher impact on a company's profitability than other traditional factors associated with a company's competitive advantage. In a later study, Reichheld and Teal (1996) state that businesses with a high rate of customer defection will face a difficult future, with reduced profits, slow growth, if any, and shorter life expectancy.

In view of this, it is essential to assess the financial potential of all customers in order to quantify their importance *vis-à-vis* corporate profitability. Kotler (1999) recommends the use of LTV (*lifetime value*) methodology, which depicts the total spending of customers, within a specific product/service category, during their lives, independently of the company with which the business is transacted. According to Peppers and Rogers (1997), LTV represents the profit generated by customers minus the costs associated with their acquisition and retention, throughout the course of their relationship with a specific company.

Stone (1984) suggests the use of RFM metrics to classify customers according to recency, frequency of sales, and amount of money spent. For this author, the best customers, namely those who have the highest likelihood of buying again, are those who have purchased more recently, those who have purchased more frequently within a given timeframe, and those who have spent a sizeable amount of money.

These metrics seek to predict the financial potential of each customer, according to the share-of-wallet concept, as the company tries to increase its share in customer spending, rather than its share in the mass market (Sheth, Sisodia, & Sharma, 2000).

A relevant issue in customer retention is client acquisition cost. Relationship marketing theory often suggests that acquisition costs associated with winning over a new customer are five times greater than the costs involved in keeping an existing client satisfied. According to Goodman (1999), this metric originated from a study developed by TARP (Technical Assistance Research Program), in 1984, which sought to examine customer acquisition costs in relation to customer retention costs in an automobile company in the USA.

In the industry under scrutiny in this chapter (e-retailing one), the acquisition costs are mainly concentrated on advertising, which belongs to the "promotion" dimension of the traditional marketing mix (McCarthy, 1960). A report from CrossRoads (2001) indicates that the growth of advertising spending worldwide has been 30% greater than worldwide economic growth. According to the report, this pattern results from the belief companies have that continuous investment in advertising allows them to keep their market share in their industry.

In marked contrast with the authors quoted, very recent research has challenged the traditional methods adopted by most executives for retaining customers as well as the resulting managerial implications involved. Schultz and Hayman (1999) warn that if all the benefits accrued from customer retention claimed by companies were true, customer loyalty would not be to their advantage, as they would be paying higher prices and advertising the company for free, in addition to receiving worse attention from the company.

Dowling and Uncles (1997) suggest that customer loyalty is probably a consequence of the industry within which the company operates, as well as the strength of the company's brand name. According to them, investments in customer retention do not reap the desired benefits for the strategic positioning and brand equity of the company. Moreover, it is quite possible that these investments neither generate a significant rise in the number of frequent customers nor an increase in the customers' profitability to the company.

Some of Dowling and Uncles' (1997) ideas tally with an empirical study conducted by Reinartz and Kumar (2000) in a catalogue-based retailing company in the USA. In this study, evidence was found that ran counter to some traditional concepts regarding relationship marketing, such as:

a. The relationship between customer lifetime and the corresponding company's cumulative profitability was only verified, in a moderate way, with frequent higher-income customers – that is, merely a small percentage of all customers. Sporadic clients with higher incomes have higher LTV than those of frequent customers with lower incomes.
b. The commercial transaction value diminishes during the course of the relationship between a company and its customers. On the basis of this statement, the notion that the profits generated by frequent customers increase over the course of time is duly challenged.
c. As commercial transactions were analysed individually, frequent customers were considered less profitable, both in terms of higher- and lower-income clients. In contrast with traditional relationship marketing literature, Reinartz and Kumar (2000) suggest that frequent customers tend to purchase cheaper products than sporadic purchasers, as time goes by.
d. The concept that attendance costs are lower for frequent customers was rejected in the article quoted (Reinartz & Kumar, 2000). In order to back their theory, the authors used the ratio between mailing costs and customer revenues. The differences observed in the ratio between frequent and sporadic customers were not statistically significant.

In an even more recent study, Reinartz and Kumar (2002) concluded that companies should not focus exclusively on their frequent customers. These authors warn that mismanagement of customer retention can lead a company to make excessive investments in an attempt to retain incidental customers, as well as undervalue the financial potential of such customers.

This evidence is even more relevant when applied to e-commerce. In this area, customer defection is impressive due to the reduced asymmetry of information provided by electronic markets. Customers are therefore far more aware of their options, which leads to lower transaction and acquisition costs for products and services (Smith, Bailey, & Brynjolfsson, 1999).

RESEARCH DESIGN

In order to gather relevant input to carry out this research, two of the largest e-retailing groups in Brazil were investigated. The databases were analyzed quantitatively to assess the transaction profitability derived from sporadic and frequent customer purchases.

Due to the characteristics of the products commercialized, namely home appliances, this research is based on the premise that customers may only be considered frequent buyers if they make at least one purchase within a 12-month period (see, for instance, Santos & Costa, 1997). It should be stressed that this is the same criteria adopted by the firms under investigation to categorize their frequent consumers.

The customers were divided into two main groups, namely sporadic and frequent buyers. Each one of them was classified by their average ticket and segmented according to a "Pareto level," as suggested by Roos (cited in Chatzkel, 2002, p.111) and Reinartz and Kumar (2000), as presented in Table 1.

From the theoretical background presented, four hypotheses were developed to be tested quantitatively. These hypotheses draw mainly on the research of Kotler (1999), Day (1999), Peppers and Rogers (1993), McKenna (1993), Seybold (1998), Reichheld and Sasser (1990), and Reichheld and Teal (1996), whose ideas were presented earlier in this work. Thus, the following hypotheses are generated and presented as follows:

H1: The transaction profit derived from frequent customers increases as they purchase more frequently (from Day, 1999; Kotler, 1999; Peppers & Rogers, 1993; Reichheld & Teal, 1996);

H2: The ticket value of frequent clients increases as they buy more frequently (from Day, 1999; Kotler, 1999; Peppers & Rogers, 1993; Reichheld & Teal, 1996);

H3: Frequent customers purchase more profitable products than sporadic consumers (from Kotler, 1999; McKenna, 1993; Reichheld & Teal, 1996);

H4: Frequent clients purchase more expensive products than sporadic buyers (from Kotler, 1999; McKenna, 1993; Reichheld & Teal, 1996).

The statistical tests used to verify whether or not the hypothesis were viable, were based on variance analysis (ANOVA) and bivariate linear

Table 1. Customer segmentation

Category	Description
Sporadic 20%	Sporadic consumers with the highest 20% average ticket
Sporadic 80%	Other sporadic consumers
Frequent 20%	Frequent customers with the highest 20% average ticket
Frequent 80%	Other frequent customers

regressions of the data collected, developed with a significance level of 5% ($\alpha = 0.05$) (for more information about the adequacy of these tests to this problem, see Stevenson, 1978 and Wonnacott & Wonnacott, 1972).

This quantitative analysis dealt with the following selected attributes:

a. Customer purchasing frequency: number of purchases made by customers;
b. Transaction profit: profit accrued from purchases made by clients;
c. Ticket value: value of purchases made by customers.

The analysis included a sample of 10% of all customers who made purchases during the 42 months under investigation, for both e-retailers. In other words, 14,906 buyers at "Company A" and 12,786 clients at "Company B" were assessed. The real value of all monetary amounts were calculated using the inflation rate during the time frame assessed, that is, the value of every purchase was discounted using the inflation rate between the purchase date and the day of data extraction from the company databases. In this field study, individualized transaction profit margins, discounted taxes, and cost of capital were accessed by the author.

DATA ANALYSIS AND FINDINGS

In line with the empirical and theoretical background herein described, it was tested, in quantitative fashion, the four hypotheses listed concerning the financial behavior of transactions made by sporadic and frequent customers in the e-retailing realm, as presented below.

Hypothesis 1: *The transaction profit derived from frequent customers increases as they purchase more frequently.*

In order to test this hypothesis, it was used bivariate linear regressions to analyze the commercial transaction mark-up as being dependent on the purchasing frequency of each frequent buyer (Stevenson, 1978 and Wonnacott & Wonnacott, 1972). The regressions took the two segments of frequent customers into account (Pareto 20% and 80%). Table 2 summarizes this analysis.

From the regressions it can be seen that the coefficients are negative in both firms (-6.18 and -33.06, respectively) for the segment of frequent customers with the highest average ticket (Pareto 20%), indicating an inverse relationship between transaction profit and customer purchasing frequency. In the other segment of frequent buyers (Pareto 80%), the coefficients are positive (0.34 and 5.43, respectively), indicating that transaction profit increases as more purchases are made by customers. In other words, this proposition cannot be supported for frequent consumers with the highest average ticket (Pareto 20%).

This finding challenges the contention that customer retention always enables companies to obtain a premium price, as suggested by relationship marketing theory (Day, 1999; Kotler,

Table 2. Regressions of transaction profit as a function of purchasing frequency

	Firm	R^2	Coefficients	Std Error	t Stat	P-value
Frequent 20%	A	0.74	-6.18	1.38	-4.46	< 0.01
	B	0.71	-33.06	10.46	-3.16	< 0.05
Frequent 80%	A	0.56	0.34	0.12	2.76	< 0.05
	B	0.61	5.43	5.43	2.81	< 0.05

1999; Peppers & Rogers, 1993; Reichheld & Teal, 1996).

Hypothesis 2: *The ticket value of frequent clients increases as they buy more frequently.*

To test this hypothesis, bivariate linear regressions were used to analyze the ticket value as dependent on the purchase frequency of each frequent client (Stevenson, 1978 and Wonnacott & Wonnacott, 1972). The regressions took the two segments of frequent customers into account (Pareto 20% and 80%). Table 3 summarizes this analysis.

From the regressions, it can be seen that the coefficients are negative in both companies (-17.86 and -72.84) for the segment of frequent customers with the highest average ticket, indicating an inverse relationship between ticket value and customer purchasing frequency. In the other segment of frequent buyers (Pareto 80%), the coefficients are -0.02 and 14.18, indicating that the ticket value decreases very slightly in "Company A" as more purchases are made by clients, while it increases in "Company B." In other words, this proposition cannot be supported for frequent buyers with the highest average ticket (Pareto 20%).

This finding runs counter to some conceptual evidence from standard relationship marketing theories that claim that frequent clients are always inclined to buy more expensive products over the course of the relationship (Day, 1999; Kotler, 1999; Peppers & Rogers, 1993; Reichheld & Teal, 1996).

Hypothesis 3: *Frequent customers purchase more profitable products than sporadic consumers.*

For this test, it was compared the average transaction mark-ups associated with both frequent and sporadic consumers within each segment. The variance analysis (ANOVA) is presented in Table 4 (Stevenson, 1978 and Wonnacott & Wonnacott, 1972).

In both firms, the low value of "F Calc" (0.62 and 0.93) for the segment of buyers with the highest average ticket (Pareto 20%) indicates that the difference between averages is not statistically significant. In the other segment of consumers, frequent clients present a higher transaction mark-

Table 3. Regressions of the ticket value as a function of purchasing frequency

	Firm	R^2	Coefficients	Std Error	t Stat	P-value
Frequent 20%	A	0.63	-17.86	5.12	-3.48	< 0.05
	B	0.70	-72.84	23.78	-3.06	< 0.05
Frequent 80%	A	0.51	-0.02	0.01	-2.49	< 0.05
	B	0.71	14.18	4.06	3.49	< 0.05

Table 4. ANOVA - Average tansaction profit of frequent and sporadic buyers

	Firm	Frequent Customers	Sporadic Customers	F Calc	P-value
Pareto 20%	A	US$26.78	US$28.69	0.62	0.43
	B	US$123.26	US$128.48	0.93	0.33
Pareto 80%	A	US$5.47	US$4.97	31.61	< 0.01
	B	US$32.97	US$28.77	98.73	< 0.01

up (US$5.47 and US$32.97) than the respective value associated with sporadic buyers (US$4.97 and US$28.77). This evidence does not support hypothesis 3 fully, as the statement that frequent customers buy more profitable products than sporadic purchasers could not be verified for those consumers with the highest ticket value (Pareto 20% segment).

This shows that it is not true in all cases to say that frequent clients always purchase more profitable products than sporadic consumers, as claimed in relationship marketing literature (Kotler, 1999; McKenna, 1993; Reichheld & Teal, 1996).

Hypothesis 4: *Frequent clients purchase more expensive products than sporadic buyers.*

For this test, the average tickets of frequent and sporadic consumers within each segment are compared. The variance analysis (ANOVA) is presented in Table 5 (Stevenson, 1978 and Wonnacott & Wonnacott, 1972).

In the Pareto 20% segment of "Company A," the high value of "F Calc" (34.05) indicates that the average ticket of frequent buyers is significantly lower than the tickets observed for sporadic clients (US$125.18 and US$151.81). In the Pareto 20% segment of "Company B," the difference between the averages is not significant ("F Calc" = 1.13 and "P-value" = 0.28). The analysis of "F Calc" in the Pareto 80% segment (449.61 and 122.56) shows that the average ticket of frequent customers (US$42.21 and US$79.66) is statistically greater than the tickets observed for sporadic consumers (US$34.57 and US$68.37). This evidence does not support Hypothesis 4, as the statement that frequent customers buy more expensive products than sporadic purchasers could not be verified for the consumers with the highest ticket value (Pareto 20%).

This finding challenges traditional marketing literature, which contends that frequent customers always purchase more expensive products than sporadic buyers (Kotler, 1999; McKenna, 1993; Reichheld & Teal, 1996).

FINAL REMARKS

The empirical evidence revealed by this study ratifies most of the findings of research that have challenged the idea that frequent customers are either always increasingly profitable or always more profitable than sporadic purchasers (Reinartz & Kumar, 2000 and Reinartz & Kumar, 2002).

The analysis of Hypothesis 1, regarding the relationship between transaction mark-up and purchase frequency, showed that the mark-up associated with the transactions made by the top 20% of frequent customers decreases progressively over the course of their purchasing history. This finding allows the researchers to challenge the contention that customer retention always enables companies to obtain a premium price, as suggested by marketing relationship theories (Brondmo, 2000; Kotler, 1999).

Table 5. ANOVA - Average ticket of frequent and sporadic customers

	Firm	Frequent Customers	Sporadic Customers	F Calc	P-value
Pareto 20%	A	US$125.18	US$151.81	34.05	< 0.01
	B	US$343.13	US$360.05	1.13	0.28
Pareto 80%	A	US$42.21	US$34.57	449.61	< 0.01
	B	US$79.66	US$68.37	122.56	< 0.01

The analysis of Hypothesis 2 showed that it is not true to say that the average ticket of frequent customers always increases as they purchase more frequently. This test was not accepted for the top 20% frequent customer segments.

The test of Hypothesis 3 demonstrates that frequent customers can sometimes purchase cheaper products than the sporadic purchasers, with the passing of time. This evidence challenges traditional marketing literature, which contends that frequent customers always purchase more expensive products than sporadic purchasers (see Kotler, 1999; Reichheld & Teal, 1996). This hypothesis was not accepted for the top 20% frequent customer segment. Although, for the other segment (80%), it was observed that frequent customers are associated with a higher average ticket than that associated with sporadic purchasers.

Finally, the test of Hypothesis 4 demonstrates that the consumers with the highest ticket value (Pareto 20%). can buy more expensive products than sporadic purchasers

The evidence presented here does not invalidate the importance of frequent customers for companies. The key question is to recognize the importance of sporadic purchasers. This study demonstrated that the profitability associated with sporadic customers can be higher than that derived from frequent purchasers.

At this juncture, it is important to link these conclusions with the intellectual capital realm and formulate a question: How are the indicators used to measure the different capitals (constructs) that are embedded into the intellectual capital chosen?

This is not a new issue. Roos *et al.* (1997, p. 82) said: " ... most measures used in companies and prescribed by scholars and consultants tend to lack a solid theory justifying their existence and specifying the cause and effect relationship involved ... ". Furthermore, Hussi & Ahonen (2002, pp. 279) ask: "Which intangibles contribute more strongly to the financial performance of the company? ... What indicators does the company use to measure these intangibles?"

Moreover, Mavrinac and Siesfield (1997), for instance, state that some customer capital indicators depend on the nature of the business.

There are several techniques to define possible indicators, which are analysed during the testing of the proposed model ("purification," as named by Churchill, 1979, p. 66). Furthermore, multivariate data analysis (Hair, Anderson, Tathan, & Black, 1998) is available to analyse the internal consistency of the construct, the causal relationship between constructs, and their influence on the financial performance of the company. Besides, the influence of each indicator can be evaluated in order to verify whether there is causality between the indicator in question and business performance.

It is important to note that some articles are bringing rigor to bear on this analysis, such as Bontis *et al.* (2000), Chua (2002), Bontis and Fitz-enz (2002), to name just a few.

Hence, the main target of this chapter was not to discard "customer retention" as an actual indicator to evaluate external capital. Most of the time, rigorous analytical techniques will prove that this is a reliable and valid indicator that has a positive impact on a company's intellectual capital. In other situations, this indicator must be discarded or considered as having a negative influence on a firm's intellectual capital. There are no indicators that can be taken for granted, without using rigorous data analysis techniques.

Thus, the main purpose of this chapter is to highlight a very important issue, namely that it is important to remember that practitioners and consultants introduced the intellectual capital concept to the business realm. Shortly thereafter, scholars began to study it as a new knowledge field. Hence, the relevance of intellectual capital is still greater than the rigour some researchers have used to deal with this concept. The same phenomenon occurred earlier in the information management realm (Robey & Markus, 1998), as well as in the marketing domain (Jacoby, 1978). So, rigor and relevance are both necessary for the intellectual capital theory. The latter is well established, though the former still needs to be fully applied.

REFERENCES

Alle, V. (2000). The value evolution: Addressing larger implications of an intellectual capital and intangible assets perspectives. *Journal of Intellectual Capital, 1*(1), 17-32.

Bontis, N., & Fitz-enz, J. (2002). Intellectual capital ROI: A causal map of human capital antecedents and consequents. *Journal of Intellectual Capital, 3*(3), 223-247.

Bontis, N., Keow, W. C. C., & Richardson S. (2000). Intellectual capital and business performance in Malaysian industries. *Journal of Intellectual Capital, 1*(1), 85-100.

Brondmo, H. P. (2000). *The engaged customer. The new rules of Internet direct narketing.* New York: Harper Business.

Chatzkel, J. (2002). A conversation with Göran Roos. *Journal of Intellectual Capital, 3*(2), 96-117.

Chua, A (2002). The influence of social interaction on knowledge creation. *Journal of Intellectual Capital, 3*(4), 375-392.

Churchill, Jr., G. A. (1979). A paradigm for developing better measures of marketing constructs. *Journal of Marketing Research, XVI,* February, 64-73.

Crossroads. (2001). *A sector report: Consumer products.* Retrieved September 12, 2002, from http://www.xroadsllc.com/pdf/cp_report.pdf

Day, G. S. (1999). *The market driven organization.* New York: The Free Press.

Dowling, G., & Uncles, M. (1997). Do customers loyalty programs really work? *Sloan Management Review, 38*(4), 71-82.

Drucker, P. (1993). *Post-capitalist society.* HarperCollins.

Edvinsson, L., & Malone, M. (1997). *Intellectual capital.* HarperBusiness.

Eisenhardt, K. M. (1989). Building theories from case study research. *Academy of Management Review, 14,* 532-550.

Gibbert, M., Leibold, M., & Voelpel, S. (2001). Rejuvenating corporate intellectual capital by co-opting customer competence. *Journal of Intellectual Capital, 2*(2), 109-126.

Goodman, J. (1999). Basic facts on customer complaint behavior and the impact of service on the bottom line. *TARP - Technology Assistive Resource Program.*

Guthrie, J. (2001). The management, measurement and the reporting of intellectual capital. *Journal of Intellectual Capital, 2*(1), 27-41.

Guthrie, J., & Petty, R. (2000). Intellectual capital: Australian annual reporting practices. *Journal of Intellectual Capital, 1*(3), 241-251.

Hair, J. F., Anderson, R. E., Tathan, R. L., & Black W. C. (1998). *Multivariate data analysis* (5th ed.). Upper Saddle River, NJ: Prentice Hall.

Hayek, F. (1945). The use of knowledge in society. *The American Economic Review, 35*(4), September.

Hunt, D. P. (2003). The concept of knowledge and how to measure it. *Journal of Intellectual Capital, 4*(1), 100-113.

Hussi, T., & Ahonen, G. (2002). Managing intangible assets – A question of integration and delicate balance. *Journal of Intellectual Capital, 3*(3), 277-286.

Jacoby, J. (1978). Consumer research: A state of the art review. *Journal of Marketing, 42*, April, 87-96.

Johnson, W. H. A (1999). An integrative taxonomy of intellectual capital: Measuring the stock and flow of intellectual capital components in the firm. *International Journal of Technology Management, 18*(5/6/7/8), 562-575.

Joia, L. A (2000). Measuring intangible corporate assets: Linking business strategies with intellectual capital. *Journal of Intellectual Capital, 1*(1), 68-84.

Kaplan, R., & Norton, D. (1997). *The balance scorecard.* Boston: Harvard Business School Press.

Kotler, P. (1999). *Kotler on marketing: How to create, win, and dominate markets.* New York: Free Press.

Liebowitz, J., & Suen, C. Y. (2000). Developing knowledge management matrics for measuring intellectual capital. *Journal of Intellectual Capital, 1*(1), 54-67.

Lim, L. L. K., & Dallimore, P. (2002). To the public-listed companies, from the investment community. *Journal of Intellectual Capital, 3*(3), 262-276.

Low, J. (2000). The value creation index. *Journal of Intellectual Capital, 1*(3), 252-262.

Mavrinac, S., & Siesfield, G. A, (1997). *Measures that matter: An exploratory investigation of investors' information needs and value properties.* Cambridge, MA:

Ernst & Young Center for Business Innovation.

McCarthy, E. J. (1960). *Basic marketing: A managerial approach.* IL: R. D. Irwin.

McKenna, R. (1993) (reprint). *Relationship marketing: Successful strategies for the age of the customer.*. Cambridge: Perseus Publishing.

McPherson, P. K., & Pike, S. (2001). Accounting, empirical measurement, and intellectual capital. *Journal of Intellectual Capital, 2*(3), 246-260.

Nunnally, J. C. (1967). *Psychometric theory.* New York: McGraw-Hill Book Company.

Pablos P. O. (2002). Evidence of intellectual capital measurement form Asia, Europe, and Middle East. *Journal of Intellectual Capital, 3*(3), 287-302.

Peppard, J., & Rylander, A. (2001). Leveraging intellectual capital at APION. *Journal of Intellectual Capital, 2*(3), 225-235.

Peppers, D., & Rogers, M. (1993). *The one to one future: Building relationships one customer at a time.* New York: Doubleday.

Peppers, D., & Rogers, M. (1997). *Enterprise one to one: Tools for competing in the interactive age.* New York: Doubleday.

Reichheld, F. F., & Sasser, W. E., Jr. (1990). Zero defections: Quality comes to services. *Harvard Business Review*, September-October, 105-111.

Reichheld, F. F., & Teal, T. (1996). *The loyalty effect: The hidden force behind growth, profits, and lasting value.* Boston: Harvard Business School Press.

Reinartz, W., & Kumar, V. (2000). On the profitability of long-life customers in a noncontractual setting: An empirical investigation and implications for marketing. *Journal of Marketing, 64*, 17-35.

Reinartz, W., & Kumar, V. (2002). The mismanagement of customer loyalty. *Harvard Business Review*, July, 86-94.

Robey, D., & Markus, L. M. (1998). Beyond rigor and relevance: Producing consumable research about information systems. *Information Resources Management Journal, 11*(1), 7-15.

Rodov, I., & Leliaert, P. (2002). FiMIAM: Financial method of intangible assets measurement. *Journal of Intellectual Capital, 3*(3), 323-336.

Roos, J., Roos, G., Dragonetti, N., & Edvinsson, L. (1997). *Intellectual capital*, Macmillan Business.

St. Leon, M. V. (2002). Strategic intellectual capital creation: Decontextualizing strategy process research. *Journal of Intellectual Capital, 3*(2), 149-166.

Sánchez, P., Chaminade, P., & Olea M. (2000). Management of intangibles: An attempt to build a theory. *Journal of Intellectual Capital, 1*(4), 312-327.

Santos, A. M., & Costa, C. S. (1997). Características Gerais do Varejo no Brasil. *BNDES – Banco Nacional de Desenvolvimento Econômico e Social,* Setorial nº 5, March.

Schultz, D., & Hayman, D. (1999). The two sides of loyalty. *Interactive marketing*, April.

Seybold, P. B. (1998). *Customers.com: How to create a profitable business strategy for the Internet and beyond.* Auckland: Random House Publishing.

Sheth, J. N., Sisodia, R. S., & Sharma, A. (2000). The antecedents and consequences of customer-centric marketing. *Journal of the Academy of Marketing Science*, 28, (2), Winter.

Smith, M. D., Bailey, J., & Brynjolfsson, E. (1999). Understanding digital markets: Review and assessment. Retrieved August 4, 2001, from http://ecommerce.mit.edu/papers/ude/ude.pdf Stevenson, W. J. (1978). *Business statistics: Concepts and applications.* Harper & Row Publishers, Inc.

Stewart, T. A (1997). *Intellectual capital.* Doubleday/Currency.

Stone, B. (1984). *Successful direct marketing methods* (3rd ed.). Lincolnwood: NTC Publishing.

Sullivan, Jr., P. H., & Sullivan, Sr., P. H. (2000). Valuing intangible companies: An intellectual capital approach. *Journal of Intellectual Capital, 1*(4), 328-340.

Sveiby, K. E. (1997). *The new organisational wealth.* Berret-Koehler Publishers, Inc.

Wonnacott, T., & Wonnacott, R. (1972). *Introductory statistics for business and economics* (2nd ed.). NY: John Wiley & Sons, Inc.

Chapter VI
The Multicultural Organization:
A Historic Organizational Theory for Gaining Competitiveness in Global Business Environment

Tongo Constantine Imafidon
Covenant University, Nigeria

ABSTRACT

This chapter avers that over the past years, monolithic organizations, as opposed to multicultural organizations, have been created by many top business executives in order to attain their corporate visions and missions. One particular feature of the monolithic organization is that its leaders psychologically impose the culture of the organization on their subjects (employees). Their expectation is that a business organization should be able to satisfy the diverse needs of its various stakeholders (customers, suppliers, shareholders, etc.), when a unique set of covert and overt behaviour is revered by a homogenous workforce. Oftentimes, the imposed "organizational culture" is nothing but a mere derivative or microcosm of the wider societal culture in which the organization is domiciled. This was conceivable in yesteryears, given the fact that most organizations only operated within their domestic business enclaves. However, with globalization and the increasing need for organizations to develop businesses and cooperation across their national boundaries; it has become imperative for business organizations to solicit for more dynamic cultural models. Consequently, the validity of the monolithic organization is fast waning, and managers, especially those of multinational corporations, are beginning to recognize the dividends to be derived in accepting, valuing, and celebrating the differences that exist in a workforce with inherent heterogeneous human attributes. It is based on this backdrop that this chapter identifies three organizational phenomena (i.e., organizational learning, organizational creativity, and organizational justice) that confer competitive edge on multicultural organizations in relation to specific sectors of today's global business environment. The chapter also presents the historical relevance of the multicultural organization to the academic field of organizational theory.

INTRODUCTION

The importance of culture in the conduct of organizational life is well established in the literature of organizational theory (Jackson, 2004; Kuada, 2007; Okpara, 2007). According to Wren (1994), organizational practices have never been developed in a cultural vacuum. Stakeholders of organizations have always been affected by the cultures of their organizations.

For instance, the fact that organizational members in the West and East, and more specifically, the United States and Japan, are influenced by their cultures is well acknowledged. The U.S. organization is characterized by such cultural values as assertiveness, decisiveness, innovativeness, and risk taking, which stem from the frontier- conquering history of the U.S. (Hall & Hall, 1990). The culture of U.S. organizations is also characterized by individualism; the belief in the power and autonomy of the individual (Yeh, 1995).

However, Easterners, particularly the Japanese, complain that Americans are too legalistic and less willing to be flexible (Thorton, 1993). Hence, Japanese organizations, as compared to U.S. organizations, are more likely to have cultures characterized by flexibility, and people and detail orientation. Possibly, these cultural factors are the driving force behind the competitiveness of Japanese organizations. That is, Japanese organizations may rely heavily on the virtues of flexibility, people orientation, detail orientation, and team orientation to achieve greater business performance and customer satisfaction. Relative to Japanese organizations, U.S. organizations are more likely to have cultures characterized by innovation, outcome orientation, and aggressiveness. Further, these cultural values, which characterize the U.S. organization, are likely to impact on their performance because their business strategies and the resulting successes are attributable to their cultural values. Just as Japanese organizations utilize the cultural values that characterize them to achieve greater competitiveness, U.S. organizations will exercise the characteristics of innovation, outcome orientation, and aggressiveness as their competitive weapon to achieve greater business performance and customer satisfaction. Thus, it is expected that the relationship between organizational culture and business competitiveness should vary across national cultures.

Therefore, aside from the fact that many studies have already recognized the importance of culture to organizational life; there is also a common consensus amongst them with regards to the impact of national culture on organizational culture. Precisely, these studies have found out that the culture of a work organization is nothing but a mere derivative or microcosm of the wider national culture (Tongo, 2005). According to them, managerial jobs are carried out within organizational cultures that are akin to the national cultures in which these organizations are domiciled. As Hofstede (2001, p. 374) observed in his monumental cross-cultural study:

...organizations are culture bound. This applies not only to the behaviour of people within organizations and to the functioning of organizations as a whole; even the theories developed to explain behaviour in organizations reflect the national culture of their author, as do the methods and techniques that are suggested for the management of organizations. In the management literature, there are numerous unquestioning extrapolations of organizational solutions beyond the border of the country in which they were developed. This is especially true for the exportation of management theories from United States to the rest of the World, for which the non United States importers, are at least, as responsible as the United States exporters. However, the empirical basis for American management theories is American organizations; and we should not assume without proof that they apply elsewhere. This assumption is found not only in the popular literature; in scholarly journals-even in those explicitly addressing an

international readership- the silent assumption of universal validity of culturally restricted findings is frequent...

This quotation therefore implies that as long as a national culture is monolithic in nature, all organizations within the boundaries of such a nation should inherit the monolithic culture of the host nation. Also, for organizations located within a multicultural society, it is expected that these organizations should reflect the cultural diversity of the society.

However, there are two flaws associated with these deductions from Hofstede's analysis. The first flaw has to do with the fact that organizational activities and relationships are now being uprooted from local origins and cultures by globalization (Gray, 1999). **Information technology** has now created the possibility and even likelihood of a global culture. The Internet is sweeping away cultural boundaries. Global entertainment companies now shape the perceptions and dreams of individuals and organizations, wherever they live. The sum effect of all of these happenings is that, the cultural boundaries of most nation states are being dissolved, and there is presently a transfer of foreign beliefs and values into indigenous work organizations. Consequently, in this globalization process, there is a built-in dialectical tension between global and local cultures. Today's competitive organizations are now forced to meet with global standards rather than local standards. Thus, the supposedly reactive posture, taken by previous organizational/national culture interface theorists, which posits that organizations must derive their cultures from those prevailing in their respective national boundaries, may soon become a thing of the past. As Castells (2001) has noted, business organizations that are organized around networks of production, management, and distribution, must respond quickly to changes in the global business environment. In other words, they must, first of all, take up the initiative of transforming their own organizational cultures to conform with standards presented by the global economy, irrespective of the culture of the nations in which they are domiciled. For one thing, any form of national culture transformation is an onerous task and can take as long as many dozens of years. Therefore, business organizations cannot afford to wait for such a long time before they themselves can become culturally transformed.

The second flaw associated with the deductions from Hofstede's analysis is based on the fact that multicultural societies do not always reproduce multicultural organizations. For instance, in spite of the multicultural nature of most African societies, leaders of African organizations psychologically impose a particular form of culture that typifies their own whims and caprices on African employees (Jackson, 2004). In the case of South Africa, the track record of its organizations, in relation to employment equity, suggests that affirmative action may be the only means for ensuring that black employees do not perpetually remain marginal in managerial and professional categories (Human, 1996). Through affirmative action, the tendency for African managers to create **monolithic organizations** that fail to acknowledge, understand, accept, and celebrate the diversities that exist in a typical African workforce is expected to decline.

Nevertheless, the use of affirmative action may be needless if modern managers perceive diversity and inclusion as a strategic imperative for effective utilization of their intellectual capital. For instance, in Sodexho (a leading integrated food and facilities management services company in the U.S. with $ 7.3 billion in annual revenue and 125,000 employees), managers are held accountable for diversity results with a direct link to their incentive compensation (Sodexho, 2007).

Sodexho is proud to be ranked fourteenth among the top 50 multicultural organizations that are committed to managing diversity in the United States. Sodexho joined distinguished companies such as Coca Cola Co., Colgate-Palmolive, Ford Motor Co., Hewlett Packard, JPMorgan Chase,

Starbucks, and Verizon Communications/Wireless, in developing corporate visions that focus on **managing diversity** in multicultural corporations (Sodexho, 2007).

Sodexho believes that embracing the concept of multiculturalism and diversity management is essential to the company's growth and long-term success. By acknowledging and valuing diversity at work, Sodexho has been able to leverage the skills, knowledge, and abilities of all employees to increase employee, client, and customer satisfaction (Sodexho, 2007).

Sodexho posits that management's ability to respect and manage employee differences is essential to attracting diverse employees and building diverse, high-performing work teams that will allow the intellectual capital, at all levels of the organization, to be unleashed. This will result in innovative solutions that contribute to the company's competitive advantage in the market place (Sodexho, 2007).

Consequently, apart from the theoretical and practical advantages already ascribed to the multicultural organization in its literature, it is the objective of this chapter to identify three organizational phenomena (i.e., organizational learning, organizational creativity, and organizational justice) that confer competitive edge on multicultural organizations in relation to specific sectors of today's global business environment. It is believed that in establishing the nexus between these organizational phenomena and the specified environmental contexts, a framework for understanding the historical relevance of the multicultural organization to the academic field of organizational theory would have been provided.

For the purpose of achieving this objective, the chapter shall be divided into three sections. The first section shall present discussions on the nature of monolithic and multicultural organizations. The second section shall deal with the competitiveness of **multicultural organizations**. The third and final section specifies the historical relevance of the multicultural organization to the academic field of organizational theory.

The thrust of these sections is hinged on the creation of multicultural corporations for unlocking intellectual capital and gaining competitiveness in the modern world of business.

NATURE OF MONOLITHIC AND MULTICULTURAL ORGANIZATIONS

Since the early 1980s, when the significance of culture to organizational studies burst onto the scene, scholarly attention has been focused on the hypothesis that strong cultures, defined as "a set of norms and values that are widely shared and strongly held throughout the organization enhances firm performance (O' Reilly & Chatman, 1996).

According to Sorensen (2002), this hypothesis is based on having highly motivated employees dedicated to common goals. In particular, the performance benefits of a strong corporate culture are thought to derive from three consequences of having widely shared and strongly held norms and values; enhanced coordination and control within the firm, improved goal alignment between the firm and its members, and increased employee effort (Sorensen, 2002). It is against this background that CEOs from the early 1980s sought to create organizations that collectively program the minds of members. In order to attain this objective, these CEOs embarked on recruitment, selection, and induction programs that enabled them to employ only persons that can fit into the culture of their organizations.

Consequently, these CEOs were able to establish what is now termed as "monolithic organizations." Typically, monolithic organizations are always devoted to maintaining the dominance of one group over all others on factors such as age, education, religion, gender, or race. The monolithic organization is characterized by exclusionary hiring practices and other forms of discrimination that lead to ethnocentrism. Ethnocentrism amounts to little or no adoption of minority cultural norms by majority group members. Women and ethnic minority men tend to be segregated into low-status jobs, reflecting a low degree of integration and inclusiveness into the organizational culture (Konopaske, & Ivancevich, 2004).

However, the success story recorded by monolithic organizations was conceivable in time past, given the fact that these organizations only operated within their domestic business enclaves. Nevertheless, in the last 17 years (1990 to be precise), organizations have been seriously confronted with certain environmental forces occasioned by **globalization**. As globalization continues, organizations have had to expand into new international markets. This expansion has brought the organizations into more direct contact with diverse sets of host-country employees and alliance partners, customers, suppliers, government officials, and union representatives. These individuals are characterized by a variety of ages, religions, ethnicities, languages, and skin colours (Konopaske & Ivancevich, 2004). Therefore, in order to develop productive relationships with these stakeholders, managers of organizations will need to have empathy, and develop a thorough understanding of how to relate with these individuals (Konopaske & Ivancevich, 2004).

Consequently, the ability of monolithic organizations to cope with these prevailing exigencies has been found wanting. This stems from the cultural rigidity embedded in these organizations, and their perceived inadequacy in responding to these global issues. Hence, organizational theorists have held that the ideal organizational type to handle these global issues should have a reflection of the highly dynamic and diverse environmental context in which organizations currently operate in. This ideal organizational type is often referred to as "the multicultural organization" in the literature of organizational theory.

According to Patricia et al. (Patricia, Nemetz, & Sandra, 1996), the foundation and point of departure for effectively managing diversity is the development of a truly multicultural organization. A multicultural organization reflects the contributions and interests of diverse cultural and social groups in its mission, operations, product, or service; acts on a commitment to eradicate social oppression in all forms within the organization; includes the members of diverse cultural and social groups as full participants, especially in decisions that shape the organization; and follows through on broader external social responsibilities, including support of other institutional efforts to eliminate all forms of social oppression (Bailey, Frank, Henry, & Don, 1992). In summary, the multicultural organization not only contains different cultural groups, but also values the diversity that these groups bring to the table (Konopaske & Ivancevich, 2004).

Therefore, the next section of the chapter shall direct our attention to the competitive advantage conferred on the multicultural organization by three organizational phenomena in today's global business environment.

COMPETITIVENESS OF MULTICULTURAL ORGANIZATIONS IN GLOBAL BUSINESS ENVIRONMENT

The competitive advantages of multicultural organizations in the global business environment have been well elucidated by many organizational theorists. For instance, Cox and Blake (1991) have argued that the multicultural organization's ability to recruit, select, retain, and motivate individuals from diverse backgrounds (age, gender, ethnicity, etc.) helps it achieve and sustain competitive advantage in a variety of key ways, such as:

i. **Cost savings:** In modern organizations, turnover and absenteeism rates are higher while job satisfaction levels are lower among women and minorities. Diversity management initiatives, such as flexible work scheduling, mentoring, and equal access to training and development opportunities, will help a multicultural organization retain these valuable human resources, especially in times of labour shortages.

ii. **Resource acquisition:** Competitive advantage in human resources can come from hiring and retaining top talent from different demographic groups. Multicultural organizations are increasingly turning to creative advertisements that focus on diversity.

iii. **Marketing:** Having a workforce that is representative of an organization's customers and other stakeholders can add value in a variety of ways. First, global managers who are from the country or region in which operations are located are able to communicate with and understand the needs and preferences of the host-country customers. Possessing the appropriate intercultural communication skills is important for managing culturally diverse relationships with customers (Victoria, Gregory, Faye, & Thomas, 2001). The same holds true for marketing to customers and customers that are part of a subculture within the same country.

iv. **Creativity and problem solving:** Research is in support of the idea that multicultural organizations tend to generate ideas and solutions to problems that are more creative and innovative compared to monolithic organizations (William, 2000). Although, too much diversity can lead to a decrease in organizational cohesiveness, companies that foster diversity and openness internally may do better in attracting talented, creative people who can collaborate and produce innovative ideas and solutions (Richard, Robert, & Gary, 2002). Also, the global nature of business today increasingly requires people to collaborate in teams that transcend cultural and geographical boundaries.

v. **System flexibility:** A successfully managed multicultural organization enhances the ability to react to changes in the environment faster and at less cost.

In spite of the identification of the competitive advantages that accrue to multicultural organizations in the **organizational theory** literature, little or no attempts have been made to relate them with specific sectors of today's global business environment. The failure to recognize how these advantages directly relate with the environmental context of global business obscures the potential benefits derivable from embracing the concept of multiculturalism in organizations and its overall relevance to the academic field of organizational theory.

Consequently, the chapter explores three organizational phenomena that typify the multicultural organization and their relationships with some specific sectors of the global business environment. The three organizational phenomena and their respective environmental contexts are organizational learning and the global economic environment; organizational creativity and the global technological environment; and organizational justice and the global politico- legal environment. These are discussed next.

Organizational Learning and the Global Economic Environment

The global economic environment in which organizations currently function is changing rapidly. Its unpredictability is increasing by the day, as both local and foreign competitions are becoming highly unrestricted. However, one factor that has accelerated the rate of change in the global economy is the fact that knowledge now constitutes the most important factor of production.

Knowledge has played an important role in the development of economies throughout history. The transformation from agrarian to industrial and now to the **knowledge economy** has been brought about by the accumulation of knowledge and advances in information technology (Al-Hawamdeh, 2003).

However, today's knowledge economy is unique in the way by which it drives change in every area of business and industry. Consequently, change has been so intense and continuous that research and development have become major components in the infrastructure of every organization (Joel, 1995). According to Joel (1995), to persist in viewing a service or product in terms of labour and material is now self defeating, negating the vital resources necessary to keep pace with times and competition.

This, therefore, implies that knowledge must be seen as an additional factor of production in this new economy. However, just as not all forms of labour and material are required by every organization; the type of knowledge needed by an organization must be tailored towards its own unique peculiarities. Thus, in order to effectively harness knowledge as a factor of production, each business organization must be able to accumulate certain "intangible knowledge assets" that are relevant and specific to its diverse operations. These "intangible knowledge assets" are often referred to as intellectual capital, in current business literature (Tongo, 2008).

The need to build the intellectual capital of organizations within the knowledge economy has had a great impact on the learning process. Changes in work patterns and mobility and the increased emphasis on skills and competences demand that workers and knowledge professionals adopt learning as a survival tool (Al-Hawamdeh, 2003). A country's capacity to take advantage of the knowledge economy depends on how quickly it can become a "learning economy." In the "learning economy," organizations will be able to create wealth in proportion to their capacity to learn.

However, modern research has shown that multicultural organizations have more capacity to imbibe organizational learning than monolithic organizations. According to Sorensen (2002), monolithic organizations (i.e., organizations with strong cultures) incur a tradeoff with respect to their adaptive ability in the face of environmental change. Monolithic organizations facilitate reliable performance in relatively stable environments, but as volatility increases, these benefits are dramatically attenuated. This pattern is consistent with the fundamental tradeoff between exploration and exploitation noted by March (1991), and suggests that monolithic organizations excel at exploiting established competences, but have difficulty exploring and discovering new competences that better suit changing environmental conditions.

Also, Lam (2003) found out that, relative to many Japanese multinational enterprises, the United States organizations have developed a greater organizational capacity for coordinating globally dispersed learning and embedding themselves in local innovation networks, because the multicultural environment, within which the United States multinational enterprises have developed, enables them to extend their organizational and human resource systems across institutional and geographical boundaries. By contrast, Japanese multinational enterprises, which are more monolithically oriented, appear to be more limited in their transnational learning because of the much more tightly integrated organizational culture within which they are embedded.

Organizational Creativity and the Global Technological Environment

There is no gainsaying that dramatic movements in the history of industrial change have always been characterized by the successful exploitation of new ideas and the achievements of innovators. For instance, the East Asian economies were able to transform rapidly due to their investment in creativity and innovation, which led to the creation of new high technology industries. Therefore, to say that the global technological environment is driven by the twin forces of creativity and innovation will amount to restating the obvious (Iwuagwu, 2007).

In recent past, global dispersion of research and development (i.e., R and D) has been propelled by organizations' needs to acquire new knowledge and capabilities, and to gain access to unique human resources that can add real value to their creativity and innovation (Cantwell, 1995).

Since the mid-1980s, the overseas R and D units of many multinational enterprises no longer confine themselves to transfer parent-company technology to host countries, but are developing major innovations for the global market by leveraging the unique knowledge resources of some host-country environments. Gerybadze and Reger (1999) argue that the proliferation of national innovation systems and knowledge centres at various locations throughout the world has strengthened the incentives for multinationals to go for global knowledge sourcing. When deciding to establish or expand R and D abroad, firms are increasingly motivated by the wish to gain access to sophisticated resources that cannot be found anywhere else.

These changes are clearly demonstrated in Pearce and Papanasatassiou's (1999) survey of the evolution of overseas R and D labs in the UK. The authors distinguish three different roles of laboratories: support, locally integrated, and internationally interdependent categories. The study shows that the internationally interdependent type, whose aim is to generate new scientific knowledge that can underpin the technological distinctiveness of the multinational enterprise, has emerged as the most prevalent type of laboratory in multinational enterprises' units in the UK.

Consequently, as organizations seek to use knowledge and innovation generated on a global scale, the development of international R and D organization becomes a central issue. Zanfei (2000) describes the new organizational mode of transnational innovation as "a double network" comprising the internal and external networks. The internal networks refer to the organizational mechanisms for the coordination and integration of distributed R and D units, while external networks are constituted by relations with actors outside the firm.

A number of authors argue that a subsidiary's ability to gain access to local knowledge sources is dependent upon its embeddedness in the host country context and the social relations of technological innovation (Blanc & Sierra, 1999; Frost, 2001; Zanfei, 2000). What makes multinational enterprises unique as knowledge acquiring organizations is their ability to generate "transnational social spaces" for organizational creativity. This is achieved by linking their internal networks with their external and locally embedded knowledge networks spanning diverse organizational and institutional contexts.

Going by these views, only the multicultural organization would have the capacity to creatively engage in relating with diverse organizational and institutional contexts for the development of new products and services.

The most significant problem encountered by monolithic organizations in relating with the global technological environment is that these organizations have cultures that restrict the management of diversity. The result is that they will be unable to create internal and external cultural linkages that foster organizational creativity in a technologically diverse environment.

Organizational Justice and the Global Politico-Legal Environment

With the collapse of the Soviet Union, we now seem to have a unipolar world driven by the free-market system. For the reinforcement of a free-market system, there has to be political reforms that align with the functionality of such a system on a global scale. This political-economic alignment has been accentuated by the policies of supranational organizations (i.e., the IMF, World Bank, and World Trade organizations), which necessitate member nations to conform to a liberal political culture.

Liberalism, as the name implies, is the fundamental belief in a political culture that allows individuals to pursue their own goals in their own ways provided they do not infringe on the equal liberty of others. Therefore, in order to entrench this liberal political ideology, there has been a convergence of laws regulating businesses in nations that have strong affiliations with these supranational organizations. These business laws promote commitment to the fundamental human rights, equality, rule of law, individual freedom, private property, and a free market.

For these business laws to have a full impart on organizational settings, there has been global legislative efforts to deal with discrimination in the workplace. In addition, organizations have considerable incentive to not only follow the laws that prohibit discrimination, but also voluntarily design and implement diversity management programs that lead to greater inclusion of all types of individuals into informal social networks and formal company programs (Konopaske & Ivancevich, 2004).

But, to adequately deal with discrimination in the workplace, CEOs must be able to study people's perceptions of fairness in organizations. This is what is termed "organizational justice" in the organizational-theory literature. Organizational justice has been decomposed into three parts; these are distributive justice, procedural justice, and interactional justice.

Distributive justice considers perceptions of fairness of outcomes (equity, equality, and needs). Procedural justice emphasizes the importance of fairness of the methods or procedures used in making decisions. Interactional justice is based on the perceived fairness of the interpersonal treatment received, whether those involved are treated with sensitivity, dignity, and respect, and also the nature of explanations given.

Therefore, based on the nature of multicultural organizations, it is important to note that all forms of organizational injustices would have no place in them, because the multicultural organization acts on a commitment to eradicate social oppression within the organization. However, expecting that the monolithic organization would one day embrace the concept of organizational justice would amount to wishful thinking. This therefore implies that the multicultural organization is most apt for today's global politico-legal environment.

Figure 1 summarizes the competitive nature of monolithic and multicultural organizations in relation to organizational learning, organizational

Figure 1.

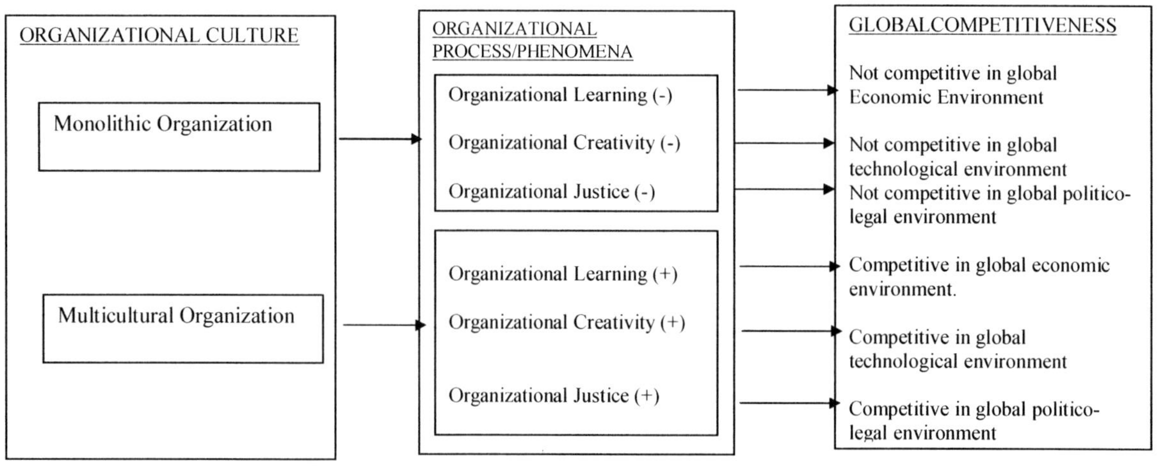

creativity, and organizational justice in the aspects of the global business environment presented in this chapter.

The negative signs attached to these organizational phenomena with respect to the monolithic organization suggest that it is not competitive in the global business environment. Conversely, the positive signs held by these organizational phenomena, with regards to the multicultural organization, depict its competitiveness in the global business environment.

THE MULTICULTURAL ORGANIZATION: A HISTORIC ORGANIZATIONAL THEORY

Theories about organization do not develop in a vacuum. They always reflect what is going on in the environmental contexts of organizations. Therefore, to understand the significance of the multicultural organization to the academic field of organizational theory, we must appreciate the historical contexts through which this academic discipline developed and the environmental milieus during and in which important contributions were made to its body of knowledge (Shafritz & Ott, 1996).

Although no single date can be pinpointed as the beginning of serious thinking about how organizations work and how they should be structured and managed, we can trace writings about organizations as far back as the known origins of commerce. A lot can be learned from the early organizations of Muslims, Hebrews, Greeks, and Romans. After all, it was Aristotle who first wrote about the importance of culture to organizational systems; ibn Taymiyyah who used the scientific method to outline the principles of administration within the framework of Islam; and Machiavelli who gave the world the definitive analysis of the use of power (Shafritz & Ott, 1996).

However, even though it may be useful to delve into the wisdom of the ancients, most analysts of the origins of organizational theory view the beginnings of the factory system in Great Britain in the 18th century as the birth-point of complex economic organizations and, consequently, of the academic field of organizational theory (Shafritz & Ott, 1996; Wren, 1994).

Prior to the industrial revolution in Britain, goods were made, or grown, in the home for family's use. Other products, however, came from two basic methods of industrial organization: the guilds and the domestic system. Guilds consisted of two types: merchant guilds, which were the buyers and sellers of goods; and craft guilds, which were the makers of the goods.

Within the craft guilds, there was a hierarchy of authority of masters, journeymen, and apprentices. There was also division of labour and devices to control who did certain types of work. Merchants were intermediaries in trade, buying raw materials to sell to producers or taking finished products for resale. A merchant procured raw materials and farmed them out to individual workers or families who, using their own equipment, would complete the product in their homes and then return it to the merchant for a wage.

During these times, economies were essentially static, and they were managed via unilateral decision making by some central authority. Although some early ideas of organizational theory appeared, however, they were largely localized. Organizations could be run on the divine right of the king on the appeal of dogma to the faithful, and on the rigorous discipline of the military. There was little or no need to develop a formal body of knowledge that could help predict how organizations function under these nonindustrialized circumstances (Wren, 1994).

Economic theory during this time focused on two factors of production, land and labour, and recognized capital as an input factor. The physiocrats recognized a farmer as an entrepreneur, but held that manufacturing and commerce were sterile and unable to produce surplus. Adam Smith recognized the entrepreneur as a factor, but treated the return or the surplus created as return to capital. Jean Baptiste Say (1767-1832), a French economist, was the first to recognize explicitly a fourth factor of production, which was referred to as management. Say noted that some "adventurers" (entrepreneurs) owned the undertaking, but more frequently than not, they owned only a share, having borrowed from others or having formed a partnership. The adventurer thus became a manager for others, and assumed an additional risk in combining the factors of land, labour, and capital.

Within this period in which the concept of management, as the fourth factor of production, emerged, the faults of the domestic system of production were becoming conspicuous. This system relied on the use of simple tools and technology, with little incentive to improve them, and in the inefficiencies of small-scale production with a limited division of labour. As the volume of trade grew, the domestic system proved inefficient, and the need for more capital, the benefits of specializing labour, and the economies of scale of centralized workplace led to the factory system of production.

The emerging factory system of production, which catalyzed the industrialization process in Britain, posed organizational problems different from those encountered before. With the factory system, the need for a rational, formalized, systematic body of knowledge about how to manage organizations became inevitable. The emergence and refinement of the market economy required managers to become more creative, and to be better informed about how best to utilize resources. People began thinking of individual gain, and had to be accommodated in some rational managerial framework. The emergence of larger organizations had to be based on rational ways of making decisions; no longer could the organization be operated on the whims of a few.

In order for organizations, during this time, to cope with the pressure for growth, the need came for economies of scale to compete more effectively. Following this problem, Frederick Taylor, and the other forerunners of classical organizational theory, had to develop principles that can help managers effectively and efficiently utilize their human resources.

Although, classical organizational theory proved successful, particularly during the period when industry was straining to meet the production demands of World War I, it was widely criticized for treating the worker as a "living tool" with little discretion or variety in work. The excesses of classical organizational theory, sometimes leading to industrial unrest, are invoked to explain the emergence of the human resource theory or the organizational behaviour perspective. Mayo's classic experiments at the Hawthorne plant in Chicago led to the conclusion that human interaction and the attention paid to the workers by the researchers caused their productivity to increase.

This contravened Taylor's dour philosophy of self interest, suggesting that social factors and the relationship of working groups to management were keys to performance.

However, the full acceptance of the human resource theory in most nations must have been facilitated by the economic depression of the World War II, which placed workers in highly unfavourable working conditions.

This economic depression was the start of a bifurcation in organizational practices in the United States and Japan (Evans, Pucik, & Barsoux, 2002). The depth of the economic depression in the United States meant that organizations had no option except to repudiate these implicit welfare arrangements, which were perpetuated by the human resource theorists. Organizations in the United States therefore turned to a path of explicit and instrumental contracts between employee and employer (performance management, pay-for-performance, and short–term contracts).

Due to the militarization of the Japanese economy, the impact of the economic depression was much less severe on the other side of the Pacific. Under legislation fostering "social peace" in the name of national unity, Japanese organizations maintained these welfare experiments, leading step-by-step to an HRM orientation built around implicit contracts (lifetime employment, corporate responsibility for the development of staff, low emphasis on formalized performance evaluation). Endorsed by the strong labour unions that emerged in postwar Japan, these practices became institutionalized, reinforcing and reinforced by cultural differences (Evans et al., 2002).

The environmental context in which organizations operated from the 1960s can be characterized as one of burgeoning masses of physical and human resources growing into ever more and more complex patterns and relationships; management is faced with advancing technology, a global market place, and people of diverse needs, educational backgrounds, and degrees of specialized knowledge. The changing means of producing goods and services have had an increasing effect on organizations (Wren, 1994).

Confronted with pervasive economic uncertainties, as well as increasing organizational complexity, organizations began a search for theories that can deal with these external shocks. Organizational theorists began to challenge the dominance of the human resource theory, and so, the systems and contingency theories of organization were propounded. These organizational theories viewed organizations as complex systems of people, tasks, and technology. They recognized that organizations were part of a larger environment with which they interacted.

The summary of this section is that the advent of the factory system of production, the economic depression occasioned by World War II, and the pervasive economic uncertainties ushered in after World War II, were mainly responsible for the paradigm shifts in organizational theorizing during these different periods. Thus, each time organizations are confronted with new environmental settings, theories of organizations emerge to deal with these settings.

Therefore, with the birthing of the knowledge economy, a technologically diverse environment, and a neoliberal political ideology that now constitute integral parts of the 21st century global business environment, the theory of the multicultural organization becomes invaluable in dealing with these environmental exigencies as long as they persist.

CONCLUSION

Even though the multicultural organization has been perceived as the most ideal form of organization to deal with workforce diversity (Cox & Blake, 1991), nevertheless, the importance of the multicultural organization to the global business environment has not been given sufficient attention by the literature of organizational theory.

Focusing on three aspects of the global business environment (i.e., global economic environment, global technological environment, and the global politico-legal environment) and three organizational phenomena (i.e., organizational learning, organizational creativity, and organizational justice) that characterize the multicultural organization, this chapter clearly articulates the competitiveness of multicultural organizations in today's global business environment.

It is suggested that future studies on the subject matter should be directed to investigating the relevance of the multicultural organization to other aspects of the global business environment, for example, the global demographic and the global socio-cultural environments. It is believed that findings from such studies would further reveal the competitive edge of multicultural organizations vis-à-vis monolithic organizations in the environmental landscape of global business.

REFERENCES

Al-Hawamdeh, S. (2003). *Knowledge management: Cultivating knowledge professionals.* Oxford: Chandos Publishing.

Bailey, W., Frank, L., Henry, G., & Don, K. (1992). Diversity. *Human Resource Management,* Spring/Summer, 22.

Blanc, H., & Sierra, C. (1999). The internationalization of R and D by multinationals: A trade off between external and internal proximity. *Cambridge Journal of Economics, 23,* 187-206.

Cantwell, J. (1995). The globalization of technology: What remains of the product cycle model? *Cambridge Journal of Economics, 19,* 155-174.

Castells, M. (2001). Information technology and global capitalism. In W. Hutton, & A. Giddens (Eds.), *On the edge, living with global capitalism.* London: Vintage.

Cox, T., & Blake, S. (1991). Managing cultural diversity: Implications for organizational competitiveness. *The Academy of Management Executive 5,* 92-100.

Evans, P., Pucik,V., & Barsoux, J. (2002). *The global challenge: Frameworks for international human resource management.* Boston: McGraw-Hill.

Frost, T. (2001). The geographic sources of foreign subsidiaries' innovations. *StrategicManagement Journal, 22,* 101-123.

Gerybadze, A., & Reger, G. (1999). Globalization of R and D: Recent changes in the management of innovation in transnational corporations. *Research Policy, 28,* 251-274.

Gray, J. (1999). *False dawn: The delusion of global capitalism.* London: Granta.

Hall, E., & Hall, R. (1990). *Hidden differences: Doing business with the Japanese.* New York: Double Day Anchor Books.

Hofstede, G. (2001). *Culture's consequences: Comparing values, behaviours, institutions, and organizations across nations* (2nd ed.). London: Sage Publications.

Human, L. (1996). Managing workforce diversity: A critique and example from South Africa. *International Journal of Man Power, 17,* (4 & 5), 46-64.

Iwuagwu, O. (2007). Creativity and innovation in business success. *Business Day,* December 23, .8.

Jackson, T. (2004). *Management and change in Africa.* London: Routledge.

Joel, L. (1995). Leverage, exploitation, and intellectual capital. *The American Journal of Nursing, 83,* 1-7.

Konopaske, R., & Ivancevich. (2004). *Global management and organizational behaviour.* New York: McGraw Hill.

Kuada, J. (2007). Cultural impacts on employee goals and behaviour in Africa. In J. Okpara (Ed.), *Management and economic development in sub-Saharan Africa: Theoretical and applied perspectives,* (pp. 28-43). London: Adonis and Abbey Publishers Ltd.

Lam, A. (2003). Organizational learning in multinationals: R and D networks of Japanese and US multinational enterprises in the UK. *Journal of Management Studies, 40,* (3), 673-703.

March, J. (1991). Exploration and exploitation in organizational learning. *Organization Science, 2,* 71-87.

O' Reilly, C., & Chatman, J. (1996). Culture as social control: Corporations, culture, and commitment. In B. Staw & L. Cummings (Eds.), *Research in organizational behaviour, 18,* (pp. 157-200). Greenwich, CT: JAI Press.

Okpara, J. (2007). Cultural influences on the work attitudes: A theoretical perspective. In J. Okpara

(Ed.) *Management and economic development in sub-Saharan Africa: Theoretical and applied perspectives,* (pp. 209-223). London: Adonis and Abbey Publishers Ltd.

Patricia, L., Nemetz, C., & Sandra, L. (1996). The challenge of cultural diversity: Harnessing a diversity of views to understand multiculturalism. *Academy of Management Review,* April, 434-462.

Pearce, R., & Papanastassiou, M. (1999). Overseas R and D and the strategic evolution of multinational enterprises: Evidence from laboratories in the UK. *Research Policy,28*, 23-41.

Richard, F., Robert, C., & Gary, G. (2002). When social capital stifles innovation. *Harvard Business Review, 80*, 20-26.

Shafritz, J., & Ott, S. (Eds.). (1996). Classical organizational theory. In J. Shafritz, & S. Ott, *Classics of organizational theory.* FL: Harcourt Brace and Company.

Sodexho. (2007). *Corporate diversity.* North America: Sodexho.

Sorensen, J. (2002). The strength of corporate culture and the reliability of firm performance. *Administrative Science Quarterly, 47*, (1), 70-91.

Thorton, E. (1993). Thailand: Japan vs. the U.S. *Fortune*, *28,* 145-149.

Tongo, C. (2005). *Re-assessing the organizational and national culture interface*. Paper presented at the International Conference of Human Development, Covenant University, June 27-30, 2005.

Tongo, C. (Forthcoming). Building the intellectual capital of African enterprises in a knowledge economy: Impediments and requirements. *International Journal of Learning and Intellectual Capital*, *5*(1), 33-47.

Victoria, D., Gregory, M., Faye, G., & Thomas, N. (2001). Managing culturally diverse buyer-seller relationships: The role of intercultural disposition and adaptive selling in developing intercultural communication competence. *Academy of Marketing.Science*, *29,* 391-404.

William, B. (2000). Global work force: The new world labour market. In C. Mary. (Ed.) (1994), *Differences that work: Organizational excellence through diversity.* Cambridge, MA: Harvard Business Review.

Wren, D. (1994). *The evolution of management thought*. New York: John Wiley and Sons.

Yeh, R. (1995). Downward influence styles in the cultural diversity settings. *International Journal of Human Resources Management, 6,* 625-641.

Zanfei, A. (2000). Transnational firms and the changing organization of innovation activities. *Cambridge Journal of Economics, 24,* 515-542.

Chapter VII
Developing a Corporate Memory as a Competitive Advantage in the ICT Sector

Arla Juntunen
Helsinki School of Economics, Finland

ABSTRACT

This chapter focuses on the challenges of developing a knowledge management platform to support organizational memory and knowledge transfer. The study is based on a qualitative study in the ICT sector. First, the chapter discusses the development of the KM platform. Second, the benefits, and a competitive advantage of such a platform, are discussed. Finally, the conclusions are made, based on the case study.

INTRODUCTION

Increased value of knowledge, technological complexity, global competition, and the availability of Internet and other emerging, digital technologies are key drivers in this change from information society to knowledge society (Castells, 1996). Managing the data, information, and knowledge within the organization, as well as using it to gain a sustainable competitive advantage, is a challenging task for both public and private sector organizations. Knowledge management essentially consists of tools, practices, and processes to efficiently capture, store, and share data and knowledge of individuals within an organization.

The last decade has witnessed a growth of information generated within organizations due to the increase use of technology and Web. During the 1990s, a concept of knowledge management (See, e.g., Davenport, 2001; Möller and Svahn, 2006; Nonaka & Takeuchi, 1995, Nonaka, Toyama, & Konno, 2001; Teece, 2000) emerged, and both the public and private sector researchers accepted it in the information technology and management literature. Sharing, transferring, and storing organizational knowledge has stressed the idea of further developing a data warehouse to support organizational learning and knowledge management within the organization. Exploiting the information and knowledge within data warehouses is one method to attain industry-leading performance (Juntunen, 2008; Matusik & Hill, 1998; Törmänen, 2003) and competitive advantage in markets. Organizations that develop and leverage knowledge resources achieve success more likely than organizations that are more dependent on tangible resources (Autio, Sapienza, & Almeida, 2000; Teece, 2000; Yli-Renko, Autio, & Tontti, 2002). This knowledge is embedded and carried through multiple entities, including organizational culture and identity, policies, routines, documents, systems, and employees. Moreover, the life cycles of technologies, products, and platforms are getting shorter, placing greater pressure on the speed of response and strategic renewal of the organization. The intangible resources drive value, and innovations are crucial for any firm to create a sustainable competitive advantage in markets.

This study is based on the knowledge-based view of the firm, and also the resource-based view of the firm theories. Originating from the strategic management literature, the knowledge-based view of the firm perspective builds upon and extends the resource-based view of the firm (RBV) initially sponsored by Penrose (1959) and later expanded by others (Barney, 1991; Conner, 1991; Wernerfelt, 1984). Although the latter theory recognizes the important role of knowledge in firms that gain a competitive advantage, supporters of the knowledge-based view claim that the resource-based perspective does not go far enough. Particularly, the RBV treats knowledge as a generic resource, rather than having unique characteristics. Consequently, it does not distinguish between different categories of knowledge-based capabilities. Information technologies can play a significant role in the knowledge-based development in the organization in that information systems can be used to synthesize, enhance, and speed up large-scale intra- and interorganizational knowledge management efforts (Alavi & Leidner, 2001) and knowledge repositories.

Also, the spirit of the knowledge-based view must be understood to understand the value of knowledge to the organization that operates in dynamically changing environment like the ICT sector is. The increasing importance of innovations, rapid product development in the ICT sector has made the understanding of organizational knowledge creation and innovative organizational transformations a critical issue in an organization. Therefore, knowledge management is not a narrow information technology (IT) related function within an organization, but rather an integration of strategic management, learning, R&D, use of different technologies, human capital, and business management. From this perspective, knowledge creation and management in an organization is not mainly a problem of product development, but rather a question of mastering the renewal and information transfer within all hierarchic levels of an organization and between different communities of practice, a continuous organizational development process, and a way to rapidly capitalize innovations. An organization with valuable, rare, inimitable, and nonsubstitutable resources can generate a sustainable competitive advantage over its rivals, thus resulting in better financial performance (See e.g., Barney, 1991; Conner, 1991; Hatch & Dyer, 2004; Wernerfelt, 1984).

Moreover, the introduction of the Internet and Web-based tools has given rise to many forms of online sociality, including e-mail, instant messaging, blogging, and community-based online services. In addition to descriptive personal profiles, members of such online communities publicly articulate mutual friendship links with other members, creating a browseable network of social relations (Heer & Boyd, 2005). The KM platform concept in the case corporation included tools for different communities, like, for example, for work projects, teams, or for leisure-time-related online societies, and for individuals.

The following sections will begin with an overview of the development of knowledge management platform (KM platform) concept, and then proceed to explain the development, benefits, and consequences of the implementation of the KM platform as a basis of organizational memory and competitive advantage in a turbulent competitive environment.

BACKGROUND

The study is based on a qualitative study in the ICT sector. The preliminary study of the development of KM platform concept was part of a longitudinal qualitative study (Juntunen, 2005). Research documentation consisted of both information about the telecommunication industry and the case corporation's development during 1990-2003. Interviews were made in 1999-2005. Interviews included personnel from different levels of the organization as well as from the network partners and main competitor. Data gathered consists of articles, project documents, memorandums concerning strategy, businesses, and competence laboratories in different communities of practice. It also has to be noted that this study focuses on the experiences of a large company with multibusiness organization.

The case organization is Elisa. It is a leading Finnish communications and ICT solutions company offering a comprehensive range of communications services, including voice and data services, connections to the Internet, customised ICT solutions, and network operator services. Elisa is a forerunner of new mobile and content services (Elisa's annual report 2006). Its core business areas are fixed network mobile network, including Internet-based services (Juntunen, 2005). Elisa's organization was integrated from several subsidiaries of different names into one Elisa in 2003. Elisa continued its corporate restructuring in 2006: Tikka Communications Plc and Jyväsviestintä Plc merged with Elisa. Saunalahti Group became a wholly owned subsidiary of Elisa, and Lounet company was also acquired. Elisa's mission is to offer its customers fast, effective, and secure communication telecommunication services. Its vision is to be the most attractive and effective operator. Elisa operates in Finland and in carefully selected international market areas, and provides international services in association with its partners, Vodafone and Telenor. (Elisa's annual report 2006). During the years 2003-2007, Elisa has unified its organizational structure, strengthened its market position in chosen core markets, added new services in its service portfolio, and entered to new markets (Elisa, 2007).

The case corporation's approach to organizational learning and to knowledge management was based on the KM platform concept (see Figure 1). The KM platform concept included different areas of information, and knowledge sharing for communities, individuals, and for work and leisure time. The community part of the KM platform concept consisted of tools for business management and learning, like, for example, benchmarking information, best practices, memorandums of different competence laboratories, and projects. It also included internal surveys, news of competitors and products, and access to e-libraries. The individual part of the platform concept consisted of tools for self-learning, education, recruitment, and job rotation.

The initial development process of the KM Platform concept, during the years 1999-2001, was explored and evaluated, and an attempt was made to understand the factors and events affecting the development. The KM platform concept, developed in 1990-2001, still supports the current strategy of the case corporation and its knowledge management initiatives and needs.

It can be claimed that the conceptualized findings have more general relevance, particularly for organizations operating in dynamic, rapidly changing fields characterized by several interlinked technologies. It is also claimed that the relevance of this study reaches beyond the limited historical period. The research design is a logical sequence that connects the empirical data to the initial research questions (Miles & Huberman, 1994; Yin, 1994). The qualitative methods make it possible to develop a thorough understanding of a complex and a multidimensional phenomenon in a specific context. The case design here is a single case study and conducted within one corporation. The reason for choosing a case study approach lies in the in-depth knowledge needed regarding the evolution of different collaborative forms and their managerial processes. Information about these phenomena requires good access to an organization in order to be able to identify them (Heide & John, 1995; Yin, 1994). While a case study is claimed to increase understanding of the complexity of process and change (see Cassel & Symon, 1994; Pettigrew, 1990; Van de Ven & Poole, 1990). Hartley (1994) emphasized the tailor-made nature of a case study, because it allows observation within the context of a real-life situation.

Moreover, in this study, the two diverse fields of research were synthesized and the interaction between the KM technology and inter- and intra-organizational relationships were also examined as part of understanding multibusiness synergies. The ICT sector is a turbulent and rapidly changing environment. It is challenging for any organization to pursue major innovations or systemic product offerings because of the dispersion of knowledge and technological resources. Organizations try to overcome this by seeking knowledge transfer and, more ambitiously, joint ventures to create knowledge and innovations through collaboration (Kogut & Zander, 1997; Teece, 2000). The knowledge can be transferred directly through education and training, or indirectly (See Norman & Ramirez, 1993). The knowledge-based theory of the firm considers the firm as a repository of knowledge-based resources and capabilities (see e.g., Teece, 2000). The inimitable and unique resources and capabilities represent the continuous competitive advantage for the organization. Thus, in these approaches of knowledge-based view and resource-based view of the firm, the performance differences within and between organizations are a result of different reserves of knowledge, resources, and capabilities, and how organizations can efficiently use and benefit them.

Because this chapter will discuss the capabilities, resources, and competences, it is necessary to clarify the meaning of these concepts first. The previous literature on capabilities, assets, and resources is somewhat diversified concerning the terminology and definitions of these concepts, and therefore, in this study, the author identifies the resources of companies as assets and capabilities. Figure 1 presents the definition of the concepts of resource, asset, and capabilities in this study. Resources can be divided into capabilities and assets (see e.g., Grant, 1996). Capabilities can be defined as intangible knowledge resources, and physical and nonphysical resources as tangible and intangible assets (see e.g., Metcalfe & James, 2000). Also, capabilities can be divided to ordinary and dynamic capabilities. Eisenhardt and Martin (2000, p. 1107) defined dynamic capabilities as the firm's processes to integrate, reconfigure, gain, and release resources to match and even create market change.

An organization must be capable of continuously creating new, and thus, temporary, competitive advantages based on different resource combinations than those of the incumbent competitors. In doing so, a company has also enhanced its value creation. (of dynamic capabilities, see, e.g., Amit & Zott, 2001, 2002; D'Aveni, 1994; Eisenhardt & Martin, 2000; Teece, 2003; Teece,

Pisano, & Shuen, 1997; Thomas, 1996; Zollo & Winter, 2002) These developments refer to changes that are a result of actions of a focal actor. These changes can be organizational, network structural, network positional, strategical, or operational changes in a business network. Capabilities are described and analyzed, in this study, when considering performance and learning within the case organization. Moreover, capabilities are linked to the firm's strategy (see Gadde & Håkansson, 2001; Håkansson & Snehota, 1995). Managerial capabilities in this study refer to the organizational-level capabilities significant in either operative or strategic management.

DESCRIPTION OF THE KM PLATFORM

The KM platform concept (Figure 2) was developed to support the organization in the identification of KM tools and methods used within the organization. Also, it aimed to assist the different parts of organization to identify its knowledge base, its competences, and capabilities. The KM methods mentioned here were, for example, the plans, technologies, and incentives to support knowledge exchange between different organizational levels and collaborative partners, like universities. It represented a new approach for the company to manage the rapid organizational, technological, and competitive environment changes. It was developed with the help of the Helsinki University professors and their knowledge of knowledge management concept and organizational learning. The KM platform represented the different views of knowledge sharing and exchange within the different levels of the organization. It also represented the different knowledge management perspectives and roles of different actors involved, so as to develop a shared view of KM within the organization and between different communities of practice. Professor Engeström (1998), of the Helsinki University, defined the communities of practices and their organizational learning and development as follows: *"Communities of prac-*

Figure 1. Definition of the concepts resource, asset, and capabilities

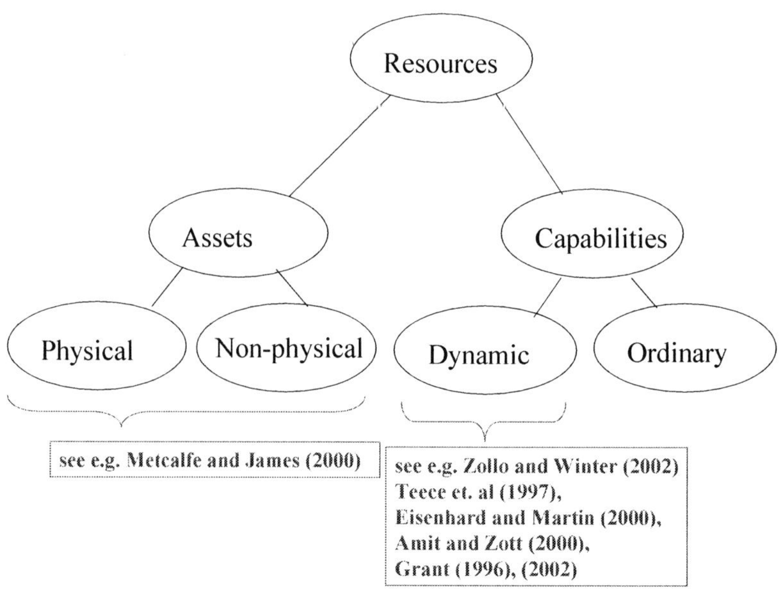

tice may be analyzed as object-oriented, socially distributed and artifact-mediated activity systems. As communities of practice perform cycles of practice-based competency maintenance and innovative knowledge creation, they also change and transform themselves, creating and realizing collective zones of proximal development." The case organization understood that the innovativeness of the communities of practice were the key to organizational success, and also, a competitive advantage.

Initially, the technological architecture did not support the knowledge management within the case organization and between its strategic partners in R&D and business. However, even if the technology base varied from one business area to another, the existing legacy systems had a lot of information from different business processes, although not all the information was used, or it was not analyzed to guide the business or to predict the business trends. The developers of the KM platform wanted to ensure that the existing legacy systems would be able to capture and encode knowledge for further business applications. The technological architecture was combined from multitechnology solutions that consisted of several products from different parties, built-in systems and components, tailored systems, and platforms from different technology internal or external partners. The modularity of the solution allowed easy replacement of the KM platform parts. The complexity and modularity of the technology architecture required the formation of a model of control and coordination so that the "plug-in" solutions would work together. There was also a requirement of compliance to the

Figure 2. KM-platform in Elisa (© Liisa Varjokallio, Elisa) (published in Juntunen, 2005,p.141)

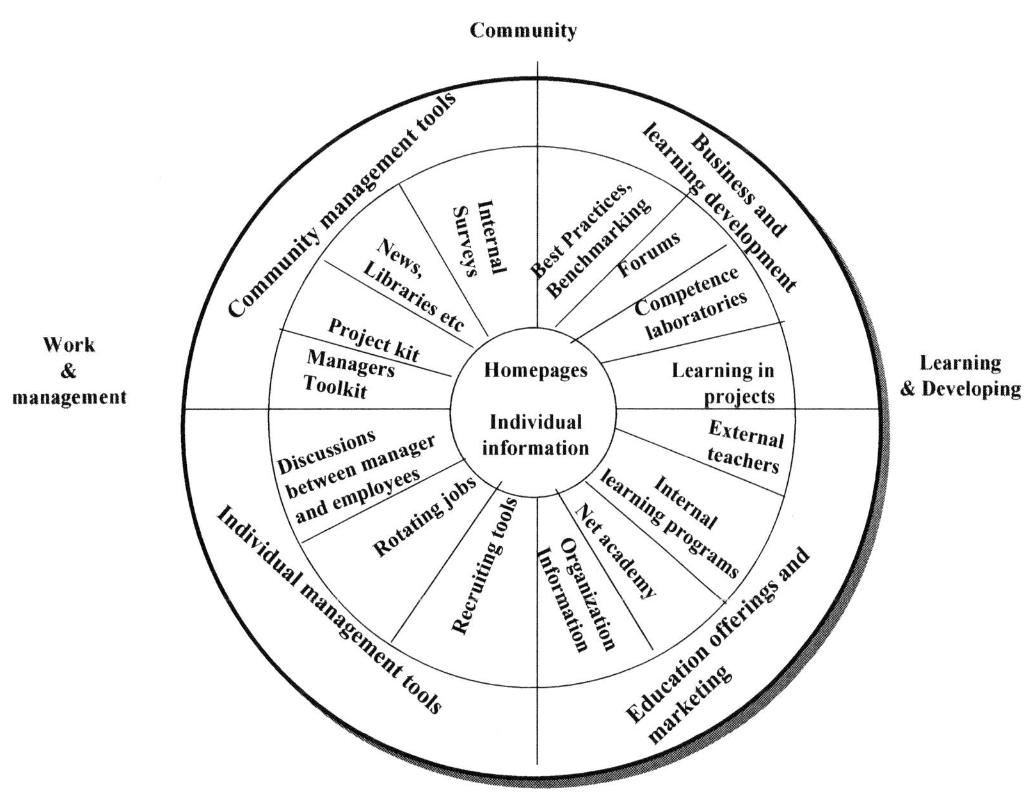

overall technology architecture of the case organization. Using a common middleware assisted in making the platform more suitable for multiple partners. Information technology architecture in the KM platform concept assisted in codifying the knowledge, storing, and delivering it to different organizational parts. KM tools also assisted in locating the knowledge and information within the company, and accelerated the creation and acquisition of knowledge within the case organization. The idea behind the KM platform concept was to leverage and enhance the organizational knowledge and knowledge transfer, within the organization and between the strategic partners of the firm. The shortening life cycles of products and services made it crucial to innovate and transfer knowledge and information more efficiently between the different communities of practice to cope with the growing competition. However, the existing businesses had fixed organization structures, processes, and infrastructure that were either a barrier or an asset in the new product development (NPD). They were an obstacle if they were slowing down or hindering new products to be in time in markets, and they were an asset if the existing infrastructure, knowledge, and capabilities could be reused in NPD. Therefore, the case corporation's top management saw that the need for a common KM platform was essential to coordinate the knowledge and information transfer within the organization.

The KM platform was divided in four parts (see Figure 2): community (*C*), individual (*I*), work and management (*WM*), and learning and developing (*LD*). These consisted of the following:

- (*I*) consisted of personal-level information such as recruitment possibilities, organizational information, and course-possibilities.
- (*LD*) was the corporate e-learning platform in which Efodi was used. There was *a net academy* that was created in conjunction with universities and allowed employees to take e-courses and e-exams in telecommunications- and technology-related subjects. The net academy was a virtual academy in Internet.
- *(WM)* consisted of a managers' toolkit in which there were essential documents and information, including HRM-issues and budgeting.
- (*C*) consisted of libraries, news, business intelligence (BI) information, and industry-level surveys, useful material to develop and ease the knowledge flow within a diversified organization.

Internal knowledge resources included employees, particularly known experts, internal libraries, internal databases, best practice and other manuals, internal yellow pages, internal summaries of lessons learnt from prior projects, GroupWare, and intranets. (Wiig, 1999)

External knowledge resources included experts, academics, customers, suppliers, external libraries, informal networks and external databases, and expert networks, like, for example, professional associations.

The competence laboratories model was part of the KM platform and its community tools. The competence laboratories model was developed at the University of Helsinki. It was a bottom-up approach to facilitate the learning process within and between the communities of practices within an organization (cf. Ahonen, Engeström, & Virkkunen, 2000). In the competence laboratories model, roots of recurrent disturbances and problems occurring in daily work were traced and conceptualized as inner contradictions of the activity system. The model was also used to analyze potential for change, and to construct a visionary model for the activity in the future. (Virkkunen & Ahonen, 2000) The competence laboratories were tested in several functional areas between 1990 and 2001 in the case organization. Particularly, this model was undertaken in customer service and help desks areas to tune the interaction between different elements of help desk functionality and associated processes, from sales to delivering the service to customers. The competence laboratory model was helpful in change management and transferring existing knowledge within the team or across the organizational boundaries when organizational changes happened. Nevertheless, it did not seem to have a long-term effect in the organization. It required repetition.

The HRM organization within the case company was responsible for the platform development and the KM program within the case organization. The trained KM network personnel held training sessions as well as the competence laboratories within the organization. The management board was interested in KM development and supported it. The human resources director, Liisa Varjokallio, was the KM champion within the organization and she boosted the KM development with enthusiasm.

Knowledge creation, exchange, and transfer had a crucial role in the various collaborative forms. Different types of knowledge bases had been created over time in the case corporation: some were based on mobile technologies, some on the Internet, and some from the integration of several technologies. These were incorporated with the KM platform.

The case company had several business areas and various business models, services, products, and technologies within the organization. The development of the KM platform assisted in tuning some of the managerial practices and processes. Often, the use of this platform was unintentional, unrecognized, or intermittent. During the development phase in 1999-2001, there were no fixed processes or guidelines in place within the case corporation as to how a business, a team, a community, or an individual should use this platform. Many parts of this platform were used out of personal interest when searching for new information and knowledge. Use of the KM platform was not pushed from the corporate level. This was partly due to a lack of resources to be able to set up a project to launch the platform within the corporation.

BENEFITS OF THE KM PLATFORM: CREATING COMPETITIVE ADVANTAGE

Different forms of competence seemed to arise from various activities within an organization. Some specific organizational competences seemed to take place mainly from the capabilities of an organization to create and produce specific kinds of products and services, e.g., R&D function and product maintenance function, and communities-of-practice related to these functions. Other competences seem to develop mainly from the abilities of some communities of practice to organize and coordinate existing internal and external resources in innovative and effective ways, like, for example, R&D, marketing, and knowledge management program in human resources management (HRM). Also, other competences seem to depend predominantly on top management's ability to vision new market possibilities of creating value for customers, like, for example, new business development and new business start-ups, like, for example, the Helsinki Arena Concept and Kotiportti™. Kotiportti™ service and platform concept consists of various subscriber connections and community services (see, e.g., Kaasinen, 2001, p. 51), like, for example, household monitoring and security systems. Helsinki Arena was an infocity multimedia platform developed in 1999-2000 in the case organization. The future home concept followed it in 2000-2003. The future home concept offered technological platforms for various DSL, mobile, and Web-based services for the case organization. It is still the basis of the case organizations' services. Helsinki Arena and future home concepts[1] were marketed internationally in the United Kingdom and in Germany to increase the case organization's market value and to get more investors interested in the case organization.

The business creation and development was seen as a collective process that required interaction and cooperation with internal and external partners, especially because of the managerial challenges in fast-changing technology environment. Therefore, it was necessary for the case corporation to process the managerial experience throughout the organization. The case organization believed that managers should not be bound by past experience, but they should, instead, uncover the implications of possible future business scenarios and encourage innovativeness. In addition, the managers had an important role within the organization in enhancing the organizational know-how within the employees, and supporting the vision and strategies chosen by the management. The managers understood the value of customer relationships and the feedback from customers in new product development (NPD). The mentoring between the managers was equally important to support the common goals and gain the information of best practices and methods used by other managers. The case organization used the so-called manager's toolkit to assist young/new managers to enhance their knowledge of how to function as a manager effectively, and how to network within the organization.

Nevertheless, access to knowledge and information still required the users of the KM platform to have both the capacity and competence for understanding, assimilating, compiling, and using the retrieved knowledge, and to adapt the information and knowledge to their specific daily problems. For example, it seemed to be very difficult to provide any kind of fixed managerial toolkits for handling the business-network management issues. In a way, all strategic business decisions and arising business situations are unique, and they could only be understood in the context of the business network situation, and from the perspective of the business history that has produced the current partners and services. The management toolkit therefore consisted of best practices, known solutions, and documentation rules and procedures.

Cognitive aspects of social capital can be seen as human-related aspects and motivation for collaboration (see e.g., Anderson & Jack, 2002; Nahapiet & Ghoshal, 1998). From the case organization's perspective, this study shows that in the relationships involving research and development activities, as well as in/out-sourcing of components required in software and platform development and implementation, the cognitive aspects of social capital providing value to software vendors include capabilities in both current technologies, as well as in emerging, future technologies. In addition, innovativeness, flexibility, and adaptability seem to be linked to cognitive capabilities of the participants and users of the KM platform.

Knowledge exchange was limited in some of the collaborative networks because the participants were unwilling to share crucial information, especially in situations where competitors were acting as coopetitors. Adapting the existing knowledge and learning within the context of partnerships happened via mutual experiences. Knowledge and information sharing happened with known and trusted partners. These formed the basis for the future competitive advantage. The historical development and experiences affected the actors' use of new technologies and solutions, and also, the partners chosen. If past experiences in projects had been good with some actors, those actors were likely to be used again. If the experiences had been less positive, those actors were stringently assessed before being selected to participate in projects. However, they were not completely out of consideration, as there were a limited number of actors with the requisite knowledge of home networking and related technologies. It was essential to keep solid working relationships with everyone. These different experiences of partners and collaboration were also recorded in the KM platform as best practices or lessons learned.

The KM platform seemed to support the creation of a new business and business networking within the case corporation satisfactorily. The most successful new service and technology platform ideas were created while the KM platform was being developed. Personnel in the R&D and in the new business development understood that cooperation and using corporate synergy was, in most cases, a benefit for any new starting business. The R&D personnel that took part of the KM development were also successful in product development and innovating. These ideas, processes, and platforms were the most profitable ones in Elisa in 2000-2007. These were, for example, Elisa's DSL solutions and Kotiportti™, which consists of various subscriber connections and community services, household monitoring, and security systems; Efodi, the learning space; and the technical solutions used in mobile and DSL services offered to consumers and business customers today.

The role of business and R&D synergies with KM platform development was, by no means, insignificant, as many of the ideas and Web and mobile technology-based tools support networking and provide new possibilities for deeper collaboration between partners and customers. For example, one of the e-learning platforms developed to support intraorganizational learning was also commercialized in 1999-2000, and sold to several external customers by the end of 2001.

Moreover, the management noticed that there were different reasons to use the KM platform in new business development and in collaborative business networking. There appeared to be different types of knowledge and information requirements relating to capability creation and utilization of capabilities in the business development and in R&D. These were categorized as follows: *Capability-driven R&D,* which required specific capabilities for research and business development; *Requirement-driven knowledge and information search* for specific business networks, like for example, mobile payment and secure money transfer issues; *Breakthrough R&D* for creating and entering the market as a pioneer and having first mover advantage on markets; and *Incremental technology requirements* for existing businesses. In *breakthrough R&D,* radically new technologies and when implementing them, the learning was learning by doing and gaining experience. However, knowledge created, for example, in breakthrough R&D, was difficult to transfer without repeated and face-to-face contacting. In *incremental technology improvement,* either an existing business sought out future business opportunities through the KM platform and networking, or R&D was looking for ideas for a technology to be applied in a new way to meet the specific commercial challenges of individual business areas.

The key objectives common to the R&D alliances during 1999 to 2000 included the utilization and development of core capabilities in both network and communication technologies (Hölttä, 2000). The case company had realized that the competitive advantage of companies relied on its managerial and organizational processes, supported by dynamic capabilities. They had also collaborated with universities to access the recent studies of dynamic capabilities (See Juntunen, 2005). These dynamic capabilities reflected organization's ability to integrate, build, reconfigure, and renew internal and external competences to address changes in its competitive environment (cf. Teece, 2003; Teece et al., 1997). Elisa's particular goal in the R&D alliances was to fine-tune product concepts generated from earlier R&D projects in 1990-1999. These ideas related to educational platforms in the Internet, self-learning in the Internet, home automation, data security issues, and VOIP-technology. The case organization also tried to establish a best practice method, with which they could manage either several concurrent R&D processes in different business units, or R&D projects concerning multiple products and services within the case company (Hölttä, 2000, Juntunen, 2007). The

R&D projects formed so-called collaborative innovation networks (COINs) (cf. Gloor, Laubacher, Dynes, & Zhao, 2003). They consisted of self-motivated individuals from different business areas of the case company, and also, sometimes from multiple organizations, and they were driven by an idea or a vision. By locating and analyzing the work methods and processes of COINs in the organization with the help of the KM platform concept, the case company was able to streamline the R&D processes of different strategic business areas in 1999-2001, and also managed to create competitive advantage in markets. In addition, according to Timo Simula (2003), who was a manager in several new business networks and involved in R&D, those people who were doing business and who were involved in projects and business networks learned, and were capable of finding, using, and adapting the new knowledge, but it also seemed as if the company itself did not learn, or that the learning cycle was unbelievably slow.

CONCLUSION

As Powell (1998, p. 228) stated: *In technologically intensive fields, where there are large gains from innovation and steep losses from obsolescence, competition is best regarded as a learning race.* Learning new technologies, integrating and implementing them into a business context, underlay the main learning race within the ICT sector during the 1990s. The capabilities and knowledge developed around these new technologies and the businesses based on them were the source for the case organization's competitive advantage. The KM platform assisted in coordinating and transferring the knowledge, information, experiences, and capabilities within the organization.

As a conclusion, the creation of a KM platform to support organizational memory and knowledge transfer within and between organizations is clearly a combination of the evolution of technological factors and organizational needs that are not totally controllable by any one actor within the organization. Rather, it is an accumulation of the intentional strategy of developing collaborative efforts and working methods, as well as alliances, partnerships, and strategic networks with other organizations that has relevant knowledge or capabilities for R&D or business development. First, this study shows that a case organization could clearly promote its business by developing an organizational memory (KM platform) and promoting social networks, as seen in this case study. Without this strong intention or strategy, the case organization would not have been able to develop its position in the emerging new e-service and mobility-related services. Second, the results show that an innovative actor has to be able to develop capabilities.

The idea behind the KM platform was that to increase the feedback and value of R&D and other organizational units, the successful innovators must complement in-house development with the know-how and technologies from external sources. At the same time, the shift from in-house R&D made it possible to increase the networking, external contacts, and access to R&D networks comprised of universities, coopetitors, competitors, and other organizations from private and public sector. (cf. Chesborough, 2003; Chesbrough & Schwartz, 2007)

Knowledge management (KM) encompassed management and communication practices designed to improve the creation and transfer of knowledge in the organizational setting. The developers and users of the KM platform were interested in retooling their organizational structures, processes, technologies, and work cultures to generate more efficient processes, practices, more creative and engaged employees, and a culture of innovating and sharing knowledge. The managers' role in enhancing the organizational know-how and knowledge sharing culture, and supporting the vision and strategies, was important (cf. Senge, 1990). Also, the employees' capability for understanding and using the retrieved knowledge, and adapting the information and knowledge to their specific daily problems, was essential (See Nonaka & Takeuchi, 1995).

The development of the KM platform was due to the need of knowledge sharing and transfer between and within different organizational units. Elisa's management clearly understood that knowledge transfer could create or surface synergies between different businesses and business networks, thus, creating competitive advantage in markets. Therefore, either finding or creating the cross-business synergies was central to the performance of multiunit and multibusiness organization with diverse business models, technology platforms, and service portfolios (See also, Goold & Luchs, 1993). The cross-business synergy arose from similarities in work processes, rules, practices, and relatedness of certain functional resources like, for example, products (See Rumelt, 1974), or technological relatedness (See Robins & Wiersema, 1995), similarities in customer base and customer interaction (See Von Hippel & Katz, 2002), R&D knowledge between businesses and business network partners (Batt & Purchase, 2004; Harrison, Hitt, Hoskisson, & Ireland 2001; Juntunen, 2005; See also Hitt & Ireland, 2002, of value of social networks), marketing relatedness (Capron & Hulland, 1999), managerial knowledge and similarities in the business governing (Ilinitch & Zeithaml, 1995; Prahalad & Bettis, 1986), human resource relatedness (Farjoun, 1994), knowledge resource relatedness (See Juntunen, 2005; Tanriverdi & Venkataraman, 2005), or closeness of strategy or small strategic distance between the businesses (See Juntunen, 2005). Increasing collaboration as an interaction strategy and a knowledge-management strategy, instead of intraorganizational rivalry, was the ultimate goal, and it was identifiable both in operations, in general, and in growing e-business and mobile business, particularly.

According to Ahonen *et al.* (2000), the first KM theories took the individual as the unit of analysis and defined knowledge and competence in terms of discrete skills that could be codified and measured. They also argued that the following KM research focused more on networking, communication and collective practices, and that knowledge is embedded in, and becomes constructed in, collective practices. This view of knowledge, embedded in the organizational practices and working groups, was also the view that the case organization wanted to enhance and support. The management strongly believed in capability and knowledge-driven competition and creating competitive advantage by superior skills and knowledge (cf. Heene & Sanchez, 1997; Stalk, Evans, & Shulman, 1992). It seemed that when the case company aimed at leveraging its capabilities and finding synergies in a multibusiness environment, the KM focused more on learning within groups and teams, and management focused on efficiency of the practices and processes. Moreover, the development and implementation of the KM platform seemed to enhance the knowledge and capability generation, business-specific architectural development and planning.

Moreover, to maintain adaptiveness, organizations need to maintain themselves in a continuous state of change in structure, processes, functions, and goals in order to achieve an optimal adaptative state (cf. Hedberg, Dahlgren, Hansson, & Olve, 1997). Operating this way is essential within organizations that operate in turbulent and rapidly changing environments, the ICT sector (cf. Hedberg et al., 1997; Juntunen, 2005). The self-renewal of the organization and the coevolution of knowledge and competence management are essential in a rapidly changing competitive environment (cf. Hong & Ståhle, 2005). Firms often face rapid technology changes with limited ability to react due to the fast pace of technological development, financial commitments, or managerial decision processes. In these situations, firms should have the ability to innovate. By focusing on knowledge management, an organization can find out that it can come upon new innovations and breakthrough technologies that can be a new competitive advantage. Simply having KM processes to produce knowledge and information of a certain product or service could assist enough to sustain an existing competitive advantage. According to Mintzberg, Ahlstrand, and Lampel (1998, pp. 175-231), in professional organizations that operate in highly complex environments, collective learning and knowledge management are essential, as the knowledge required to create strategy is widely dispersed, and further, organizations facing new situations usually have to engage in a process of learning in order to understand emerging change, as exemplified by the introduction of technological breakthroughs like the Internet and mobile technologies.

As this chapter discussed about the issue of creating competitive advantage with a KM platform, it managed to touch on several important factors, including the benefits of corporate-level knowledge management program, strategy planning, management roles in this process, and synergies with the R&D and knowledge transfer within the organization. Horizontal and vertical collaboration within the organization is important, especially in a new business development and finding and developing business synergies. These findings have important theoretical and methodological implications. First, they support the industrial network approach (see e.g., Håkansson & Waluszewski, 2002) and the resource-based view in emphasizing the key role of combining the heterogeneous resources controlled by various actors in order to be able to create new technological and business solutions. They also support the knowledge-based view of the firm, and that information technologies can play a significant role in the knowledge-based development in the organization in that information systems can be used to synthesize, and boost up large-scale intra- and interorganizational knowledge management efforts (Alavi & Leidner, 2001) and knowledge repositories.

At the organizational level, the findings emphasize two interrelated perspectives, the role of management in boosting the knowledge management efforts to gain competitive advantage and the managerial capabilities related to it, and the role of organizational learning, in the development of new business. Finally, the study suggests that organizational and interorganizational learning and knowledge management has a crucial role in network management. This is logical as capabilities are, to a great extent, created through learning processes. The results indicated that learning was both exploitative and explorative (March, 1991) in the development of the KM platform. Exploitative learning means here that the organization is constantly monitoring its competitors and the field of technology. Explorative learning means here that the organization was capable of identifying new technologies and business opportunities, and conceptualizing these into practice. By applying knowledge management tools, the case organization was also able to turn its learning into organizational routines and capabilities. A specific capability that should be singled out was the cognitive ability of the case organization to renew itself. This is a good example of a so-called dynamic capability.

FUTURE RESEARCH DIRECTIONS

Opportunities for further research are numerous, ranging from coordination issues with external partners to strategy planning of interorganizational knowledge transfer systems, because new linkages between public and private sector are forming, and innovations extend beyond traditional industry border lines. However, this also creates new challenges for organizations: how to keep the capable employees and business-critical information and knowledge within the organization and out of competitors' reach. Also, concerns about the effectiveness of providing services and products fast and efficiently have mushroomed in the past decade. In part, this was due to the fast pace of technology development, globalization, and increasing networking between the private and public sector. The collaborative networking that is increasingly emerging in our society requires efficient knowledge sharing and transferring, which can be done by using KM-tools like, for example, data mining.

The current evidence emphasizing the role of learning in new knowledge and business creation suggest that it would be useful to apply the theories of organizational and interorganizational learning more explicitly to studies investigating knowledge transfer and exploitation in collaborative networks and network management in turbulent environments. The results achieved in this study provide several articulated contributions towards this direction.

REFERENCES

Ahonen, H., Engeström, Y., & Virkkunen, J. (2000). Knowledge management – The second generation: Creating competencies within and between work communities in the competence laboratory. In Y. Malhotra (Ed.), *Knowledge management and virtual organizations*. London: Idea Group Publishing (IGP).

Alavi, M., & Leidner, D. E. (2001) . Review: Knowledge management and knowledge management systems. *MIS Quarterly, 25*(1), 107-136.

Amit, R., & Zott, Ch. (2001). Value creation in e-business. *Strategic Management Journal, 22*, 493-520.

Amit, R., & Zott, Ch. (2002). Value drivers of e-commerce business models. In M. Hitt, R. Amit, E. Autio, H. J. Sapienza, & J. G. Almeida (2000), Effects of age at entry, knowledge intensity, and imitability on international growth. *Academy of Management Journal, 43*(5), 909-924.

Anderson, A. R., & Jack, S. L. (2002). The articulation of social capital in entrepreneurial networks: A glue or lubricant? *Entrepreneurship and Regional Development, 14*, 193-210.

Barney, J. B. (1991). Firm resources and sustained competitive advantage. *Journal of Management, 17*(1), 99–120.

Batt, P. J., & Purchase, S. (2004). Managing collaboration within networks and relationships. *Industrial Marketing Management, 33*, 169-174.

Capron, L, & Hulland, J. (1999). Redeployment of brands, sales forces, and general marketing management expertise following horizontal acquisitions: A resource-based view. *Journal of Marketing, 63*(2), 41–54.

Cassel, C., & Symon, G. (Eds.). (1994). *Qualitative methods in organisational research: A practical guide*. London: Sage.

Chesbrough, H. (2003). *Open innovation: The new imperative for creating and profiting from technology*. Harvard Business School Publishing Corporation.

Chesbrough, H., & Schwartz, K. (2007). Innovating business models with co-development partnerships. *Research-Technology Management*, Jan-Feb.

Conner, K. R. (1991). A historical comparison of the resource-based theory and five schools of thought within industrial organization economics: Do we have a new theory of the firm? *Journal of Management, 17*(1), 121-154.

D'Aveni, R. A. (1994). *Hypercompetition: Managing the dynamics of strategic maneuvering*. New York: Free Press.

Davenport, T. H. (2001). *From data to knowledge*. San Jose, CA: Oracle Inc.

Elisa. (2006). *Annual report*. Retrieved 6/12/2007, from http://www.elisa.com/english/docimages/attachment/Elisa_vk2006_uk.pdf

Elisa. (2007). *Presentation*. Retrieved 6/12/2007, from http://www.elisa.com/english/docimages/attachment/Q2%202007%20English.pdf

Engeström, Y. (1998). Innovative learning in work teams: Analyzing cycles of knowledge creation. In Y.Engeström, R. Miettinen, & R-L. Punamäki (Eds.), *Perspectives in activity theory* (pp. 377-404). Cambridge University Press.

Farjoun, M. (1994). Beyond industry boundaries: Human expertise, diversification and resource-related industry groups. *Organization Science, 5*(2), 185–199.

Freeman, L. (2000). Visualizing social networks. *Journal of Social Structure, 1*(1).

Gadde, L-E., & Håkansson, H. (2001). *Supply network strategies*. IMP group. John Wiley and Sons Ltd.

Gloor, P., Laubacher, R., Dynes, S., & Zhao, Y.(2003). Visualization of communication patterns in collaborative innovation networks: Analysis of some W3C working groups. In *Proc. ACM CIKM 2003*, New Orleans, November 5-6, 2003.

Grant, R. M. (1998). *Contemporary strategic analysis: Concepts, techniques, applications*. Oxford: Blackwell.

Grant, R. M. (2002). *Contemporary strategy analysis*. Blackwell: Cambridge, MA.

Hartley, J. F. (1994). Case studies in organisational research. In C. Cassel & G. Symon, (Eds.), *Qualitative methods in organisational research: A practical guide*. London: Sage.

Håkansson, H., & Waluszewski, A. (2002). *Managing technological development. IKEA, the environment and technology. Routledge Advances in Management and Business Studies*. London: Routledge.

Harrison, J. S., Hitt, M. A., Hoskisson, R. E., & Ireland, R. D. (2001). Resource complementarity in business combinations: Extending the logic to organizational alliances. *Journal of Management, 27*, 679–690.

Hatch, N. W., & Dyer, J. H. (2004). Human capital and learning as a source of sustainable competitive advantage. *Strategic Management Journal, 25*, 1155–1178.

Hedberg, B. L. T., Dahlgren, G., Hansson, J., & Olve, N. G. (1997). *Virtual organizations and beyond: Discover imaginary systems*. London: Wiley and Sons.

Heene, A., & Sanchez, R. (Eds.). (1997). *Competence-based strategic management*. Chichester: John Wiley and Sons.

Heer, J., & Boyd, D. (2005). Vizster: Visualizing online social networks. In *InfoVis 2005, IEEE Symposium on Information Visualization*.

Heide, J .B., & John, G. (1995). Measurement issues in research on interfirm relations. In K. Håkansson, & I. Snehota (Eds.), *Developing relationships in business networks*. London: Routledge.

Hitt, M. A., & Ireland, R. D. (2002). The essence of strategic leadership: Managing human and social capital. *Journal of Leadership and Organizational Studies, 9*, 3-12.

Hölttä, P. (2000). *Piimäki 2000: Laajakaistaisen alueverkon uudet palvelut. tuotekehityshakemuksen liite 2*. Tutkimus- ja kehitysprojektisuunnitelma TEKESin 'Tietoliikenteellä maailmalle' teknologiaohjelmaan. HPY Tutkimuskeskus.

Hong, J., & Ståhle, P. (2005). The coevolution of knowledge and competence management. *Int. Journal of Management Concepts and Philosophy,*1(2).

Ilinitch, A. Y., & Zeithaml, C. P. (1995). Operationalizing and testing Galbraith's center of gravity theory. *Strategic Management Journal, 16*(5), 401–410.

Juntunen, A. (2005). *The emergence of a new business through collaborative networks: A longitudinal study in the ICT sector.* Acta Universitatis Oeconomicae Helsingiensis. Printed in HSEPrint. A-series, no 256, ISSN 1237-556X. ISBN: 951-791-957-3/1.

Juntunen, A. (2007). Creating competitive advantage: The emergence of a new business through collaborative networks – An empirical case study in the ICT sector. In H. Rahman (Ed.), *Developing successful ICT strategies: Competitive advantages in a global knowledge-driven society.* Idea Group Publishing. Information Science Reference.

Juntunen, A. (2008). Data warehouse in the Finnish police - A case study. In J. Wang (Ed.), *Encyclopedia of data warehousing and mining* (2nd ed.). Idea Group Publishing. Forthcoming.

Kaasinen, K. (2001). *Describing business concept based on partnership network.* Thesis. Lappeenranta University of Technology.

Kogut, B., & Zander, U. (1997). Knowledge of the firm, combinative capabilities, and the replication of technology. In N. J. Foss (Ed.), *Resources, fims and strategies – A reader in the resource-based perspective.* Oxford: Oxford University Press.

Matusik, S. F., & Hill, C. W. L. (1998). The utilization of contingent work, knowledge creation, and competitive advantage. *Academy of Management Review, 23*(1), 680–697.

Metcalfe, J. S., & James, A. (2000). Knowledge and capabilities: A new view of the firm. In N. J. Foss & P. L. Robertson (Eds.), *Resources, technology, and strategy - Exploration in the resource-based perspective.* New York: Routledge.

Miles, M. B., & Huberman, A. M. (1994). *Qualitative data analysis: An expanded sourcebook* (2nd ed.). CA: SAGE Publications.

Mintzberg, H., Ahlstrand, B., & Lampe, J. (1998). *Strategy safari. The complete guide through the wilds of strategic management.* London: Prentice Hall Financial Times.

Möller, K., & Svahn, S. (2006). Role of knowledge in value creation in business nets. *Journal of Management Studies, 43*(5), 985-1007.

Nahapiet, J., & Ghoshal, S. (1998). Social capital, intellectual capital, and the organizational advantage. *Academy of Management Review, 23*, 242-266.

Nonaka, I., & Takeuchi, H. (1995). *The knowledge-creating company. How Japanese companies create the dynamics of innovation.* NY: Oxford University Press.

Nonaka, I., Toyama, R., & Konno, N. (2001). SECI, Ba and leadership: A unified model of dynamic knowledge creation. In I. Nonaka & D. J. Teece (Eds.), *Managing industrial knowledge. Creation, transfer, and utilization* (pp. 13-43). London: Sage.

Norman, R., & Ramirez, R. (1993). From value chain to value constellation: Designing interactive strategy. *Harvard Business Review, 71*, 65-77.

Penrose, E.T. (1959). The theory of the growth of the firm. New York: Wiley.

Pettigrew, A. M. (1997). What is a processual analysis? *Scandinavian Journal of Management,13*, 337-348.

Powell, W. W. (1998). Learning from collaboration: Knowledge and networks in the biotechnology and pharmaceutical industries. *California Management Review, 40*(3), 228-340.

Prahalad, C. K., & Bettis, R. A. (1986). The dominant logic: A new linkage between diversity and performance. *Strategic Management Journal, 7*(6), 485–501.

Robins, J. A, & Wiersema, M. F. (1995). A resource-based approach to the multibusiness firm: Empirical analysis of portfolio interrelationships and corporate financial performance. *Strategic Management Journal, 16*(4), 277–299.

Senge, P.M. (1990). The leader's new work: Building learning organizations. *Sloan Management Review, 3*(1), 15–26.

Stalk, G., Evans, P., & Shulman, L. E. (1992). Competing on capabilities: The new rules of corporate strategy. *Harvard Business Review, 90*(2),.57–69.

Tanriverdi, H., & Venkatraman, N. (2005). Knowledge relatedness and the performance of multibusiness firms. *Strategic Management Journal, 26*, 97–119.

Teece, D. J. (2000). *Managing intellectual capital.* Great Britain: Biddles Ltd., Guildford and King's Lynn.

Teece, D. J. (2003). Explicating dynamic capabilities: Asset selection, coordination, and entrepreneurship. *Strategic Management Theory* (August).

Teece, D. J., Pisano, G., & Shuen, A. (1997). Dynamic capabilities and strategic management. *Strategic Management Journal, 18*(7), 509-533.

Thomas, L. G. (1996). The two faces of competition: Dynamic resourcefulness and the hypercompetitive shift. *Organization Science, 7*(3), 221–242.

Van de Ven, A. H., & Poole, M. S. (1990). Methods for studying innovation development in the Minnnesota innovation research program. *Orga nization Science, 1*(3), 313-335.

Virkkunen, J., & Ahonen, H. (2000) *Knowledge management as creative dialogue about the future.* Paper presented in Knowledge Management Conference in Sao Paulo, Brazil, 7/2000.

Wernerfelt B. (1984). A resource-based view of the firm. *Strategic Management Journal, 5*(2), 171–180.

Wiig, K. M. (1999). Introducing knowledge management into the enterprise. In J. Liebowitz (Ed.), *Knowledge management handbook* (pp. 3.1- 3.41). Boca Raton: CRC Press.

Yin, R. K. (1994). *Case study research: Design and methods.* Sage, Thousand Oaks.

Yli-Renko, H., Autio, E., & Tontti, V. (2002). Social capital, knowledge, and the international growth of technology-based firms. *International Business Review, 11*, 279-304.

Zollo, M., & Winter, S. G. (2002). Deliberate learning and the evolution of dynamic capabilities. *Organization Science, 13*(3), 339-351.

ADDITIONAL READING

Argote, L., McEvily, B., & Reagans, R. (2003). Managing knowledge in organizations: An integrative framework and review of emerging themes. *Management Science, 49*(4), 571-582.

Bartlett, C. A., Kanter, R. M., Kaplan, R. S., & Jensen M. C. (2003). *Best practice: Ideas and insights from the world's foremost business thinkers.* Cambridge, MA: Perseus Publishing.

Baum, J. (2002). *Blackwell companion to organizations.* New York: Blackwell Publishers.

Bolton, P., & Dewatripont, M. (1994). The firm as a communication network. *Quarterly Journal of Economics, 109*(4), 809- 839.

Card, S. K., Mackinlay, J. D., & Shneiderman, B. (1999). *Readings in information visualization: Using vision to think.* San Francisco: Morgan-Kaufmann.

Carrillo, J. E., & Gaimon, C. (2004). Managing knowledge-based resource capabilities under uncertainty. *Management Science, 50*(11), 1504-1518.

Garud, R., Kumaraswamy, A., & Langlois, R. (Eds). (2002). *Managing in the modular age: Architectures, networks, and organizations.* Blackwell Publishers.

Giles, J. (2005). Internet encyclopedias go head to head. *Nature*: 900-901.

Johnson, R. A., & Greening, D. W. (1999). The effects of corporate governance and institutional ownership types on corporate social performance. *Academy of Management Journal,* 42(5), 564–576.

Keele, L., & Kelly, N. J. (2006). Dynamic models for dynamic theories: The ins and outs of

lagged dependent variables. *Political Analysis,* 14(2),186-205.

Nadler, D., & Tushman, M. (1998). *Competing by design: The power of organizational architectures.* NY: Oxford University Press.

O'Reilly, C. A., III, & Tushman, M. L.(2004). The ambidextrous organization. *Harvard Business Review, 82*(4), 74-81.

Schoonhoven, K., & Romanelli, E. (Eds). (2001). *The entrepreneurship dynamic: The origins of entrepreneurship and its role in industry evolution.* Stanford University Press.

Simon, H. (1991). Bounded rationality and organizational learning. *Organization Science, 2,* 125-134.

Smith, W., & Tushman, M. (2005). Managing strategic contradictions: A top management model for managing innovation streams. *Organization Science, 16*(5) (September-October 2005).

Tushman, M. L. (2004). From engineering management/R&D management, to the management of innovation, to exploiting and exploring over value nets: 50 years of research initiated by IEEE-TEM. *IEEE Transactions on Engineering Management, 51*(4), 409-411.

Tushman, M. L. (in press). On the co-evolution of knowing and doing: A personal perspective on the synergies between research and practice. *Journal of Management Inquiry.*

Tushman, M., & O'Reilly, C. (1997). *Winning through innovation: A practical guide to leading organizational change and renewal.* Boston, MA.: Harvard Business School Press.

Tushman, M. L., &. O'Reilly, C. (2002). *Winning through innovation: A practical guide to leading organizational change and renewal.* Boston, MA.: Harvard Business School Press.

Tushman, M. L., O'Reilly, C. A., Fenollosa, A. E. K., Adam, M., & McGrath, D.. (in press). Relevance and rigor: Executive education as a lever in shaping practice and research. *Academy of Management Learning & Education* (Special Issue: Challenges and Opportunities for Executive Education.)

Varun, G., & Lynne, M. M. (Eds.). (in press). Business process transformation. In *the Advances in Management Information Systems (AMIS) serial.* M.E. Sharpe.

Viégas, F. B., & Wattenberg, M. (2006). Communication-minded visualization: A call to action. *IBM Systems Journal, 45*(4).

von Hippel, E. (1994). "Sticky information" and the locus of problem solving: Implications for innovation. *Management Science,* 40, 429-439.

von Hippel, E. (2005). *Democratizing innovation.* Cambridge, MA: MIT Press.

Walsh, J. P., & Hong, W. (2003). Secrecy is increasing in step with competition. *Nature, 422,* 801-802.

Wattenberg, M., & Kriss, J. (2006). Designing for social data analysis. *IEEE Transactions on Visualization and Computer Graphics, 12*(4), 549–557.

ENDNOTE

[1] Helsinki Arena, Future Home, Megahouse and Megahome concepts are presented in Chapters III and IV.

INTERVIEWS

Name (Interviewee)	Position	Organization	Interview	Time
Ahlstrand, Klaus	Business Development Manager	Datatie	in person	February 11th 2001, October 31st 2001, November 1st 2001
Ahlstrand, Klaus	Business Development Manager	Datatie	e-mails	March 29th 2000, October 31st 2001, November 1st 2001, November 12th 2001, December 5th 2001, January 5th 2002
Arhi, Mika	BI, Analyst	Elisa Corporation	in person	May 2001
Arhi, Mika	BI, Analyst	Elisa Corporation	e-mails	July 7th 2002, August 1st 2002
Buuri, Marko	Product Development	Elisa, HCB	in person, cooperation meeting	September 7th, 2001
Grönroos, Timo	Development Manager	Radiolinja	in person	May 5th, 1999
Hakanen, Seppo	Marketing Manager	Elisa, PCS	in person	March 30th 2000
Hakanen, Seppo	Marketing Manager	Elisa, PCS	cooperation meeting	April 17th 2000
Hedberg, Nina	Voice Services, Manager	Elisa, Traffic and Subscriber connections	in person, cooperation meeting	June 2nd 1999, November 20th 1999
Hedberg, Nina	Manager	Elisa, PCS	in person, cooperation meeting	,March 30th 2000, April 17th 2000
Hietanen, Petri	Development Manager	Elisa, HCB	in person, cooperation meeting	September 2nd 2001, October 3rd 2001
Hölttä, Pertti	Research Center	Elisa, Research Center	in person, cooperation meeting	January 31st 2000, January 21st, 2001, January 25th 2001
Jokinen, Juha	Manager (IM)	Elisa, BS	in person, cooperation meeting	September 5th 2001, September 27th 2001, June 18th 2004, January 12th 2005
Jokinen, Juha	Manager (IM)	Elisa, BS	e-mail updates	October 20th 2001, May 15th 2002, January 12th 2003, March 10th 2004
Jäntere, Kirsi	Development Manager	Elisa, PCS	in person, cooperation meeting	March 3rd 2000, April 5th 2000
Kaasinen, Katariina	Student	Elisa, HCB	in person	November 30th 2001
Kaasinen, Katariina	R&D developer	Nokia, R&D	e-mail	August 4th 2003
Karjalainen, Ismo	Product Manager (Kotiportti™)	Elisa, PCS	in person, cooperation meeting	June 1st 2001
Kautto, Antti	Management Consultant	Comptel	in person	December 18th 2001

continued on following page

INTERVIEWS CONTINUED

Lehmus, Pasi	Director	Elisa	in person, cooperation meeting	January 15th 2002 March 3rd 2003
Malmberg, Juha	Director	Elisa, Traffic and Subscriber connections	in person	May 1999
Malmberg, Juha	Director	Elisa, PCS	in person	March 30th 2000, April 17th 2000, November 20th 2001, December 17th 2001
Masala, Sami	Business Development Manager	Elisa, HCB	e-mails	March 30th 2000, April 17th 2000, November 26th 2002, December 12th 2002, January 23rd 2003, February 27th 2003, November 13th 2003, December 16th 2003
Masala, Sami	Business Development Manager	Elisa, HCB	in person	March 29th 2000, April 18th-19th 2000, November 24th 2002, December 12th 2002, January 20th 2003, February 25th 2003, November 10th 2003, December 15th 2003, January 12th 2004, May 21st 2004, August 18th 2004, May 13th 2005, June, 12th 2006
Peltola, Hannu	Product Development	Elisa, Traffic and Subscriber connections	in person, cooperation meeting	May 20th 1999
Pohtola, Raili	Director	Elisa, PCM	in person	May 15th 2002
Rasia, Olli	Multimedia Access, Manager	Elisa, Traffic and Subscriber connections	in person, cooperation meeting	May 5th 1999
Rasia, Olli	Department Manager	Elisa, PCS	in person, cooperation meeting	March 30th 2000, April 17th 2000, April 9th 2001, August 28th 2001
Riipinen, Jarmo	Business Manager	Elisa, BS	phone	November 7th 2001
Simula, Timo	Head of Development, HCB's Manager	Elisa, HCB	in person, cooperation meeting	March 30th 2000, April 17th 2000, November 7th 2001, December 2nd 2001, December 20th 2001
Simula, Timo	Head of Development, HCB's Manager	Elisa, HCB	e-mails	November 26th 2002, December 12th 2002, January 30th 2003, March 14th 2003, September 9th 2003, October 13th 2003, November 3rd 2003, December 18th 2003, January 12th 2004, February 13th 2004,

continued on following page

INTERVIEWS CONTINUED

Simula, Timo	GIGA program director	TEKES The National Technology Agency	e-mails, updates in meetings	June 18th 2005, September 30th 2005, May, 15th 2006, June 12th 2006, January 12th 2007, March 3rd 2007
Tirkkonen, Piia	Student	Elisa, HCB	in person	November 22nd 2002
Tirkkonen, Piia	R&D	Nokia	e-mail	July 22nd 2003
Yli-Äyhö, Janne	Manager	Telia-Sonera	e-mail	June 24th 2002
Varjokallio, Liisa	Manager	Elisa, HR	in person	January 25th 2001
Vainionpää, Sami	Multimedia Access, Development Manager	Elisa, PCS	in person, cooperation meeting	January 15th 2001
Viitala, Erkki	Customer Service Manager	Comptel	in person	December 2001
Viitala, Erkki	Customer Service Manager	Comptel	in person	July 7th 2003
Vuolteenaho, Petri	Product Development, Manager	Elisa, PCS	in person, cooperation meeting	March 30th 2000
Vuolteenaho, Petri	Product Development, Manager	Elisa, PCS	in person, cooperation meeting	April 17th 2000
Weckström, J-P.	Manager	Telia-Sonera, BI	e-mail	June 18th 2002

Chapter VIII
Learning Organizations or Organizations for Learning? How Small Firms can Learn from Planned and Random Technical Problem Solving:
Implications for Technical Education

Corrado lo Storto
Universitá di Napoli Federico II, Italy

ABSTRACT

This chapter reports the findings of an empirical study whose purpose is to identify the attributes of the organization infrastructure that support organizational learning in small manufacturing firms through the creation of procedural knowledge. The study is based on the following assumptions: a) organizations are cognitive systems that process information and knowledge; b) knowledge is a by-product of technical problem solving; c) innovation occurs as a stream of random or planned problem solving; d) many attributes of the organization infrastructure that foster innovation also foster knowledge generation during technical problem solving. Findings show that three dimensions of the organization infrastructure have an influence on learning: openness, innovativeness, and leadership. These attributes identify two typologies of organization infrastructures that differently affect the generation of procedural knowledge and learning. In particular, it was found that the organization infrastructure has a moderating effect on the relationship between some context factors (environment diversity, problem complexity, context ambiguity, and uncertainty) and the amount of procedural knowledge generated during technical problem solving. Implications for technical education are also discussed.

BACKGROUND

In the last years, the business environment has dramatically changed. This new environment demands that firms perform their operations with greater speed, flexibility, dynamism, and superior quality. Global competition imposes higher, global standards of customer service, creativity, and innovation that even those firms having no global market goals are forced to meet to protect their market share. Knowledge and the capability of firms to learn developing new knowledge are two main strategic issues that hold the highest potentials for gaining efficiencies, and creating value.

The learning organization and organizational learning have emerged as metaphors and models for the adaptation and growth for successful and competitive organizations (Argyris & Schon, 1978; Senge, 1990). Models of organizational learning are developed from models of human learning (Bandura, 1986; Kolb, 1984; Postman, 1976; Schein, 1993). Like the individual learner, organizations draw on experience, interpret and process information transforming it into knowledge, and purposefully use knowledge. Scholars distinguish between personal knowledge that an individual possesses by virtue of education or experience and collective or organizational knowledge, identified as organizational memory or a publicly documented body of knowledge (Nevis, DiBella, & Gould, 1995). As an individual learner does, a learning organization accumulates experience, leveraging on feedback about past decisions to incrementally adjust its reactions to similar problems (Pennings, Barkema, & Douma, 1994). However, an organization by itself cannot develop, learn, grow, or take action independently of its members. Organizations have to capture tacit knowledge of individuals and make it explicit and/or shared in the organizational structure to create and manage organizational knowledge (Lynn, 2000). Moreover, in order to learn, it must apply knowledge. Indeed, organizational learning links cognition to action (Crossen, Lane, & White, 1999). Ideally, learning organizations are communities of learners, all working toward common goals. Some activities characterize learning organizations (Garvin, 1993): systematic problem solving, experimentation with new approaches, incentives for risk taking, steady flow of new ideas, learning from their own experiences and past history, learning from the experiences and best practices of others, transferring knowledge quickly and efficiently throughout the organization. Even though knowledge can also be brought in from the outside, either through market intelligence activities or by hiring people with a particular expertise, the outside knowledge has to be absorbed internally by the firm to be utilized in its operations, and the capability to do that depends on the knowledge resources the firm already holds within its boundaries, primarily knowledge embedded as organizational knowledge in the minds and routinized behaviours of its employees (i.e., its human and structural intellectual capital, see Bontis, Dragonetti, Jacobsen, & Roos, 1999). Human knowledge is created through social interaction between the explicit and the tacit knowledge, and in the organizational knowledge environment (consisting of the numerous interacting and interdependent social, cultural, cognitive, political subsystems that shape the creation, accumulation, flow, and use of knowledge within the organization), the organizational infrastructure is an important part of the overall organizational knowledge ecology, as it influences how people interact within the organization and with the external environment (i.e., the customers, the technology sources, the norms, and standard framework, etc.).

The idea that some attributes of the organizational infrastructure (i.e., culture and attitudes of people relative to certain behaviours, communication environment, climate, etc.) may be supportive to information processing and knowledge management and, in the same time, to innovation, has been largely explored, discussed, and now is well accepted in the literature. However, a few number of scholars focused their attention on the fact that the attributes of organization infrastructure that support innovation processes may also influence organizational processes leading to the creation of new knowledge and learning. As knowledge and learning are an outcome of a socialization process, diffusion, and sharing of tacit knowledge (Nonaka, 1994), the same mechanisms and attributes of the organization infrastructure that play a role in the information processing and innovation management may have not a secondary weight in the creation of new organizational knowledge and learning.

The notion of the learning organization has generated tremendous debate and several definitions have been proposed in literature. In spite of the multiple perspectives that exist about the learning organization, there is a pressing need to understand "whether such ideas and practices genuinely create fitter and better organizations for both the people who work in them and the society they seek to serve" [or whether this concept is] "simply yet another 'vision' propounded by management and educational idealists or whether it is an ideal capable of reality" (Jones & Hendry, 1992, p. 58).

A great amount of the literature on the learning organization, both in the form of theoretical considerations and case studies, is concerned with large firms. However, learning and knowledge management remain critical activities for small firms too, and as in large firms, they can support competitiveness and success. There is no doubt that there exist differences between large and small firms (Julien, 1993; Welsh & White, 1981), and, consequently, the latter develop and implement innovation and knowledge management models that differ from those typical of larger firms. For instance, studies carried on, relative to innovation management within small firms, emphasized how these have a larger dependence on the environment compared to large firms, and the networking effects have a substantial weight in the innovation activity and information and knowledge collection (Saxenian, 1991), and different interaction and collaboration models, more or less formalized, may even affect innovation success (Imai, Nonaka, & Takeuchi, 1985; Lundval, 1988; Maidique & Zirger, 1988; Rothwell, Freeman, Horsley, Jervis, Robertson, & Townsend, 1974; Saxenian, 1991; Teece, 1986; Van Kooji, 1990; von Hippel, 1987). The dominance of the entrepreneur/manager and the scarce formalization of the organization structure are also elements that give a specific character to knowledge management and learning models adopted in small firms. New knowledge is usually created discontinuously in the life of a small firm, when it has to deal with unusual situations, such as the development of a new product or the entrance into a new market, and, not in a formal way, as it happens in large firms, during the institutionalised R&D activity. Moreover, small firms are frequently founded and managed by people having a technical background, more oriented to solve technical problems rather management problems. Technical problem-solving cycles, both at an individual and a collective level, random or planned, occurring during innovation, are a primary source for the creation of technical knowledge (Corti & lo Storto, 1997; von Hippel & Tyre, 1993), and often it happens that a large amount of organizational knowledge (even the management knowledge) accumulates as a by-product of technical problem solving. Putting technical problem solving in a central position of the process leading to the creation of new knowledge in small firms allows us to construct a contingent model of the learning process in which the attributes of the organization infrastructure that affect how technical problem-solving proceeds have also a weight on the typology and amount of knowledge generated in specific situations. Consequently, small organizations differ as to their capability to generate knowledge and learn when they carry on innovation, and some attributes of their infrastructure may be more effective to support knowledge generation in some contexts rather than in others. The organizational infrastructure is the complex system that links together the social system of human relationships interacting in many ways, the cultural, beliefs, and value system that provide people with the ability to understand and respond to a given situation, the norms and not written rules system that encompasses people's action, the interdependencies system that sets constraints to how work has to be done, and the management style. It determines the type of leadership, communication, and group dynamics within the organization, substantially addressing how learning occurs. For instance, if the organization has an infrastructure supporting teamwork, stimulating and enabling effective collaboration and social interaction, the capability of the organization to carry out distributed and collective problem solving may be enhanced, and, consequently, its learning capability results improved. Teams are able to deal with more complex problems because they have usually a larger range of skills and expertise than a single individual. Team dynamic generally produces better solution outputs than individual analysis can do. When people work together to achieve their shared understandings, they exchange ideas to clarify issues and reach consensus, put in place the knowledge and insights that team members should have to achieve the team goal, make a collective decision, create such intellectual outputs as situations assessment, courses of action, plans, analyses, recommendations, and action.

This chapter reports the findings of an empirical study aimed at identifying the attributes of a small firm organization infrastructure that support organizational learning through the creation of routine knowledge during technical problem solving performed in the innovation activity. The study is based on the following assumptions: a) organizations are cognitive systems that process information and knowledge; b) knowledge is a by-product of technical problem solving; c) innovation occurs as a stream of random or planned problem solving; d) many attributes of the organization infrastructure that foster innovation also foster knowledge generation during technical problem solving. Implications are also driven relatively to how address technical education to support learning, both at the high school and the university level. A large part of the roles in small manufacturing firms are indeed covered by people that possess a technical education.

A contingent framework is adopted, as there are no universal attributes of an organization infrastructure that make possible, in every context, the effective creation of organizational knowledge during innovation. Rather, it is the fit between the organization infrastructure attributes and context nature that determines the amount and quality of knowledge created. This is the relevant research problem addressed in this chapter.

Figure 1 shows the logical flow of the research approach.

The chapter has the following structure. First, the main characters of technical problem solving, and the relationship between problem solving and learning and knowledge, are discussed. Next, the organization infrastructure attributes are identified, and the conceptual model and a set of hypotheses are constructed. Finally, the data are analysed, testing hypotheses, and conclusions are driven.

TECHNICAL PROBLEM SOLVING AS A SOURCE OF LEARNING DURING INNOVATION ACTIVITY

When organizations undertake innovation, information and knowledge processing becomes a frantic activity during the cycles of technical problem solving. Technical problem solving has a critical importance in generating learning (Fisher, 1980; Johnston & Gibbons, 1975; Maidique & Zirger, 1988; Torrance & Myers, 1970; Utterback, 1971; von Hippel, 1994; von Hippel & Tyre, 1993). Argyris (1982, p. 38) defines learning how: "[...] a process in which people discover a problem,

Figure 1. The flow of the research approach

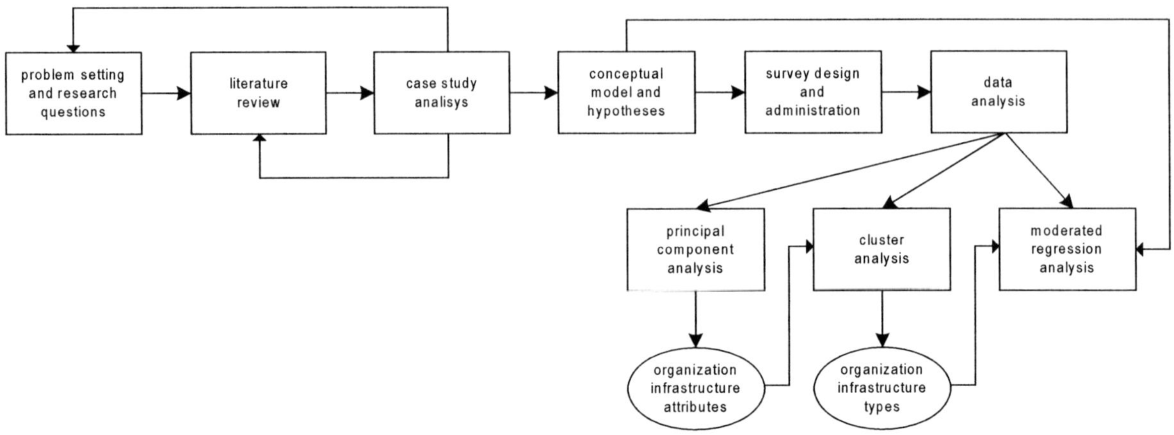

invent a solution to the problem, produce the solution, and evaluate the outcome, leading to the discovery of new problems [...]," while von Hippel and Tyre (1993, p. 5) suggest that "[...] learning by doing is simply a form of problem solving that involves application of a production process (or product, service or technique) in its intended use environment."

The most critical phase of problem solving is "problem formulation." In fact, Getzels and Csikszentmyhalyi (1976) have shown how problem formulation is more intimately linked to creativity and interaction between individuals than the other phases of problem solving (diagnosis and solution). The solution to a problem can be easier or not depending on the representation and classification of a problem that individuals produce during formulation (Hayes, 1978). For instance, a problem can be represented in an abstract or real shape by using mathematical formulae, logical symbols, or by using words or drawings. Problems can be indeed "ill framed" or "well framed." Newell et al. (Newell, Shaw, & Simon, 1979) maintain that problems that require a creative approach to be solved are, at the beginning, ill framed and generally ambiguous, and a great part of the problem-solving activity reduces to formulate a correct frame of the problem. The novelty, the complexity, and the ambiguity of the problem are all features that influence the individual capability to frame a problem correctly (Mintzberg, Duru, & Theoret, 1976).

One of the major tasks of problem-solving activity is to define the boundaries between these variables. Complexity, ambiguity, and uncertainty individuals perceive during problem solving are indeed the outcome of a choice, either explicit or implicit, that the problem solver makes when he/she frames or reframes the problem according to a convenience analysis of his/her experience, knowledge, and cognitive limitations, and henceforth, are not objectively and exogenously defined. This choice has strong implications on the prosecution of problem solving, as it addresses the following diagnosis and solution, while providing insights relative to the mental model to adopt (Brief & Downey, 1983; Clement, 1989; Larkin & Simon, 1987, 1991; Mintzberg et al., 1976). Individuals use existing mental models when they perceive that the environment is fundamentally uncertain or they attempt to bring complexity to a manageable level; they build new mental models when ambiguity increases or complexity cannot be reduced.

Firms undertake learning each time they invent, develop, and implement new products, programs, services, or adopt new management practices, new procedures, new organizational settings, new policies, or enter new markets. Most of times, in these occurrences, their entrepreneurial group/CEO faces situations that he/she is not familiar with. In this case, individuals embark upon a stream of problem-solving activities during which new knowledge emerges in different shapes. This activity is characterized as being inherently full of uncertainty and ambiguity.[1] Uncertainty reduction and ambiguity alleviation are usually achieved through a process of trial and error learning, during which people build and rebuild the reference domain of the problem, and sense making, in which they develop new categories for the interpretation of the real world or use old categories to interpret new information. People reduce uncertainty about states and linkages between actions and outcomes by collecting new useful information, and alleviate ambiguity by identifying new meanings and approaching the problem-solving activity from a different perspective, moving from local to diffused problem solving. In local problem solving, initial problem formulation remains unchanged all over problem solving, and causes and solution are identified within the original problem domain. As a consequence, problem is solved by eliminating direct causes that determined the drawback that originated the problem. When individuals involved in problem solving fail to identify causes or solution, they abandon the attempt to find a solution. In diffused problem solving, vice versa, they reformulate the problem, either introducing new variables or eliminating some of the old ones, or, further, assuming new relations between problem variables. That happens when it clearly appears that current problem formulation neither can lead to an acceptable solution, nor to any solution; for instance, when causes that generated problems are not under the organization control. As a consequence, the problem-solving cycle comes to an end when the initial state of the system is redefined and altered, modifying the value of the parameters (e.g., a product is enriched with new features to satisfy latent needs of the customer) and a solution to the new problem is found that can eliminate the original drawback, even though not in a direct manner. The reformulation of the old problem is particularly critical, because it questions the reference pattern of the organization. The problem-solving activity, started within a specific domain, transfers to other domains, generating other problems to be solved, not necessarily of technical type. The locus of problem solving thus migrates from a domain to another (see Figure 2a and Figure 2b) (Corti & lo Storto, 1997).

Frequently, when problems are too complex, and ambiguity and uncertainty are, as a consequence, very high, the innovation process assumes an indeterminate nature, and characters of randomness. The problem-solving activity is

Figure 2a. Local problem-solving

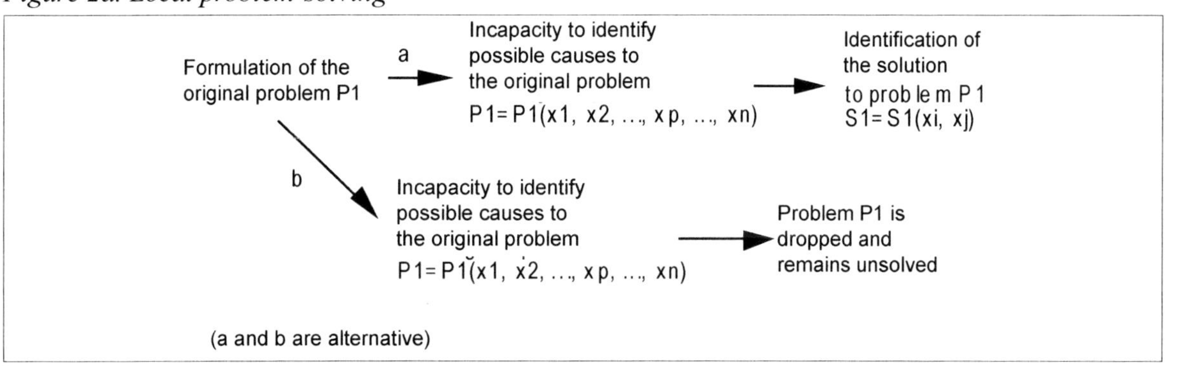

Figure 2b. Diffused problem-solving

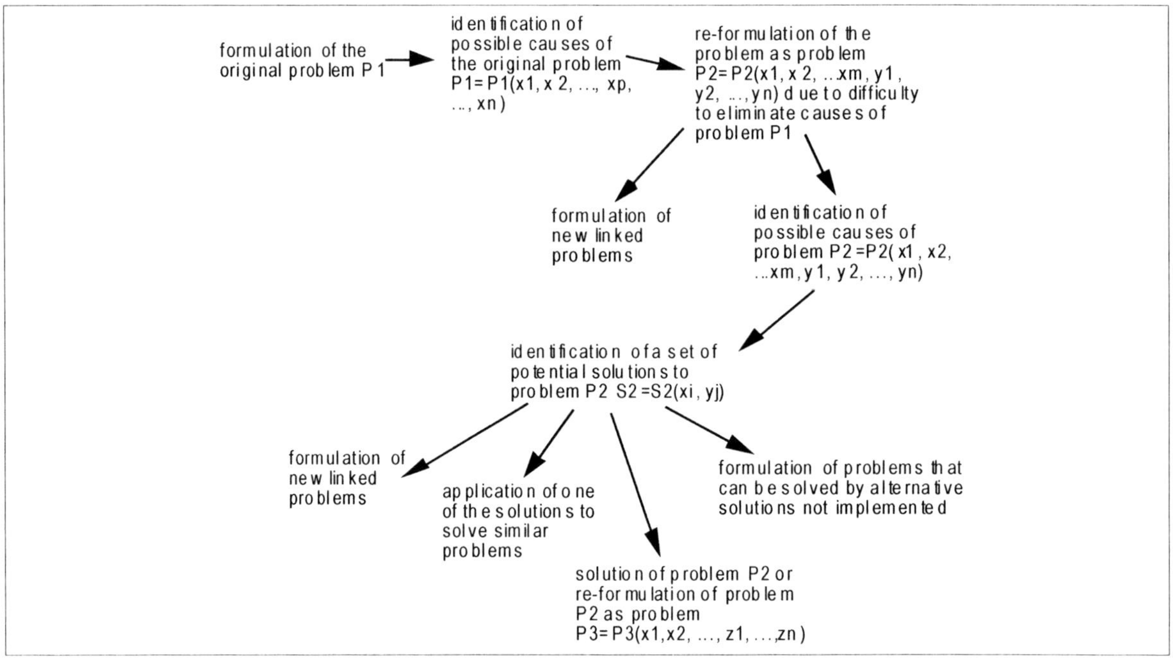

extremely sensitive to the different initial conditions and constraints of the organization where it occurs, and a number of factors affect how technical problem solving proceeds (West & Farr, 1989). These factors, indirectly, influence how knowledge is generated during problem solving. Literature has identified three types of factors: a) factors describing the characters and the attitudes of individuals involved in problem solving; b) factors describing the attributes of the organization infrastructure where problem solving occurs, that is to say, the set of attributes that develop a climate more or less favourable to carry out problem solving as they positively influence interaction among individuals, new idea generation, exchange and flows of expertise, and socialization[2]; c) environment and context factors, such as problem complexity, the diversity of knowledge domains needed to carry on problem solving, and ambiguity and uncertainty perceived by actors.

A major outcome of learning is knowledge. Knowledge differs from information. While information is objective, knowledge is associated with a particular cognitive structure of the individuals who develop and use it. Knowledge at the individual and organizational level derives from the interpretation of either new or existing information (Daft & Weick, 1984) that is, through developing, consciously or not, a new understanding of surrounding events (Fiol, 1994; Weick, 1995). Knowledge is not independent, but fundamentally situated, being, in part, a product of the activity, context, and culture in which it is generated. The transformation of individual knowledge into organizational knowledge critically depends on the organizational culture. Shared norms, values, interpretive categories, and behaviours are an indicator of organizational knowledge. According to Hedberg (1981, p. 3): "[...] although organizational learning occurs through individuals, it would be a mistake to conclude that organizational learning [...henceforth, knowledge...] is nothing but the cumulative result of their members' learning. Organizations do not have brains, but they have cognitive systems and memories [...]. Members come and go, and leadership changes, but organizations'memories preserve certain behaviours, mental maps, norms, and values over time." The creation of organizational knowledge is, therefore, the result of a social interaction between individuals that share and develop individual knowledge (Nonaka, 1994). Organization infrastructures that allow socialization, interaction among individuals, and communication, positively affect the generation of organizational knowledge.

A large amount of the organizational knowledge remains in an informal form, as tacit knowledge that is created and used when formal results leading to formal knowledge are generated. Tacit knowledge is made of facts, ideas, opinions, judgements, assumptions, meanings, questions, decisions, guesses, stories that cannot be stored in some physical support, and most of times, it emerges through people action. It is almost invisible, transitory, and ephemeral (Corti & lo Storto, 2000). Organizational knowledge can also be classified in terms of its being linked to action or not, as routine or procedural knowledge and declarative knowledge. While declarative knowledge only provides the means for interpreting facts, we need procedural knowledge to use it in order to change a situation. Procedural knowledge is indeed the organizational capability to use, proficiently and effectively, knowledge. Therefore, it has a strong behavioural orientation. Organizational procedural knowledge emerges from the behaviours of the individuals within the organization and exists in the form of routines (Nelson & Winter, 1982). Routines acquire a particular importance in shaping the organization knowledge (Nelson & Winter, 1982), as they make declarative knowledge and organization memory operative and useful for the organization. They include (Levitt & March, 1988, p. 320): "[...] the forms, rules, procedures, conventions, strategies, ad technologies around which organizations are constructed and through which they operate. They also include the structure of beliefs, frameworks, paradigms, codes, cultures and knowledge that buttress, elaborate, and contradict the formal routine.". Organizational routines are a particular way of doing that an organization has developed and learned. As organizations, groups, and individuals gain experience, they tend to adopt habitual modes of behaviour (i.e., routines), devoting, as a consequence, only occasionally, attention and effort to modify them. Routines can be viewed as a concatenation of actions stored in the organization memory. Behind these routinized behaviours there lie particular features in terms of mental models. Individuals and organizations follow a set of rules, sedimented in the organizational memory, that enable them to perform their actions with a reduced mental effort. They may or may not be equivalent to its official standard operating procedures, which are more explicitly formulated and have normative standing (Cohen & Bacdayan, 1994). Usually, these routines have a strong tacit dimension that makes them difficult to imitate or change (Johnson-Laird, 1983). But, even though routines are believed to be difficult to change, so that stability is usually used as an attribute to characterize them, most organizational routines can undergo substantial change after learning (Feldman, 2000). Pentland and Rueter (1994) use the metaphor of grammar to explain how routines can change. As a grammar allows people to produce a variety of sentences that make sense to others who know the grammar by combining elements of the language according to rules, in the same way, routines allow people to select elements from a repertoire (the language) to put together sequences of actions that make sense to others in the organization. Recent field work, done by Feldman (2000), has further revealed that "grammar" also changes in the organizations, as members do not only use common rules to combine the elements of a repertoire, but they also develop a new repertoire of interpretative categories and develop new rules, that is to say, new ways to put elements together. Similar findings were found in previous field analysis (Corti & lo Storto, 1997; Corti & lo Storto, 2000). This perspective of routines is perfectly consistent with the idea of two-level organizational learning, proposed in literature (Argyris & Schon, 1978). Therefore, both for its potential of change, and the impact that this change can have on organization performance, routine knowledge merits a particular attention for further investigation.

THE CONCEPTUAL MODEL AND THE RESEARCH HYPOTHESES

Literature on problem solving has identified a set of factors that affect the way all the problem-solving activity proceeds. If we analyse innovation in an organizational perspective through the metaphor of organization as a cognitive system, we find a coincidence between factors that foster innovation and factors that affect technical problem solving within a group (Amabile, 1983; Nystrom, 1979). Most of these factors are attributes of the organization infrastructure: good communication inside groups, decentralized decision making, a diffused approach to problem solving, strong leadership, attitude to innovation and change, the tolerance for ambiguity, collaboration, and participative management. Factors that work as stimuli come both from outside the organization and from inside. The first kind of factors are usually denominated "environment" and include some attributes of the market (i.e., the customer typology, the geographical area where the firm sells its products, the products, competition, etc.), of the technology that is incorporated in the product, of the political and social setting. The environment is usually described in terms of its diversity, turbulence, uncertainty, dynamics, and so on. Aiken and Alford (1970) affirm that a high level of environment turbulence, in terms of instability and unpredictability, provides the organization with strong stimulations and suggestions relative to innovation as technical problem to solve. The second kind of factors relates to the nature of the information and knowledge context in which problem solving occurs, and is regarded as being, or not, complex, uncertain, and ambiguous.

With reference to factors describing the organization infrastructure characters, research has shown how participation in the decision-making process is associated to a lower resistance to change and to a higher probability to generate innovative ideas (Wall & Lischeron, 1977). When individuals participate in decision making by exerting influence, they interact, and exchange information; henceforth, they can offer ideas useful to improve all the problem-solving activity. A decentralized structure enables individuals to consider several perspectives, and with great probability, to produce a greater diversity of ideas enhancing individual and group creativity (West & Farr, 1989). The variety of perspectives, relative to a problem, improves the quality of the solution as it enriches the set of possible interpretations of facts and meanings. The decentralisation of decision making fosters autonomy, a greater commitment of individuals, and a diffused flow of information within the problem-solving group, and from the group to the rest of the organization. On the contrary, a strong centralization of decision making works as an inhibitor of innovative behaviours (Burns & Stalker, 1961; Shepard, 1967; Thompson, 1965). Centralization, indeed, limits the use and the effectiveness of communication channels, thus reducing the amount of available information (Hage & Aiken, 1967). Organization procedure formalization and rigid task and activity design are also inhibitors for the generation of new ideas, as rigid rules and procedures can impede individuals from searching new sources of information. Zaltman et al. (Zaltman, Duncan, & Holbeck, 1973) suggest that the combination of organizational formalization and centralization, on the one side, and context complexity, on the other side, have different effects on the generation and implementation of innovative ideas. A high level of context complexity, combined with a low organization formalization and centralization, stimulates and makes the collection and processing of information and knowledge, and the generation of ideas, easier; vice versa a low level of complexity joined to a high level of organization formalization and centralization reduces role conflicts and ambiguity, henceforth, making easier the implementation of new ideas. But, even though a high level of discretion stimulates new ideas at all levels (Amabile, 1983), it remains also true that the effect of the discretion is amplified by the presence of a moderated control on the group involved in the problem-solving activity by the leader (Pelz & Andrews, 1976). Empirical research has indeed shown that the leadership style has a critical weight in affecting the performance of innovative behaviours and problem solving.

A participative, collaborative, and democratic management style also encourages the generation of new ideas Kanter, 1983; (Nystrom, 1979; Peters & Waterman, 1982). An organization climate that supports independent action, autonomy, and interaction is an important issue in the innovation process (Andrews, 1975; Taylor, 1972). When investigating the influence of specific resources on innovation, scholars focused on the availability either of slack or idiosyncratic and specialized resources (Mohr, 1969; Rogers, 1983). Information and knowledge are critical resources, the lack of which, during technical problem solving, can seriously be an obstacle, and compromise innovation (Bell, 1982; Tushman, 1979). When individuals involved in problem solving perceive a state of uncertainty consequent to the lack of useful information, or a state of ambiguity, as the available information appears meaningless, they undertake an intense activity of information collecting, knowledge sharing, and sense making by building several kinds of networks in the organization. Collaboration at different levels becomes a necessary means to feed these informative networks, while socially shared or distributed problem solving elicits the dynamic development of an individual's expertise. Social interaction, and joint problem solving as well, foster the emergence of new ideas and innovation.

A number of factors affect the resistance to change of the individuals inside the organization: selective perception, conformity to rules and norms, habitual modes of behaviour, scarce tolerance for change, dogmatism, scarce tolerance for ambiguity, and a low attitude for risk (Watson, 1973). With reference to individual factors, research in the field of organization innovation suggests that some traits of the individual personality are critical, as they can foster or inhibit innovation. Kirton (1976) affirms that the "adaptation-innovation" dimension of human personality is critical in the analysis of the organization change. Indeed, some individuals adapt (for instance, to do things better), while others tend to innovate (for instance, to do things differently). Differences across two groups of individuals is in the style rather than in the degree of creativity. Beside the use of general problem-solving strategies, it seems clear that the capability to solve a problem efficiently is dependent on the availability of deep, well-organized knowledge, specific of the problem domain. Some factors can, vice versa, affect negatively the problem-solving activity: inertia, conservativism, assumptions, beliefs, old knowledge. Past successful experience can decrease the productivity of problem solving and learning (Adamson & Taylor, 1954; Birch & Rabinowitz, 1951; Glucksberg & Weisberg, 1966), because individuals tend to apply procedures for problem solving that are consolidated, even when other procedures could work better (Cyert & March, 1963; Luchins & Luchins, 1959). The initial assumptions can set boundaries to the search for a fruitful solution (Scheerer, 1963). Entrepreneurial myopia can suggest to select the first identified solution that provides the minimum standard of satisfaction (Luchins & Luchins, 1959). Groups that move from a local approach to problem solving to a diffused approach can get better results, both in terms of problem solution and learning.

Figure 3. The conceptual model

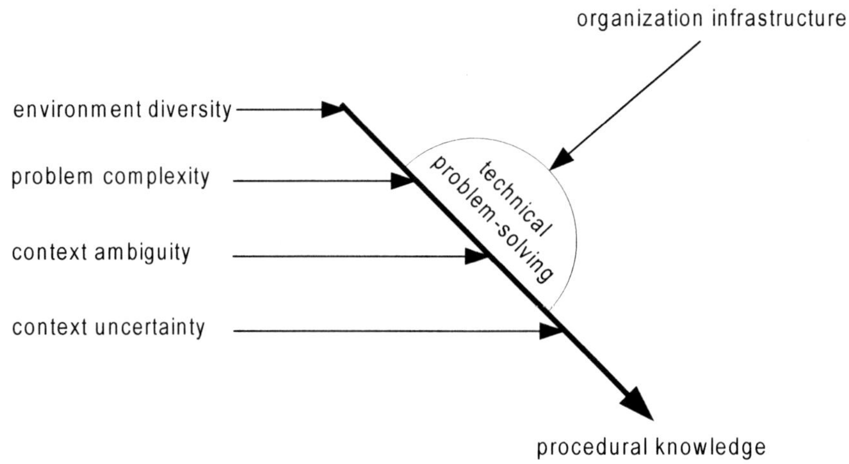

The foregoing reviews of the literature reinforce the importance of addressing the research question posed at the beginning of the chapter. Figure 3 reports the conceptual model of the study. It is assumed that the following set of contextual factors have a direct effect on the generation of procedural knowledge during technical problem solving: (a) environment diversity, (b) problem complexity, (c) context ambiguity, (d) context uncertainty, while the organization infrastructure has a moderating effect on the relationship between these factors and procedural knowledge. Table 1 shows the list of variables considered in the study, and the respective value of Cronbach index calculated to assess construct reliability.

The conceptual model can be restated as a sequence of specific hypotheses incorporating the contingency effects of the organization infrastructure:

Hypothesis 1: *An organization infrastructure that presents attributes that foster innovation also supports the generation of procedural knowledge during technical problem solving when environment diversity is high.*

Hypothesis 2: *An organization infrastructure that presents attributes that foster innovation also supports the generation of procedural knowledge during technical problem solving when problem complexity is high.*

Hypothesis. 3: *An organization infrastructure that presents attributes that foster innovation also supports the generation of procedural knowledge during technical problem solving when context ambiguity is high.*

Hypothesis 4: *An organization infrastructure that presents attributes that foster innovation also supports the generation of procedural knowledge during technical problem solving when context uncertainty is high.*

SAMPLE AND METHODOLOGY

Data Collection

The main study was preceded by an exploratory study to identify categories and constructs. A number of in-depth semistructured interviews

Table 1. Variables of the model and Cronbach index

Variable	*Cronbach*
1) Attributes of the organization infrastructure	
collaborative climate	0.70
participative climate	0.86
decentralized decision-making	0.55
orientation to change	0.73
communication quality	0.89
customer orientation	0.86
entrepreneurial style (adaptive vs innovative)	0.86
procedure formalization	0.77
ambiguity tolerance	0.58
leadership	0.87
accurate task and activity design	0.64
problem-solving approach (local vs diffused)	0.79
2) Context factors stimulating knowledge creation	
environment diversity	0.60
problem complexity	0.85
context ambiguity	0.79
context uncertainty	0.85
3) output of knowledge creation	
procedural knowledge	0.74

were carried out in nine small firms in the food equipment manufacturing industry located in the area close to Naples, southern Italy. Several topics were covered during the interviews: the model adopted in product development, technical problem-solving management, common practices and behaviours adopted during technical problem solving to deal with familiar and unfamiliar problems, knowledge management practices (storage, retrieval, use), and learning strategies.

The outcome of this exploratory study was used to develop a structured questionnaire. The constructs of the study were operationalized along multiple dimensions, most of which were measured using multi-item scales. Questions required the respondents to give a subjective judgement. In this case, a 7-points Likert anchor grid was used. For every variable, a set of statements encircling the underlying concept was designed as a measuring tool. Measures were obtained as summation of the scores given to the single items of each scale after standardizing the value distribution for every item. Both the sets of scales for measuring the environment and context attributes (diversity, problem complexity, context ambiguity and uncertainty), and organization infrastructure (collaborative climate, participative climate, decentralized decision making, orientation to change, communication quality, customer orientation, entrepreneurial style, procedure formalization, ambiguity tolerance, leadership, task and activity design, problem-solving approach) were derived from the theory and similar scales proposed in the literature. In particular, the scale for measuring the problem-solving approach adopted (local vs. diffused) was derived by the author from previous field analysis (Corti & lo Storto, 1997), while the scale for measuring the entrepreneurial style (adaptive vs. innovative) was developed from the Kirton (1976) theoretical framework. One form of organizational knowledge was considered, in the study, that was simply denominated "routine or procedural knowledge," denoting the capability to properly execute a set of actions aimed at modifying situations. To resolve the conceptual/operative difficulty of assessing the emergence of new routines, routinized behaviour was associated to a set of condition-action rules prescribing the actions to be made for every condition. The change in a routine is thus identified by the change in the corresponding set of behavioural rules or components of a rule. A scale for knowledge was, therefore, built following a logical-deductive reasoning and case study research (Corti, lo Storto, & Trombetta, 1996). Perceptual measures were considered to be very appropriate for this kind of study, even for assessing the rate of knowledge generation. In this case, it would be difficult to measure actual generation, especially with the nature and variety of routines used during product development. The link between perceptions of knowledge acquisition and actual learning has been demonstrated in industrial training research (Hicks & Klimoski, 1987).

In the next step of data collection, the survey questionnaire was administered, face-to-face, to a sample of 35 small firms in the food-processing-equipment manufacturing industry. The sample is not a random sample, but it was designed to cover a broad range of types of equipment manufactured in the area close to Naples, Salerno, and Caserta, in the south of Italy. At the time of the survey, it almost covered one third of the population of small firms in the industry located in this area. The study focused on a single industry in order to control for the influence of industry specificity. These firms manufacture products on order for an industry where processes and products are neither based on sophisticated and complex technologies, nor carry on any formalized R&D activity. They are low-technology firms and their markets are local and of niche. Generally, these firms resort to technological innovation (of product or process) to face market pressure coming from their competitors, either due to a change in the technology used in the industry or to market size decrease. Technological innovation allows them to keep a competitive advantage and increase profit. Many times, they have a reactive behaviour to market change. The size of firms is very small, 14 employees on average, but these figures do not take into account the "black economy" phenomenon of the geographical area.

Respondents were asked to nominate three problems occurred during the development of a new product, ranked according to the level of perceived complexity. Ninety-one cases of technical problem solving were studied in-depth. Only ill-structured or partially structured problems were considered. Technical problems have a various nature, but all of them are linked to the ill or non-functioning of a new machine or equipment. All problems are of mechanical type.

Data Analysis

Cluster analysis was performed to uncover homogeneous groups of similar organization infrastructures using the K-means technique (Arabie & Hubert, 1994). These groups were used as moderating variables to test how the fit between typologies of organization infrastructures and external and internal environment attributes determines a better outcome in terms of new

Table 2. Factorial analysis output

	Factor 1	Factor 2	Factor 3
collaborative climate	0.808	0.028	0.329
participative climate	0.900	-0.004	-0.029
decentralized decision-making	0.025	-0.133	0.443
orientation to change	0.338	0.679	0.146
communication quality	0.696	0.077	0.135
customer orientation	0.669	0.168	0.235
entrepreneurial style (adaptive vs innovative)	-0.044	0.948	-0.083
procedure formalization	0.189	-0.212	0.124
ambiguity tolerance	-0.144	0.171	0.037
leadership	0.408	-0.068	0.686
accurate task and activity design	0.195	-0.136	0.194
problem-solving approach (local vs diffused)	0.156	0.598	0.476
percent of total variance explained	23.31	15.45	9.67

organizational routines after problem solving. Preliminarily, the sample was first examined in order to discover outliers in the data. Because it was found not to have strong candidates for deletion, all the data were considered. Further, factor analysis was used to identify common factors and reduce the number of variables determining clusters (Kim & Mueller, 1978). Variables describing the organization infrastructure were considered as inputs in factor analysis.

Adopting a contingency perspective, fit between organization infrastructure and environment was operationalized as an interaction between the two sets of variables (Covin & Slevin, 1988; Schoonhoven, 1981; Venkatraman, 1989). According to this view, the higher the fit, the higher the amount of knowledge generated (henceforth, the width of the substitution of old routines with new ones). To test the existence of fit, moderated regression analysis was implemented, following the procedure suggested by Sharma et al. (Sharma, Durand, & Gur-Arie, 1981).

RESULTS

Table 2 shows the outcome of factor analysis.

Three factors emerged with eigenvalues at least 1, and explaining few less than 50% of total variance. In the table, boldface indicates largest loadings on each factor. The names of factors, based on highly loading items, were "Openness," "Innovativeness," "Leadership." Composites were formed for each factor by averaging items with the highest loadings and scaling them so that larger values meant a higher organizational openness or innovativeness or leadership. The first factor indicates the attitude of the small organizations to offer a climate that fosters communication and collaboration among individuals, and to be open and receptive of useful insights coming from the customer. The second factor is an indicator of the innovative behaviour of the firm. Extremes of scale are an adaptive/reactive behaviour, an inclination to perform local problem solving, with a scarcity of new products developed or with some minor improvements of existing products and, on the other end, a proactive/innovative behaviour, more inclined to widen problem-solving activity, with a number of new products developed, or with major improvements or complete redesign of the existing products to include new features and performance. The third factor simply reveals the leadership dimension of the entrepreneurial group/CEO of the firm.

Table 3 shows the results of cluster analysis performed with the composite variables, Openness, Innovativeness, Leadership, as inputs. Two clusters of firms clearly emerged from the analysis, denoting two prevailing attitudes diffused among the firms of the sample. The first cluster which was called "Type 1 firms," includes 23 firms having a relatively reduced openness, attitude to perform innovative behaviours, and leadership. The second cluster, "Type 2 firms," is made of 12 firms having a relatively higher openness and innovativeness with a slightly higher attitude to leadership of the entrepreneurial group/CEO.

Table 4 reports the outcome of the moderated regression analysis. Four regression models were analysed and all times, procedural knowledge was considered as the dependent variable. The variables problem complexity, context ambiguity, context uncertainty, and procedural knowledge, considered critical for the prosecution of the analysis, were treated further on. With this aim, four composite variables were built to measure, for each firm, the relative change of the construct, assuming, as a reference, the change in the perceived familiarity with problem faced. For instance, in the case of context ambiguity measurement, for each firm, the relative change of context ambiguity was calculated as a difference between the perceived levels of ambiguity passing from the problem solving of familiar problems to the problem solving of unfamiliar problems. The same procedure was implemented for the remaining three constructs. In this way, by measuring relative changes, the influence of respondents' judgement subjectivity was attenuated[3].

The moderation effect, due to the nature of the organization infrastructure, was introduced in the analysis, including a dummy variable that, in the codification of the statistical software utilized, assumes the values 1 for "Type 1" cluster and –1 for the "Type 2" cluster. To test the contingency effect, for each model, two regression analyses were performed. The first regression assessed the main effects of the independent variables (the dummy variable and the environment/context variable), which were included separately. The second one entered the cross-product term (the product of the dummy variable and the environment/context variable). According to this procedure, a moderation effect exists if the coefficient of the product term significantly differs from 0, and there is a substantial increase in the value of R-squared. Table 4 shows that only in Model 1, the existence of fit between the environment diversity and the typology of the organization infrastructure was not ascertained. In Model 2, a change in perceived problem complexity positively correlates with an increase in the amount of

Table 3. Cluster analysis output

	Cluster 1 (Type 1)		*Cluster 2 (Type 2)*		*t-value*	*prob.*
	mean	*std.dev*	*mean*	*std.dev*		
openness (Factor 1)	4.81	0.48	5.76	0.57	-5.301	0.000
innovativeness (Factor 2)	3.51	0.57	4.67	0.65	-5.465	0.000
leadership (Factor 3)	5.11	0.41	5.56	0.58	-2.698	0.011

Table 4. Moderated regression analysis

	Model 1		*Model 2*		*Model 3*		*Model 4*	
constant	0.301	0.301	0.203	0.183	0.171	0.108	0.183	0.094
environment diversity	0.077	0.076						
problem complexity change			0.264	0.655°				
ambiguity change					0.874*	1.239*		
uncertainty change							0.522^	0.836*
dummy (1)	-0.077	-0.077	-0.040	0.082	-0.081	0.029	-0.075	0.059
environment diversity x dummy		0.001						
problem complexity change x dummy				- 0.747°				
ambiguity change x dummy						-0.620^		
uncertainty change x dummy								-0.476^
R-squared	0.058	0.058	0.110	0.157	0.361	0.461	0.218	0.295

* prob.≤0.01, ^prob. ≤0.05, °prob. ≤0.10

routine knowledge change after problem solving. The "Type 2" infrastructure amplifies this effect. In Model 3 and in Model 4, similar findings were found, as both cross-effects are significant. However, the first order effects of a change in context ambiguity, or uncertainty on the generation of new routine knowledge, are also significantly positive. Hypotheses Hp. 2, Hp. 3, and Hp. 4 have, thus, been confirmed.

From these findings clearly emerges that the organization infrastructure works as an amplifier in the process of knowledge generation during technical problem solving.

DISCUSSION AND CONCLUSION

The results of this study provide substantial support for the hypothesis of a contingency relationship between environment/context and organization infrastructure also in the perspective of learning and knowledge generation.

The outcome of the statistical analysis shows that an increase, both in the level of ambiguity and uncertainty of the context in which individuals move, induced by the perceived nature of available information and knowledge during technical problem solving, will be conducive to a more consistent change in routine knowledge, with a greater probability if the organization infrastructure presents attributes of high openness, innovativeness, and leadership. Findings also show that a similar behaviour is apparent when small firms'entrepreneurial group/CEO faces a high complex problem. However, the research shows that a hierarchy exists in the magnitude of effects between the different attributes of context determined by the perceived nature of problem upon the generation of new routine knowledge through the mediating effect of the organization infrastructure. Uncertainty, and much more ambiguity, independently of the moderation effect of organization infrastructure, have also a stronger effect on knowledge generation than problem complexity. This outcome should not be surprising, as it is consistent with what is reported in literature (Weick,1995).

Knowledge creation occurs, indeed, as a paradoxical play between the need to reduce the level of uncertainty, and alleviate the level of ambiguity in the organization, in order to carry on the innovation activity, on one hand, and the need to enhance the level of uncertainty and ambiguity necessary to generate new knowledge, on the other one (Corti & lo Storto, 2000). New knowledge is created when individuals face ambiguous situations. Weick (1995) gave early insights into the importance of ambiguity, rather than uncertainty, in fostering learning. While ambiguity has a direct effect in stimulating the process of knowledge generation, as it requires efforts from the members of the organization to find meaningful interpretations of old or new circumstances, facts, information, and causal relationships, uncertainty influences knowledge generation only in an indirect way, as it induces individuals to search for new information to process. Insofar, uncertainty produces a favourable condition to the development of a state of necessary ambiguity to produce new organization knowledge. These findings are also consistent with what was found in previous work investigating in-depth technical problem solving in small firms. Henceforth, there is evidence that the organization infrastructure practices an amplification effect in the process of generation of new knowledge. The attributes of the organization infrastructure, openness, innovativeness, and leadership, work as levers that amplify the positive effect of social behaviours and cognitive efforts of individuals involved in technical problem solving[4].

Implications that these findings may have on the organization of technical education curricula are relevant. Methods and techniques to deal with technical problem solving, people attitudes, and orientation toward collaboration and teamwork, creative thinking, are all factors that enhance organization capability for learning. Problem solving is an important component of technical education curriculum. Current thinking seems to strongly support the importance of problem solving. Problem solving is indeed the core activity of professional technical and engineering work. As much of what students need to know with a great probability has not yet been created, it does not make sense to try to teach students the most up-to-date technology if they do not leave school with the ability to continue learning by themselves. Developing problem-solving capabilities in technicians and engineers is a crucial factor to support future organizational learning. Technical skills remain still essential, but poor communication and interpersonal skills, inability to work in teams, and lack of creative thinking, can limit business opportunities. Further, experience shows that project outcomes are improved by the ability to reduce stress, resolve conflicts, increase motivation, and develop positive attitudes and team unity.

Formal education usually does not support the enhancement and refining of problem-solving skills. Most technical problems are open by nature, and require estimating, evaluating, and making choices. Common textbook problems are, however, mostly closed problems with one definite answer, and ask the students "to find the answer" rather than "to solve the problem." Further, closed mathematical problems have the same solution regardless of the person solving them and thus, can be considered to be totally value free. In the opposite end of the spectrum, there are the real-world problems that require plenty of creativity and decision making. Curricula should henceforth be revised in order to include integrated learning environments that encourage learners to use higher-order thinking skills, and in particular, problem-solving skills, considering problem solving as a complex mental activity consisting of a variety of cognitive skills and actions, rather than a mechanical systematic and decontextualized set of skills. Students must be challenged, to analyse critically, problem situations that include technical, economic, social, environmental, and ethical factors. General problem-solving skills are more important than being able to solve specific problems. Creativity plays a central role in problem solving and in particular, in fostering divergent thinking, which is required to come up with proper solutions to problems (Thomas & Litowitz, 1986). The question is whether creativity can be taught, in particular, whether an educational system profoundly steeped in convergent thought encourages or even tolerates divergent thinking. Some techniques can be transferred to students to enhance creativity. These techniques, together with working in a cross-disciplinary setting, can help students to use convergent and divergent thinking. Education for problem solving not only enhances problem-solving skills, but also develops complementary attitudes, such as ambiguity tolerance.

As always, limitations in this research should be taken into account. The dimensions used to measure the nature of organization infrastructure are limited in scope, although they represent the dominant constructs common in the innovation, problem solving, and knowledge-management-literature domains. A major focus should be addressed to the individual attributes, rather than only to the organization ones as a whole. Indeed, individuals learn and unlearn. Organizations provide an environment that favours individual learning, socialization, sharing and diffusion of information, beliefs, and meanings. Individuals' experience, knowledge, expectations, motivation, and attitudes are all attributes that could have a weight in the process of generation of organization knowledge.

When factor analysis was performed, with surprise, not all the items were loaded in the discovered factors. These items indicate procedure formalization, accurate task and activity design, decentralized decision making, and tolerance for ambiguity. Literature on innovation foresees that low values of the first two attributes, and high values of the last two, are positively correlated to innovation. A linkage between tolerance for ambiguity and change in procedural knowledge might be manifest, but the small size of sample partially hides the existence of other factors that could further shape the organizational infrastructure. The discrepancy between literature and field results, as to the other three correlations, are probably a sign of the difference between large and small firms. On the one side, as in small firms, the entrepreneur group/CEO is dominant, decision making is usually centralized, while, on the other side, formalization and rigid organization design are typically attributes of large bureaucratic firms rather than small organic ones. For these reason, these attributes, as they were defined, become meaningless and not discriminating in the small firm sector. Anyhow, a further investigation of these constructs is necessary.

Some issues also merit further analysis. First, although the fit between the nature of the environment and problem-solving context, on the one hand, was explored, and organization infrastructure, on the other, new sets of variables should be considered as having impacts on knowledge creation during technical problem solving. One of this is industry typology. Findings are idiosyncratic, as management practices and organization cultures are very dependent on the typology of industry considered. Environment diversity was considered as fundamentally dependent on the number of customers and products developed by the firm. The idea implicit in this definition is that there is only one kind of environmental diversity, as firms included in the sample design and manufacture products only in the food equipment manufacturing industry, but, there are different kinds of environment diversity, for instance, diversity due to structural or technological differences across industries. Working in different industries offers an effective means for knowledge transfer and creativity enhancement.

A static perspective of learning in small firms was fundamentally adopted. Organizational learning or, what is the same in the study, organizational knowledge generation, is a multidimensional concept. Learning rate, learning amount, learning flexibility, and learning recurrence are important dimensions that depict the nature of learning within an organization. The learning amount was only considered in this research. This dimension alone, perhaps, is unable to effectively describe learning modes and measure the impact of the organization infrastructure typology on knowledge creation. Two firms can show different learning modes, as the first can develop small amount of knowledge very frequently, while the second can develop large amount of knowledge every now and then. In this context, learning persistence and unlearning capabilities become critical.

This study remains exploratory in its nature. The number of firms considered in the sample is small, even though it is very representative of the population of firms in the specific industry studied. Nevertheless, the research has several important implications. First, although there has been a prodigious amount of theorizing about many issues in the area of the learning organization, knowledge management, and learning, empirical research is still very limited, and, what is more important, very little has been explored about these topics and their implications to small firms, primarily those ones in less dynamic industries. Therefore, in an academic perspective, this study has the merit to have shed new light as to knowledge management in small manufacturing firms. In the practitioner perspective, findings suggest how to intervene to support the entrepreneurial group/CEO to enhance the knowledge asset of the organization during technical problem solving, as they have identified organization openness, innovativeness, and leadership as the levers of learning and the knowledge creation process.

REFERENCES

Acs, Z. J., & Audretsch, D. B. (1990). *Innovation and small firms*. Cambridge: The MIT Press.

Adamson, R. W., & Taylor, D. W. (1954). Functional fixedness as related to elapsed time and to set. *Journal of Experimental Psychology, 47*, 122-126.

Aiken, M., & Alford, R. (1970). Community structure and innovation: The case of urban renewal. *American Sociological Review, 35*, 650-665.

Amabile, T. M. (1983). *The social psychology of creativity*. New York: Springer-Verlag.

Andrews, F. M. (1975). Social and psychological factors that influence the creative process. In I. A. Taylor & W. Getzels (Eds.), *Perspectives in creativity* (pp. 37 – 59). Chicago, IL: Aldine.

Arabie, P., & Hubert L. (1994). Cluster analysis in marketing research. In R. P. Bagozzi (Ed.), *Advanced methods of marketing research* (pp. 160-189). Cambridge, MA: Basil Blackwell.

Argyris, C. (1982). *Reasoning, learning, and action: Individual and organizational*. San Francisco, CA: Jossey-Bass.

Argyris, C., & Schon, D. A. (1978). *Organizational learning: A theory of action perspective*, Reading, MA: Addison-Wesley.

Bandura, A. (1986). *The social foundation of thought and action: A social cognitive theory*. Englewood Cliffs, NJ: Prentice-Hall.

Bell, M. A. (1982). Phases in group problem solving. *Small Group Behaviour, 13*, 475-495.

Birch, H. G., & Rabinowitz, H. S. (1951). The negative effect of previous experience on productive thinking. *Journal of Experimental Psychology, 41*, 121-125.

Bontis, N., Dragonetti, N. C., Jacobsen, K., & Roos, G. (1999). The knowledge toolbox: A review of the tools available to measure and manage intangible resources. *European Management Journal, 17*, 391–402.

Brief, A. P., & Downey, H. K. (1983). Cognitive and organizational structures: A conceptual analysis of implicit organizing theories. *Human Relations, 36*, 1065-1090.

Burns, T., & Stalker, G. (1961). *The management of innovation*. London: Tavistock.

Clement, J. (1989). Learning via model construction and criticism: Protocol evidence on sources of creativity in science. In J. Glover, R. Ronning, & C. Reynolds (Eds.), *Handbook of creativity: Assessment, theory and research* (pp. 341 – 381). NY: Plenum.

Cohen, M. D., & Bacdayan, P. (1994). Organizational routines are stored as procedural memory: Evidence from a laboratory study. *Organization Science*, *5*, 554-568.

Corti, E., & lo Storto, C. (1997). Technical problem solving and learning processes during product innovation: Some empirical evidence for the development of a theoretical framework of knowledge creation in small firms. In *Proceedings of the PICMET'97*, Portland (Oregon).

Corti, E., & lo Storto, C. (2000). Knowledge creation in small firms during product innovation: An empirical analysis of cause-effect relationships among its determinants. *Enterprise & Innovation Management Studies*, *1*, 245-263.

Corti, E., lo Storto, C., & Trombetta, A. (1996). Fattori critici nell'innovazione di prodotto all'interno delle piccole imprese nelle aree deboli: apprendimento, competenze, e risorse ambientali.In *Proceedings of the AiIG Workshop*, Potenza.

Covin, J. G., & Slevin, D. P. (1988). The influence of organization structure on the utility of an entrepreneurial top management style. *Journal of Management Studies*, *25*, 3, 217-234.

Crossen, M. M., Lane, H. W., & White, R. E. (1998). An organizational learning framework: From induction to institution. *Academy of Management Review*, *24*, 522-539.

Cyert, R. M., & March, J. G. (1963). *A behavioral theory of the firm*. Englewood Cliffs, NJ: Prentice-Hall.

Daft, R. L., & Lengel, R. H. (1986). Organizational information requirements, media richness, and structural design. *Management Science*, *32*, 554-571.

Daft, R. L., & Macintosh, N. B. (1981). A tentative explanation into the amount and equivocality of information processing in organizational work units. *Administrative Science Quarterly*, *26*, 207-224.

Daft, R. L., & Weick, K. E. (1984). Toward a model of organizations as interpretation systems. *Academy of Management Review*, *9*, 284-295.

Feldman, M. S. (2000). Organizational routines as a source of continuous change. *Organization Science*, *6*, 611-629.

Fiol, C. (1994). Consensus, diversity, and learning in organizations. *Organization Science*, *5*, 403-420.

Fisher, W. A. (1980). Scientific and technical information and the performance of R&D groups. *TIMS Studies in the Management Sciences*, *15*, 67-89.

Galbraith, J. K (1952). *American capitalism: The concept of countervailing power*. Boston: Houghton Mifflin.

Galbraith, J. R. (1973). *Designing complex organizations*, Reading. MA: Addison-Wesley.

Garner, W. R. (1962). *Uncertainty and structure as psychological concepts*. New York: John Wiley & Sons.

Garvin, D. (1993). Building a learning organization. *Harvard Business Review*, August, 78-90.

Getzels, F., & Csikszentmyhalyi, M. (1976). *The creative vision: A longitudinal study of problem solving in art*. New York: Wiley.

Glucksberg, S., & Weisberg, R. W. (1966). Verbal behavior and problem solving: Some effects of labeling in a functional fixedness problem. *Journal of Experimental Psychology, 71*, 659-664.

Hage, J., & Aiken, M. (1967). Program change and organizational properties: A comparative analysis. *American Journal of Sociology, 72*, 503-519.

Hayes, J. R. (1978). *Cognitive psychology. Thinking and creating*. Homewood, IL: Dorsey Press.

Hedberg, B. (1981). How organizations learn and unlearn. In P. C. Nystrom & W. H. Starbuck (Eds.), *Handbook of organizational design* (pp. 3 – 27), vol. 1. New York: Oxford University Press.

Hicks, W. D., & Klimoski, R. J. (1987). Entry into training programs and its effects on training outcomes: A field experiment. *Academy of Management Journal, 30*, 542-552.

Imai, K, Nonaka I., & Takeuchi H. (1985). Managing the new product development process : How Japanese companies learn and unlearn. In K. B. Clark, R. H. Hayes, & C. Lorenz (Eds.), *The uneasy alliance: Manging the productivity-technology dilemma* (pp. 337 – 376). Boston, MA: Harvard Business Press.

Johnson-Laird, P. N. (1983). *Mental modes*. Cambridge, MA: Harvard University Press.

Johnston, R., & Gibbons, M. (1975). Characteristics of information usage in technological innovation. *IEEE Transaction on Engineering Management, 22*, 27-34.

Jones, A. M., & Hendry, C. (1992). *The learning organization: A review of literature and practice*. The HRD Partnership.

Julien, P. A. (1993). Small businesses as a research subject: Some reflections on knowledge of small businesses and its effects on economic theory. *Small Business Economics, 5*, 157-166.

Kanter, R. M. (1983). *The change masters*. New York: Simon and Schuster.

Kim, J., & Mueller, C. W. (1978). *Factor analysis. Statistical methods and practical issues*. Sage University Paper series on Quantitative Applications in the Social Sciences, 07-014. Beverly Hills and London: Sage Publications.

Kirton, M. J. (1976). Adaptors and innovators: A description and measure. *Journal of Applied Psychology, 6*, 622-629.

Kolb, D. A. (1984). *Experiential learning: Experience as the source of learning*. Englewood Cliffs, NJ: Prentice-Hall.

Larkin, J. H., & Simon H. A. (1987). Why a diagram is (sometimes) worth 10,000 words. *Cognitive Science, 11*, 65-100.

Levitt, B., & March, J. G. (1988). Organizational learning. *Annual Review of Sociology, 14*, 319-340.

Luchins, A. S., & Luchins, E. H. (1959). New experimental attempts in preventing mechanization in problem solving. *The Journal of General Psychology, 42*, 279-291.

Lundval, B. A. (1988). Innovation as an interactive process: From user-producer interaction to the national systems of innovation. In G. Dosi, C. Freeman, R. Nelson, G. Silverberg, & L. Soete (Eds.), *Technical change and economic theory* (pp. 349 – 369). London: Pinter.

Lynn, B. E. (2000). Intellectual capital. *Ivey Business Journal, 64*, 48- 51.

Machlup, F., & Mansfield, U. (1983). *The study of information: Interdisciplinary messages*. New York: John Wiley & Sons.

Maidique, M. A., & Zirger, B. J. (1988). The new product learning cycle. In K. Gronhaug, & G. Kaufmann (Eds.), *Innovation: A cross-disciplinary perspective*. Norwegian University Press.

March, J. G. (1988). *Decisions and organizations*. Oxford: Basil Blackwell.

March, J. G., & Olsen, J. P. (1975). The uncertainty of the past: Organizational learning under ambiguity. *European Journal of Political Research, 3*, 147-171.

March, J. G., & Simon, H. A. (1958). *Organizations*. New York: John Wiley and Sons.

Mintzberg, H., Duru, R., & Theoret, A. (1976). The structure of unstructured decision process. *Administrative Science Quarterly, 21*, 246-275.

Mohr, L. B. (1969). Determinants of innovation in organizations. *American Political Science Review, 63*, 111-126.

Nelson, R. R., & Winter, S. G. (1982). *An evolutionary theory of economic change*. Cambridge, MA: Harvard University Press.

Nevis, E. C, DiBella, A. J., & Gould, J. M . (1995). Understanding organizations as learning system. *Sloan management review, 36*, 73-92.

Newell, A., Shaw, J. C., & Simon, H. A. (1979). The processes of creative thinking. In H. A. Simon (Ed.), *Models of thought*. New Haven: Yale University Press.

Nonaka, I. (1994). A dynamic theory of organizational knowledge creation. *Organization Science, 5*, 14-36.

Nystrom, H. (1979). *Creativity and innovation*. Chichester: John Wiley & Sons.

Pelz, D. C., & Andrews, F. M. (1976). *Productive climates for research and development*. Ann Arbor, MI: Institute for Social Research, University of Michigan.

Pennings, J. M., Barkema, H., & Douma, S. (1994). Organizational learning and diversification. *Academy of Management Journal, 37*, 608-640.

Pentland, B. T., & Rueter, H. H. (1994). Organizational routines as grammar of actions. *Administrative Science Quarterly, 39*, 484-510.

Peters, T. J., & Waterman, R. H. (1982). *In search of excellence: Lessons from America's best run companies*. New York: Harper and Row.

Postman, L. (1976). Methodology of human learning. In W. K. Estes (Ed.), *Handbook of learning and cognitive processes* (pp. 11 – 69), vol. 3. New York: John Wiley.

Rogers, E. M. (1983). *The diffusion of innovations*. New York: The Free Press.

Rothwell R., Freeman C., Horsley A., Jervis, V. T. P., Robertson A., & Townsend J. (1974). SAPPHO updated – Project SAPPHO phase II. *Research Policy, 3*, 259-291.

Saxenian, A. L. (1991). The origins and dynamics of production networks in Silicon Valley. *Research Policy, 20*, 423-437.

Scheerer, M. (1963). Problem solving. *Scientific American, 208*, 118-128.

Schein, E. H. (1993). On dialogue, culture, and organizational learning. *Organizational Dynamics, 22*, 40-51.

Schein, E. H (1996). *Organizational learning as a cognitive redefinition: Coercive persuasion revisited*. Retrieved from http:/learning.mit.edu/res/wp/10010.html

Schoonhoven, C. B. (1981). Problems with contingency theory: Testing assumptions hidden within the language of contingency "theory." *Administrative Science Quarterly, 26*, 349-77.

Senge, P. (1990). *The fifth discipline: The art and science of the learning organization*. New York: Doubleday.

Sharma, S., Durand, R. M., & Gur-Arie, O. (1981). Identification and analysis of moderator variables. *Journal of Marketing Research, 18*, 291-300.

Shepard, H. A. (1967). Innovation-resisting and innovation-producing organizations. *Journal of Business, 40*, 470-477.

Simon, H. (1991). Bounded rationality and organizational learning. *Organization Science, 2*(1), 125-134.

Taylor, C.nW. (1972). Can organizations be creative too?. In C. W. Taylor (Ed.), *Climate for creativity* (pp. 1 – 15). New York: Pergamon Press.

Teece, D. J. (1986). Profiting from technological innovation: Implication for integration, collaboration, licensing, and public policy. *Research Policy, 15*, 285-305.

Thomas, R. G., & Litowitz, L. (1986). *Vocational education and higher-order thinking skills: An agenda for inquiry.* St: Paul, MN: Research and Development Center for Vocational Education.

Thompson, J. D. (1967). *Organizations in action.* New York: McGraw-Hill.

Thompson, V. A. (1965). Bureaucracy and innovation. *Administrative Science Quarterly, 10*, 1-20.

Torrance, E. P., & Myers, R. E. (1970). *Creative learning and teaching.* New York: Dodd.

Tushman, M. L. (1979). Managing communication networks in R&D laboratories. *Sloan Management Review*, 37-49.

Utterback, J. M. (1971). The process of innovation: A study of the origination and development of ideas for new scientific instruments. *IEEE Transaction on Engineering Management, 18*, 124-131.

Van Kooji, E. H. (1990). *Technology transfer in the Japanese electronics industry, Economic Research Institute for Small and Medium Sized Business.* The Netherlands, Zoertmeer.

Venkatraman, N. (1989). The concept of fit in strategy research: Toward verbal and statistical correspondence. *Academy of Management Review, 14*, 423-444.

von Hippel, E. (1987). Cooperation between rivals: Informal know-how trading. *Research Policy, 16*, 291-302.

von Hippel, E. (1994). «Sticky information» and the locus of problem solving: Implications for innovation. *Management Science, 40*, 429-439.

von Hippel, E., & Tyre, M. (1993). *How learning by doing is done: Problem identification in novel process equipment.* Massachusetts Institute of Technology, SSM Working Paper#BPS 3521-93.

Wall, T. D., & Lischeron, J. H. (1977). *Worker participation: A critique of the literature and some fresh evidence.* Maidenhead (England): McGraw-Hill.

Watson, G. (1973). Resistance to change. In G. Zaltman (Ed.), *Processes and phenomena of social change* (pp. 117 – 131). New York: John Wiley & Sons.

Weick, K. E. (1995). *Sensemaking in organizations.* SAGE Publications.

Welsh, J., & White, J. (1981). A small business is not a little big business. *Harvard Business Review,* July-August, 18-32.

West, M. A., & Farr, J. L. (1989). Innovation at work: Psychological perspectives. *Social Behaviour, 4*, 15-30.

Zaltman, G., Duncan, R., & Holbeck, J. (1973). *Innovations and organizations.* Chichester: John Wiley & Sons.

ENDNOTES

1 A great amount of literature on decision making and problem solving has dealt with uncertainty. However, uncertainty differs from ambiguity, and both of them affect the cognitive work of problem solvers. Uncertainty is the consequence of the perceived lack of information, or factual knowledge, about the present or future states, preferences, goals, and actions (Daft & Lengel,

1986; Galbraith, 1973; Garner, 1962; March, 1988). Individuals are able to reduce or eliminate uncertainty by collecting or developing information (e.g., through experimentation). When they are unable to collect or develop information, they adopt strategies to deal with uncertainty, either by predicting or inferring values for missing information, or using information buffers, or developing a capability allowing the organization to quickly, and flexibly, respond to unexpected events (Galbraith, 1973; March & Simon, 1958; Thompson, 1967). Ambiguity derives both from the inability of individuals to interpret the meaning of facts and actions, as they lack appropriate informational cues or perceive events so unfamiliar that they are unable to give judgements, and from the existence of multiple redundant interpretations of the same thing (Daft & Macintosh, 1981; Daft & Weick, 1984; Machlup & Mansfield, 1983; March & Olsen, 1975; Weick, 1995). Individuals alleviate ambiguity by collecting and sharing rich information, reframing the information pieces they have about a situation, identifying new interpretative categories, and changing their basic assumptions and beliefs.

2 As in most of the activities performed in small firms, the entrepreneurial group/CEO keeps a strict control of what happens in the organization, and acquires a central role all over the problem-solving activity. Factors, such as leadership and entrepreneurial style, also influence problem solving.

3 Implicitly, this procedure introduces a new moderating effect of the variable "problem familiarity."

4 Research carried on in the area of innovation, and of problem solving, has found a number of individual characters that positively correlate with the outcome of these activities, and in particular, individual's expertise, knowledge, personality traits. Even though there is the awareness that these personal factors are essential ingredients in problem solving and learning, in this study, it was decided to concentrate attention primarily at the organizational level rather than at the individual one.

Chapter IX
Learning at the Core:
Knowledge Management as an Employer Strategy for Lifelong Learning

Ernesto Villalba
Centre for Research on Lifelong Learning (CRELL, Institute for Protection and Security of the Citizen (IPSC) and European Commission)- Joint Research Centre, Italy

ABSTRACT

The present study explores the relationship between the knowledge-enabling environment and the demand of training in 18 small private companies providing educational and consultancy services in Sweden. In this way, the chapter is an exploration of the ways Swedish knowledge-intensive companies manage their knowledge. The 18 companies have participated in a European programme for employee's competence, financed by the European Social Fund. As part of this European financed programme, companies have evaluated their business activity and determined their training needs in order to remain competitive. The 18 companies, thus, are in a position of providing information on the demand for learning that is rarely available. Knowledge is understood, here, both as the structure and the content of the mental schemas. It is embodied in individuals; it differs from information and data; and it can be tacit or explicit. Knowledge is a dynamic entity that is in a constant dialectic process with the reality it represents. It is through this dialectic process that people learn. This conceptualization of knowledge implies that when looking at organizational processes for managing knowledge, it is important not only to look at formal organized activities for learning, but also informal learning activities that constitute the main source for tacit knowledge, as well as the conditions in place for knowledge creation, what is here called the knowledge-enabling environment. It is argued that through knowledge management, companies are indeed implementing strategies for the promotion of lifelong learning. Lifelong learning has been used in policy arenas as a guiding principle for educational policies and reforms.

INSIDE CHAPTER

This chapter presents a multisite case study of knowledge management in 18 Swedish companies providing educational and consultancy services. Knowledge management is understood in a broad sense, and includes more than the use of technology for sharing of information. The chapter brings some insights from educational theory into the study of intellectual capital and knowledge management in organizations, especially from the area of lifelong learning.

INTRODUCTION

Training and competence development is one of the principal activities to maintain and renew knowledge, and hence, competitiveness. At the political level, the European Union is making efforts to establish a European area of lifelong learning, promoting initiatives towards skills and competence development (see e.g., European Commission, 2005). Member states have placed lifelong learning at the center of their educational debates, and the concept has become integrated into the policy discourse (see e.g., CEDEFOP & EURYDICE, 2001; Field, 2000; Leader, 2003). The basic principle in lifelong learning is that knowledge, skills, and competencies should be constantly updated throughout life. The knowledge and skills acquired at one point in time are no longer sufficient for the entire working life (Lundvall, 2000; Tuijnman, 1999); workers are demanded to be autonomous lifelong learners, with higher levels of multiple skills, and flexibility.

Lifelong learning is an underlying principle that arguably has guided educational reforms in the last 20 years. Three main attributes define lifelong learning (Rubenson, 2001): (1) it refers to the whole life span (lifelong); (2) it takes into account different forms of learning (life-wide): and, (3) it places major emphasis on learning, which in turn emphasizes the importance of individual involvement in her/his own learning. As indicated in Aspin et al. (Aspin, Chapman, Hatton, Sawano 2001, p. xx-xxi) lifelong learning has an economic justification in that it is instrumental in maintaining competitiveness and innovation. In addition, the discourse on lifelong learning defends learning as an "intrinsically valuable activity." Finally, lifelong learning is seen as a "pre-requisite for informed and effective participation in society."

The concept of lifelong learning, thus, implies not only that learning occurs along the whole life span, but also that learning occurs in different settings and different ways. This includes formal, nonformal and informal ways of learning. Private as well as public institutions have to create opportunities for individuals to develop their competencies, both through planned training activities as well as through the design of the working conditions that promote learning while working (Hasan, 1996; Rubenson, 2003). In other words, organizations have to become learning organizations, defined as those "that encourage learning at all levels (individually and collectively) and continually transform [themselves] as a result" (European Commission, 2001, p. 33).

The importance of education and learning to increase competitiveness is not only present in policy documents (European Commission, 2000a, 2000b, 2001, 2005; OECD, 1997, 1998, 2000); management and economic literature also places a central role in learning and the creation of knowledge. Many different fields have contributed, in the last few years, to the progress of a body of knowledge in the field of management and development of competence and skills in organizations; however, communication between different approaches has not been straightforward.

The present chapter defends that these different approaches can be brought together within the framework of knowledge management (see e.g., McElroy, 2003; Stankosky, 2005a; Villalba, 2006; Wei Choo & Bontis, 2002a). Assumptions and findings from the fields of human-capital theory, intellectual capital, organizational learning, the knowledge-creating company, and human resource development are brought together to create a holistic framework to study knowledge management in small companies in Sweden.

From the early 1980s, knowledge management has been traditionally associated with the use of information technologies (IT), knowledge-based systems, search engines, portals, and data-repositories in companies. From the year 2000 onwards, knowledge management has grown to be an integrated part of the basic concepts for managing, especially in relation to knowledge-intensive organizations, including other organizational processes not related with IT. In this vein, knowledge management integrates all organizational processes that are directed towards knowledge creation and use, and information distribution and storage. Despite the central role that knowledge creation plays in knowledge management, little references to educational science and learning can be found. It is interesting, therefore, to explore how knowledge management is enhancing learning activities in organizations. Further, as Wong and Aspinwall (2004) point out, the study of knowledge management has been mainly concerned with large corporations and less attention has been paid to small and medium enterprises (SME). Studies within the human capital theory have found that small companies face more problems in providing training opportunities to their employees. In addition, it has found that certain company and work characteristics, such as size of the company or literacy practices at work, are associated with higher level of training participation (Boudard, 2000, 2001; Boudard & Rubenson, 2003; Murnane, et al. 1995; Rubensson & Xu, 1997; Rubensson & Schuetze, 2000). Zuboff (1988, p. 395) puts it this way: "The behavior that defines

Figure 1. Knowledge management and lifelong learning

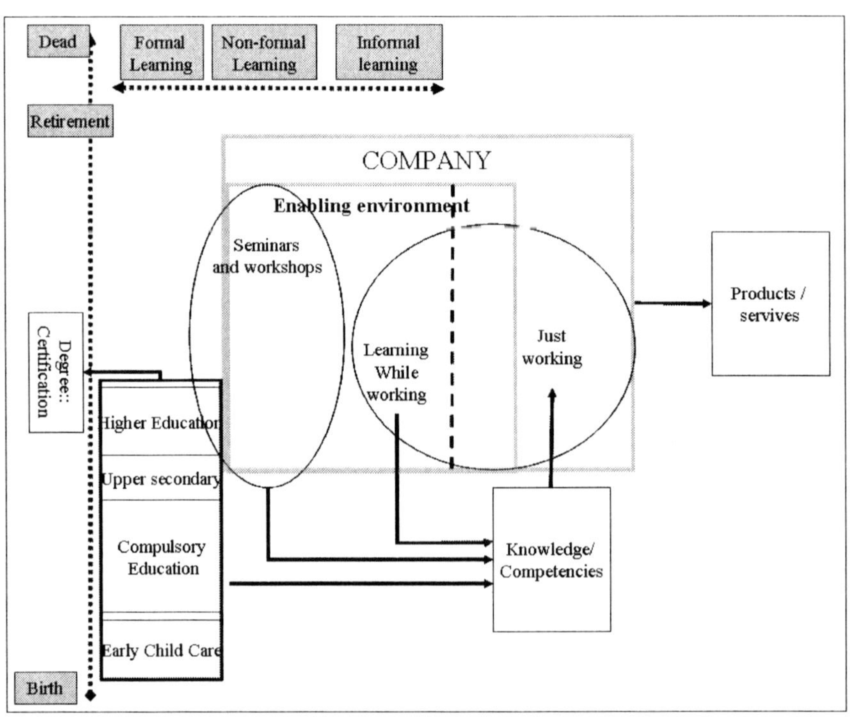

learning and the behavior that defines being productive are one and the same... to put it simply, learning is the new form of labor." In this vein, this chapter explores to what degree the way small organizations manage their knowledge is related to their demand for training. Figure 1 shows the key issues of the chapter relating lifelong learning to the knowledge-enabling environment, and hence, to knowledge management.

The chapter, thus, contributes to the overall theme of the book by providing a multidisciplinary view on the management of intellectual capital in knowledge intensive small companies. Especially interesting is the emphasis given to learning and lifelong learning. In global business, there is a clear need of constantly updating the companies' knowledge base. Professionals in global business need to be constantly updating their knowledge and skills in order to provide quality services. In other words, they need to be lifelong learners, willing to learn constantly in different ways and settings, alone and with others. The fundamental theoretical assumption maintained here is that companies have to place learning and knowledge at the centre of their business activities.

In this way, intellectual capital management becomes not an additional part of the business activities of a company, but their "modus operanti." In this way, it is not enough to have a training department, at the company, that promotes learning through seminars or organized courses; the human resources, the physical structure, the organization of the work, and the communication patterns of the company have to be directed to increasing possibilities for learning.

The chapter first presents a brief conceptualization of knowledge as the starting point to create a holistic model of knowledge management. Then it shows a small, nonexhaustive historical overview of the field. Then, the theoretical framework that guided the exploration of the 18 companies is briefly introduced. The following section presents the methodology and the data collection procedure. The chapter continues by presenting main

Figure 2. Logical flow of the research approach

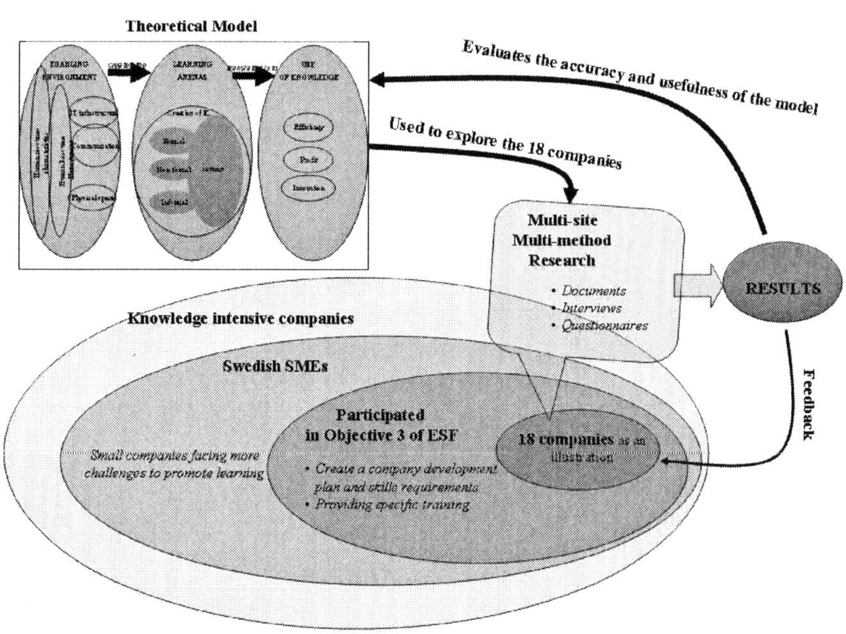

findings of the case studies. Finally, the chapter presents some conclusions and implications of the model.

THE FIELD OF KNOWLEDGE MANAGEMENT

From Knowledge to Learning

Learning can be regarded as the adaptation of mental models or schemas to the specific realities that an individual confronts. These schemas can be regarded as "highly organized set of propositions, concepts, and rules for relating them to one another" (Shute, 1996, p. 3323). When we act, new information is processed, and it will produce some kind of disequilibrium or cognitive conflict in the schema or theory. The process of adaptation (assimilation or accommodation) will tend to restore the equilibrium. Knowledge, understood both as content and as schema, will, therefore, be constructed during the process of adaptation through the individual's interaction with the environment. When we are presented with data (facts, impressions), we will examine that specific information (which has some meaning and structure for us) with the knowledge that we already have. In fact, the previous knowledge will guide the type of data that we seek, or beyond that, the information we seek and are capable of understanding. If that specific information content (either know-what, why, how, or who) appears in adequate conditions of motivation, interest, and attention, the content will be "absorbed" into the mental model (or theory, or schema) that we are applying to that specific context. The new content might not produce much change in the structure of the mental model (*alpha* answer), it might produce partial modification (*beta* answer) or it might result in a critical modification (*gamma* answer, significant learning, or conceptual change) (see or Limon, 2001; Piaget, 1975). These changes in our schema constitute, in fact, learning. Figure 3 shows that learning is the process of transforming data into knowledge, making something public (information) into something private (knowledge).

The process of transforming knowledge into data is the process of teaching, understood broadly. The information that starts the process of learning is usually the articulation of someone's knowledge that served to codify and externalize her/his knowledge. If the students (or any listener or reader) incorporate the data that has been externalized, then there is learning.

Finally, it is important to mention that knowledge might be acquired through different means. Knowledge is not only created through theoretical means (such as reading or analyzing information); learning also occurs by doing. Thus, when we act, our acts "teach" us, providing us with information on our performance. This process of learning is not necessarily a conscious one, and can occur implicitly without the individual realizing it; it is in this way that we mainly acquire tacit knowledge.

To sum up, learning and knowledge are considered here to be totally interrelated, since learning is the process of creating knowledge and knowledge guides the process of learning. Learning occurs constantly (lifelong) and throughout the entire life span (life-wide), and in this sense, the concept of lifelong learning becomes useful to be integrated into knowledge management ideas.

Historical Overview of the Knowledge Management Field

Within the last 15 years, the recognition of knowledge management has increased tremendously in the business and research communities (see e.g., Desouza, 2003, p. 25; Harris, Fleming, Hunter, Rosser, & Cushman, 1999; KPMG 1998, 2000; Quintas, 2003, p. 30). Wiig (2000) argues that the field of knowledge management will be integrated into management tools and, in this way, will eventually disappear as a separate effort. Van Winkelen et al. (Van Winkelen, Birchall, & Smith, 2004,

Figure 3. The conceptualization of knowledge for this chapter

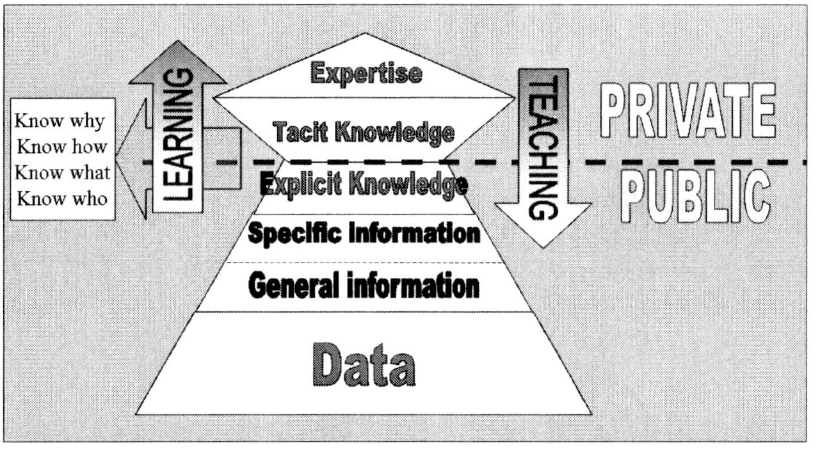

p. 32), in their study of 116 organizations, argue that knowledge management "is evolving from a separate discipline into one that is integrated into business practice." Quintas (2003, p. 31) has pointed out that knowledge management has existed informally since the "earliest incarnations of organizations." Formally as a discipline, DiMattia and Oder (1997, p. 33) trace the beginnings of knowledge management to the 1980s, when downsizing was a popular business strategy that resulted in the loss of existing company expertise. Moody and Duff (2000, p. 21) maintain that in order to retain expertise, companies looked for ways of storing "employee knowledge." A second origin can be found, according to Wiig (1997a, p. 6), when some American companies began to use knowledge-based systems (KBS) to increase their competitiveness in the market. Aguirre et al. (Aguirre, Brena, & Cantu, 2001, p. 1) maintain that the origin of knowledge management can be traced to the extensive research on artificial intelligence (AI) from the 1960s, before companies were using knowledge-based systems (KBS). Quintas (2003), on the other hand, associates knowledge management with the development of human capital theory and its focus on knowledge.

McElroy (2000, p. 200) argues that knowledge management has two distinct stages. The first generation, as he calls it, is concentrated on the "supply" of existing knowledge rather than on the demand for new knowledge. Tuomi (2002, p. 69-75) maintains that in the time period between 1993 to 1996, knowledge management developed from four different disciplines: organizational information processing; business intelligence; organizational cognition; and, organizational development. The two first would be in line with McElroy's first generation of knowledge management, or what Mårtensson (2000, p. 210) refers to as knowledge management as an information-handling tool, whereas the last two are the basis for the second generation. This first generation knowledge management is mainly interested in using information technology in the workplace, creating knowledge-based systems or other so-called knowledge management software. As understood in this chapter, the first generation of knowledge management mainly deals with information and not with knowledge (Fulmer & Keys, 1998).

In the second generation of knowledge management, which would start around 1995, the field evolves into a broader perspective, where it is seen as a management strategy (Mårtensson 2000, p. 209). The distinction between knowledge and information becomes central. The emphasis is placed particularly on tacit knowledge (see Hislop, 2002; Jasmuddin, Klein, & Connell, 2005; Polanyi, 1962, 1967, 1969, for a review on tacit knowledge). In this second generation, thus, the assumption is that knowledge is owned and controlled by individuals. Hence, knowledge management centers on people rather than on technology. In this generation, information technologies are viewed as an enabler of the knowledge management process (Allavi & Tiwana, 2003; Martiny, 1998, p. 76; Rao, 2005). Information technologies are directed towards group activities as well as allowing for a certain degree of personal communication, taking into account the tacit nature of knowledge. In addition, further development of knowledge management emphasizes the role of collaboration and culture (see e.g., Ahmed, Kok, & Loh, 2002; Bixler, 2005; Chase, 1997; Davenport & Prusack 1998; Hauschild, Licht, & Stein, 2001).

Tuomi (2002, p. 76) maintains that knowledge management is living its third generation. He characterizes it as a generation that uses software that takes into account the dynamic nature of knowledge and the importance of collaboration. For the present chapter, Tuomi's characterization does not truly differentiate between second and third generation knowledge management. It is argued here that the main feature in the current knowledge management field is that the different disciplines are coming together and being integrated (see e.g., Butler & Grace, 2005; Diakoulakis, Georgopoulos, Koulouriotis, & Emiris, 2004; Easter-Smith & Lyles, 2003b; Wei Choo & Bontis, 2002b). Different terms, such as organizational learning, intellectual capital accounting, learning organizations, and so forth, point to different perspectives within the same arena: how to treat people's knowledge to increase competitiveness. Despite the different definitions and terms, what is proposed here is that new developments in knowledge management are working towards integrating these different fields (see Villalba, 2006 for a full explanation of the concepts). Within these new developments, knowledge is a dynamic entity constructed through social interaction. Therefore, information technologies are used only as enablers, and are therefore only a small part of the knowledge management effort. Knowledge is linked with action within the overall strategy of a company. Knowledge management is not a specific small part of the organization, but a way of organizing the whole business. This could be referred to as increasing the knowledge intensiveness of the firm (see e.g., Starbuck, 1992). In a knowledge-intensive company, the organization of work has to maximize the use of its main source of revenue, the employees' knowledge. The company has to find strategies to make each employee share her/his knowledge with coworkers, both tacitly and explicitly. The company has to assure that the distribution of information is creating new insights in the mind of its employees. And finally, the company has to promote the translation of these new insights into new services or products. In other words, companies have to promote lifelong learning in their employees.

Towards a Holistic Model for Knowledge Management

The previous section revealed the complexity of the knowledge management field. As Quintas et al. (Quintas, Lefrere, & Jones, 1997, p. 387) have pointed out, the field is at a crossroad of several different disciplines, such as strategic management, information technology, and human resource development (see also Easter-Smith & Lyles 2003b; Liebowitz, 1999; Stankosky, 2005b Wei Choo & Bontis 2002b). It is the intention of this section to present a holistic model for knowledge management specifically directed towards the study of SMEs, putting a major emphasis on the lifelong learning implications of the model. The model is specifically adapted towards the study of SMEs in education and consultancy in Sweden.

Figure 4. A holistic model for knowledge management in SMEs

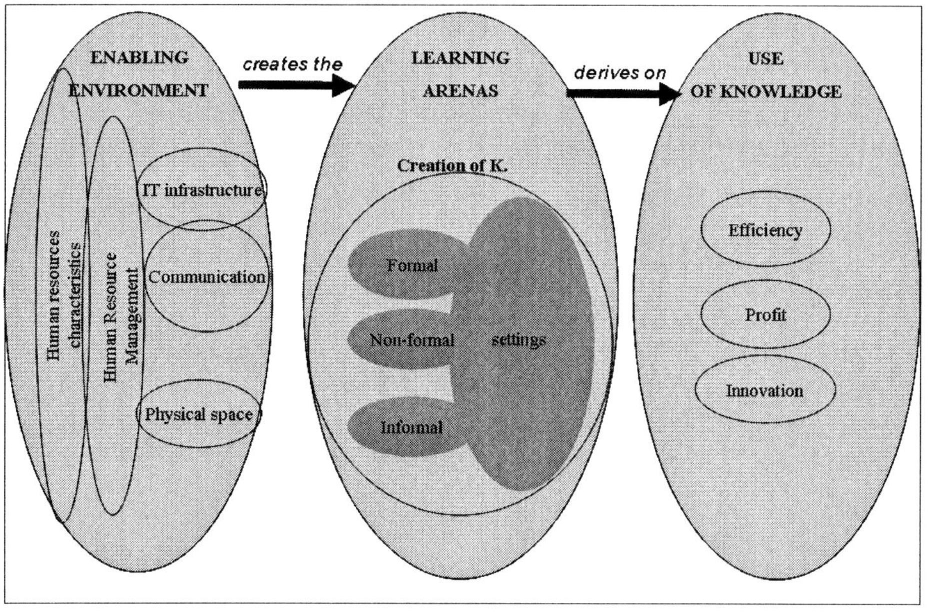

The model consists of specific characteristics that knowledge-intensive SMEs hypothetically possess. The present chapter explores to what extent these characteristics appear in SMEs and in this way, tests the accuracy of the model. The model assumes that knowledge management implies much more than the use of information technologies for internal business processes. In the model, knowledge management takes into account the tacit nature of knowledge as well as its transformation into information. The model's main foci are on human capital (or individual competences), organizational capital (or internal structure), and how the transfer between these two types of intangibles is accomplished (see e.g., Sveiby, 1997 or Sveiby, Linard, & Dvorsky, 2002 for explanation of the terms). The framework pays special attention to the processes directed toward the creation of knowledge, both formally and informally. It is important to note that the model constitutes a tentative hypothesis on how the companies under study are knowledge intensive firms.

The theoretical framework for knowledge management in SME's is presented in Figure 3. It is composed of three main areas that include the four focal processes traditionally defined within knowledge management: knowledge creation and use, and information storage and distribution (see e.g., Coleman, 1999; Hellström, Kemlin, & Malmquist, 2000; Leech & Sutton, 2002; Wiig, 1997b). It is important to mention that although the literature on knowledge management uses the expression "distribution" or "storage" of knowledge, it is information that is distributed or stored, not knowledge. Knowledge is only kept in people's minds. Knowledge-creation processes refer to the activities intentionally directed towards learning at any level of the organization. Distribution processes refer to the exchange of information and the transfer of tacit knowledge. This can occur in any kind of gathering among employees, as well as through exchange of ideas through e-mail or other means. Storage processes refer to the codification, organization, and storage into databases of explicit knowledge. It also includes the internalization among employees of working routines. Knowledge use processes refer to the application of the knowledge created, distributed, and/or stored into products or other visible outputs that create revenues directly or indirectly for the company.

It is hypothesized that knowledge intensive organizations foster knowledge creation, distribution, storage, and use processes through strategic actions directed towards the management of knowledge. These actions, which constitute the knowledge management approach of each company, have been grouped into three main areas: the knowledge-enabling environment, learning arenas, and knowledge use. These three areas are somewhat artificial since the separation of the different aspects of an organization is not uniform.

The knowledge-enabling environment refers to the organization of a company, the ways of working, and the facilities that employees have in order to deliver services and constantly upgrade their knowledge. Such an environment constitutes a knowledge-intensive organization (where knowledge is produced and sold). As it is used here, the concept of knowledge-enabling environment encompasses more features than the ones described in Von Krogh et al. (Von Krogh, Ichijo, & Nonaka, 2000, see also Ichiyo, 2004). In this framework, the knowledge-enabling environment is divided into four main areas: human resources and its management; communication activities; physical space arrangement; and, information technology infrastructure.

Learning arenas refer mainly to activities directed specifically towards the creation of knowledge, such as training events. Learning activities can be placed within the life-wide dimension, from informal learning to formal learning. The life-wide dimension of learning provides a framework to define three main types of learning: Formal, nonformal, and informal. Informal unintentional learning (as defined by Livingstone, 2000) occurs almost constantly in our daily activities. It is, thus, almost impossible to account for it. However, the assumption is that a knowledge-enabling environment will promote unintentional learning. In addition, a knowledge-enabling environment should also foster the creation of knowledge intentionally, through planning of events, time, and investments for learning activities.

The distinction between learning arenas and the knowledge-enabling environment is, to some degree, artificial. For example, informational meetings that have an information-sharing objective are considered within the enabling environment. However, it is very likely that this sharing constitutes new knowledge for many of the participants. However, for analytical purposes, only activities directed exclusively to the improvement of the human capital are considered within the learning arenas. In other words, learning arenas are made up of activities exclusively directed towards learning new knowledge or skills. Other activities, such as meetings, that might promote learning but are primarily directed toward sharing organizational information, are considered part of the enabling environment.

Finally, the use of knowledge refers to the outcomes of the knowledge-enabling environment and learning activities. Any service or product is the result of a knowledge production process, especially in knowledge-intensive companies. The services that companies provide are knowledge-products; specifically, they are professional's knowledge translated into a service for a client. The ultimate objective of knowledge management in an organization is to improve company profitability, efficiency, or effectiveness, as well as to assure quality in the service delivered. Especially interesting is how this knowledge-enabling environment facilitates product or service innovation.

In addition, the output of a knowledge-enabling environment should be that employees are willing to share their knowledge, improving the overall collaborative climate of the company. Collaborative climate of the company was measured using an adapted version of the collaborative climate index (CCI) developed by Sveiby and Simons (2002). The present chapter only attempts to relate knowledge-environment to learning arenas as an exploration of the relationship between human capital and organizational capital.

METHOD

The study is mainly explorative, and strives to understand rather than predict the management of knowledge in small knowledge intensive services. To this end, this particular work uses what Yin's (1993) typology of case studies defines as multiple and descriptive case study or a multisite case study (see e.g., Stenhouse, 1982). The unit of analysis (or the case) in this study is the management of knowledge in organizations, specifically knowledge-intensive organizations. There are 18 cases in this specific study. The study tries to gain as much information as possible from each of the cases, creating a "picture" of each company that can tell us something about how knowledge is managed in knowledge-intensive SMEs. The 18 companies are illustrative, not representative, of knowledge intensive SMEs in Sweden.

The present study is based on companies that have participated in Priority 1 (Measure 1.1 and 1.2) of the Objective 3 of the European Social Fund (ESF) Council in Sweden. The ESF constitutes the main financial tool through which the European Union implements its European Employment Strategy (Council of the European Union, 1999). In Sweden, the ESF serves as a complement to the Swedish government economic policy aimed at promoting growth and increased employment (Swedish Ministry of Finance and Ministry of Industry, Employment and Communications, 1999). Priority 1, "Competence development for the employees," is "the main trust" of the ESF program. It consists of two measures (Swedish ESF Council, 2001):

1. Measure 1.1 "support for the analysis of the competence development and support for the competence development": It consists of preparing a competence analysis plan as part of improving work organization (Verksamhets- och kompetensanalys), thereby formulating related skills development needs (kompetensutveckling). These companies, thus, provide a rare opportunity to explore aspects of the demand for training in small enterprises.
2. Measure 1.2 "general stimulus for skill development": It consists of the actual training of employees, cofinanced by the ESF.

Priority 1 follows two-step model. Measure 1.1 is a prerequisite for participation in Measure 1.2. In the 6-year programming period (2000–2006), Priority 1 has had more than one million participants (Ramboll Management, 2005) employed in 37,000 organizations, 88% of them had less than 50 employees.

In order to select the companies to study, four criteria where applied to the pool of more than 20,000 companies:

1. Size of the company (between 10 and 100)
2. Companies that are privately owned
3. Belonging to education (NACE rev. 1 80) or consultancy (NACE rev. 741, 742, 743, 744, 745)
4. Have participated in the Measure 1.1 and Measure 1.2

In order to gain the cooperation of these companies, two letters were sent to each company: one signed by the ESF-council in Sweden and the other from the Institute of International Education, which was conducting the study. Up to three reminders were sent via e-mail and telephone contact. Eighteen companies were selected because they provided rich amounts of information in terms of documents, interviews, and completed employee questionnaires. Therefore, this constitutes a self-selected convenient sample that meets certain predefined criteria.

Data Collection

The data was collected using three different methods: document analysis, semistructured interviews and questionnaires. Data triangulation provides a richer picture of the reality under study, since information on the same entity comes from different sources. The documents analyzed are copies of documents the companies sent to the ESF-council in order to gain monetary aid for employee's training. As part of the Measure 1.1, companies carried out an analysis of their business environment and an assessment of their competency needs. With the insight gained through the document analysis, a script for a semistructured interview was prepared. An interview guide was sent to the company prior to visiting it. Interviews attempted to ascertain more specific information about issues previously identified from the documents and from the theoretical framework on the company profile, and not specifically on the ESF program. Interviews collected both quantitative as well as qualitative information. All interviews were recorded and codified, and later introduced into the database; thus, combining the interview data with the documentary data. Finally, questionnaires were created from various sources that touch upon aspects of the theoretical framework.

Data Combination

The three sources of information (document analysis, interviews, and questionnaires) provide data referring to the same realities, as well as aspects covered only in a single source. It was possible to collect many different parameters and knowledge-related aspects for each company. The main dataset had a total of more than 180 variables for the 18 companies under study. It was necessary, therefore, to reduce the data to a manageable and understandable set of variables. In order to do so, 43 relevant variables were selected as indicators for eight theoretically identified constructs in the knowledge-intensive company (see table 2): (1) Size of the company, (2) workforce's stability, (3) workforce's experience, (4) professional orientation of the company, (5) tacit orientation of the recruitment process, (6) monetary reward system, (7) communication intensiveness, and (8) investment in information technologies (IT).

In a similar way, seven indicators were used to grasp the knowledge-creation effort and the demand for training of the companies: (1) training estimated time per employee each year; (2) average number of training events that each employee demands; (3) total training estimated cost per employee; (4) actual total training expenditure per employee; (5) actual expenditure as a proportion of the total estimated training cost; (6) total training cost per hour of training; and, (7) the company's average of the informal learning activities items.

These 50 indicators were recoded into binary variables using the median split method that determined low or high level of the attribute (see Table 2). This data reduction had the advantage of simplifying the sample into high achievers and low achievers for the different indicators selected. In other words, it divided the sample into companies that "have" certain characteristics (indicators) and companies that "do not have" them. It also "destroyed" the outliers, and in this way, avoided problems in associative measures. The indicators were correlated using the Pearson correlation. A joint scale was created for each construct using the arithmetical average of all the different binary indicators of that specific construct. As a general rule, indicators with more than four cases of missing values were not included in the composition of the scales. These scales were then used in order to relate the different constructs. These scales, recoded using the median split method, were related to indicators on effectiveness, innovation, as well as training.

Creating the scales, as described, has the advantage of summarizing a-priori theoretically related variables and creating a comparable scale. However, it is important to note that each scale implies that all the indicators have a similar weight. This means that the different indicators that measure a construct are treated equally. This means that companies with similar scores in a scale might actually have a slightly different knowledge-enabling environment. To some degree, the study is assuming that all the components of the knowledge-enabling environment are equally important.

RESULTS

The Knowledge-Enabling Environment

A descriptive analysis of the 18 companies shows that despite the similarities in the services they provide, companies present a high variability in the different aspects studied. Companies differ considerably in the composition of their workforce, the way they select and recruit employees, the way they provide bonuses, the way they structure their work, in their communication activities, and in their investment in IT. Based on this descriptive analysis, an exploration of the most important aspects of the knowledge-enabling environment was undertaken. These aspects were captured by the seven constructs that were created and used together with the construct of size. These constructs, with the exception of size, were grouped in a composite indicator to measure the knowledge intensiveness of a company.

Analysis of the eight constructs shows that companies present a high degree of variability in their knowledge-enabling environment (see Table 3). Each company, thus, has a unique way of managing their knowledge; it was not possible to identify similar patterns among the 18 companies. The seven constructs for a knowledge-enabling environment have a similar distribution in both sectors, or in other words, consultancy and education generally have similar knowledge-enabling environments. The relationship between the knowledge-enabling constructs was relatively weak. Only workforce stability and experience showed a positive significant relationship. The weak or nonrelationship among knowledge-enabling constructs might, in part, be due to a seeming inconsistency between the different indicators within each construct. Another way of saying this is that the constructs are composed of aspects that each company uses differently. One could say that each company is unique in their approach to managing knowledge.

The relationships between the construct indicators of size, stability of the workforce, experience, and tacit orientation of the recruitment process can be explained by the service the company provides: consultancy or education. However, other relationships do not appear to be associated with the company activity and thus, further exploration might be worthwhile. For example, the data shows that higher stability among employees is associated with lower communication intensiveness. This can be related to the idea of creative chaos defended by Nonaka and Takeuchi (1995). They suggest that less stability generates more communication among employees that, in turn, can create more innovation and insights. Also interesting to note is that the study indicated that companies with higher professionalism have less communication among employees, which is in line with the characterization of professional workers presented by Sveiby (1997). It was also found that having cross-functional teams and a mentor system is associated with having a higher level of communication in a company, which is in line with Nonaka and Takeuchi's characterization of a knowledge creating company (see Nonaka, 1991, 1994, Nonaka & Takeuchi, 1995).

Table 1. Indicators and medians

Knowledge-enabling environment			
	(1) Size		Median
		Part of a large corporation	
		Number of offices in Sweden	0
		Number of offices in other countries	0
		Monetary turnover (in million SEK)	19
		Number of employees in 2001*	21
		Total number of employees in 2003	15
	(2) Stability		
		Percentage of full-time employees	0.88
		Percentage of permanent employees	1
		Percentage of permanent part-time employees	0.45
		Percentage of employees lost in the last year (inversed scale)	0.1
		Respondent's number of years in the company in relation to companies starting date	0.43
	(3) Workforce's experience		
		Average respondent's age	42 years
		(a5) Average numbers of years working in related area	12 years
		Percentage of employees with tertiary education degree (more than 3 years)	0.4
	(4) Professionalism		
		Professional as a manager of the company	
		Main manager owns the company (totally or partially)	
		Having cross-functional teams	
		Having a middle manager	
		Specific person for human resource function	
		Number of professionals as a proportion of the total employees	0.85
	(5) Recruitment policy		
		Method for advertising available positions: Through contacts	
		Method of selecting employees: interviews	
		Criteria for personnel selection: Social skills	
		Criteria for personnel selection: Fitting into the company	
		Having a mentor for new employees	
		Policy for newly employed	
	(6) Reward system		
		Salary level	165 SEK/h.
		Salary determination individually	
		Bonus within the company	
	(7) Communication intensiveness		
		Percentage of respondents with more than 5 ...	
		...hours in informal meetings	0.23
		...hours in regular meetings	0

continued on following page

Table 1. continued

		...work related written materials in one week	0.15
		...work related materials in one week	0.36
		...telephone calls per day from other colleagues	0.11
		...e-mails per day from other colleagues	0.09
		Having regular meetings every week	
		Professionals having an scheduled meeting	
		Having a Newsletter	
	(8) IT investment		
		Number of computers per employee	1
		Investment in IT per employee in 2002	7407 SEK
		Investment in IT as a percentage of the total monetary turnover, 2001	7 per MSEK
		Investment in IT as a percentage of the total monetary turnover, 2002	8 per MSEK
		Investment in IT as a percentage of the total monetary turnover, 2003	6 per MSEK
Learning arenas			
	(A) Training effort per employee		
	1	Yearly training estimated time per employee (*trTemp*)	85 hours
	3	Total training estimated cost per employee (*trCTemp)*	30903 SEK
	4	Actual total training expenditure per employee (*trActemp)*	9074 SEK
	(B) Monetary effort in training of the company		
	5	Actual expenditure as a proportion of the total estimated training cost (*trActPer)*	0.35
	6	Total training estimated cost per hour of training (*trctT)*	378 SEK
	(C) Demand for formal learning		
	2	Average number of training events that each employee demands (*trPemp*)	6 courses
	7	Company's average of the informal learning activities items (*d17*)	3.45

The Learning Arenas

In relation to learning arenas, the study emphasized the demand for training. The study focused mainly on formal and nonformal training activities; specifically on company-identified estimated training needs. The average estimate for each employee was seven courses and around 111 hours (almost 3 working weeks) of training. The 18 companies studied invest more in training than the average for Swedish companies. However, the companies only invest around 40% of their total estimated training costs in monetary terms. On average, around 31% of the employees attend the same courses in each company. The average duration of each course is 26 hours. Consultancy and education do not differ in estimated training time, cost, or participation, except in the case of course duration, where educational employees attend longer courses. The overall cost of the courses does not differ in the two sectors, but the cost per hour is higher in consultancy. Consultancy companies pay higher direct costs, while educational companies pay higher labour costs, since more employees go to each course. The study of the purpose and subject matter of the training events indicate that the training is mainly directed towards professionals, which

Table 2. Below or above the median in each of the knowledge-enabling constructs by company

Company ID	*(1) Size*	*(2) Stability*	*(3) Experience*	*(4) Professionalism*	*(5) Recruitment*	*(6) Reward system*	*(7) Communication*	*(8) IT*	*KISall*
Median	**0.43**	**0.4**	**0.5**	**0.56**	**0.65**	**0.5**	**0.48**	**0.55**	**0.57**
Consultancy	**0.50***	**0.50***	**0.50***	**0.58***	**0.58***	**0.25***	**0.58***	**0.45***	**0.50***
58	High	High	Low	Low	Low	Low	High		Low
87	Low	Low	Low	Low	High	Low	High	High	Low
94	High	High	High	Low	High	Low	High	Low	High
02	High	Low	Low	High	Low	High	Low	Low	Low
110	Low	High	High	High	High	Low	Low	High	High
98	High	High	High	High	High	Low	Low	Low	High
11	Low	High	High	Low	High	High	High	Low	High
106	Low	High	High	High	High	Low	Low	High	High
49	Low	Low	Low	High	Low	Low	High	High	Low
82	Low	Low	Low	Low	Low	High	High	High	High
83	High	Low	Low	High	Low	Low	Low	Low	Low
24	High	Low	High	High	High	Low	High	Low	Low
Education	**0.50***	**0.33***	**0.50***	**0.17***	**0.33***	**0.50***	**0.33***	**0.50***	**0.50***
26	Low	High	Low	Low	Low	Low	Low	Low	Low
71	Low	Low	High	Low	Low	High	Low	Low	Low
33	High	Low	High	High	Low	Low	High	High	High
30	Low	Low	Low	Low	High	Low	Low	Low	Low
55	High	High	High	Low	Low	High	Low	High	High
68	High	Low	Low	Low	High	High	High	High	High
* Proportion of companies above the median									

is in consonance with their workforce composition. Companies also seem to plan for general rather than specific training. It might be that the planned training is rather general because an external body, the ESF Council in Sweden, helps finance the training. This would be in line with economic theories within the human capital framework (Becker, 1962, 1993). Some attention was also given to informal learning engagement. Employees seem to engage regularly in informal learning activities, especially in reading manuals and other written materials that are not part of a course, as well as in trying new things.

Seven indicators were selected in order to grasp the overall knowledge-creation effort of a company: (1) training estimated time per employee each year (*trTemp*, median = 85 hours); (2) average number of training events that each employee demands (*trPemp*, median = 6 courses); (3) total training estimated cost per employee (*trCTemp*,

Table 3. Pearson correlations of the knowledge-enabling constructs (above 0.20)

	(1) Size	*(2) Stability*	*(3) Experience*	*(4) Professionalism*	*(5) Recruitment*	*(6) Reward system*	*(7) Communication*	*(8) IT*
Size	1							
Stability		1						
Experience		0.49	1					
Professionalism	0.22		0.22	1				
Recruitment		0.27	0.33		1			
Reward system		-0.20		-0.40	-0.20	1		
Communication		-0.20		-0.20			1	
IT		-0.20					0.29	1

median = 30903 SEK); (4) actual total training expenditure per employee (*trActemp*, median = 9074 SEK); (5) actual expenditure as a proportion of the total estimated training cost (*trActPer*, median = 0.35); (6) total training estimated cost per hour of training (*trctT*, median = 378 SEK); and, (7) the company's average of the informal learning activities items (d17, median = 3.45).

These seven indicators were grouped into three main factors: (A) the training effort per employee, composed of (1), (3), and (4); (B) monetary effort in training of the company, composed of (5) and (6) negatively associated; and, (C) the demand for formal learning, composed of (2) and (7) negatively associated. It is important to note that labour cost is higher for consultancy companies than for educational companies. The analysis indicated that companies that estimate more training events, estimate higher costs, and invest more per employee. It also showed that companies invest less if the cost per employee is higher. And finally, employees seem to demand more formal training if they are less engaged in informal learning. This last relationship seems to indicate that formal learning compensates for lower levels of informal learning engagement, or vice versa.

The relationship between the knowledge-enabling constructs and the knowledge-creation (or learning arenas) indicators is relatively weak. This could in part be due to the differences between the consultancy and education sectors. However, generally, in both sectors, the working-environment characteristics that theoretically promote learning, that is the knowledge-enabling environment, do not necessarily promote a higher demand for learning. This is contrary to the primary assumption of this chapter, that the existence of knowledge-enabling characteristics will be related to a higher demand for training. On the other hand, it also seems that companies that have more stability and more experience in their workforce invest more in training. This is in line with previous findings on the demand and supply for learning. Also in line with previous studies on the demand for learning is that higher IT investment seems to be associated with higher levels of training demand and investment in knowledge creation activities.

Table 4. Knowledge-creation indicators binary recoded through the median split method by company and sector

Company ID	*(1) trTemp*	*(2) trPemp*	*(3) trCTemp*	*(4) trActemp*	*(5) trActPer*	*(6) trctT*	*(7) d17*
Consultancy	**0,44**	**0,70**	**0,60**	**0,67**	**0,50**	**0,75**	**0,42**
2	.	High	.	High	.	.	Low
11	High	High	Low	High	High	Low	Low
24	Low	Low	Low	High	Low	.	High
49	Low	High	.	Low	High	High	Low
58	Low	High	High	.	.	High	Low
82	.	Low	High	Low	High	.	High
83	.	High	Low	Low	Low	.	High
87	High	Low	High	High	Low	High	High
94	High	Low	High	High	Low	High	Low
98	Low	Low	Low	.	.	High	Low
106	High	High	High	High	High	Low	High
110	Low	High	High	.	.	High	Low
Education	**0,67**	**0,33**	**0,33**	**0,20**	**0,40**	**0,17**	**0,67**
26	High	High	Low	Low	Low	Low	Low
30	Low	Low	Low	Low	Low	High	High
33	High	Low	High	High	High	Low	High
55	Low	Low	Low	Low	Low	Low	High
68	High	Low	Low	Low	High	Low	High
71	High	High	High	.	.	Low	Low
Both sectors	**0,53**	**0,50**	**0,50**	**0,50**	**0,43**	**0,50**	**0,50**

trTemp: training estimated time per employee each year (median = 85 hours)
trPemp: Average number of training events that each employee demands (median = 6 courses)
trCTemp: Total training estimated cost per employee (median = 30903 SEK)
trActemp: Actual total training expenditure per employee (median = 9074 SEK)
trActPer : Actual expenditure as a proportion of the total estimated training cost (median = 0.35)
trctT: Total training estimated cost per hour of training (median = 378 SEK)
d17: Company's average of the informal learning activities items (median = 3.45).

Table 5. Bivariate Pearson correlations of the knowledge creating indicators

	trTemp	*trPemp*	*trCTemp*	*trActemp*	*trActPer*	*trctT*	*d17*
trTemp	1						
trPemp		1					
trCTemp	0.37		1				
trActemp	0.69		0.73	1			
trActPer	0.51			0.33	1		
trctT	-0.48		0.60		-0.53	1	
d17		-0.34		-0.29			1

Table 6. Bivariate Pearson correlation between knowledge-enabling constructs and knowledge-creation indicators

	trTemp	*trPemp*	*trCTemp*	*trActemp*	*trActPer*	*trctT*	*d17*
Size		-0,33					
Stability				0,32			-0,34
Experience				0,58			
Professionalism	-0,33						
Recruitment		-0,33		0,43			
Reward system					0,39	-0,63	
Communication		-0,33			0,41		
IT			0,46		0,55		0,42
kisallb		-0,33			0,55		
Collaborative Climate Index							-0,33

CONCLUSIONS AND FURTHER RESEARCH

Generalization of these results must be done cautiously. It is important to keep in mind that the 18 companies can only be an illustration of the possible theoretical relationships presented in the theoretical framework. The data collected comes from a particular set of companies in particular circumstances. It is not clear that this demand for training is representative of what companies might demand if not associated with the receipt of training assistance from an external source. In addition, it is not clear to what extent these companies are archetypical of a knowledge-intensive SME company in Sweden. It is, however, very likely that they represent companies interested in the promotion of employee's skills development.

The results seem to indicate that knowledge-intensive companies manage their knowledge in different, uniquc ways, and that there are no strong relationships among the different aspects explored. In other words, companies differ in their knowledge-enabling environments, which complicate any determination as to what extent knowledge-enabling environments affect the demand for training and knowledge creation. With regard to the sectors, education and consultancy, they are relatively similar in their knowledge-enabling environments, but differ considerably in their knowledge-creation activities.

The empirical results showed that the a-priori theoretically related indicators within each of the knowledge-enabling constructs are relatively independent from each other. Accordingly, the internal validity of such constructs is uncertain in this empirical example, and therefore, the usefulness of the constructs is questionable. This supports the idea that intellectual capital and knowledge management applications have to be tailor-made for each specific company.

The empirical results do illustrate the importance of IT infrastructure in driving both formal and informal learning. This seems to be the case because people have to learn to use IT equipment. If this is the case, it is important to study to what extent learning associated with IT can enhance effectiveness. Higher levels of human capital, as well as higher stability, are associated with higher levels of training demand. Also interesting is that a knowledge-enabling environment does not seem to necessarily promote informal learning activities.

This exploratory study has shown certain directions in the management of knowledge in SMEs that need to be further developed in order to prove additional external validity. In essence, the results put into question the idea that a knowledge-enabling environment fosters demand for training. Survey data (such as IALS or CVTS) seem to indicate that company size, and literacy practices at work, relate positively to the demand for training. However, the small sample studied here does not appear to necessarily follow this trend. Further testing of these results is recommended in a larger sample and in other business sectors.

The results indicate that informal learning and formal learning activities seem to have a compensatory relationship. This relationship has to be analyzed further. In addition, higher informal learning engagement relates negatively with an overall collaborative climate. In this vein, further studies on how the collaborative climate relates to informal learning would be interesting. Do people who engage in more intentional informal learning have less interest in sharing their knowledge and in collaborating? Do they have less interest or time to engage in formal training?

From the exploration of the 18 companies, it seems advisable for companies to create a more explicit plan for managing knowledge. In this way, companies might be able to make their different business processes work in a similar direction, creating a truly knowledge-intensive company. However, it is important to link this knowledge-intensive environment with company effectiveness and survival in order to justify it. Further studies for determining what characteristics are associated with effectiveness are necessary.

REFERENCES

Aguirre, J. L., Brena, R., & Cantu, F. J. (2001). Multiagent-based knowledge networks. *Expert Systems with Applications, 20*, 65-75.

Ahmed, P. K., Kok, L. K., & Loh, A. Y. E. (2002). *Learning through knowledge management.* Oxford: Butterworth-Heinemann.

Allavi, M., & Tiwana, A. (2003). Knowledge management: The information technology dimension. In M. Easter-Smith & M. A. Lyles (Eds.), *Handbook of organizational learning and knowledge management* (pp. 105-121). Oxford: Blackwell Publishing.

Becker, G. S. (1962). Investment in human capital: A theoretical analysis. *Journal of Political Economy, 70*, S9-S49.

Becker, G. S. (1993). *Human capital. A theoretical and empirical analysis, with special reference to education* (3rd ed.). Chicago: University of Chicago Press

Bixler, C. H. (2005). Developing a foundation for a successful knowledge management system. In M. A. Stankosky (Ed.), *Creating the discipline of knowledge management: The latest in university research* (pp. 51-66). Oxford: Elsevier.

Boudard, E. (2000). What are the main predictors of recurrent education? A five-country comparative model. In M. O'Dowd & I. Fägerlind (Eds.), *Mapping European comparative education research perspectives: The PRESTiGE TMR Network* (pp.147-167). Studies in Comparative and International Education No.52. Stockholm: Institute of International Education.

Boudard, E. (2001). *Literacy proficiency, earnings, and recurrent training: A ten country comparative study.* Studies in Comparative and International Education, No. 57. Stockholm: Institute of International Education, Stockholm University.

Boudard, E., & Rubenson, K. (2003). Revisiting major determinants of participation in adult education with a direct measure of literacy skills. In R. Desjardins & E. Boudard (Eds), *Literacy proficiency, International Journal of Educational Research, 39*, 265 –281.

Butler, T., & Grace, A. (2005). Beyond knowledge management: Introducing learning management systems. *Journal of Cases on Information Technology, 7*, 53-70.

CEDEFOP & EURYDICE. (2001). *National actions to implement lifelong learning on Europe*. Brussels: EURYDICE.

Chase, R. L. (1997). The knowledge-based organization: An international survey. *The Journal of Knowledge Management, 1*, 38-49.

Coleman, D. (1999). GroupWare: Collaboration and knowledge sharing. In J. Lebowitz (Ed.), *Knowledge management handbook*. Orlando: CRC pres LLC.

Council of the European Union. (1999). Council Regulation (EEC) No. 1784/1999 of the European Parliament and of the Council of 12 July 1999 on the European Social Fund. *Official Journal of the European Communities, L 213*, 13/08/1999, 0005–0008.

Davenport, T. H., & Prusak, L. (1998). *Working knowledge. How organizations manage what they know*. Boston: Harvard Business School Press.

Desjardins, R., Murray, T., & Tuijnman, A. (Eds). (2005). *Learning a living: First results of the adult literacy and life skills survey*. Paris & Ottawa: OECD and Statistics Canada.

Desouza, K. C. (2003). Knowledge management barriers: Why technology imperatives seldom works. *Business Horizons, 46*(1), 25-29.

Diakoulakis, I. E., Georgopoulos, N. B., Koulouriotis, D. E., & Emiris, D. M. (2004). Towards a holistic knowledge management model. *Journal of Knowledge Management, 8*, 32-46.

DiMattia, S., & Oder, N. (1997). Knowledge management: Hope, hype, or harbinger? *Library Journal, 122*, 33-35.

Easter-Smith, M., & Lyles, M. A. (Eds.). (2003a). *Handbook of organizational learning and knowledge management*. Oxford: Blackwell Publishing.

Easter-Smith, M., & Lyles, M. A. (2003b). Introduction: Watersheds of organizational learning and knowledge management. In M. Easter-Smith & M. A. Lyles (Eds.), *Handbook of organizational learning and knowledge management* (pp. 1-17). Oxford: Blackwell Publishing.

European Commission. (2000a). *Towards a European research area*. Luxemburg: Office for Official Publications of the European Communities.

European Commission. (2000b). *A memorandum on lifelong learning*. Luxembourg: Office for Official Publications of the European Communities.

European Commission. (2001). *Making a European area of lifelong learning a reality*. Luxembourg: Office for Official Publications of the European Communities.

European Commission. (2005). *Progress towards the Lisbon objectives in education and training, 2005 report*. Commission staff working paper, Luxemburg: Office for Official Publications of the European Communities.

Field, J. (2000). *Lifelong learning and the new educational order*. Trent: Trentham Books.

Fulmer, R. M., & Keys, J. B. (1998). A conversation with Argyris: The father of organizational learning. *Organizational Dynamics, 27*. 21-33.

Harris, K., Fleming, M., Hunter, R., Rosser, B., & Cushman, A. (1999). *The knowledge management scenario: Trends and directions for 1998 –2003*. London: Gartner.

Hasan, A. (1996). Lifelong learning. In A. C. Tuijnman (Ed.), *The international encyclopedia of adult education and training* (2nd ed.) (pp. 33-41). Oxford: Pergamon Press.

Hauschild, S, Licht, T., & Stein, W. (2001). Creating a knowledge culture. *The McKinsey Quarterly, 1*, 74-81.

Hellström, T., Kemlin, P., & Malmquist, U. (2000). Knowledge and competence management at Ericsson: Decentralization and organizational fit. *Journal of Knowledge Management, 4*, 99-110.

Hislop, D. (2003). Linking human resource management and knowledge management via commitment: A review and research agenda. *Employee Relations, 25*, 182-202.

Ichijo, K. (2004). From managing to enabling knowledge. In H. Takeuchi & I. Nonaka (Eds.), *Hitosubashi on knowledge management* (pp. 125-153). Singapore: John Wiley and Sons.

Jasimuddin, S. M., Klein, J. H., & Connell, C. (2005). The paradox of using tacit and explicit knowledge: Strategies to face dilemmas,.*Management Decision, 43*, 102-112

KPMG. (1998). *Knowledge management: Research report.* London: KPMG Management Consulting.

KPMG. (2000). *Knowledge management: Research report.* Retrieved October 2002, from http://www.kpmg.nl/Docs/Knowledge_Advisory_Services/KPMG%20KM%20Research%20Report %202000.pdf

Leader, G. (2003). Lifelong learning: Policy and practice in further education. *Education + Training, 45*, 361-370.

Leech, S. A., & Sutton, S. G. (2002). Editorial: Knowledge management issues in practice: Opportunities for research. *International Journal of Accounting Information Systems, 3*, 60-73.

Liebowitz, J. (Ed.). (1999). *Knowledge management handbook.* London: CRC Press.

Limón, M. (2001). On the cognitive conflict as an instructional strategy for conceptual change: critical appraisal. *Learning and Instruction, 11*, 357-380.

Livingstone, D. W. (2000). Researching expanded notions of learning and work and underemployment: Findings for the first Canadian Survey of informal learning practices. *International Review of Education, 46*, 491-514.

Lundvall, B. Å. (2000). Understanding the role of education in the learning economy: The contribution of economics. In OECD, *Knowledge management in the learning society* (pp. 11-35). Paris: OECD.

Mårtensson, M. (2000). A critical review of knowledge management as a management tool. *Journal of Knowledge Management, 14*, 204-216.

Martiny, M. (1998). Knowledge management at HP consulting. *Organizational Dynamics, 27*, 71-77.

McElroy, M. W. (2000). Integrating complexity theory, knowledge management and organizational learning. *Journal of Knowledge Management, 4*, 195-203.

Moody, M., & Duff, A. (2000). Is that public knowledge? *Director, 53*, 21-24.

Nonaka, I. (1991). The knowledge creating company. *Harvard Business Review, 69*, 96-104.

Nonaka, I. (1994). A dynamic theory of organizational knowledge creation. *Organizational Science, 5*, 14-37.

Nonaka, I., & Takeuchi, H. (1995). *The knowledge creating company: How Japanese companies create the dynamics of innovation.* Oxford: Oxford University Press

OECD. (1997). *Sustainable flexibility. A prospective study on work, family and society in the information age.* Paris: OCDE.

OECD. (1998). *Human capital investment. An international comparison.* Paris: OECD.

OECD. (2000). Knowledge management in the learning society. In OECD, *Knowledge management in the learning society. Education and Skills* (pp. 11-104). Paris: OECD.

OECD & Statistics Canada. (2000). *Literacy in the information age: Final report on the international adult literacy survey.* Paris: OECD.

Piaget, J. (1975). *L'e'quilibration des structures cognitives. Proble`me central du de'velopment.* Paris: PUF (*The development of thought: equilibration of cognitive structures.* Eng. trans. New York: Viking Press).

Quintas, P. (2003). Managing knowledge in practice. In OECD & Statistics Canada, *Measuring knowledge management in the business sector: First steps* (pp. 385-391). Paris: OECD.

Quintas, P. Lefrere, P., & Jones, G. (1997). Knowledge management: A strategic agenda. *Long RangePlanning, 30,* 385-391.

Ramboll Management. (2005). Slututvärdering Växtkraft Mål 3: Final version. Stockholm: Ramboll management. (Ramboll Management (2005). *Final evaluation of the Objective 3.* Stockholm: Ramboll management.).

Rao, M. (2005). The social life of KM tools. In M. Rao (Ed.), *Knowledge management tool and techniques: Practicioners and experts evaluate KM solutions* (pp. 1-77). London: Elsevier.

Rubenson, K. (2001). Lifelong learning for all: Challenges and limitations of public policies. In Ministry of Education and Science in Sweden (Ed.), *Adult lifelong learning in a Europe of knowledge* (pp. 29-39), Ekilstuna, Sweden, 21-23 March 2001. Stockholm: Ministry of Education and Science in Sweden,.

Rubenson, K. (2003). Adult education and cohesion. *Lifelong Learning in Europe, 8,* 32-36.

Stankosky, M. (Ed.). (2005a). *Creating the discipline of knowledge management: The latest in university research.* London: Elsevier.

Stankosky, M. A. (2005b). Advanced in knowledge management: University research toward an academic discipline. In M. A. Stankosky (Ed.), *Creating the discipline of knowledge management: The latest in university research* (pp. 1-15). Oxford: Elsevier.

Starbuck, W. H. (1992). Learning by knowledge-intensive firms. *Journal of Management Studies, 29,* 713-738.

Stenhouse, L. (1982). The conduct, analysis, and reporting of case study in educational research and evaluation. In R. Murphy & H. Torrance (Eds.), (1987), *Evaluating education: Issues and methods* (pp. 74-80). London: Paul Chapman Publishing.

Sveiby, K. E. (1997). *The new organizational wealth: Managing and measuring knowledge-based assets.* San Francisco: Berrett-Koehler Publishers.

Sveiby, K. E., Linard, K., & Dvorsky, L. (2002). *Building a knowledge-based strategy: A system dynamics model for allocating value-adding capacity.* Retrieved October 2004, from, *http://www.sveiby.com/Portals/0/articles/sdmodelkstrategy.pdf*

Sveiby, K. E. & Simons, R. (2002). Collaborative climate and effectiveness of knowledge work – An empirical study. *Journal of Knowledge Management, 6,* 420-433.

Swedish ESF Council. (2001). *Summary of the Swedish objective 3: Single program document (SPD)* 2000-2006. August 19th, 2002. Retrieved from http://europa.eu.int/comm/employment_social/esf2000/ms/s-obj-3-doc-en.pdf

Swedish Ministry of Finance and Ministry of Industry, Employment, and Communications. (1999). *Sweden's action plan for employment, 2000.* Stockholm: Government of Sweden. Retrieved November 2002, from *http://www.sweden.gov.se/sb/d/108/a/1859;jsessionid=aFVFi7RjX*

jp_Swedish Ministry of Finance and Ministry of Industry, Employment and Communications. (2004). *Sweden's action plan for employment, 2004.* Stockholm: Government of Sweden. Retrieved November 2005, from *http://www.regeringen.se/sb/d/2530/a/36642*

Tuijnman, A. C. (1999). Research agenda for lifelong learning: A report by the task force of the International Academy of Education. In A. C. Tuijnman & T. Schuller (Eds.), *Lifelong Learning Policy & Research: Proceedings of an International Symposium* (pp. 1-22). London: Portland Press.

Tuomi, I. (1999). Hierarchy for knowledge management and organizational memory. *Journal of Management Information Systems, 16*, 103-117.

Tuomi, I. (2002). Towards the third generation of knowledge management. *Lifelong Learning in Europe, 7*, 69-80.

Van Winkelen, C., Birchall, D., & Smith, G. (2004). A framework for comparing knowledge management practices. In E. Truch (Ed.), *Leveraging corporate knowledge* (pp. 23-33). Aldershot, UK: Gower.

Villalba, E. (2006). *The uniqueness of knowledge management in small enterprises: Knowledge management as an employer strategy for lifelong learning.* Studies in International and Comparative Education, No. 70. Stockholm: Stockholm University.

von Krogh, G., Ichijo, K., & Nonaka, I. (2000). *Enabling knowledge creation: How to unlock the mystery of tacit knowledge and release the power of innovation.* Oxford: Oxford University Press.

Wei Choo, C., & Bontis, N. (Eds.). (2002a). *The strategic management of intellectual capital and organizational knowledge.* Oxford: Oxford University Press.

Wei Choo, C.. & Bontis, N. (2002b). Knowledge, intellectual capital, and strategy. In C. Wei Choo, & N. Bontis, (Eds.), *The strategic management of intellectual capital and organizational knowledge* (pp. 3-19). Oxford: Oxford University Press.

Wiig, K. M. (1997a). Knowledge management: Where did it come from and where will it go? *Expert Systems with Applications, 13*, 1-14.

Wiig, K. M. (1997b). Integrating intellectual capital and knowledge management. *Long Range Planning, 30*, 399-405.

Wiig, K. M. (2000). Knowledge management: An emerging discipline rooted in long history. In C. Despres & D. Chauvel (Eds), *Knowledge horizons: The present and the promise of knowledge management* (pp.3-27). Woburn, MA: Butterworth-Heinemann.

Wong, K. Y., & Aspinwall, E. (2004). Characterizing knowledge management in the small business environment. *Journal of Knowledge Management, 8*, 44-61.

Yin, R. K. (1993). *Applications of case study research.* Applied social research methods series, volume 34. London: SAGE Publications.

Zuboff, S. (1988). *In the age of the smart machine: The future of work and power.* New York: Basic Books.

ADDITIONAL READING

Rubenson, K. (2001). The Swedish adult education initiative: From recurrent education to lifelong learning. In D. N. Aspin, J. Chapman, M. Hatton, & Y. Sawano (Eds.), *International handbook of lifelong learning* (pp. 329-339). London: Kluwer Academic Publishers.

Rubenson, K. (2003). Adult education and cohesion. *Lifelong Learning in Europe, 8*, 32-36.

Rubenson, K., & Schuetze, H. G. (1995). Learning at and through the workplace: A review of participation and adult learning theory. In D. Hirsch & D. A. Wagner (Eds.), *What makes workers learn: The role of incentives in workplace education and training*. Series on Literacy, Research, Policy and Practice (pp. 95-116). Cresskill, NJ: Hampton Press.

Svensson, L, Heraty, N., Hoogendorn, J, Madsen, P., & Tregaskis, O. (2002). *Learning environments of knowledge intensive company units in five European countries*. Final Research report of the LATIO research project (SOE2-CT96-2013) sponsored by the European Commission under the Fourth Framework Programme.

Takeuchi, H., & Nonaka, I. (Eds.). (2004a). *Hitosubashi on knowledge management*. Singapore: John Wiley and Sons.

Tuijnman, A. C., & Boström, A.-K. (2002). Changing notions of lifelong education and lifelong learning. *International Review of Education, 48*, 93-100.

Wiig, K. M., de Hoog, R, & Van der Spek, R. (1997). Supporting KM: A selection of methods and techniques. *Expert System with Applications, 13*, 15-27.

Chapter X
An Integrated Knowledge Innovation Process Management Model:
The Case of Skandia

Dimitris Bibikas
South East European Research Center, Greece

Iraklis Paraskakis
South East European Research Center, Greece

Alexandros G. Psychogios
CITY College, affiliated Institute of University of Sheffield, Greece

Ana C. Vasconcelos
The University of Sheffield, UK

ABSTRACT

The increasing pressure of today's highly globalised markets has lead organisations to continuously compete for knowledge and innovation. Despite the fact that there is extensive analysis of the concepts of knowledge and innovation management as autonomous areas of research, there is limited investigation for identifying and managing knowledge innovation as an integrated concept. The aim of this chapter is to conceptualise an amalgamation between innovation and knowledge process management models. This study is based on a single case, selected to provide description and generate theory around the introduced knowledge innovation lifecycle model. Skandia was conceived as an appropriate example, since it has significant reputation both on knowledge and innovation management strategy. The proposed conceptual model of highly interlinked and recursive knowledge and innovation processes flow is believed to offer enhanced utilisation of knowledge and innovation management in organisational settings.

INTRODUCTION

In today's increasingly unpredictable and volatile environment, organisations are obliged to ceaselessly innovate in order to survive (McAdam, 2000). Encompassing innovation from an economic perspective, it is admitted that it comprises both an important catalyst for effective competition (Christensen, 1997), as well as a vital source for global market success (Schumpeter, 1934). The growing importance of comprehending innovation has resulted in augmented interest in academia and business circles alike. Similarly, the significance of managing organisational knowledge, and the largely established recognition that intangible assets constitute a critical enterprise resource, is often cited in knowledge-management literature (Davenport & Prusak, 1998; Drucker, 1993). The recent knowledge-based view of the firm, an extension of the previous resource-based theory, suggests that knowledge constitutes a vital organisational resource and a crucial asset that enables sustainable competitive advantage (Bhatt, 2001; Davenport & Prusak, 1998; Zack, 1999).

Furthermore, there is an increasing trend for knowledge management to be associated with innovation (Chatzkel, 2007). The concept of innovation is rooted in knowledge management definitions and practices (Demerest, 1997). It was Amidon (1997) that first defined the term knowledge innovation (KI) as "the creation, evolution, exchange and application of new ideas into marketable goods and services, leading to the success of an enterprise, the vitality of a nation's economy and the advancement of society" (p. 7). However, despite the fact that there is extensive analysis of the concepts of innovation and knowledge management as autonomous areas of research, there is limited investigation for identifying and managing an integrated knowledge innovation concept (Goh, 2005).

Perhaps this derives mainly from the fact that innovation in knowledge management literature is typically approached merely as a result of successful initiatives of the former. Generally, the emphasis is placed on the utilisation of knowledge, in order for an organisation to gain enhanced innovation capabilities. Additionally, despite the fact that there is a plethora of research studies on innovation, it is cited that the relevant literature is usually only case study specific (Kusiak, 2007), and the concept of innovation management remains poorly understood (Birkinshaw & Mol, 2006). Insofar as innovation management is concerned, and despite the fact that knowledge and innovation are two highly and increasingly interlinked concepts (Chatzkel, 2007; du Plessis, 2007; McAdam, 2000; Nonaca & Takeuchi, 1995), there seems to be a gap in the relevant literature and lack of investigating innovation as a discipline in an equal level of significance to knowledge management.

Due to the fact that very little clarity exists in relation not only to the innovation process, as such, but also towards an integrated management procedure of knowledge innovation, this chapter has a two-fold target. The first objective is to conceptualise an integrated model of innovation and knowledge process management. Innovation, in this chapter, is approached as a systematic management discipline and not as an *ad hoc* and random organisational procedure. It utilises experiences and well-established models of knowledge lifecycle, and juxtaposes these principles with innovation process management. The second objective of the chapter is to present a new value proposition of organisational knowledge management. Recent research proposes that the association of knowledge management with innovation will lead the former to a next stage (Chatzkel, 2007). However, these links are somehow tenuously researched. The proposed conceptual model of highly interlinked and recursive knowledge and innovation process flow is believed to offer enhanced utilisation of knowledge management in organisational settings.

This chapter explicitly addresses the "global business and intellectual capital management" objective of the book. Namely, it explores the means by which a globalised company (i.e., Skandia) harmonised its knowledge and innovation management models in order to pioneer on the field of intellectual capital. Furthermore, the chapter comprehensively investigates the "knowledge and innovation" objective of the book, by presenting a novel approach of amalgamating these concepts at process level on organisational settings. On a more broadly defined scope, this chapter contributes to the overall target of the book by studding how organisational knowledge and innovation management processes operate in ever increasingly connected, decentralised, and

Figure 1. The basic structure and flow of the chapter

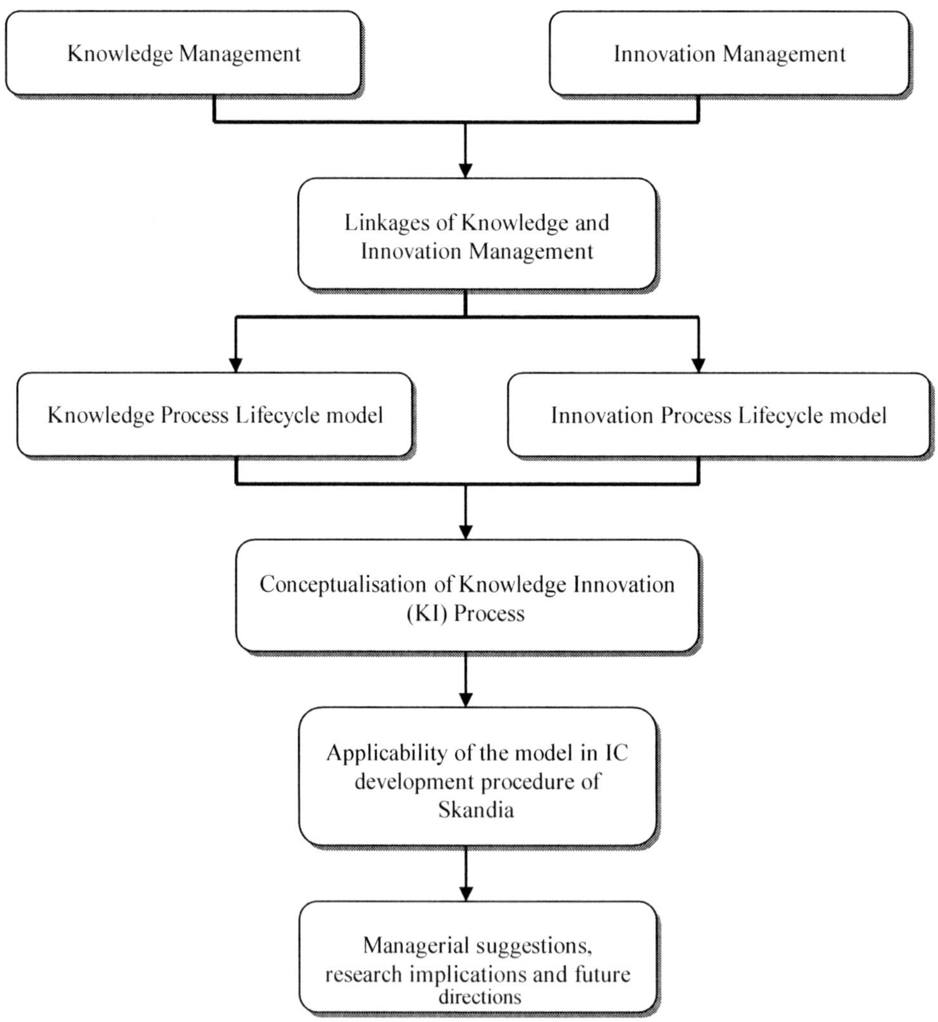

action-oriented corporate environments. This chapter expects to constitute a useful resource for enterprise executives, knowledge and innovation management officers, and people interested in implementing knowledge and innovation management initiatives. Moreover, this chapter will offer a preliminary model that can be used in order to contribute to academics' and practitioners' understanding of organisational knowledge and innovation management capabilities. Finally, it is hoped that this chapter will set the theoretical grounds and invoke further research in the area of knowledge innovation.

The remainer of this chapter is structured as follows (*see Figure 1*). It begins with the description of the research methodology employed in this study. It continues with an overview of existing literature on the relationship of knowledge and innovation management research strands. Subsequently, the chapter merges existing knowledge and innovation lifecycle models and proposes an integrated schema for a knowledge innovation process. The applicability of this model is investigated through an explorative analysis of the case study of Skandia, an international insurance company with strong reputation in the field of intellectual capital. Through the suggested model, the chapter aims to contribute to the establishment and understanding of knowledge innovation as an applicable and systematic management process.

RESEARCH APPROACH

This chapter employs a deductive qualitative research approach. It uses a combination of critical literature review on knowledge and innovation management in order to conceptualise an integrated knowledge innovation process model. Subsequently, this model is applied to a single case study (i.e., Skandia). This research was performed using a desk study method, exclusively, using secondary sources.

Although desk research approaches are usually regarded as mere literature reviews in order for the researcher to be familiarised with background knowledge (Gill & Johnson, 1991; Remenyi, Williams, Money, & Swartz, 1998), this chapter aims at having the desk study as the main method of research. The objective of this chapter is to adopt a deductive argument in order to conceptualise an integrated knowledge innovation lifecycle model. This is materialised through critical analysis of relevant literature and the subsequent model's applicability examination with available secondary data sources of the Skandia case study. Therefore, this study adopts a deductive desk research approach, and involves the development of a theory that is later subjected to a test (Collis & Hussey, 2003).

Developing a hypothesis is typically the initial stage in a deductive research approach (Robson, 2002), which is then followed by expressing the hypothesis in operational terms. Under this perspective, it is suggested that the analysis and preliminary validation of this hypothesis is performed employing a qualitative approach in order to examine the specific outcome of the inquiry (Saunders et al., 2007). The selection of meaningful and representative secondary data sources of the Skandia case were thought to assist in the investigation of the conceptualised model's applicability. Another important characteristic of the followed deductive research approach is its appropriateness in explaining causal relationship between concepts (Saunders et al., 2007). Since it is the aim of this chapter to integrate and explore the dialogic relationship between the concepts of knowledge and innovation management, a qualitative and deductive research approach was considered as the most suitable. An overview of the methodological framework utilised in this chapter is shown in Figure 2.

This methodological approach encompasses the following five deductive and qualitative research steps:

Figure 2. The selected methodological approach

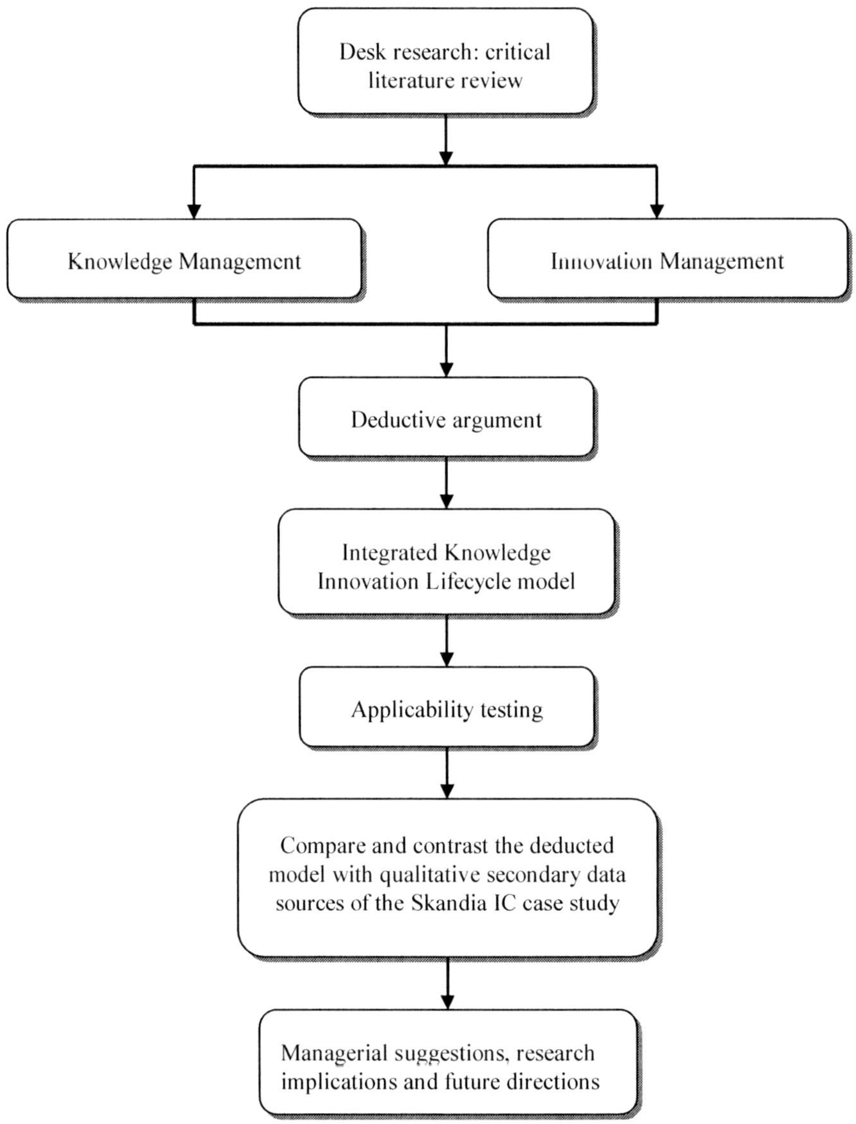

- Performing a critical literature review on the linkages of knowledge and innovation management, in order to establish an initial theoretical background on the subject;
- Deploying a critical analysis of these studies and proposing an integrated knowledge innovation lifecycle model;
- Expressing the conceptual knowledge innovation model in operational terms, indicating the relationships of knowledge and innovation at a process level;
- Testing the conceptualised knowledge innovation model through qualitative secondary data sources in order to investigate the applicability of the proposed knowledge innovation process management model;
- Examining the findings and proposing further research objectives.

The approach adopted in this study uses case-study findings as secondary data, due to the contextualised and applied nature of this type of research. Therefore, secondary data sources external to Skandia were used (see *References with descriptions of Skandia*). The company has attracted much interest, both in business and academic circles alike. There is a rich mixture of book chapters, business magazines articles, and journal papers investigating a variety of aspects of the particular company. These sources provided valuable secondary data with respect to details of stages in the development of the intellectual and social capital programmes.

Finally, the chapter does not intend to analyse the value of intellectual capital reporting *per se*, the area in which Skandia is widely known, but rather to focus on the *process* in which the particular innovation took place. Through this exploratory investigation, it is proposed that the knowledge innovation model can be employed to describe the generation and lifecycle management of the IC concept initiated by Skandia. However, one cannot neglect the limitations of this particular approach, and emphasise on the need to further investigate the suggested theoretical model to other companies and industry sectors employing primary data and field investigation methods.

LINKAGES OF KNOWLEDGE AND INNOVATION MANAGEMENT

In knowledge management literature, innovation is mainly approached as an effect of knowledge management initiatives. In other words, innovation is often cited to derive from managing organisational knowledge; hence, knowledge management is seen as a vehicle for enhancing innovation. In particular, Nonaka and Takeuchi (1995) suggest that innovation should be an ongoing organisational process and associate the transformation procedure from tacit to explicit knowledge with the increased innovation capabilities of knowledge workers. Additionally, they posit that knowledge dissemination activities act in essence as enablers for continuous and systematic innovation. Demerest (1997) advises that knowledge creation and application processes can act as vehicles for enhanced organisational innovation.

Furthermore, McAdam (2000) emphasises on the role of knowledge management in strengthening innovation organisational capabilities. He proposes a knowledge management model which incorporates innovation. This model is based mainly on the social constructionist knowledge management approach of Demerest (1997) and suggests that the interactive knowledge flow among four main knowledge processes (knowledge construction, embodiment, dissemination and use/benefit) can lead to enhanced levels of innovation.

On the other hand, Goh (2005) stresses the importance of an integrated view of knowledge and innovation management and refers to the notion of knowledge innovation in an attempt to bridge the two concepts. He investigates knowledge utilisation as a catalyst for advancing innovation inside organisational settings and suggests an integrated strategic management model focused on knowledge-centred principles, knowledge-sharing infrastructures and knowledge-initiatives. However, although he suggests that innovation management should be a "discipline that deals primarily with issues relating to how the innovation process could be managed effectively" (Goh, 2005, p. 6), a specific innovation process is not depicted, but rather is implied as an outcome from knowledge management practices.

The role of knowledge management in innovation realm is also exhibited by du Plessis (2007), who suggests that knowledge management plays five main roles in fostering innovation: a) enabling the sharing of tacit knowledge as a resource for innovation, b) making explicit knowledge available for novel transformations into innovations, c) providing collaborative experiences which have a positive effect on fostering innovation, d) integrating various knowledge management lifecycle activities for innovation, and e) creating a culture for knowledge creation and sharing for enhanced innovation performance.

In the pursuit for continuous innovation, a knowledge-intensive enterprise simply cannot address knowledge and innovation management issues independently (Goh, 2005). As a result, there is a need towards establishing innovation as a systematised organisational procedure, and the necessity to be closely interlinked with knowledge management practices.

KNOWLEDGE INNOVATION (KI) PROCESS MANAGEMENT

This chapter draws mainly upon the four-stage definition of knowledge lifecycle model of Birkinshaw and Sheehan (2002) and innovation lifecycle model of Birkinshaw and Mol (2006). It attempts to integrate these two unrelated concepts into one coherent knowledge innovation process, materialising the proposed definition of Amidon (1997). The suggested model also reinforces Goh's (2005) recommendation of an integrated knowledge innovation concept at process level.

The first stage of the innovation lifecycle is cited to be *dissatisfaction with the status quo* (Birkinshaw & Mol, 2006, p. 82). This phase of the innovation-process management is typically initiated by a necessary organisational response to a current or impeding danger. In fact, it is proposed that there are three distinct levels of threat in which a corporation usually is obliged to react upon: a current operational problem, a potential strategic threat, and an impending crisis (Birkinshaw & Mol, 2006). In an emergent manner, the social structures of the organisation (i.e., individual, team, business unit) begin to explore the environment for possible solutions. This procedure of investigating and generating new and useful ideas is linked with the capability of an organisation to create new knowledge (Bhatt, 2001). The necessity to combine and interpret information in novel means, in order to react to an impeding organisational threat, results in the creation of new knowledge. However, *knowledge creation* constitutes the first stage of the knowledge lifecycle model (Bhatt, 2001; Birkinshaw & Sheehan, 2002). Thus, the first step of the innovation process can act as an enabler for the initial phase of knowledge lifecycle, knowledge creation. On the other hand, an organisation creates knowledge through the actions of individuals who generate new "realities" and overpass existing rigid thinking and assumptions (Argyris & Schon, 1978). The process of knowledge creation is suggested to be continuously evolving, emergent, and based on the adaptive flexibility of an organisation to investigate the implementation of novel solutions to problems in different contexts (Bhatt, 2000). New knowledge creation often requires organisations to alter their current and established norms, and to perceive reality in new perspectives (Weick, 1979). These new perspectives, however, can lead to novel realisations of previously uncovered situations (Argyris & Schon, 1978), often undesirable or problematic. In other words, an organisation can apprehend formerly hidden problems deriving from the newly created knowledge. Thus, the first step in knowledge development process can result in *dissatisfaction with the status quo*, which constitutes the initial stage of the innovation lifecycle model.

The second stage of the innovation process management model is proposed to be *inspiration from external sources* (Birkinshaw & Mol, 2006). During this phase, individuals investigate, more thoroughly, similar problems and solution approaches selected in analogous external organisational settings. It is suggested that only seldom, innovation derives from the organisation's own industry paradigms and solution approaches (Birkinshaw & Mol, 2006; Chesbrough, 2003) Circumstantial evidence from working solutions, or untested but appealing ideas from the outer environment and peripheral resources, are explored. These preliminary ideas and thoughts, which are generated from other socio-technical grounds, can eventually facilitate one or more knowledge mobilisation strategies: imitation, replication, and substitution (Bhatt, 2000). Depending on business objectives, an organisation can select a knowledge adaptation strategy. Newly acquired knowledge frequently is refined and replenished, according to internal business objectives, and endeavours to extract value are initiated (Birkinshaw & Mol, 2006). However, this iterative knowledge modification cycle results in internal *knowledge mobilisation*, which forms a distinct stage in the knowledge lifecycle model (Birkinshaw & Sheehan, 2002). In contrast, knowledge mobilisation of organisational internal resources usually results in refined knowledge assets (Birkinshaw & Sheehan, 2002). These knowledge resources in highly globalised and competitive markets are quite difficult to keep proprietary and hidden from the external environment (Bhatt, 2000). The example of many Japanese firms that imitated their western counterparts, but eventually successfully modified the adopted assets to better suit their national and organisational culture is often stated in the knowledge management literature (Bhatt, 2000). As a result, the mobilisation of internal knowledge assets, acts as *external inspiration* resource to other organisations, which comprises a significant stage in the innovation process management model (Birkinshaw & Mol, 2006).

The third stage of the innovation procedure is the *invention* (Birkinshaw & Mol, 2006) of the "prototype," either that being a product, process, business model, branding strategy, and so forth (Birkinshaw & Mol, 2006; Keeley, In press; Sawhney, Wolcott, & Arroniz, 2006). The distinctive phase of invention consists of the problematic situation's systematic investigation, the exploration of various elements of possible solutions from both the external environment, as well as the internal organisational context (Birkinshaw & Mol, 2006). This procedure is rarely spontaneous and momentary, but rather iterative and gradual. Admittedly, organisations engaged in the invention stage are increasingly wishing for fast realisation and propagation of their eventual "prototype." Thus, customers, partners, suppliers, and even competitors are increasingly thought of as collaborative members in the value chain of organisations (Bonabeau & Meyer, 2001; Chesbrough, 2003; Gloor & Cooper, 2007; Hargadon, 2003). The initiating company attempts to multiply the value of the invention by diffusing it to the internal, as well as the external environment (Birkinshaw & Sheehan, 2002). However, *knowledge diffusion* comprises the fourth phase of the knowledge process management model; hence, the invention stage of innovation lifecycle can advance the knowledge diffusion stage. On the other hand, during the knowledge diffusion stage of the knowledge development process, organisations typically propagate and market their idea in broad audiences in search of network economies (Birkinshaw & Sheehan, 2002). This holds especially true in the knowledge-based services sector (i.e., software development, consulting services, etc.), where ideas flow with fast pace from one company to another. However, when a concept becomes widely accessible, a challenge becomes evident, that

Figure 3. The interplay between knowledge and innovation lifecycles at the first stage

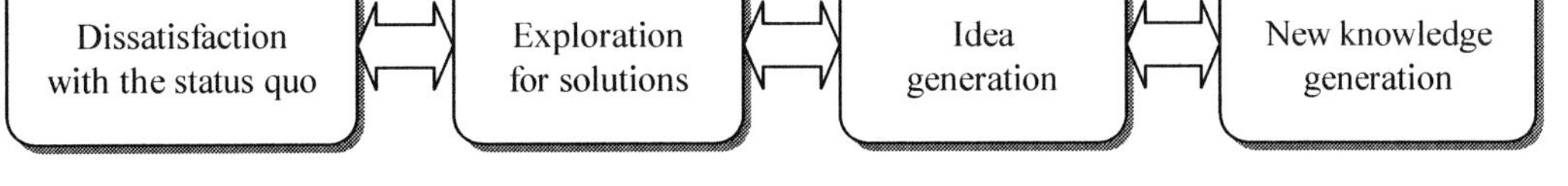

Figure 4. The interplay between knowledge and innovation lifecycles at the second stage

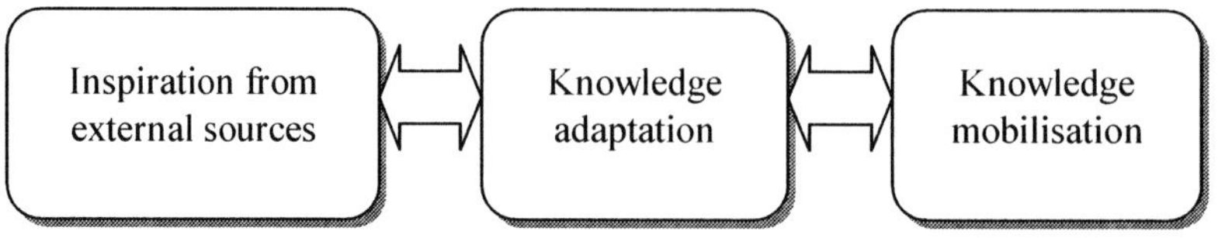

Figure 5. The interplay between knowledge and innovation lifecycles at the third stage

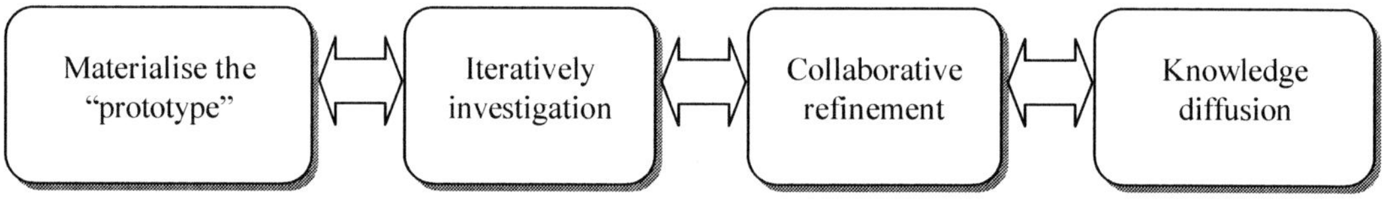

is, to differentiate from competitors. Therefore, other organisations engage in modification and refinement of the "prototype" idea according to their own contexts and capabilities (Bhatt, 2001). This requires a thorough and iterative analysis of the internal organisational situation, as well as investigation of external sources of inspiration. Nevertheless, this gradual and analytical process reflects the *invention phase* of the innovation lifecycle (Birkinshaw & Mol, 2006). Thus, the diffusion procedure of the knowledge-process management model can progress the realisation the innovation lifecycle's invention stage.

The final step of the innovation process management is to gain *internal and external validation* (Birkinshaw & Mol, 2006). In order for an organisation, or part thereof, to undertake the risk to implement an innovative concept (i.e., either that being the development of a product, business process, branding strategy, customer experience aspects, etc.), strong internal managerial support is imperative. This holds especially true when one considers the fact that very few inventions ultimately prove to be successful (Fleming, 2007; Keeley, In press). In contrast to technological innovation, where the output of such an initiative is somewhat more codifiable and tangible (e.g., an innovative product), the value of managerial innovation (e.g., processes and strategies) may seem rather generic, thus difficult to perceive (Birkinshaw & Mol, 2006; Keeley, In press). Innovation endeavours need not only a "champion" to put forward internal publicity, and eventually acceptance of the value offered by the "prototype" invention, but also senior management individuals to clearly support the initial concept and allocate proper resources for the required experimentation (Birkinshaw & Mol, 2006). External validation from "independent observers" (Birkinshaw & Mol, 2006, p. 86) is also of pivotal significance. This outward looking process tends to reinforce the value of the innovation, both within as well as without the initiating organisation (Birkinshaw & Mol, 2006). Ultimately, the innovative concept becomes well known among partners, clients, and eventually competitors. Notions and aspects of the particular innovation are widely spread and diffused. Thus, knowledge of the particular topic becomes *commoditized*. However, *knowledge commoditization* constitutes the final stage of the knowledge-process management model (Birkinshaw & Sheehan, 2002). On the other hand, the fact that commoditized knowledge is broadly communicated, and perhaps commonly exploited, does not mean that it has lost its value, but rather quite the opposite (Birkinshaw & Sheehan, 2002).

Due to continuously shifting and dynamic market conditions, knowledge should be constantly reviewed, revised, reconfigured, and organisations should adapt their strategy accordingly (Bhatt, 2000; Birkinshaw & Sheehan, 2002; Spender, 1996). Knowledge review and revision procedures are important to respond to external environmental stimuli and solve existing organisational problems (Bhatt, 2001). In order to assess and evaluate the applicability of knowledge resources for particular organisational contexts, knowledge should be validated both from internal as well as external sources. *Internal validation* often focuses on the factors that influence the possible internal fit of a widely known knowledge asset, while *external sources of validation* (e.g., academics, consultancies, and media) usually investigate more broad perspectives of knowledge assets and their generic application impact. Management typically considers both validation sources in order to assess the risk of internal applicability (Bhatt, 2000; Birkinshaw & Sheehan, 2002). However, this particular procedure reveals the final stage of the innovation lifecycle, thus, the last step of the knowledge process management can assist in the progression of the innovation lifecycle.

Overall, one can observe the highly interlinked and interdependable relationship between innovation and knowledge-process management models. This interplaying flow among these procedures can lead to a conceptual model that integrates them both. Particularly, commencing from dissatisfaction with an existing organisational situation, new knowledge can be generated in the form of an initial and often abstract idea. This novel concept typically gets mobilised and investigated for preliminary reactions. The selected feedback usually provides with more inspiration for refinement. In case that the newly created idea/knowledge obtains the required support, a "prototype" for testing purposes is employed, and the resulting invention ultimately becomes diffused, both within, as well as without the initiating company. This is realised mainly through the collaboration with partners and customers during the pilot phase. Finally, the well-known invention gets validated from both internal and external sources and, in the case that proves to be successful, the end result becomes widely accepted and commoditized in the industry.

This procedure reflects an integrated view of knowledge innovation (KI) process, and establishes a direct interdependent link between the two lifecycle models. Thus, a merged process management model is proposed with two distinct characteristics:

- It recognises both knowledge and innovation as two inseparable and equally important core components.
- It depicts an integrated flow and use of discrete stages.

In particular, the proposed knowledge innovation process management model consists of the following stages:

- **Creative dissatisfaction:** It is the first phase of the knowledge innovation lifecycle. An organisational challenge, which is usually imposed from outside, is recognised. Initial investigation of the characteristics of the

Figure 6. The interplay between knowledge and innovation lifecycles at the fourth stage

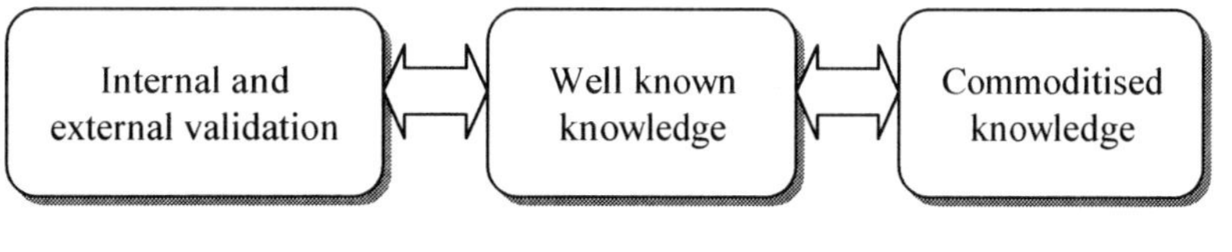

Figure 7. The interplay between knowledge and innovation lifecycles

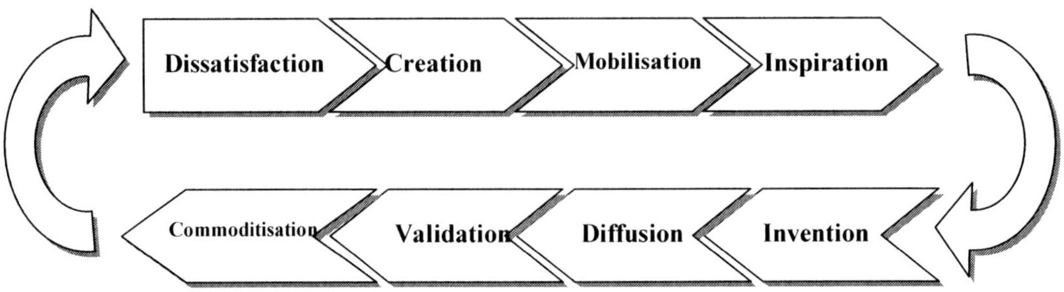

situation and possible means of reaction commence, resulting in preliminary ideas and new knowledge.

- **Mobilised inspiration:** During the second stage of knowledge innovation process, similar problems domains and solution approaches, selected from analogous external organisational settings, are investigated more thoroughly. Experimental ideas are being developed that are inspired from the previously mentioned sources. Knowledge is mobilised from the outer environment of the organization, and is gradually refined and replenished according to internal contexts.
- **Diffused invention:** A "prototype" of the idea is materialised in an iterative and gradual manner, employing continuous interaction with the external environment of the organisation. Idea propagation and knowledge diffusion, regarding the invention, are core components of this particular stage. Partners, clients, and perhaps even competitors are collaboratively refining the "prototype."
- **Validated commoditization:** The final step in knowledge innovation lifecycle is the internal and external validation. Senior management support for internal acceptance is vital. External validation from independent observers is also of pivotal significance. Knowledge about the specific innovation outcome ultimately becomes commoditized, eventually generating the need for review, revisit, and reconfiguration.

This model is consistent with the emerging role of social networks in relation to innovation. Networked innovation is seen as an increasingly important factor for enhanced organisational performance (Gloor & Cooper, 2007; Scarbrough, 2003; Swan & Scarbrough, 2005). Ideas and knowledge are continuously dispersed across organisational boundaries. Through these interstices distributed concepts are brought together and are integrated into innovative solutions (Swan and Scarbrough, 2005). In each stage of the model, there is an interactive flow of ideas and acquired knowledge between the internal organisation and its external environment. Hence, innovation occurs through iterative negotiations that are seldom based on marker or hierarchical control functions. In the proposed knowledge innovation lifecycle model, innovation and knowledge sharing are not depended on top-down organisational initiatives, but rather they emerge from the social structures of the organisation through exploratory investigation for senior management support and internal/external acceptance. This is inline with the notion that innovation and knowledge are not shaped by command-and-control supply-chain relationships; rather, they surface through open and dialectic relationship between partners, clients, and competitors. In this model, innovation

Figure 8. The knowledge innovation lifecycle

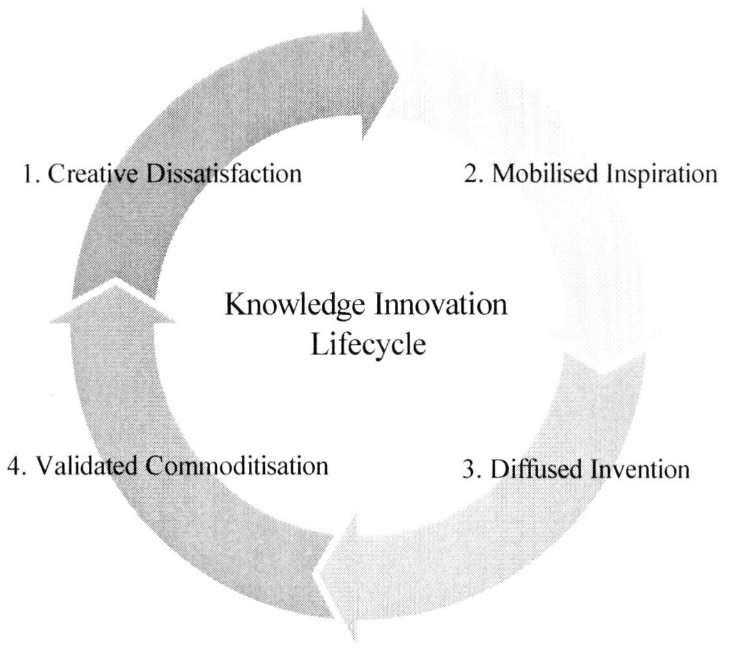

and knowledge encompass both intra-, as well as interorganisational relationships, and competitive as well as collaborative relationships (Swan & Scarbrough, 2005).

KNOWLEDGE INNOVATION PROCESS MANAGEMENT AT SKANDIA

Background

Skandia is a multinational insurance and financial services company based in Stockholm, Sweden. The company was established in 1855 as an international insurance corporation. In 1900, Skandia founded a New York office, and became the first non-British reinsurer to have a subsidiary in United States. Today, the company has five divisions: Skandia Norden, Direct Insurance Nonlife, Assurance and Financial Services (AFS), Skandia Investment Management, and Reinsurance.

Skandia, an international knowledge-intensive company, has focused since 1991 on highlighting the "hidden value" of the company (Edvinsson & Malone, 1997). It uses, in addition to the standard book value of the official balance sheet, a new systematised approach to quantify intangible values the company possesses. Skandia introduced the innovation of intellectual capital reporting. Intellectual capital (IC) encompasses all employees' knowledge and applied experience, organisational structure, technology, and professional competences within a firm. These elements were translated into competitive advantage and monetary gains for the corporation.

The following paragraphs do not analyse the value of IC reporting *per se*, but focus on the process in which the particular innovation took place. Through an exploratory investigation, it is proposed that the knowledge innovation model can be employed to describe the generation and lifecycle of the IC concept initiated by Skandia.

Knowledge Innovation Process

Creative Dissatisfaction

Traditionally, the book value of a company was assumed to reflect its market valuation. This assessment, which is frequently referenced in traditional accounting reporting, is based on the financial worth and the confidence in the company. However, these methods typically focus solely on tangible resources (e.g., land, buildings, equipment, etc.) and neglect intangible ones (e.g., value creating processes, knowledge level and competences of employees, collaborative networks of partners, etc.).

By the early 1990s, Skandia recognised an externally imposed threat, which acted as a catalyst for the first stage of knowledge innovation process. The Swedish real estate market suffered a crisis, and Skandia's land assets, one of its core business focuses back then, were significantly devaluated (Whipple, 2006). As a result, and by employing only traditional accounting methods, the company was threatened by serious undervaluation. This was a clear potential strategic threat. Skandia, in order to effectively react to this impending danger, had to shift focus from traditional organisational financial reporting means towards new value-assessment techniques. The problem seemed to be predominantly severe in the early days of the development of the Assurance and Financial Services (AFS) unit , a "hollowed out organisation" whose future potential was very difficult to assess employing standard reporting methods (see Edvinsson & Malone, 1997; Nahapiet & Earl, 2000).

This *externally imposed threat,* and the subsequent *dissatisfaction with the status quo,* generated new knowledge; the realisation of inadequate book value accounting techniques. Scott Hawkins, of American Skandia unit, mentioned: "We needed a way to explain that we had a lot more value than just real estate" (Whipple, 2006). The CEO of Skandia, Bjorn Wolrath, stated that "Within Skandia, processes that create value for customers, shareholders, and the staff are carried out on a daily basis. Many of these are invisible. Nevertheless, they are innovative, and they create value." This *creative dissatisfaction* produced the early steps towards the financial reporting of "hidden values" inside organisations (Edvinsson & Malone, 1997).

Mobilised Inspiration

In the fall of 1991, Skandia employed Leif Edvinsson, an action that later proved to be a significant source of *mobilised inspiration.* Edvinsson mentions that he was aware of a global growing interest in the area of intellectual capital. He states that he followed the preliminary work of Tom Stewart, who had begun writing about the value of knowledge in the United States, and his Swedish compatriot, Karl-Erik Sveiby, who had also started to investigate the importance of intangible assets in corporate settings (Lelic, 2003). The idea of focusing on intangible assets reporting, *which stemmed from the outer globalised environment outside Skandia's industry,* seemed not only lucrative, but perhaps, more importantly, a source of potential solution for the problematic representation of intangible assets by conventional accounting measures (Nahapiet & Earl, 2000).

The externally acquired knowledge began to be *internally mobilised* and explored. President of Skandia, Bjorn Wolrath, stated that "Commercial enterprises have always been valued according to their financial assets and sales, their real estate holdings, or other tangible assets... The service sector has few visible assets, however." Moreover, the CEO of the company, Lars-Eric Peterson, mentions that "One of the principal tasks is to continue creating long-term, sustainable growth in shareholder value. This includes nurturing and developing Skandia's Intellectual Capital – capital that is seen in the difference between the company's market value and its book value" (Nahapiet & Earl, 2000).

Evidently, the idea to develop a set of tools to define, measure, and report on intellectual capital was starting to grow inside the organisation. This idea that was initially mobilised from the outer environment of the organisation was gradually refined and replenished according to internal contexts, and attempts to extract value were investigated. Under this context, Skandia commenced the intellectual capital programme, a project undertook in order to implement a methodology to identify, quantify, and account organisation's intellectual capital.

Diffused Invention

The invention of the "prototype" was initiated by the appointment, in 1991, of Leif Edvinsson as *director of intellectual capital* for AFS. Edvinsson was given the opportunity to be the first person to combine the intellectual capital theory with a specific organisational operation. He credits Skandia's CEO at the time, Bjorn Wolrath, for his foresight and belief in what Edvinsson was trying to accomplish (Lelic, 2003).

The appointment of Leif Edvinsson as director of intellectual capital for AFS, triggered a *systematic, iterative, and gradual development* of a formal process, and an integrated programme for defining, measuring, and accounting for intellectual capital. Edvinsson felt that the value of a company's intellectual assets was much greater than the value of tangible resources that typically appeared on a balance sheet. By developing sophisticated tools to measure intellectual capital, such as its Dolphin Navigator and Intellectual Capital Index, Skandia was able to illustrate the means by which the company's knowledge could be converted into value. According to Leif Edvinsson, these hidden values differentiate companies and give them competitive advantage. He mentioned that "for companies in the knowledge area, development of new measurement approaches and indicators, in addition to traditional financial indicators, has become critical" (Nahapiet & Earl, 2000).

Skandia attempted to *multiply the value of the invention* by diffusing it into the internal as well as the external environment. In 1993, Skandia took the IC theory one step further, and began supplementing its annual report, which reflects the company's traditional assets, with an IC supplement statement. Intellectual capital statements combined various elements, such as numbering, visualization, and narration, to account for organisational value creation. It is cited that the number of issues provided to interested readers outperformed the demand of Skandia's Annual Financial Report tenfold (Mouritsen, Larsen, & Bukh, 2001). IC supplements communicated more effectively, in a narrative manner, the mechanisms of value creation. This communication was directed not only to the *external audience* (e.g., shareholders, analysts, investors, etc.), but also, or perhaps mainly, to the *internal audiences* of the company. This novel representation was employed in order to communicate the employees' roles and obligations in the firm and how they should contribute to value creation (Mouritsen, et al., 2001). Employees, customers, partners, and even competitors were part of the value chain of the organisation (Nahapiet & Earl, 2000). The endeavour proved to be highly successful: between 1993 and 1999, Skandia's share price quadrupled. Having an early sign of victory and timely engagement of all actors in the value chain, Skandia's IC report was a *diffused invention.*

Validated Commoditization

The last step of the knowledge innovation process in Skandia was IC reporting to gain *internal and external validation* and subsequently, to be *commoditized.* In order to gain internal validation, Edvinsson himself played a leading role in publicising his idea (Edvinsson & Malone, 1997; Nahapiet & Earl, 2000). He spent much of his time to *increase awareness* and share his insights within the organisation. As part of his responsibility, he had regular meetings with his colleagues from the information technology, human resources, accounting, and operations departments. This activity, internally called "missionary," was of outmost importance, as communication technology and networking, culture refinement and cultivation, hidden value measurement and intellectual capital ratios creation, and finally, project initiation and implementation were thought to be critical success factors (Bucklew & Edvinsson, 1999).

As already stressed, *senior management acceptance* is vital. Edvinsson mentions that "senior managers have been very supportive. They agree with the concept, appreciate the new insights, and promote key activities related to intellectual capital. Middle managers have also been supportive. They have experienced a growing need for a formal approach to intellectual capital issues in recent years. Frontline staff and the union agree with the concept and actively participate" (Bucklew & Edvinsson, 1999). Top management support is reflected in the words of Bjorn Wolrath, president of Skandia of that period: "... That is why we have made substantial efforts in recent years to visualize and more concretely describe those assets that are difficult to distinguish in the overwhelming mass of financial information..... A clearer and more balanced reporting of Skandia not only makes it easier for the world around us to value our operations – it also gives us more effective instruments to better manage and develop our hidden values. And the more tangible we can make our hidden values, the better for all of us" (Nahapiet & Earl, 2000). Lars-Eric Peterson, Skandia's CEO, adds, "At Skandia we have long maintained that our truly sustainable earnings are derived from the interaction between our intellectual capital and financial capital. Through measurement tools like the Skandia Navigator and through continued work on developing – and, not least, applying – new work methods, competencies and value-creating processes, we are making the invisible capital visible" (Nahapiet & Earl, 2000). Evidently, *internal acceptance* was assured.

External validation of IC reporting came from many sources. Media offered valuable publicity of the idea. Skandia's IC reporting method was publicised in popular management magazines, such as *Fortune* (Mouritsen et al., 2001). The Danish government has published a version of IC accounting guidelines, and the Association of Financial Analysts in Norway released a similar document (Lelic, 2003). Consulting companies (e.g., Ernst & Young) started to experiment with notions of IC reporting (Bucklew & Edvinsson, 1999). Moreover, the concept of IC developed as an increasingly important research field in academia.

Ultimately, intellectual capital was beginning to become *commoditized*. Edvinsson mentions: "We try to develop knowledge for our alliance partners by having a Leader's College which is a kind of training program for them. It is a concept developed by America Skandia. Training is in economics, finance, as well as management. Then they take that knowledge to the ultimate customer" (Merline, 1997). The innovative concept of IC reporting was well known and diffused among partners, clients, and eventually competitors. Many companies around the world followed the example of Skandia (see Ordonez de Pablos, 2002, 2005).

Yet, as stressed, the fact that commoditized knowledge is broadly communicated, and perhaps commonly exploited, does not mean that it has lost its value. Therefore, Skandia looked for *new ways of utilising its innovation*. The company established, in 1996, the Future Centre, a type of laboratory for research into the future of organisational development. It is mentioned that the centre attracted some 20,000 visitors during the first 2 years of its operation, and acted as an organisational development model. Both Denmark Ministry of Finance, and the major European energy company Eon/Sydkraft, have realised similar institutes. "In that sense, we became a prototype for the rest of the world, as we had been for accounting," Edvinsson said (Lelic, 2003).

Knowledge about the innovation of IC reporting should be constantly reviewed, revised, and reconfigured. Ordonez de Pablos (2005, p. 143) states that "we should not forget that there is a long way ahead still to cover in the field of the intellectual capital report. It is necessary to design intellectual capital report guidelines which are accepted and carried out by those firms that decide to measure and report their intellectual capital or in a not-so-distant future may be enforced by regulatory bodies..." Knowledge review and revision procedures are important in order to react to external environmental stimuli and solve organisational problems.

Edvinsson founded, in 1999, the Universal Networking Intellectual Capital organisation devoted to the application of IC-based tools and methods. Also, he is active in researching this field as a professorship at the University of Lund and the Royal Institute of Technology in Stockholm. As such, his work in the area of organisational development and intellectual capital theory continues to evolve (Lelic, 2003).

CONCLUSION AND IMPLICATIONS

The aim of this chapter was to conceptualise an integrated model between innovation and knowledge-process management. The review of the literature has shown that there appears to be a lack of comprehension about innovation process management, as well as an integrated approach towards a knowledge innovation notion. This study contributes to the establishment of an amalgamation between innovation and knowledge process management, investigating the similarities between the two concepts and proposing an integrated knowledge innovation process management model. The model consists of four distinct phases: i) creative dissatisfaction, in which an imposed threat is recognised and reaction is initiated; ii) mobilised inspiration, where experimental ideas are being developed that are inspired from other industries; iii) diffused invention, in which a "prototype" of the idea is materialised in an iterative and gradual manner with continuous interaction from the external environment; iv) validated commoditization, where internal and external validation of the prototype takes place.

The applicability of the suggested knowledge innovation process management model was investigated in the single case of Skandia, a multinational insurance and financial services company. This knowledge-intensive company focused on highlighting the "hidden value" of the company and used, in addition to the standard book value of the official balance sheet, a new systematised approach to quantify intangible values. Skandia introduced the innovation of intellectual capital reporting. The case study analysed the process in which the particular innovation took place. Through an exploratory investigation, it was suggested that the knowledge innovation model can be employed to describe the generation and lifecycle of the IC innovative concept initiated by the company.

This model opens the possibility for organisations to embody both knowledge and innovation processes as of equal importance, and encourages the implementation of integrated knowledge innovation management initiatives. To further increase the level of understanding in the area of knowledge-innovation process management, it is recommended that further research should be carried in order to apply the model in different sectors and sizes of organisations, and analyse the case studies employing this generic approach.

REFERENCES

Amidon, D. M. (1997). *Innovation strategy for the knowledge economy: The ken awakening.* Boston: Butterworth-Heinemann.

Argyris, C., & Schon, D. (1978). *Organisational learning: A theory of action perspective.* Reading, MA: Addison-Wesley.

Bhatt, G. D. (2000). Organizing knowledge in the knowledge development cycle. *Journal of Knowledge Management, 4*(1), 15-26.

Bhatt, G. D. (2001). Knowledge management in organizations: Examining the interaction between technologies, techniques, and people. *Journal of Knowledge Management, 5*(1), 68-75.

Birkinshaw, J., & Mol, M. (2006). How management innovation happens. *MIT Sloan Management Review, 47*(4), 80-88.

Birkinshaw, J., & Sheehan, T. (2002). Managing the knowledge life cycle. *MIT Sloan Management Review, 44*(1), 74-83.

Bonabeau, E., & Meyer, C. (2001). Swarm intelligence: A whole new way to think about business. *Harvard Business Review, 79*(5), 106-114.

Chatzkel, J. (2007). Conference report: 2006 KM-World Conference review. *Journal of Knowledge Management, 11*(4), 159-166.

Chesbrough H. (2003). The era of open innovation. *Sloan Management Review, 44*(3), 35-41.

Christensen, C. (1997). *The innovator's dilemma: When new technologies cause great firms to fail.* Boston: Harvard Business School Press.

Collis, J., & Hussey, R. (2003). *Business research: A practical guide for undergraduate and postgraduate students.* New York: Palgrave Macmillan.

Davenport, T. H., & Prusak, L. (1998). *Working knowledge: How organizations manage what they know.* Boston: Harvard Business School Press.

Drucker, P. (1993). *Post-capitalist society.* New York: Harper & Collins.

du Plessis, M. (2007). The role of knowledge management in innovation. *Journal of Knowledge Management, 11*(4), 20-29.

Fleming, L. (2007). Breakthroughs and the "long tail" of innovation. *MIT Sloan Management Review, 49*(1), 69-74.

Gill, J., & Johnson, P. (1991). *Research methods for managers.* London: Paul Chapman.

Glesne, C., & Peshkin, A. (1992). *Becoming qualitative researchers.* New York: Longman.

Gloor, P. A., & Cooper, S. M. (2007). The new principles of a swarm business. *MIT Sloan Management Review, 48*(3), 81-84.

Goh, A. L. S. (2005). Harnessing knowledge for innovation: An integrated management framework. *Journal of Knowledge Management, 9*(4), 6-18.

Hargadon, A. (2003). *How breakthroughs happen: The surprising truth about how companies innovate.* Boston: Harvard Business School Press.

Ordonez de Pablos, P. (2002). Evidence of intellectual capital measurement from Asia, Europe, and the Middle East. *Journal of Intellectual Capital, 3*(3), 287-302.

Ordonez de Pablos, P. (2005). Intellectual capital reports in India: Lessons from a case study. *Journal of Intellectual Capital, 6*(1), 141-149.

Keeley, L. (In press). *Taming the new: The emerging discipline of innovation.* Boston: Harvard Business School Press.

Kusiak, A. (2007). Innovation: The living laboratory perspective. *Computer-Aided Design & Applications, 4*(6), 863-876.

McAdam, R. (2000). Knowledge management as a catalyst for innovation within organizations: A qualitative study. *Knowledge and Process Management, 7*(4), 233-241.

Nonaka, I., & Takeuchi, H. (1995). *The knowledge creating company: How Japanese companies create the dynamics of innovation*, New York: Oxford University Press.

Remenyi, D., Williams, B., Money, A., & Swartz, E. (1998). *Doing research in business and management: An introduction to process and method.* London: SAGE Publications.

Robson, C. (2002). *Real world research: A resource for social scientists and practitioner-researchers.* Oxford: Blackwell.

Saunders, M., Lewis, P., & Thornhill, A. (2000). *Research methods for business students.* Harlow: Pearson Education Limited.

Sawhney, M., Wolcott, R. C., & Arroniz, I. (2006). The 12 different ways for companies to innovate. *MIT Sloan Management Review, 47*(3), 75-81.

Schumpeter, J. (1934). *The theory of economic development.* Cambridge, MA: Harvard University Press.

Swan, J., & Scarbrough, H. (2005). The politics of networked innovation. *Human Relations, 58*(7), 913-943.

Weick, K. E., & Roberts, K. H. (1993). Collective mind in organizations: Heedful interrelating on flight decks. *Administrative Science Quarterly, 38*, 357-381.

Zack, M. H. (1999). Managing codified knowledge. *MIT Sloan Management Review, 40*(4), 45-58.

References with Descriptions of Skandia

Bucklew, M., & Edvinsson, L. (1999). *Intellectual capital at Skandia.* Retrieved December, 30, 2007, from http://www.fpm.com/cases/el3.html

Daum, J. (2001). Interview with Leif Edvinsson: Intellectual capital: The new wealth of corporations. *The new New Economy Analyst Report.* Retrieved December, 30, 2007, from http://www.juergendaum.com/news/11_13_2001.htm

Edvinsson, L. (2000). Some perspectives on intangibles and intellectual capital 2000. *Journal of Intellectual Capital, 1*(1), 12-16.

Edvinsson, L., & Malone, M. (1997). *Intellectual capital.* New York: HarperCollins Publishers.

interKnowledge Technologies. *Interview with Leif Edvinsson.* Retrieved December, 30, 2007, from http://www.interknowledgetech.com/brainovation.html

Lelic, S. (2003). The knowledge: Leif Edvinsson. *InsideKnowledge Magazine, 6*(6). Retrieved December, 30, 2007, from http://www.ikmagazine.com/xq/asp/sid.0/chapterid.9942D3E4-534F-44D4-B8A4-2207F95A8174/eTitle.The_knowledge_Leif_Edvinsson/qx/display.htm

Merline, K. (1997). Leading lights. Interview with Leif Edvinsson. *Community Intelligence Labs.* Retrieved December, 30, 2007, from http://www.co-i-l.com/coil/knowledge-garden/ic/edvinsson.shtml

Mouritsen, J., Larsen H. T., & Bukh, P.,N. (2001). Valuing the future: iltellectual capital supplements at Skandia. *Accounting, Auditing & Accountability Journal, 14*(4), 399-422.

Nahapiet, J., & Earl, M. (2000). *Creating organizational capital through intellectual and social capital.* Working chapter for presentation at the Organization Science Winter Conference. Retrieved December, 30, 2007, from http://faculty.fuqua.duke.edu/oswc/2000/papers/wednesday/JanineNahapiet.doc

Whipple, L. (2006). *Skandia Insurance Company Ltd.* Retrieved December, 30, 2007, from http://www.answers.com/topic/skandia-insurance-company-ltd?cat=biz-fin

Chapter XI
Intellectual Capital Reporting: Can a Strategy Perspective Solve Accounting Problems?

Christian Nielsen
Aalborg University, Denmark

Robin Roslender
Heriot-Watt University, UK

Per Nikolaj Bukh
Aalborg University, Denmark

ABSTRACT

During the last decade, many calls for improving disclosure practices, in relation to intellectual capital and intangibles, have been uttered in the standard setting, academic, and business communities. There seem to be two types of solutions to this problem. One angle of attack is to seek to improve transparency through implementation of global accounting standards, and moving from historic value to fair-value practices. Another way of dealing with the problem is to step outside the accounting paradigm to see if transparency and relevance problems can be solved by way of supplementary disclosures. For some, this is a logical step. However, for many, this represents shaky ground. It is ironic that while supplementary information has been shown to reduce investors' uncertainty, it is not being acknowledged as a key element in solving the existing problems by standard setters and academics. This chapter is a wake-up call to the drowsy constituents of academia and policy making, asking them to see beyond their normative accounting paradigm and in turn, showing them how far the strategy-oriented solutions they choose to ignore have come. In this chapter, we thus illustrate for the reader how reporting and management of companies' knowledge resources and intellectual capital is possible through the strategic ideas of the Danish guideline for IC statements.

INTRODUCTION

There has been a lot of discussion in recent years of whether or not both accounting standards and firms' reporting of their assets of intellectual capital to the business environment are sufficient. This discussion is often coupled with the emergence of the knowledge society and the so-called "new economy," where intellectual capital, rather than physical capital, has become the pivotal factor underlying value creation. These changes, associated with the developments in the business environment, such as globalisation and faster innovation rates, have also altered the demands for organizational communication, because traditional financial reporting seemingly is unable to meet the information requirements of users. Hence, it is argued that the prerequisites for transparency have changed.

As such, this chapter promotes a link between the ongoing developments in global business and the necessity of managing intellectual capital; a link that can be attained through the strategic focus of the Danish guideline for intellectual capital reporting. Hence, the notion put forth here is that "accounting" for intellectual capital is a strategic management issue rather than an accounting-based measurement issue.

It is widely accepted that intellectual capital, strategy, and other drivers of value creation constitute strategically important elements for the future profitability and survival of companies. Many firms already disclose much supplementary information in their management commentary regarding strategy, market competition, technological developments, and products in the pipeline. Also, in the Nordic countries and, more recently, in a number of other European countries, companies have been experimenting with disclosing such voluntary and forward-looking disclosures through intellectual capital statements.

The problem, as well as the prospect, with strategy, is that it is about being different. Hence, the bundle of indicators on strategy, intellectual capital, and so forth, that will be relevant to disclose, will differ among firms. For such information to make any sense at all, it should be inserted in the particular firms' strategic context, thereby determining their relevance in relation to the company's value-creation process. In other words, it does not make sense to insert such information into a standardized accounting regime.

Therefore, further elaborations will need to move on from the accounting agenda, and at the least, recognize that these differing perspectives exist. It can be argued that the accounting agenda initially spurred the interest in supplementary business reporting (cf. American Institute of Certified Public Accountants [AICPA], 1994), but that the debate, in recent years, has moved on, and is now more preoccupied with visualizing strategy and the business model rather than measuring for example companies' intangible assets in monetary terms. There have been a number of attempts at constructing business reporting models inherently concerned with strategy, and about showing future-oriented perspectives on the company, which accounting cannot.

Business reporting is the generic term used to identify the type of reporting that the accountancy profession has come to recognise as, if not a direct successor to its highly successful corporate reporting approach, then at least a complement. Because of this, like corporate reporting, business reporting is, at base, a further manifestation of financial reporting, the practice upon which a major part of the reputation of the accountancy profession is based. Assuming that the accountancy profession, one well known for its collective conservatism, is unlikely to willingly reconstitute itself in a radically different guise, it is reasonable to expect that a business-reporting approach is unlikely to depart significantly from the predecessor corporate-reporting approach.

A key motivation for rethinking the latter approach to financial reporting was the recognition that the principal users (Jenkins' "customers") of such reports, investors and analysts, were no longer sufficiently well informed about the performance of businesses. As a result of this situation, the actions of investors and analysts might prove detrimental to the future performance of business, perhaps resulting in a measure of self-fulfilling prophecy. For example, investors might decide to sell doubtful stock, encouraged by the assessments of their analysts, which in turn might influence other investors to follow suit. As a consequence of this chain of events, businesses might find their commercial credibility called into question, resulting in precisely the underperformance supposedly portended in the initial financial information. Alternatively, given the increasingly close links between the cost of investment funds and the assessment of ongoing financial performance, any shortcomings in reports of the latter might cost a business dearly in the medium to long-term. In order to circumvent these problems, "customers" were to be better served by a revitalised reporting approach.

Compounding this situation was the realisation that in many instances, business performance was critically dependent on the success with which a novel category of resources was managed. Intellectual capital (or intangibles) was increasingly recognised as the foundation for long-term value creation in many businesses. As such, it demanded to be accounted for by the accountancy profession, that is, taken into account in some way. Like intangible assets before them, the many constituents of intellectual capital posed major problems for the profession. As assets that promised long-term value creation, the preferred solution is the determination of their financial value, enabling them to be included alongside the other bases of value creation. Leaving aside the not inconsiderable difficulty of identifying the totality of any business's stock of intellectual capital, the obstacle was a lack of objective valuations. All too many examples of intellectual capital defied such valuation, and so their place within the principal financial statements that formed the corporate report was, at best, contestable.

A possible solution, promised by a business reporting approach to financial reporting, was to make more extensive use of statements that were characteristically narrative in format rather than numerical. Such information promised to both supplement and complement the conventional representations that had long served the accountancy profession, and those whose patronage they relied upon. The opportunity to extend the account provided in a business report was seen as a means of addressing some of the issues that worried users. This was particularly the case in respect of intellectual capital, for two interconnected reasons. First, talking about intellectual capital seemed a more appropriate way to proceed, especially where the narrative incorporated quantitative, albeit nonfinancial, metrics. Second, such narratives also provide a means of conveying information about the future prospects of the business, that is, the long-term value creation

Figure 1. Illustration of the chapter's argumentation

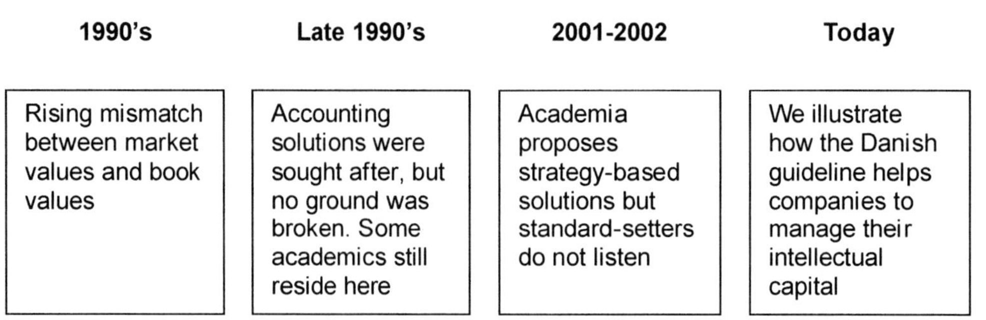

capacity associated with the various constituents of its intellectual capital.

Figure 1 illustrates the argumentation of this chapter. The timeline indicates that it is time to issue a wake-up call to the drowsy constituents of academia and policy making, asking them to see beyond their normative accounting paradigm and, in turn, showing them how far the strategy-oriented solutions they choose to ignore have come. Thus, we show how reporting and management of companies' knowledge resources and intellectual capital is possible through the strategic ideas of the Danish guideline for IC statements.

The remainder of this chapter is structured as follows: We start off by identifying core evidence in relation to the value-relevance problem of the existing accounting regime. This leads to a review of the activities and lines of reasoning applied by the proponents who stand steadfast in the accounting paradigm. We discuss the prevailing ideas, and use these as a point of departure from which we leap to a strategy perspective. We juxtapose the accounting and strategy perspectives, in turn, illustrating how the recent developments of the strategy-oriented solutions refute the concerns stemming from the accounting paradigm.

THE LIMITED SPHERE OF ACCOUNTING SOLUTIONS

The empirical research on disclosure of IC tends to be divided into two branches. The first branch focuses mostly on the value relevance of specific IC indicators, for example, research and development expenses (Lev & Sougiannis, 1996), possibly even with the purpose of showing how intangibles could be capitalized (e.g., Gu & Lev, 2001), while the second branch of research focuses on the interconnectedness of the specific parts of IC, with the purpose of showing how integrated reports on IC could be designed and used both for disclosure purposes (e.g., Collier, 2001; Mouritsen, Larsen, Bukh, & Johansen, 2001c) and for management control purposes (Mouritsen & Larsen, 2005).

From the "traditional" accounting perspective, the first branch of literature often focuses on how various categories of intangible assets, often classified as traditional intangibles, for example, goodwill, brand names, or patents, and deferred charges, for example, advertising, research and development, or training costs (cf. Hendriksen & van Breda, 1992) relates to financial performance and decision making based on this. Cañibano, García-Ayuso, and Sánchez (2000) review a number of studies where the value relevance of other elements of IC, for example, research and development expenses, advertising, patents, brands, customer satisfaction, and human resources, are studied

The value of a firm can be referred to its physical and monetary assets, as well as its intangible assets, which can be in the form of patents, customer relations, organizational structure, and knowledge resources. There have been a number of attempts that seek to value intellectual capital from a stock perspective; most notable is Lev's "return on knowledge capital" (2001) and the VAIC approach (cf. Nazari & Herremans, 2007). These "stock oriented" approaches, concerned with calculating the dollar value of intangibles, however, are still in their infancy and at the present, their methodologies are weak and inconsistent.

In recent years, companies have become aware of the importance of managing their external communications more systematically, due to the growing importance of investor relations activities. Various studies of investors and analysts' request for information indicate a substantial difference between the type of information found in companies' annual reports and the type of information demanded by the market (cf. Beattie & Pratt, 2002; Eccles & Mavrinac 1995).

The perceived stability of intangibles and strategy statements, for example, due to their historical performance, may affect the way they are included or excluded in the market for information participants' valuation process. Sakakibara, Hansson, and Yosano (2005) seem to suggest that the capital market is suspicious towards the cash-flow-generating abilities of intangibles, and thus they pay more attention to the types of intangibles that are more closely related to value creation, or have a historically proven ability to generate cash flows. A good example of such a proxy is the attention that is paid to the track record of top management.

Gelb (2002) argues that providing supplementary disclosures is especially important for firms with significant levels of intangible assets. This can be done through supplementary business reporting, like, for example, an intellectual capital statement. There are previous attempts at reviewing and comparing approaches to business reporting. A recent report from the Institute of Chartered Accountants in England and Wales [ICAEW] (2004) project for improving the existing model of corporate reporting sums up most of the problems we are facing. It is concerned with reviewing the present status and literature of the business reporting debate. However, the present report seems to fail in going beyond the "intangibles measurement debate" of the late 1990s; a debate that primarily took an accounting perspective to the intangible debate (cf. Aboody & Lev 2002), rather than a strategy perspective (cf. Bontis, Dragonetti, Jacobsen, & Roos 1999).

In general, companies, investors, and analysts are becoming more aware of the importance of factors not included in the financial statement, although traditional financial information is still considered to be of greatest importance. Users request more reliable information on, for example, managerial qualities, expertise, experience and integrity, customer relations, and personnel competencies, all factors related to intellectual capital, since these factors are considered important for the company's ability to generate value.

According to Bontis et al. (1999), intellectual capital is the collection of intangible resources and their flows. Hence, the point made here, is that merely depicting the company's stock of intellectual capital in a cost-based asset fashion is insufficient. Regardless of the construction of global standards and the introduction of fair-value valuation practices, historical accounting measures are still not going to be able to convey a fair enough view of the economic potential of intellectual capital. Because intellectual capital is a strategic resourcc, accounting for it in financial terms is difficult. Perhaps for this reason, most recent contributions turn to a more narrative orientation (cf. Fincham & Roslender 2003) when it comes to accounting for intellectual capital, something which is not particularly regarded by the traditional accounting institutions like, for example, the London-based Institute of Chartered Accountants in England and Wales (ICAEW 2004).

HELP FROM THE IASB?

Previous reviews of developments within the intellectual capital reporting agenda seem to paint a rather rosy picture. A more realistic assessment can be gleaned from looking at what might reasonably be regarded as the leading edge of practitioner thinking at this time, the Management Commentary discussion paper issued in October 2005 by the International Accounting Standards Board (IASB). It draws on over a decade of narrative reporting, including the US Management Discussion and Analysis requirement, the UK Operating and Financial Review experience, the German Business Report, and similar initiatives in the European Union, Australia, Canada, and New Zealand, as well as the position adopted by the International Organization for Securities Commissions. The definition proposed by the IASB is that:

Management commentary is information that accompanies financial statements as part of an entity's financial reporting. It explains the main trends and factors underlying the development, performance and position of the entity's business during the period covered by the financial statements. It also explains the main trends and factors that are likely to affect the entity's future development, performance and position. (IASB, 2005, para19).

The primacy of financial reporting is clearly evident here, with Management Commentary being commended as serving to enhance the traditional financial statements. The IASB's proposal is that while the inclusion of such a commentary is mandatory, its content is to be determined by those who manage the business entity, in ways that they deem to be relevant to their own situation. Quite how practitioners will respond to this freedom to choose what to comment on will be interesting, since it markedly contrasts with the very prescriptive manner in which they are called upon to construct their financial statements. A sceptic might conclude that despite all the talk of Management Commentary providing complementary and supplementary information in the discussion paper, for many practitioners, the real accounting information will continue to be found in the financial statements.

What makes the Management Commentary project particularly important, however, is that it emphasises the significance that now needs to be accorded to "future developments" in any financial (business) report. In principle, such information is incommensurate with the historical information that has characterised the generality of financial reporting for generations. Future information is more the province of management reporting (accounting), traditionally the poor relation of financial reporting. Although the volume of prospective information has increased within financial statements in recent times, it has often been contained within those pages not subject to the same levels of attestation by the audit profession. Again, this may be taken to signify that such information is not to be regarded as having equal importance to that contained within those (financial) statements that are subject to the highest levels of attestation. Management Commentary, if embraced by the accountancy profession, may become subject to rigid scrutiny (IASB, 2005, para 194).

The term "future developments" is a potentially broad one, which can encompass many different things. It is clear from the IASB discussion paper that the strategies of any business are viewed as being of critical importance in the context of such developments and, therefore, likely to be the major feature of any Management Commentary. To those working in the strategy field, this belated acknowledgement of the importance of "strategy" by the accountancy profession, and more particularly the dominant financial reporting constituency, will be welcome. As such, it provides the basis for a long overdue dialogue. For despite its considerable success as a business function throughout the greatest part of the past century, there are very few signs that the accountancy profession has ever been much interested in strategic issues. Consequently, it seems reasonable to conclude that the profession will be able to accommodate such issues either readily or painlessly.

The IASB is not in the business of identifying problems in respect to encouraging a greater degree of narrative reporting in the guise of Management Commentary. Its role is to promote practical solutions through a process of debate among interested parties. It falls to accounting academics to identify and debate such problems; in this case the observation that accounting, in the specific guise of financial reporting, has traditionally exhibited few signs of being able to account for strategy. Financial reporting is not focused on strategic issues. It is principally about the provision of a detailed account of the historical performance of a business. While it is true that this information may be of value to senior management in their deliberations on the future direction (strategy) of the business, this entails bringing many more information sets to bear, something that is increasingly evident in the manner in which such reports are presently framed within the broader set of financial statements. The business report concept is underpinned by recognition that an enhanced approach to financial reporting is now needed, with the accountancy profession itself embracing the challenge of accounting in a more strategically relevant way.

There have been a number of initial attempts to develop business reporting, dating back to the Jenkins' Report in 1994 (AICPA 1994). Many of these approaches have not addressed the strategy issue directly, although they have drawn attention to the growing importance of a range of factors that now need to be taken into account, and which merit the designation "strategic." A recent ICAEW report (ICAEW 2004) identified 11 examples of new (business) reporting models, including the Balanced Scorecard, the Jenkins' Report, the Global Reporting Initiative, and PwC's ValueReporting initiative (ICAEW, 2003). The ICAEW acknowledges that this set of developments is very much a work in progress, much the same as Management Commentary/narrative reporting developments that the IASB has focused on (IASB 2005). Both organisations would, with some justification, retort that it is still very early days in the process of developing what, in truth, is likely to be a very different approach to financial reporting.

Nevertheless, it is difficult to avoid the conclusion that, to date, the omens are not too promising. Neither the ICAEW nor the IASB make any reference to the various frameworks that have recently emerged to report on intellectual capital. Several of these are potentially promising, including the Intellectual Capital Statement and Intellectual Capital Report frameworks developed in the Danish Ministry of Science, Technology and Innovation (2003), and EU's Meritum projects (2002) respectively, together with Sveiby's (1997) earlier Intangible Assets Monitor, Lev's (2001) Value Chain Scoreboard, and the IC-index developed by Roos *et al.* (Roos, Roos, Dragonetti, & Edvinsson, 1997).

What is particularly interesting about these developments is that they have, in large part, emerged as a response to the difficulties involved in using a valuation approach to report intellectual capital in financial statements, identified earlier as being a critical factor informing deliberations about the need to develop a business reporting approach to financial reporting. All these intellectual-capital reporting approaches have the capacity to incorporate a considerable narrative content and consequently, may provide some lessons for the IASB Management Commentary project, which only refers to intellectual capital in passing (para A40). It may be considered problematic that institutions, by many regarded as leaders in global thinking, are so narrow-sighted that they are not aware of the developments within intellectual capital and business reporting that have taken place elsewhere over the last decade.

FROM STOCKS OF ASSETS TO ILLUSTRATING STRATEGY AND FLOWS

The point of departure for many of the recent developments in IC reporting, especially the so-called narrative models, is to illustrate the flows of value creation by linking indicators to strategy, and supporting an understanding of them by providing a context-giving narrative. Mouritsen and Larsen (2005) label this a process of "entangling" the indicators, arguing that individual pieces of IC information and measurements, by themselves, can be difficult to relate to any conception of value creation. As such, this "flow" approach is concerned with identifying which knowledge resources drive value creation, instead of assigning a specific dollar value to those resources (Bukh, 2002).

Even though the precise definition of an intellectual capital report in the literature is connected with some ambiguousness, the statements that have been disclosed in Denmark over the past few years do have similarities, which can also be found in the literature. In relation to IC reports, intellectual capital is often thought of as intangible value drives systematized under the headings employees, organisation, and customers (e.g., Edvinsson & Malone, 1997; Roos et al., 1997; Sveiby, 1997). In practice, intellectual capital statements contain a number of financial and nonfinancial information, that is, staff turnovers and job satisfaction, in-service training, turnover split on customers, customer satisfaction, precision of supply, and so forth (cf. Bukh *et al.*, 2001; Mouritsen *et al.,* 2001a), as well as a substantial narrative part positioning the indicators within a strategic framework. See Guthrie (2001), Petty and Guthrie (2000), and Andriessen (2004) for an overview of the literature and approaches to measuring intellectual capital.

Most literature on intellectual capital suggests that it grasps the key value drivers of the company and that it is strategically important. But, strategy, at least competitive strategy, in Porter's sense, "is about being different," which means "deliberately choosing a different set of activities to deliver a unique mix of value" (Porter, 1996; see also Sandberg, 2002). Thus, the bundle of IC indicators that would be relevant for disclosing intellectual capital are likely to differ among firms, and likely to be difficult to interpret by analysts and investors, unless they are inserted in the strategic context that determined their relevance. Hence, the main point in this commentary is that the intellectual capital report should, actually, communicate management's understanding of strategy and value creation, and not only indicators of general interest. This implicates that an intellectual capital report cannot be read only by comparing indicators between firms because strategies and value creation models are likely to differ between firms, and that disclosure of intellectual capital should be done in the framework of the firm's strategy for value creation, that is, the value creation model should also be disclosed.

From a strategy theory point of view, such a framework for disclosure is offered by the concept of a *business model*. Business models have been intimately connected with e-business (e.g., Kodama 1999; Sweet 2001), see Hedman and Kalling (2001) for a review. However, the concept, as such, has a much more general meaning in recent management literature, where Magretta sees business models as "stories that explain how enterprises work" (Magretta, 2002, p. 4). A business model not only shows how the firm makes money but also how - by answering the fundamental questions: "Who is the customer? And what does the customer value" (Magretta 2002, 4). Further, a basic idea of the business model concept is that it should spell out what the unique value proposition of the firm is, and how it should be implemented. For customers, the value creation could be related to "solving a problem, improving performance, or reducing risk and cost" (Sandberg, 2002, p. 4), which might require specific value configurations (cf. Sweet, 2001), including relationships to suppliers, access to technologies, insight in the users needs, and so forth.

Accounting for intellectual capital has been associated with the coming of a new economy or a knowledge society, where knowledge and information "have become the economy's primary raw material and its most important outcome" (Stewart, 1997, p. 39). Understanding what this implies at firm level demands, as Sweet (2001, p. 71) states, a focus on the logic of how value is configured. New forms of value configurations and thus, new business models, are emerging. New knowledge-based business models that identify knowledge resources are needed in order to show how knowledge-based resources have become key elements in value creation and accordingly, managers, as well as analysts, must recognize that business models are made up of asset portfolios, but not traditional physical and financial assets alone, since these asset portfolios include intangibles. Therefore, "Every company needs to create a business model that links combinations of assets to value creation" (Boulton, Libert, & Samek, 1997, p. 33).

The main point here is that value creation based on knowledge resources, that is, intellectual capital, are brought forward, and that new value creation models are linked with an understanding of who the customers are, what they need, and how value is created for the customers, that is, the business model. When uniqueness, and hence, competitive advantage from a management point of view, is to be found in the development and implementation of the business model, it becomes natural to take this as a starting point for structuring the disclosure of the company's intellectual capital.

When it comes to information on the business model, including the specific value creation processes, an integral reporting of intellectual capital is more likely to convey relevant information. The recent research interest for new value configurations (Ramirez, 1999; Stabell & Fjeldstad, 1998; Sweet, 2001) reflects a change in the competitive landscape towards more variety in value creation models within industries where, previously, the "name of the industry served as shortcut for the prevailing business model's approach to market structure" (Sandberg, 2002, p. 3); competition now increasingly stands between competing business concepts (Hamel, 2000). If firms within the same industry operate on the basis of different business models, different competencies and knowledge resources are key parts of the value creation, and mere benchmarking of intellectual capital indicators does not provide insight in the profit or growth potential of the firm. A comparison of the specific firm with its peer group requires interpretation within an understanding of differences in business models.

If firms only disclose intellectual capital indicators without disclosing the business model that explains the interconnectedness of the indicators, and why the bundle of indicators is relevant for understanding firms strategy for value creation, this interpretation must be done by the analysts. Currently, there exists no research-based insight into how this reading and interpretation is conducted, and it is very likely that this understanding of firms' value creation would be facilitated if companies disclosed the information on intellectual capital as an integral part of strategy disclosure.

Despite the Jenkins' Report identifying that a significant element of any business report might be constituted by what is normally regarded as management (accounting) information, the general emphasis of extant business reporting approaches has not reflected this. The ICAEW report identifies the balanced scorecard as its first exemplar of a business reporting model, but refers to it as "one of the most important management ideas of the past 15 years" (2004, p. 23) without ever acknowledging its origins in management accounting. The IASB discussion paper makes no reference to the balanced scorecard, presumably on the basis that it is most readily understood to offer a solution to the problems associated with developing a more inclusive approach to internal reporting rather than external reporting. Although the balanced scorecard is most commonly associated with the use of a combination of financial and nonfinancial performance metrics, chosen to best represent the past, present, and future performance of the business, a more narrative-based format is, by no means, precluded. For this reason, some observers regard the balanced scorecard to be suitable for intellectual-capital reporting purposes, as an alternative to the Skandia Navigator, the Intangible Assets Monitor, and the Value Chain Scoreboard (Fincham & Roslender, 2003).

The merits of the balanced scorecard as a potential business-reporting framework are further strengthened when one recalls that, for the past decade, its principal advocates, Kaplan and Norton, have identified it as being more than simply a performance measurement and reporting system. In their view, the balanced scorecard forms the "foundation of an integrated and iterative strategic management system." (Kaplan & Norton, 1996, p. 85). It is an enabling mechanism that allows management to translate strategy into action, and as such, can be understood to constitute a "strategic" management accounting development. In this way, it is the sort of development that has allowed management accounting to make a higher-level contribution to the management process, the level that Anthony (1965) designated strategic planning in contrast to management control and operational (or task) control. Consequently, the balanced scorecard would seem to promise the accountancy profession a credibility within the highest echelons of management that financial reporting, despite its centrality to the management (control) process, has not achieved. The observation that the balanced scorecard originated within the "poor relation" internal reporting branch of accounting that, for much of the twentieth century, was essentially subordinate to financial reporting (Johnson & Kaplan, 1987), only serves to reinforce our belief that, while financial reporting might wish to retain its primacy in the guise of business reporting, for the latter to be truly successful, business reporting requires to be based on fundamentally different foundations.

The balanced scorecard is not a panacea, however, and has been widely criticised in recent years. One criticism has been that in the second phase of thinking about the balanced scorecard, Kaplan and Norton are guilty of only crudely linking it with the strategy process (Roslender & Hart, 2002). With the emergence of the strategy map concept in their subsequent output, the potential for a more robust marriage between accounting and strategy is potentially on offer, although worries remain about the centrality that Kaplan and Norton accord the cause and effect relationship between the different levels (formerly the four perspectives of the balanced scorecard). In this regard, the business model concept might offer much needed assistance in clarifying the way of seeing that is a strategy map.

It is thus evident that illustrating stocks and flows is not something completely new. In the intellectual capital literature, and the much-related fields concerning business models and performance measurements, that is, balanced scorecard, we find notions of illustrating flows, albeit in slightly different ways. The next section describes the framework of an intellectual capital statement in terms of the Danish guideline, thereby illustrating an example of how it is possible to entangle individual indicators of intellectual capital into a narrative of strategic flows.

INTELLECTUAL CAPITAL STATEMENTS: ENTANGLEMENT OF INDICATORS

Some observers regard the balanced scorecard as offering a means of reporting management's success in growing their stocks of intellectual capital or intangibles. Kaplan and Norton have acknowledged this since their 1996 monograph, although to date, they have not provided a detailed discussion of the connection. As a possible intellectual-capital-reporting framework, the balanced scorecard exhibits a number of similarities with the Skandia Navigator (Edvinsson & Malone, 1997, Mouritsen, Larsen ,& Bukh, 2001a), the Intangible Assets Monitor (Sveiby, 1997), and the Value Chain Scoreboard (Lev, 2001). All seek to provide a set of relevant indicators of intellectual capital growth, using a combination of financial and noninformation organised in some form of scorecard (Fincham & Roslender, 2003; Starovich & Marr, 2004).

An intellectual capital statement is best understood as being the next step in developing a framework for intellectual capital reporting. The most widely discussed example of such a framework is the intellectual capital statement developed in Denmark (DATI, 1999; Mouritsen et al., 2003). The Meritum Report (2002) also provides a variation on the same model, not least as a result of extensive participation by a number of Danish researchers in that project (Bukh & Johanson, 2003). More recently, a comparable set of principles for fabricating intellectual capital statements has been proposed in Australia (Boedker, 2005). The principal difference between the intellectual capital statement approach to intellectual capital reporting and the scorecard approach is that the former is based in narrative rather than numerical indicators. This said, advocates of the use of such statements commend the incorporation of a wide range of qualitative forms of reporting, and sometimes talk in terms of visualising intellectual capital rather reporting on it. Equally, there is always a place for relevant indicators, confirming the view that as a 21st century accounting development, an intellectual capital statement is underpinned by a very extensive interpretation of what "accounting" entails.

Following the Danish Ministry of Science, Technology, and Innovation (Mouritsen et al., 2003), the purpose of an intellectual capital statement is to communicate the use value, knowledge resources, and most important challenges for the management of a company to overcome in the process of value creation. The use value outlines, in a narrative form, the ambition of the company's knowledge management activities. In doing so, it not only accounts for present performance, but also formulates a strategy for the company's know-how in the future. The structure of this model is presented in Figure 1.

The founding knowledge narrative is a story about how the company seeks to create value for its customers through the utilisation of its knowledge resources. The knowledge narrative pinpoints the ambition of the company's knowledge management, because it not only accounts for present performance, but also formulates a strategy for the company's know-how in the future. The knowledge narrative fulfills this objective by describing three elements: how the customer is taken into account by the company's products or services, called the use value; which knowledge resources in the form of employees, customers, processes, and technologies, it must possess in order to deliver the described use value; and lastly, the particular nature of the product or service in question. In order to formulate the knowledge narrative, companies need to provide answers to a number of key questions. Among these questions are what product or service does the company provide; what makes a difference for the customer; what knowledge resources are necessary to be able to supply the product or service; and what is the relationship between value and knowledge resources?

Figure 2. The Danish guideline for intellectual capital statements model (Mouritsen et al., 2003, p. 13)

The company's management challenges are necessarily informed by its knowledge narrative. Management challenges are a set of meaningful and lasting elements in the managerial agenda that provide continuity in handling the development and composition of knowledge resources. Thus, these management challenges relate to the needs for knowledge management that can be derived from the knowledge narrative and which the company must address in order to fulfill the ambition defined in it. This activity involves a number of strategic choices in implementing the knowledge narrative, and is informed by the answers to a further set of questions, including what are the challenges that the organisation is experiencing; which of the organisations' existing knowledge resources should be strengthened; and what new knowledge resources are required?

In combination, the knowledge narrative and management challenges have to take on the form of a coherent tale. In this way, they constitute a coherent knowledge management strategy designed to explain how the company seeks to enact its ongoing value creation activities. They therefore communicate the company's ambition for knowledge management, and how the company intends to realise this. To develop and compose knowledge resources and the key management challenges, a series of initiatives are derived about "knowledge containers" such as employees, customers, processes, or technologies. In addition to initiatives designed to increase or decrease the extent of the latter, management is also required to adopt positions on launching particular initiatives and in this context, which initiatives should be prioritised.

The first three elements of an intellectual capital statements assume a narrative form, where necessary being embellished using appropriate qualitative modes of visualistion, for example, illustrations. In the final element, the effects of the initiatives and management challenges described are monitored using quantitative indicators, as in scorecard approaches. As ever, the precise choice of indicators is informed by the information needs believed to be most relevant to users. A number of key indicators have been identified, including staff turnover and job satisfaction, in-service training, turnover split on customers, customer satisfaction, precision of supply, and so forth (cf. Bukh, Larsen, & Mouritsen, 2001; Mouritsen, Larsen, & Bukh, 2001b), indicating the extent these have been implemented and thus, the status for the company's realisation of its management challenges.

Like the earlier scorecard approaches to intellectual capital reporting, intellectual capital statements were initially devised for internal reporting purposes. The type of information that is disclosed in intellectual capital statements is only to a limited degree present in financial reports, which mainly focus on financial information reflecting the tangible value of the company, and they thus represent knowledge resources relatively poorly (Barth, Kasznik, & McNichols, 2001). In the case of the Danish initiative, the researchers, supported by the government, were keen to promote a measure of external reporting of such information. Throughout the research project, the audit profession was represented and provided a range of insights on how to make such a reporting framework more credible for external reporting purposes. The principal outcome of the project was a detailed guideline for the development and use of intellectual capital statements, intended to assist those companies interested in such activities. To date, in excess of 150 Danish organisations have expressed some degree of interest in using intellectual capital statements, with a number of them, including Coloplast, the Carl Bro Gruppen, and Maxon Telecom A/S, making extensive use of this approach.

The guideline also provides a series of practical inputs relating to the communicating and construction of the intellectual capital statement to external stakeholders. Among the important points that might be considered are who is the target audience; what is the principal message to be communicated; which media should be used to deliver the message; should the intellectual capital statement be part of the annual report or should it be a separate document; and what are the relevant legal requirements? The final part of the guideline addresses the work process involved in preparing an intellectual capital statement, and provides suggestions for how to organise an intellectual capital reporting project and project team by raising questions such as who should be a part of the project team; what is the role of senior management; how can management commitment ensured; and how can companies ensure that their intellectual statements will become embedded in the organisation?

Examples of Intellectual Capital Reporting

In order to provide an impression of how the guideline described is applied in practice, a couple of examples are provided in the Tables 1 and 2 according to the model presented in Figure 2. The first example is a medical technology company listed on the Copenhagen Stock Exchange. The example illustrates how this company, through insights into patient needs and employee competences, seeks to strengthen its research and development activities. As such, the management challenges lead to the deliverance of the proposed use value, while the activities and indicators leverage the management issues and performance measurement necessary for managing the intellectual capital.

The second example is from a medium-sized advertising agency that had problems in retaining the best employees. In addition to this, onc of thc main management challenges became knowledge sharing and ensuring the documentation of existing knowledge and solutions across several branches of the firm. The example illustrates how the company mobilized its strategy for knowledge management through a series of performance measures.

CONCLUDING REMARKS

It is often argued, both in the accounting and management literature, that voluntary information is important for understanding value creation, and that such disclosures would improve, for example, investment and credit decision making. From the

Table 1. Managing the intellectual capital of a medical technology company

Knowledge narrative	Management challenges	Activities	Indicators
Use value of products is delivering quality of life by helping a reducing the effects of a physical handicap	Product development	Investing in R&D New patents New products	R&D spending Total number of patents Number of patents pr. year New products' revenue share
	Gathering knowledge about the users situation	Measuring satisfaction of users Focus group activities	No. of meeting with users and nurses
	Excellence in product quality	Quality control systems and processes	Index for complaints Internal auditing Documentation costs Total customer satisfaction
	Employee development	Self-controlled groups in production Jobrotation Employee development progammes	Employee loyalty Employees with more than 3 year education Jobrotation and overseas job exchanges Employee satisfaction index

Table 2. Managing the intellectual capital of an advertising company

Knowledge narrative	Management challenges	Activities	Indicators
Delivering effective communication which creates results for the customers	Attracting and retaining competent and innovative employees and developing them professionally and personally	Employee satisfaction survey Training programmes for employees	Pct. of employees looking forward to going to work every day Education costs pr. employee No. of employees engaged in training Pct. of employees able to work form home
	Retaining and developing customer relationships	Surveying reasons for customer loyalty	Customer satisfaction Image Customer dependency
	Knowledge management	Knowledge sharing via Intranet Documenting customer solutions	Intranet activity No. of solutions applying shared knowledge
	Optimizing information technology		IT-costs pr. employee

accounting perspective, improved disclosure is more or less about including the asset values of intellectual capital resources in the balance sheet of the company's financial accounts, that is, capitalizing the value of intangibles. From a business reporting perspective, like, for example, that of intellectual capital statements, improved disclosure is rather concerned with illustrating the flows in the company that create value, benchmarking performance of specific value creation metrics, such as strategy, IC, future prospects, and so forth. Rather than integrating IC in financial accounts, the suggestion made here is that it ought to be entangled in the strategic statements, or management commentary, of the company.

It is, however, questionable whether this would improve anything. The analysts and professional investors already have deep insight in a lot of details, and the most important information on intellectual capital is likely to be related to the specific strategies of the firms and hence, difficult to compare and interpret unless it is disclosed as an integral part of a framework that explains how value is created. Since understanding the importance of intellectual capital, in terms of value configurations and customer value creation, is more of interest from the strategy side of the world, a possible reconciliation of the reporting-understanding gap could, for the firm, be to disclose the business model, that is, the story that explains how enterprises work, who the customer is, what does the customer value; based on this, how the firm is supposed to make money. Exactly how this disclosure should be reported is maybe not easy to say. Some experiments by proactive firms are needed, and the business climate in some countries, for example, Denmark, might be more favourable for firms' experiments with reporting.

Experiences from Danish firms issuing intellectual capital reports (cf. Bukh *et al.*, 2001; Mouritsen *et al.*, 2001a, 2001b, 2001c, 2002) show that intellectual capital is not only about knowledge resources in the form of human capital, customer capital, structural capital, and so forth, as separate categories. It is just as much about their complementarities; the productivity of one resource may improve by investments in another resource. It may be that investments in employee development will improve effectiveness of IT technology, or effectiveness of customer-relations. If this is the case, human capital is neither separate from organizational capital, from customer capital, nor is there a causal relationship between them, because overall effectiveness is a collective effect that cannot be explained by the sum of its parts. This is what Nielsen and Dane-Nielsen (2008) denote; the emergent properties of intellectual capital.

Hence, intellectual capital reports are, as argued in Mouritsen et al. (2001c), not to be read simply by analyzing the indicators and imposing an explanatory model linking the elements in a causal relationship. As there is more to an intellectual capital report than just the numbers, the reading is different than reading a traditional financial statement. Textual representation, indicators, and pictures about the knowledge management activities of the firm compose intellectual capital reports, and there are no specifically stated ways of reading and interpreting IC reports. This makes the comparison of different IC reports difficult.

Another way of dealing with the problem is to step outside the accounting paradigm to see if transparency and relevance problems can be solved by way of supplementary disclosures. For some, this is a logical step. However, for many, this represents shaky ground. It is ironic that while supplementary information has been shown to reduce investors' uncertainty, it is not being acknowledged as a key element in solving the existing problems by standard-setters and academics.

From the analyst point of view, IC indicators disclosed in the annual report, or in a supplementary intellectual capital report, are only one part, maybe even an inferior part, of the information needed to make recommendations to clients, because they are in a privileged position to "get more information – and sooner – than all except the very largest investors" (Eccles, Herz, Keegan, & Phillips 2001, p. 274). It might be that the information has value relevance, but the analysts have already a much more detailed understanding about, for example, the research and development activities, than what could be gained from reading about the aggregate research and development expenses.

Since private investors do not have the same access to information, greater disclosure of intellectual capital information could, however, at least for them, be an improvement. Despite the fact that such improvements undoubtedly would improve "market fairness," most private investors would still be left with little clue about how the IC indicators should be interpreted. This is because there exist few rules of thumb from which to interpret such new information. Future research should denote attention to such problems.

This chapter has constituted a wake-up call to the drowsy constituents of academia and policy making, asking them to see beyond their normative accounting paradigm and, in turn, showing them how far the strategy-oriented solutions they choose to ignore have come. Especially the Danish guideline for intellectual capital statements has the ability of illustrating the strategic imperatives of the firm and entangling intellectual capital indicators into a story of value creation.

REFERENCES

Aboody, D., & Lev, B. (2002). Information asymmetry, R&D and insider gains. *The Journal of Finance, 55*(6), 2747-2766.

American Institute of Certified Public Accountants [AICPA]. (1994). *Improving business reporting – A customer focus: Meeting the information needs of investors and creditors; and Comprehensive report of the special committee on financial reporting.* New York: American Institute of Certified Public Accountants.

Andriessen, D. (2004). IC valuation and measurement: Classifying the state of the art. *Journal of Intellectual Capital, 5*(2), 230-242.

Anthony, R. N. (1965). *Planning and control systems: A framework for analysis.* Boston: Harvard University Press.

Barth, M. E., Kasznik, R., & McNichols, M. F. (2001). Analyst coverage and intangible assets. *Journal of Accounting Research, 39*(1), 1-34.

Beattie, V., & Pratt, K. (2002). *Voluntary annual report disclosures: What users want.* Institute of Chartered Accountants of Scotland.

Boedker, C. (2005). *Australian guiding principles on extended performance management: A guide to better managing, measuring and reporting knowledge intensive resources.* Society for Knowledge Economics, Grosvenor Place.

Bontis, N., Dragonetti, N. C., Jacobsen, K,. & Roos, G. (1999). The knowledge toolbox: A review of the tools available to measure and manage intangible resources. *European Management Journal, 17*(4), 391-402.

Boulton, R. E. S., Libert, B. D., & Samek, S. M. (1997). *Cracking the value code: How successful businesses are creating wealth in the new economy.* New York: Harper Collins Publishers.

Bukh, P. N. (2002). *Disclosure of intellectual capital – Indicators or models? A matter of accounting or strategy.* Working paper, Aarhus School of Business.

Bukh, P. N., & Johanson, U. (2003). Research and knowledge interaction: Guidelines for intellectual capital reporting. *Journal of Intellectual Capital, 4*(4), 572-583.

Bukh, P. N., Larsen, H. T., & Mouritsen, J. (2001). Constructing intellectual capital statements. *Scandinavian Journal of Management, 17*(1), 87-108.

Cañibano, L., García-Ayuso, M., & Sánchez, M. P. (2000). Accounting for intangibles: A literature review. *Journal of Accounting Literature, 19*, 102-130.

Collier, P. M. (2001). Valuing intellectual capital in the police. *Accounting, Auditing & Accountability Journal, 14*(4), 437-455.

Danish Agency for Trade and Industry (DATI). (1999). *Developing intellectual capital accounts. Experiences from 19 companies.* Ministry of Business and Industry, Copenhagen.

Eccles, R. G., Herz, R. H., Keegan, E. M., & Phillips, D. M. (2001). *The value reporting revolution: Moving beyond the earnings game.* New York: John Wiley & Sons.

Eccles, R., & Mavrinac, S. (1995). Improving the corporate disclosure process. *Sloan Management Review,* Summer, 11-25.

Edvinsson, L., & Malone, M. S. (1997). *Intellectual capital.* London: Piatkus.

Fincham, R., & Roslender, R. (2003). *The management of intellectual capital and its implications for business reporting.* The Institute of Chartered Accountants of Scotland.

Gelb, D. S. (2002). Intangible assets and firms' disclosures: An empirical investigation. *Journal of Business Finance & Accounting, 29*(3-4), 457-476.

Gu, F., & Lev, B. (2001). *Intangible assets: Measurement, drivers.* Usefulness. working paper. Boston University.

Guthrie, J. (2001). The management, measurement and the reporting of intellectual capital. *Journal of Intellectual Capital, 2*(1), 27-41.

Guthrie, J., & Boedker, C. (2006). Perspectives on "new" models of business reporting: A reflective note. *Accounting, Auditing & Accountability Journal, 19*(6), 785-792.

Hamel, G. (2000). *Leading the revolution.* Boston: Harvard Business School Press.

Hedman, J., & Kalling, T. (2001). *The business model: A mean to understand the business context of information and communication technology.* Working paper 2001/9, Institute of Economic Research, School of Economics and Management, Lund Universitet.

Hendriksen, E. S., & van Breda, M. F. (1992). *Accounting theory* (5th ed.). Burr Ridge: Irwin.

Institute of Chartered Accountants in England and Wales (ICAEW). (2004). *Information for better markets: New reporting models for business.* Institute of Chartered Accountants in England and Wales, London.

International Accounting Standards Board [IASB]. (2005). *Discussion paper: Management commentary.* London: IASCF Publications Department

Johnson, H. T., & Kaplan, R. S. (1987). *Relevance lost: The rise and fall of management accounting.* Boston: Harvard Business School Press.

Kaplan, R. S., & Norton, D. P. (1996). *The balanced scorecard - Translating strategy into action.* Boston: Harvard Business School Press.

Kodama, M. (1999). Customer value creation through community-based information networks. *Journal of Information Management, 19,* 495-508.

Lev, B. (2001). *Intangibles – Management, measuring and reporting.* Brookings Institution Press.

Lev, B., & Sougiannis, T. (1996). The capitalization, amortization, and value relevance of R&D. *Journal of Accounting and Economics, 21,* 107-138.

Magretta, J. (2002). Why business models matter. *Harvard Business Review,* May, 3-8.

Meritum. (2002). Guidelines for managing and reporting on intangibles. L. Cañibano, Sanchez, M. Garcia-Ayuso, & C. Chaminade (Eds.), *Fundación Airtel Móvil.*

Mouritsen, J., Bukh, P. N., Flagstad, K., Thorbjørnsen, S., Johansen, M. R., Kotnis, S., Larsen, H. T., Nielsen, C., Kjærgaard, I., Krag, L., Jeppesen, G., Haisler, J., & Stakemann, B. (2003). *Intellectual capital statements – The new guideline.* Copenhagen: Danish Ministry of Science, Technology and Innovation. Retrieved from http://www.vtu.dk/icaccounts

Mouritsen, J., Bukh, P. N., Larsen, H. T., & Johansen, M. R. (2002). Developing and managing knowledge through intellectual capital statements. *Journal of Intellectual Capital, 3*(1), 10-29.

Mouritsen, J., & Larsen, H. T.. (2005). The 2nd wave of knowledge management: The management control of knowledge resources through intellectual capital information. *Management Accounting Research, 16*(4), 371-394.

Mouritsen, J., Larsen, H. T., & Bukh, P. N. (2001a). Valuing the future: Intellectual capital accounts at Skandia. *Accounting, Auditing & Accountability Journal, 14*(4), 399-422.

Mouritsen, J., Larsen, H. T., & Bukh, P. N. (2001b). Intellectual capital and the "capable firm": Narrating, visualising and numbering for managing knowledge. *Accounting, Organisations and Society, 26*(7), 735-762.

Mouritsen, J., Larsen, H. T., Bukh, P. N., & Johansen, M. R. (2001c). Reading an intellectual capital statement: Describing and prescribing knowledge management strategies. *Journal of Intellectual Capital, 2*(4), 359-383.

Nazari, J. A., & Herremans, I. M. (2007). Extended VAIC model: Measuring intellectual capital components. *Journal of Intellectual Capital, 8*(4), 595-609.

Nielsen, C., & Dane-Nielsen, H. (2008). *The emergent properties of intellectual capital: A conceptual offering.* Working paper submitted to Accounting, Organizations and Society.

Petty, R., & Guthrie, J. (2000). Intellectual capital literature review: Measuring, reporting and management. *Journal of Intellectual Capital, 1*(2), 155-176.

Porter, M. E. (1996). What is strategy? *Harvard Business Review*, November-December, 61-78.

Ramirez, R. (1999). Value co-production: Intellectual origins and implications for practice and research. *Strategic Management Journal, 20*, 49–65.

Roos, J., Roos, G., Dragonetti, N. C., & Edvinsson, L. (1997). *Intellectual capital: Navigating the new business landscape*. London: Macmillan Press Ltd.

Roslender, R., & Hart, S. J. (2002). Integrating management accounting and marketing in the pursuit of competitive advantage: The case for strategic management accounting. *Critical Perspectives on Accounting, 13*, 255-277.

Sakakibara, S., Hansson, B., & Yosano, T. (2005). *Japanese analysts' perception of intellectual capital information*. Working paper presented at the EIASM workshop on "Visualising, measuring and Managing Intangibles and Intellectual Capital" in Ferrara, Italy, October 2005.

Sandberg, K. D. (2002). Is it time to trade in your business model? *Harvard Management Update*, January, 3-5.

Stabell, C. B., & Fjeldstad, Ø. D. (1998). Configuring value for competitive advantage: On chains, shops, and networks. *Strategic Management Journal, 19*, 413–437.

Starovic, B. & Marr., D. (2003). *Understanding corporate value: Managing and reporting intellectual capital.* Cranfield School of Management, Chartered Institute of Management Accountants.

Stewart, T. A. (1997). *Intellectual capital.* London: Nicholas Brealey Publishing.

Sveiby, K. E. (1997). *The new organizational wealth: Managing and measuring knowledge-based assets.* San Fransisco: Berrett-Koehler.

Sweet, P. (2001). Strategic value configuration logics and the "new" economy: A service economy revolution? *International Journal of Service Industry Management, 12*(1), 70-83.

Chapter XII
Managing the Information Technology:
Knowledge Transfer in Virtual Teams

Huei-Chen Hsu
Transworld Institute of Technology, Taiwan, R.O.C.

ABSTRACT

The main points of this chapter are probing for the combination of information technology and virtual work, and how to change the distribution of different types of knowledge across individuals, teams, and even the organization. The discussion in the chapter will assess the dynamics between the individual, the organization, and information technology in the context of teams that vary in their virtualness. Information technology can make convenient spread of knowledge across the organization; even the point of making virtual teams a viable alternative to face-to-face work. However, unless managed, information technology may destabilize the relationship between organizations and their employees when it comes to the transform of knowledge. Therefore, this chapter advances theory and informs practice by illustrating the dynamics of knowledge development and transfer in more and less virtual teams.

INTRODUCTION

The rapid proliferation of the Internet and information technology has dramatically increased the speed of knowledge creation and information distribution. As a result, the global business has entered a new era of the knowledge ecology, in which knowledge has become the driving force for productivity improvement and economic growth.

The knowledge ecology, which treats knowledge as a valuable asset in economic development, has changed industrial structures and business operations. On the one hand, the Internet has changed the nature of the supply chain, and creates significant needs for electronic markets.

Electronic commerce has become the most popular business function and almost a necessity for service-oriented enterprises. On the other hand, traditional industries are facing a great pressure to reengineer and digitize their information process in order to survive.

With this understanding, it is natural that many researchers have devoted their effort to investigating this new global trend of applying information technologies to facilitate the development of knowledge ecology. Even after the burst of the Internet bubble, intellectual capital (IC) management in businesses is still a central theme for research and practical applications. In fact, it is only until the bubble burst that managers made a closer examination of what is the real value of managing intellectual capital for business and economics.

Academic research also helps in building fundamental theory from the observed phenomena, and suggests a better use of the knowledge technology transfer. Thus, intellectual capital (IC) of a business's knowledge technology transfer has been a very critical issue within this research field. Intellectual capital (IC) is also commonly accepted as the basis for knowledge technology learning for organization.

Teams and knowledge management are two areas that are often providing increased value when carefully managed. Teams can increase capability, flexibility, and responsiveness (Leavitt, 1996), while knowledge management is believed to be crucial to organizational performance (Berman, Down, & Hill, 2002; Kogut & Zander, 1992; Liebeskind, 1996).

Technology may provide a means of structuring teamwork, enhance the information available to the team, and/or provide a communication system (McGrath & Berdahl, 1998). The growth of virtual teams in organizations is the example on which we will focus here. Organizations can form teams regardless of the physical location of the members, providing further opportunity and flexibility in building the best teams (Griffith & Neale, 2001). Organizations can also take advantage of the ability of such virtual teams.

Modern organizational teams have access to a variety of communication and work process technologies. More and less virtual teams use technology in ways that capture more and less knowledge for the organization. More virtual teams seem to use technology to do their work as a matter of course, passively collecting knowledge and perhaps sidestepping many of the motivational problems of knowledge management (e.g., Goodman & Darr, 1998) found in more traditional settings. Equivalent levels of knowledge capture in less virtual teams might require added work. The added work, even the straightforward task of documentation, may cause such efforts to fail, regardless of the benefit of knowledge management (Goodman & Darr, 1998; Majchrzak, Rice, King, Malhotra, & Ba, 2000).

There may also be negative effects related to virtual teams and knowledge. If the perspective is that of increasing value to the organization, our analysis seems to suggest that the use of more virtual teams provides an opportunity for knowledge capture to occur at a low marginal cost. However, individuals who hold this knowledge to be captured may experience a considerable loss, even as the organization gains.

The organization possibly forms the virtual team, no matter member's physical location, creation opportunity, and flexibility (e.g., Griffith & Neale, 2001). The modern organization virtual team can work by various communications. Originally belongs to the virtual network imagination, the man-machine surface is mutually dependent, and it creates the virtual team culture. That is, this report attempts to inspect the knowledge transfer in virtual team, and some discussion subjects are proposed.

Studies mainly lie in the discussion of the knowledge types in virtual team, and on the different stratification plane evolution in knowledge transfer. The establishment in research model will transform the tacit knowledge in virtual team for explicit knowledge.

To take full advantage of the virtual team knowledge management, we need to understand the experts' view in literature, using deductive research method to discuss knowledge types and the team organization relations in detail.

The discussion below will assess the dynamics between the individual, the organization, and information technology in the context of teams that vary in their virtualness. First, we address the role communication and information technologies play in the form and function of teams. We then make the critical link between types of knowledge and knowledge transfer in more and less virtual teams. Finally, implications are considered, including the possibility that information technology may play the role of a jealous mistress when it comes to the development and ownership of valuable knowledge in organizations; that is, information technology may destabilize the relationship between organizations and their employees when it comes to the transfer of knowledge.

LITERATURE REVIEW

Context: Virtualness and Knowledge

Team context and technological support are keys to our analysis. Technology enables these variations in context in two ways. First, communication technology (such as e-mail, voice mail, etc.) make it feasible for work teams to be formed with members who do not necessarily work in close proximity. The reduction in physical and temporal boundaries subsequently diminishes the likelihood that homogenous teams are formed for convenience, or due to other factors that might collocate members in either space or time (Griffith & Neale, 2001). In addition, group support technology may provide additional functionality by structuring the team's tasks, enabling analysis of the team's information.

Clearly, the functionality of such technologies is mutable and socially constructed (Barley, 1986;

Figure 1. character between more virtual team and less virtual team

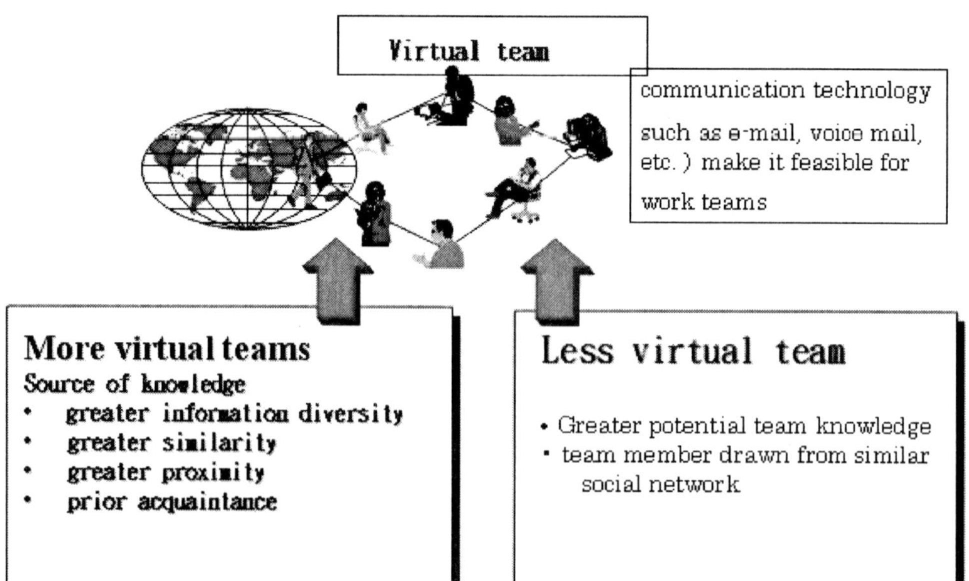

Griffith, 1999). Different configuration may provide communication, and/or support and teams may choose to appropriate different technology features, or not. As a result, we will speak in terms of more or less virtual rather than technological, physical, or temporal structures. More virtual teams may be able to draw upon a larger network for sources of knowledge due to their expected greater informational diversity (Griffith & Neale, 2001). Similarity (e.g., Ancona & Caldwell, 1992), proximity (e.g., Festinger, Schachter, & Back, 1950), and prior acquaintance (e.g., Goins & Mannix, 1999) are all factors that may bring particular members into a team. However, such forces serve to reduce potential team knowledge, as the knowledge and perspective of team members drawn from similar social networks are likely to be redundant (Granovetter, 1973). In fact, virtual teams are likely to be formed when needed skills are not available locally (Boutellier, Gassmann, Macho, & Roux, 1998), suggesting that more virtual teams are less likely to be drawn from similar social networks. As a result, we assume members of virtual teams will have access to a potentially greater base of knowledge through their individual team members than collected teams. Further, as teams differ in their amount of virtualness, so too do they differ in critical ways regarding the transfer of knowledge from their members to the team and to the organization. In the next section, we present a model of knowledge transfer, and highlight the areas where virtualness may play a role in how knowledge is transferred among individuals, to the team, and the organization.

Knowledge in Organizations

The scientific understanding of knowledge in organizations is still in an explorative stage, in spite of a large and growing literature focused on organizational knowledge, organizational learning, knowledge creation, and knowledge management. Beyond common concepts, such as tacit knowledge and organizational knowledge, the many theoretical frameworks offer diverse concepts, terminology, hypotheses, and evidence (Nonaka & Nishiguchi, 2001).

A thorough review of the knowledge literature is beyond the scope of this manuscript. We wish to focus on the distinction between individual and social knowledge for differing types of knowledge development in the context of virtual teams. Individual knowledge is composed of the psychological components that reside within the individual. Social knowledge is a collective type of knowledge that is publicly available or embedded within the routines, culture, or norms of the team (Spender, 1996). A group's repertoire of decision-making approaches is an example of such social knowledge. We detail the components of individual and social knowledge as we focus on how knowledge transfers among individuals and becomes available to the team. Figure 2 provides a stylized model of this transformation.

This model is presented from a perspective of virtual teams where membership is relatively stable. Leave the possibility of teams with more fluid membership (e.g., Gruenfeld et al., 2000) for future consideration. The propositions will be stated in terms of more and less virtual. This allows for consideration of more virtual teams that spend little time on task together, use a great deal of technology for their communication and work, and are geographically distributed, as well as slightly less virtual teams that might have more face-to-face interaction, or subgroups (some collocated members), and less virtual teams with greater amounts of face-to-face interaction, more collocated members, and less dependence on technology for communication and work.

Knowledge and its Transfer in Virtual Teams

In the next sections, we will use Figure 2 as a road map for examining different types of knowledge; the moderating effects of absorptive capacity,

Figure 2. Determinants of usable team knowledge

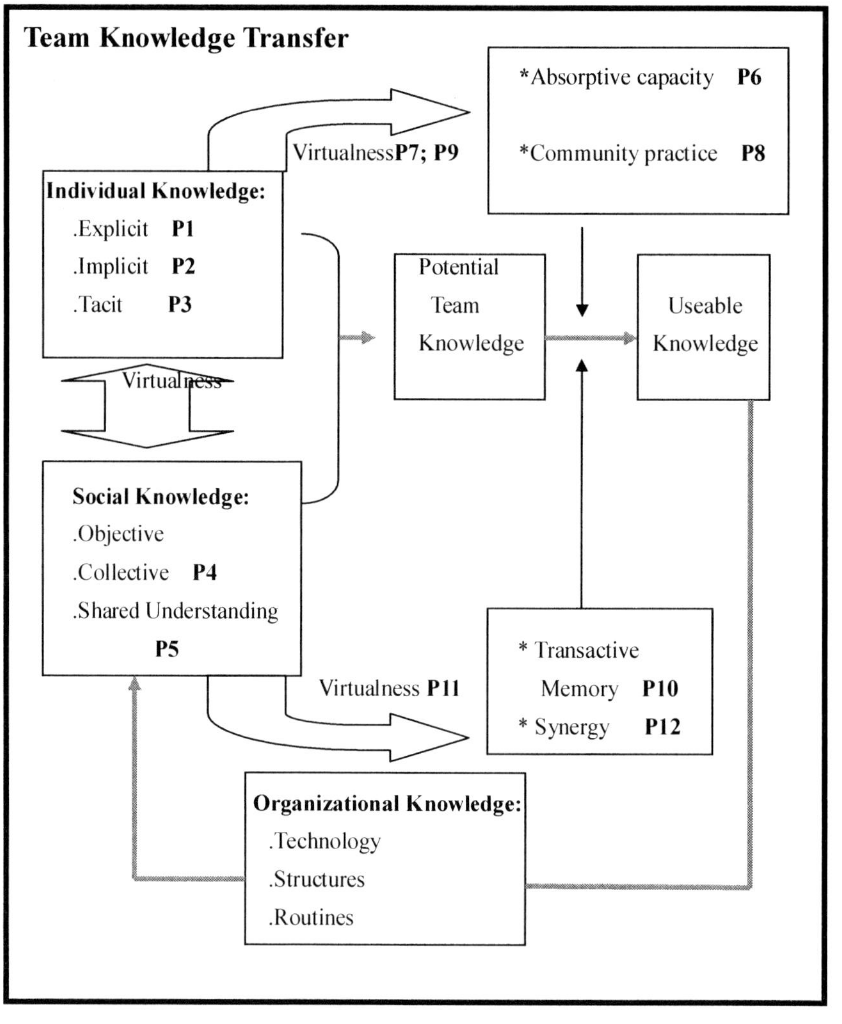

communities of practice, transitive memory, and synergy; and the recursive link from the resulting usable knowledge. We use the term usable knowledge here to reflect the notion that while knowledge may exist within the team (potential team knowledge), it is not usable unless the team possesses the necessary tacit knowledge, both at the individual and social level, to know when and how to use that knowledge. This model is largely drawn from extant literature, as we will point out as we discuss the model, and is intended to reflect how knowledge comes to and is used by the team. We assume that the virtualness of team plays a role where potential team knowledge is (or is not) transformed into usable knowledge. Individual absorptive capacity, communities of practice, transitive memory, and synergy are all affected by the team context, for example, the virtualness of the team.

Individual Knowledge Types

In Figure 2, we begin by recognizing that knowledge is embedded in individuals, the social context, and the organization. Individual knowledge is conceptualized as a continuum from explicit to tacit.

Hard distinctions between tacit and explicit knowledge are more often a convenience than a theoretical requirement. Some knowledge will seem to be a particularly clear example of tacit, some of explicit, while other knowledge will seem to share elements of both tacit and explicit. Polanyi (1966) pointed out that tacit knowledge cannot be articulated. Spender (1996) further clarified that some tacit knowledge could be articulated, but has yet to be so, while other tacit knowledge is incapable of being articulated. Explicit knowledge can be articulated and is, thus, accessible to others (Leonard & Sensiper, 1998).

Leonard and Sensiper suggest that instead of separate constructs, tacit and explicit may signify a continuum, noting that Polanyi's discussion allows that all knowledge has tacit dimensions. Thus, we consider these forms of individual knowing as ranges along a continuum, although they are easier to discuss as discrete points. To simplify the discussion of this continuum, we will use the term *explicit* to refer to the most objective or declarative end of the continuum, *implicit* to refer to the midrange of the continuum in which knowledge is not currently declarative but could be made so, and *tacit* to refer to the extreme end of the knowledge continuum in which knowledge has never been, and could not likely be, made declarative.

Explicit knowledge has been referred to in the literature variously as objective (Schultze, 2000), information (Zander & Kogut, 1995), or declarative or fact-based (Berry, 1987) knowledge. Distinctions along this continuum can be made on the basis of how knowledge is transferred and how it is initially created or acquired. Researchers, working on the development of expert systems, have acknowledged the difficulty of transferring knowledge (Berry, 1987; Gammack & Yong, 1985; Olson & Rueter, 1987; Swartout & Smoliar, 1987). For example, in constructing expert systems, researchers generally consider three types of knowledge: terminological knowledge, domain descriptive knowledge, and problem-solving knowledge (Swartout & Smoliar, 1987). They consider terminological and domain knowledge to be relatively explicit, while problem-solving knowledge tends to have more tacit components. They find that problem-solving knowledge is more difficult to transfer than terminological or domain-descriptive knowledge. (This difficulty with transferring more tacit knowledge will be a theme throughout our examination.)

In an applied sense, explicit knowledge can be captured in e-mail, discussion groups, or knowledge databases, and can be transferred to others within or outside the team. In making a distinction between tacit and explicit knowledge, Berry (1987) uses a three-stage model of learning based on cognitive (learning from instruction or observation), associative (learning from practice), and autonomous (practice to the point that actions occur without thinking) stages. For example, someone could learn how to use a word processor by attending a class where the rules are taught (cognitive), then by working with the word processor to create different kinds of documents (associative), and finally, through extensive practice, reach the stage where typing errors are corrected seemingly without thought, the fingers immediately hitting the right keys (autonomous). In the most extreme form of autonomous learning, it will actually be difficult for the learner to recall exactly what they have done to make the action occur.

Berry suggests that these different stages of learning differentially support the ability to obtain explicit vs. tacit knowledge. In the cognitive and associative stages, individuals learn through instruction, observation, and practice. In these stages, explicit knowledge can be effectively transferred in written form, through training programs, and through other media such as databases.

We believe that the virtualness of the work plays a key role in understanding the transfer of knowledge. Teams, who spend less time together on task, are located further apart, and who make greater use of technological tools (i.e., more virtual teams) will be more likely to transfer knowledge in explicit rather than tacit forms because the technology supports the declarative nature of explicit knowledge. Tacit knowledge is more "sticky," more difficult to transfer in a usable form (Von Hipple, 1994). Members of more virtual teams have a greater need to transform tacit knowledge into more explicit forms if they are to transmit this knowledge to their teammates. For example, Tidwell and Walther (2002) found that subjects who used computer-mediated communication used a more direct communication approach than subjects in face-to-face conditions. We believe that it is also possible that more virtual teams, having made their knowledge more explicit and having used technological tools for communicating this knowledge (e.g., e-mail) will have permanent (and searchable) access to this knowledge. More virtual teams may also choose technologies with such capabilities over less permanent and searchable tools (e.g., voice mail). It is not that less virtual teams do not use similar tools; rather, it is that more virtual teams are likely to rely more on such systems, and so the effect will be more dominant. Consider an experienced team member trying to transfer their best practices regarding customer presentations. In a face-to-face setting, this implicit knowledge could be demonstrated. Depending on whether or not the team chose to record the presentation, there might or might not be a record. In a more virtual setting, there might be stronger emphasis on creating a framework or set of rules about giving such presentations (e.g., Tidwell and Walther's finding that computer-mediated communication may be more direct). The emphasis on verbalization (vs. demonstration) helps to recapture implicit knowledge in an explicit form.

In summary,

Proposition 1: *More virtual teams are more likely to transform implicit knowledge into explicit knowledge than are less virtual teams.*

Implicit knowledge refers to knowledge that is made tacit through practice. In the later autonomous stage of learning, explicit knowledge may become tacit as "relationships are compiled through practice to the point where they can be donc 'without thinking'" (Berry, 1987, p. 145). Thus, as expertise develops, individuals "lose awareness of what they know." However, this is not necessarily a permanent transition.

Research on building expert systems has found that rules, terminology, and descriptions that have been lost through autonomous processing may be recaptured. Once recaptured, this knowledge is capable of being transferred to other individuals in the form of explicit knowledge (Berry, 1987) Thus, in the virtual team that relies heavily on verbal (word-based, such as telephone or e-mail) forms of communication, implicit knowledge can be captured in relatively explicit forms and transferred to others. Because virtual teams must rely more on technologies, much of which transfers information in verbal modes, these teams may find it more useful to convert and transfer knowledge in explicit forms.

Proposition 2: *Implicit knowledge can be transferred to explicit knowledge to the extent that a proactive effort is made to verbalize rules, terminology, and descriptions.*

At the opposite end of the knowledge continuum from explicit knowledge is tacit knowledge, knowledge that has been formed through experience and that has never been represented explicitly. With this type of knowledge, experience is necessary for new, tacit knowledge to take shape, as new patterns, associations, and processes are formed. Patterns, if-then relations, and instrumental processes, which cannot be effectively taught through instruction, form through trial-and-error learning (Sawyer, 1990, 1991), but once learned often cannot be directly described and, thus, are tacit. Specifically, this type of knowledge has been described as *deep tacit* knowledge (Leonard & Sensiper, 1998).

It is unlikely that such tacit knowledge can be made explicit (Berry, 1987). Structured processes fail to transfer the less tangible elements of tacit knowledge (Pfeffer & Sutton, 1999), and significant information loss can be experienced when trying to articulate some experientially derived forms of tacit knowledge. According to some, deep tacit knowledge can only be shared among individuals through a network of individuals (Leonard & Sensiper, 1998; Venzin et al., 1998). In this case, knowledge does not actually transfer among members of the network. Instead, the network is used to apply the individual knowledge to the task. Others suggest that tacit knowledge is transferred among individuals working closely together through socialization processes, such as on-the-job training, apprenticeship, and direct observation (Nonaka, 1994). The members of more virtual teams work in an environment where their relationships are more filtered (by communication technologies) and they have fewer direct physical connections with team members. More virtual teams would thus seem to be at an overall disadvantage, relative to more traditional teams, when it comes to tacit knowledge transfer. In more virtual teams, it is unlikely that the degree of direct interaction possible through electronically mediated communication would allow the transfer of tacit knowledge.

Proposition 3: *Individual members of more virtual teams are less likely to acquire tacit knowledge from their teammates than are members of less virtual teams.*

Social Knowledge Types

In Figure 2, there is a double-ended arrow between individual knowledge and social knowledge. This arrow reflects two dynamics. First, social knowledge, knowledge that is either *objectified* (explicit and known among team members, such as the due date for a particular task), *collective* (explicit knowledge that has been internalized by the team members, such as the steps to take for moving through a particular process), or has formed as a *shared* understanding among team members (such as the identity of the emergent leader for different parts of the team's task), flows from individual knowledge as team members interact. The flow is affected by the degree of virtualness. Second, as individual members work within the team, their own knowledge is developed and enhanced as individual and team knowledge is combined. This combinatorial process is influenced, as well by the degree of team virtualness.

SECI Knowledge Transfer Model

According to the knowledge creation of four transformations pattern that Nonaka and Takeuchi (1995) proposed, Nonaka, Ikujiro, and Noboru Konno (1998) made the renewal pattern of SECI knowledge transforms.

The SECI model described the pattern that four kinds of knowledge transforms, included individual, the team, and organization's self-surmounting, these four kinds of transformations to the knowledge creation all was the essential process.

1. **Socializations:** It refers to the tacit knowledge transform between the member in organizes, it is to share experience during the process thus to create tacit knowledge. The shared experience is mainly understood for other people's ideas. Consciously, the tacit knowledge is only willing to share to the neighbor also the identical association's people.
2. **Externalization:** Tacit knowledge can become explicit knowledge. There are

Figure 3. SECI knowledge transform model

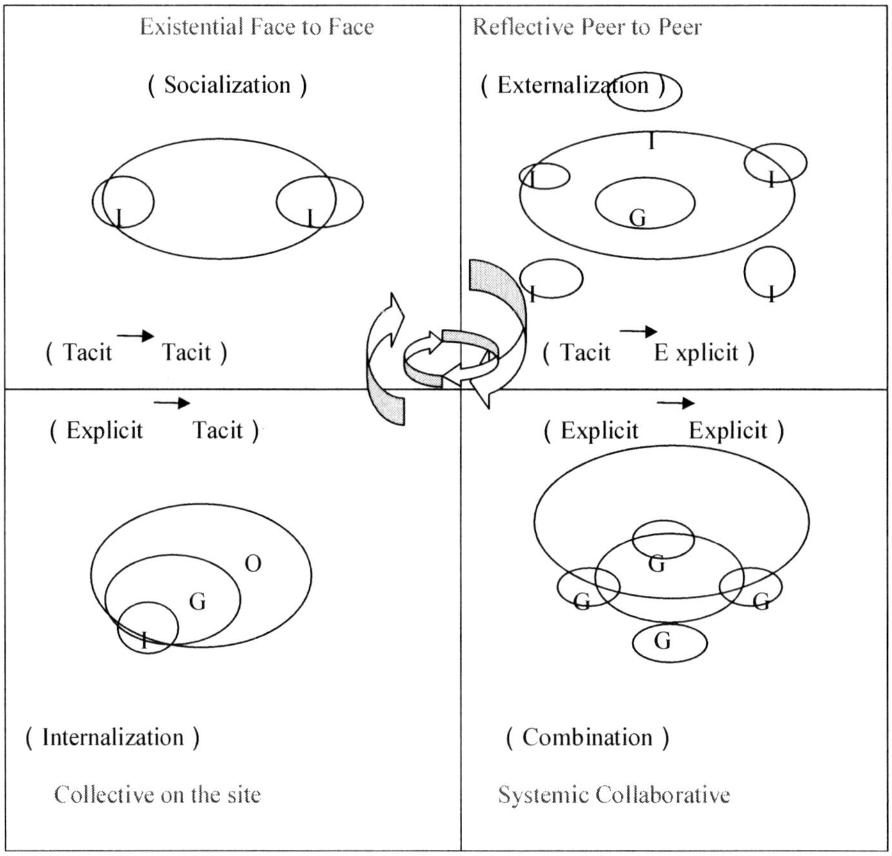

written down data source from memory to understand the expression for the tacit knowledge.

3. **Combination:** Explicit knowledge becomes explicit knowledge, Apparently, it refers the systematization to be performed to form the knowledge system, but this kind of knowledge transformation involves to the different explicit knowledge system, by way of the classification can increase the information and create the new knowledge.
4. **Internalization:** Explicit knowledge becomes tacit knowledge, In this process, "learning while practicing" can catch the detail of tacit experiences.

Nonaka (1994) suggested a "spiral of knowledge" (p. 18) in which individuals' explicit and tacit knowledge transforms and builds upon one another to form social- and organization-level knowledge. Individual-level explicit knowledge becomes objectified knowledge at the social level of analysis, while individual-level tacit knowledge becomes collective knowledge at the social level of analysis (Spender, 1996).

Nonaka suggested that interaction among individuals converts knowledge in various ways. Tacit knowledge at the individual level is converted to tacit knowledge at the team level through socialization. Explicit knowledge is combined with other explicit knowledge to form new explicit knowledge. As tacit knowledge is externalized through interactions among individuals, it becomes explicit knowledge. Mutual interaction among individuals can have the effect of causing explicit knowledge to be internalized within the team and thus become tacit. This form of tacit team knowledge is what Spender (1996) refers to as collective knowledge.

Collective knowledge is embedded in the team's routines, norms, and culture. Because mutual interaction is necessary for the implicit combination of various elements of explicit knowledge into collective knowledge, anything that reduces the level of interpersonal interaction in the team may impede the development of collective knowledge. Thus, highly virtual teams may not be able to form collective knowledge unless they are able to use highly enriched forms of media, or at least experience their communication as enriched through greater experience with the task, their teammates, and the technology (Carlson & Zmud, 1999).

Proposition 4: *More virtual teams will have greater difficulty forming collective knowledge than will less virtual teams. This effect will be moderated by their experienced richness of communication.*

Shared understanding is the third type of social knowledge identified in Figure 3. Social knowledge may be considered a continuum from objectified knowledge, through collective knowledge, to shared understanding in a manner similar to the continuum of individual knowledge. Greater shared understanding is more likely to develop in tasks where there is a high level of interdependence (Janz, Colquitt, & Noe, 1997). If teams break tasks into less interdependent, additive parts, such interaction may be impeded; thus, limiting the extent to which shared understanding is formed (Hollingshead, 2001). Interdependence requires a high level of communication (Tschan & von Cranach, 1996). To the extent that the communication technology employed by virtual teams constrains the richness of communication, those teams may break their task into less interdependent pieces as a way of managing their separation. As a result, we expect

Proposition 5: *More virtual teams have a greater likelihood of enacting an independent approach to their tasks and, therefore, are expected to have less shared understanding of these tasks than less virtual teams.*

So far, our discussion of team effects has been independent of the organizational context in which these teams function. Yet, this context can be critical. Argote (1999) and others (Levitt & March ,1988; Starbuck & Milliken, 1988; Walsh & Ungson, 1991) identify various organizational repositories of knowledge and productivity-enhancing improvements: individual workers, an organization's *technology*, and an organization's *structures* and *routines*. Argote (1999) provides evidence that each of these repositories is suited for the development, retention, and transfer of different types of knowledge. Individuals are the most effective media for acquiring and storing tacit knowledge; technology, best for explicit knowledge; while structures and routines are most effective for transferring knowledge.

Organizational knowledge provides a basis and context for the development and transfer of individual and social knowledge. The more knowledge is modifiable (in our model, the more explicit individual or objectified social knowledge), the greater the flow of knowledge both vertically and horizontally in the organization (Schulz, 2001). Shultz studied interunit knowledge flow by surveying subsidiary leaders about three domains of organizational knowledge. The dependent variables were the volume of knowledge provided by a subunit to other subunits in each of the knowledge domains. Independent variables included exposure to internal and external sources of new experiences, the uniqueness of a unit's experiences compared to peers, the level of codification of knowledge in the domain, and the amount of inflow of knowledge from both peer and supervising units. Schulz found that horizontal inflow of information was positively related to the horizontal outflow of information. Peer groups shared information more readily with peer groups when there was an expectation of information flowing in from peers. Unit autonomy was also positively related, and distances to peers negatively related to horizontal flow of information.

An important finding by Schulz was that horizontal knowledge flow consisted mainly of incremental knowledge, while new knowledge tended to flow vertically. Schulz interpreted this finding by suggesting that new knowledge has uncertain relevance. Uncertainty is best resolved centrally where the exposure to remote and different knowledge is greatest. In contrast, horizontal knowledge flow depends on the absorptive capacity of the peer groups to receive and understand the relevance of the knowledge. This is best done with incremental knowledge, as peer groups are more likely to share the necessary knowledge to make sense of the incremental knowledge. Organizational knowledge is created through the enactment of knowledge that occurs as peer groups utilize the knowledge available.

Potential Team Knowledge

In teams, individual knowledge and social knowledge combine to form potential team knowledge. This is the total pool of explicit, implicit, and tacit knowledge residing in the individual members of the team, as well as the objectified, collective, and shared understanding residing as the social knowledge of the team. Potential knowledge is only realized if the individuals within the team, and the team itself, can utilize the potential knowledge. We expect that the level of usable knowledge will be moderated by the absorptive capacity (Cohen & Levinthal, 1990) of members of the team, the availability of relevant communities of practice, and the team's transitive memory and synergy. In the next three sections, we will discuss both individual level absorptive capacity and communities of practice, and the two group-level phenomenon: transitive memory and synergy.

Absorptive Capacity and Communities of Practice

Absorptive capacity refers to the individual's ability to utilize available knowledge. Absorptive capacity is a function of the individual's preexisting stock of knowledge and is heavily dependent on tacit knowledge (Szulanski, 1996). The more complex and ambiguous the knowledge, the more tacit and explicit knowledge must exist together for knowledge to be usable (Schultze, 2000). For example, Nambisan et al. (Nambisan, Agarwal, & Tanniru, 1999) examine organizational mechanisms for enhancing user-based innovations for information technology. In their review and conclusions, they note that users must have a combination of both explicit knowledge (e.g., an understanding of available technologies and their basic capabilities) and tacit knowledge (e.g., context dependent knowledge perhaps gained from association with the technology vendors) for effective development of new technology application ideas. Thus, the ability to make use of even quite explicit knowledge may be dependent on more tacit elements.

Proposition 6: *The transition of potential team knowledge to usable knowledge is positively moderated by individual absorptive capacity.*

Absorptive capacity can be enhanced through the social transfer of tacit knowledge from one individual to another (Nonaka, 1994). Thus, for the team to be able to utilize members' knowledge, all members of the team must have some degree of related tacit knowledge. Because tacit knowledge transfers among team members through social interaction, virtual teamwork may impede that social interaction, thus the transfer of necessary tacit knowledge, as represented by the shaded arrow from individual knowledge to absorptive capacity in Figure 2.

We assume that virtualness has a direct effect on the level of absorptive capacity among team members. Over time, the members' further development of absorptive capacity may be hampered because their ability to develop new tacit knowledge is constrained. While it is possible that members of more virtual teams could develop absorptive capacity from collocated others who are not on the team, the development of absorptive capacity would be relatively lower and less specific to the team tasks than that of an equivalent, but less virtual, team. As such, we propose,

Proposition 7: *To the extent that more virtual work limits the social interaction of the team members, virtual teamwork will reduce the absorptive capacity of team members.*

These social networks may or may not be part of the team structure (thus our inclusion in the individual knowledge section of the model: individuals may bring with them memberships in various communities of practice). Communities of practice are broader than transitive memory, the group level construct we will discuss, in that they extend beyond the team. The communities are fluid, interpretive, and often incorporate people from outside the team or organization (Brown & Duguid 1991). The knowledge is more about a common language or point of view than about particular rules. We suggest that the team can utilize the potential team knowledge to the extent that team members are also members of the communities of practice relevant to the team's task.

Proposition 8: *The transition of potential team knowledge to usable knowledge is positively moderated by individuals' connections to relevant communities of practice.*

Communities of practice develop when there are ample opportunities for informal contact. Informal, voluntary users' groups focus on sharing of relevant experiences that enable acquisition or transfer of tacit knowledge about technology applications (Nambisan et al., 1999). An environment of frequent and intensive interactions among members forms a high-density field of interactions (Nonaka & Takeuchi, 1995). A certain level of personal intimacy (Leonard & Sensiper, 1998) is necessary to establish communication of tacit knowledge. Transfers of best practices in firms were significantly impeded when arduous relationships between the sources and recipients reduced the transfer of both tacit and explicit knowledge (Szulanski, 1996).

This highlights the possibility of two dynamics related to communities of practice. More virtual teams, by virtue of their members' more diverse social connections, may have access to a wider range of communities of practice outside of the team. However, the arrow in Figure 2 relating individual knowledge to communities of practice reflects the notion that while access to communities of practice may be greater in more virtual teams, team virtualness may impede informal interaction among members. This suggests that there is less possibility that tacit knowledge from relevant communities of practice will transfer from team member to team member in more virtual teams.

Proposition 9: *More virtual teams will have greater access to communities of practice than will less virtual teams.*

The previous discussion focused on individual knowledge that is brought to the team, how that knowledge is affected by more virtual work, and the role that moderating factors play at the individual level of analysis as we look at the transition from potential team knowledge to usable knowledge.

Transactive Memory and Team Synergy

Argote (1999) describes team learning as a process where members share their own knowledge, generate new knowledge, and evaluate and combine this knowledge. The ability to turn tacit and explicit individual knowledge into team-level knowledge should be associated with the development of transitive memory (e.g.,Wegner, 1986). Recall that potential team knowledge resides differentially among the members of the team. Groups need a transitive memory system to help them effectively apply potential knowledge toward performance (e.g., Liang, Moreland, & Argote, 1995). Argote (1999) notes that group learning combines knowledge that individual members bring to the group with the knowledge developed by these individuals within the group. Levine and Moreland (1991, cited in Argote, 1993) describe the kinds of knowledge that groups acquire: knowledge about the group (culture, structure, norms); knowledge of each other (who is good at which tasks); and knowledge about the work (what kinds of work the group does, how it should be done). The development of transitive memory (Wegner, 1986, 1995) and its importance to group performance is an underlying theme in much of this work.

Transferable memory moderates the transformation of potential team knowledge to usable knowledge by allowing the members to be more efficient in their processes (Liang et al., 1995; Moreland et al., 1998; Wegner, 1986, 1995). Potential team knowledge is more directly transformed into usable knowledge when transitive memory forms within the group.

Proposition 10: *The transfer of potential team knowledge to usable team knowledge will be positively moderated by team transitive memory.*

Hollingshead (1998) argues that shared experiences, common language, and joint decision making facilitate the development of transitive memory. Argote, Moreland, and their colleagues have shown that groups who train together on the task they are to perform develop transitive memory relevant to the task and so, are able to outperform teams who train apart or who do not train together on their given task. These conditions for the development of transitive memory would seem to argue against effective transitive memory development in more virtual groups. We agree that transitive memory development may be more difficult in situations where groups work apart and are located in different environments. However, we also believe that technology or organizational systems may be able to support transitive memory development in such a way as to mitigate the difficulties otherwise experienced.

Moreland and Myaskovsky (2000) experimentally examined groups who were provided with exogenously generated evaluations of members' levels of performance. These groups were able to perform as effectively as groups who trained together on the task. We believe this is support for the idea that transitive memory can be artificially created through technologies, or other organizational systems, that supply the building blocks of transitive memory: directory updating, information allocation, and retrieval coordination.

Proposition 11: *More virtual teams will have less effective transitive memory development than less virtual teams.*

The transformation of potential team knowledge to usable knowledge is also moderated by team synergy (e.g., Watson, Michaelsen, & Sharp, 1991). Synergy speaks to the generation of additional knowledge once the members are in the team. This is the knowledge behind the idea that teams are greater than the sum of their parts. Whereas transitive memory speaks to the efficient use of the information brought to the team (and eventually, that knowledge developed by the team), *synergistic knowledge* is developed through the team's interaction. Synergistic knowledge is defined as knowledge created within the team, beyond the potential knowledge initially held by the team's individuals (*emergent* knowledge; Argote, 1999). For example, two members each know one, different way to solve a problem (information that could be stored as an aspect of transitive memory); yet together they are able to develop a third, new solution (synergy). Popular presentations (Corning, 1986), as well as experimental research (Reagan-Cirincione, 1994; Watson et al., 1991; Weldon & Bellinger, 1997), have shown that team performance can exceed that of the average performance of the team's members, and often that of the team's most proficient member. Thus, the moderating relationship between potential team knowledge and usable knowledge is expected to be positive.

Proposition 12: *The transition of potential team knowledge to usable knowledge is positively moderated by the level of synergy in the team.*

Organizational Knowledge: Technology, Structures, and Routines

Many authors suggest that as knowledge is enacted in organizations, it is captured through the organization's technologies, structures, and routines (Leonard & Sensiper, 1998). We believe that knowledge can be useful to organizations while it resides in the organization's individuals and teams. However, if others hold that knowledge, then it must be captured in a repository that is not dependent on individuals before it can be of value to the organization (Levitt & March ,1988). Our perspective is consistent with that of Huber (1991) and his colleagues, who describe three repositories for information and knowledge that organizations have acquired and retained: the minds of organizational members, organizational records (hardcopy or electronic), and the embodiment of the organization in its equipment, procedures, routines, and physical layout (Huber et al., 1998). The technology, structure, and routines of the organization embody the past actions of the organization, and provide the context and foundation for knowledge within the individuals and teams. Change or learning in organizations comes from the knowledge that individuals bring into the organization and/or that teams create through the combination and synergy of knowledge held within the team. We note this on the bottom of Figure 1 as the recursive flow from usable knowledge to organizational standards and routines, through to the initial knowledge types that feed into potential team knowledge.

DISCUSSION

Figure 2 illustrates a way of thinking about the forms of knowledge and their transfer within teams and the organization. Figure 2 also makes it explicit that virtualness impacts knowledge transfer at three key points: (1) transfer and development of knowledge among team members; (2) formation of absorptive capacity and community of practice; and (3) formation of transitive memory and synergy.

Theoretical Contribution

The individual benefits from retaining knowledge as tacit knowledge that cannot easily be assimilated by others. Thus, if the individual allows s/his tacit knowledge to be converted into explicit knowledge, s/he loses the benefit of retaining that knowledge; but if that tacit knowledge is used by the individual within the team (remaining tacit), the tacit knowledge increases a special status to its holder.

As discussed, in the case of teams working across a range of traditional (face-to-face), hybrid (both face-to-face and electronically supported communication), and more virtual (large electronically mediated and supported) settings, the distribution and form of knowledge may vary.

For example, proposition four suggests that media richness must be considered to understand how teams may form their own structure of the media to meet team communication needs. Proposition five suggests that task interdependence is also an important moderator of the relationship between individual and team knowledge. As shown in appendix, measures for these constructs also exist.

Having worked through the knowledge transfer processes depicted in Figure 2, it is now time to turn our attention to the implications of this model for the relationship between individuals and their organizations. Does information technology in virtual teams increase the transformation of tacit knowledge to explicit, while at the same time reducing the development of new, individually held tacit knowledge? Do such dynamics increase value to the organization while decreasing value to the individual? The answers may be yes, unless certain safeguards are put in place. Without such safeguards, we believe that organizations may achieve short-term gains by this symmetry, although in the long-term, organizations will also lose as knowledge generation and the resulting transformation slows.

Organizational Implications

In the long-term, organizations would appear to have two choices. In a Machiavellian world, organizations might develop systems where they quickly turn over employees after any unique knowledge has been stripped away (simulations in March (1991) describe such a process). Alternatively, information technologies and the organizational systems within which they exist could be managed to improve the transmission of more tacit knowledge (e.g., Carlson & Zmud, 1999), or the individual development of tacit knowledge based on more broadly available explicit knowledge. Richer media facilitating the communication of intuition through personal, nonverbal, and other rich communication forms would characterize these systems. These systems may support the levels of personal experimentation and learning-by-doing those are necessary to transfer tacit knowledge among individuals (Sternberg & Frensch, 1993).

Research Limitations

The discussion assesses the dynamics between the individual, the organization, and information technology in the context of teams that vary in their virtualness. The model is presented from a perspective of virtual teams, where membership is relatively stable, leaving the possibility of teams with more fluid membership for future consideration. The identification of these constructs is consistent with recurring themes in the literature, and it needs to be identified considering their different virtualness.

Future Research

Through further research, the field should be able to identify the limiting conditions for effective learning and knowledge transfer across the range of traditional, hybrid, and virtual teams. Such conditions may include the stability of group membership (e.g., Gruenfeld et al. 2000), magnitude of geographical dispersion (e.g., Festinger et al., 1950), types of technological support, and/or timing of face-to-face interaction (Mannix et al., in press). Observations, such as those presented here, serve as a starting point for critical organizational and technological design decisions.

The model and propositions we have suggested are potentially testable. In appendix, we catalogue the constructs and assessments necessary to test our model. While there are good measures of some of the antecedent and moderator variables in our model, other measures need to be modified or further developed.

As another research related the tacit knowledge, we will suggest studies in individual tacit knowledge level that belong to the general wisdom knowledge, or perhaps belong to the decision-making ability? (Chan & Schmitt, 2002) Nevertheless, in this research model, it provides the knowledge transfer types, further surveys should be suggested for order of priority to obtain knowledge in virtual team.

CONCLUSION

The importance of knowledge technology transfer, however, lies not only on providing opportunity to gain better return, but also to enhance its ability of technical innovation through the process. In other words, knowledge transfer in organization, individuals, and information technology may significantly influence the value of intellectual capital.

We construct a theoretical model suggesting that teams in more virtual settings will process their knowledge such that eventually, they will focus on, and be better able to transfer, explicit rather than tacit knowledge. This focus may unfortunately reduce the team's ability to utilize much of the available knowledge (i.e., tacit knowledge) in the team. Similarly, it is unlikely that much of the knowledge available through the individuals will be effectively converted to organizational knowledge. Organizational knowledge is dependent on more tacit processes, such as enactment, to be transferred into the technology, structures, and routines that retain knowledge for future organizational use. We suggest a variety of organizational actions that may mitigate these limitations to knowledge transfer in more virtual teams, including:

- Verbalization of rules, terminology, and descriptions
- Experience-building opportunities with team members, technology, and task
- Access to tools that support highly interdependent work
- Development of communities of practice
- Development of strategies and technologies that support transitive memory
- Development of strategies and technologies that support the transfer of tacit knowledge
- Focus on continued development of individual-level tacit knowledge

Without such actions, the combination of information technology and more virtual work may change the dynamics of knowledge transfer in organizations in unintended ways. The effectiveness of virtual knowledge transfer in organization depends not only upon the characteristics of the individuals' cooperative relationship; but it also depends upon how both ends align with each other in terms of intellectual capital in order to ensure effective internationalization and efficient mobilization. Thus, it may be interesting topics for future studies to include the variables in this research; future research could be formulated survey measures to tap the idea of communities of practices with empirical steps.

REFERENCES

Argote, L. (1993). Group and organizational learning curves: Individual, system, and eEnvironmental components. *British Journal of Social Psychology, 32*, 31-51.

Berman, S. L., Down, J., & Hill, C. W. L. (2002). Tacit knowledge as a source of competitive advantage in the National Basketball Association. *Academy of Management Journal, 45*(1), 13-31.

Berry, D. C. (1987). The problem of implicit knowledge. *Expert Systems, 4*(3), 144-150.

Boutellier, R., Gassmann, O., Macho, H., & Roux, M. (1998). Management of dispersed product development teams: The role of information technologies. *R&D Management, 28*(1), 13-25.

Brown, J. S., & Duguid, P. (2000). *The social life of information.* Boston: Harvard Business School Press.

Burt, R. S. (1992). *Structural holes: ThesSocial structure of competition.* Cambridge, MA: Harvard University Press.

Chan, D., & Schmitt, N. (2002). Situational judgment and job performance. *Human Performance, 15*(3), 233-254.

Davenport, T. H., De long, D. W., & Beers, M. C.(1998). Successful knowledge management projects. *Sloan Management Review*, 443-57.

Eierman, M. A., Niederman, F., & Adams, C. (1995). DSS theory: A model of constructs and relationships. *Decision Support Systems, 14*, 1-26.

Ellen, K. (1997). Know-how's not easy. *Computerworld, 31*(11), L1-L11.

Festinger, L., Schachter, S., & Back, K. W. (1950). *Social pressures in informal groups: A study of human factors in housing.* New York: Harper Brothers.

Frappaolo, C. (1998).Defining knowledge management: Four basic functions. *Computerworld.* Retrieved from http://www.computerworld.com/home/featu

Glasser, P. (1998). The knowledge factor knowledge management. *CIO Magazine.* Retrieved from http://www.cio.com/archive/010199_know_content.htm

Goodman, P. S., & Darr, E. D. (1998). Computer-aided systems and communities: Mechanisms for organizational learning in distributed environments. *MIS Quarterly, 22*(4), 417-440.

Granovetter, M. (1973). The strength of weak ties. *American Journal of Sociology,78*(6), 1360-1379.

Griffith, T. L., Mannix, E. A., & Neale, M. A. (2003). Conflict in virtual teams. In S. G. Cohen & C. B. Gibson (Eds.),*Virtual teams that work* (pp. 335-352). San Francisco: Jossey-Bass.

Hannabuss, S. (1987). Knowledge management. *Library Management, 8*(5), 1-50.

Holsapple, C., & Whinston, A. (1983). Software tools for knowledge fusion. *Computerworld, 17*(15),11-18.

Janz, B. D., Colquitt, J. A., & Noe, R. A. (1997). Knowledge worker team effectiveness: The role of autonomy, interdependence, team development, and contextual support variables. *Personnel Psychology ,50*(4), 877-904.

Kogut, B., & Zander, U. (1992). Knowledge of the firm, combinative capabilities, and the replication of rechnology. *Organization Science, 3*(3), 383-397.

Leavitt, H. J. (1996). The old days, hot groups, and manager's lib. *Administrative Science Quarterly, 41*(2), 288-300.

Leonard, D., & Sensiper, S. (1998). The role of tacit knowledge in group innovation. *California Management Review, 40*(3), 112-132.

Levitt, B., & March, J.(1988). Organizational learning. *Annual Review of Sociology,* (14), 319-340.

Liang, D. W., Moreland, R., & Argote, L. (1995). Group vs. individual training and gGroup performance: The mediating role of transactive memory. *Personality and Social Psychology Bulletin, 21*(4), 384-393.

Maglitta, J. (1996). Know-how, Inc.. *Computerworld*, 74-76.

Majchrzak, A., Rice, R. E., King, N., Malhotra, A., & Ba, S. (2000). Computer-mediated interorganizational knowledge-sharing: Insights from a virtual team innovating using a collaborative rool. *Information Resources Management Journal, 13*(1), 44-53.

Mannix, E. A., & Griffith, T. L. (Eds.), (2000). Stamford, CT: JAI Press.

Mayor, T. (1999). What dreams may come. *CIO Magazine.* http://www.cio.com/archive/011599_wish_content_open.htm

Moreland, R. L., Argote, L., & Krishnan, R. (1998). Training people to work in groups. In *Applications of Theory and Research on Groups to Social Issues,* (4), 37-60. New York: R. S. Plenum Press.

Myers, P. S., & Swanborg, R. W., Jr. (1998). Packaging knowledge. *CIO Enterprise Magazine.,* Retrieved from http:/www.cio.com/archive/enterprise/041598_intellectual_content.htm

Nambisan, S., Agarwal, R., & Tanniru, M. (1999). Organizational mechanisms for enhancing user innovativeness in information technology. *MIS Quarterly, 23*(3), 365-395.

Nonaka, I. (1994). A dynamic theory of organizational knowledge creation. *Organization Science, 5*(1), 14-37.

Nonaka, I., & Noboru, K. (1998). The concept of "Ba": Building a foundation for knowledge creation. *California Management Review.*

Nonaka, I., & Takeuchi, H. (1995). *The knowledge-creating company.* New York: Oxford University Press.

Polanyi, M. (1996). *The tacit dimension.* New York: Doubleday.

Reuber, R. (1997). Management experience and management expertise. *Decision Support Systems, 21*(2), 51-60.

Schatz, B. R. (1991). Building an electronic community system. *Journal of Management Information System, 8*(3), 87-107.

Schultze, U. (2000). A confessional account of an ethnography about knowledge work. *MIS Quarterly, 24*(1), 3-41.

Schulz, M. (2001). The uncertain relevance of newness: Organizational learning and knowledge flows. *Academy of Management Journal, 44*(4), 661-681.

Simon, H. A. (1977). *The new science of management decision, Chapter2* . Englewood Cliffs, NJ: Prentice-Hall.

Spender, J. C. (1996). Making knowledge the basis of a dynamic theory of the firm. *Strategic Management Journal, 17*(2), 45-62.

Stein, E. W., & Zwass, V. (1995). Actualizing organizational memory with information systems. *Information Systems Research, 6*(2), 85-117.

Swartout, W. R., & Smoliar, S. (1987). On making expert systems more like experts. *Expert Systems, 4*(3), 196-207.

Szulanski, G.. (1996). Exploring internal stickiness: Impediments to the transfer of best practices within the firm. *Strategic Management Journal, 17*(10), 27-43.

Tidwell, L. C., & Walther, J. B. (2002). Computer-mediated communication effects on disclosure, impressions, and interpersonal evaluations. *Human Communication Research, 28*(3), 317-348.

Tschan, F., & Von Cranach, M. (1996). Group structure, process, and outcome. In M. E. West (Ed.), *Handbook of Work Group Psychology* (95-121). New York: John Wiley & Sons.

Walsh, J. P., & Ungson, G. R. (1991). Organizational memory. *Academy of Management Journal, 16*(1), 57-91.

Watson , S. (1998). Getting to "aha"! *Computerworld, 32*(4), S1-S2.

Watson, W. E., Michaelsen, L. K., & Sharp, W. (1991).Member competence, group interaction, and group decision making: A longitudinal study. *Journal of Applied Psychology, 76*(6), 803-809.

Wegner, D. M. (1995). A computer network model of human transactive memory. *Social Cognition, 13*(3), 319-339.

Zuboff, S. (1988). *In the age of the smart machine.* New York, Basic Books.

APPENDIX

Table 1. Operationalization of constructs to test the theoretical model

CONSTRUCT	ASSESSMENT	REFERENCES
Team Characteristics		
• **Team Virtualness:** Time spent interacting with Team members via various media and face-to- face, location • **Task Interdependence:** Task, goal and outcome interdependence • **Media Richness:** Multiple channels, immediacy of feedback, language variety, personality		Griffith et al. (2003) Campion et al. (1993) Carlson and Zmud (1999) Ferry et al. (2001)
Individual Knowledge Types		
• Explicit, implicit and tacit	Extent to which individuals rely on codified knowledge, versus knowledge which could be codified but has been made automatic by practice, versus knowledge gained through direct experience	Measures to be developed
Social Knowledge Types		
• Objectified, collective and	Extent to which team has shared understanding objectified or collective knowledge or relies on shared understandings.	Measures to be developed
Individual Moderators		
• Absorptive Capacity • Communities of Practice	Recipient capacity to utilize information Survey assessing external and internal sources of communities of practice (Paradigms, practice norms, etc.)	Adaptation of Szulanski (1996) Measures to be developed
Team Moderators		
• Transactive Memory • Synergy	Specialization, credibility, and coordination Synergistic group processes	Lewis (in press) Watson and Michaelsen (1988)
Knowledge Utilization		
• Ratings of knowledge outflow from the team • Evidence of knowledge production of new, unique, and useful knowledge	Ratings by horizontal and produced by the team vertical teams Ratings by supervisors of the generation within team by the team	Adaptation of Schulz (2001) Adaptation of measures of creative output. Amabile (1982)

Section I

Selected Readings

Chapter XIII
The Building of Intellectual Capital Statements in Multinationals:
Challenges for the Future

Miltiadis D. Lytras
University of Patras, Greece

Patricia Ordóñez de Pablos
University of Oviedo, Spain

ABSTRACT

Multinational companies (MNCs) are facing important challenges within the current economic context. Rapid technological changes, the globalization of the economy, the existence of increasingly demanding consumers are, among other factors, the origin of the difficulties involved in achieving and sustaining a competitive advantage in the long term. One of the keys for overcoming these difficulties is to manage knowledge-based resources appropriately. However, in order to be able to manage these resources, the multinationals need to know, with complete transparency, just what these resources are, and this is achieved by quantifying them. The quantification of knowledge-based resources and the preparation of intellectual capital statements represent two strategic challenges for the MNCs.

INTRODUCTION

The resource-based view of the firm and the literature on knowledge management and organizational learning state that knowledge-based resources are a source of sustained competitive advantage due to their distinctive characteristics: causal ambiguity, social complexity, organizational path dependence, time compression diseconomies, and idiosyncratic value (Barney, 2001; Dierickx & Cool, 1989; Mahoney, 1995; Ordóñez de Pablos, & Peteraf, 2004, 2005; Peteraf,

1993; Reed & DeFillippi, 1990; Wernerfelt, 1984; 1995). These special features of knowledge-based resources require that the organization develops new strategies to manage them.

Knowledge management and intellectual capital literature respectively provide both a conceptual framework and specific tools for the management of intraorganizational and interorganizational knowledge flows in multinational companies (MNCs). Multinational companies consider that the transfer of knowledge flows at the international level represents a source of opportunities and risks.

This chapter has two basic aims. First, it analyzes the complex dynamics of knowledge flow transfers in multinational firms. Second, it addresses the measuring and reporting of knowledge-based resources in MNCs.

INTELLECTUAL CAPITAL

Concept and Constructs

Managing knowledge-based resources is not a new problem, and there have been other theories that have tried to tackle it. As Roos et al. (1998) state, intellectual capital is the latest development in this line of research. In particular, the theoretical roots of intellectual capital come from two different streams of research: strategy and measurement. While the first stream studies knowledge management—knowledge creation, acquisition, diffusion, capitalization, conversion, transfer, and storage—the second stream of research focuses on the measuring of intellectual capital. This stream has advanced towards the building of *intellectual capital statements* and the development of international standards on intellectual capital measuring and reporting. Now we are going to focus on the second stream of research: measuring and reporting intellectual capital (Lytras & Pouloudi, 2006).

A broad definition of intellectual capital states it is the difference between the company's market value and its book value. Knowledge-based resources that contribute to the sustained competitive advantage of the firm form intellectual capital. However these resources are not registered in the financial accounts. In contrast with tangible resources, the payoff and value of investments in a firm's current stock of knowledge (intellectual capital) will not appear in the financial accounting until later on. For all these reasons, knowledge-based resources must now being identified, dissected, and analyzed.

An accepted idea in the field is that intellectual capital is formed by three components or subconstructs: human capital (HC), structural capital (SC), and relational capital (RC) (Skandia, 1996).

Human capital reflects the set of knowledge, capabilities, skills, and experience of the employees of the company. It represents the accumulated value of investments in employee training, competence, and the future. It also includes an even more intangible element: employee motivation (Becker, 1964; Skandia, 1996).

Structural capital represents organizational knowledge that has moved from individuals or from the relationships between individuals to be embedded in organizational structures, such as organizational routines, policies, culture, or procedures. Generally, structural capital is divided into technological capital and organizational capital. Technological capital represents industrial and technical knowledge, such as results from R&D and process engineering. Organizational capital includes all aspects that are related to the organization of the company and its decision-making process, for example organizational culture, organizational structure design, coordination mechanisms, organizational routines, planning and control systems, among others (Bontis, Chong, & Richardson, 2000; Skandia, 1996).

Finally, relational capital reflects the value of organizational relationships. In general, it has been accepted that these relationships were mainly focused on customers, suppliers, shareholders, and the administrations, among others, without including the employees, and therefore adopting an external perspective (Ordóñez de Pablos, 2005). However, it is clear that the relationship of a company with its employees creates value, and for this strategic reason it is necessary to bear them in mind. To advance in the study of relational capital, it is convenient to differentiate between internal relational capital and external relational capital. Internal relational capital includes the value of the strategic relationships created between the company and its employees. External relational capital represents the external perspective of relational capital and includes social relations of the company with key agents: customers, suppliers, shareholders and stakeholders, current and potential, regional and national administrations, and the environment, among others.

Intellectual Capital Measuring Tools

Among these tools for managing a company's stock of knowledge is the Skandia Navigator (Skandia, 1996), the Intellectual Assets Monitor (Sveiby, 1997), and Balanced Scorecard (Kaplan & Norton, 1992, 1993, 1996).

The Skandia Navigator

In 1991, Leif Edvinsson started to work on the building of intellectual capital tools at Skandia. With the help of Professor Edvinsson, Skandia become world's first company to publish the intellectual capital statement. He also developed two major intellectual capital managing and measuring tools: Skandia Value Scheme and Skandia Navigator (Bounfour & Edvinsson, 2005; Edvinsson, 1997; Edvinsson & Malone, 1997).

The well-known Skandia Value Scheme and the Skandia Navigator are two models for highlighting and describing the evolution of intellectual capital within Skandia. These models visualize value components that make up intellectual capital, as well as the method of managing them and reporting on their development.

Skandia Navigator is designed to provide a balanced picture of the financial and intellectual capital. Its greatest advantage is "the balanced total picture it provides of the operations" (Skandia, 1994, p. 15). The focus on financial results, capital, and monetary flows is complemented by a description of intellectual capital and its development. Indicators that specify both the level and change are highlighted. At Skandia, the intellectual capital ratios are grouped into major focus areas: the customer focus, the process focus, the human focus, and the renewal and development focus.

Intangible Assets Monitor

The Intangible Assets Monitor represents a theory of stocks and flows which aim to guide managers in the utilization of intangible assets, the identification and renewal of these flows and stocks, and the avoiding of loss. This tool is focused on three types of intangible assets: external structure assets, internal structure assets, and employee competence assets (Sveiby, 1997).

The Swedish firm Celemi uses this intangible assets measuring tool. In its Invisible Balance, Celemi classifies its assets in three main categories: "our clients" (external structure assets), "our organization" (internal structure assets), and "our people" (employee competence assets). Celemi has also developed different tools that assess and better understand its intangible assets. Tango is one example of this. This simulation tool identifies key intangible assets, and measures and manages them in coordination with a firm's tangible assets. Intangible assets are studied at three different levels: (1) growth and renewal, (2) efficiency, and (3) stability of a firm's parameters.

Balanced Scorecard

It is one of the first tools that aim to create an integral vision of measurement systems for management, including not only financial elements but those non-financial elements (market, internal processes, and learning) that influence organizational performance.

The Balanced Scorecard (BSC) complements the information provided by traditional tools with three additional views: clients, internal and business processes, and learning and growth. They allow controlling the building of capacities and the acquisition of intangible assets needed for future growth. The BSC model proposes that an organization must meet the requirements of three groups of people if it wants to achieve success: investors, customers, and employees (Kaplan & Norton, 1992, 1993, 1996).

THE DYNAMICS OF KNOWLEDGE FLOWS IN MULTINATIONAL COMPANIES

Introduction

Multinational corporations have different reasons for global expansion, largely aiming to increase competitive advantage by realizing economies of scale or economies of scope (Harzing & van Ruysseveldt, 2004).

There are stages in the internationalization process and choices in the strategies and related structures adopted by multinational corporations. The range of MNC subsidiary strategies are (Bartlett & Ghoshal, 1989; Perlmutter, 1969):

- **Ethnocentric, Global Strategy:** The control is centralized. Subsidiaries resemble the parent company.
- **Polycentric, Multi-Domestic Strategy:** Control is decentralized. Subsidiaries conform to local practices.
- **Geocentric, Transnational Strategy:** Subsidiaries and headquarters alike adhere to worldwide standards.

Internal Knowledge Flows in MNCs

Knowledge management in any organization is a complex task. The complexity of this activity increases substantially in the case of a multinational. With respect to the management of knowledge flows within MNCs, we are able to differentiate four dimensions of analysis:

1. Internal knowledge flows within the parent company of the MNC.
2. Internal knowledge flows within the subsidiaries of the MNC.
3. External knowledge flows between parent company-subsidiaries and vice versa.
4. External knowledge flows between subsidiaries.

Managing internal knowledge flows is always easier—obviously within the complexity inherent to the knowledge transfer process—than managing the flows of knowledge between two organizational units (be they parent company-subsidiary or subsidiary-subsidiary).

Basically speaking, the factors that determine the complexity of the knowledge transfer process are:

1. *The tacit character of the knowledge to be transferred:* The greater the tacit component, the more difficult it is for the multinational to carry out this transfer successfully (Nonaka & Takeuchi, 1995; Szulanski, 2003).
2. *Causal ambiguity:* Not knowing the relationships involved in the body of knowledge in question, the relationships between units of knowledge, make transferring it difficult (Dierickx & Cool, 1989; Lippman & Rumelt, 1982).
3. *A "knowledge hoarding" culture:* If the MNC, by way of its organizational policies

and style of leadership, has fostered the development of an organizational culture that rewards the hoarding of knowledge as a source of power, the difficulties involved in the knowledge transfer process will be greater.

4. *Cultural distance:* Here a differentiation must be made between organizational cultural distance and the cultural distance of the country where the MNC is located. The greater the cultural differences between the country of the parent company and the country where the subsidiary is based, for example, the more obstacles there will be to hinder the transfer of knowledge (Hofstede, 1991).
5. *The capacity of absorption:* This is also going to be a determining factor when it comes to receiving or transferring flows of knowledge. If both the parent company and subsidiary company have a good capacity for learning and experience in receiving and sending knowledge flows, this will undoubtedly make transferring knowledge between units easier (Reed & DeFillippi, 1990).

Organizational knowledge transfer is a complex process that faces many obstacles. The tacit nature of knowledge and the diversity of national and organizational cultures are good examples.

There is a correlation between the degree of knowledge transferability and the type of organizational knowledge (Ordóñez de Pablos, 2004a, 2006). Nonaka and Takeuchi (1995) differentiate two knowledge dimensions: epistemological level and ontological level. The first level proposes the existence of explicit and tacit knowledge. Explicit knowledge is knowledge articulated and codified in handbooks, computer programs, databases, and training tools, among other elements. Therefore this type of knowledge is transmissible. However some knowledge-based resources, such as skills—competences, know-how, and experience, for example—cannot be completely codified knowledge, while other resources can be fully codified through standard procedures, computer algorithms, predicting models and theories, formulae, or programs, for example. Tacit knowledge is personal, context specific, and difficult to regularize. It includes cognitive elements—that is, "mental patterns" (diagrams, paradigms, prospects, beliefs, points of view, etc.)—that help individuals to perceive and define their environment. The second level of analysis highlights the existence of knowledge at individual, group, organizational, and interorganizational levels respectively.

Combining these dimensions, we can say that organizations are considered to be depositary of several types of knowledge (explicit and tacit) existing on different levels (individual, group, organizational, and interorganizational). Literature and empirical evidence emphasizes the "stickiness" of tacit knowledge: the transfer of knowledge has more difficulties if the knowledge exhibits a high degree of tacitness.

MEASURING AND REPORTING KNOWLEDGE-BASED RESOURCES IN MULTINATIONALS

Brief Historical Review of Intellectual Capital Reporting

MNCs must quantify their available stocks of knowledge. These stocks include the organizational resources based on the knowledge of the parent company and the subsidiaries. At any given moment within each one of these units, there exists a knowledge stock level that, with the passing of time, will subsequently move on to another level as a result of the knowledge flows that exist not only within each organizational unit, but also between them.

Midway through the '90s, a number of innovative companies began, on their own initiative, to publish intellectual capital statements. These are a new type of corporate report that seeks to reflect the company's knowledge map or inventory.

Current accounting standards allow a very small number of intangible resources to be posted if and when these comply with certain conditions, for example, goodwill and patents. However, what happens to the knowledge of the employees? Is it an organizational resource? Does it appear posted in the company's financial statements?

The intangible resources that do not appear reflected in the company's accounting process are not merely limited to the knowledge of the employees. Other knowledge-based resources exist, such as the value of the relationships developed with customers, suppliers, shareholders, competitors, and other agents. Neither must we forget the knowledge that goes into certain organizational policies, structures, culture, and routines.

These intangible resources do not figure into the financial statements. But does that mean that companies should forget to manage them? Is it that they, unlike tangible assets, are unimportant?

Without doubt, knowledge-based resources are a key factor in achieving and sustaining long-term competitive advantage. In order to be able to manage them appropriately, firstly it is necessary to have a clear vision of the stocks of knowledge that exist within the organization, in this case, within the MNC. To achieve this objective, it is vital to measure and quantify these resources.

The Intellectual Capital Statement

The result of the measurement of knowledge-based resources is a key element for building the intellectual capital report of the company. What is an *intellectual capital statement or report?* According to the Danish Agency for Trade and Industry (2003), the intellectual capital report is:

...an externally published document, which communicates the company's knowledge management goals, efforts and results. [It] forms an integral part of working with knowledge management within a company. Its statements on the company's efforts to obtain, develop, share and anchor the knowledge resources required to ensure future results. The intellectual capital can contribute to creating value for the company by improving the basis for growth, flexibility and innovation. Its merits lie in expressing the company's strategy for what it must excel at in order to deliver satisfactory products or service. (p. 13)

An Austrian nanotechnology firm called Nanonet (2003) states that the aim of the intellectual capital report is "to provide a transparent, verifiable overview of the effects of the research funds invested in nanotechnology...it provides a modern communication and control instrument for knowledge-intensive issues" (pp. 2-3). Having a knowledge map of the organizational knowledge is a key issue for MNCs.

Where MNCs are concerned, quantifying knowledge-based resources (intellectual capital) is more complex, in so much as it entails measuring the existing knowledge stock levels not only within the parent company, but also those in the possession of the subsidiaries.

What indicators can be used to quantify the knowledge that exists in an MNC? Two analysis dimensions need to be considered when studying these indicators:

1. The level of knowledge (at the individual, group, and organizational level); and
2. The location of the knowledge (within the parent company or within the subsidiary).

The intellectual capital statement will include a table with two entries. The vertical plane shows the different knowledge stock levels (individual, group, and organizational). In the horizontal plane we shall show the knowledge stocks that exist within the parent company and within the subsidiary, both for the current financial year and for the previous one, thereby providing a comparison of magnitudes.

The type of indicators for MNCs depends on the type of sector in which the company operates. Following recent empirical research on intellectual capital reports published by world leading pioneer firms (Ordóñez de Pablos, 2004b; Ordóñez de Pablos & Edvinsson, 2006), we can propose the indicators listed in Table 1.

Choosing intellectual capital indicators is a complex task. As neither official indicators nor an official intellectual capital guideline exist, companies use those indicators that they deem most opportune to quantify their intellectual capital.

Given the fact that no official directive exists, the MNC is free to decide which specific indicator to use. To do so, it will take into account, among other factors, the sector in which it operates, its activity, the size of the company, and the number of subsidiaries.

If we follow the recommendations for the drawing up of the Intellectual Capital Statement laid down by the 3R Model—developed by Patricia Ordóñez de Pablos at the University of Oviedo, Spain—the MNC should also present the intellectual capital flows account and the intellectual capital memo report (Ordóñez de Pablos, 2004b, 2005a, 2005b).

The intellectual capital flows account will reflect both the increases and the reductions of intellectual capital that occurred during the financial year, with the difference between these being the result. This information will be compiled for each indicator, indicator category, and intellectual capital component as well as at an aggregated level (intellectual capital). Likewise, the objectives for each of the indicators, indicator categories, and intellectual capital components will be specified (Ordóñez de Pablos, 2004b).

The intellectual capital memo shall have to complement and explain the information contained in the intellectual capital statement and in the intellectual capital flows account. In line with traditional accounting plans, the report will include information regarding the company's activity or activities, the standards used to evaluate intellectual capital, as well as events occurring after the closure of the accounts that do not affect these, but knowledge of which will be useful to the users of the intellectual capital accounts.

What advantage does quantifying and reporting on its knowledge-based resources bring to an MNC?

1. Evaluation of the type of existing stocks (strategic knowledge, basic knowledge, residual knowledge, idiosyncratic knowledge).
2. Improved management of these resources, given the fact that they have been quantified and we know where they are located throughout the different organizational units.
3. Knowing the results of the different organizational policies. For example, the influence human resources policies have on the creation of human capital.

Intellectual Capital and Accounting Policies

Intellectual capital does not appear in the traditional financial report. The explanation is the following. An asset—under *International Accounting Standard Committee* (IASC) literature—is a resource controlled by an enterprise as a result of past events and from which future economic benefits are expected to flow to the enterprise. According to International Accounting Standard (IAS) 38, the list of items that will not make it onto the balance sheet include expenditure on the following items: (a) research, starting-up a business, training, and advertising; and (b) generating internally customer lists, brand names, mastheads, customer loyalty, customer relationships, human capital, structural capital, and publishing titles. These items will not meet the definition of an intangible asset and the recognition criteria. Expenditures on these items will therefore be expended when incurred.

Table 1. Intellectual capital report (Sources: Ordóñez de Pablos, 2004b; Ordóñez de Pablos & Edvinsson, 2006)

UNIT	PARENT COMPANY		SUBSIDIARY$_i$	
	Year $_t$	Year $_{t-1}$	Year $_t$	Year $_{t-1}$
HUMAN CAPITAL				
Indicators • Number of employees • Number of graduate employees • Number of employees holding a doctorate • Total investment in training • Hours of training per employee per year • Number of employees who permanently work abroad • Number of new employees • Number of waivers/relinquishments • Number of competence development plans • Number of career development plans • Average length of service • Number of permanent contracts • Number of employees who have received awards/prizes • Employee job satisfaction index/ratio				

RELATIONAL CAPITAL				
Indicators • Domestic/international market share • Number of strategic customers • Amount invoiced to the five most important customers • Length of the existing customer relationships • % of customers who would recommend the company • New strategic customers gained during the financial year • Investments in relational marketing • Number of relationships with business schools and/or universities • Number of suggestions made by customers • Number of offices equipped with customer satisfaction quantifying systems • Number of management conferences attended • Number of employees speaking/presenting at scientific conferences • Sponsorship agreements • Professional networks • Employees on advisory boards (corporate, political, scientific) • Number of countries in which the company operates • Average number of employees per office • Number of commercial alliances				
STRUCTURAL CAPITAL				

continued on following page

Table 1. continued

Indicators				
• Investment in office equipment • Investment in IT equipment • IT expenditure per employee • Number of visits paid to the organization's Web site on a daily basis • Number of visits paid to the organization's Web site on a monthly basis • Number of employees with a teleworking option • Number of best working practices "posted" on the organization's intranet • Number of employees with intranet access out of total number of employees • Number of documents shared/distributed via the intranet • Number of employees with Internet access out of total number of employees • Number of shared-knowledge databases • Number of participants in best working practice processes • Number of knowledge management projects • Number of products/services • Number of new products/services • Sales volume linked to new products/services introduced over last year • Total innovation • Accreditations and certifications (environmental and quality) • Number of ISO-9000 certifications • Number of quality committees • Number of improvement groups • Number of employees who participate in round tables • Environmental investment • Number of occupational audits of the company's installations • Investment in cultural support projects and solidarity projects				

As there are no generally accepted accounting policies for the presentation of the intellectual capital accounts, this is a field currently under development where everything is left to be done in following years.

Additionally, as there are no standards and/or general accounting policies for the intellectual capital accounts, the reliability of intellectual capital accounts depends on quality data and accumulation methods.

CHALLENGES FOR REPORTING KNOWLEDGE-BASED RESOURCES IN MNCs

An important challenge is that of the development of official directives—either by the corresponding accounting bodies or by other institutions—that will enable the intellectual capital reporting models drawn up by the companies to be standardized, thereby making it easier to compare and audit them.

The MNCs that still do not quantify their knowledge-based resources must become aware of the importance of these strategic actions and observe the experience and results of those pioneering companies that have been preparing intellectual capital statements for years.

In short, the drawing up of an intellectual capital statement will enable the MNCs to possess a map of their knowledge-based resources that will in turn serve as a route map for making the strategic decisions that will enable them to survive successfully in competitive, complex, and dynamic environments.

CONCLUSION AND IMPLICATIONS FOR MANAGEMENT

Managers know that managing and measuring knowledge-based resources are key strategic processes for achieving a long-term competitive advantage. These tasks are even more complex in an international context with multiple intra- and interorganizational knowledge flows. The first step towards the management of knowledge-based resources must be the measurement of these resources as well as the building of the intellectual capital statement.

Measuring knowledge stocks in multinational companies is not easy. On the one hand, there are knowledge stocks—as well as flows—within the headquarters of the MNC. On the other, there are knowledge flows and stocks within each subsidiary of the MNC. Additionally there are knowledge flows among the headquarters and the subsidiaries, and among the companies' own subsidiaries.

However, the path to building intellectual capital statements is not easy. Is there an official model for intellectual capital statements? The answer is "No...at least not yet." Then how can MNCs build this report? Should they learn from pioneer firms? Definitely yes!

REFERENCES

Barney, J.B. (2001). Is the resource-based view a useful perspective for strategic management research? Yes. *Academy of Management Review, 26*(1), 41-56.

Bartlett, C.A., & Ghoshal, S. (1989). *Managing across borders: The transnational solution.* Boston: Harvard Business School Press.

Becker, G.S. (1964). *Human capital.* New York: Columbia University Press.

Bontis, N., Chong, W., & Richardson, S. (2000). Intellectual capital and business performance in Malaysian industries. *Journal of Intellectual Capital, 1*(1), 85-100.

Danish Agency for Development of Trade and Industry (DATI). (2003). *Intellectual capital statements—the new guideline.* Author.

Dierickx, I., & Cool, K. (1989a). Assets stock accumulation and sustainability of competitive advantage. *Management Science, 35*(12), 1504-1511.

Dierickx, I., & Cool, K. (1989b). Assets stock accumulation and sustainability of competitive advantage: Reply. *Management Science, 35*(12), 1512-1513.

Edvinsson, L. (1997). Developing intellectual capital at Skandia. *Long Range Planning, 30*(3).

Edvinsson, L., & Malone, M.S. (1997). *Intellectual capital. Realizing your company's true value by finding its hidden brainpower* (1st ed.). HarperCollins.

Ferner, A. (1997). Country of origin effects and HRM in multinational companies. *Human Resource Management Journal, 7*(1), 19-37.

Gooderham, P.N., & Nordhaug, O. (2003). *International management: Cross-boundary challenges.* Oxford: Blackwell.

Harzing, A., & van Ruysseveldt, J. (Eds.). (2004). *International human resource management* (2nd ed.). London: Sage.

Hofstede, G. (1991). *Cultures and organizations: Intercultural cooperation and its importance to survival.* Glasgow: HarperCollins.

Kaplan, R.S., & Norton, D.P. (1996). Using the balanced scorecard as a strategic management system. *Harvard Business Review,* (January-February), 76.

Kaplan, R.S., & Norton, D.P. (1993). Putting the balanced scorecard to work. *Harvard Business Review,* (September-October), 134-147.

Kaplan, R.S., & Norton, D.P. (1992). The balanced scorecard—measures that drive performance. *Harvard Business Review, 70*(January-February), 72-79.

Lippman, S., & Rumelt, R.P. (1982). Uncertain imitability: An analysis of interfirm differences in efficiency under competition. *Bell Journal of Economics, 13,* 418-438.

Lytras, M., & Pouloudi, N. (2006). Towards the development of a novel taxonomy of knowledge management systems from a learning perspective. *Journal of Knowledge Management, 10*(6), 64-80.

Mahoney, J.T. (1995). The management of resources and the resource management. *Journal of Business Research, 33,* 91-101.

Nanonet. (2003). *Nanonet–Styria intellectual capital report.* Retrieved from *www.nanonet.at*

Nonaka, I., & Takeuchi, H. (1995). *The knowledge-creating company.* Oxford: Oxford University Press.

Ordóñez de Pablos, P. (2001). Relevant experiences on measuring and reporting intellectual capital in European pioneering firms. In N. Bontis & C. Chong (Eds.), *Organizational intelligence: The cutting edge of intellectual capital and knowledge management.* Butterworth-Heinemann.

Ordóñez de Pablos, P. (2004a). Knowledge flow transfers in multinational corporations: Knowledge properties and implications for management. *Journal of Knowledge Management, 8*(4), 105-116.

Ordóñez de Pablos, P. (2004b). A guideline for building the intellectual capital statement: The 3R model. *International Journal of Learning and Intellectual Capital, 1*(1), 3-18.

Ordóñez de Pablos, P. (2005a). Intellectual capital accounts: What pioneering firms from Asia and Europe are doing now. *International Journal of Knowledge and Learning, 1*(3), 249-268.

Ordóñez de Pablos, P. (2005b). Intellectual capital reports in India: Lessons from a case study. *Journal of Intellectual Capital, 6*(1), 141-149.

Ordóñez de Pablos, P. (2006). Transnational corporations and strategic challenges: An analysis of knowledge flows and competitive advantage. *The Learning Organization.*

Ordóñez de Pablos, P., & Edvinsson, L. (2006). *The intellectual capital statements: Evolution and how to get started.* Working Paper.

Ordóñez de Pablos, P., & Peteraf, M. (2004). Managing and measuring knowledge-based resources. *International Journal of Learning and Intellectual Capital, 1*(4), 377-379.

Ordóñez de Pablos, P., & Peteraf, M. (2005). Organizational learning, innovation and knowledge: The creation of a sustained competitive advantage. *International Journal of Learning and Intellectual Capital, 2*(2), 111-113.

Perlmutter, H.V. (1969). The tortuous evolution of the multinational corporation. *Columbia Journal of World Business, 4*(1), 9-18.

Perlmutter, H.V., & Heenan, D.A. (1974). How multinational should your top managers be? *Harvard Business Review, 52*(6), 121-132.

Peteraf, M.A. (1993). The cornerstone of competitive advantage: A resource based-view. *Strategic Management Journal, 14,* 179-191.

Reed, R., & DeFillippi, R. (1990). Causal ambiguity, barriers to imitation and sustainable competitive advantage. *Academy of Management Review, 15*(1), 88-102.

Skandia. (1994). *Visualizing intellectual capital at Skandia.* Supplement to Skandia's 1994 Annual Report.

Skandia. (1996). *Customer value.* Supplement to Skandia's 1996 Annual Report.

Szulanski, G. (2003). *Sticky knowledge: Barriers to knowing in the firm.* London: Sage.

Wernerfelt, B. (1995). The resource-based view of the firm: Ten years after. *Strategic Management Journal, 5*(2), 171-174.

Wernerfelt, B. (1984). A resource based view of the firm. *Strategic Management Journal, 5,* 171-180.

Zahra, S.A., & George, G. (2002). Absorptive capacity: A review, reconceptualization and extension. *Academy of Management Review, 27*(2), 185-203.

This work was previously published in Strategic Knowledge Management in Multinational Organizations, edited by K. O'Sullivan, pp. 195-206, copyright 2008 by Information Science Reference, formerly known as Idea Group Reference (an imprint of IGI Global).

Chapter XIV
Intellectual Capital in Knowledge-Intensive Firms:
Exploring the Concept and Main Components in Boston's Route 128

Pedro López Sáez
Complutense University of Madrid, Spain

José Emilio Navas López
Complutense University of Madrid, Spain

Gregorio Martín de Castro
Complutense University of Madrid, Spain

ABSTRACT

During more than a decade, the literature has provided several intellectual capital models. Nevertheless, empirical evidence is still necessary in the field, and empirically supported models for classification and measurement of intellectual capital are not very common. This work finds the main components or building blocks of an intellectual capital balance sheet, taking the three most common components of intellectual capital (human capital, structural capital, and relational capital) and testing empirically if this grouping of intangible assets is supported by the evidence obtained from a sample of knowledge-intensive firms from Boston's Route 128. Findings suggest a classification of intellectual capital according to four categories: human capital, structural capital, relational business capital, and strategic alliances.

INTRODUCTION

More than a decade has passed since the publication of the first proposals about the concept and measurement of intellectual capital. Until now, literature has provided several intellectual capital models (Brooking, 1996; Bueno, 1998; CIC, 2003; Edvinsson & Malone, 1997; Kaplan & Norton, 1996; among others). Nevertheless, the need for adapting theoretical and empirical models to the new social and economic trends justifies an effort in improving previous proposals. Empirical evidence is still necessary, and empirically supported models for classification and measurement of intellectual capital are not very common.

At the international level it is accepted that there are three basic components of intellectual capital: human capital, structural capital, and relational capital. In a wide sense, these represent all expressions of firm's knowledge stocks. This triple nature of intellectual assets is being revisited by different lines of research, which are trying to reconcile the concept of intellectual capital (CIC, 2003).

In this chapter, an empirical research about knowledge-intensive firms is presented, based on the dominant stream of the theoretical proposals of intellectual capital, thus adopting these basic three components:

Human capital, which includes values and attitudes, aptitudes and know-how Structural capital, which contains both organizational and technological elements that pursue integration and coordination within the firm Relational capital, which gathers the value of the relationships that the firm maintains with external agents (close to business activity or with other more distant social agents).

The purpose of this empirical research is to test the previously extant models, and provide a configurative definition of intellectual capital from the different components that it comprises.

BACKGROUND: MAIN COMPONENTS OF INTELLECTUAL CAPITAL AND COMPETITIVE ADVANTAGE

Although for a long time it has been recognized that economic wealth comes from knowledge assets—intellectual capital—and its useful application (Teece, 1998), the emphasis on it is relatively new. Managing the intellectual capital of the firm has become one of the main tasks in the executive agenda. Nevertheless, this work is especially difficult because of the problems involved in its identification, measurement and strategic assessment. In this situation, the models of intellectual capital become highly relevant, because they not only allow one to understand the nature of these assets, but also to carry out their measurement.

The term intellectual capital is used as a synonym for intangible or knowledge assets since the work by Stewart (1991). The fact of calling it "capital" makes reference to its economic roots, because it was described in 1969 by the economist Galbraith as a process of value creation and as a bundle of assets at the same time. The definition by Bueno-Campos (1998, p. 221), "basic competencies of intangible character that allow to create and maintain competitive advantage," argues how we can tie intellectual capital to the resource-based view (RBV).

A joint perspective for intellectual capital (understood as strategic resources and capabilities) led to us to raise its assessment in order to state its own consistency. The different types of intellectual capital represent different types of intangible resources and capabilities. Nevertheless, in spite of their strategic nature, all of these assets would not have the same value for the firm, as it seems to suggest in the works of Hall (1992, 1993), Itami and Roehl (1987), Aaker (1989), or Prahalad & Hamel (1990) that emphasize the importance of certain intangibles. Setting this kind of difference can be considered as a useful help for strategic management. They can help in making decisions about the actions that the firm must perform and about the implementation of programs that allow it to protect, maintain or develop those more valuable intangible assets. Nevertheless, in order to explore the relation between any specific kind of intellectual asset and competitive advantage, a clear identification of the main components of intellectual capital is required.

In this way, several contributions have provided different frameworks for classifying the different components of intellectual capital, as well as for establishing series of indicators for intellectual capital measurement. Thus, according to most of the theoretical proposals, in a first step, three main components can be found: (i) human capital; (ii) structural capital; and (iii) customer or relational capital (Kaplan & Norton, 1992; Bontis, 1996; Saint-Onge, 1996; Sveiby, 1997; Edvinsson & Malone, 1997).

Nevertheless, a more detailed classification is needed in order to reach a better understanding. In this sense, Brooking (1996) highlights the differences between intellectual property assets–focused on technological knowledge—and infrastructure assets – focused on organizational knowledge— and gives a broader concept of market assets—that include customer assets.

Following the identification and classification of intellectual capital assets, during 2002 and 2003 a group of academics—including the authors—and expert practitioners developed a series of workshops at the Spanish Knowledge Society Research Center in Madrid. In those workshops, based on previous literature as well as on professional experience, a model of intellectual capital—called Intellectus (CIC, 2003)—was developed. It includes five components:

- Human capital (makes reference to the tacit or explicit knowledge which people possess, as well as their ability to generate it, which is useful for the mission of the organization and includes values and attitudes, aptitudes and know-how),
- Technological capital (refers to the combination of knowledge directly linked to the development of the activities and functions of the technical system of the organization, responsible for obtaining products and services),
- Organizational capital (as the combination of explicit and implicit, formal and informal knowledge, which in an effective and efficient way structure and develop the organizational activity of the firm, that includes culture—implicit and informal knowledge, structure—explicit and formal knowledge, and organizational learning—implicit and explicit, formal and informal renewal knowledge processes),
- Business capital (refers to the value to the organization of the relationships which it maintains with the main agents connected with its basic business processes—customers, suppliers, allies, and so forth),
- Social capital (as the value to the organization of the relationships which it maintains with other social agents and its surroundings).

As it can be seen, due to its heterogeneous nature, structural capital was divided into technological and organizational capital. In the same way, relational capital was divided into business and social ones. This more detailed classification allows a better understanding of these types of organizational factors. The Intellectus Model (CIC, 2003) is a good example that theoretical proposals about intellectual capital are becoming more complex and detailed every day. This encourages analytical reflection among managers and chief knowledge officers, but it can also be seen as a too extensive proliferation of criteria and categories of intangible assets.

This way, empirical evidence is needed in order to determine the level of aggregation that intellectual capital components must adopt in practice. This is the purpose of this work: to find out the main components or building blocks of an intellectual capital balance sheet. Bearing this aim in mind, we take the three most common components of intellectual capital (namely human capital, structural capital, and relational capital) and test empirically if this grouping of intangible assets is supported by the evidence obtained from a sample of knowledge intensive firms.

SAMPLE AND METHOD

Taking into account the previously mentioned theoretical proposal, we empirically test the presented simple model of intellectual capital in knowledge-intensive firms. With this purpose, we have carried out a survey in firms operating within NAICS 334 (Computer and Electronic Product Manufacturing), 516 (Internet Publishing and Broadcasting), 517 (Telecommunications) and 518 (Internet Service Providers, Web Search Portals, and Data Processing Services) from Boston's Route 128 (Massachusetts, U.S.) during 2005. The selection of industries was guided by the purpose to have a homogeneous sample (Rouse & Daellenbach, 1999).

From a population of 422 firms, 52 firms took part in our survey, so we reached a response rate of 12.32 % (see Figure 1 for a general description of the fieldwork).

The questionnaire employed for the survey included 12 items for measuring different intellectual capital aspects according to the three main constructs that it involves. Four items were devoted to report human capital (HC), three addressed structural capital (SC), and five tried to analyze relational capital (RC). Firms had to answer in a seven positions Likert-style scale, showing their level of agreement about the sentences present in the survey. The 12 items employed in the questionnaire were taken from general insights about the pre-defined components of intellectual capital taken into account (see Figure 2). The items were ungrouped in the questionnaire, and one of them was reversely written ("our relations with suppliers are sporadic and punctual"). These facts granted attention and sense-making from the respondent. Assessing the intellectual capital in a homogeneous scale is not very easy to do; nevertheless, the survey allows one to perform these comparison applying a same framework for assessment from each respondent.

RESULTS

A factor analysis was developed in order to identify the main dimensions of intellectual capital for these type of industries as well as their main elements and variables, although in the following paragraphs, as a preliminary approach to the data analysis performed after data gathering, a comment on the descriptive statistics about the items of the questionnaire is provided. This analysis

Figure 1. Research resume

Research focus	Knowledge Creation Processes
Criteria defining sample	Knowledge-intensive firms From industries NAICS 334, 516, 517 & 518 Placed on "Route 128" (Massachusetts, U.S.) 50 employees or bigger Included in CareerSearch Database
Sample	422 firms
Response rate	52 firms (12.32%)
Method for data gathering	Survey
Process for data gathering	Ordinary mail Follow up on the phone Backup with second ordinary mail, FAX, Web page and e-mail
Statistical software used	SPSS 12.0S for Windows (version 12.0.1)

Figure 2. Intellectual capital elements: Descriptive statistic

Questionnaire items	Mean	Standard Deviation
HC2 - Our employees are among the most experienced in the industry	5.92	1.074
HC1 - Our employees develop new ideas and knowledge	5.81	1.049
HC4 - Our employees have a long experience in the firm	5.67	1.232
HC3 - Our employees do team work	5.67	1.098
RC5 - Our firm is recognized by the external agents (customers, suppliers, competitors, and the general public) as one of the best firms in the industry	5.61	1.297
RC2 - Our customers are highly loyal to our firm	5.35	1.341
RC4 - Our collaboration agreements are held during long periods of time	5.19	1.394
SC1 - Our efforts in creating and sustaining an organizational culture are among the highest in our industry	5.02	1.651
SC2 - Our firm develops more ideas and products than any other firm in our industry	4.75	1.671
SC3 - We perform a lot of actions to spread our corporate values and beliefs	3.96	1.703
RC3 - Our relations with suppliers are sporadic and punctual (R)	3.81 (R)	1.313
RC1 - Our firm devotes an important part of its budget to funding community and green actions	2.60	1.796

(R) Reversed item. Un-reversed mean would be 4.19. Standard deviation remains the same.

allows us to detect the most and less common aspects of intellectual capital that firms possess (see Figure 2).

As it can be seen, the items related to human capital show the higher means (close to 6 in a scale with 7 as the maximum value). This reports that firms operating in the chosen industries are highly focused on having a strong human capital. And these data are quite robust, as the low standard deviation figures show. Almost every firm values so strongly its human capital. Employees with high experience in the industry, ability to develop new ideas and knowledge, as well as experience within the firm and the involving in teamwork appear as key assets for competing in the industries analysed.

The surveyed firms agree considerably (reduced standard deviations) about recognizing as next important in the list of intellectual strengths and assets the renown among customers, suppliers, competitors and the general public, the effective customer loyalty, and the long-lasting collaboration agreements sealed by the firm. All of these issues are tied to relational capital in the fashion of reputation-based and operationally based relationships with the environment.

The item "our relations with suppliers are sporadic and punctual" (RC3) deserves special attention. Its right mean will place it as an intermediate power asset. This is consistent with the literature, which confers less relevance to the relation with the suppliers in respect to other external agents as customers or allies. This is backed by the obtained results, because the items devoted to these agents show higher values as firm strengths than relations with the suppliers.

When firms assessed their intellectual capital positions, the issues tied to structural capital ranked among the less common element. Organizational culture emerges as the most employed element of internal coherence, but firms differ considerably among them about this issue (see the standard deviation figure). The effective flow of ideas and products delivered to the market is a slightly common asset, but we must take into account that it has been posed in industrial-competition terms. Finally, the relevance of actions for spreading and reinforcing corporate values and beliefs differ considerably for each particular firm (see standard deviations in Figure 2).

In order to end this preliminary descriptive analysis of our results, we must highlight that there are very few firms in the studied industries investing in community and green actions. Funding these actions was posed as an indicator for relational capital focused on community, social and green care agents. The average position in this kind of relation is actually low.

After descriptive statistics, an exploratory factor analysis was carried out in order to identify the factors or latent phenomena that lie in the data about intellectual capital provided by the studied firms.

For deciding if factor analysis is an appropriate technique in this case, several preliminary tests are needed: the analysis of correlations and communalities, the Bartlett test, and the Kaiser-Meyer-Olkin. Figures 3, 4 and 5 show the results of them for the set of items contained in the questionnaire employed in the research.

Figure 3. Correlation matrix (a)

		SC1	RC1	SC2	SC3	RC2	RC3	RC4	HC1	HC2	HC3	HC4	RC5
Correlation	SC1	1.000	.387	.318	.596	.074	.070	-.101	.153	.400	.331	.581	.410
	RC1	.387	1,000	.249	.600	-.039	-.030	.043	-.178	-.024	.079	.273	.140
	SC2	.318	.249	1.000	.375	.241	.277	.021	.296	.404	.082	.153	.419
	SC3	.596	.600	.375	1.000	.067	.025	.050	-.003	.057	.094	.448	.296
	RC2	.074	-.039	.241	.067	1.000	.250	.227	.280	.271	.150	.378	.312
	RC3	.070	-.030	.277	.025	.250	1.000	.192	.081	.065	-.128	.111	.063
	RC4	-.101	.043	.021	.050	.227	.192	1.000	.373	.130	.031	.071	.285
	HC1	.153	-.178	.296	-.003	.280	.081	.373	1.000	.528	.319	.446	.713
	HC2	.400	-.024	.404	.057	.271	.065	.130	.528	1.000	.566	.422	.540
	HC3	.331	.079	.082	.094	.150	-.128	.031	.319	.566	1.000	.254	.445
	HC4	.581	.273	.153	.448	.378	.111	.071	.446	.422	.254	1.000	.522
	RC5	.410	.140	.419	.296	.312	.063	.285	.713	.540	.445	.522	1.000
Sig.	SC1		.006	.020	.000	.321	.331	.263	.167	.004	.016	.000	.003
(Unilat.)	RC1	.006		.056	.000	.402	.425	.392	.130	.439	.310	.040	.188
	SC2	.020	.056		.007	.062	.038	.447	.029	.004	.303	.167	.003
	SC3	.000	.000	.007		.336	.437	.376	.494	.360	.277	.001	.029
	RC2	.321	.402	.062	.336		.055	.074	.036	.041	.171	.007	.022
	RC3	.331	.425	.038	.437	.055		.111	.305	.342	.209	.243	.347
	RC4	.263	.392	.447	.376	.074	.111		.007	.206	.423	.328	.034
	HC1	.167	.130	.029	.494	.036	.305	.007		.000	.020	.002	.000
	HC2	.004	.439	.004	.360	.041	.342	.206	.000		.000	.003	.000
	HC3	.016	.310	.303	.277	.171	.209	.423	.020	.000		.052	.002
	HC4	.000	.040	.167	.001	.007	.243	.328	.002	.003	.052		.000
	RC5	.003	.188	.003	.029	.022	.347	.034	.000	.000	.002	.000	

Figure 4. Communalities

	Initial	Extraction
SC1	1,000	.734
RC1	1,000	.728
SC2	1,000	.627
SC3	1,000	.811
RC2	1,000	.433
RC3	1,000	.705
RC4	1,000	.826
HC1	1,000	.761
HC2	1,000	.752
HC3	1,000	.634
HC4	1,000	.583
RC5	1,000	.752

Extraction Method: Main Components Analysis

Figure 5. KMO and Bartlett tests

Kaiser-Meyer-Olkin index		.618
Bartlett's Test	Aprox. Chi-squared	191.200
	FD	66
	Sig.	.000

As it can be seen in those figures, the tests advise to perform the factor analysis, rejecting the null hypothesis that the correlation matrix is an identity matrix (there are several correlations among the considered variables). Besides, the KMO index is above 0.6, so it can be considered acceptable for exploratory studies (as this), and the factor analysis becomes appropriate.

From the factor analysis we obtained four components of intellectual capital. Jointly they explained almost a 70% of the total variance contained in the original data (see Figure 6).

The first component found was labeled as "human capital" because it gathered all the items originally developed for measuring this construct, as well as one of the elements initially designed for relational capital. The five items included in this component explained the 25% of the total intellectual capital of the firm. The element that better characterizes "human capital" is the experience in the industry that employees hold. Nevertheless, the experience in the firm also presents important factorial weight. Besides, this

Figure 6. Explained variance

Component	Inicial Autovalues			Sum of saturation at extraction squared			Sum of sturation at rotation squared		
	Total	% of variance	Acumul. %	Total	% of variance	Acumul. %	Total	% of variance	Acumul. %
1	3.921	32.674	32.674	3.921	32.674	32.674	3.009	25.078	25.078
2	2.003	16.688	49.363	2.003	16.688	49.363	2.400	20.000	45.078
3	1.408	11.736	61.099	1.408	11.736	61.099	1.587	13.224	58.302
4	1.014	8.451	69.550	1.014	8.451	69.550	1.350	11.248	69.550
5	.880	7.331	76.881						
6	.708	5.903	82.784						
7	.677	5.643	88.427						
8	.412	3.431	91.858						
9	.392	3.265	95.123						
10	.260	2.168	97.292						
11	.193	1.609	98.901						
12	.132	1.099	100.000						

component of intellectual capital includes the abilities of the employees for developing ideas and new knowledge, and for team-working, as well as the recognition as a leading firm by the external agents (see Figure 7 for factorial loadings).

The second component found in the factor analysis represents 20% of the intellectual capital of the firm and includes three elements. The most important of them is the set of actions devoted to spread corporate values and beliefs. Due to the fact that this item was clearly representing structural capital, and because this component of intellectual capital includes two of the three items originally designed for structural capital it was named "structural capital." The other two items that appear within this component are the investments on community and green initiatives, as well as the efforts that the firm makes for creating and sustaining its organizational culture.

The third component of intellectual capital found weighted at 13% of the total variance contained in the original data and it was shaped by three items. The strongest of them was representing the relations with suppliers, showing content clearly tied to relational capital. In this vein, this component also included the relations with the customers. The factorial loadings of two relational capital items in this component, as well as the clear dominance of one of them led us to label it simply as "relational capital," although it also contained one of the items originally designed for structural capital (see the composition of this component through the factorial loadings shown in Figure 7).

The last component of intellectual capital that provided the factor analysis was designated "strategic alliances" because it contained only one item, initially developed for measuring relational capital along with the collaboration agreements held by the firm. This component emerged as an own entity, representing the 11% of the intellectual capital of the firm (see *Figure 6*), which highlights the relevance that special partners can have for a firm of the industries analyzed.

Figure 7. Rotated components matrix (a)

	Component			
	1	2	3	4
HC2	.836			
HC3	.760			
RC5	.739			
HC1	.716			.448
HC4	.527	.500		
SC3		.892		
RC1		.844		
SC1	.446	.681		
RC3			.821	
SC2			.660	
RC2			.507	
RC4				.903

Extraction method: Main components analysis
Rotation method: Normalization Varimax with Kaiser
(a) Rotation has converged after 5 iterations

FINDINGS AND FUTURE TRENDS

According to the obtained data, the average balance sheet of intellectual capital that could be found in a firm of the knowledge-intensive industries of computer and electronic product manufacturing, Internet publishing and broadcasting, telecommunications, and Internet service providers, Web search portals, and data processing services operating in Boston's Route 128 at the beginnings of 2005 would show something similar to Figure 8.

In this configuration of intellectual capital, human capital appears as the most influential component. It includes the experience, creativity and teamwork of the employees, but when the firm holds a strong position in these areas, an image of leading firm is projected towards the external agents (customers, suppliers, competitors, and the general public) present in the environmental set-

Figure 8. Components of intellectual capital obtained from the empirical research

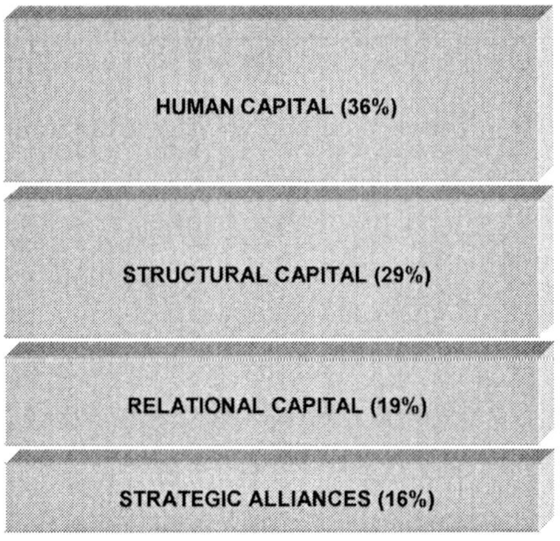

ting. Thus, the quality of the workforce seems to be the main indicator of leadership in the industry. Probably, due to the important knowledge base of the studied industries, the role of key engineers or experts could determine that "the best people make the best firm."

Structural capital represents almost a 30% of the total intellectual capital of a typical firm. The purpose of structural capital is to provide an appropriate context for communication, cooperation, adhesion and identity (Kogut & Zander, 1996). Issues related to organizational culture, values and beliefs are gathered within the label of structural capital, although we have found that investments on green care or community initiatives hold a strong relation to corporate culture and structural capital. This is nothing strange, because when a positive mission and values are stated for the company, probably the best way to legitimize them is with subsequent actions that reinforce the declared principles. Respect for the natural environment and the active involvement in the community life are two of the most common aspects that can be included in the documents about organizational mission, vision and values, and this explains the configuration obtained for structural capital.

Nevertheless, one of the most appealing findings of this research has been the fact that relational capital did not appeared as initially supposed. Although according to the literature we expected to found grouped all the relations with external agents (customers, suppliers, allies, competitor...), two components of intellectual capital were found in regard to these issues: the one that we have named "relational capital" and the one that has been labeled "strategic alliances."

Our block of relational capital includes the relations with customers and suppliers, as well as the capability of the firm to deliver ideas and products in its industrial setting. Although this characteristic was originally planned as an indicator of structural capital, the development process of ideas and products appears intertwined with its industrial environment, involving external aspects because it has been written with a comparison to the rest of competitors of the firm. This way, the factor named relational capital represents the set of general relations that a firm holds in its industrial setting, taking into account the interconnections with customers, suppliers and competitors. These agents are very close to the business activities, and it can be compared easily to the concept of "business capital" that can be found in other models (CIC, 2003).

The rising of and independent relational component of intellectual capital for allies and partners of the firm points out that certain collaboration agreements deserve a special interest. The presence of strategic partners could make the management and nature of this component considerably different from the management of the rest of the relations with the environmental agents. Although we have taken into account firms from different industries, or even from different sectors, there are common patterns about the possible interactions with key partners. Thus, firms born in a certain industry can learn to operate in another one with the help of an appropriate ally, or simply form alliance networks (Kogut, 2000) to reinforce its competitive position.

It is not strange to find a computer manufacturer partnering with a firm that develops and updates contents for manuals, or distributing its product with the Web-searching software of other firm, or providing special reduced conditions for accessing the Internet through a specific company, which surely will need communication equipment for undertaking its operations. These are some examples of how strategic alliances can strengthen the competitive position in the firm's own industry, thanks to the ties with firms from other industries. This kind of alliances can be a key for success and require specialized management, so that is what the results reveal when "strategic alliances" appear as an independent component of intellectual capital.

Further research is needed in order to improve knowledge about any of these building blocks of intellectual capital, bridging the extant advances in the fields of human resource management, organization theory and design, supply chain management or collaborative agreements, with the literature of intellectual capital. With empirical researches as the one presented in this chapter, managers can discover the components of intellectual capital that can be found in their industry. Then, they must apply the strategies and advice already developed for other fields of management research in order to develop and strengthen each kind of capital. Research efforts are welcome: (a) in analyzing the configuration of intellectual capital for different industries, building models from empirical findings, so theoretical proposals in the field could be supported or improved, and (b) in providing guidance for practitioners in the complex process of reinforcing the intangible endowments of the firm, improving each of the different components of intellectual capital.

CONCLUSION

We want to highlight the contribution of our research to the field of intellectual capital, where empirical works are very scarce. This way, although several proposals about intellectual capital classification, identification and measurement can be found in the literature, this work provides an evidence-driven classification and configuration of intangible assets.

We must not forget that, although the traditional concept of relational capital has been split up, adding both obtained components, it would represent a 35% of the intellectual capital of the firm. This makes the sum of relational capital and strategic alliances as important than human capital, leaving a supporting role for structural capital. It is not difficult to find a theoretical interpretation for this. The keys or main components of intellectual capital (for the surveyed firms) are at the very heart of the organization (human capital) as well as in its "osmosis" with the environment (relational capital and strategic alliances). Structural capital provides support for leveraging human capital and designing a coherent map of interconnections with external agents.

We must highlight that the empirically driven model for classifying intellectual capital that has been obtained in this research (see Figure 8) does not differ very much from the three main components that have been traditionally and theoretically discussed. Strategic alliances emerge as an intellectual capital component probably due to its relevance in the industries of the sample. Thus, we can argue that intellectual capital is a construct shaped by four different components, two of them with an internal nature and two more devoted to relating the firm with its environment.

This way, managers face four important challenges in managing intellectual capital: (1) granting access and development of human capital as the origin of its intellectual capital; (2) providing a structure for supporting strategy, connecting properly the different elements of human capital, and designing the desirable map of relationships and alliances needed for running business successfully; (3) relating the firm with its environmental setting and the different key agents that can be found on it (as customers or suppliers); and (4) finding and connecting properly with key partners that allow a special leverage of service, operative, and financial performance.

REFERENCES

Aaker, D. (1989). Managing assets and skills: The key to a sustainable competitive advantage. *California Management Review, 31*, 91-106.

Brooking, A. (1996). *Intellectual capital: Core asset for the third millennium enterprise*. London: International Thomson Business Press.

Bueno-Campos, E. (1998). El capital intangible como clave estratégica en la competencia actual. *Boletín de Estudios Económicos, 53*, 207-229.

CIC. (2003). *Modelo intellectus: Medición y gestión del capital intelectual* (Serie Documentos Intellectus No. 5). Madrid: Centro de Investigación sobre la Sociedad del Conocimiento (CIC).

Edvinsson, L., & Malone, M. (1997). *Intellectual capital: Realizing your company's true value by finding its hidden brainpower*. New York: Harper Collins Publishers, Inc.

Hall, R. (1992). The strategic analysis of intangible resources. *Strategic Management Journal, 13*, 135-144.

Hall, R. (1993). A framework linking intangible resources and capabilities to sustainable competitive advantage. *Strategic Management Journal, 14*, 607-618.

Itami, H., & Roehl, T. (1987). *Mobilizing invisible assets*. Cambridge, MA: Harvard University Press.

Kaplan, R., & Norton, D. (1992). The balanced scorecard: Measures that drive performance. *Harvard Business Review, 70*, 71-79.

Kogut, B. (2000). The network as knowledge: Generative rules and emergence of structure. *Strategic Management Journal, 21*, 405-425.

Kogut, B., & Zander, U. (1996). What firms do? Coordination, identity, and learning. *Organization Science, 7*(5), 502-518.

Prahalad, C., & Hamel, G. (1990). The core competence of the corporation. *Harvard Business Review, 90*, 79-91.

Rouse, M.J., & Daellenbach, U.S. (1999). Rethinking research methods for the resource-based perspective: Isolating sources of sustainable competitive advantage. *Strategic Management Journal, 20*, 487-494.

Saint-Onge, H. (1996). Tacit knowledge. The key to the strategic alignment of intellectual capital. *Strategy & Leadership, 24*, 10-14.

Stewart, T. (1991). Brainpower. *Fortune, 123*, 44-50.

Sveiby, K. (1997). *The new organizational wealth*. San Francisco: Berrett-Koeheler Publishers, Inc.

Teece, D. (1998). Capturing value from knowledge assets: The new economy, markets for know-how, and intangible assets. *California Management Review*, *40*, 55-79.

This work was previously published in Strategies for Information Technology and Intellectual Capital: Challenges and Opportunities, edited by L. Joia, pp. 29-39, copyright 2007 by Information Science Reference, formerly known as Idea Group Reference (an imprint of IGI Global).

Chapter XV
Organizations and Learning Process:
Its Antecedents and Consequences in Enterprise System Implementation

Weiling Ke
Clarkson University, USA

Kwok Kee Wei
City University of Hong Kong, Hong Kong

ABSTRACT

This chapter uses organizational learning as a lens to study how firms implement the enterprise system. The core research questions are: What are the critical organizational factors affecting organizational learning in ES implementation? How do these elements shape the learning process and thereby influence ES implementation outcomes? To address these questions, we conducted comparative case study with two organizations that have recently adopted ES and achieved significantly different results. Based on the empirical findings, we propose a framework that describes how organizational factors affect the four constructs of organizational learning in ES implementation context — knowledge acquisition, information distribution, information interpretation and organizational memory.

INTRODUCTION

Over the past few years, Enterprise Systems (ES) have generated much interest among researchers and practitioners as a potential means to enhance organizational agility (Davenport, 1998; Sambamurthy, Bharadwah, & Grover, 2003). While interest and investment in ES have been rising steadily, actual experiences with ES have exhibited more ambiguity. Some studies report improvements in efficiency and effectiveness from ES adoption, yet others find that the expected gains are far beyond reach (Al-Mashari & Zairi, 2000). It is imperative to conduct research that can make sense of the apparently-inconsistent ES adoption results.

Most of extant research on ES focuses on discrete critical success factors leading to on-time and within budget implementation (e.g., Bingi, Sharma, & Godla, 1999; Holland & Light, 1999; Parr & Shanks, 2000; Sumner, 2000). Yet, to leverage the business value of ES, it is not sufficient to simply adopt and install the system. Rather, employees and the organization as a whole must learn how to apply the technology effectively while they are implementing the system (Argyris & Schon, 1978; Attewell, 1992; Cooper & Zmud, 1990; Fichman & Kemerer, 1997; Purvis, Sambamurthy, & Zmud, 2001). The learning process plays a critical role in shaping IT adoption results (Tippins & Sohi, 2003). Hence studying how different forces affect the organizational learning process allows us to understand what leads to different ES implementation outcomes.

In this chapter, we use organizational learning as a lens to study how firms implement ES. Extant ES literature alludes to organizational learning sporadically and most of them do so in a cursory fashion, except the work of Robey, Ross, and Boudreau (2002) and Scott and Vessey (2000). Different from these studies, this chapter studies all four constructs of the underlying learning process involved in ES implementation - knowledge acquisition, information distribution, information interpretation and organizational memory (Huber, 1991). The core research questions are: What are the critical organizational factors affecting organizational learning in ES implementation? How do these elements shape the learning process and thereby influence ES implementation outcomes? To address these questions, we collect data by conducting case studies with two firms that have implemented ES within budget and on-time, but with significant different outcomes.

This chapter makes three principal contributions. First, drawing on the rich data of two organizations' experiences, the chapter generates an understanding of the organizational learning associated with ES implementation. Second, dealing with the complex links traced in context, this chapter adds substantive content to our understanding of the central role played by organizational factors in the organizational learning enacted in ES implementation. Such an understanding has been absent from the research and practice discourses on ES. Third, the chapter integrates our research findings with the more formal insights available from the IS implementation and organizational learning literature. It facilitates researchers and practitioners to explain, anticipate, and evaluate the organizational learning process associated with the ES adoption. This chapter is organized as follow: First, we briefly describe theoretical background of this study. Second, we discuss our research methodology. Third, we present the empirical findings that emerged from our case study. Last is our discussion and conclusion.

THEORETICAL BACKGROUND

Firms' ability to apply IT effectively in their business activity explains the different outcomes of their IT adoption (Armstrong & Sambamurthy, 1999; Boynton, Zmud, & Jacobs, 1994; Cooper & Zmud, 1990; Feeny & Willcocks, 1998; Sethi & King, 1994). When technologies are first introduced, they impose a substantial burden on the adopter in terms of the knowledge needed to understand and use them effectively (Argyris & Schon, 1978; Attewell, 1992; Fichman & Kemerer, 1997; Purvis, Sambamurthy, & Zmud, 2001). Organizations must undergo an intensive learning process to bridge the gap between what they have known and what the new technology requires them to know. Thus, the effectiveness of the organizational learning process plays a critical role in shaping IT adoption results. Indeed, this argument has been widely tested to be valid by the IS implementation literature (e.g., Boynton et al.,

1994; Ciborra & Lanzara, 1994; Fichman & Kemerer, 1997; Lyytinen & Robey, 1999; Pentland, 1995; Purvis et al., 2001; Wastell, 1999).

Organizational learning is defined as a process enabling the acquisition of, access to and revision of organizational memory, thereby providing direction to organizational action (Robey et al., 2002). As cognitive entities, organizations are capable of observing their own actions, experimenting to discover the effects of alternative actions, and modifying their actions to improve performance (Fiol & Lyles, 1985). The breadth and depth of organizational learning are positively related to its four constructs — knowledge acquisition, information distribution, information interpretation and organizational memory (Huber, 1991). Knowledge acquisition is the process by which knowledge is obtained (Huber, 1991; Robey et al., 2002; Tippins & Sohi, 2003). Information distribution is the process by which knowledge obtained is shared through formal and informal channels (Maltz & Kohli, 1996; Slater & Narver, 1995). Information interpretation is the process by which functional units reach a consensus with regard to the meaning of information (Daft & Weick, 1984; Slater & Narver, 1995; Tippins & Sohi, 2003) and organizational memory refers to organizations' storing knowledge for future use (Huber, 1991; Walsh & Ungson, 1991).

Extant ES literature alludes to organizational learning sporadically, and most of them do so in a cursory fashion, except the work of Robey et al. (2002) and Scott and Vessey (2000). In addition, the literature suggests a list of critical success factors for ES implementation, such as leadership (Lee & Sarkar, 1999), top management support and change management (Al-Mashari & Zairi, 2000). But there is no study explicitly linking these factors with organizational learning enacted in ES implementation. Different from the extant studies, our research studies how organizational factors affect the learning process, which determines ES implementation outcomes.

RESEARCH METHODOLOGY

To address our research questions, we employ a case study methodology. As an empirical inquiry investigating a contemporary phenomenon within its real-life context, a case study is particularly appropriate when examining "how" and "why" research questions (Yin, 1994). Given the nature of our research question and desire to obtain rich explanations of organizational learning process in ES implementation, a case study methodology is the most appropriate.

We selected two organizations for their similarities as well as their differences (Glaser & Strauss, 1967), paying attention to theoretical relevance and purpose. With respect to relevance, our selection process ensured that the substantive area addressed — the on-time and within budget implementation of ES — was kept similarly. As the purpose of the research is to generate insight into how organizational factors affect organizational learning enacted and thereby ES implementation outcomes, differences were sought in organizational conditions, such as the motivation of adopting ES, user training methods, and adoption outcomes. We first conducted a study with CPM — a PC and computer peripheral manufacturing company with 800 employees located in South China. The second company we studied was MEM which was a division of a publicly listed multinational electronic manufacturing company. This division had 750 employees and was located in North China.

In both research sites, we collected data by using multiple methods: unstructured and semi-structured interviews, archival sources, and observation. This triangulation across various techniques of data collection provides multiple perspectives on an issue, supplies more information on emerging concepts, and yields stronger substantiation of constructs and allows for cross-checking (Eisenhardt, 1989; Pettigrew, 1990; Yin, 1994).

In this study, we had both investigators make visits to the case study sites together so that we could avoid biases due to one single researcher's perception. In particular, we followed Eisenhardt and Bourgeois' (1988) strategy and had one researcher handling the interview questions, while the other recording notes and observations. This tactic allows the interviewer to have the perspective of personal interaction with the informant, while the other investigator retains a different and more distant view. The interviews we conducted are shown in Table 1. Each interview lasts between one and one-and-a-half hours. They were all tape-recorded and transcribed within 24 hours after the interview.

Data Analysis

We analyzed data within each site as well as across the two sites. Given the qualitative nature of the data collected, we avoided biases by using the iterative approach of data collection, coding, and analysis. Within CPM, the first site, we relied more on open-ended and generative interview questions. After these interviews, both authors independently read the transcripts of interviews and categorized data into concepts of salient organizational factors, major organizational learning activities, and implementation outcomes. The lists of concepts were compared and contrasted. Any difference was further examined and verified with the informants. This process yielded a broad set of concepts, which guided our second field study conducted in MEM.

Following the constant comparative analysis method suggested by Glaser and Strauss (1967), we systematically compared MEM's experiences with those of CPM. Data collected from MEM were first sorted into concepts generated by CPM's data. However, the list of concepts did not accommodate some findings emerging from MEM. For example, the mistrust among mid-level managers led us to study the organizational culture's effect, which did not seem to be salient to us in CPM's case. In this kind of situation, we went back to CPM to collect data related with these new concepts. The iteration between data and concepts ended when we had enough concepts to explain experiences of both sites.

RESEARCH FINDINGS

Organizational Factors and Organizational Learning in CPM

ES Vision. The vision of adopting ES was formulated when CPM was in a crisis. Its management decision-making and inter-departmental coordination became ineffective due to its fast

Table 1. Amount of interviewees

CPM		MEM	
Interviewee's Title	**Count**	**Interviewee's Title**	**Count**
Senior VP in Marketing	1	Senior VP	1
Senior VP in Manufacturing	1	General Manager	1
CIO	1	Vice General Manager	1
Departmental Manager	4	Departmental Manager	5
Line Worker	5	Line Worker	4

business expansion – more than 25% annual growth rate for four years in a row. As described by the CIO:

Our management encountered severe difficulties due to the lack of information support. The business data located in fragmented systems were inconsistent and difficult to reconcile… The coordination between departments was chaotic. For example, our accounting system didn't record the sales long after the goods were delivered and we didn't detect these mistakes until we did [a] physical count.

In addition to the internal difficulties, CPM faced a more and more competitive market, and profit margins of its major products were diminishing. To cope with these problems, the top management decided to expand its business scope and adopt the advanced packaged software — enterprise system. As explained by the CIO:

The packaged software in the market was a solution to integrate our system and streamline our business processes… It (ES adoption) is part of our business strategic plan… In addition [to] adopting an integrated system, we expected to change our practices and organizational structure in the light of ES functionalities.

With a "transform" vision of ES adoption, CPM treated it as an investment and was committed to it with slack resources. These resources allowed CPM to acquire ES knowledge by hiring consultants (the Consulting Group in our later description), whose service cost USD$400,000. The consultant group transferred its system knowledge to CPM by helping the firm choose the right software/hardware, configure the system, and train end users. In addition, the consultants transferred the knowledge of process-oriented methodology to CPM and taught CPM managers how to use tools to draw business process diagrams. The external knowledge provided by the Consulting Group was critical to jump start CPM's ES project, as commented by the IT manager:

ES is much more complicated than our old systems. Without the external knowledge from the consultants, I don't think we would be able to get it implemented successfully.

Also, as described by the Senior VP of Manufacturing:

Though I had heard of the concept of process-oriented thinking, but I didn't know how to describe our business practices by using the tools until I attended the classes… These business process diagrams were really helpful and greatly facilitated our sharing of business process ideas.

Equipped with process-oriented knowledge and graphically describing business process techniques, CPM managers were able to discuss business practices by representing business processes with a uniform set of notations. It enhanced the effectiveness of communications and facilitated information interpretation – another construct of organizational learning (this sub-process is described in later sections).

Advocacy of ES Vision

The necessity of adopting ES was first perceived by the CEO who had led the firm since it was first set up in 1988. In a top management meeting, CEO presented his idea about ES adoption and asked for attendants' comments. After studying the feasibility of adopting ES for two weeks, the top management formulated its ES vision and started to communicate the vision with mid-level managers. The managers were called upon to embrace this vision and influence their subordinates by articulating the vision as much as possible. In addition, flyers, posters, and brochures about ES were widely distributed. Within two weeks, the message of adopting ES was disseminated across the organization. As described by a line worker about employees' reaction to ES adoption decision:

Some people thought it would be a good opportunity for the firm and individuals to learn, while others were worried about losing their jobs after ES adoption. It took a while for us to be convinced that we would benefit from ES adoption.

Employees' concerns were addressed by the CEO in an assembly meeting, in addition to the departmental meetings. By clearly explaining the rationale for ES adoption, the CEO assured employees that their jobs would be secure as long as the firm grew healthily, which required employees to endeavor as a unit toward a common goal – enhancing the firm's competitiveness and make ES adoption a success. As explained by a line worker:

Since implementing ES was a must-do project for our company's survival, it didn't make sense for us to resist it ... If we accepted the project positively and tried to gain some ES knowledge, mostly likely we would keep our jobs and upgrade ourselves. Especially, a lot of firms were adopting ES. With the ES knowledge gained from the project, we would be more competitive in the job market.

His comments were conferred by another line-worker:

It was a good opportunity for us to learn this advanced technology ... Being positive and supportive was a smarter choice than being worried and resistant.

The advocacy of ES vision allowed CPM to win the majority's support. It also motivated the employee to contribute, receive, and capture ES knowledge. This was revealed by the employees' passion and persistence in learning ES after work twice a week for nearly two months. In recalling the learning experience, one line worker described to us that:

Though we had to perform our job duty as before, staying overtime to learn ES was not unbearable. Since we were excited about this learning opportunity and looking forward to seeing the system implemented successfully. [Those] kind of feelings made us .. take a positive approach and [be] better able to put up with the fatigue.

The employees' endeavor in learning ES allowed CPM to distribute knowledge to the right people. The system knowledge was first transferred to the IT group, which would be responsible for the maintenance and support of the system. Also, knowledge on each module adopted was transferred to all relevant employees by formal training courses. Though the users were mainly trained to master the knowledge on the modules related to their work, a lot of employees proactively studied other modules and how different modules were inter-related. In addition, power users were formally assigned in each business unit. These power users learned about "why" and "how", in addition to "what". Such knowledge empowered them to be able to re-configure the system and make necessary adjustments of parameters to meet the requirements of special events.

Administrative Structure Support

CPM set an administrative structure for the project, which included a steering committee, working committee, project function groups, IT group, and Consulting Group. The steering committee was consisted of the members of the top management team, while the working committee consisted of senior managers who were respected and trusted in the organization. The project function groups were made up by the managers and key employees of every department. The six members of the Consulting Group were from a highly-reputable consulting firm specializing in ES adoption. These committees/groups were delegated with appropriate responsibility and authority to make decisions related to ES implementation. For example, the responsibilities of the working committee included formulating project plans and ensuring the progress of the project, guiding, organizing, and promoting the interaction among function groups, analyzing and proposing solutions to problems of business process optimization, organizing managerial and technical training courses, and being in charge of job specifications and standardizing work procedures.

The administrative structure served as a formal communication channel in CPM's learning ES, which was especially important for the acquisition of business knowledge and information interpretation. It called for regular/irregular meetings that allowed people to have formal and informal information exchange. For example, the function groups met four times a week to generate the diagrams of the business process status quo and redesigning the firm's business processes. According to the Inventory Manager:

Being a member of the function group made me better understand what role I should play in this project... The meetings and social gatherings provided us chances to communicate with each other. In addition to getting jobs done, they also enhanced cohesion and trust among us, which made coordination and cooperation issues much easier... It helped a lot with our reaching consensus on the business processes spanning departmental boundaries.

Control Scheme

To ensure that employees would learn and master knowledge required to apply ES effectively, the firm made employees' performance in the ES implementation an important part of individuals' and business units' annual evaluation. For example, it accounted for 60% of the CIO's annual evaluation. As commented by the Manufacturing Manager:

This evaluation scheme made it clear to everyone that he must be responsible for what he did and how he performed throughout the ES implementation process... I think this evaluation scheme was really helpful in encouraging people to put in their effort... As we would also be evaluated as a business unit, we were encouraged to help each other in learning how to use the system.

In addition, CPM formulated strict controlling rules, that is, only when the employees passed skill tests on ES, would they be allowed to take up jobs using the system. Employees who failed these tests would have to undergo the training again or be assigned to do some other jobs. In addition to providing incentives to learning ES, these control schemes ensured minimum operation and manufacturing disruptions after the system went live.

Top Management Involvement

The committee members attended all business process-redesign meetings and training workshops on process-oriented methodology. Also, the steering committee evaluated and approved the refined business process and ES implementation plan. As commented by a mid-level manager:

They worked together with us, even though we had to work overtime continuously for months. Their personal involvement in the project made us well aware of the importance of the project and inspired us to work hard on it... Also, with their presence in the meetings, we could make decisions on business process changes on the spot, which facilitated the project's progress.

In addition to enhancing employees' morale and facilitating the project progress, top management brought constructive ideas and sound judgments on the refined business processes. Due to their possession of knowledge that was not available to mid-level managers, top management was able to challenge the business model proposed by the groups and evaluate different proposals, which ensured that the most suitable model was adopted.

Organizational Structure and Culture

CPM was organized divisionally with business units representing its major business areas. It had a culture that emphasized cooperation among employees and across functional units. Especially, the management emphasized employees' job satisfaction and career development. The firm organized many formal and informal social gatherings every year, in addition to providing free lunches for employees in its canteen. As commented by the Senior VP of Marketing:

These social gatherings allowed employees from different, maybe not directly-related, departments to know each other... It helped us build cohesive and trusting culture.

The firm's culture enabled people to share different opinions openly, which was critical for the organizational learning in ES implementation. In the sub-process of information interpretation, all groups and committees came together to discuss about the possibilities of redesigning the organization's business processes. The discussions mainly focused on further improvement of business processes within the department and the management of activities spanning departmental boundaries and ad hoc business events. Trusting and cohesive culture facilitated the reaching of the consensus on how to get jobs done, as described by the Marketing Manager:

We benefited a lot from the innovative ideas provided by people from other departments... We freely expressed our opinion and discussed in greater details when there was any disagreement. While trying to fight for our department, we also tried to put ourselves in others' shoes. There was nothing that couldn't be worked out. Especially, we could always pass controversial issues to the Boss. He had the last say.

With the shared understanding about what the best business practices were after ES implementation, CPM was able to update its organizational memory according to changes in its organizational structure, business processes, and management white paper. The information distribution and interpretation sub-processes decided the types of organization memory for this project. First, all the activities happened during the ES implementation were recorded in the computer system as part of the project. These documents facilitated the review, coordination and communication during and after the ES implementation. Second, the organization memory had humans as carriers. All end users and power users passed ES tests and became carriers of knowledge on how to interact with the system. They served as instructors to new comers of their departments, using the operation documentation of each module compiled by IT group. In addition, function group and committee members are the carriers of knowledge on business processes.

Organizational Factors and Organizational Learning in MEM

ES Vision. Aiming to cut purchasing cost and reduce lead time, the headquarters of MEM decided to integrate the databases in different sites located in different countries. Following this strategy, MEM was required to adopt ES which had been implemented in the headquarters and some other sites. ES implemented in MEM had its configuration and business processes exactly the same as those in other sites.

With the aim to cut costs by ES adoption, MEM was tight with resources contributed to ES project. The knowledge about the new business processes and system was acquired by learning from the Expert Team sent by headquarters. The experts spoke different languages from MEM employees. Due to the language barrier, it was difficult for MEM employees to capture the knowledge transferred by the experts, just as described by the Personnel Manager:

Language barrier was a big problem. I couldn't understand them clearly. Even worse, it was hard for them to understand my questions. Sometimes it became so frustrating that I just kept silent. And that might have passed a wrong message, and made them [think] that I didn't have any problems in understanding what they said.

Though the employees complained about the difficulties in learning and suggested hiring native speaking consultants, the top management decided not to do so due for two main reasons: (1) the high consulting fee; and (2) the consultants' lack of knowledge about business processes to be adopted. The Senior VP believed that as long as employees in MEM put in enough effort, they could get around the language barrier problem. Hiring consultants was regarded as a waste of money and violated the principle of ES adoption - cost saving.

Advocacy of ES Vision

In one meeting, the General Manager informed the top and mid-level managers of the headquarter's decision on implementing ES at MEM and explained the rationale for this adoption. Different from CPM, the vision was not passed to employees at lower levels. Neither did all of the mid-level managers align with this vision. As told by the Sales Manager:

With all the data shared among different sites, it meant that the discount we offered to our clients would be monitored by other sales people. That would lead us (sales representatives) to compete against each other by offering higher discount rates. It would harm both the interests of our division and the company as a whole. In my opinion, the adoption of ES was a big strategic mistake.

Some employees were against ES adoption because of their fear of losing jobs after ES adoption. As described by the Purchasing Manager:

The system was bad for each division. With central sourcing, we would lose autonomy in selecting our own supplies... Since the Boss emphasized cost saving, most likely we would be replaced by the system.

Overall, employees regarded the project owned by headquarters and stayed distant from it. With the lack of support from employees, especially some key mid-level managers, the morale of learning ES was low. MEM employees received knowledge transferred by the Expert Team passively and did not endeavor to capture the knowledge, which was reflected in their making excuses for skipping or postponing ES lessons.

Administrative Structure Support

MEM did not set up a specific administrative structure to support the ES implementation project, but had the experts from headquarters to lead the project, with assistance of the IS department. The Expert Team was in charge of the project plan and training organization. Throughout the project, the information flew mainly from the experts to MEM, and there was an insufficiency of communication among MEM employees. This arrangement affected the effectiveness of information distribution and interpretation, due to the lack of inputs from MEM employees.

Treating MEM employees as knowledge receivers, the Expert Team adopted a hierarchical approach to transfer ES knowledge, that is, the Expert Team trained the mid-level managers and the managers trained their subordinates. In these trainings, the experts verbally explained the standardized business practices set by headquarters and showed the managers how to enter and retrieve data from the system. Each manager was shown how to use the module related to his/her work only. The managers passed what they had learned to their subordinates in a similar way. Regarding the trainings, a manager made such comments:

The experts just told me what to do, rather than why I should do it that way. So after they left, I was totally lost when I encountered problems. As I was the only one who learned this module with the experts, I couldn't seek help from others within our firm... I was not confident to give advice to my subordinates when they had problems with the system.

Also, a line worker told us:

The system was too complex to me and learning experiences were really frustrating... It seemed to me that none of the people in our division really knew the system. Basically we just learned by trial and error... So our skepticism about the system's capability in supporting our operation turned out to be right.

This training method led to little ES knowledge overlapping within the firm, and the lack of administrative structure deprived the chance for employees to share what they had learned. Thus, the firm did not have managers who knew the new business processes across department boundaries well. The low degree of information distribution made MEM encounter great problems in information interpretation, which was described as, "there was little shared understanding of business processes coming along with the system".

Control Schemes

The top management assumed that all of the employees would put in their best efforts in learning ES and participate in ES project proactively, so the firm did not set up any reward scheme for the employees' performance in the project. Neither did they formulate any control scheme to ensure that employees were able to interact with the system appropriately before the system went live. This lack of control scheme, coupled with the employees' attitude towards the project, did not provide employees enough incentive to seek for and capture ES knowledge.

Top Management Involvement

Trusting the Expert Team's capability, the top management did not participate in the project as much as in CPM. On the contrary, they almost left the project completely in the hands of the Expert Team, though they checked whether the project was progressing as expected from time-to-time. The General Manager told us:

The Expert Team from headquarter[s] was very experienced in ES implementation after undertaking many projects in other sites. Leaving the project to them was the best choice for us.

With the lack of top management involvement, MEM lost the chance to study the feasibility of copying all business processes from headquarters, as commented by one manager:

Some of the new business processes did not suit our division. I think it would be very helpful if our boss discussed with the Expert Team and got them (business processes) modified... Well, the processes implemented were so alien to us.

Organizational Structure and Culture

MEM was organized as a matrix with control coming directly from the General Manager. It had a particularly competitive culture. The employees' career path was "up or out". The turnover rate was higher than other companies in the same industry. So the employees needed to focus on excelling themselves individually. The working relationship was described as "more competitive than cooperative" by one manager.

This culture made employees concerned about what they talked about and made them unwilling to share their ideas freely. When the General Manager called for meetings after realizing the lack of knowledge overlapping and mutual understanding of business practices, the participants chose to be silent most of the time, as described by the General Manager:

I really didn't know what went wrong. They simply didn't want to share their ideas openly. If I was in the meeting, I would lead the discussion and they would talk. But without my presence, the meetings were so silent. But I was too busy to attend all their meetings.

In addition, a manager explained to us:

Some managers didn't get along well and were afraid of being backstabbed. So they wouldn't talk freely. Even with [the] General Manager's presence, they chose to avoid critical problems existing in their departments... Also, some of us just didn't feel like sharing what we had learned with each other, since our exclusive possession of knowledge made us valuable to the firm.

Due to the limited information distribution and little information interpretation, there was insufficient organizational memory to guide ES application. Humans were the main organizational learning carriers in MEM, especially the mid-level managers. In addition, the business process changes were not followed by corresponding organizational structure changes. MEM ended up having a function-oriented, organizational structure and process-oriented, business practices. This situation, coupled with insufficient understanding of business practices across the organization, caused confusion about job specification of posts spanning functional units.

To summarize our research findings described in the previous sections, we present the major differences between organizational factors (Table 2) and the organizational learning processes enacted in CPM and MEM ES implementation (Table 3).

These differences between the organizational learning processes enacted in ES implementation by CPM and MEM caused significant different implementation outcomes, though both firms managed to get the system implemented within budget and on-time. We categorized these outcomes into the following: further business process refinement, users' capability to apply the system effectively and appropriately, more effective and efficient

Table 2. Differences of organizational factors in CPM and MEM

Organizational Factor	CPM	MEM
ES Adoption Vision	Transform	Informate up
Advocacy of ES Vision	Strong advocacy across the firm	Limited dissemination
Top Management Involvement	Actively participated in key decision making	Left the decisions to the Expert Team from HQ
Administrative Structure Support	Steering and Working Committees and Functional Groups	No formal structure at MEM side
Control Scheme	Strict rules on the assignment jobs related with ES	No control scheme
Organizational Structure and Culture	Cohesive and trusting	Competitive and mistrusting
Employee's Attitude	Enthusiastic	Resistant and suspicious

Table 3. Differences between organizational learning in CPM and MEM ES implementation

Org. Learning Sub-Process	CPM	MEM
Knowledge Acquisition	- System knowledge and process-oriented methodology were acquired from the consultants - Business process status quo was acquired from organizational memory	- System knowledge and new standardized business process information were acquired from experts at headquarters
Information Distribution	- System configuration information was distributed to the IT group and power users in every business unit - System operation knowledge was distributed to all end users - Information about business processes was shared among business units	- System operation knowledge and information about business processes were distributed to the relevant mid-level managers by the experts - Mid-level managers passed what
Information Interpretation	- Function groups and the working committee worked together to streamline the business process, focusing on the activities spanning departmental boundaries and non-routine practices	- Little information interpretation during ES implementation
Organizational Memory	- All information related to the project was documented in computer-based repositories - Standard system operation manuals were compiled - Humans were certified and became organizational memory carriers	- Humans were the main organizational memory carriers -System configuration files were archived

departmental coordination, better decision making, solid organizational memory, and enhanced business performance. To avoid the complexity of presentation, we list our findings one by one, following the order of the earlier-mentioned aspects of implementation outcomes.

ES Implementation Outcomes in CPM

1. By implementing ES, CPM managers learned to evaluate different business practices by analyzing the efficiency and effectiveness of business processes. The group and committee members learned process-oriented methodology, thus they were able to change business processes without the help from the consultant after the system went live. According to the Senior VP in Marketing, "we now have a team to keep studying our business processes and continuously refine them. I think this is the most important gain from ES project."
2. The end users and power users mastered system knowledge. End users were effective in interacting with the system. The firm did not run into any chaos due to end users' operation mistakes. In addition, power users were able to reconfigure the system to cater for the requirements of ad hoc events and new business processes.
3. By solving many problems together throughout the ES implementation project, managers knew each other better and established a more trusting relationship. This relationship, coupled with their knowledge about business practices across the whole organization, made inter-departmental coordination more effective and efficient.
4. With real-time operational data stored in the central database, the management was able to make more informed decisions and respond to market changes more swiftly.
5. With many different types of organizational memory carriers and overlapping knowledge among employees, the firm was able to maintain its organizational memory integrity when some key players left for ES consulting jobs.

6. With the support of ES, the amount of bad debts was reduced by four million U.S. dollars in the year 2002. In addition, the firm succeeded in getting around the dealership and set up their own distribution channel across the country. As described by the Senior VP of Marketing:

Without the ES, it wouldn't be possible for us to manage the inventory across thc country on our own. By getting rid of the dealership, our profit margin was increased significantly.

ES Implementation Outcomes in MEM

1. There was insufficient understanding of business processes among managers. Since the business processes implemented in the system were straightforward to the Expert Team, they were not aware of the necessity of sharing the rationales for these business practices with MEM managers. This caused managers' incapability in handling ad hoc events and system errors. Thus, MEM had to turn to the Expert Team at headquarters whenever problems arose. But being located in different time zones, a difference of 13 hours, MEM couldn't get a response from the experts promptly. The efficiency promised by the ES system was greatly comprised.
2. End users could not interact with the system appropriately. The central database was often corrupted by individuals' mistaken operation. Due to the lack of knowledge about the inter-relationship between different modules, they did not take action to inform related parties of these errors immediately. This allowed the mistakes to cascade across the whole system and caused operation and manufacturing disruptions. Eight months after the within-budget and on-time implementation of the ES, MEM kept experiencing difficulties and encountered problems with this system. MEM had to limit the access privilege of most users or simply switch to manual operation for some processes.
3. With the lack of common understanding of how jobs were done across departmental boundaries, inter-departmental coordination was chaotic and relationships between some managers became distrustful.
4. Since the central database was often corrupted, managers could not make decisions based on these data. Also, since MEM abandoned the old system after ES went live, the managerial decision making could not receive the right data support for months.
5. MEM also suffered a loss of organizational memory due to the leaving of some key end users and managers. Due to the limited information distribution and little information interpretation throughout the ES project, the manager became the single carrier of knowledge transferred by the Expert Team. This knowledge structure made MEM vulnerable to personnel turnovers.
6. The operation cost was increased rather than decreased, due to the end users' inappropriate interactions with the system. For example, its inventory cost was increased by two million U.S. dollars in 2003.

The major differences between these two firm's ES implementation outcomes can be summarized by Table 4.

Developed from these two organizations' experiences, the process of organizational learning in ES implementation can be described with a model (Figure 1). This model shows the major organizational factors that emerged as salient from our data analysis. Also, it encompasses how these organizational factors affect the four constructs of organizational learning. This process is proposed as an initial formulation of the key concepts and interactions that portray organizational learning in ES implementation. No claim is made that the concepts and interactions presented here are exhaustive. Further organizational learning studies on ES implementation should modify or extend the ideas presented here.

In this model, the four organizational learning constructs are influenced by organizational factors as follows:

A. Influenced by environmental and organizational contexts, the top management formulates ES vision. Guided by this vision, the organization decides the amount of resources to be committed to the project, which leads to different ways of knowledge acquisition. The knowledge acquired directly affects the amount of knowledge that is distributed in the organization.

B. The organization takes action to distribute knowledge to its relevant employees. This sub-process is influenced by advocacy of ES vision, top management's involvement, and the control scheme mediated by employees' motivation to receive and capture knowledge. The end users' learning experiences either reinforce or change their perception about ES adoption, which in turn influences their learning motivation. On the other hand, the breadth and depth of information distribution influences information interpretation.

C. Top management's involvement, the administrative structure, and organizational culture, trust in particular, decide the effectiveness and outcomes of information interpretation. The interaction process in information interpretation may affect organizational culture.

D. With top management involvement, the consensus on business practices implemented in ES (the result of information interpretation) was institutionalized and became organizational memory. Employees equipped with ES knowledge (the result of information distribution) are another type of ES knowledge carrier. The knowledge in organizational memory can be brought forth, affecting future learning and affecting the organization.

Table 4. Differences of implementation outcomes in CPM and MEM

Implementation Outcomes	CPM	MEM
Relationship between business units	Trusting and valuing each other	Distrustful and competitive
Inter-department coordination	Became more effective and efficient	Coordination was difficult due to lack of business practice knowledge
Managerial decision making	Got timely and accurate information support	Couldn't use the information due to the inaccuracy of data
Loss due to employee turnover	Did not lose organizational memory	Big loss of organizational memory due to resignation of some key mid-level managers
End user's interaction with the system	Effective and appropriate	Their mistakes caused manufacturing and operation disruption
Capability to deal with ad hoc events	Could handle special events without help from consultant	Must turn to experts at HQ
Significant impact on business performance	Decreased bad debts by about 4 million USD in 2002 and set up distribution channels without new hiring	Inventory cost increased by about 2 million USD in 2003

Figure 1. Organizational factors affecting organizational learning in ES implementation

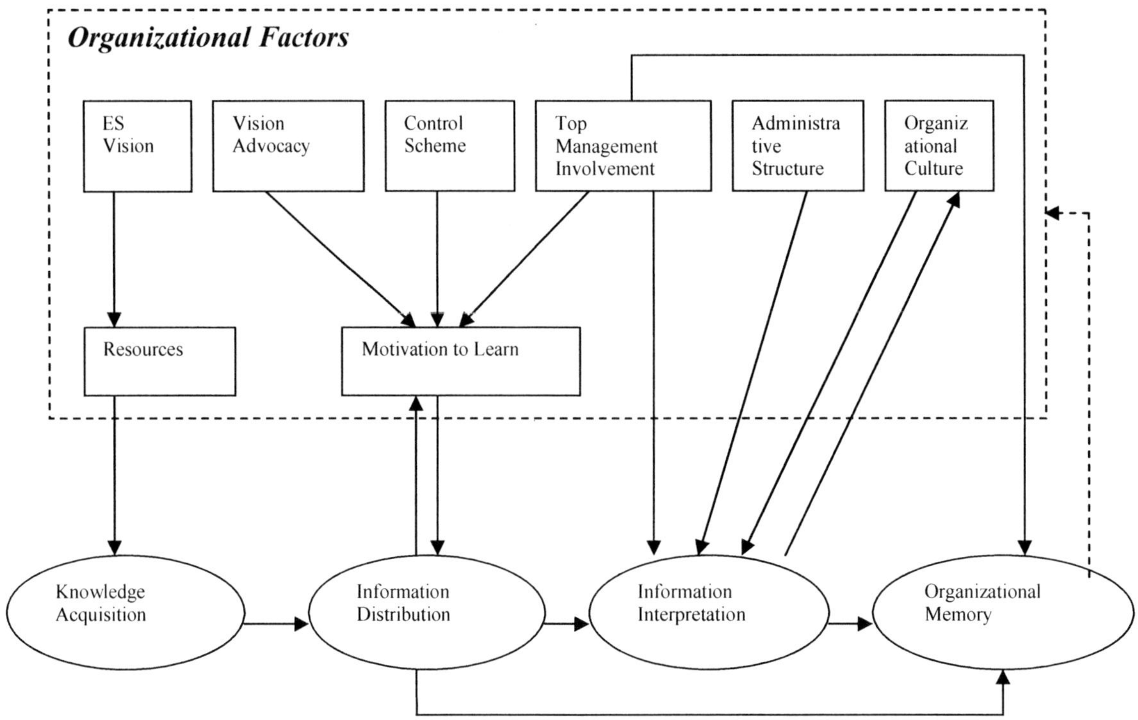

DISCUSSION AND CONCLUSION

While CPM and MEM both implemented ES on-time and within budget, their implementation outcomes differ significantly. The comparative analysis method, which allows contrasting CPM with MEM on a common set of concepts, suggests that these differences can be attributed to variations in the organizational learning process which was affected by organizational factors including the firm's ES vision, organizational culture, the ad hoc administrative structure for ES adoption, employees' motivation to learn ES, leaders' advocacy of ES vision, the top management's involvement, and control scheme. To enhance the internal validity and generality of theory building from this case study, we tie our findings to existing literature (Eisenhardt, 1989).

First, the attitude of the organization's "power elites" is important for ES implementation outcomes. Institutional leadership goes to the essence of the process of institutionalization, concurring with Armstrong and Sambamurthy's (1999) findings. It is particularly needed for ES implementation, which represents a transition to alternative ways of getting jobs done across the whole organization. The central responsibility of the top management is to ensure individuals and the organization as a whole learn how to apply ES effectively. This responsibility can be carried out through four key functions: advocacy of ES vision, personal involvement in the learning, setting up formal communication channels, and ordering internal conflicts.

Second, the firm's IT vision affects the amount of resources dedicated to the organizational learning in ES implementation. Firms with transformative IT vision would treat ES adoption as an investment and devote adequate resources to the project. In contrast, the firm with the vision of "automate" or "informate up" would try to minimize the cost of ES adoption (Scott-Morton, 1991). Thus, the vision about ES adoption affects organizational learning, mediated by the resources dedicated to the project.

Third, effective learning depends on a culture of openness, mutual trust, and a self-critical disposition. Consistent with the literature of organizational learning and learning in information system development, the accessibility to expertise and trusting working environment help the business units and individuals overcome learning anxiety and learn faster (Schein, 1993; Wastell, 1999). Anxiety and uncertainty about sharing "private" knowledge lead to the avoidance of authentic engagement in identifying and solving substantive problems.

Fourth, knowledge structure characterized by extensive knowledge overlaps, and information exchange among managers is important for successful ES implementation outcomes. The information exchange enriches organizational knowledge structure and consequently enhances the firm's absorptive capacity (Boynton et al., 1994; Cohen & Levinthal, 1990; Purvis et al., 2001). In turn, such knowledge and enhanced absorptive capacity enable rich dialogues among managers through which truly innovative ES applications arise (Lind & Zmud, 1991; Watson, 1990). Also, know-how and know-why about the innovation should be distributed to system users. Transferring why and how knowledge to the end users can instill confidence and a sense of control, which helps users to deal with ad hoc events.

In order to ensure that the study's results can be placed in an appropriate context as well as to enable future research, it is important to examine the limitations of this study. First, we neglect the socialization of the learning process from the individual to the organizational level, which might offer insights into how the learning process can be correctly managed. Second, both organizations we conducted the study with are in a culture of high collectivism. Some strategic conducts applicable in this culture might not be appropriate for another culture. Future research on the issues we do not address in this chapter can extend our understanding of organizational learning in ES implementation.

REFERENCES

Al-Mashari, M., & Zairi, M. (2000). The effective application of SAP R/3: A proposed model of best practice. *Logistics Information Management, 13*(3), 156-166.

Argyris, C., & Schon, D. (1978). *Organizational learning: A theory of action research.* Reading, MA: Addison-Wesley.

Armstrong, C. P., & Sambamurthy, V. (1999). Information technology assimilation in firms: The influence of senior leadership and IT infrastructures. *Information Systems Research, 10*(4), 304-327.

Attewell, P. (1992). Technology diffusion and organizational learning: The case of business computing. *Organization Science, 3*(1), 1-19.

Bingi, P., Sharma, M. K., & Godla, J. (1999). Critical issues affecting an ERP implementation. *Information Systems Management, 16*(3), 7-14.

Boynton, A. C., Zmud, R. W., & Jacobs, G. C. (1994, September). The influence of IT management practice on IT use in large organizations. *MIS Quarterly, 18*(3), 299.

Ciborra, C. U., & Lanzara, G. F. (1994). Formative contexts and information technology: Understanding the dynamics of innovation in organizations.

Accounting, Management and Information Technology 4(2), 61-86.

Cohen, W. M., & Levinthal, D. A. (1990). Absorptive capacity: A new perspective on learning and innovation. *Administrative Science Quarterly, 35*(1), 128-125.

Cooper, R. B., & Zmud, R. W. (1990, February). Information technology implementation research: A technological diffusion approach. *Management Science, 36*(2), 123.

Daft, R. L., & Weick, K. E. (1984). Toward a model of organizations as interpretation systems. *Academy of Management Review, 9*(2), 284.

Davenport, T. H. (1998). Putting the enterprise into the enterprise system. *Harvard Business Review, 76*(4), 121-131.

Eisenhardt, K. M. (1989, October). Building theories from case study research. *Academy of Management Review, 14*(4), 532-550.

Eisenhardt, K. M., & Bourgeois, L. J. I. (1988, December). Politics of strategic decision making in high-velocity Envi. *Academy of Management Journal, 31*(4), 734-737.

Feeny, D. F., & Willcocks, L. P. (1998). Core IS capabilities for exploiting information technology. *Sloan Management Review, 39*(3), 9-21.

Fichman, R. G., & Kemerer, C. F. (1997, October). The assimilation of software process innovations: An organizational learning perspective. *Management Science, 43*(10), 1345-1363.

Fiol, C. M., & Lyles, M. A. (1985, October). Organizational learning. *Academy of Management Review,* 10, 803.

Glaser, B. G., & Strauss, A. L. (1967). *The discovery of grounded theory: Strategies for qualitative research.* New York: Aldine Publishing.

Holland, C. P., & Light, B. (1999). A critical success factors model for ERP implementation. *IEEE Software,* May/June, 30-36.

Huber, G. P. (1991). Organizational learning: The contributing processes and the literatures. *Organization Science, 2*(1), 88-115.

Lind, M. R., & Zmud, R. W. (1991). The influence of a convergence in understanding between technology providers and users on information technology innovativenss. *Organization Science, 2*(2), 195-217.

Lyytinen, K., & Robey, D. (1999). Learning failure in information systems development. *Information Systems Journal,* 9, 85-101.

Maltz, E., & Kohli, A. K. (1995). Market intelligence dessemination across functional boundaries. *Journal of Marketing Research, 33*(1), 47.

Parr, A., & Shanks, G. (2000, December). A model of ERP project implementation. *Journal of Information Technology, 15*(4), 289-303.

Pentland, B. T. (1995). Information systems and organizational learning: The social epistemology of organizational knowledge systems. *Accounting, Management, and Information Technologies, 5*(1), 1-21.

Pettigrew, A. (1995). Longitudinal field research on change: Theory and practice. In G. P. Huber & A. H. Van de Ven (Eds.), *Longitudinal field research methods: Studying processes of organizational change* (p. 91). Thousand Oaks, CA: Sage.

Purvis, R. L., Sambamurthy, V., & Zmud, R. W. (2001, March/April). The assimilation of knowledge platforms in organizations: An empirical investigation. *Organization Science, 12*(2), 117-135.

Robey, D., Ross, J. W., & Boudreau, M. C. (2002, Summer). Learning to implement enterprise systems: An exploratory study of the dialectics of change. *Journal of Management Information Systems, 19*(1), 17-46.

Sambamurthy, V., Bharadwah, A., & Grover, V. (2003). Shaping agility through digital options: Reconceptualizing the role of information technology in contemporary firms. *MIS Quarterly, 27*(2), 237-263.

Sarker, S., & Lee, A. S. (2003). Using a case study to test the role of three key social enablers in ERP implementation. *Information & Management, 40*(8), 813.

Schein, E. H. (1993). How can organizations learn faster? The challenge of entering the green room. *Sloan Management Review, 34*(2), 85-92.

Scott, J. E., & Vessey, I. (2000). Implementing enterprise resource planning systems: The role of learning from failure. *Information Systems Frontiers, 2*(2), 213-232.

Scott-Morton, M. S. (1991). IT-induced business reconfiguration. In M. S. Scott-Morton (Ed.), *The corporation of the 1990s: Information technology and organizational transformation* (pp. 3-23). Oxford: Oxford University Press.

Sethi, V., & King, W. R. (1994). Development of measures to assess the extent to which an information technology application provides competitive advantage. *Management Science, 14*(2), 1601-1627.

Slater, S. F., & Narver, J. C. (1995). Market orientation and the learning organization. *Journal of Marketing, 59*(3), 63.

Sumner, M. (2000, December). Risk factors in enterprise-wide/ERP projects. *Journal of Information Technology, 15*(4), 317-327.

Tippins, M. J., & Sohi, R. S. (2003). IT competency and firm performance: Is organizational learning a missing link? *Strategic Management Journal, 24*(8), 745.

Walsh, J. P., & Ungson, G. R. (1991). Organizational memory. *Academy of Management Review, 16*(1), 57-91.

Wastell, D. (1999). Learning dysfunction in information systems development: Overcoming the social defenses with transitional objectives. *MIS Quarterly, 23*(4), 581-600.

Watson, R. T. (1990). Influences on the IS manager's perceptions of key issues: Information scanning and the relationship with the CEO. *MIS Quarterly, 14*(2), 217.

Yin, R. K. (1994). *Case study research: Design and methods.* Thousand Oaks, CA: Sage Publications.

This work was previously published in Journal of Global Information Management, Vol. 14, Issue 1, edited by F. Tan, pp. 1-22, copyright 2006 by IGI Publishing, formerly known as Idea Group Publishing (an imprint of IGI Global).

Chapter XVI
The Role of Organizational, Environmental, and Human Factors in E-Learning Diffusion

Kholekile L. Gwebu
University of New Hampshire, USA

Jing Wang
Kent State University, USA

ABSTRACT

Improvements in technology have led to innovations in training such as Electronic Learning (E-learning). E-learning aims to help organizations in their training initiatives by simplifying the training process and cutting cost. It also attempts to help employees in their learning processes by making learning readily accessible. Unfortunately, the diffusion of this innovation has not been as successful as was initially predicted. In this article we explore the drivers behind the diffusion of e-learning. Apart from the factors investigated by previous research, we believe that one more dimension—human factors—should be taken into account when evaluating the diffusion of a training innovation, since learners are, to a large extent, the central issue of training. In the case of e-learning we believe that motivation plays a key role in the diffusion of e-learning.

INTRODUCTION

With the rapid improvement in technology and the growing demand for a knowledge- based labor force, the demand for e-learning has grown considerably over the past few years. E-learning has provided organizations and employees with tremendous advantages over traditional training (Li & Lau, 2006). It transcends the limitation of time and space and has been reported to provide companies with time and cost saving benefits in the long run (Li & Lau, 2006; Ong, Lai, & Yishun, 2004; Zhang, 2004). In a recent report, Deloitte and Touche (2002) spell out some of the major advantages of e-learning including: increased volume of training, geographic distribution and reusability of content. E-learning gives organizations the ability to simultaneously train a larger percentage of employees than does traditional classroom-based training as employees can be trained anytime from anywhere. Moreover, it permits large dispersed organizations to train all their employees with homogeneous content. This is extremely useful for organizations that want to ensure that employees gain standardized skills and knowledge. Furthermore, it has the power to bring people together for collaborative learning (Zhang & Nunamaker, 2003).

Along with its unique advantages, the improvements in technology have also facilitated the adoption and implementation of e-learning. The wide accessibility of the internet, increased bandwidth, better delivery platforms, and the growing selection of high-quality e-learning products have all added to the feasibility and attractiveness of e-learning (McCrea, Gay, & Bacon, 2000). The strategic importance of e-learning is real and many companies have been investing heavily in this education sector (Huynh, Umesh, & Valacich, 2003). In fact, 95% of the respondents of an American Society for Training and Development survey conducted in 2003 indicated that they had used some form of e-learning in their organizations (Renée, Barbara, & Eduardo, 2005) . However, many e-learning initiatives are not living up to initial expectations. According to a study done by the Silicon Valley World Internet Center on corporate e-learning (Duggan & Barich, 2001), out of 44 respondents, only 21% indicated a very high level of executive confidence in e-learning; 58% regarded top management confidence as moderate, 15% unknown and 6% as very low. Additionally, a number of studies have suggested that a large number of e-learning initiatives fail (Hamid, 2001). Such findings have spurred research which attempts to identify factors which contribute to the success of e-learning.

One research stream has primarily focused on the effect of technology on the success of e-learning. Researchers have indicated that text-based e-learning systems tend to make learners disengaged and have proposed the use of different multimedia systems in e-learning (Merchant, Kreie, & Cronan, 2001; Zhang, 2004). Prototype systems that are multimedia integrated are also developed and tested to demonstrate the important role of technology in e-learning (Sampson, Karagiannidis, & Cardinali, 2002; Zhang, 2004). Although such studies have improved our understanding of the alignment between different technologies and e-learners, they remain hampered by one major limitation: they adopt a technological deterministic view and postulate direct links between technology and e-learning success. By its very nature, such an approach propagates technological materialism and amplifies technology specifics. Human action, interpretation, and organizational and environmental contexts play little role in this stream of research. Hence, this approach provides relatively little detail about the organizational contexts and human action that shape the observed e-learning outcome. Such a materialistic view diminishes the importance of human agency, organizational structures, and complex social environments and falls short in explaining why identical e-learning technologies succeed in some organizations but fail in others.

Hence, an adequate understanding of the factors that facilitate the success of corporate e-learning requires a more balanced view which does not privilege technology over human agency and the social context (Bruckman, 2002). Another research stream has challenged the technological deterministic view and has focused on the social aspects of e-learning. A number of studies have examined the way in which organizational culture (Harreld, 1998; Nurmi, 1999), the trainers (Chute, Thompson, & Hancock, 1999; Wagner & Reddy, 1987), and differences in individual training styles (Clariana, 1997; Cohen, 1997) influence e-learning initiatives. Although this body of literature has the potential to offer a richer understanding of the role of social forces in e-learning, it tends to employ a uni-dimensional approach, isolating the influence of human agency from the influence of organizational structures on e-learning. Following the second stream of research, this study challenges the determinist view of technology and focuses on the social factors facilitating the success of e-learning. However, it differs from prior work in that it postulates that both human agency (the e-learners) and the organizational context play an important role in the outcome of corporate e-learning initiatives. Focusing on only one dimension provides only part of the story. Therefore, the goal of this study is to develop an integrated conceptual model that explains the influences of both the organizational and the human factors on the successful diffusion of e-learning in contemporary corporations. While various organizational and individual factors can be explored, we limit the scope of our conceptualization to two organizational factors and one individual factor: organizational complexity, bureaucratic control, and motivation. Our proposed conceptual model emerges at the crossroads of four areas of inquiry: e-learning, motivation, the innovation diffusion literature, and technology-related changes. Research in technology-related organizational changes provides an overview of the limitations of the technological deterministic perspective in explaining the outcome of e-learning initiatives. The e-learning, motivation, and innovation diffusion literature helps us conceptualize the relationship between the identified organizational and individual factors and the success of e-learning.

The rest of the paper is organized as follows. The next section defines major terms used throughout the paper in order to eliminate ambiguity which may arise from differences in terminology. This is largely due to the vast number of definitions that have emerged from different fields of study over the years. A literature review on e-learning, innovation, and motivation is then conducted, followed by a set of propositions. In the methodology section of the paper, we describe the manner in which a pilot study is conducted. Subsequently, we present our findings and engage in discussion of the results of the study. Finally, conclusions are drawn from the result analysis, a discussion of the limitations of this study is presented, and areas of future research are proposed.

DEFINITIONS

E-Learning

Over the years the term "e-learning" has been used and interpreted in many different ways in the literature. Some authors use it to refer to the use of any form of electronic learning tool such as radio, television, or computers, to deliver learning materials. Urdan and Weggen (2000) describe e-learning as "the delivery of content via all electronic media, including the internet, intranets, extranets, satellite broadcast, audio/videotape, interactive TV and CD-ROM" .They also use the term synonymously with technology-based learning.

In this paper we will use the term e-learning to refer to two forms of contemporary learning. These include Web-based and computer-based learning. Web-based learning represents learning conducted via the Internet or an Intranet or Extranets or a combination of all three. Computer-based learning on the other hand only includes learning which utilizes CD-ROM or other training technology on a stand alone personal computer.

Diffusion

Rogers (1995) described the diffusion of innovations as "the process by which an innovation is communicated through certain channels over time among members of a social system". Based on this definition, the major players in any innovation diffusion process should be the participants, also referred by Roger as adopters. This has lead to many researchers and practitioners using the "number" of adopters as a measure of successful diffusion. However, research in information systems and organizational change has long suggested that adoption differs from the real usage of a technology. Using only the number of adopters as the measure of e-learning diffusion success neglects one important principle of e-learning—its goal is to enable organizations to enhance their effectiveness and competitive position (Phillips, 1997). Therefore, rather than solely considering the number of adopters as the indicator of success, we use a perceptional measure, in other words, managers' perception of how successful the companies' e-learning initiative is, as an indicator for the success of e-learning diffusion.

LITERATURE REVIEW

The literature is examined in three distinct sections: (1) e-learning, (2) innovation theories, and (3) motivation theories. The purpose is to first investigate the research that been done in these three fields then to explore how innovation, motivation and e-learning interact in an organizational context.

E-Learning

With its increasing popularity and strategic importance, e-learning has received ample attention both from practitioners and scholars. In the industry, companies have and continue to invest heavily and deploy various technologies including learning management systems, learning content management systems, and reusable learning objects. In the academia, a considerable number of studies have investigated the effects of different technologies on e-learning outcomes. For examples, some studies have examined the effects of text-based systems versus multimedia systems on e-learning success (Merchant et al., 2001; Zhang, 2004). Different prototypes and architectures have also been developed in order to improve the outcome of e-learning (Sampson et al., 2002; Zhang, 2004).

Although technology plays an important role in e-learning, one should not presume that if a learning system is built, learners will quickly begin to use it. Studies primarily focusing on the materialistic attributes of e-learning systems assume technology to be an objective, external, and independent force that has relatively deterministic impact on e-learning outcomes. Such studies yield seemingly universal claims as "introduction of good e-learning technology will lead to more successful diffusion of e-learning." But as management in many organizations has discovered, the availability of sophisticated e-learning technologies does not guarantee success (Servage, 2005) and a large number of organizational e-learning endeavors failed in the past (Hamid, 2001). A major concern with the deterministic view of technology is that it downplays the role of human action, interpretation, and organizational and environmental contexts in e-learning and provides little insight into how e-learning success is shaped by such social forces. Such a view is insufficient in explaining why identical e-learning technologies yield divergent outcomes in different organizations.

Researchers in information technologies and organizational studies have long pointed out that an identical technology can be enacted differently in different organizational context (Boudreau & Robey, 2005; Orlikowski, 1992, 1993). They adopt a less deterministic view and propose that both human agency and the social context within which a technology operates play an important role in the outcome of the technology. Similar arguments can be made in the case of e-leaning. Adopting this less deterministic view, a number of studies have focused on the social aspects e-learning. For instance, Harreld (1998) pointed out that it is prohibitive for management to impose new technology and management process changes in an organization where the organization culture is not ready to embrace the changes. Other researchers shift their focus from the organization aspect to the human aspect of e-learning. They address this issue by tackling the trainer's role or individual training styles. They accentuate that to ensure the successful implementation of e-learning, trainers should assume different roles in e-training to those they typically assume when they engage in classroom-based training. Typical additional roles include instructional designer, instructional developer, materials supporter, technology supporter, facility supporter, and distance-site facilitator (Abernathy, 1998; Chute et al., 1999).

Another school of researchers attempts to identify the role of individual learning styles on the effectiveness of e-learning. For example, Clariana (1997) use Kolb, Rubin, and McIntyre's (1979) Learning Style Inventory (LSI) to study training styles in Computer Assisted Learning (CAL). He found that learning style dimensions shifted after a certain period of exposure to CAL. The degree of the shift varies with a learner's ability and the length and extent of exposure to CAL. However, another study done by Cohen (1997) did not reveal a learning style shift after one year of exposure to CAL. Other studies also have mixed results. Gunawardena and Boverie (1992) found that there was no significant correlation between learning style and how students interact with media and methods of instruction, but a correlation did exist between learning style and students' satisfaction. However, Larsen (1992) concluded from her study that both effectiveness and satisfaction are independent of students' learning styles.

While this stream of research has shed valuable insights into some of the social factors that may contribute to the successful implementation of e-learning in organizations, one limitation is that they only focus on a single dimension at a time, isolating the role of organizational factors from that of the human agents. This one-dimensional approach fails to reflect the complexity of reality and may also partly explain their inconsistent results. This paper proposes an integrated model that incorporates different dimensions—organizational structure, environmental factors and human factors (motivation in particular) and provides an in-depth theoretical discuss on how those dimensions work together to influence the diffusion of e-learning.

CONCEPTUAL FOUNDATION

To identify organizational factors that may contribute to the successful diffusion of e-learning, we draw on the rich stream of research on diffusion of innovation. As we limit the scope of our conceptualization to one human factor, in other words, motivation, literature on motivation will be used as the foundation for our theoretical discussion of the relationship between individual motivation and e-learning success.

Innovation

Innovation literature is broad and diverse. According to Wolfe (1994), during the five years foregoing his study on organization innovation, 351 dissertations and 1299 journal articles addressing organizational innovation were written. The most basic questions at the heart of most researchers in the field of innovation adoption and diffusion are questions such as "What organizational structures and management processes facilitate or inhibit innovation?" and "Why are some organizations more innovative than others?"(Damanpour, 1991; Fichman, 2001, 2004). Researchers have also attempted to answer questions such as "Why do certain innovations diffuse successfully in certain organizations and not in others?"(Chen, 1983; Fichman, 2001, 2004). E-learning can be conceptualized as an innovation in learning and the rich innovation literature furnishes conceptual tools that aid in the identification of key organizational factors that may contribute to the success of e-learning diffusion.

Organizational Structural Theories

Extant literature on innovation is replete with hypotheses, models, and theories that seek to identify organizational structural factors that facilitate the diffusion of innovations. The theories can all be categorized under the umbrella term Organizational Structural Theories. Structural theories have evolved over the years from uni-dimensional to middle-range theories. As explained by Damanpour and Gopalakrishan (1998), uni-dimensional theories use organization structural variables such as vertical differentiation (the number of levels in an organization hierarchy) to explain innovation adoption and diffusion. For instance, some researchers posit that vertical differentiation is negatively associated with innovation adoption and diffusion as it increases links in communication channels, thereby inhibiting the flow of innovative ideas (Damanpour & Gopalakrishnan, 1998; Hull & Hage, 1982). Other variables which are commonly considered in these theories are: functional differentiation (the number of different functional units in an organization), specialization (different areas of expertise in an organization), professionalism (professional knowledge including employees' education and experience), formalization (the degree to which rules and procedures are followed in an organization), and centralization (whether decision making is centralized or distributed) (Damanpour, 1987).

One limitation with uni-dimensional theories is that they neglect other dimensions and do not reflect the complexity of the real world (Damanpour & Gopalakrishnan, 1998). Researchers also criticize them due to the inconsistencies between their prediction and the results gathered from empirical studies (Downs & Mohr, 1976). This limitation in uni-dimensional theories leads to the development of Middle- range theories.

Middle range structural theories incorporate other contingency factors as an explanation of the contradictory findings in prior work. Examples of middle range structure theories include the dual core theory, which focuses on differentiation between types of innovation (Daft, 1978; Damanpour, 1991), the theory of innovation radicalness which examines incremental versus radical innovations (Dewar & Dutton, 1986), the ambidextrous theory of innovation which focuses on the various stages of the innovation process (Damanpour & Gopalakrishnan, 1998; Zmud, 1982). These theories postulate that the relationship between organization structural variables studied by uni-dimensional theories and diffusion of innovation is contingent on the different types of innovation, or radicalness of innovation, or stages of innovation.

In the following section, we will only examine the ambidextrous theory in greater detail. This is because depending on the organization using e-learning, it could be categorized as either an administrative innovation or a technical innovation, or it could be categorized as either a radical innovation or an incremental innovation. This relativity in categorization has made the findings in the dual-core theory and radicalness theory of little value to our study. The ambidextrous theory on the other hand, is of more interest to us since there is no relativity regarding two stages of e-learning innovation. The ambidextrous theory categorizes organizational innovation into two distinct stages, the initiation stage and the implementation stage (Duncan, 1976). The initiation stage consists of all the activities pertaining to problem perception, information gathering, attitude formation and resource development leading to the decision to adopt (Rogers, 1995). This is synonymous with the term adoption which we use in this paper. The implementation stage is composed of all events and actions relating to change in both the innovation and the organization (Duncan, 1976; Rogers, 1995). This stage also incorporates the diffusion of innovation.

The ambidextrous theory explores the relationship between organization structural variables and the two stages of the adoption process. Based on its finding, high organization complexity (specialization, functional differentiation, and professionalism) and low bureaucratic control (formalization, centralization, and vertical differentiation) facilitate the adoption of an innovation, while low complexity and high bureaucratic control facilitate the diffusion of innovations (Damanpour & Gopalakrishnan, 1998).

Uni-dimensional theories suggest that organizational complexity is positively related to innovation adoption and diffusion whereas the degree of bureaucratic in an organization is negatively associated with innovation adoption and diffusion (Damanpour & Gopalakrishnan, 1998). When applied to e-learning, this would mean that organizations with high organization complexity should expect e-learning to be adopted and diffused while in organizations with a high level of bureaucratic control adoption and diffusion are unlikely.

The ambidextrous theory adds one more dimension (stages of innovation) to the uni-dimensional theory. Besides pointing out that organization complexity has a positive effect while bureaucratic control has a negative impact on both the adoption and diffusion of innovation, the ambidextrous theory also examines the correlation between structural variables and the two stages of innovation. According to the theory, the correlation between organization complexity and initiation of innovation is high while the correlation between organization complexity and diffusion is low. On the other hand, the correlation between organization bureaucracy and initiation of innovation is low while the correlation between bureaucracy and diffusion of innovation is high (Damanpour, 1991).

As seen in the above discussion, uni-dimensional as well as middle-range structural theories of innovation usually aim to specify organizational structural characteristics that lead to the adoption and diffusion of innovation. However, most results from empirical studies using structural theories tend to conflict (Damanpour, 1991). The problem with these theories is that they do not take into account other variables such as the business environment and human factors when attempting to explain how innovations diffuse into an organization.

Other Dimensions

Environmental Dimension

To explain the variance between the findings in empirical studies conducted using middle-range theories, innovation scholars have attempted to develop more sophisticated and more comprehensive models, which take into consideration multiple dimensions of innovation. For example, Damanpour and Gopalakrishnan (1998) added the environmental context into their framework to investigate how organizational structures and environmental factors influence the adoption of innovation. Damanpour and Gopalakrishnan focus on the dynamism of the environment and further classify environmental dynamism into two components: environmental stability and environmental predictability. These two components have resulted in four combinations of environment characteristics: stable and predictable, stable and unpredictable, unstable and predictable, unstable and unpredictable. They argue that organizations in environments which are stable and predictable tend to adopt few innovations slowly in contrast to organizations in environments which are unstable and unpredictable. Additionally, organizations in both unstable and unpredictable environments tend to have cultivated a culture of innovation. Employees in such organizations are continuously encouraged to make use of new innovations and to be creative. Moreover, the organizational structure, culture, and administrative system encourage employees to be innovative and also make use of innovations. Thus, when it comes to innovations such as e-learning one would expect that organizations in an environment characterized by instability and unpredictability, most members would have at some point experimented with e-learning packages. However, the sustained use of this innovation would largely be dependent on the human factors which are discussed below.

Human Factors

Although organization structural variables and the environment provide important insights into various factors which may influence the adoption and in some cases the diffusion of innovations, they cannot fully explain why certain innovations such as e-learning tend to diffuse in some organizations and not in others. We believe that when analyzing the diffusion of innovations that involve the transformation of human resources such as e-learning, human factors need to be taken into consideration. This argument is consistent with the recent development in information systems research and organizational change. While earlier work in these two fields tends to privilege technology over human agency, there is an increasing tendency to emphasize the importance of human agents in enacting technologies (Boudreau & Robey, 2005; Orlikowski, 1992, 1993). This human agency position suggests that individuals do not passively accept and use technology. In contrast, they actively enact technologies in different ways. They can use it minimally, maximally, or improvise in ways that are hard to anticipate. Hence, it stands to reason that human factors should be incorporated in order to have a complete understanding of e-learning success. In particular, we focus on one human factor, motivation. Motivation has been suggested as being one of the key drivers of users' technology acceptance and subsequent usage behavior.

Motivation

Motivation theories seek to identify and explain the factors that influence human behavior, particularly the way in which individuals react to the actions of others around them and the stimuli in their environment (Wilkinson, Orth, & Benfari, 1986). Over the years several general theories on motivation have emerged, the most discussed being Maslow's Hierarchy of Needs theory, Alderfer's ERG Theory, Herzberg's Two Factor Theory and McClelland's Learned Needs Theory.

Motivation theories can be categorized into three broad categories namely, Content Theories, Process Theories, and Reinforcement Theories. Content theories advocate that individuals are motivated to fulfill needs. As stated by Knoop (1994), Content Theories focus on identifying values conducive to, but not necessarily causal to, job satisfaction. Maslow's hierarchy of Needs Theory, Alderfer's ERG Theory and Herzberg's Two-Factor Theory, all fall under the category of content theories. Process theories on the other hand are mainly concerned with explaining the manner in which people think and behave to get what they want. Motivation Theories included under this category include the Equity Theory and the Expectancy Theory. Reinforcement Theories are concerned with the effects of rewards upon motivated behavior. McClelland's Acquired Needs Theory is an example of such a theory. Although these theories differ in how they define motivation, they all agree that if people are not motivated they will not engage in certain behavior.

Drivers of Motivation

Drawing from Motivation Theory we were able to identify two broad drivers of motivation for human behavior, namely, intrinsic motivation and extrinsic motivation. Davis, Bagozzi, and Warshaw (1992) found intrinsic and extrinsic motivation to be key drivers of behavioral intention to use a technology. Vallerand (1997) mentions that intrinsic motivation refers to the pleasure and inherent satisfaction derived from a specific activity. Intrinsic rewards are those that come from the work itself, for instance, the feeling of accomplishment and success one experiences from performing a task they enjoy. Both the nature of the task and the compatibility of the person with the task primarily influence intrinsic rewards. Venkatesh (1999) states that research in psychology advocates that intrinsic motivation during training leads to favorable outcomes. However, individuals tend to determine intrinsic motivation thus organizations cannot have a huge impact on various outcomes determined by intrinsic motivation.

Extrinsic motivation highlights performing a specific behavior in order to achieve a specific goal (Deci & Ryan, 1987). Extrinsic rewards are those that have are not necessarily related to a task, but have strong motivational effects. Examples of these include pay, benefit, and recognition programs, and are influenced primarily by the organization. Organizations may make use of extrinsic rewards to attempt to motivate employees to achieve or perform various tasks and activities.

E-Learning and Motivation

People in organizations differ from one another in their motivation to learn and participate in training programs (Ukens, 2001). Most motivational theories have not been able to agree on whether people are primarily motivated by intrinsic or extrinsic factors. Bruno and Osterloh (2002) argue that intrinsic and extrinsic motivation are interlinked and as such companies cannot opt for one or the other in isolation. It is therefore imperative that both be considered when attempting to assess whether or not employees are motivated to perform certain tasks, in this case e-learning.

Research suggests that motivation in general (whether it is intrinsic or extrinsic) is an important factor driving perceptions and behavior, even in a training context (Bruno & Osterloh, 2002; Pierce & Delbecq, 1977). Compared to traditional classroom-based learning initiatives, corporate e-learning initiatives are particularly susceptible to high dropout rates because participation is typically voluntary and often goes unsupervised. Oftentimes, companies require that e-learning courses be taken outside the work environment during one's own time. However, studies have shown that most employees not only prefer to take e-courses during work hours but they also prefer to take them in the workplace (ASTD, 2006). If employees are not self-motivated to work outside the work environment because they cannot perceive any meaningful benefits to such work, they are likely to drop out of e-learning programs. Previous research has found that individuals tend to persist at activities that are intrinsically motivating (Rieber, 1991). Rosenberg (2001) argues that employees will only embrace learning when they perceive direct relevance and benefit (extrinsic motivation) of the learning program for themselves and when they sense support from the firm. It is therefore imperative that firms understand the factors which motivate employees (such as firm support in terms of time and sponsorship) to engage in e-learning in order to ensure its successful diffusion into the organization.

When applied to the context of e-learning adoption, the theories of motivation are consistent with other technology adoption theories. The Technology Acceptance Model (TAM) proposed by Davis (1989) suggests that when users are presented with a new technology, the factors that influence their decision on whether or not to use it include the perceived usefulness of the innovation, in other words. The degree to which the innovation would enhance that employee's job performance and perceived ease of use, or, the degree to which an employee believes that using a particular innovation would be free of effort. Perceived enjoyment, otherwise known as the extent to which an activity is perceived as being enjoyable in its own right (Davis et al., 1992), has also been found to significantly influence perceived ease of use (Hwang & Yi, 2003). Perceived ease of use of a system and perceived usefulness of the system are both extrinsic motivators whereas the enjoyment derived from using the system is an intrinsic motivator (Igbaria &

Livari, 1995). Therefore, several factors will influence an employee's perception about a particular technology which in turn will influence actual usage of that technology. Together these factors contribute to an employee's motivation to make use of a particular technology.

To this end, we have seen from the literature that organizational structural variables (Daft, 1978; Nord & Tucker, 1987; Zmud, 1982) and the environment (Damanpour & Gopalakrishnan, 1998) in which an organization operates are key drivers of the diffusion of innovations in general. In the case of e-learning however, we believe that human factors such as motivation of people within an organization also plays a critical role in whether or not e-learning will diffuse. If the majority of the employees of an organization do not feel motivated to engage in e-learning, the e-learning initiative of that organization will not diffuse. This leads to our first proposition:

P1. The diffusion of leaning innovations such as e-learning in organizations is not only a function of organizational and environmental factors, but also a function of human factors such as motivation.

Furthermore, we believe that human factors such as motivation may in fact moderate the relationship between organizational and environmental variables and the diffusion of e-learning. We therefore propose that the following:

P2. Human factors such as motivation will moderate the relationship between organizational factors and e-learning diffusion.

P3. Human factors such as motivation will moderate the relationship between environmental factors and e-learning diffusion.

PROPOSED FRAMEWORK

Our proposed framework stems from the above discussion. According to our argument, human factors such as motivation, organizational variables, and the environment all influence e-learning diffusion. The Figure 1 summarizes the proposed relationship between motivation, organizational variables, and environment.

The function in Figure 1 suggests that motivation is a key factor in e-learning diffusion. If employee motivation is low or non existent (zero), then e-learning diffusion will not occur (it will also be zero). However, if organizational structural or structural variables alone are poor/low or zero, diffusion may still occur if motivation is high.

Figure 2 graphically illustrates the propositions presented above. If motivation to engage in e-learning is high among employees and organization structural variables and environmental variable are positive, then successful e-learning diffusion will be highly likely. If motivation is positive but structural and environmental variables are negative, then diffusion is still likely. However, if motivation is low and structural and environmental variables are positive diffusion is unlikely, and if motivation is low and structural and environmental variables are negative then e-learning diffusion will be highly unlikely.

Therefore, the desirable state for organizations engaged or wishing to engage in e-learning

Figure 1. The relationship between e-learning, motivation, structural variables and the organizational operating environment

E-learning Diffusion = *f* [motivation (Organizational Variables + Environment)]

Figure 2. The relationship between e-learning, motivation, structural variables and the business operating environment-the likelihood of e-learning diffusion

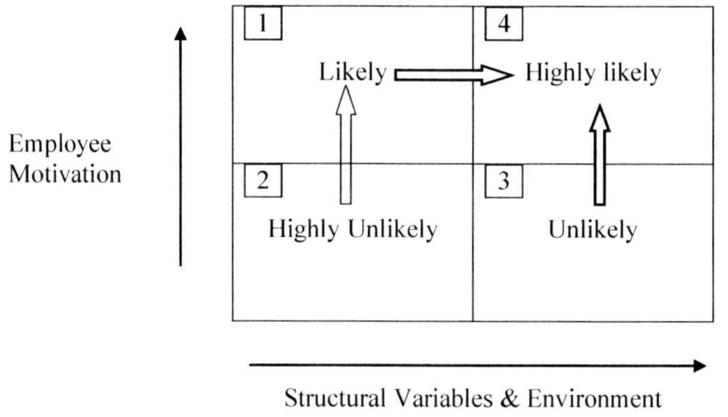

Figure 3. Activities that improve employee motivation to engage in e-learning

<u>Corporate Support</u>

- Top management participation and involvement
- Flexible learning hours
- Relevant content

<u>Incentives</u>

- Monetary
  - Cash Bonuses
  - Base salary increase
  - Stock options
- Non-monetary
  - Promotion to higher profile position
  - Recognition
  - Accolades

<u>Technology</u>

- Easy to use
- Enjoyable to use
- Readily Accessible
- Technical support

initiatives is to be in the top right-hand portion of the quadrant where employee motivation is high and structural and environmental variables are positive. If an organization is in the top left-hand section (1) of the diagram it needs to focus on structural variables in order to move toward 4. Activities that focus on building organization complexity (specialization, functional differentiation, and professionalism) and reducing organization bureaucratic control (formalization, centralization, and vertical differentiation) are necessary to push such organizations to 4. If an organization is in the bottom right-hand portion of the quadrant (3), it needs to focus on activities which cultivate employee motivation in order to move to 4. These and other activities are summarized in Figure 3 and include actively, providing flexible learning hours for employees, involving top management, providing relevant content, attaching financial and non financial incentives for completing e-learning modules or programs, providing easy to use technology, and making the technology readily accessible for employees.

Finally, organizations in the bottom left-hand portion of the quadrant (2) need to improve both the structural variables and the employee motivation in order to move to 4. However, trying to improve both simultaneously may in many cases prove too much of a challenge. Therefore, an organization may wish to first focus on first improving employee motivation which will move them to 1. Thereafter they may focus of techniques for improving structural elements in order to move to 4.

PILOT STUDY

Although the purpose of the study was to develop rather than empirically test the conceptual framework presented above, we had the opportunity to conduct a pilot study to assess some of the above stated conceptual propositions. Of interest to us was the role of motivation (a human factor) on e-learning diffusion in corporate environments. Data for this study was collected from four corporations based in North East Ohio from both the employees and management.

Instrumentation

The instruments used included two questionnaires. One was specifically for the management and the other was specifically for employees. The questionnaire for managers was developed by the researchers based on the literature review on e-learning, innovation theories, and motivation theories. The questionnaire for employees was based on an instrument formed by Wherry and South (1977) and the literature review. The questions in both questionnaires regarding employee motivation, organization structure, and effectiveness of e-learning were formulated to be answered using a five-point Likert scale with 1=strongly disagree, 2= disagree, 3= neutral, 4= agree, and 5=strongly agree.

The Management Questionnaire

Considering that management would have better knowledge about the aggregate information of the company, we designed a questionnaire specifically for the management. The aim of the management questionnaire was to assess organizational structural variables such as Organizational Complexity (specialization, function differentiation, professionalism) and Bureaucratic Control (formalization, centralization, vertical differentiation). Based on the literature review on innovation theories, 6 questions were designed to measure the organization structural variables. Although, the main thrust of the management questionnaire was to determine the various structural variables in the solicited organization, we also added a second dimension to assess the effectiveness of e-learning diffusion and management's perceptions about the benefits of e-learning. Additionally, a question was also included to assess the environment in which the organizations are currently operating in. This question asked about the level of competition perceived by management. The final part the management questionnaire sort general personal information about the manager, such as their age, gender, and educational background.

The Employee Questionnaire

The employee questionnaire aimed to address the issue of employee motivation to engage in e-learning. The questionnaire was based on an instrument formed by Wherry and South (1977) to evaluate employee motivation.

The instrument evaluates eight broad categories of intrinsic and extrinsic motivation namely:

(1) responsibility, (2) challenge vs. boredom, (3)high level of activity, (4) goal orientation, (5) social recognition, (6) being appreciated, (7) being judged reliable, and (8) immediate gratification.

The first four items in the above list cover intrinsic motivation while the last four cover extrinsic motivation (Wherry & South, 1977).

Seventy sample questions are given in the Wherry and South (1977) instrument which, may be used to evaluate the eight broad categories of intrinsic and extrinsic motivation. We took some of these questions and used them in an e-learning context. Our questionnaire was divided into two distinct sections. A five-point Likert scale was used in the first section to assess questions about intrinsic and extrinsic motivation, while the second part of the employee questionnaire was comprised of general questions such as employee age, gender, years of working experience, and level of education.

FINDINGS

The Demographic data of the respondents is summarized in Table 1. Table 2 outlines some of the findings of the pilot study, regarding the independent variables motivation, environment, organizational structure and the dependent variable successful diffusion of e-learning.

The second column in Table 2 (Motivation x_1) shows the mean motivation levels of employees to engage in e-learning. For all companies on average employees seem motivated to engage in e-learning but the degree of motivation varies from company to company. The next column (Environment x_2) shows the environment in which each of the firms operates. Recall from the literature that an organization can either be in a stable and predictable environment or an unstable and predictable environment or a stable and unpredictable environment or an unstable and unpredictable environment. If an organization is in an unstable and unpredictable environment a score of +1 was assigned. If an organization is in an unstable and predictable or stable and unpredictable environment the environment is considered neutral and a score of 0 was assigned. Finally if an organization was in an environment that is stable and predictable environment a score of -1 was assigned. On average all the companies appear to be operating in an unstable and unpredictable environment.

Next, organizational complexity and bureaucratic control variables were considered. Two companies, (1 and 4) were not complex in structure, while company 3 was complex and company 2 was somewhere in the middle. Previous research (Damanpour, 1991; Hull & Hage, 1982) suggests that there is a negative relationship bureaucratic control and innovation, therefore a score of -1 was given to companies that are displayed high levels of bureaucratic control and a score of 1 was given to those which displayed low levels of bureaucratic control. Half the companies appear to have some level of bureaucratic control.

Table 1. Employee demographics

Gender		Industry		Education Level	
Male	**Female**	**Service**	**Manufacturing**	**Bachelor Degree**	**No Bachelor Degree**
65%	35%	43%	57%	81%	19%

Table 2. Descriptive statistics

Variable / Company	Motivation (x_1)	Environment (x_2)	Organization Structure (x_3)	Diffusion (x_4)
1	0.46	1	C = -0.33 B = 0.00	0.5
2	0.54	1	C = 0.00 B = -0.67	0.75
3	0.51	1	C = 0.67 B = 0.67	0.5
4	0.54	1	C = 1.00 B = 0.33	1
Range of values for variables	$-1 \leq x_1 \leq 1$	$-1 \leq x_2 \leq 1$	$-1 \leq x_3 \leq 1$ $-1 \leq C \leq 1$ $-1 \leq B \leq 1$	$0 \leq x_4 \leq 1$

Finally, successful diffusion of e-learning was assessed. The diffusion of e-learning could either be successful or unsuccessful. If fully successful a score of 1 was assigned while if unsuccessful a score of 0 was assigned. Companies scoring 0.5 and below were considered to be unsuccessful in their e-learning diffusion initiative while those scoring above 0.5 were considered successful in the diffusion of their e-learning initiative. Company 2 and 4 appear to be successful while company 1 and 3 appear to be unsuccessful in the diffusion of their e-learning initiative.

DISCUSSION

The pilot study yielded some interesting results. Although a small and convenient sample was used, which subsequently prevents the research from making any probability statements, the descriptive statistics offered some interesting insights into the various variables examined in the study. Upon examination of the data it is evident that all companies reported that they have been operating in an unstable and unpredictable environment, so it is difficult to determine the impact of the environment on the successful diffusion of e-leaning. No pattern is evident from the relationship between organizational variables and the successful diffusion of e-learning, however due to the small sample size it is difficult to draw generalized conclusions from this. A very interesting finding from the pilot, however, is that there seem to be some differences in the motivation levels of the employees to engage in e-learning. Company 1 and 3 had the lowest employee motivation levels and also the lowest levels of e-learning diffusion, while company 2 and 4 which had the highest levels of employee motivation and the highest levels of e-learning diffusion.

CONCLUSIONS AND DIRECTIONS FOR FUTURE RESEARCH

The purpose of this study was to conceptually explore the factors that influence e-learning diffusion in contemporary corporations. We treated e-learning as an innovation in learning and applied concepts from literature on organizational change, innovation diffusion, and motivation to assess the factors that influence the diffusion of e-learning in organizations. Among these factors are organizational variables such as Organizational Complexity (specialization, function differentiation, professionalism) and Bureaucratic Control (formalization, centralization, vertical differentiation). Previous literature has also looked into the effect of the environment, so we also factored this into the analysis. However, in the case of e-learning we believe that human factors may play a crucial role in the determination of whether or not an innovation such as e-learning will successfully diffuse into an organization. We considered just one human factor (employee motivation) and suggested that motivation may not only be a factor that contributes towards the successful diffusion of e-learning, but without employee motivation e-learning initiatives in an organization could fail.

Armed with this framework, future researchers could empirically explore the relationships between these three factors. We conducted a pilot study to get insights into relationships between employee motivation, organization variable, and the environment and found that in organizations which had lower levels of employee motivation the diffusion of e-learning was not as successful as organizations with higher levels of employee motivation.

Clearly the pilot study has several limitations which future research could address. The first major limitation to the study was the small sample size. For the results to be generalized it's necessary to substantially increase the sample size. A second limitation with the pilot study is the sampling procedure used. A convenient sample of companies is used. Ideally, a random sample should have been used. Without a random sample we cannot and do not make any probability statements and are obliged to only report descriptive statistics.

Despite the above limitations of the pilot study, the main contribution of this paper, the conceptual framework, offers researchers the opportunity to investigate a myriad of research questions related to the successful diffusion of e-learning, by considering e-learning as an innovation in learning and factoring in human factors. In this paper the human factor considered was motivation. Future researchers may wish to look into the role of other human factors. For example they may consider issues such as the impact of the level of technological expertise among employees on e-learning diffusion. This approach of considering organizational, environmental, and human factors together rather than in isolation as have some previous studies, has the potential to advance knowledge on factors which contribute to the successful diffusion of e-learning.

REFERENCES

Abernathy, D. J. (1998). The WWW of distance learning: Who does what and where? *Training and Development, 52*(1), 29-30.

ASTD. (2006). *State of the industry report (Online).* Available at www.astd.org

Boudreau, M.-C., & Robey, D. (2005). Enacting integrated information technology: A human agency perspective. *Organization Science, 16*(1), 3-18.

Bruckman, A. (2002). The Future of e-learning communities. *Communications of the ACM, 45*(4), 60-63.

Bruno, S. F., & Osterloh, M. (2002). *Successful management by motivation: Balancing intrinsic and extrinsic incentives.* Berlin Herdelberg: Springer-Verlag

Chen, E. K. Y. (1983). Multinational corporations and technology diffusion in hong kong manufacturing. *Applied Economics, 15*(3), 309-312.

Chute, A. G., Thompson, M. M., & Hancock, B. W. (1999). *The Mcgraw-Hill handbook of distance learning.* New York: McGraw-Hill.

Choo, C.W. and Bontis, N. (Ed.) (2002), *The strategic management of intellectual capital and organizational learning.* Oxford University Press.

Clariana, R. B. (1997). Considering learning style in computer-assisted learning. *British Journal of Education Technology, 28*(1), 66-68.

Cohen, V. L. (1997). Learning styles in a technology-rich environment. *Journal of Research on Computing in Education, 29*(4), 339-350.

Crossan, M., Lane, H. and White, R. (1999), An organizational learning framework: from intuition to institution. Academy of Management Review 1999,Vol. 24 No 3 522-537

Daft, R. L. (1978). A dual-core model of organizational innovation. *Academy of Management Journal, 21*(2), 193-210.

Damanpour, F. (1987). The adoption of technological, administrative, and ancillary innovations: Impact of organizational factors. *Journal of Management, 13*(4), 675.

Damanpour, F. (1991). Organizational innovation: A meta-analysis of effects of determinants and moderators. *Academy of Management Journal, 34*(3), 555-590.

Damanpour, F., & Gopalakrishnan, S. (1998). Theories of organizational structure and innovation adoption: The role of environmental change. *Journal of Engineering and Technology Management, 15*(1), 1-24.

Davis, F. D. (1989). Perceived usefulness, perceived ease of use, and user acceptance of information technology. *MIS Quarterly, 13*(3), 318-340.

Davis, F. D., Bagozzi, R. P., & Warshaw, P. R. (1992). Extrinsic and intrinsic motivation to use computers in the workplace. *Journal of Applied Social Psychology, 22*(14), 1111-1132.

Deci, E. L., & Ryan, R. M. (1987). The support of autonomy and the control of behavior. *Journal of Personality and Social Psychology, 53*(6), 1024-1037.

Deloitte Research. (2002). *From e-learning to enterprise learning, becoming a strategic organization*. Retrieved from www.dc.com/research

Dewar, R. D., & Dutton, J. E. (1986). The adoption of radical and incremental innovations: An empirical analysis. *Management Science, 32*(11), 1422-1433.

Downs, G. W., & Mohr, L. B. (1976). Conceptual issues in the study of innovation. *Administrative Science Quarterly,* (21), 700-714.

Duggan, S., & Barich, S. (2001). *The knowledge economy and corporate e-learning.* CA: The Silicon Valley World Internet Centre.

Duncan, R. B. (1976). The ambidextrous organization: Designing dual structures for innovation. In R. H. Kilmann, L. R. Pondy & S. D. P. (Eds.), *The Management Of Organization: Strategy And Implementation* (Vol. 167-188). New York: North- Holland.

Fichman, R. G. (2001). The role of aggregation in the measurement of it-related organizational innovation. *MIS Quarterly, 25*(4), 427-455.

Fichman, R. G. (2004). Going beyond the dominant paradigm for information technology innovation research: Emerging concepts and methods. *Journal of the Association for Information Systems, 5*(8), 314-355.

Gunawardena, C. N., & Boverie, P. E. (1992). *Impact of learning styles on instructional design for distance education.* Paper presented at the World Conference of the International Council of Distance Education,, Bangkok Thailand.

Hamid, A. A. (2001). E-Learning-Is it the"E"or the learning that matters? *The Internet and Higher Education, 4*(3-4), 311-316.

Harreld, J. B. (1998). Building faster, smarter organizations. In D. Tapscott, A. Lowy & N. Klym (Eds.), *Blueprint the digital economy: Creating wealth in the era of e-business.* New York: McGraw Hill.

Hull, F., & Hage, J. (1982). Organizing for innovation: beyond burns and stalker's organic. *Sociology, 16*(4), 564-577.

Huynh, M. Q., Umesh, U. N., & Valacich, J. S. (2003). E-Learning as an emerging entrepreneurial enterprise in universities and firms. *Communications of the Association for Information Systems, 12*, 48-68.

Hwang, Y., & Yi, M. Y. (2003). Predicting the use of web-based information systems: Self-efficacy, enjoyment, learning goal orientation, and the technology acceptance model. *International Journal of Human-Computer Studies, 59*(4), 431-449.

Igbaria, M., A., & Livari, J. (1995). The effects of self-efficacy on computer usage. *OMEGA International Journal of Management Science., 23*(6), 587-605.

Knoop, R. (1994). Work values and job satisfaction. *Journal of Psychology, 128*(6), 683.

Kolb, D. A., Rubin, I. M., & McIntyre, J. M. (1979). *Organizational Psychology:An Experiential Approach* (3rd ed.). Englewood Cliffs, NJ: Prentice-Hall.

Larsen, R. E. (1992). Relationship of learning style to the effectiveness and acceptance of interactive video instruction. *Journal of Computer-based Instruction, 19*(1), 17-21.

Li, F. W. B., & Lau, R. W. H. (2006). On-demand e-learning content delivery over the internet. *International Journal of Distance Education Technologies, 4*(1), 46-55.

McCrea, F., K. , Gay, R., & Bacon, R. (2000). Riding the big waves: A white paper on the B2B

e-learning industry. In (pp. 1-51.). San Francisco: Thomas Weisel Partners.

Merchant, S., Kreie, J., & Cronan, T. (2001). Training end users: Assessing the effectiveness of multimedia CBT. *Journal of Computer Information Systems, 41*(3), 20-25.

Nord, W. R., & Tucker, S. (1987). *Implementing routine and radical innovation*. Lexington, MA: Lexington Books.

Nurmi, R. (1999). Knowledge-intensive firms. In J. W. Cortada & J. A. Woods (Eds.), *The knowledge management yearbook*. Boston: Butterworth-Heinemann.

Ong, C.-S., Lai, J., & Yishun, W. (2004). Factors affecting engineers' acceptance of asynchronous e-learning systems in high-tech companies. *Information, 41*(6), 795-804.

Orlikowski, W. J. (1992). The duality of technology - Rethinking the concept of technology in organizations. *Organization Science, 3*(3), 398-427.

Orlikowski, W. J. (1993). Case tools as organizational-change - Investigating incremental and radical changes in systems-development. *MIS Quarterly, 17*(3), 309-340.

Phillips, J. J. (1997). *Handbook of training evaluation and measurement methods* (3rd ed.). Houston, TX: Gulf Publishing.

Pierce, J. L., & Delbecq, A. (1977). Organization structure, individual attitudes and innovation. *Academy of Management Review, 2*(1), 27.

Renée, E. D., Barbara, A. F., & Eduardo, S. (2005). E-Learning in organizations. *Journal of Management, 31*(6), 920-940.

Rieber, L. R. (1991). Animation, incidental learning, and continuing motivation. *Journal of Educational Psychology, 83*(3), 318.

Rogers, E. M. (1995). *Diffusion of innovations* (Vol. 4th). New York: The Free Press.

Rosenberg, M., 2001. . (2001). *E-learning: Strategies for delivering knowledge in the digital age*. Toronto: McGraw-Hill.

Sampson, D., Karagiannidis, C., & Cardinali, F. (2002). An architecture for Web-based e-learning promoting re-usable adaptive educational e-content. *Educational Technology and Society, 5*(4), 27-36.

Servage, L. (2005). Strategizing for workplace e-learning: Some critical considerations. *The Journal of Workplace Learning, 17*(5-6), 304-317.

Ukens, L. (2001). *What smart trainers should know: The secrets of success from the world's foremost experts.* San Francisco: John Wiley & Sons, Inc.

Urdan, T. A., & Weggan, C. C. (2000). *Corporate e-learning: exploring a new frontier.* New York: Hambrecht & Co.

Vallerand, R. J. (1997). Toward a hierarchical model of intrinsic and extrinsic motivation. *Advances in Experimental Social Psychology, 27*, 271-360.

Venkatesh, V. (1999). Creation of favorable user perceptions: Exploring the role of intrinsic motivation. *MIS Quarterly, 23*(2), 239-260.

Wagner, E. D., & Reddy, N. L. (1987). Design considerations in selecting teleconferencing for instruction. *The American Journal of Distance Education, 1*(3), 49-56.

Wherry, R. J., & South, J. C. (1977). A Worker Motivation Scale. *Personnel Psychology, 30*(4), 613-636.

Wilkinson, H. E., Orth, C. D., & Benfari, R. C. (1986). Motivation theories: An integrated operational model. *SAM Advanced Management Journal, 51*(4), 24.

Wolfe, R. A. (1994). Organizational innovation: review, critique and suggested research. *Journal of Management Studies, 31*(3), 405-431.

Zhang, D. (2004). Virtual mentor and the lab system—Toward building an interactive, personalized, and intelligent e-learning environment. *Journal of Computer Information Systems, 44*(3), 35-43.

Zhang, D., & Nunamaker, J. F. (2003). Powering e-learning in the new millennium: An overview of e-learning and enabling technology. *Information Systems Frontiers, 5*(2), 207-218.

Zmud, R. W. (1982). Diffusion of modern software practices: Influence of centralization and formalization. *Management Science, 28*(12), 1421-1431.

This work was previously published in International Journal of Web-Based Learning and Teaching Technologies, Vol. 2, Issue 2, edited by L. Esnault, pp. 59-78, copyright 2007 by IGI Publishing, formerly known as Idea Group Publishing (an imprint of IGI Global).

Chapter XVII
Supporting Innovation Through Knowledge Management in Extended Enterprise

Mikel Sorli
Fundación LABEIN, Derio, Spain

Dragan Stokic
ATB, Bremen, Germany

ABSTRACT

Managing of knowledge for innovation in an extended enterprise (EE) environment is a key issue. This in turn requires effective utilization of information and communication technologies (ICT). This chapter addresses the application of ICT for knowledge management (KM) needed for innovation in industry. An ICT-based KM system to support innovation process in EE environment (i.e., to support mastering of the innovation process) is presented. The main objective of the new AIM system is to provide the means of stimulating the creation of innovative ideas in general, and specifically on potential product/process improvements and on problem solving. The AIM system supports collection of such ideas throughout EE from people involved with the products and processes, as well as a development of the collected ideas into innovations.

INTRODUCTION

In current global markets, **innovation** is generally one of the most critical factors for success in industrial firms. Former advantages based on aspects such as costs reduction, natural resources, and geographical situation are no more valuable since globalization is flattening these issues and furthermore, needed natural resources are usually coming from outside. One must always be meaningful of the need of fostering innovation fighting against usual themes as: "cut your costs," "get focused." Nowadays the motto should be "innovate or lose." This new situation imposes changes in the way the companies work. One of these changes has to be accomplished in the field of new product development that is the basis of the success of manufacturing companies (Sawaguchi, 2001; Sorli, 1999).

New ways of working move ineluctably toward the **extended enterprise**. The extended enterprise (EE) concept in parallel with the concurrent enterprising looks for how to add value to the product by incorporating to it knowledge and expertise coming from all participants on the product value chain. Manufacturers need to benefit from "extended enterprise" techniques (Dyer, 2000) by involving all people from throughout the product life cycle (suppliers, customers, design, production, and servicing) to provide their product knowledge to enhance product development and support. This new paradigm implies a quite new scenario: knowledge capturing and sharing, new forms of interrelationship between companies and persons.

Innovation is important for all companies, and just as important is the need to get innovative products to the market place quickly. Therefore, it is important to talk about "Management of **product development time and process improvement/innovation time within EE**." Under this new paradigm, companies able of "mastering" the development time can launch the product/service into the market or improve their processes (e.g., shop-floor process, maintenance processes etc.) just spending the planned time and resources and at the right moment, meaning at the exact date when the product achieves the higher and faster market penetration. This will give back to the company higher market share and better returns.

As it has been previously mentioned, knowledge useful to design engineers comes in many forms and it can come from many sources inside and outside the company. A common need among companies is to be able to acquire and process this knowledge so that a greater, richer, centralized source of knowledge and information is available to produce better designs, faster, with greater innovation, and with less re-inventing the wheel. Therefore, ICT based systems to support management of knowledge related to product/process innovation is of key importance.

This chapter presents one ICT based solution of effective management of knowledge for product/process innovation.

BACKGROUND

On this framework industry in the XXI century has to face these challenges by using techniques to deal with aspects as:

- **Extended enterprise (EE) (Davis & Spekman, 2003):** Enterprises are surpassing physical boundaries and establishing durable links with other companies: engineering, sub-contractor, providers, but are mostly at a loss on how to deal with customers in both ends of the chain. The customer is clearly a very relevant actor at the conceptual phase of the product life where the designer has to understand customer's needs and feelings as well as at the other end of it when the extended product has to live together with the user along its operating live.
- **Concurrent enterprising:** As the idea of EE refers to a longer time frame, concurrent enterprising focus more in the specific relationship among companies to set up new operations: new product development and launch, marketing activities covering a wider range than only the physical product by itself (extended product) and others.
- **Extended product:** Product is rapidly changing from physical tangible product to a plus of intangible assets related to fulfill-

ing requirements, fitting the right product to the right needs, servicing the product and maintaining it through its life, empowering the user to get the best from it and last but not lest facilitating the product retrieval and eventual replacement in a environmental friendly manner.

- **Support of ICTs (Levy, Rajaraman, & Ordille, 1996):** Besides some psychosocial changes, the technical challenge is related to the massive use and incorporation to industry of the new IT and Internet based technologies. There is a strong human implication in the users about getting used to the new technologies and changing the way the work has to be performed, especially related to knowledge management (KM) in an EE environment, leading to a number of problems which have to be considered when applying ICTs in industry.
- **E-working:** A newly issued term that implies working at a distance by using information and communication technologies (ICT). It covers not only the software/hardware tools but goes beyond physical aspects including social behavior and cultural change. The old ways of working change in a great amount since e-working allows workers such things as interacting on real time with people in distant locations or working on round-the-clock modus passing the token on from one to another through different time zones
-

From this basis, the new trends should be to extend the e-Working systems to the whole life cycle of the extended product. In such way, new working methods will be able of supporting the "extended enterprise" to monitor and capture knowledge from the "extended product" all through its life cycle. This will cover from the conception of the product/service to its disposal and back to "re-incarnation," that's to say: launching improved new extended products based on the knowledge collected from the existing ones.

PROBLEMS ADDRESSED

The new system described in this chapter—AIM system—supports the collection of innovative ideas and relevant knowledge (AIM, 2005) throughout the EE for new and existing process and product developments. These ideas and knowledge will later be developed in a collaborative way fostering industrial innovations as team work will be enhanced by cooperation between manufacturers, customers, and suppliers by means of the Internet facilities provided by the AIM system, "accelerating" innovation into the market.

As stated, one of the most important targets for the AIM tool is the collection of ideas throughout all the EE. For this, every worker is called to provide ideas and opinions on how improving the productive process and product quality. The problem to be solved here is the motivation for the workers to use a tool to which they are not familiar. A system of incentives could be tried, which must be decided by the companies, and the assumption that any initiative coming from each actor is always well considered must be acquired.

It must be assured, therefore, that all operators can introduce ideas easily. This poses the problem of structuring of user interface for introduction of ideas into the system in such a way that people not trained in using the tool are able to quickly do it. To achieve this, the distinction of the AIM users in three categories (administrator, process designer, and standard user) is done. For the standard user, the introduction of ideas must be friendly and easy, only needing to relate them to the product, unit, or process for which the idea could be useful.

The rational followed to support innovation process in EE is based on the following assumptions:

- The ideas for product/process innovations have to be collected throughout an EE in order to use all potentials for innovation available in an EE

- The ideas are proved either as possible solutions to identified problems in products/processes or as potential improvements of products/processes
- The ideas generation and gathering can be stimulated by provision of knowledge on:
  - Problems related to processes/products
  - "Similar" ideas on products/processes.
  - All other available knowledge on (extended) products/processes
- Ideas have to be effectively assessed to select those, which are most likely to lead to innovative solutions (process or product innovations)
- Ideas may need to be combined to achieve innovations

AIM system has very much based on TRIZ concepts (Altshuller, 1988; Kohnhauser, 1999; Terninko, Zlotin, & Zusman, 1996), from which the general concepts and the methodology for innovation using the innovation algorithm (Altshuller, 1999) have been integrated.

The main objectives of using AIM solution are:

- To develop a means of stimulating the creation of innovative ideas for innovation in broad sense, and specifically on problems solving and on potential product/process improvements and collecting them from people involved with the products and processes.
- To provide aids to efficiently gather information/knowledge on problems and improvement potentials regarding products and processes as a base for required innovation.
- To provide an approach to combine (experience based) knowledge on products/processes and innovation ideas.
- To develop a way of processing these ideas and storing them into a structured knowledge repository. To ensure that all useful knowledge (innovative information) is saved and made available.
- To develop a means of analysing innovative ideas to determine which are useful, and which are not, that is, to enable the viability of ideas to be assessed.
- To develop the best means of delivering the innovative ideas to the product and process designers for maximum effect.

In order to meet above listed objectives and baseline scenarios the analysis of the state-of-the-art relevant for the addressed system has been carried out. The state-of-the art involves the following aspects:

- Methods which can be used to develop innovative ideas
- Extended enterprise
- Methods for ontologies building
- ICT Tools which support the innovations process
- ICT Tools for gathering knowledge on problems and product/processes
- Innovation assessment

Although the main technologies mentioned are available in the market, the results of the analysis of the state of the art revealed that:

1. Practical means for developing ideas into innovations in products and processes are still missing. This will involve taking what is currently available and producing methods of rapidly taking many creative ideas, and assisting people to work together in a structured manner to develop these ideas into innovations.
2. Methods and tools for capturing and structuring innovative ideas, over EE, in a way that enables the best use for product/process innovation are still missing.
3. Providing means for team development of innovative ideas over EE is a high challenge

and asks for a generic approach for development of ontologies applicable in the context of specific products/processes.

Methods Which Can Be Used to Develop Innovative Ideas

The only known and proved ways of generating innovative ideas are currently based on generic means helping human brains to open their focus, use the lateral thinking, and try to be creative. Some creative tools have been developed along the years: Brainstorming, lateral thinking, 6-3-5, think-tank, affinity diagrams, etc. based on the psychological sciences upon the works and ideas of known people as Osborne (creator of the brainstorming and the innovation checklist), De Bono (Six Thinking Hats, The Lateral Thinking) and others.

On the other hand, tools extensively used in design such as QFD, VM, FMEA, and others give a very valuable help in identifying where innovation is needed either by market pressure (QFD), high cost (VM) or potential failures (FMEA) but have few if any hint on how actually innovate.

The most important method for the new CAI system is TRIZ (theory of inventive problem solving). TRIZ is a recently developed methodology giving a more systematic and technological approach promoting not only idea generation, but also a consistent comprehensive method to convert ideas into feasible concepts.

Extended Enterprise

Extended enterprise (Duffy & Tod) concept in parallel with the concurrent enterprising looks for how to add value to the product by incorporating to it knowledge and expertise coming from all participants on the product value chain.

The concept of EE has been defined in similar ways as can be seen in the following two samples:

- **Extended enterprise** (GlobePro Project. Helsinki University of Technology; Laboratory of Information Processing Science) is a set of real organizations. EE is the competence pool, resource pool, infrastructure and means for doing business. It is the base set from which organizations are tied in formation of functional consortia.
- **EE** (Anthony R. Sukdeo, TECHNOCORP. August 22, 2006 in Wikipedia) is a concept that is derived from the Enterprise terminology in application to both internal and external business relationships and associated services extended across multiple divisions (the holding, subsidiaries and branch offices) in one or more countries. With the evolution of networked technologies, efforts have been made to integrate and consolidate all business resources (humans and systems) for improved management and operations within a global competitive environment. This generalized effort is termed EE resources management.

As previously indicated, manufacturers need to benefit from "**extended enterprise**" (Burton & Shaw, 2005; Hagel & Singer, 1999; Short & Venkatraman, 1992) techniques by involving all people from throughout the product life cycle to provide their product knowledge. This knowledge needs to be saved and managed. Loss of this knowledge results in increased costs, longer time-to-market, reduced quality of products and services. By improving products and customer support manufacturing companies will be more competitive, and employment will increase. Manufacturing companies have to shift towards the use of EE technologies and KM for customer/product support. This new paradigm implies a quite new scenario in which aspects as knowledge capturing and sharing and the new forms of interrelationship between companies and persons result of very high relevance.

The key idea behind the EE concept is to develop means supporting the collection of all useful knowledge throughout the EE for new and existing process and product developments, and to develop this knowledge into a means of fostering industrial innovations. Innovation by combining the ideas and feedback from all parts of the product life cycle, including customer interaction with existing products and new product ideas, and including customer service and field engineers, including suppliers, and including pooling of knowledge between multiple sites.

Companies need to be able to extend their own enterprises (by removing barriers of geographic location and human resource problems) to encompass the customer's operations where the supplied industrial products are being used. They need to provide the expertise to support the products in situ (including problem solving support, and diagnostic analysis of customer feedback) just as though the company expert was there with the customer solving the problems. This will involve EE model of the technical expertise of the companies in supporting their products at the customers' site.

This new paradigm addresses issues of significant importance to industry: the use of e-business technologies for EE product knowledge systems permitting ubiquitous human interaction, across and beyond industrial organizations, getting organizations to work better with each other. The novelty of the approach is to focus on product knowledge, which is not managed today, and which comes from suppliers, customers and employees (and tacit or informal knowledge generated by internal staff) involved in the development, support and use of products. It represents the next evolution of product information systems, taking standards and practices forward to support co-operative working and partnerships.

Methods for Ontologies Building

Methods for ontology building (Gruninger & Uschold, 1996) are of a special relevance for the AIM system, since they have to serve as a basis to put together and re-use innovative ideas from different actors within an extended enterprise. An overview of the ontologies building approaches and tools relevant for innovation management is provided in Kirchhoff, Kuczynski, and Stokic (2005). This overview indicates that ontologies attract high intention of RTD community. However, their application in practice is not still wide spread and additional RTD activities are needed to provide application oriented method for product and process innovation domain. Especially what is needed is a means for continuous update of ontologies enabling long life of knowledge systems.

ICT Tools Which Support the Innovations Process

There are two software tools based in the TRIZ methodology for inventive problem solving: IBW (Innovation Work Bench) and TECH OPTIMIZER (Both based in USA). Both software packages use schematic representation of problems and automated analysis of generated diagrams that guides the user to the abstract solution. Technical information and examples are included for helping the user in the particularization of the solution. However, these are both aimed at the scientist level of user, and not at the industrial manufacturing level.

Ideafisher, Inspiration professional edition, is another tool for helping to generate ideas. However, again this is aimed at the specialist level, and is not appropriate for industrial companies.

However, some tools exist to support application of other methodologies (QFDCapture from ITT for QFD, GAMDEC/GAMTREE from France for the FMEA, CDCF for Function Analysis according to French standard AFNOR X50-X51, DECIDOR and EXPERT CHOICE supporting decision-making for concept evaluation, etc).

ICT Tools for Gathering Knowledge on Problems and Product/Processes

There are many commercially available products providing means to capture knowledge on problems and product/processes, which are relevant for the development of certain AIM modules. The tools analyzed primarily address heuristic (case base reasoning and rule base reasoning) and model based reasoning approaches. Some examples are listed here:

- Good examples of CBR tools are KATE, Easy Reasoner, ReCall, Know How. They all are tool kits to develop case-based reasoning applications. For example, the KATE Software Suite is an Internet based tool-kit.
- TER includes a rule-based system, which supports forward and backward chaining.
- GRADE contains tools to assist in the diagnosis and repair process. It captures and automates the knowledge from the process. Diagnostics rely on model-based reasoning and case-based reasoning.
- RODON contains simulation and diagnosis software.
- Diagnostician provides a development tool and a run-time tool.

The main problems with these reasoning methods/tools is a re-use and sharing of knowledge among different experts and partners within distributed and extended industrial companies, since the most of the existing tools are missing capabilities to provide presentation of the captured knowledge in appropriate form to different actors.

Innovation Assessment

Some tools already exist to help assessing innovation capacity:

- Innovation styles for groups from the Innovation Group Consulting Inc. According to its description, the product is unique and focus on evaluating *how are you innovative* rather than *how innovative are you.* It is based on the fact that all people are unique individuals and while everyone has the capacity to be creative and innovative, each of us expresses this potential differently
- Innovation system architecture (ISA) from the same company. Assess your team's or organization's "infrastructure" to cultivate, support and sustain innovation. It incorporates the innovation group model for creating the framework or architecture for sustaining organizational innovation
- The innovation assessment program by United Inventors Association. It is an inventor/innovator assistance service that provides inventors, entrepreneurs, and product marketing/manufacturing enterprises with an honest and objective third-party analysis of the risks and potential of their ideas and inventions. This is why it focuses on invention evaluation

SOLUTIONS AND RECOMMENDATIONS

The approach for the development of the AIM system as a KM system to support innovation in EE is based on three business cases, used to ensure that the system concept and development is driven by industrial needs, and that these needs are met. The business cases use the AIM system in different ways enabling to develop and test AIM system for different scenarios, ensuring its general applicability.

Technological Solution Description

Based on the previous analysis of the state-of-the art and the end-users requirements it was decided to base the AIM system upon TRIZ concepts from which the general concepts and the methodology for innovation using the Innovation algorithm has been integrated. As indicated above, existing methods aim at the scientist level of user, and not at the industrial manufacturing level. AIM intends to provide methods and tools, which are applicable in the industrial environment.

A combination of TRIZ, RBR, and CBR as well as repositories of ideas and knowledge on product/processes (included in models) is applied, which is currently not available for innovations development domain. TRIZ methodology refers to the use of past knowledge to overcome problems and both RBR and CBR use past information, gathered in rules or cases, to reach a result. The necessary knowledge to realise these reasoning methods will be provided in the AIM system, either as innovations, ideas, or product and process knowledge. The reasoning methods are very adequate to present a possible solution for problems (i.e. new ideas or previous solutions), because the system contains information on past experiences. All three reasoning approaches are used to combine the ideas into innovation concepts by providing set of ideas that may fit together, providing previous appropriate combinations.

The AIM system is thought as a process of innovation (Zlotin & Zusman, 1999), which means that an Idea will undergo a complete cycle, in order to be collected, documented, classified and used in the AIM system. Ultimately, ideas turn into innovations, which is one of the main objectives of the system. This section provides a rough overview of the life cycle of an idea. Figure 1 shows the complete path that an idea undergoes in the system.

This life cycle is the basis of the innovation process, containing the activities to be realised to achieve innovations in the concurrent enterprise. The life cycle starts with data acquisition, where ideas are collected using an appropriate graphical user interface, accompanied by knowledge acquisition methods. The users of EE will use

Figure 1. AIM innovation life cycle

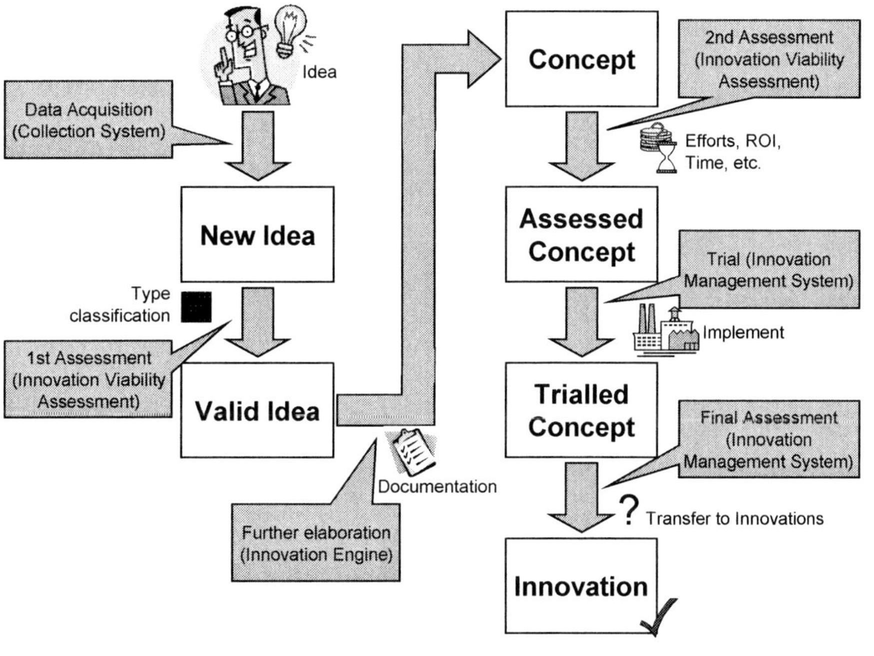

remotely the system to document their thoughts and viewpoints concerning the products and services of a company.

The AIM system performs a first assessment of the **new ideas**, with the purpose of making a rough classification. This classification will be an identification of the idea type, according to the information that it contains: improvement, potential cause, action, or new product/process. The main objective of this first classification is to attribute a type to each **new idea**, enabling its fast identification by the appropriate staff members of the company.

With all the ideas classified by type, a responsible staff member will develop **valid ideas** further, by first collecting any additional information that might be relevant for the **valid idea**, and further elaborate it. All the information can be useful to enable the best possible assessment. This step also includes relating the idea to any other ideas, innovations, and information stored, such as products, processes, problems, causes, actions. The result of this step is a more elaborated idea: **Concept**.

The company's staff members responsible for ideas' evaluation will realise a detailed assessment of each **concept**, with the objective of supporting a decision of trying or not the idea (i.e., implementing it). Several issues must be considered here, such as material, machines, staff members, implementation cost, profit, efforts, ROI. The result of the assessment will be documented in the repository, together with the concept, defining an **assessed concept**.

If the result of the assessment expresses an expensive and unworthy implementation, the **assessed concept** will probably not be implemented, and this has to be documented. It is then possible to keep the concept in the repository to reuse part of its information, or delete it. When the assessment provides positive results, the **positively assessed concept** is tried, and the complete development process is documented in the repository. The most important part of this documentation is the result obtained from the trial implementation, which expresses the success of the concept or not, and defines a **trialled concept**. The complete documentation of the concept (i.e., **trialled concept)**, collected until this step, enables the final classification of the initial ideas. Based on the assessments and the trial implementation is possible to identify if the idea is successful, and therefore constitutes an **innovation**.

Developments

The AIM system follows a component-based architecture, enabling an easy extensibility, robustness and customization, and supporting the activities identified in the idea life cycle.

Main RTD challenges contemplated basically the combination of advanced methods for generating innovative ideas with "classical" methods for collection of knowledge on products/processes and their problems. It also includes the development of specific ontologies needed to enable efficient exchange of ideas between different experts/actors within an EE. The AIM system comprehends several modules, as presented in Figure 2. In the text to follow these modules are briefly described.

Main components are:

- **Innovation repository:** This repository allows classifying ideas and corresponding data in a way common to all AIM modules, and stores them for rapid access.
- **Collection of innovative ideas and product/process knowledge:** This module is based on a combination of 'classical' approaches/ commercial tools and new developments required to provide means to efficiently collect ideas, but also to collect knowledge on product and process problems for which ideas are needed. In order to optimally support users in introducing their ideas different Graphical User Interfaces (GUIs) were implemented to add or edit ideas. Any

Figure 2. AIM system and relation to innovation life cycle

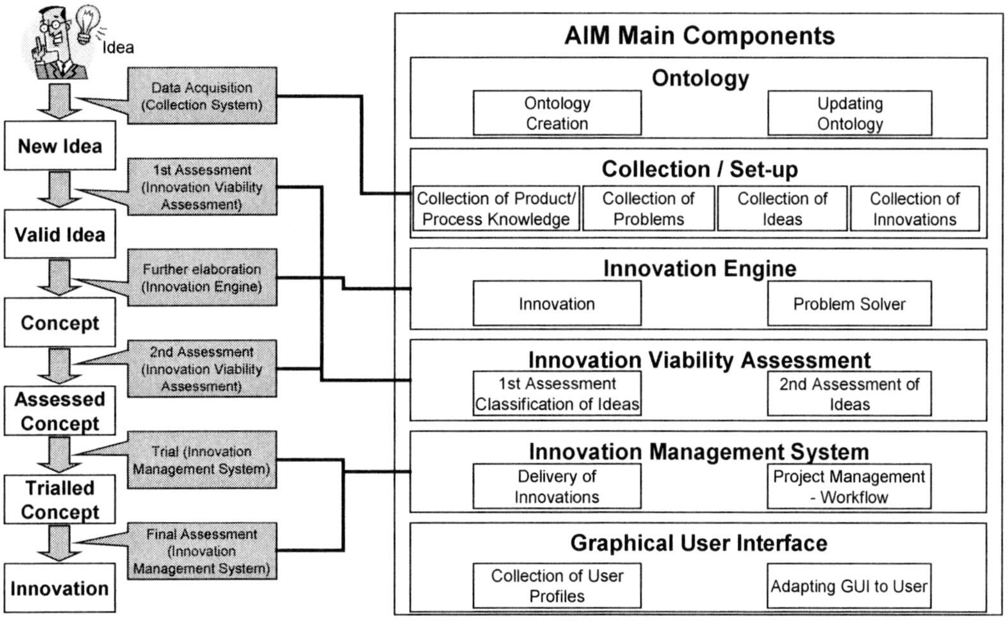

user can choose the most appropriate GUI, and this choice can be modified at any moment. The simplest GUI implemented is the Easy GUI, which is represented in Figure 3 (Campos, da Silva, & Stokic, 2004).

The so-called advanced GUI contains more information on the idea, as can be seen from Figure 4. In this GUI, besides the information contained in the Easy GUI, it is also possible to see or edit documents, Internet links, and problems related to the idea.

- **Innovation engine:** This module provides a systematic methodology for the development of ideas into innovation concepts, by sharing and working on these ideas in a structured framework. TRIZ methodology serves as a baseline approach (Kohnhauser, 1999) for this module, where the in-depth analysis of technical requirements and manufacturing failure situations is performed, structured knowledge is delivered, and graphical aids for team working and creation of concepts are provided.
- **Innovation viability assessment:** This module provides a structure (based on rapid consulting within the company of evaluation of developments and risks, combined with a multi-criteria decision support—DSS) to assist users in assessing the feasibility of new ideas at the collection stage, and innovation assessment facilities for design teams. It is important to focus on feasible, good innovative knowledge, and develop this.
- **Innovation management system:** This is a means of providing an efficient way for planning and monitoring the use of the innovation knowledge during design activities and a structured delivery of thc innovations/ideas to the process and product design teams.

The **main features** of the AIM system are:

Figure 3. Easy GUI

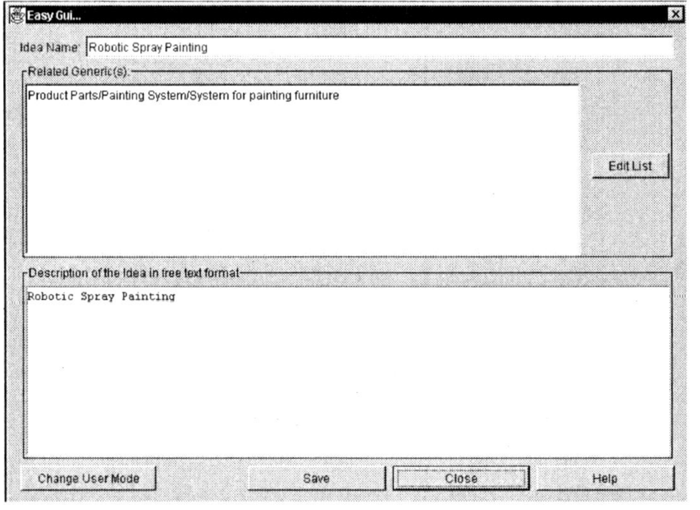

Figure 4. Advanced GUI

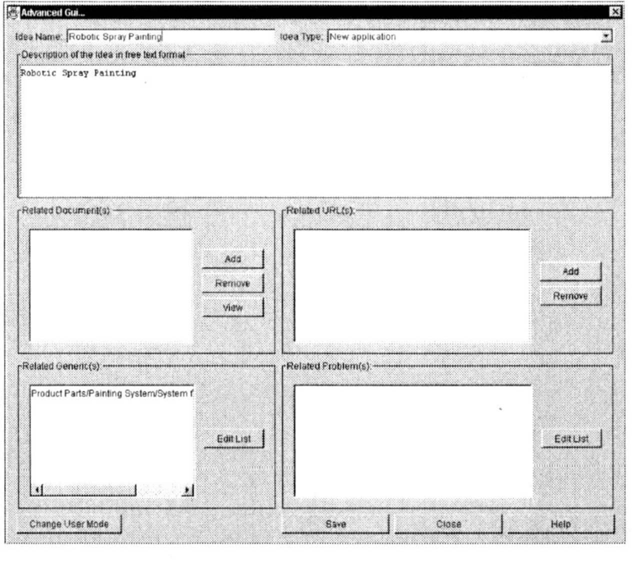

- AIM enables users along the EE to introduce ideas and report problems.
- AIM enables the complete modelling of the EE (i.e., the departments, staff, processes, products, customers, innovations), in order to support an appropriate and efficient structure and classification of ideas and problems.
- AIM provides functionality to validate the ideas, classifying them by type.
- AIM includes an extensive search system for ideas, using all possible attributes as search parameters, in order to support definition, elaboration, and combination of ideas and further development of innovative concepts.
- AIM supports users in the technical development of ideas, following a TRIZ-based

methodology, for in-depth analysis of technical contradictions.
- AIM supports users, following a TRIZ-based methodology, in depth-analysis and solving of problems and failure situations.
- AIM supports the assessment of the ideas developed in terms of technical viability, resources, costs, benefits.
- AIM comprehends innovation management functionality to determine and monitor the process of innovation.
- AIM enables functionality to maintain a common ontology used in several sites, by comparing local and global ontologies.
- AIM allows online monitoring and access to innovation processes through Web-services providing statistics on system's use and success (e.g., new ideas, status of innovation process, users, number of innovations, number of problems solved).

One of the key aspects of the AIM KM system is **ontology**, which enables sharing and reuse of knowledge and reasoning behavior across different users, domains, and tasks. Ontology can be seen as complementary reusable components to construct knowledge bases. The AIM system is going to be used by a wide spectrum of users with different technical backgrounds and sometimes with different languages. Therefore, it is highly important to have a common dictionary that makes evident to avoid misunderstandings. By adding and retrieving innovative ideas, it is essential to ensure that certain words or keywords really mean that the users are going to enter. Ontology is used in the AIM system to enable knowledge exchange among different subsidiaries of an EE (Davis et al., 2003). It can even help in the translation of words between different languages. The ontology supports searching for ideas and problems and other knowledge stored in the system. After analysing three ontology tools, it has been decided to use the tool Protégé-2000, which seems to be the most suitable one to satisfy the end user requirements (Kirchhoff et al., 2005).

Results

This section presents findings and achievements of the integrated system validation by the industrial end-users. In order to ensure reliable validation of the AIM methods and tools, metrics were defined to enable a quantitative assessment of the system development progress and the results achieved. These metrics include business metrics—benefits for the end-users and technical metrics—fulfilment of the requirements upon the tools.

Aiming to provide appropriate procedures for self-assessment throughout the system development, the system prototypes were installed in the industrial environment enabling the tools testing under real conditions. The prototypes tests carried aimed at a definition of new workflow flows to be realized using the AIM system and allowed the end-users to provide valuable feedback regarding the AIM system. This feedback was used to improve prototype of the modules.

Business Case 1: Innovation Process in SME

The business line selected for the scenario is the development of new products and cutting methods, and maintenance of cutting tools, which is the process where the most off-site involvement of personnel happens, and is the one where innovation is most needed. Therefore, the business case focuses on innovation generation, to achieve new products and processes, and also on solving problem occurred with cutting machines supplied to customers. The main business targets were to increase the number of ideas generated by the company for new products or cutting processes by 50-70%, to reduce the time for solving the product problems by 25%, and to use the improved innovation process, supported by the AIM system, as a marketing tool to show existing and new customers that this is a high-tech company.

The tests of the prototypes involved the managing director of the company, the works and sales manager, and one shop floor tool designer. In future tests, when the full prototype is installed, the entire shop floor will be involved. In addition, sales will also be involved in testing the AIM system. The works manager, supported by the managing director, defined the company model of the company, and introduced it in the AIM repository, using the set-up tool provided. The model included several tools designed by the company, and problems collected in the past, with respective solutions. Afterwards, problems reported by customer were introduced in the AIM repository, using the collection system, with the complete description. In several cases, ideas were collected to help solving these problems. The application of the AIM system to elaborate these ideas into innovation was tested as well.

Business Case 2: Innovation in Service and Engineering Medium Company

The business case area is the business of providing a complete air compressor system solution to customers, and then supporting this air compressor system (extended product). The selection of the air compressor business is because it involves (and needs to innovate and enhance this involvement) significant interactions with suppliers and customers. The main focus of the company business case is to collect information from customers about needed solutions. This information can be seen as problems, which need solutions to be provided by the company. The main objectives were to increase the number of innovative suggestions on products from customers and suppliers by 50% (specifically by 60% with large suppliers and customers), to increase the number of innovative ideas on products from employees by 50% and to increase the number of implemented innovation/new concepts of offers to customers by at least 30%.

The tests of AIM's prototype were realised by the managing director, one account manager, and one service manager. This group will be extended during the tests of the full prototype, to include sales engineers, service engineers, management, suppliers and customers. Customers and suppliers were indirectly involved, as they did not use the tool yet, but information provided by them was introduced in the repository by the company employees. The company model was defined by the three users involved in the tests, using the set-up tool provided by AIM. This model included several air compressor systems developed by the company and provided to several customers. In addition, the problems related to these systems were also introduced. With this basic information defined, it was possible to begin collecting problems regarding actual and future air compression systems, using AIM collection system. The process of solving these problems included also the collection of ideas and transformation of these ideas into solutions (innovations).

Business Case 3: Innovation in Multiple Site Manufacturing Process

The third company business case focuses upon innovation in multiple site manufacturing process based on the identified problems.

The selected business case area is the manufacturing process of cans in two plants. In one plant, the process selected to test AIM system is a bottleneck machine called "Necker." This machine in the production floor requires a generation/collection of innovative ideas in order to improve the process as well as the quality of the products. Since this bottleneck machine (Necker) creates a number of complex problem/failure causes asking for complex activities to remove these causes, the AIM tools should support a collection of ideas on this production step. To solve the problems, an innovation management system is needed which gives the staff members in the shop floor, as well as engineers, a consolidated overview on problems in production and proposals of causes/actions to remove these problems. The similar process (with similar problems) is selected in the other plant. The testing process at this company was realized by the process engineers and plant managers and selected maintenance workers who defined the plant model, especially the necker machine, using the set-up tool provided. This information was the basis to collect problems and ideas. Afterwards, about 350 problems and solutions registered in paper forms in both plants were introduced in the AIM system. In addition, ideas to solve these problems and improve the manufacturing processes were collected. The solving of new problems, with special emphasis on re-use of knowledge between two plants, was considerably improved, with an increased number of ideas collected from the employees on how to solve these problems (by 25%—see Table 1).

The AIM tools provide information on problems identified, in different forms, depending on the expertise of actors, and gather ideas from shop-floor workers as well as process design experts and support collaborative work on evaluation of these ideas. The tools provide 'similar' ideas in order to support ideas gathering and evaluation. The challenging task is how to motivate shop floor workers to provide their ideas and collaborate on innovative solutions for process improvements. The objective is to support cross regional teams building within different subsidiaries including international teams (cooperation between subsidiary in Germany and subsidiary in Poland), where one of the key problem is appropriate (multilanguage) ontology. Once fully introduced in the first two plants, it is expected to bring improvement in productivity and reduction in waste due to effective process improvements by about 5-7% but once introduced in at least eight plants world wide, the benefits (due to exchange of ideas

Table 1. Validation results of the prototype (n.a.—not applicable, n.m.—not measured)

Requirement	Objective	Assessment of prototype		
		BC1	BC2	BC3
Increase the number of innovative suggestions on products from customers and suppliers by a structured Web link.	50%	50%	50%	n.a.
Increase the number of innovative ideas on products from employees, by means of easy to use facilities.	70%-100%	60%	50%	n.a.
Collect the corporate knowledge from the company.	n.m.	OK	OK	OK
Establish a classification scheme for product/process knowledge to be used for further development.	n.m.	Yes	OK	OK
Increase the number of implemented innovation/ new concepts of offers to customers.	at least 30%	30%	30%+	-
Increase the number of innovative ideas on processes from employees within an EE, making easy the introduction of information.	50%	50%	50%	25%
Increase number of innovative solutions of the identified problems within processes.	at least 30%	30%	30%	10%
Reduce time and efforts to solve product/process problems.	at least 25%	25%	25%	20%
Have a managed way of developing ideas into new practical concepts.	n.m.	Yes	OK	-
Have a structure to record and classify ideas.	n.m.	Yes	OK	OK
Reduce wastes and costs associated with problems, and supporting customers.	12 %	12%+	25%+	Ca. 10%
Shorten the time needed to collect and implement new ideas in the manufacturing process.	n.m.	Yes	OK	OK

on common problems) may bring improvements of over 12%.

Table 1 presents validation results obtained, where the current measures are compared against the objectives defined in the system development start. Each company measured different values depending on its own specificity (e.g., number of ideas collected, number of problems solved in a time period, number of innovations implemented in the products or processes, costs reduction arising from AIM innovations) after the introduction of the AIM system and compared with the records before the introduction of the system. Some of the requirements are not measurable (n.m.) or were not at the point of starting using the system (nº 12) and some measures were not available (n.a.) for several reasons. Basically two types of indicators can be found: those that can be measured with real figures (1, 2, 5, 6 , 7, 8, & 11) and those that are not measurable but give a feeling of real advantage for users (3, 4, 9, 10, & 12).

The results of tests led to the conclusion that the modules developed are satisfactory from functionality point of view. The functionality implemented was working without major problems, and in a robust and reliable way. The results presented in the Table clearly indicate that the main expected improvements were successfully achieved.

FUTURE TRENDS

Innovation is a serious job that cannot rely only on software tools as sophisticated as they could be; there is a real need of methodologies helping people to innovate. Creativity and innovation do not arise directly from any tool itself. In fact, creativity steams only from the human's brain and becomes an innovation only when applied to solve specific technical problems that will increase the added value to the final consumer. One should remind that only combination of the three factors (new idea, implementation on product and market success) is the real way of achieving innovation.

Besides that, innovation means team working which means sharing information. People are in general very reluctant to share information unless they will obtain something in change.In that sense, the most important actual drawback is related to the reluctance of human beings to share experience, expertise, information, etc. that's to say: "Knowledge." Then a very important line of research is starting in the psycho-social fields providing mechanisms helping to override this barrier. The most convincing arguments will come by showing the unquestionable benefits and the enormous possibilities for the employees in sharing and inter-changing knowledge with their peers in order to achieve a "win-win" environment.

Within this scope, new products design, and development is a key area on which these new approaches will provide to industrial companies new methodologies enabling them to develop products including differentiating performances at very low prices. The problem of the management of distributed innovation knowledge in complex manufacturing systems, often spreading over many countries should be addressed. This problem is of a general nature, widely applicable and of essential significance in the worldwide manufacturing industry, both in large and small companies. These new EE and KM approaches are expected to be a good help to push manufacturing companies moving towards increasing innovation rates throughout these new paradigms.

Very promising research lines in the near future should be:

- Combination of methodologies to promote innovation, techniques for team working, creativity, and fostering information sharing by creating "win-win" situations will be really a must in the short term in order to enhance the possibilities of the emerging Web based collaborative working environments

- Integration of engineering tools and human sciences tools in the previously mentioned way
- Migration of tools to the Web based collaborative environments
- Development of new ICTs focusing on the new working paradigm and even shifting it in order to enhance and empower their possibilities
- Systems for comprehensive Product KM System enabling to manage the overall life-cycle of manufactured "Extended products"

On a general basis, the future research on the area of "product KM" will continue to explore the possibilities arising from ICT tools in order to capture implicit knowledge from the persons in a way enabling its storage and re-use. Since the modern approaches for products/processes innovation in industry require involvement of many different teams in EE context, it is of particular importance to provide ICT solutions, which support collaborative work on innovation. The increasing trend of globalised manufacturing environments and a radical increase in number of product variants in modern manufacturing industry (e.g., build-to-order) requires new forms of collaboration among teams involved along product/process innovation life cycle (e.g., design, planning, production scheduling, manufacturing, after sales services etc.), as well as seamless knowledge and experience sharing among these teams, often distributed geographically and in time. There is a clear need to efficiently support different collaboration patterns (synchronous, asynchronous, multi-synchronous collaboration etc.). This is especially a challenge for manufacturing industry in many leading industrial countries facing massive migration of manufacturing facilities towards Eastern European and Asian countries.

There is a strong trend to provide advanced ICT solutions for collaborative work on innovation. So-called collaborative working environments (CWE) may support innovation processes in manufacturing industry. The objectives are to develop new collaborative working platform to support collaboration among teams in manufacturing industry (regarding different collaboration patterns, semantically enriched contents for collaborative work etc.) enabling more effective innovation processes (Stokic, 2006). The platforms are intended to support collaborative work on innovation within organised teams in industry in EE context, but there is a trend to provide platforms to support collaboration between teams in industry and ad-hoc groups and wider communities (e.g., RTD communities, customers etc).

In this subject field, there are some facts that have to be taken into consideration:

- Collaborative working among distributed teams is becoming a "must" due to globalization.
- ICT technologies (mainly Web based) are the key enablers of this new working paradigm.
- CWE have to focus in product knowledge captured from the whole value chain no matter how geographically dispersed they may be.
    - **Manufacturing:** Designers, manufac turers, suppliers, customers, maintenance, etc.
    - **Business:** Vendors, buyers, intermediar ies, after-sales services, logistics, financials, etc.

CONCLUSION

Innovation is a critical factor in the success of industrial companies, and just as important is the need to get innovative products to the market quickly, as well as to innovate processes with minimum efforts and time. Such innovation must happen within an EE context. Managing of knowledge for innovation in an EE environment is a key issue. This in turn requires effective utilization of ICT.

This chapter presents an example of a successful ICT based system for effective management of knowledge needed within innovation processes in an EE context. The overall objective of the AIM system is twofold: (i) Increasing Innovation and (ii) accelerating their introduction to the Market. From the system validation through Industrial scenarios, it can be concluded that systematic approaches applied to incremental innovation lead to increased efficiency within innovation development process, confirming the basis and assumptions of the work. Specific achievements of the AIM system may be listed as:

- Developing means of stimulating the creation of innovative ideas and collecting them from people at EE level involved with the products and processes.
- Developing ways of processing these ideas and storing them into a structured knowledge repository. To ensure that all the useful knowledge (innovative information) is saved.
- Developing means of analysing innovative knowledge to determine which is useful, and which is not. That is, to enable the viability of ideas to be assessed.
- Developing means of delivering the innovative ideas to product and process designers for maximum effect.

The AIM system is targeted at industrial companies with complex products and processes, which have to provide significant product and process knowledge/information throughout the product life cycle, and which need to harness the product and process innovation with knowledge from their staff, suppliers and customers. The AIM system, thus, leads to important business benefits on the fields of:

- Reduction of process/product innovation cycle-time.
- Reduction of time and efforts for solving product/process problems.
- Improvement of process efficiency and reduction of wastes.

However, the solution presented has certain limitations: the AIM tools do not fully support collaborative work on innovations regarding e.g., different collaboration patterns (which is a strong trend as previously indicated), the reasoning methods used do not efficiently utilise semantics to support knowledge sharing. The current work on new, upgraded versions of the tools is, therefore, focused on solving several fundamental RTD problems, such as "cooperativity" of tools and semantic based KM.

ACKNOWLEDGMENT

The previously described work has been partly carried out in the project AIM (Acceleration of Innovative Ideas to Market) co-funded by the European Commission (EC) under contract (Ref. n° IST-2001-52222). The authors would like to acknowledge the EC for the support as well as all members of the consortium in the AIM Project for their contribution during the development of the various ideas and concepts presented in this work.

REFERENCES

AIM. (2005). IST-2001-52222: *Acceleration of innovative ideas to market.* Project public report, EC.

Altshuller, G. (1988). *Creativity as an exact science.* New York: Gordon and Breach Science Publishers.

Al'tshuller, G. S., Shulyak, L., & Rodman, S. (1999). *The innovation algorithm.* Worcester, MA: Technical Innovation Center.

Blake, A., & Mann, D. (2000). *Making knowledge tangible.* CMC and DuVersity, September 2000.

Brazil, K., Serdella, A. (2005). *Next generation extended enterprise.* Juniper Networks, USA.

Browne, J., Sackett, P. J., & Wortmann, J. C. (1995). Future manufacturing systems—Towards the Extended Enterprise. *Computers in Industry.*

Busby, J. S., & Fan, I. S. (1993). The extended manufacturing enterprise: Its nature and its needs. *International Journal of Technology Management*, Special Issue on Manufacturing Technology: Diffusion, Implementation and Management.

Burton, T. T., & Shaw, T. E. (2005). *Building the lean extended enterprise through adaptive supply chain networks.* LAI (Lean Aeronautics Imitative).

Campos, A. R., da Silva, R., & Stokic, D. (2004). Integrated approach for innovation and problem solving in dynamic virtual enterprises. *Proceedings of the INDIN 04*, Berlin.

Caskey, K. R. (1995). *Co-operative distributed simulation and optimization in extended enterprise.* IFIP WG5.7 Conference Proceedings.

Davis, E. W., & Spekman, R. E. (2003). The extended enterprise: Gaining competitive advantage through collaborative supply chains. *Financial Times Prentice Hall.*

Davis, G., Wilt, C., Dillon, P., & Fishbein, B. (1997). *Extended product responsibility: A new principle for product-oriented pollution prevention.* The University of Tennessee. The Gordon Institute, INFORM.

Dynes, S., Breschbühl, H., & Johnson, M. (2005). *Information security in the extended enterprise.*

Duffy, J., & Tod, M. (2004). *The extended enterprise: Eliminating the barriers.* CIO Magazine. Retrieved from http://www2.cio.com/analyst/report2118.html

Dyer, J. H. (2000). *Collaborative advantage: Winning through extended enterprise supplier networks.* Oxford University Press.

Gruninger, M., & Uschold (1996). Ontologies: Principles, methods, and applications. *Knowledge Engineering Review, 11*(2).

Hagel, J., & Singer, M. (1999). Unbundling the corporation. *Harvard Business Review, March-April 1999.*

Harrington, L. (1995). Taking Integration to the next level, *Transportation and Distribution.*

Haskell, D. (2005). *What is extended product responsibility?* NZ2000 Plastics, Otaki, New Zealand.

Hunt, I., Pereira Klen, A., & Zhang, J. (1997). Cross border enterprises: Virtual or extended! *ISIP'97 OE/IFIP/IEEE International Conference on Integrated and Sustainable Industrial Production*, Lisboa, Portugal.

Johanson M. *White Paper: Sharing Product Data Through Life in the Extended Enterprise –the share-A-space™ solution.* Eurostep Commercial Solutions AB, Sweden.

Kirchhoff, U., Kuczynski, A., & Stokic, D. (2005). *Set-up and maintenance of ontologies for innovation support in extended enterprises.* Int J Adv Manuf Technol, Published online: 12 October 2005

Kohnhauser, V. (1999). Use of TRIZ in the Development Process. *Triz Journal, June 1999.*

Kühule H, Wagenhaus G (2005) *Extended Enterprise Architectures (E2A)-Towards a powerful Mode of Production.* Otto-von-Guericke-University Magdeburg.

Levy, A., Rajaraman, & Ordille, K. (1996). Querying heterogeneous information sources using source descriptions. *Proceedings of the 22nd VLDB Conference.*

O'Neill, H., & Sackett, P. J. (1994). *The extended manufacturing enterprise paradigm.* Management Decision.

Rabelo, R., & Camarinha-Matos, L. (1996). Towards agile scheduling in extended enterprise. In L. M. Camarinha-Matos, H. & Afsarmanesh (Eds.), *Proceedings of BASYS'96: Balanced Automation Systems II—Implementation Challenges for Anthropocentric Manufacturing.* Chapman & Hall.

Sawaguchi, M. (2001). Study of effective new product development activities through combination of patterns of evolution of technological systems and VE. *Triz Journal. March 2001.*

Schekkerman, J. (2004). *Another View at Extended Enterprise Architecture Viewpoints.* Institute For Enterprise Architecture Developemets.

Short, J., & Venkatraman, N. (1992). *Beyond business process redesign: Redefining Baxter's business network.* Sloan Management Review, *34*(1), Fall 1992

Sorli, M. (1999). Innovación en el Diseño de Productos. *Forum Calidad Journal.*

Sorli, M., Stokic, D., Gorostiza, A., & Campos., A. (2006). Fostering innovation in practice through TRIZ-based CAI tool. *International Journal of Computer Applications in Technology (IJCAT),* special issue on Computer Aided Innovation (CAI).

Sorli, M., Stokic, D., Gorostiza, A., & Campos, A. (2006). *Managing product/process knowledge in the concurrent/simultaneous enterprise environment.* Robotics and Computer Integrated Manufacturing. Elsevier (2006) p. 399–408. Volume 22, October-December 2006. ISSN 0736-5845.

Sorli, M., Mendikoa, I., Barbero, J. I., & Carrillo, A. (2006). *Distributed product design and manufacturing based on KBE. Computer Supported Cooperative Work in Design II;* Lecture Notes in Computer Science 3865. Springer-Verlag Berlin Heidelberg, 2006, ISSN 0302-9743.

Stokic, D. (2006). *A New Collaborative Working Environment for Concurrent Engineering in Manufacturing Industry.* Proc. CE 2006, 13th ISPE International Conference on Concurrent Engineering, Juan-les-Pins, France.

Szgeo, O., & Andersen, B. *Modeling the Extended Enterprise: A comparison of Different Modeling Approaches.*

Terninko J, Zlotin B. & Zusman A (1996). *Step by Step TRIZ. Creating Innovative Solution Concepts.* Responsible Management Inc.

Zlotin B. & Zusman A. (1999). Managing Innovation Knowledge. *Triz Journal.*

This work was previously published in Information Technology Entrepreneurship and Innovation, edited by F. Zhao, pp. 310-328, copyright 2008 by Information Science Reference, formerly known as Idea Group Reference (an imprint of IGI Global).

Chapter XVIII
Government Innovation Through Knowledge Management

Luis Felipe Luna-Reyes
Universidad de las Américas-Puebla, Mexico

INTRODUCTION

Contemporary organizations face the challenge of growing and advancing in a complex and changing environment (Johannessen, Olaisen, & Olsen, 2001; Malhotra, 2000). In order to accomplish this objective, private organizations continuously innovate to attract customers (Johannessen et al.). Competition has been accelerated by information technology, which allows the appearance of new business models, introducing new competitors in the business arena (Rayport, 2001). Under these circumstances, it appears that innovation is one of the most valuable activities for any organization (Nonaka, 1996). Furthermore, the management of intangible assets such as knowledge is one of the critical factors to promote innovation and sustainable competitive advantage (Davenport, 2001; De Long & Fahey, 2000; Malhotra; Nonaka).

The need for innovation in government does not respond directly to competition, but to several intertwined factors, such as the complexity of the problems being faced by government, the emergence of new organizational forms such as networks, the pressure to improve service to the citizens, and the need to learn about new information technology.

Government faces complex social problems that require collaboration from different levels of government, private organizations, and nonprofits (Snyder & de Souza Briggs, 2003; Snyder, Wenger, & de Souza Briggs, 2004). These new collaboration patterns challenge the traditional hierarchical government organization, deriving on the need to innovate in the structure of institutions (Gascó, 2004) and the creation of networks of public and/or private organizations needing to share what they know about a specific problem domain (Fountain, 2001a; Snyder & de Souza Briggs; Zhang, Cresswell, & Thompson, 2005). Innovation is also needed to respond to citizens demanding from government levels of service similar to the ones they are used to getting from private companies (Kannabiran, Xavier, & Anantharaaj, 2004). Additionally, movements such as the New Public Management or the Reinvention of Government are also adding pressure to improve these levels of service (Fountain, 2001b).

IT is being used to respond to these challenges, and public-sector organizations are using IT to promote better relationships between government and citizens (Gil-García & Helbig, 2006; Heeks, 2006; Lee, Tan, & Trimi, 2005; Rocheleau, 2006). However, introducing IT in government poses the challenge of continuous learning and education of government employees, promoting also the need for sharing knowledge (Heeks, 2006). In several countries, additional pressures promoting knowledge management (KM) come from personnel turnover from retirements (Bontis, 2007).

In this way, promoting innovation and managing knowledge is becoming increasingly important for public agencies. As with many other public information technologies, knowledge management and knowledge management systems require the integration of technical design in a series of social processes and interactions among government, citizens, and private organizations, where knowledge is continuously created or transformed (Awad & Ghaziri, 2003; Barrett, Cappleman, Shoib, & Walsham, 2004; Fountain, 2001a).

The purpose of the present chapter is to discuss the process involved in managing knowledge and innovation in government, considering some critical factors in the process. To accomplish this objective, the chapter is organized in four different but conceptually interrelated sections. In the first of them, I describe some of the main concepts of knowledge management. The second section is a description of the knowledge management process, and the next one is a brief discussion about the impact of the four critical factors identified by Arthur Andersen and Company on the main stages in the KM process. The last sections of the chapter constitute a description of future trends and conclusions.

BACKGROUND: THE CONCEPT OF KNOWLEDGE AND KNOWLEDGE MANAGEMENT

Knowledge management is the activity of administering knowledge. De Long and Fahey (2000) consider that the purpose of knowledge management "is to enhance organizational performance by explicitly designing and implementing tools, processes, systems, structures, and cultures to improve the creation, sharing and use of all types of knowledge that are critical for decision making."

Although knowledge is an abstract concept difficult to define, there are two common ways of conceptualizing knowledge. Some experts consider knowledge as an accumulation of actionable information (Davenport, de Long, & Beers, 1998; Nonaka, 1994) or intellectual capital (Becerra-Fernandez, Gonzalez, & Sabherwal, 2004; Bontis, 2007). Some others consider knowledge as a dimension of practice (Black, Carlile, & Repenning, 2004; Levina & Vaast, 2005; Walsham, 2005).

In this way, knowledge management projects take two different forms, characterized as person to person and person to document, responding to each of these views (Dennis & Vessey, 2005). Although both perspectives recognize that knowledge resides in people, person-to-document projects consider knowledge as a codifiable asset to manage. Examples of person-to-document projects include knowledge repositories, decision support systems, expert systems, data warehouses, or executive information systems. The federal Mexican government, for instance, maintains a public repository of government procedures known as Tramitanet (http://www.tramitanet.gob.mx). The e-Mexico program, on the other hand, has invested part of its resources to create knowledge portals in areas such as education, health, economy, and government (Luna-Reyes, Gil-García, & Cruz, 2006).

Person-to-person projects assume that knowledge is embedded in practice, and they look to promote innovation and knowledge sharing by establishing means to connect people. Knowledge directories, groupware, customer relationship management (CRM), workflow management tools, and communities of practice are examples of this kind of projects. In Argentina, for instance, CIOs (chief information officers) have created an interorganizational network to share knowledge and solve IT-related problems in government (Kaufman, 2004). Similarly, the New York State Office of the State Comptroller (NYS-OSC) has developed and consolidated a workflow management and CRM tool known as Multi-Purpose Access for Customer Relations and Operational Support (MACROS; Luna-Reyes, Zhang, Gil-García, & Cresswell, 2005). In the next two sections, I will discuss some basic ideas associated with these two perspectives, linked in an interesting way on a matrix (Belardo, 2001).

THE KNOWLEDGE MANAGEMENT PROCESS

Although there are different ways of conceptualizing the knowledge management process (Awad & Ghaziri, 2003), this section follows a four-activity approach in which managing knowledge involves its identification, elicitation, dissemination, and utilization.

Identification

Knowledge identification involves the activities associated with answering the questions of who knows what, where the knowledge is, and what type of knowledge it is (Awad & Ghaziri, 2003). The intelligence quadrant is a tool to help during the identification process (Hall, 2000). The quadrant has four cells (Table 1). The first cell contains the items we know that we know, and the second cell has the items we know that we do not know. The third and fourth cells contain knowledge we do not know that we know and we do not know that we do not know, respectively. The first two cells in the quadrant contain knowledge that is possible to identify through knowledge fairs, networks, communities of practice, decision conferences, talk rooms (Gray, 2001), and interactions with clients and providers (Davenport, 2001). For instance, e-Mexico participants identified knowledge categories to include in the portals in the context of face-to-face meetings. Similarly, NYS-OSC has continuously defined and redefined the main characteristics of MACROS on the basis of input from users and managers. In both cases, a critical factor to succeed is getting involved with the main stakeholders and domain experts.

The third and fourth cells, on the other hand, constitute places to use tools developed to build

Table 1. Intelligence quadrant (Adapted from Hall, 2000)

	...That We Know	... That We Don't Know
We Know...		
We Don't Know...		

Figure 1. Example of a concept map based on Dennis and Vessey (2005)

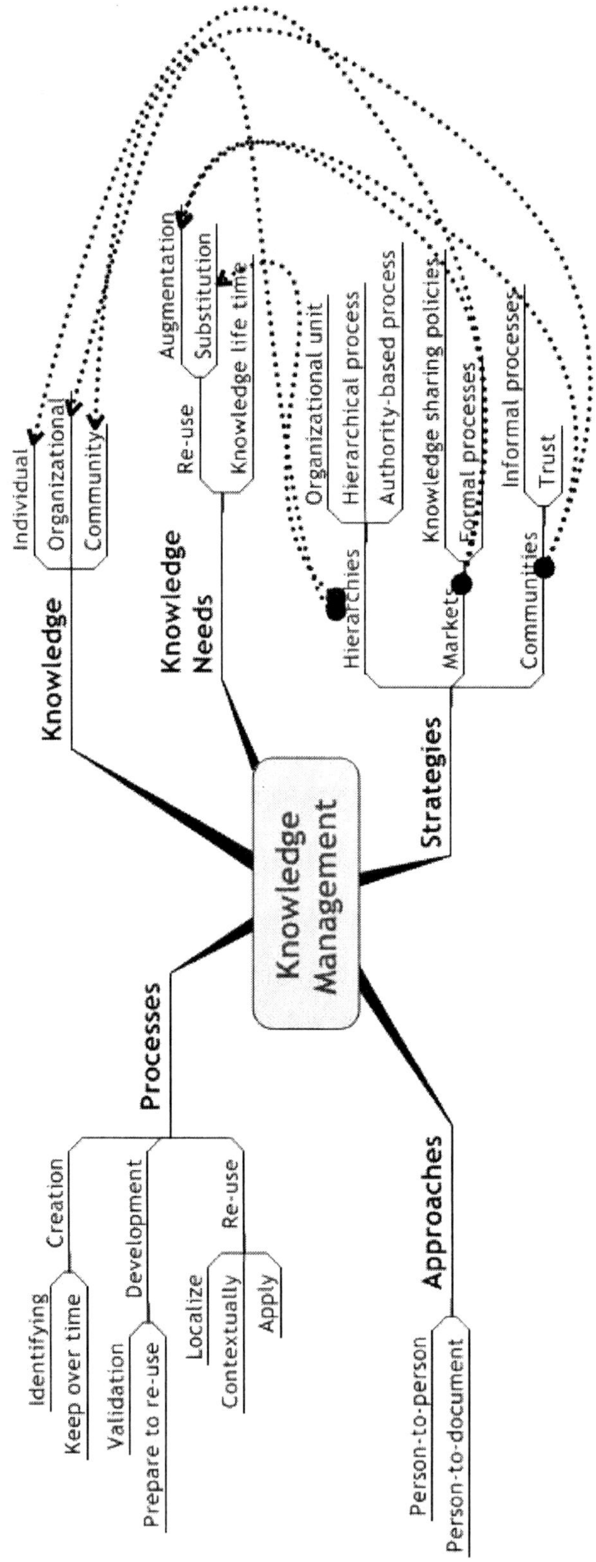

business intelligence, such as data warehousing, data mining, customer relationship management, and so forth. For example, the e-health group from the e-Mexico initiative is mining electronic health records to identify health trends and risks in some pilot communities.

Elicitation

Knowledge elicitation is associated with protocols and tools used to acquire and codify knowledge (Byrd, Cossick, & Zmud, 1992; Eriksson, 1992). From a problem-solving point of view, knowledge is acquired during the process of problem solving, particularly the new or unique kind of problems (Gray, 2001).

From the accumulation view of knowledge, the purpose of knowledge elicitation is to obtain and codify knowledge from domain experts. From the practice point of view, the processes associated with acquiring or creating knowledge can also be conceptualized as the result of the interaction of the knowledge that resides in our heads, the one associated with the context of our physical and social context and the proper act of knowing (Cook, 1999): "The source of new knowledge and knowing lies in the use of knowledge as a tool of knowing within situated interaction with the social and physical world" (p. 383).

The acquisition and codification of knowledge are difficult tasks. Even when companies have access to a rich set of tools such as surveys, interviews, decision conferences, teaching, counseling, repertory grids, or talk rooms, the characteristics of practice-embedded knowledge poses several challenges for the process (Black et al., 2004). These kinds of knowledge are context related, embedded in a tacit level of understanding difficult to make explicit and charged with power, having the potential of create conflict during the acquisition of knowledge across organizational or departmental boundaries (Bechky, 2003; Black et al.; Carlile, 2002). In such cases, the use of objects to facilitate knowledge sharing at the boundary is recommended. For instance, concept maps are becoming a standard to represent specific problems or content domains in group sessions. In fact, the e-Mexico group has intensively used concept maps to define knowledge domains associated with each of the e-Mexico portals (see Figure 1 for an example of a concept map).

Dissemination

The process of dissemination involves the creation of knowledge representations that allow the processing and storage of knowledge. Additionally, the main concerns for managers are related to the problem of making knowledge available to the right people at the right time (Belardo, 2001). Depending on the project, dissemination of knowledge is related to one of two main purposes: knowledge augmentation or knowledge substitution (Dennis & Vessey, 2005).

Knowledge augmentation projects look to incrementally build over existing knowledge and innovation. These projects usually involve the creation of repositories and making more accessible the knowledge kept in these repositories. Repositories keep internal, external, and informal knowledge (Davenport et al., 1998). Improving-access projects have as their most common purpose the creation of a catalog or other artifact intended to find the person who knows how to deal with specific problems (expert networks).

The MACROS system at the NYS-OSC is an example of a knowledge augmentation system. The purpose of MACROS is to help several divisions of the Office of the State Comptroller to manage their relationships with customers by keeping a record of the interactions with them, and to give advice and technical support. Knowledge substitution systems have the purpose of substituting expert knowledge such as in expert systems.

Knowledge transfer and dissemination is also a difficult task. The problems associated with this process have led some researchers to characterize it as a "sticky" process (Szulanski, 1999). There is a conflict between the knowledge created by a community of practice and the knowledge needed to promote collaboration between communities (Carlile, 2002). From this point of view, knowledge is a barrier and a source of innovation and collaboration.

Utilization

Knowledge utilization involves not only the actual internalization processes (Nonaka, 1994, 1996), but also an assessment of the benefits that the organization is obtaining through the use of this knowledge. Under these assumptions, knowledge utilization is related to both knowledge internalization and evaluation processes.

The internalization process has aroused the interest of researchers who conclude that knowing what to do is not enough (Pfeffer & Sutton, 2000). Actually, it is possible to identify several knowing-doing barriers such as the tendency to substitute action with talking or the substitution of thinking with memory (Pfeffer & Sutton, 2000).

A MODEL TO INTEGRATE KNOWLEDGE MANAGEMENT APPROACHES

Interpretations of the knowledge management process can be integrated with descriptive models involving critical success factors as shown in Table 2 (Belardo, 2001). The purpose of this part of the chapter is to make some comments and to stress the role of each of the four factors during the different stages in the KM process. Instead of discussing the role of the critical factors across all the stages in the process, I will focus on the shaded cells in Table 2. That is to say, I will discuss the role of technology in the dissemination process, the role of measurement on the identification process, and so on.

Technology

Technology is an important factor that can influence positively the dissemination of knowledge, as well as the other stages in the process. It is important to point out that technologies, broadly defined, include not only computer hardware and software, but a rich set of hard and soft technologies that can be used in the process of dissemination of knowledge. Examples of hard technologies are whiteboards, bulletin boards, overhead projectors, and computers. On the other hand, soft technologies include Post-its, overhead transparencies, and software used with hardware, but also the technologies developed to design and manage this series of artifacts.

From this point of view, "[k]nowledge management tools are technologies, broadly defined, which enhance and enable knowledge generation, codification and transfer" (Ruggles, 1997), and they include among others data warehouses, search engines, and visualization tools.

An interesting set of technologies for the dissemination process are the tools associated with the development of knowledge repositories or

Table 2. A matrix approach to knowledge management (Adapted from Belardo, 2001)

	Identification	Elicitation	Dissemination	Utilization
Technology				
Measurement				
Leadership				
Culture				

knowledge bases. They are different from databases or information bases in the sense that they contain interrelationships, history, and past usage of the knowledge inside them. Three technologies are changing the way in which this kind of repositories can be organized and accessed. First, the extensible markup language (XML) offers the possibility to create a meaningful syntax for a community of practice, and to embed this syntax inside documents, making possible to have the contents of these documents self-describing (Bosak & Bray, 1999). On the other hand, there is the resource description framework (RDF), which encodes meaning in sets of triplets with each triple being like the subject, verb, and object of an elementary sentence (Berners-Lee, Hendler, & Lassila, 2001). Finally, recent developments in ontology engineering add to these basic technologies the capability to develop documents that formally define the relation among terms (or ontologies). This triplet of technologies makes possible the development of software to help people find information and services called agents. From my personal point of view, this powerful combination of technologies will revolutionize the way in which knowledge repositories are used nowadays.

Some other technologies used in the dissemination of knowledge are portals, component- or modular-based products (integration of knowledge tools, legacy systems, enterprise resource planning [ERP], and CRM systems), e-mail based solutions, expert systems, and collaborative working environment servers (Silver, 2000). All these technology-based solutions have the potential of increasing the ways in which knowledge is transferred and communities of practice acquire new knowledge.

However, it is important to be aware that technological solutions are not enough, and the extensive use of them without taking into account a set of soft technologies has the potential to overemphasize person-to-document over person-to-person initiatives (Johannessen et al., 2001).

Measurement

Measurement is another critical factor along the knowledge management process, and projects involving the development of better ways to measure intangible assets are very common across organizations (Davenport et al., 1998). Moreover, there exist several systems to measure the impact of knowledge and knowledge management programs (Martin, 1999). Some of these approaches focus on accounting methods (market-to-book ratios or Sveiby invisible balance sheets), some of them focus on the output of the system (peer-reviewed performance or customer appraisal), and some of them involve a more integral approach (balance scorecard or intangible assets monitor).

However, some problems have been identified in measurement practices in organizations (Martin, 1999). The first one is that organizations do not measure what they perceive as important. For example, 76% of the organizations included in a survey rated morale as important, but only 37% measure it. The second problem is that even when organizations collected relevant data, most of them did not use it for anything.

Interesting approaches to identify and measure what we think is actually relevant can be found in the education literature. Core-competencies identification to identify e-learning and training initiatives can be guided, for example, by Bloom's taxonomy of learning objectives (Belardo, 2001). This statement makes a lot of sense if we think that Bloom developed this taxonomy to help educators think about what was really important to teach as an aid to setting objectives and as the basis of the creation of learning measurement instruments.

Bloom's taxonomy (Bloom, Messia, & Krathwohl, 1964) involves three domains of knowledge: cognitive, affective, and psychomotor. For each domain, he developed a hierarchy of levels of skill (see Table 3). Both tacit and explicit dimensions of knowledge are present in the taxonomy. The tacit dimension is present particularly in the levels of

Table 3. Bloom's taxonomy of learning objectives

COGNITIVE DOMAIN	AFFECTIVE DOMAIN	PSYCHOMOTOR DOMAIN
Knowledge	Receiving phenomena	Perception
Comprehension	Responding to phenomena	Readiness to act
Application	Valuing	Guided response
Analysis	Organization	Mechanism
Synthesis	Characterization	Complex overt response
Evaluation		Adaptation

skill that imply knowledge embedded in practice (particularly in the affective and psychomotor domains).

In this way, we can use this framework to think about the kinds of knowledge and core competencies that we really want to promote and leverage, as well as key skills and attitudes.

Finally, it is important to stress the importance of taking care of the reliability and validity of our measurement systems, thinking of reliability as the consistency of an assessment device and validity as the extent to which the instrument measures what it was designed to measure (Aiken, 1994).

Leadership

The role of the leader is important in knowledge management, particularly in the world of public administration where complex problems need to be solved by networks of public and private organizations in which power is shared (Crosby & Bryson, 2005; Frederickson, 2005).

The leader in this environment has new roles to play. First, the leader is a designer of vision, policies, and learning processes that enable knowledge utilization. Additionally, the leader is a teacher who helps people get more insightful views of a current problem. Finally, the leader is a steward of the people's needs and the broader mission (Bertucci, 2006; Senge, 1996).

Building a shared vision is particularly important in network environments where no actor has full control or jurisdiction over a problem or resources for potential solutions (Crosby & Bryson, 2005; Frederickson, 2005). Encouraging people to have a personal vision, to communicate and ask for support when needed, and to bring the external views to blend them with internal practices and activities constitutes an important activity for the leader.

Crosby & Bryson (2005) propose the Leadership for the Common Good framework for public-sector leaders. The framework includes four components: attention to the dynamics of a shared-power world, the wise design and use of forums, effective navigation of the policy change cycle, and the exercise of leadership capabilities.

Complex public-sector problems require from leaders to understand that collaboration is needed to solve problems. The main challenge is to get together key stakeholders with different and complementary expertise in the problem domain. A wise design of forums involves the leader's capabilities to design a place to share meanings and knowledge about the problem and its solutions. Leader activities should rest on the principle of creative tension, that is, "from seeing clearly where we want to be and telling the truth about where we are" (Senge, 1996). This principle promotes actions to close the gap between what we know and what we do. Navigating the policy change cycle involves project management activities needed to push the shared vision of a solution forward, from problem identification to implementation and evaluation. Leadership, in fact, has played a key role in several projects that I have observed in Mexico and the United States such as the e-Mexico program or specific projects like MACROS.

Culture

Organizational culture is a major barrier (or facilitator) to knowledge management projects (De Long, 1997; De Long & Fahey, 2000), and it is critical in the acquisition and creation of knowledge involved in the elicitation stage.

First of all, it is important to state that culture is reflected in values (tacit preferences about objectives and relevant issues), norms (informal rules inside the organization), practices (individual and collective behaviors), and artifacts shared by the people across an organization (Beer & Eisenstat, 2000; De Long, 1997; De Long & Fahey, 2000). Values and assumptions are commonly referred to as the ideational components of culture, while norms, practices, and artifacts constitute the material components of culture (Leidner & Kayworth, 2006). Establishing these values, norms, and common understandings are recognized as important components in a KM program (Snowden, 1999). Although values are difficult to observe directly, they are linked to observable practices and artifacts. That is to say, values shape norms, which in turn determine specific practices. De Long (1997) found four different ways in which organizational culture shapes knowledge management initiatives. First, culture mediates how knowledge is to be distributed between the organization and the individual, and what is to be shared. Norms about status and trust among individuals are crucial for knowledge acquisition given that it is very difficult to acquire knowledge from a distant or distrusted source (Szulanski, 1999). In this way, although government agencies encourage the transfer of knowledge and best practices to reduce the costs of innovation, differences in norms or shared meanings about how work must be done between government agencies represent a barrier to facilitate knowledge sharing. On the other hand, culture creates the rules and practices of communication (vertical vs. horizontal, and opened vs. closed) and social interaction, both critical in the creation of knowledge. In the e-Mexico project, for example, differences between the centralized Ministry of Transportation and Communications and the highly decentralized Ministry of Education or the professional-oriented Ministry of Health have been important challenges to facilitate knowledge sharing. Finally, culture determines how we gather information from the environment or internal sources, shaping directly the creation and adoption of new knowledge. Public-sector organizations are, for instance, much more cautious and risk averse in their decisions about IT investments than private firms (Rocheleau, 2006).

FUTURE TRENDS

Most of the existing research favors an epistemology of possession (knowledge as an asset) over an epistemology of practice (knowledge as practice). In this way, current and future research trends call for developing such epistemology of practice that differentiates knowledge from the act of knowing, and recognizes the differences between knowledge that is part of practice and knowledge that resides or is possessed in the heads of the members of a group (Cook, 1999; Walsham, 2005). This practice approach is particularly important in understanding interorganizational networks like the ones emerging in the public sector to innovate and solve complex problems.

Associated with this practice approach to knowledge, knowledge transfer across boundaries is an area future research should try to better understand (Bechky, 2003; Black et al., 2004; Carlile & Rebentisch, 2003; Levina, 2005; Levina & Vaast, 2005). Carlile (2002), for example, identifies three approaches to analyze knowledge transfer: syntactic (common syntax to communicate), semantic (shared meanings), and pragmatic approaches (communities are reluctant to change their own knowledge through interaction across boundaries). To solve the problem, boundary objects can be used to clarify meaning and specify dependencies (Carlile, 2002). Boundary objects are "objects that are shared and shareable across different problem solving contexts" (p. 451). Moreover, boundary objects will play an important role in identifying and eliciting knowledge from groups of stakeholders playing the role of domain experts analyzing public problems and policies.

Finally, another important trend is associated with the use of social network analysis to better understand the social relations among members of an organization to develop better strategies and channels to share knowledge (Borgatti & Cross, 2003), and to better understand relationships in communities of practice (Wenger & Snyder, 2000).

CONCLUSION

I want to finish this chapter by remarking again that all efforts in identifying, eliciting, disseminating, and using knowledge are closely related to increasing individual and collective capabilities to innovate. Innovation is without a doubt one of the core competencies of public organizations in order to improve governance and create public value. Although it is possible to create new ideas by contemplation or by encouraging serendipity, most of the creative efforts came from reorganizing, challenging, or taking different points of view about the things that we actually know. In the face of complex problems, innovation also involves bringing together a diversity of stakeholders in a creative way to build and negotiate shared meanings about the problem and its solutions. This very nature of the innovative process pinpoints the importance of identifying, acquiring, sharing, and using the knowledge that we already have.

FUTURE RESEARCH DIRECTIONS

There are a lot of knowledge-related phenomena that are yet to be explored. We need to understand and find better ways to share knowledge that forms part of practice. It is important also to get a better understanding of the act of knowing, and the ways in which the act of knowing interacts with our actual knowledge in the creation or innovative process.

Although information technologies have a great potential to facilitate both the administration of knowledge and the innovation processes, understanding the social relationships of networks of individuals and looking for better organizational designs need attention to truly improve the way of doing government. Leaders in this process are the architects of the technological and organizational designs that will increase the innovative processes.

ACKNOWLEDGMENT

The research reported here is supported by the Consejo Nacional de Ciencia y Tecnología (CONACYT-Mexico) Grant No. SEP-2004-C01-46507. The views and conclusions expressed in this chapter are those of the authors alone and do not necessarily reflect the views or policies of CONACYT.

REFERENCES

Aiken, L. (1994). *Psychological testing and assessment* (8th ed.). Boston: Allyn & Bacon.

Awad, E. M., & Ghaziri, H. M. (2003). *Knowledge management.* Upper Saddle River, NJ: Prentice Hall.

Barrett, M., Cappleman, S., Shoib, G., & Walsham, G. (2004). Learning in knowledge communities:

Managing technology and context. *European Management Journal, 22*(1), 1-11.

Becerra-Fernandez, I., Gonzalez, A., & Sabherwal, R. (2004). *Knowledge management: Challenges, solutions, and technologies.* Upper Saddle River, NJ: Pearson Prentice Hall.

Bechky, B. (2003). Sharing meaning across occupational communities: The transformation of understanding on a production floor. *Organization Science, 14*(3), 312-330.

Beer, M., & Eisenstat, R. (2000). The silent killers of strategy implementation and learning. *Sloan Management Review, 41*(4), 29-40.

Belardo, S. (2001). *Learning organizations and knowledge management: A conventional view and an alternative view.*

Berners-Lee, T., Hendler, J., & Lassila, O. (2001). The semantic Web. *Scientific American.*

Bertucci, G. (2006). Unlocking the human potential for public sector performance. *Public Personnel Management, 35*(3), 175-179.

Black, L. J., Carlile, P. R., & Repenning, N. P. (2004). A dynamic theory of expertise and occupational boundaries in new technology implementation: Building on Barley's study of CT scanning. *Administrative Science Quarterly, 49*(4), 572-607.

Bloom, B., Messia, B., & Krathwohl, D. (1964). *Taxonomy of educational objectives.* New York: David McKay.

Bontis, N. (2007). Mining the nation's intellectual capital: Knowledge management in government. In S. Borins, K. Kernaghan, D. Brown, N. Bontis, P. 6, & F. Thompson (Eds.), *Digital state at the leading edge* (pp. 155-182). Toronto, Canada: University of Toronto Press.

Borgatti, S. P., & Cross, R. (2003). A relational view of information seeking and learning in social networks. *Management Science, 49*(4), 432-445.

Bosak, J., & Bray, T. (1999). XML and the second-generation Web. *Scientific American.*

Byrd, T. A., Cossick, K. L., & Zmud, R. W. (1992). A synthesis of research on requirements analysis and knowledge acquisition techniques. *MIS Quarterly, 16*(1), 117-138.

Carlile, P. (2002). A pragmatic view of knowledge and boundaries: Boundary objects in new product development. *Organization Science, 13*(4), 442-455.

Carlile, P., & Rebentisch, E. (2003). Into the black box: The knowledge transformation cycle. *Management Science, 49*(9), 1180-1195.

Cook, S. J. B. (1999). Bridging epistemologies: The generative dance between organizational knowledge and organizational knowing. *Organization Science, 10*(4), 381-400.

Crosby, B., & Bryson, J. (2005). A leadership framework for cross-sector collaboration. *Public Management Review, 7*(2), 177-201.

Davenport, T. (2001). How do they know their customers so well? *Sloan Management Review, 42*(2), 63-73.

Davenport, T., de Long, D., & Beers, M. (1998). Successful knowledge management projects. *Sloan Management Review, 39*(2), 43-57.

De Long, D. (1997). *Building the knowledge-based organization: How culture drives knowledge behaviors.* Unpublished manuscript.

De Long, D., & Fahey, L. (2000). Diagnosing cultural barriers to knowledge management. *The Academy of Management Executive, 14*(4), 113-127.

Dennis, A. R., & Vessey, I. (2005). Three knowledge management strategies: Knowledge hierarchies, knowledge markets and knowledge communities. *MIS Quarterly Executive, 4*(4), 399-412.

Eriksson, H. (1992). A survey of knowledge acquisition techniques and tools and their relationship to software engineering. *The Journal of Systems and Software, 19*, 97-107.

Fountain, J. E. (2001a). *Building the virtual state.* Washington, DC: The Brookings Institution.

Fountain, J. E. (2001b). Paradoxes of public sector customer service. *Governance: An International Journal of Policy and Administration, 14*(1), 55-73.

Frederickson, H. G. (2005). Transcending the community: Local leadership in a world of shared power. *Public Management, 87*(10), 8-15.

Gascó, M. (2004). E-gobierno en Bolivia y Paraguay. In R. Araya Dujisin & M. A. Porrúa Vigon (Eds.), *América Latina puntogob: Casos y tendencias en gobierno electrónico* (pp. 125-150). Santiago, Chile: FLACSO-Chile/AICD-OEA.

Gil-García, J. R., & Helbig, N. (2006). Exploring e-government benefits and success factors. In A.-V. Anttiroiko & M. Malkia (Eds.), *Encyclopedia of digital government* (pp. 803-811). Hershey, PA: Idea Group Reference.

Gray, P. (2001). A problem-solving perspective on knowledge management practices. *Decision Support Systems, 31*, 87-102.

Hall, H. (2000). Online information sources: Tools of business intelligence? *Journal of Information Science, 26*(3), 139-143.

Heeks, R. (2006). *Implementing and managing egovernment: An international text.* London: Sage Publications.

Johannessen, J., Olaisen, J., & Olsen, B. (2001). Management of tacit knowledge: The importance of tacit knowledge, the danger of information technology, and what to do about it. *International Journal of Information Management, 21*, 3-20.

Kannabiran, G., Xavier, M. J., & Anantharaaj, A. (2004). Enabling e-governance through citizen relationship management: Concept, model and applications. *Journal of Services Research, 4*(2), 223-240.

Kaufman, E. (2004). E-gobierno en Argentina: Crisis, burocracia y redes. In R. Araya Dujisin & M. A. Porrúa Vigon (Eds.), *América Latina puntogob: Casos y tendencias en gobierno electrónico* (pp. 151-188). Santiago, Chile: FLACSO-Chile/AICD-OEA.

Lee, S. M., Tan, X., & Trimi, S. (2005). Current practices of leading e-government countries. *Communications of the ACM, 49*(10), 99-104.

Leidner, D. E., & Kayworth, T. (2006). A review of culture in information systems research: Toward a theory of information technology culture conflict. *MIS Quarterly, 30*(2), 357-399.

Levina, N. (2005). Collaborating on multiparty information systems development projects: A collective reflection-in-action view. *Information Systems Research, 16*(2), 109-130.

Levina, N., & Vaast, E. (2005). Competence in practice: Implications for implementation and use of information systems. *MIS Quarterly, 29*(2), 335-363.

Luna-Reyes, L. F., Gil-García, J. R., & Cruz, C. B. (2006, August). *Collaborative digital government in Mexico: Some lessons from federal Web-based inter-organizational information integration initiatives.* Paper presented at the 12th Americas Conference on Information Systems, Acapulco, Mexico.

Luna-Reyes, L. F., Zhang, J., Gil-García, J. R., & Cresswell, A. M. (2005). Information systems development as emergent socio-technical change: A practice approach. *European Journal of Information Systems, 14*(1), 93-105.

Malhotra, Y. (2000). Knowledge management for e-business performance: Advancing information strategy to "Internet time." *Information Strategy, The Executive's Journal, 16*(4), 5-16.

Martin, W. (1999). Approaches to the measurement of the impact of knowledge management programs. *Journal of Information Science, 26*(1), 21-27.

Nonaka, I. (1994). A dynamic theory of organizational knowledge creation. *Organization Science, 5*(1), 14-37.

Nonaka, I. (1996). The knowledge-creating company. In K. Starkey (Ed.), *How organizations learn* (pp. 18-31). London: International Thompson Business Press.

Pfeffer, J., & Sutton, R. (2000). *The knowing-doing gap* (1st ed.). Harvard Business School.

Rayport, J. B. J. (2001). *E-commerce* (1st ed.). New York: McGraw-Hill.

Rocheleau, B. (2006). *Public management information systems.* Hershey, PA: Idea Group Publishing.

Ruggles, R. (1997). *Using technology to manage knowledge better.* Unpublished manuscript.

Senge, P. (1996). The leader's new work: Building learning organizations. In K. Starkey (Ed.), *How organizations learn* (pp. 288-315). London: International Thompson Business Press.

Silver, C. (2000). Where technology and knowledge meet. *The Journal of Business Strategy, 21*(6), 28-33.

Snowden, D. (1999). Three metaphors, two stories and a picture. *Knowledge Management Review, 7*, 30-33.

Snyder, W. M., & de Souza Briggs, X. (2003). *Communities of practice: A new tool for government managers.* Retrieved March 20, 2007, from http://www.businessofgovernment.org/pdfs/Snyder_report.pdf

Snyder, W. M., Wenger, E., & de Souza Briggs, X. (2004). Communities of practice in government: The case for sponsorship. *The Public Manager, 32*(4), 17-21.

Szulanski, G. (1999). The process of knowledge transfer: A diachronic analysis of stickiness. *OBHDP.*

Walsham, G. (2005). Knowledge management systems: Representation and communication in context. *Systems, Signs & Actions, 1*(1), 6-18.

Wenger, E., & Snyder, W. (2000). Communities of practice: The organizational frontier. *Harvard Business Review, 78*(1), 139-145.

Zhang, J., Cresswell, A. M., & Thompson, F. (2005). Participants' expectations and the success of knowledge networking in the public sector. In W. Huang, K. Siau, & K. K. Wei (Eds.), *Digital government: Strategies and implementation from developing and developed countries* (pp. 260-281). Hershey, PA: Idea Group Inc.

FURTHER READING

Andersen, D., & Dawes, S. (1991). *Government information management: A primer and casebook.* Englewood Cliffs, NJ: Prentice Hall.

Argote, L., McEvily, B., & Reagans, R. (2003). Managing knowledge in organizations: An integrative framework and review of emerging themes. *Management Science, 49*(4), 571-582.

Bechky, B. (2003). Sharing meaning across occupational communities: The transformation of understanding on a production floor. *Organization Science, 14*(3), 312-330.

Black, L. J., Carlile, P. R., & Repenning, N. P. (2004). A dynamic theory of expertise and occupational boundaries in new technology implementation: Building on Barley's study of CT scanning. *Administrative Science Quarterly, 49*(4), 572-607.

Bontis, N. (2007). Mining the nation's intellectual capital: Knowledge management in government.

In S. Borins, K. Kernaghan, D. Brown, N. Bontis, P. 6, & F. Thompson (Eds.), *Digital state at the leading edge* (pp. 155-182). Toronto, Canada: University of Toronto Press.

Carlile, P. (2002). A pragmatic view of knowledge and boundaries: Boundary objects in new product development. *Organization Science, 13*(4), 442-455.

Carlile, P., & Rebentisch, E. (2003). Into the black box: The knowledge transformation cycle. *Management Science, 49*(9), 1180-1195.

Dawes, S. S. (1996). Interagency information sharing: Expected benefits, manageable risks. *Journal of Policy Analysis and Management, 15*(3), 377-394.

Dawes, S. S., Pardo, T. A., Simon, S., Cresswell, A. M., LaVigne, M. F., Andersen, D. F., et al. (2004). *Making smart IT choices: Understanding value and risk in government IT investments.* Retrieved March 20, 2007, from http://www.ctg.albany.edu/publications/guides/smartit2

Fountain, J. E. (2001). *Building the virtual state.* Washington, DC: The Brookings Institution.

Gascó, M. (2004). E-gobierno en Bolivia y Paraguay. In R. Araya Dujisin & M. A. Porrúa Vigon (Eds.), *América Latina puntogob: Casos y tendencias en gobierno electrónico* (pp. 125-150). Santiago, Chile: FLACSO-Chile/AICD-OEA.

Gherardi, S. (2001). From organizational learning to practice-based knowing. *Human Relations, 54*(1), 131-139.

Gil-García, J. R., & Helbig, N. (2006). Exploring e-government benefits and success factors. In A.-V. Anttiroiko & M. Malkia (Eds.), *Encyclopedia of digital government* (pp. 803-811). Hershey, PA: Idea Group Reference.

Heeks, R. (2006). *Implementing and managing egovernment: An international text.* London: Sage Publications.

Levin, D., Cross, R., & Abrams, L. (2002). *Why should I trust you? Antecedents of trust in a knowledge transfer context.* Unpublished manuscript.

Levina, N. (2005). Collaborating on multiparty information systems development projects: A collective reflection-in-action view. *Information Systems Research, 16*(2), 109-130.

Levina, N., & Vaast, E. (2005). Competence in practice: Implications for implementation and use of information systems. *MIS Quarterly, 29*(2), 335-363.

Luna-Reyes, L. F., Cresswell, A. M., & Richardson, G. P. (2004). *Knowledge and the development of interpersonal trust: A dynamic model.* Paper presented at the Hawaiian International Conference on System Sciences, HI.

Luna-Reyes, L. F., Zhang, J., Gil-García, J. R., & Cresswell, A. M. (2005). Information systems development as emergent socio-technical change: A practice approach. *European Journal of Information Systems, 14*(1), 93-105.

Orlikowski, W. (2002). Knowing in practice: Enacting a collective capability in distributed organizing. *Organization Science, 13*(3), 249-273.

Pardo, T. A., Cresswell, A. M., Thompson, F., & Zhang, J. (2006). Knowledge sharing in cross-boundary information system development in the public sector. *Information Technology and Management, 7*(4), 293-313.

Polanyi, M. (1966). *The tacit dimension.* Garden City: Doubleday & Company.

Rocheleau, B. (2006). *Public management information systems.* Hershey, PA: Idea Group Publishing.

Snyder, W. M., & de Souza Briggs, X. (2003). *Communities of practice: A new tool for government managers.* Retrieved March 20, 2007, from http://www.businessofgovernment.org/pdfs/Snyder_report.pdf

Snyder, W. M., Wenger, E., & de Souza Briggs, X. (2004). Communities of practice in government: The case for sponsorship. *The Public Manager, 32*(4), 17-21.

Walsham, G. (2005). Knowledge management systems: Representation and communication in context. *Systems, Signs & Actions, 1*(1), 6-18.

Zhang, J., Cresswell, A. M., & Thompson, F. (2005). Participants' expectations and the success of knowledge networking in the public sector. In W. Huang, K. Siau, & K. K. Wei (Eds.), *Digital government: Strategies and implementation from developing and developed countries* (pp. 260-281). Hershey, PA: Idea Group Inc.

KEY TERMS

Customer Relationship Management (CRM): CRM is an IT-supported process that has as its objective to increase value to customers or citizens. There are two common ways in which public organizations are approaching CRM. The first of them involves improving customer support and service through one-step shopping through the Internet, toll-free numbers, or in some countries through service kiosks. The second approach consists of mining data to better understand citizens' needs in areas such as health or education.

Decision Conferences: These are computer-supported meetings where a group negotiates a shared meaning about a policy problem and alternative solutions to it.

E-Learning: E-learning is a process to improve knowledge dissemination and sharing through the application of information technologies to learning programs such as mentoring or on-the-job training. The concept is also used to refer to formal distance education programs offered through the Internet or other electronic means.

Expert Systems: These are computer programs that codify expert knowledge associated with a specific problem domain. An expert system is formed by a set of rules and an inference engine with the capability to reach a conclusion by combining and applying the rules to a set of facts or statements.

Groupware: Groupware is a computer program that offers services to support group collaboration such as e-mail, meeting scheduling, shared libraries, forums, and chat rooms.

Knowledge Management (KM): KM is a professional field committed to innovation and improved organizational performance by identifying, eliciting, disseminating, and using knowledge and other intangible assets within an organization.

Knowledge Portal: A knowledge portal is an Internet-based computer program that constitutes a single point of access to organizational knowledge, integrating knowledge repositories, expert directories, collaboration tools, and other knowledge-intensive applications.

This work was previously published in Handbook of Research on Public Information Technology, edited by G. Garson & M. Khosrow-Pour, pp. 493-507, copyright 2008 by Information Science Reference, formerly known as Idea Group Reference (an imprint of IGI Global).

Chapter XIX
A Technology-Focused Framework for Integrating Knowledge Management into Strategic Innovation Management

Marc Henselewski
Deloitte Consulting GmbH, Germany

Stefan Smolnik
European Business School, Germany

Gerold Riempp
European Business School, Germany

ABSTRACT

Today's business environment is characterized by highly transparent markets and global competition. Technology life cycles are decreasing due to the fast pace at which development of new technologies is progressing. To compete in this environment, it is necessary to identify upcoming innovations and trends as early as possible to decrease uncertainty, implement technology leadership, and create competitive advantage. In a parallel development, the amount of information available is already vast and increasing daily. As a result of these developments, strategic innovation management has become increasingly challenging. The goal of our chapter is to investigate to what extent knowledge management technologies support and improve strategic innovation management to face the aforementioned problems successfully. Consequently, we will develop a characterization scheme which works as a framework for the subsequent evaluation of knowledge management technologies and apply this to a real-world case.

INTRODUCTION

Competition in today's business environment is intense. The influences of the rapid pace of globalization, and of national and international markets' on-going liberalization lead to the emergence of new problem settings and, consequently, increased pressure on companies. Companies therefore face greater risks due to the higher number of players in the market. However, environmental influences created outside the market are not the only factors that have an impact on companies' complexity. The increasing speed at which innovations and new developments occur, the resultant shorter product life cycles, and decreasing production costs also add to the pressure felt by firms and their decision-makers. High technology companies that have high research and development (R&D) expenditures, have to specifically plan their research programs more carefully, because they run a higher risk of losing the competitive advantage when "going the wrong way". Consequently, decision-makers have a greater need to anticipate or forecast future developments and apply these insights in business strategies and strategic innovation management in order to keep risk levels low and the company competitive. According to Bright (1979), all "firms and governments dealing with technology have been and are doing technology forecasting. This is because each decision to explore, support, oppose or ignore a technological prospect incorporates the decision-maker's assumptions about that technology and its viability in the future" (p. 228).

Over the last few years, firms have increasingly realized that knowledge plays a key role in the development of strategies for future success and stronger market positions. The most striking examples of such firms are technology and service-oriented companies, but retailers also engage in activities to use knowledge as factors of competitive advantage. A paradigm shift can be observed in business strategies: from a focus on tangible assets to one that prioritizes intangible assets (Drucker, 1996, p. 203; Stewart, 1997, p. 23). However, information and information sources' quantity is continuously increasing, and what at first seemed to be the solution to several business problems has itself become a unique problem for today's companies—too much information. In order to gain from information and to facilitate knowledge creation within a company, new ways of filtering and selecting information have to be applied. Furthermore, the nature of knowledge is highly dynamic. The value of knowledge is difficult to measure and can change from one moment to another. Companies try to control this uncertainty to some extent and to obtain as much advantage as possible from their knowledge by integrating knowledge management paradigms into competitive strategies.

The question arises if it is possible to successfully support knowledge and strategic innovation management alignment on an operational level. With technology forecasting being an essential discipline of today's innovation and innovation management processes, it is of specific interest to know whether technology forecasting can be improved by integrating knowledge management—particularly by means of current knowledge management technologies. In the following, we understand the latter as instruments of information and communication technologies that support knowledge management processes.

In order to answer the stated question, this chapter's objective is to develop a characterization scheme that integrates aspects of both fields: knowledge management as well as innovation management process's technology forecasting. Furthermore, selected knowledge management technologies will be evaluated by applying this scheme to derive conclusions regarding the most promising solutions with which to support technology forecasting.

The section following this one introduces and defines technology forecasting and illustrates the associated standard technology forecasting process, which is tailored to comply with strategic innovation management. Thereafter, an overview of several forecasting methods is given. The section *Knowledge Management Needs Within Technology Forecasting* explains the motivation for knowledge management's integration into technology forecasting and describes the strategic and organizational reasons. The subsequent section leads to the development of a characterization scheme in order to evaluate the knowledge management technologies data mining, case-based reasoning, information retrieval, topic maps, and ontologies. The next section comprises the actual evaluation of the mentioned technologies and is followed by an integrative discussion of the findings to close the evaluation. The transfer of the developed insights to the real world through discussion of an example case is covered in the section *Towards an Exploratory Case Study*. This is taken from an innovation project at DETECON Inc., conducted for Deutsche Telekom AG. The subsequent section summarizes the main results and the concluding section suggests fields for further research.

DELIMITATION AND CONCEPTUAL DEFINITIONS

Technology Forecasting

As Granger points out, technology forecasting evolved from the argument that, in the long run, technological change is one of the most important influencing factors of economies (Granger, 1989, p. 209). Thus, technology forecasting seems to be most valuable when applied to long time horizons, which becomes even more important in strategic innovation management. For example, decisions pertaining to general strategic business planning are often based on a forecast time horizon of three to twenty years (DeLurgio, 1998, p. 8).

Besides longer time horizons, the scope of the results is another specific property of technology forecasting. Such forecasts "are generally concerned with the characteristics of a technology rather than how these are achieved" (Granger, 1989, p. 210). It was Bright (1979) who incorporated this fact into a definition of technology forecasting:

Technology forecasting is a quantified statement of the timing, the character or the degree of change in technical parameters and attributes in the design, production and application of devices, materials and processes, arrived at through a specified system of reasoning. (p. 235)

Other authors (for example, DeLurgio, 1998, p. 10) stress that uncertainties about future developments can be modeled with the help of probabilities that help decision-makers plan for a variety of contingencies and scenarios. For this reason and the fact that technology forecasting mostly deals with long time horizons, we revised Bright's definition to attain a more rigorous and precise definition of technology forecasting:

Technology forecasting is a probabilistic, long-term estimate of the timing, the character or the degree of change in technical parameters and attributes in the design, production, and application of devices, materials, and processes, arrived at through a system of reasoning consciously applied by the forecaster and exposed to the recipient.

In different situations, the exact technology-forecasting process can vary from a relatively simple process with just a few stages, to a process comprising a complex structure of stages and subprocesses (DeLurgio, 1998, p. 26). Armstrong (2001) divides the process into six basic steps: formulate problem, obtain information, select methods, implement methods, evaluate methods, and use forecasts (p. 8). These steps also appear in other literature, in the same or a very similar order (DeLurgio, 1998, p. 27; Reger, 2001, p.538), sometimes in combination with additional stages.

In addition to this process structure, DeLurgio (1998) mentions that on-going maintenance and verification are necessary to ensure that the results are valid and effective (p. 27). Hence, it is recommended that reality be monitored and compared to the forecasting results in order to respond to possible inaccuracies. In the context of innovation management, the suggested on-going monitoring becomes even more important, since companies have to respond to changes as quickly as possible to stay competitive. Moreover, it can be assumed that in a large company, the individuals who conduct the forecast and the decision-makers are not the same persons. Additional steps to prepare and make decisions are therefore necessary for a complete view of the process. To include these thoughts into the process, the last step of the process has to be split and a more detailed structure created. The resulting technology-forecasting process for strategic innovation management is shown in Figure 1.

Overview of Forecasting Methods

For the later discussion of technology forecasting, it is important to get a basic understanding of available classes of forecasting methods. This section is based on the "Methodology Tree" by Armstrong which illustrates the characteristics of forecasting methods and their relationships. Figure 2 depicts the Methodology Tree.

Armstrong begins with a separation of judgmental and statistical methods. He mentions, however, that judgment pervades all aspects of forecasting (Armstrong, 2001, p. 9). The further down a method is positioned in the tree, the higher the amount of judgmental and statistical integration. On the judgmental side of the tree, the methods are split into those predicting one's own behavior and those predicting the behavior of others, mostly by including experts into the forecasting process. On the side of method types predicting one's own behavior, the methods are characterized by the influence of a role. If a role influences the decision to make, *role playing* is a valuable tool for forecasting the outcome of the decision through the simulated interaction of roles affected by the decision. In case there is no influence of a role, the *intentions method* can be used in which people predict their own behavior in different situations. *Conjoint analysis* goes a step further than the *intentions method* by trying to create a connection between personal intentions and certain features of a situation through statistical analysis. For example, "a forecaster could show various designs for a computer and ask people about their intentions to purchase each version" (Armstrong, 2001, p. 9).

Forecasting methods within the *others* branch are based on *expert opinions* about how organizations or others will behave. There is a broad number of forecasting methods which belong to this type, with the Delphi method being the most famous one. In this method, questionnaires are sent out to experts in the targeted fields who answer the questions by the use of their subjective judgment. Once the questionnaires are sent back and analyzed, they are sent out again to the same experts together with the results of the first round in order to get a second estimation. The reason for this is to share the results and create a common knowledge base among all

Figure 1. The technology-forecasting process (following Armstrong, 2001)

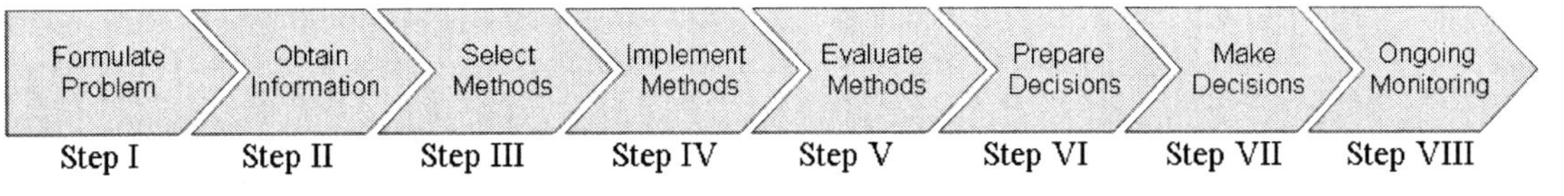

Figure 2. Methodology tree by Armstrong (2001, p. 9); dotted lines present possible relationships

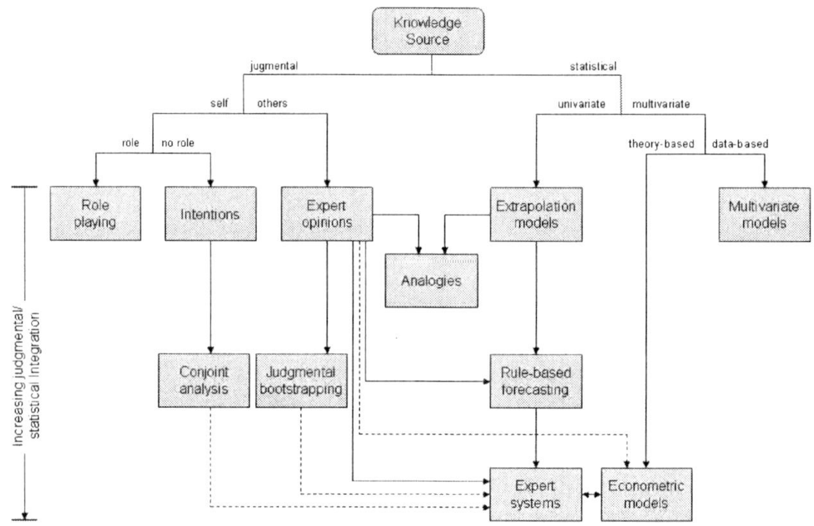

participants of the forecast. This process can be repeated for one or two more rounds after which the final conclusions are drawn and the forecast is created. Further information about the Delphi method can be found in the forecasting literature (e.g., Armstrong, 2001; DeLurgio, 1998; Granger, 1989; Martino, 1983). *Judgmental bootstrapping* refers to methods which use regression analysis in order to draw conclusions and rules from expert opinions and, to a certain extent, belongs to the class of expert systems.

Judgment and statistics are merged into one method type when *analogies* are used. Based on statistical data, experts try to forecast the development of a situation. The success of such an approach depends on the degree of similarity between the situation which has to be predicted and the one the statistical data are taken from.

The statistical side of the tree is split into univariate and multivariate methods. The *univariate* part of the tree contains extrapolation methods (Armstrong, 2001, p. 10); that is, values are predicted by the use of older values within a (time-) series. The simplest method of this type is using today's number of sales to predict tomorrow's number. When domain knowledge and knowledge about forecasting procedures is combined in a type of expert system to achieve this task, one speaks of *rule-based forecasting*. Full *expert systems* utilize an even greater integration of expert rules (rules which are similar to the way experts create their judgments) in order to support forecasting.

Multivariate forecasting methods are distinguished whether they are based on statistical data or theory. The latter leads to *econometric models* which base on domain knowledge or findings from prior research. "Econometric models provide an ideal way to integrate judgmental and statistical sources" (Armstrong, 2001, p. 10).

In general, one can argue that the focus of the following sections lies within the area of quantitative or statistical forecasting methods. However, it is the goal of this chapter to identify possible knowledge management technology support throughout the entire technology forecasting process as introduced in the section before and not only for a specific type of forecasting method. Therefore, the dedicated analysis of specific statistical and nonstatistical methods with regards to knowledge management needs could lead to further improvements of the forecasting quality and is suggested as an area of future research.

KNOWLEDGE MANAGEMENT NEEDS WITHIN TECHNOLOGY FORECASTING

There are three major perspectives that have to be considered in order to determine the need for knowledge management within technology forecasting. First, knowledge management needs within technology forecasting can be considered natural implications emerging from business and knowledge strategies which companies formulate to sustain or increase their competitive advantage. Second, the topic can be approached from an inside-the-company view: which other strategic, technological, or organizational factors within a company necessitate integrating knowledge management into the technology-forecasting process? Third, a company's forecasting process is obviously influenced by the company's environment. Therefore, an analysis from an outside-the-company perspective is also crucial to achieve a complete view of the need for knowledge management within technology forecasting.

Business and Knowledge Strategy Implications

As business strategies are formulated to set the overall company goals and define a company's unique strategy to gain profits, one needs to understand that these strategies are built from different components, each delivering a fundamental part to realize a company's objectives. Various authors, for example, Geschka (1992), broadly accept that "the innovation strategy is one means to achieve overall strategic company goals" (p. 70). Therefore, innovation is becoming increasingly important within companies and is moving from an activity often conducted solely within marketing or research and development departments to a process spanning several departments steered by dedicated innovation management. Furthermore, the nature of innovation is such that it can be the sole source of a company's competitive advantage and business success. O'Hare (1988) states that "truly successful innovation does not just lead to some extra sales volume, or a temporary improvement in performance. ... Rather, it is about achieving fundamental improvement in competitive position, about re-establishing the competitive equilibrium at a new, more favorable point" (pp. 39-40). However, the value of innovation and, therefore, its ability to function as a basis for competitive advantage, declines over time. This can be observed on a daily basis and examples can be found everywhere, from food to consumer technology and from health care to aviation; what seems to be a unique and exclusive product justifying a premium price today becomes a commodity product tomorrow.

It is essential to continue the development of further innovations to successfully build and sustain competitive advantage based on innovation. This undertaking is, however, influenced by many factors that determine the future of a company as well as the economy and society to which the company belongs. These factors could, for example, belong to political regulations, trends, and hypes within a society, or technological and scientific breakthroughs. Therefore, the development of innovation faces risks and uncertainty that are all future related and with which the company needs to cope through stringent innovation management. It is essential to recognize that this uncertainty with regard to future developments is the main reason for technology forecasting being a core part of current companies' efforts to plan innovation roadmaps and business strategies in keeping with future challenges. Armstrong (2001) says that:

We have no need to forecast whether the sun will rise tomorrow. There is also no uncertainty when events can be controlled; for example, you do not need to predict the temperature in your home. Many decisions, however, involve uncertainty, and in these cases, formal forecasting procedures ... can be useful. (p. 2)

A knowledge management strategy defines the basic direction of an organization's knowledge management structures and activities (Riempp, 2004, p. 77). The overall aim of these structures and activities is the improved utilization of knowledge that contributes to the better achievement of an organization's goals; that is, the knowledge management strategy is part of the overall business strategy. When thinking about technology forecasting and transferring it to the domain of knowledge strategies, technology forecasting can be regarded as a means to define and evaluate what Abou-Zeid (2005) calls the Knowledge-Scope (K-Scope); "K-Scope deals with the specific domains of knowledge that are critical to the firm's survival and advancement strategies" (p. 100). In other words, technology forecasting helps a company to understand which path technological innovations will follow to identify the implications for the company's own innovation roadmap and its overall competitive strategy. According to Abou-Zeid (2005), this is part of the Knowledge Strategy External Domain (p. 100). Thereby, technology forecasting is a means to support knowledge strategy creation by supporting the Knowledge-Scope definition as well as an essential part of a company's innovation management by being a driver for innovation strategy formulation.

Needs Emerging from Inside the Company

Inside a company, technology forecasting is closely linked with decision-making processes. It is part of the activities incorporated in strategic innovation management in order to support planning of innovation and R&D programs. DeLurgio (1998) argues that "it is important to recognize the role of forecasting in expanding the knowledge base of organizations and whole societies" (p. 6). Thus, technology forecasting itself can be regarded as a knowledge-creating activity; that is, knowledge in the sense of enabling managers to make strategic decisions, plan a technological innovation path for the company, and adjust business strategies. Therefore, decision-makers need an as comprehensive view of future developments as possible, which cannot be achieved with the help of technology forecasting alone. The end product of forecasting activities is, in most cases, some sort of study or report that represents all analyzed future developments. However, it can be assumed that this report does not contain enough information for a decision-maker to recreate all the knowledge that has been created by participants through the entire forecasting process. Knowledge, like perspectives and prior experiences shared by forecasters, might be valuable for a decision-maker. This facilitates interpretation of the information contained within the reports in a more efficient and comprehensive fashion, thus leading to decreased uncertainty and better-informed decisions. Moreover, reports cannot contain all the information available to the forecasters. In order to provide precise information and to reduce the document's complexity, some information has to be omitted. However, this information might become useful later in the decision process. Without efficient ways of recovering the missing information, the decision process is either slowed down, due to the additional time spent analyzing or acquiring the missing information for a second time, or it becomes less accurate.

In summary, from an inside-the-company perspective, two major reasons can be identified for the emerging need of knowledge management support for technology forecasting within strategic innovation management. Moreover, the last two major reasons have the potential to improve the quality and efficiency of the process:

- Technology forecasting is itself a knowledge-creating process.
- Knowledge that has been created during the process is not transferred to decision-makers due to, for example, the limited amount of information that can be conveyed via documentation.

Needs Emerging from Outside the Company

Making the right decisions with respect to future developments and technologies is vital for a company's competitiveness. One reason for this is the decreasing length of technological life cycles as "technological change is one of the most important forces affecting a firm's competitive position" (Burgelman, Maidique & Wheelwright, 1996, p. 6). Additional dynamics and uncertainty are created by the phenomenon of unexpected, disruptive innovations with which a company has to cope and which can never be fully excluded. Another factor that increases the pressure felt by decision-makers is cost. Vanston (1996) states that "under pressure to contain these [higher] costs, it has become increasingly important for R&D programs to focus on projects that will result in enhanced profits and sustainable competitive advantage" (p. 57). All these factors are evidence of how crucial it is for a company to make the right decisions in a constantly decreasing time frame.

On the other hand, the same reasons lead companies to face increasing uncertainty with respect to future developments. In order to deal with this uncertainty, companies have to collect and assess more information swifter and more efficiently than they used to. This is also true in the context of technology forecasting within strategic innovation management. It can be assumed that more information leads to a reduced uncertainty and thus to a better-informed decision. At the same time, however, more information also leads to greater complexity and, consequently, to a decrease in efficiency and a slower process. The amount of information required to decrease uncertainty and the time needed to collect, assess, and process information are in inverse proportion to each other. As far as possible, companies should therefore find equilibrium on the information side to keep uncertainty low, while keeping complexity on a level that the forecaster can still handle.

Hence, two main factors—related to a technology-forecasting process's efficiency and emerging from outside the company—that influence a company's competitive advantage and business strategy, and create a need for knowledge management within technology forecasting, are:

- Decisions have to be made faster to stay ahead of competition.
- More information with an increasingly complex relational structure has to be collected, assessed, and processed to decrease uncertainty.

DEVELOPMENT OF A CHARACTERIZATION SCHEME FOR KNOWLEDGE MANAGEMENT TECHNOLOGIES

In this chapter, we will develop a characterization scheme to evaluate and delineate knowledge management technologies. Since these technologies differ with respect to knowledge management as well as technology forecasting, the scheme will combine these two fields by integrating a dimension for each of them.

We have shown that one can argue that technology forecasting itself is a knowledge-creating process. A second look at the forecasting process reveals that each step can be regarded as a transformation process with specific inputs and outputs. Step II, for example, needs the definition of the forecasting objectives, the scope, and the time horizon as inputs. This information is utilized within the process step's activities and transformed into information of a greater complexity by combining the input with new information. New relations are identified between certain information objects, leading to the observed information structure's greater complexity. The subsequent step III also requires input from the preceding steps. It is, however, different from step II with respect to the transformation of information. While the activities of process step II increase the information structure's overall complexity, the complexity remains constant during step III, because the information is only analyzed to select suitable forecasting methods. An analysis of the other process steps reveals that the technology-forecasting process's steps can be characterized by their varying degree of complexity; in other words, either the level of complexity is increased or it remains unaltered. Figure 3 illustrates this relation on an abstract level without claiming to represent the actual degree of complexity increase.

On examining Figure 3, it is possible to identify four steps that cause the information structure's increasing complexity within the forecasting process. These steps are: obtain information, implement methods, prepare decisions, and ongoing monitoring. Reasons can be found for these four steps' contribution to the complexity when comparing each step's activities. They all have the combination of previous steps' results and newly acquired information in common, which leads to the creation of new knowledge. Such knowledge is needed to complete each process step's tasks.

Accordingly, the level of the information structure's complexity is chosen as a dimension of technology forecasting and is expressed by the four process steps identified. This dimension enables knowledge management technologies to be classified according to their capability to support these four process steps, and allows an implicit description of the level of information complexity within the technology-forecasting process that a knowledge management technology supports.

While the development of the technology forecasting dimension is based on the analysis of the forecasting process, a different approach has to be found to define the knowledge management dimension. As a starting point, the definitions of data, information, and knowledge should be considered. Since there is a defined difference between these terms, one can argue that data, information, and knowledge's definitions could be used as a structure with which to categorize knowledge management technologies; for example, the category "information" contains all those technologies that target information. Furthermore, transformation processes are required to turn data into information and information into

Figure 3. Information-structure complexity

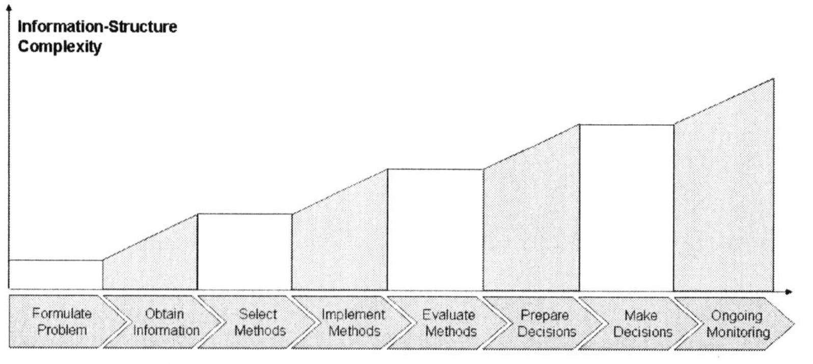

knowledge. A categorization structure based only on the definitions of the three terms is not capable of integrating such transformation processes, and it is obvious that there are knowledge management technologies that, for example, specifically support the transformation of data into information. Aamodt and Nygård (1995) propose a model for data, information, and knowledge that takes the three terms' specific relationships into account (p. 8). The model explains the processes that are needed to transform, for example, data into information, in addition to providing data, information, and knowledge's basic structure. However, with regard to the development of a dimension for knowledge management technologies' characterization from a knowledge management point of view, it can be argued that this model is not applicable. Knowledge, as understood in this chapter, is closely linked with human action and the human mind, with learning being one way of creating knowledge. While there might be a number of knowledge management technologies that support learning, it is impossible for technologies to target knowledge itself.

Another disadvantage of such a model is its granularity. It can be assumed that there are several types of knowledge management technologies that target information, but each with a different focus or different application areas. Consequently, a finer granularity is needed which, in an optimal case, can be based on a single and continuous criterion to facilitate adoption and the development of a knowledge management dimension for the characterization scheme as stated previously.

Smolnik et al. (2005) suggest an approach called "the continuum of context explication", which fulfills the mentioned requirements and is based on the importance of context. Here, context explication means "discovering implicit meanings and expressing those meanings explicitly" (p. 28). The authors stress that context is an important aspect that many definitions of knowledge have in common (Smolnik et al., 2005, p. 30) and they compare several definitions of context. Dey and Abowd (2000), for example, define context as follows:

Context is any information that can be used to characterize the situation of an entity. An entity is a person, place, or object that is considered relevant to the interaction between a user and an application, including the user and applications themselves. (pp. 3-4)

Besides its role in the definition of knowledge, context also plays an important role in the definition of information. Nonaka and Takeuchi (1995) argue that "knowledge, like information, is ... context-specific and relational" (p. 58). Smolnik et al. (2005) found that knowledge management technologies "focus on contextual information in different ways and with varying intensity" (p. 36). Consequently, the authors present five approaches to "find and use information objects and contextual information ..., each with a differing degree of context and explication ease" (Smolnik et al., 2005, p. 36). The continuum distinguishes the following five approaches:

- **The data approach:** Data are symbols or signs without a meaning or context. Thus, context cannot be explicated. Nevertheless, technologies can be applied to transform data into information or domain-specific knowledge. The data approach encompasses these methods.
- **The information approach:** Most important for the definition of information is that information includes meaning and a specific context. However, the "context is ... interwoven with the content and difficult to conceptualize, which means that the methods implemented to find requested information objects have to rely on the content and cannot access contextual information" (Smolnik et al., 2005, p. 37).
- **The descriptor approach:** The addition of explicit contextual information to infor-

mation objects, thereby providing context-aware methods for information search and discovery, is called a descriptor approach.

- **The metacontext approach:** This approach extends the descriptor approach, as explicit contextual information no longer resides only within information objects, but is integrated into a metalayer that lies above and spans a variety of information.
- **The knowledge approach:** The knowledge approach focuses on the human being and considers characteristics of knowledge. It is about knowledge creation through actions like communication, construction, or cognition.

The continuum's consideration of context and its explication offers a continuous criterion through which it is possible to distinguish different knowledge management technologies. This makes the continuum of context explication an ideal basis for the development of a knowledge management dimension. Each approach forms one category that can be used to classify knowledge management technologies. The only exception is the knowledge approach. Since it is closely linked to the human mind and human action, knowledge management technologies cannot explicate the person-specific context. This approach is therefore not used within the knowledge management dimension.

The combination of the developed technology-forecasting dimension with the knowledge management perspective dimension results in the context-complexity matrix. This matrix allows the characterization of knowledge management technologies with regard to the degree of context as well as to the technology-forecasting process's degree of information structure complexity. The background of each dimension implicitly provides further characteristics of the classified knowledge management technologies. A categorization of, for example, the metacontext approach within the knowledge management domain and step VIII of the technology-forecasting domain means that the knowledge management technology is capable of supporting step VIII's great information structure complexity and also comprises a high level of explicit contextual information.

EVALUATION OF KNOWLEDGE MANAGEMENT TECHNOLOGIES

The breadth of available knowledge management technologies ranges from very simple to very complex. The set of knowledge management technologies for the following evaluation has therefore been selected to represent this breadth, namely, data mining, case-based reasoning, information retrieval, topic maps, and ontologies. We evaluate these technologies in the following with respect to the presented characterization scheme.

Data Mining

Authors in the field of data mining often state that the identification of specific patterns enables the extraction of knowledge embedded within databases (e.g., Han & Kamber, 2001, p. 4; Lusti, 2002, p. 260). This view is not absolutely precise. The consideration of data-mining applications like market basket analysis, fraud detection, or risk analysis leads to the thought that data-mining functionalities enrich data through the identification of patterns or classes in a way that a person familiar with the domain is capable of deriving a meaning from the presented results. Hence, domain-specific information is generated, which can then be combined with other information and knowledge to create new knowledge. But data mining contains no functionality that specifically supports this combination of information. By considering the continuum of context explication as a dimension for a knowledge management categorization, the discussion above can be summarized by assigning data mining to the category "data approach".

With respect to technology forecasting, Armstrong (2001) argues that "an immense amount of research effort has so far produced little evidence that data-mining models can improve forecasting accuracy" (p. 10). Thus, the quality of forecasts that are solely based on data mining is debatable and, consequently, so is the support of step IV. However, it is our opinion that with the exception of the implementation of forecasting methods, data mining can be successfully utilized to facilitate specific tasks within the technology forecasting process's steps. As we explained in the previous section, step II and step VIII require the analysis of great amounts of information with respect to specified criteria. In step II, information is needed that can be associated with the forecast's objectives as defined during step I, while an on-going analysis of information based on the results of a forecast is required within step VIII. In combination with other technologies, data mining might be a suitable way to improve the efficiency of identifying interesting information objects through classification and association analysis. Data mining can therefore be assigned to the categories "step II" and "step VIII" of the technology-forecasting dimension.

Case-Based Reasoning

Compared to data mining, case-based reasoning is a concept which targets information rather than data. A case provides the solution to some problems, which can basically be viewed as providing domain-specific information (Riesbeck & Schank, 1989, p. 24). Case-based reasoning comprises certain functionalities that allow the emulation of cognitive processes in order to generate solutions (Riesbeck & Schank, 1989, p. 24). These functionalities are the capability to adapt old cases to suit the needs of new cases and the fact that a system enlarges its case base by evaluating and retaining cases that have either been solved, or provide information about faults. Systems following the structural case-based reasoning approach (Bergmann, Althoff, Breen, Göker, Manago, Traphöner & Wess, 2003, p. 21) integrate these functionalities and apply general domain knowledge to a model to improve case storage and retrieval, thereby putting the different cases into a certain context. The context is defined by a set of features that are used to index a case and to determine similarity between different cases (Aamodt & Plaza, 1994, p. 50). Thus, features are descriptors of information objects and the corresponding context.

On the other hand, there are also case-based reasoning systems that do not have an underlying domain model, like those that use the textual case-based reasoning approach (Bergmann et al., 2003, p. 21). Such systems work directly on the information and utilize certain algorithms to compare and match new cases with those contained in the case base. Consequently, with respect to the knowledge management dimension, case-based reasoning belongs equally to the category "information approach" and to the category "descriptor approach".

With regard to the dimension for technology forecasting, an appropriate characterization and the corresponding identification of the potential for supporting the technology-forecasting process is a more difficult task. Gaines and Shaw (1986) argue that as far as technology and innovations are concerned, it seems that the past is not appropriate for predicting the future (p. 3). Case-based reasoning is, however, designed around previous experiences. This leads to the conclusion that case-based reasoning cannot be applied to technology-forecasting activities. It cannot therefore be assigned to the category "step IV" of the technology-forecasting dimension. Moreover, taking the requirements of step II and step VIII into account, it is doubtful that case-based reasoning is a useful method with which to support these activities. Both steps need to handle a great amount of new information and need to put this information into context to achieve a clearer perspective of the forecast's scope as well as to collect information with which to monitor the forecast's results. Case-based reasoning is not a method that is intended for the identification of new information. It cannot therefore be assigned to the categories "step II" or "step VIII" of the technology-forecasting dimension.

Nevertheless, it is case-based reasoning's purpose to support decisions and to solve problems. Therefore, it is an appropriate technology for application during step VI. More precisely, case-based reasoning can be used to support planning activities (Lenz, Bartsch-Spörl, Burkhardt & Wess, 1998, p. 14). A company that has a long experience of pursuing and developing innovative technologies might profit from its knowledge when a new technology is about to be developed or integrated.

Information Retrieval

On considering the definitions of each single category of the knowledge management dimension, it seems obvious that information retrieval belongs to the category "information approach'. In general, such a categorization appears to be reasonable since information retrieval targets raw information. Smolnik et al. (2005) argue that although information itself comprises content and context, the context is interwoven with the content and thus difficult to explicate (p. 37). As a result, technologies that do not include additional explicit contextual information only rely on content or its representation within search functionalities. Clearly, this is true of most conceptual information retrieval models.

On the other hand, one can argue that some forms of information retrieval also integrate explicit contextual information into search and retrieval methods. While Smolnik et al. (2005) state that "authors have to provide [explicit contextual] information at the time of creation" (p. 37), the consideration of the concept of aboutness, as introduced by Ingwersen (1992, p. 50), allows an additional perspective. On considering the fact that some information retrieval systems are based on the creation of index terms through document analysis and alignment with a specific domain by individuals, we argue that such indexes represent the indexer's aboutness and therefore also the context of the individual who analyzes the documents and creates the index. Nevertheless, in the same way that indexer aboutness differs from author aboutness, the author and indexer's contexts vary. In general, the characterization of information retrieval by assigning it to the category "information approach" within the knowledge management dimension is a reasonable outcome; however, the exceptions as discussed previously should be taken into account. Information retrieval will therefore be categorized by mainly assigning it to the category "information approach" as well as partially to the category "descriptor approach".

Within technology forecasting, certain process steps include the need to identify information when a large amount of it is available, namely in step II, step IV, and step VIII. The difference between these steps' information need is that the first two steps require a broad range of new information with respect to the selected forecasting scope, while the latter step utilizes specific information that is closely linked with the developed technology forecasts in order to compare them to reality. Therefore, an efficient way to identify and assess relations and derive consequences from specific information objects is more important than the mere retrieval of interesting information from a large amount and variety of information. It is a common assumption among information retrieval researchers that searching within such systems is an iterative process (Salton & McGill, 1983, p. 3). A user starts with some sort of query and evaluates his or her own understanding of the information needed with the help of the first result set. Either the information is sufficient—it results in the retrieval of additional information through references or the like—or a user realizes that the request has to be completely revised. Reasons for this can be found when taking into account that users are only able to describe what they need, which is in turn based on what they already know. These arguments lead to the conclusion that information retrieval is not applicable to step VIII of the technology-forecasting process and, instead, can be characterized as able to support steps with a need for a wide range of new information, thus step II and step IV.

Topic Maps

Topic maps provide methods with which to navigate associatively across large amounts of information in a conscious manner, enabling a systematic identification of information and creation of new knowledge by the user. This is possible by detaching the information source from the context used to find the information, which results in topic maps being "information assets in their own right, irrespective of whether they are actually connected to any information resources or not" (Rath & Pepper, 1999, p. 9). Moreover, topic maps support "managing the meaning of the information, rather than just the information" (Garshol, 2002, p. 2). An explicit context, called metacontext, is used to organize available information in such a way that more efficient search methods can be applied. Hence, the metacontext is the most characterizing aspect when discussing topic maps; they thus clearly belong to the category "metacontext approach" when considering the knowledge management dimension of the context-complexity matrix.

Because a topic map describes certain domain knowledge, it can be very useful when created to represent the forecast's scope. Such a topic map comprises the different technologies and research areas within the focus of the company that conducts the forecast. Associations can be used to link technologies to express their influences and relations. Any information, to which the topic map is applied, can then be categorized with respect to the forecast's scope, facilitating identification of valuable information. Furthermore, once there is a comprehensive information repository, the topic map can be used to relocate information and to relate it to the forecasting activities' results. Hence, topic maps also provide additional value when used within step IV and step VI. Identifying specific information that correlates with the forecasting activities' results is especially important within step VIII. Topic maps' filtering and localization capabilities help to achieve a more precise analysis of available information and, hence, a more efficient monitoring process overall. In general, topic maps have the potential to increase the efficiency of each technology-forecasting step in the context-complexity matrix, because they can be tailored to a forecast's scope and thereby reduce the available information's complexity to a manageable level.

Ontologies

Ontologies are a means to provide a resource that unambiguously determines the meaning of terms and their relations to other terms within a certain domain (Benjamins, Fensel, & Gómez Pérez, 1998, p. 2). This structure is an autonomous construct without links to specific information resources. With respect to the knowledge management dimension of the context-complexity matrix, it is quite obvious that ontologies belong to the category "metacontext approach", as explicit context structures are created that are independent of specific information resources and can themselves be viewed as an information resource. Therefore, relations have to be created between an information resource and ontologies by means of explicit contextual information and specific references that are added to the information resource. This methodology clearly does not fit into any other category on the knowledge management dimension than the metacontext approach.

The same reasons that lead to the obvious characterization of ontologies as a metacontext approach hamper categorization with regard to technology forecasting. The question arises: which of the technology-forecasting process's steps and activities benefit from the development and application of an ontology? Following the premises regarding the benefits of ontology application as presented by Zelewski (2001, p. 4), possible applications can be derived for ontologies within technology forecasting. Zelewski (2001) argues that the knowledge intensity of the tasks to be accomplished and the degree to which the knowledge backgrounds of the parties involved in an interaction differ both influence ontologies' importance as a means to improve the considered process tasks' efficiency (p. 4). When conducted for strategic innovation management, many technology-forecasting methods such as, for example, the Delphi method (e.g., Armstrong, 2001; DeLurgio, 1998), are aimed at transforming individuals with different backgrounds' specific knowledge into statements about future technological innovations and developments. Thus, Zelewski's premises are true with regards to technology forecasting. As a result, only the category "step IV" seems to be suitable for ontology application's characterization within technology forecasting for strategic innovation management, but it is limited by the chosen technology-forecasting methods.

DISCUSSIONS

Obviously, some of the technology-forecasting process's steps can be supported by more than one knowledge management technology. Therefore, the question arises: which single technology or which combination appears to be the most promising with which to support and improve this process? To answer this question, it is helpful to consider technology forecasting for strategic innovation management with respect to the type of input each process step requires. We have shown that the complexity of the information structure within the technology-forecasting process increases in the course of the process. We argue that context too becomes more and more

Figure 4. The context-complexity matrix

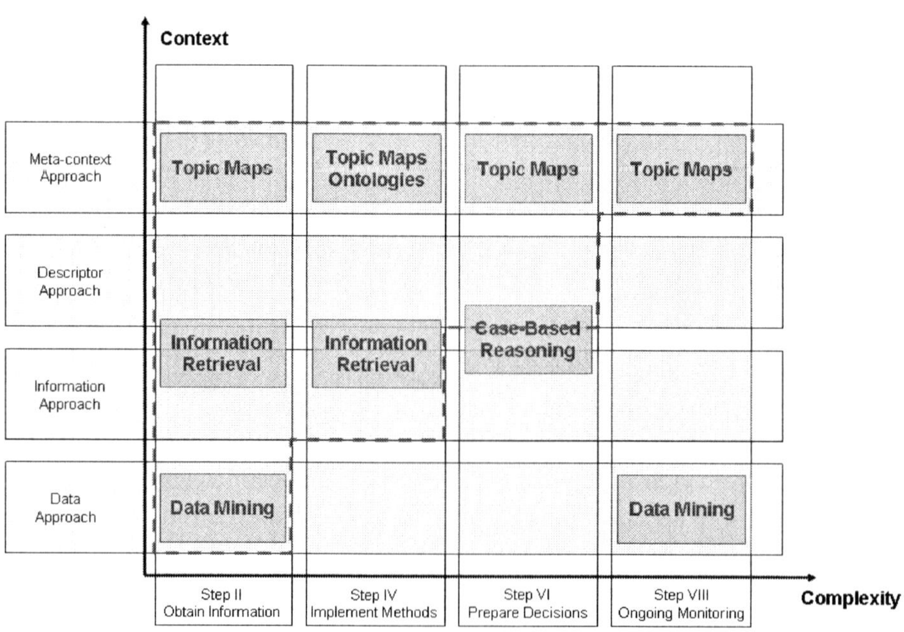

important. At the beginning of the process, the importance of context as well as the information structure's complexity is rather modest, but in the end, the degree of complexity and context importance reaches a maximum. As a result, the context-complexity matrix has to be refined to integrate strategic innovation management's focus in such a way that only the upper left triangle represents possible solutions, which are promising ways of supporting technology-forecasting steps through knowledge management technologies as presented in Figure 4.

A striking point of the context-complexity matrix is the fact that topic maps are capable of supporting each process step in a certain way. However, topic maps require some knowledge about the domain and its topics for their generation, while information retrieval provides functionalities that require less prior knowledge and can be used to gather a first broad variety of information. This can be especially helpful during the first phases of technology-forecasting research efforts. Such information can then be analyzed to generate the needed topic map, which corresponds with a technology forecast's scope. Later on, the topic map can be used to classify and organize further information and, hence, allows a more systematic way of discovering additional information.

In summary, we can state that a knowledge management system that is based on topic map technologies and integrates information retrieval functionalities as extensions to those provided by the topic map, is the most promising solution with which to support technology forecasting for strategic innovation management. In order to verify the theoretical results, we test them within a real-world scenario.

TOWARDS AN EXPLORATORY CASE STUDY

We applied our findings to a project conducted for Deutsche Telekom AG at DETECON Inc., a technology and management consulting company with a focus on innovation engineering. The main objectives of the project were the identification of technology trends and developments that are able to open new opportunities and the assessment of their innovation potential in order to define innovation strategies and achieve company goals. The technology forecasting process at DETECON Inc. differs in two main aspects from the generic process as presented in this chapter. First of all, people at DETECON Inc. distinguish between *inductive* and *deductive* approaches toward innovation and trend identification. This is comparable to what Reger (2001) calls "core technologies" and "white spaces" (p. 539). Inductive methods begin with the identification and formulation of a certain problem setting. In this case, the term *problem* refers to certain needs which emerge from inside Deutsche Telekom and are derived from, for example, internal developments or processes.

After problem formulation, specific information is obtained which is related to the problem and helps finding innovative solutions. In other cases the appearance of information about certain technology developments and innovations precedes the identification of a problem. Emerging trends and innovations are monitored by DETECON Inc. and assessed with respect to their potential influence on Deutsche Telekom AG's business or innovation strategy. An example for technological trends which lead to an innovation need from outside Deutsche Telekom is Voice-over-Internet protocol (VOIP) which, in the long run, can be considered a threat to Telekom's integrated services digital network (ISDN) landline product.

In summary, a forecasting process at DETECON Inc. can be initiated in basically two ways (Figure 5): either problem precedes information or information precedes problem. Furthermore, the technology forecasting process for Deutsche Telekom AG can be considered an iterative process. A first iteration gives a broad overview of potential interesting technologies which are then communicated on a very high level towards

Figure 5. Technology-forecasting process at DETECON, Inc. for Deutsche Telekom AG

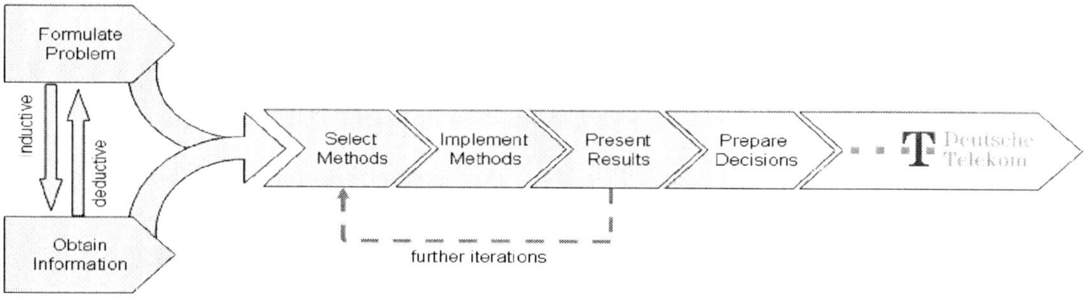

Deutsche Telekom AG. On the base of interest, Deutsche Telekom AG requests an additional iteration with an increased analysis depth and a more precise technology scope which results in the development of *technology profile documents*. The process leaves DETECON Inc. in a phase comparable to step VI of the general process of technology forecasting for innovation management. From this point on, Deutsche Telekom AG is responsible for the remaining steps and activities and the integration of the acquired knowledge into its innovation strategy.

In the light of the previous section's results, a system based on the central utilization of topic maps seems most promising to improve technology forecasting's efficiency.

One characterizing aspect of technology forecasting at DETECON Inc. is the flexible scope required by the different steps and activities inside the process. Topic maps can be tailored to suit this flexible use. Regarding the process at DETECON Inc., the development of a single comprehensive topic map that represents the applied domain knowledge's basic structure as, for example, technologies and their relations and influences, could offer a solution. Sophisticated methods, like a topic map concept called scope, can then be used to restrict this topic map to the necessary range for single activities. This is sufficient because all DETECON Inc.'s forecasting activities deal with technology and innovation developments and their influences on Deutsche Telekom's technology and business situation. A topic map that has been built and maintained for the corresponding domain, and which can be tailored to represent only the available information's subparts through the exploitation of topic maps' scope attribute, provides an efficient solution to the flexibility requirement.

Obviously, the nature of a topic map also facilitates the organization and reuse of information, and therefore fulfills another requirement with respect to technology forecasting at DETECON Inc.: information that has been used once can be stored in a repository and can be accessed through the topic map. It is also associated with analyses, contacts, or other related information. Therefore, knowledge structures, once generated, can be represented by the topic map, facilitating the recovery of these structures. In addition, a topic map can be used to categorize new information by determining the topics that occur in the new information. This functionality can be combined with automated information retrieval methods. The information is retrieved from a source (most likely within the WWW); it is analyzed with respect to the occurring topics, and then added to the information repository. This process facilitates the identification of valuable new information without the need to analyze all new information manually. Because the information is available through the topic map, it can be accessed when needed.

Switching control of and responsibility for the process from DETECON Inc. to Deutsche Telekom AG, leads to knowledge transfer being facilitated—another requirement of a system to support technology forecasting at DETECON Inc. Once Deutsche Telekom AG considers a technology interesting and relevant, a more detailed technology profile is created, which is then sent to Deutsche Telekom AG. The integration of the mentioned profile documents into the structure of a topic map, as well as their association with the main topics and further relevant information about the corresponding technologies, facilitates this task. The technology-related knowledge can be transferred with the help of the topic map by allowing access to the profile documents and their related information. Personal meetings can then be used to discuss the technology and business consequences, creating additional knowledge that goes beyond the technology itself.

The challenge of such a system is, however, maintaining the topic map. A fully manual maintenance implies the awareness of new developments. Therefore, methods have to be found that can facilitate this task by suggesting new topics and associations. Statistical methods as applied within automatic indexing can provide a useful starting point to solve this problem.

It is obvious that the intense communication and collaboration between the two organizations cannot only rely on an underlying knowledge management system. Therefore, it can be considered valuable future research to include non-codified knowledge management processes into the analysis of knowledge management support within technology forecasting. One starting point can be to map the socialization, externalization, internalization and combination (SECI) model as presented by Nonaka and Takeuchi of organizational knowledge creation with the technology forecasting process to determine those stages which rely on non-codified knowledge creation to improve the overall forecasting process (Nonaka & Takeuchi, 1995, p. 70).

In summary, topic maps provide the needed degree of flexibility, facilitate information organization and reuse as well as knowledge transfer. Therefore, a system that is based on topic maps will be considered the solution to the increasing difficulties with technology forecasting at DETECON Inc.

CONCLUSION

As shown, knowledge management technologies play an important role in supporting the technology forecasting process as a part of strategic innovation management and overall competitive strategies. As there are several possible knowledge management technologies, the real task for technology forecasting begins with the selection of the appropriate technologies for each process step. We have therefore evaluated several knowledge management technologies, each explained according to its main characteristics, benefits, and constraints, focusing on its support of the technology forecasting process's different steps. We have furthermore aligned them all in the proposed context-complexity matrix. The successful application of our theoretical findings was revealed by the case study, realized at DETECON Inc. and Deutsche Telekom AG.

FUTURE RESEARCH DIRECTIONS

To enrich our proposed context-complexity model, we envisage the following areas of future research:

- First, within innovation management, most forecasting is done via the analysis of information as exemplified by DETECON Inc. and Deutsche Telekom AG. We have to determine whether the integration of other forecasting methods, for example, extrapolation methods, into the supporting system could lead to a higher forecasting quality and decreased uncertainty, with the aim of automating a major part of the forecasting process and achieving improved decision support.

- Second, we have to determine whether knowledge management technologies are also capable of supporting single technology forecasting methods.
- Third, we have to validate and expand our findings in further real-world cases in order to verify the theoretical results and ideas of this chapter and to identify further aspects that could potentially increase technology forecasting efficiency, improve innovation strategy formulation, and thus create and sustain competitive advantage.
- Fourth, efficient knowledge management also depends on organizational issues to a certain extent. While this chapter considers knowledge management technologies to be the focal point for knowledge management support within technology forecasting, we have to determine to what extent organizational knowledge management concepts influence technology forecasting. We assume that organizational concepts depend on the structure of a forecasting process. Processes which are conducted completely inside a single company might benefit more from organizational knowledge management concepts than processes which a scattered over one, two, or more companies. Further research in this area should discuss which combination of technological and organizational process support results into the highest value for competitive advantage and company success.
- Fifth, the main objective of this chapter is to introduce a technology focused framework for integrating knowledge management into quantitative technology forecasting. However, further research should also focus on the support of qualitative technological forecasting, for example, using methods such as scenarios, as well as on the support by noncodified knowledge management processes like those defined by Nonaka and Takeuchi's SECI model and respective technologies such as collaboration supporting tools.

The development of the context-complexity matrix and its application to selected knowledge management technologies has shown that, within technology forecasting, increasing information structure complexity leads to an increasing need for context explication. Information repositories are less useful without the application of explicit metacontexts that facilitate the discovery of needed information. While technologies like data mining or case-based reasoning provide only a marginal efficiency increase, topic maps possess a broad applicability and have the potential to increase efficiency greatly.

By returning the conclusion to the level of innovation and knowledge strategies, we can state that technology forecasting, which was originally a means of supporting an innovation strategy definition, simultaneously supports a knowledge strategy definition by presenting a basis for knowledge-scope determination. The integration of knowledge management technologies and technology forecasting by applying the proposed framework, can therefore be considered a method with which to support business and knowledge strategy alignment on an operational level.

REFERENCES

Aamodt, A., & Nygård, M. (1995). Different roles and mutual dependencies of data, information, and knowledge: An AI perspective on their integration. *Data and Knowledge Engineering, 16*, 191-222.

Aamodt, A., & Plaza, E. (1994). Case-based reasoning: Foundational issues, methodological variations, and system approaches. *AI Communications, 7*(1), 39-59.

Abou-Zeid, E. (2005). Alignment of business and knowledge management strategies. In M. Khosrow-Pour (Ed.), *Encyclopedia of information science and technology* (Vol. 1, pp. 98-103). Hershey, PA: Idea Group Publishing.

Armstrong, J.S. (2001). *Principles of forecasting: A handbook for researchers and practitioners.* Boston: Kluwer.

Benjamins, V.R., Fensel, D., & Gómez Pérez, A.G. (1998). Knowledge management through ontologies. In *Proceedings of the 2nd International Conference on Practical Aspects of Knowledge Management (PAKM98) (pp. 5.1-5.12).* Basel, Switzerland.

Bergmann, R., Althoff, K., Breen, S., Göker, M., Manago, M., Traphöner, R., & Wess, S. (2003). *Developing industrial case-based reasoning applications* (2nd ed.). Berlin: Springer-Verlag.

Bright, J.R. (1979). Technology forecasting as an influence on technological innovation: Past examples and future expectations. In M.J. Baker (Ed.), *Industrial innovation* (pp. 228-255). Basingstoke, UK: The Macmillan Press Ltd.

Burgelman, R.A., Maidique, M.A., & Wheelwright, S.C. (1996). *Strategic management of technology and innovation* (2nd ed.). Boston: Irwin/McGraw-Hill.

DeLurgio, S.A. (1998). *Forecasting principles and applications.* Boston: Irwin/McGraw-Hill.

Dey, A.K., & Abowd, G.D. (2000). *Towards a better understanding of context and context-awareness.* Atlanta: Graphics, Visualization and Usability Center and College of Computing, Georgia Institute of Technology.

Drucker, P.F. (1996). *Managing in a time of great change.* Boston: Butterwort-Heinemann.

Gaines, B.R., & Shaw, M.L.G. (1986). A learning model for forecasting the future of information technology. *Future Computing Systems, 1*(1), 31-69.

Garshol, L.M. (2002). What are topic maps? Retrieved May 22, 2007, from http://www.XML.com

Geschka, H. (1992). The strategic aspect in the process of innovation. In H. Geschka & H. Hubner (Eds.), *Innovation strategies: Theoretical approaches - experiences - improvements* (pp. 69-78). Amsterdam: Elsevier Science Publishers.

Granger, C.W.J. (1989). *Forecasting in business and economics.* San Diego: Academic Press.

Han, J., & Kamber, M. (2001). *Data mining: Concepts and techniques.* San Diego: Academic Press.

Ingwersen, P. (1992). *Information retrieval interaction.* London: Taylor Graham Publishing.

Lenz, M., Bartsch-Spörl, B., Burkhardt, H., & Wess, S. (1998). *Case-based reasoning technology: From foundations to applications.* Berlin: Springer-Verlag.

Lusti, M. (2002). *Data warehousing und data mining: Eine Einführung in entscheidungs-unterstützende Systeme.* Berlin: Springer-Verlag.

Martino, J.P. (1983). *Technological forecasting for decision making.* New York: Elsevier Science Publishers.

Nonaka, I., & Takeuchi, H. (1995). *The knowledge-creating company: How Japanese companies create the dynamics of innovation.* New York: Oxford University Press.

O'Hare, M. (1988). *Innovate! How to gain and sustain competitive advantage.* Oxford: Basil Blackwell Ltd.

Rath, H.H., & Pepper, S. (1999). Topic maps: Introduction and Allegro. In *Proceedings of the Markup Technologies, 99.* Philadelphia, USA.

Reger, G. (2001). Technology foresight in companies: From an indicator to a network and process perspective. *Technology Analysis & Strategic Management, 13*(4), 533-553.

Riempp, G. (2004). *Integrierte wissensmanagement-systeme—Architektur und praktische anwendung.* Berlin: Springer.

Riesbeck, C.K., & Schank, R.C. (1989). *Inside case-based reasoning.* Hillsdale: Lawrence Erlbaum Associates.

Salton, G., & McGill, M.J. (1983). *Introduction to modern information retrieval.* New York: McGraw-Hill.

Smolnik, S., Kremer, S., & Kolbe, L. (2005). Continuum of context explication: Knowledge discovery through process-oriented portals. *International Journal of Knowledge Management, 1*(1), 27-46.

Stewart, T.A. (1997). *Intellectual capital: The new wealth of organization.* Currency New York: Doubleday.

Vanston, J.H. (1996). Technology forecasting: A practical tool for rationalizing the R&D process. *The New Telecom Quarterly, 4*(1), 57-62. Technology Futures Inc.

Zelewski, S. (2001). Ontologien—ein Überblick über betriebswirtschaftliche Anwendungsbereiche. In Workshop Forschung in schnellebiger Zeit", Beitrag 5, Appenzell.

ADDITIONAL READING

Alavi, M., & Leidner, D.E. (1999). Knowledge management systems: Issues, challenges, and benefits. *Communication of the AIS, 1*(2), Article 7.

Alavi, M., & Leidner, D.E. (2001, March). Review: Knowledge management and knowledge management systems: Conceptual foundations and research issues. *MIS Quarterly, 25*(1), 107-136. MIS Quarterly and The Society for Information Management, Minneapolis, Minnesota.

Allesch, J. (1986). Situative model of the innovation process in the area of tension between market and technology. In H. Hubner (Ed.), *The Art and Science of Innovation Management* (pp. 3-13). Amsterdam: Elsevier Science Publishers.

Baeza-Yates, R.A., & Ribeiro-Neto, B. (1999). *Modern information retrieval.* Boston: Addison-Wesley Publishing.

Berners-Lee, T., Hendler, J., & Lassila, O. (2001). The Semantic Web. *Scientific American, 284*(5), 34-43. Stuttgart: Verlagsgruppe Georg von Holtzbrinck.

Bruckner, R.M., Ling, T.W., Mangisengi, O., & Tjoa, A.M. (2001). A framework for a multidimensional OLAP model using topic maps. In *Proceedings of the Second International Conference on Web Information Systems Engineering (WISE 2001), Web Semantics Workshop* (Vol. 2, pp. 109-118), Kyoto, Japan. Los Alamitos CA: IEEE Computer Society Press.

Davenport, T.H., & Prusak, L. (1998). *Working knowledge: How organizations manage what they know.* Boston: Harvard Business School Press, Boston (Excerpt from the ACM Digital Library). Retrieved May 22, 2007, from http://www.acm.org/ubiquity/book/t_davenport_1.html

David, F.R. (1986). Fundamentals of strategic management. London: Merrill Publishing Company.

Dussauge, P., Ramanantsoa, B., & Hart, S. (1992). *Strategic technology management: integrating product technology into global business strategies for the 1990s.* Hoboken, NJ: John Wiley & Sons Ltd.

Fayyad, U.M., Piatetsky-Shapiro, G., Smyth, P., & Uthurusamy, R. (1996). Advances in knowledge discovery and data mining. Menlo Park,

CA: American Association for Artificial Intelligence.

Fensel, D. (2001). *Ontologies: A silver bullet for knowledge management and electronic commerce.* Berlin: Springer.

Fensel, D., Wahlster, W., Lieberman, H., & Hendler, J. (2003). *Spinning the Semantic Web: Bringing the World Wide Web to its full potential.* Cambridge, MA: MIT Press.

Frakes, W.B., & Baeza-Yates, R.A. (1992). *Information retrieval: Data structures & algorithms.* Upple Saddle River, NJ: Prentice Hall.

Gallupe, B. (2001, March). Knowledge management systems: Surveying the landscape. *International Journal of Management Reviews, 3*(1) 61-77. Oxford: Blackwell Publishing Limited.

Gruber, T.R. (1993). A translation approach to portable ontology specifications. *Knowledge Acquisition, 5*(2), 199-220.

Gruninger, M., & Lee, J. (2002). Ontology applications and design. *Communications of the ACM, 45*(2), 39-41.

Hovy, E. (2003). Using an ontology to simplify data access. *Communications of the ACM, 46*(1), 47-49.

Kolodner, J. (1993). *Case-based reasoning.* San Mateo, CA: Morgan Kaufmann Publishers.

Loveridge, D. (1997). *Technology forecasting and foresight: Pedantry or disciplined vision?* The University of Manchester, Policy Research in Engineering, Science and Technology.

Lyles, M.A., & Schwenk, C.R. (1992, March). Top management, strategy and organizational knowledge structures. *Journal of Management Studies, 29*(2), 155-174. Oxford: Blackwell Publishing Limited.

Maedche, A., Motik, B., Stojanovic, L., Studer, R., & Volz, R. (2003). Ontologies for enterprise knowledge management. *IEEE Intelligent Systems, 18*(2), 26-33.

Maier, R. (2002). *Knowledge management systems: Information and communication technologies for knowledge management.* Berlin: Springer.

Martin, B.R. (1995). Foresight in science and technology. *Technology Analysis & Strategic Management, 7*(2), 139-168.

McInerney, C. (2002). Knowledge management and the dynamic nature of knowledge. *Journal of the American Society for Information Science and Technology, 53*(12), 1009-1018.

Nonaka, I. (1994, February). A dynamic theory of organizational knowledge creation. *Organization Science: A Journal of the Institute of Management Sciences, 5*(1), 14-37. Linthicum, MD: Institute for Operations Research (INFORMS).

Nonaka, I., Toyama, R., & Konno, N. (2001). SECI, ba and leadership: A unified model of dynamic knowledge creation. In I. Nonaka & D.J. Teece (Eds.), *Managing industrial knowledge* (pp. 13-43). London: SAGE Publications.

Pao, M.L. (1989). *Concepts of information retrieval.* Englewood, CO: Libraries Unlimited.

Park, J., & Hunting, S. (2003). *XML topic maps: Creating and using topic maps for the Web.* Boston: Addison-Wesley.

Pearce II, J.A., & Robinson, R.B., Jr. (2000). *Strategic management: Formulation, implementation, and control.* Boston: Irwin/McGraw-Hill.

Polanyi, M. (1966). *The tacit dimension.* Gloucester: Routledge & Kegan Paul.

Rumelt, R.P., Schendel, D., & Teece, D.J. (1991). Strategic management and economics. *Strategic Management Journal, 12*, 5-29.

Russell, S.J., & Norvig, P. (2003). *Artificial intelligence: A modern approach* (2nd ed.). Upper Saddle River, NJ: Pearson Education.

Sanchez, R., & Heene, A. (2004). *The new strategic management: Organization, competition, and competence*. New York: John Wiley & Sons.

Smolnik, S., & Erdmann, I. (2003). Visual navigation of distributed knowledge structures in groupware-based organizational memories [Special Issue: Knowledge Management and Organizations: Process, System, and Strategy]. *Business Process Management Journal, 9*(3), 261-280. West Yorkshire, UK: Emerald, Bradford.

Sowa, J.F. (1991). *Principles of semantic networks*. San Mateo, CA: Morgan Kaufmann Publishers.

Sowa, J.F. (2000). *Knowledge representation: Logical, philosophical, and computational foundations*. Pacific Grove, CA: Brooks/Cole.

Tsoukas, H. (2003). Do we really understand "tacit knowledge"? In M. Easterby-Smith & M.A. Lyles (Eds.), *The Blackwell handbook of organizational learning and knowledge management* (pp. 410-427). Malden, MA: Blackwell Publishers.

Tsoukas, H., & Vladimirou, E. (2001). What is organizational knowledge? *Journal of Management Studies, 38*(7), 973-993.

Von Krogh, G., Ichijo, K., & Nonaka, I. (2000). *Enabling knowledge creation: How to unlock the mystery of tacit knowledge and release the power of innovation*. New York: Oxford University Press.

Von Krogh, G., & Roos, J. (1996). The epistemological challenge: Managing knowledge and intellectual capital. *European Management Journal, 14*(4), 333-337. Amsterdam: Elsevier B. V.

Weiss, S.M., Indurkhya, N., Zhang, T., & Damerau, F. (2004). *Text mining: Predictive methods for analyzing unstructured information*. New York: Springer.

Wiig, K.M. (1993). *Knowledge management foundations: Thinking about thinking—How people and organizations create, represent, and use knowledge*. Arlington, TX: Schema Press.

Wiig, K.M. (1999). *Knowledge management: An emerging discipline rooted in a long history*. Knowledge Research Institute, Inc.

Zack, M.H. (1999). Managing codified knowledge. *Sloan Management Review, 40*(4), 45-58.

This work was previously published in Knowledge Management and Business Strategies: Theoretical Frameworks and Empirical Research, edited by E. Abou-Zeid, pp. E. Abou-Zeid, copyright 2008 by Information Science Reference, formerly known as Idea Group Reference (an imprint of IGI Global).

Compilation of References

Aaker, D. (1989). Managing assets and skills: The key to a sustainable competitive advantage. *California Management Review, 31*, 91-106.

Aamodt, A., & Nygård, M. (1995). Different roles and mutual dependencies of data, information, and knowledge: An AI perspective on their integration. *Data and Knowledge Engineering, 16*, 191-222.

Aamodt, A., & Plaza, E. (1994). Case-based reasoning: Foundational issues, methodological variations, and system approaches. *AI Communications, 7*(1), 39-59.

Abernathy, D. J. (1998). The WWW of distance learning: Who does what and where? *Training and Development, 52*(1), 29-30.

Aboody, D., & Lev, B. (2002). Information asymmetry, R&D and insider gains. *The Journal of Finance, 55*(6), 2747-2766.

Abou-Zeid, E. (2005). Alignment of business and knowledge management strategies. In M. Khosrow-Pour (Ed.), *Encyclopedia of information science and technology* (Vol. 1, pp. 98-103). Hershey, PA: Idea Group Publishing.

Ackerman, L. S. (1986). Development, transition, or transformation: The question of change in organizations. *Organizational Development Practicioner*, December, 1-8.

Acs, Z. J., & Audretsch, D. B. (1990). *Innovation and small firms*. Cambridge: The MIT Press.

Adamson, R. W., & Taylor, D. W. (1954). Functional fixedness as related to elapsed time and to set. *Journal of Experimental Psychology, 47*, 122-126.

Adler, P. A., & Adler, P. (1994). Observational techniques. In N. Denzin & Y. Lincoln (Eds.), *Handbook of qualitative research* (pp. 377-392). London: Sage.

Agor, W. H. (1997). The measurement, use, and development of intellectual capital to increase public sector productivity. *Public Personnel Management, 26*(2), 175-186.

Aguirre, J. L., Brena, R., & Cantu, F. J. (2001). Multiagent-based knowledge networks. *Expert Systems with Applications, 20*, 65-75.

Ahmed, P. K., Kok, L. K., & Loh, A. Y. E. (2002). *Learning through knowledge management*. Oxford: Butterworth-Heinemann.

Ahonen, H., Engeström, Y., & Virkkunen, J. (2000). Knowledge management – The second generation: Creating competencies within and between work communities in the competence laboratory. In Y. Malhotra (Ed.), *Knowledge management and virtual organizations*. London: Idea Group Publishing (IGP).

Aiken, L. (1994). *Psychological testing and assessment* (8th ed.). Boston: Allyn & Bacon.

Aiken, M., & Alford, R. (1970). Community structure and innovation: The case of urban renewal. *American Sociological Review, 35*, 650-665.

AIM. (2005). IST-2001-52222: *Acceleration of innovative ideas to market*. Project public report, EC.

Al'tshuller, G. S., Shulyak, L., & Rodman, S. (1999). *The innovation algorithm*. Worcester, MA: Technical Innovation Center.

Alas, R., & Sharifi, S. (2002). Organizational learning and resistance to change in Estonian companies. *Human Resource Development International, 5*(3), 313-331.

Alavi, M., & Leidner, D. E. (2001) . Review: Knowledge management and knowledge management systems. *MIS Quarterly, 25*(1), 107-136.

Al-Hawamdeh, S. (2003). *Knowledge management: Cultivating knowledge professionals*. Oxford: Chandos Publishing.

Allavi, M., & Tiwana, A. (2003). Knowledge management: The information technology dimension. In M. Easter-Smith & M. A. Lyles (Eds.), *Handbook of organizational learning and knowledge management* (pp. 105-121). Oxford: Blackwell Publishing.

Alle, V. (2000). The value evolution: Addressing larger implications of an intellectual capital and intangible assets perspectives. *Journal of Intellectual Capital, 1*(1), 17-32.

Al-Mashari, M., & Zairi, M. (2000). The effective application of SAP R/3: A proposed model of best practice. *Logistics Information Management, 13*(3), 156-166.

Altshuller, G. (1988). *Creativity as an exact science*. New York: Gordon and Breach Science Publishers.

Amabile, T. M. (1983). *The social psychology of creativity*. New York: Springer-Verlag.

American Institute of Certified Public Accountants [AICPA]. (1994). *Improving business reporting – A customer focus: Meeting the information needs of investors and creditors; and Comprehensive report of the special committee on financial reporting*. New York: American Institute of Certified Public Accountants.

Amidon, D. M. (1997). *Innovation strategy for the knowledge economy: The ken awakening*. Boston: Butterworth-Heinemann.

Amit, R., & Zott, Ch. (2001). Value creation in e-business. *Strategic Management Journal, 22*, 493-520.

Amit, R., & Zott, Ch. (2002). Value drivers of e-commerce business models. In M. Hitt, R. Amit, E. Autio, H. J. Sapienza, & J. G. Almeida (2000), Effects of age at entry, knowledge intensity, and imitability on international growth. *Academy of Management Journal, 43*(5), 909-924.

Anand, V., Manz, C. C., & Glick, W. H. (1998). An organization memory approach to information management. *Academy of Management Review, 23*(4), 796-809.

Andersen, M. M. (1999). Market institutions and interorganisational learning, In *Proceedings from Druid Winter Seminar.*

Andersen, P. H. (1995). Managing market resources. In L. Nørreklit, & H. M. Schoenfeld (Eds.), *Resources of the firm, creating, controlling, and cccounting*. DJØF Publishing Company.

Andersen, P. H., & Christensen, P. R. (2000). Interpartner learning in global supply chains: Lessons from NOVO nordisk. *European Journal of Purchasing and Supply Management, 6*, 105-116.

Andersen, P. H., & Kristensen P. H. (1999). The systemic qualities of Danish industrialism. In

Anderson, A. R., & Jack, S. L. (2002). The articulation of social capital in entrepreneurial networks: A glue or lubricant? *Entrepreneurship and Regional Development, 14*, 193-210.

Andrews, F. M. (1975). Social and psychological factors that influence the creative process. In I. A. Taylor & W. Getzels (Eds.), *Perspectives in creativity* (pp. 37 – 59). Chicago, IL: Aldine.

Andriessen, D. (2004). IC valuation and measurement: Classifying the state of the art. *Journal of Intellectual Capital, 5*(2), 230-242.

Anthony, R. N. (1965). *Planning and control systems: A framework for analysis*. Boston: Harvard University Press.

Arabie, P., & Hubert L. (1994). Cluster analysis in marketing research. In R. P. Bagozzi (Ed.), *Advanced methods of marketing research* (pp. 160-189). Cambridge, MA: Basil Blackwell.

Argote, L. (1993). Group and organizational learning curves: Individual, system, and eEnvironmental components. *British Journal of Social Psychology, 32*, 31-51.

Argyris, C. (1982). *Reasoning, learning, and action: Individual and organizational.* San Francisco, CA: Jossey-Bass.

Argyris, C., & Schon, D. (1978). *Organisational learning: A theory of action perspective.* Reading, MA: Addison-Wesley.

Armstrong, C. P., & Sambamurthy, V. (1999). Information technology assimilation in firms: The influence of senior leadership and IT infrastructures. *Information Systems Research, 10*(4), 304-327.

Armstrong, J.S. (2001). *Principles of forecasting: A handbook for researchers and practitioners.* Boston: Kluwer.

Arrow, K. (1974). *The limits of organisation.* New York: Norton & Company.

Arrow, K. (1994). Methodological Individualism and social knowledge, Richard T. Ely Lecture. In *AeA Papers and Proceedings, 84*, 2.

ASTD. (2006). *State of the industry report (Online).* Available at www.astd.org

Attewell, P. (1992). Technology diffusion and organizational learning: The case of business computing. *Organization Science, 3*(1), 1-19.

Awad, E. M., & Ghaziri, H. M. (2003). *Knowledge management.* Upper Saddle River, NJ: Prentice Hall.

Bailey, W., Frank, L., Henry, G., & Don, K. (1992). Diversity. *Human Resource Management,* Spring/Summer, 22.

Bandura, A. (1986). *The social foundation of thought and action: A social cognitive theory.* Englcwood Cliffs, NJ: Prentice-Hall.

Barney, J. B. (1991). Firm resources and sustained competitive advantage. *Journal of Management, 17*(1), 99-120.

Barney, J. B., & Hansen, M. H. (1994). Trustworthiness as a form of competitive advantage. *Strategic Management Journal, 15*, 175–190.

Barney, J.B. (2001). Is the resource-based view a useful perspective for strategic management research? Yes. *Academy of Management Review, 26*(1), 41-56.

Barrett, M., Cappleman, S., Shoib, G., & Walsham, G. (2004). Learning in knowledge communities: Managing technology and context. *European Management Journal, 22*(1), 1-11.

Barth, F. (1971). *Ethnic groups and boundaries: The social organization of cultural difference.* Bergen: Universitetsforlaget.

Barth, M. E., Clement, M. B., Foster, G., & Kasznik, R. (2003). Brand values and capital market valuation. In J. Hand, & B. Lev (Eds.), *Intangible assets: Measures, values, rnd Risks.* NY: Oxford University Press.

Barth, M. E., Kasznik, R., & McNichols, M. F. (2001). Analyst coverage and intangible assets. *Journal of Accounting Research, 39*(1), 1-34.

Bartlett, C.A., & Ghoshal, S. (1989). *Managing across borders: The transnational solution.* Boston: Harvard Business School Press.

Bartunek, J. M. (1993). The multiple cognitions and conflicts associated with second-order organizational change. In J. K. Murnighan (Ed.), *Social psychology in organizations: Advances in theory and research* (pp. 322-349). NJ: Prentice Hall.

Batt, P. J., & Purchase, S. (2004). Managing collaboration within networks and relationships. *Industrial Marketing Management, 33*, 169-174.

Beamer, L., & Varner, I. (2001). *Intercultural communication in the global workplace.* New York: McGraw-Hill Irvin.

Beattie, V., & Pratt, K. (2002). *Voluntary annual report disclosures: What users want.* Institute of Chartered Accountants of Scotland.

Becerra-Fernandez, I., Gonzalez, A., & Sabherwal, R. (2004). *Knowledge management: Challenges, solutions, and technologies.* Upper Saddle River, NJ: Pearson Prentice Hall.

Bechky, B. (2003). Sharing meaning across occupational communities: The transformation of understanding on a production floor. *Organization Science, 14*(3), 312-330.

Becker, G. S. (1962). Investment in human capital: A theoretical analysis. *Journal of Political Economy, 70*, S9-S49.

Becker, G. S. (1993). *Human capital. A theoretical and empirical analysis, with special reference to education* (3rd ed.). Chicago: University of Chicago Press

Becker, G.S. (1964). *Human capital.* New York: Columbia University Press.

Beer, M., & Eisenstat, R. (2000). The silent killers of strategy implementation and learning. *Sloan Management Review, 41*(4), 29-40.

Belardo, S. (2001). *Learning organizations and knowledge management: A conventional view and an alternative view.*

Bell, M. A. (1982). Phases in group problem solving. *Small Group Behaviour, 13*, 475-495.

Benjamins, V.R., Fensel, D., & Gómez Pérez, A.G. (1998). Knowledge management through ontologies. In *Proceedings of the 2nd International Conference on Practical Aspects of Knowledge Management (PAKM98) (pp. 5.1-5.12).* Basel, Switzerland.

Bergmann, R., Althoff, K., Breen, S., Göker, M., Manago, M., Traphöner, R., & Wess, S. (2003). *Developing industrial case-based reasoning applications* (2nd ed.). Berlin: Springer-Verlag.

Berman, S. L., Down, J., & Hill, C. W. L. (2002). Tacit knowledge as a source of competitive advantage in the National Basketball Association. *Academy of Management Journal, 45*(1), 13-31.

Berners-Lee, T., Hendler, J., & Lassila, O. (2001). The semantic Web. *Scientific American.*

Berry, D. C. (1987). The problem of implicit knowledge. *Expert Systems, 4*(3), 144-150.

Bertucci, G. (2006). Unlocking the human potential for public sector performance. *Public Personnel Management, 35*(3), 175-179.

Bhatt, G. D. (2000). Organizing knowledge in the knowledge development cycle. *Journal of Knowledge Management, 4*(1), 15-26.

Bhatt, G. D. (2001). Knowledge management in organizations: Examining the interaction between technologies, techniques, and people. *Journal of Knowledge Management, 5*(1), 68-75.

Bierly, P., & Chakrabarti A. (1996). Generic knowledge strategies in the US pharmaceutical industry. *Strategic Management Journal, 17*, Winter Special, 123-135.

Bingi, P., Sharma, M. K., & Godla, J. (1999). Critical issues affecting an ERP implementation. *Information Systems Management, 16*(3), 7-14.

Birch, H. G., & Rabinowitz, H. S. (1951). The negative effect of previous experience on productive thinking. *Journal of Experimental Psychology, 41*, 121-125.

Birkinshaw, J., & Mol, M. (2006). How management innovation happens. *MIT Sloan Management Review, 47*(4), 80-88.

Birkinshaw, J., & Sheehan, T. (2002). Managing the knowledge life cycle. *MIT Sloan Management Review, 44*(1), 74-83.

Bixler, C. H. (2005). Developing a foundation for a successful knowledge management system. In M. A. Stankosky (Ed.), *Creating the discipline of knowledge management: The latest in university research* (pp. 51-66). Oxford: Elsevier.

Black, L. J., Carlile, P. R., & Repenning, N. P. (2004). A dynamic theory of expertise and occupational boundaries in new technology implementation: Building on Barley's study of CT scanning. *Administrative Science Quarterly, 49*(4), 572-607.

Blake, A., & Mann, D. (2000). *Making knowledge tangible*. CMC and DuVersity, September 2000.

Blanc, H., & Sierra, C. (1999). The internationalization of R and D by multinationals: A trade off between external and internal proximity. *Cambridge Journal of Economics, 23*, 187-206.

Bloom, B., Messia, B., & Krathwohl, D. (1964). *Taxonomy of educational objectives*. New York: David McKay.

Boedker, C. (2005). *Australian guiding principles on extended performance management: A guide to better managing, measuring and reporting knowledge intensive resources*. Society for Knowledge Economics, Grosvenor Place.

Boisot, M. H. (1995). Is your company a creative destroyer? Competitive learning and knowledge flows in the technological strategies of firms. *Research Policy*, 485-506

Boisot, M. H. (1998). *Knowledge assets*. New York: Oxford University Press.

Bonabeau, E., & Meyer, C. (2001). Swarm intelligence: A whole new way to think about business. *Harvard Business Review, 79*(5), 106-114.

Bonache, J., & Brewster, C. (2001). Knowledge transfer and the management of expatriation. *Thunderbird International Business Review, 43*(1), 3-20.

Bontis, N. (2007). Mining the nation's intellectual capital: Knowledge management in government. In S. Borins, K. Kernaghan, D. Brown, N. Bontis, P. 6, & F. Thompson (Eds.), *Digital state at the leading edge* (pp. 155-182). Toronto, Canada: University of Toronto Press.

Bontis, N., & Fitz-enz, J. (2002). Intellectual capital ROI: A causal map of human capital antecedents and consequents. *Journal of Intellectual Capital, 3*(3), 223-247.

Bontis, N., Chong, W., & Richardson, S. (2000). Intellectual capital and business performance in Malaysian industries. *Journal of Intellectual Capital, 1*(1), 85-100.

Bontis, N., Dragonetti, N. C., Jacobsen, K,. & Roos, G. (1999). The knowledge toolbox: A review of the tools available to measure and manage intangible resources. *European Management Journal, 17*(4), 391-402.

Borgatti, S. P., & Cross, R. (2003). A relational view of information seeking and learning in social networks. *Management Science, 49*(4), 432-445.

Bosak, J., & Bray, T. (1999). XML and the second-generation Web. *Scientific American*.

Boudard, E. (2000). What are the main predictors of recurrent education? A five-country comparative model. In M. O'Dowd & I. Fägerlind (Eds.), *Mapping European comparative education research perspectives: The PRESTiGE TMR Network* (pp.147-167). Studies in Comparative and International Education No.52. Stockholm: Institute of International Education.

Boudard, E. (2001). *Literacy proficiency, earnings, and recurrent training: A ten country comparative study*. Studies in Comparative and International Education, No. 57. Stockholm: Institute of International Education, Stockholm University.

Boudard, E., & Rubenson, K. (2003). Revisiting major determinants of participation in adult education with a direct measure of literacy skills. In R. Desjardins & E. Boudard (Eds), *Literacy proficiency, International Journal of Educational Research, 39*, 265 –281.

Boudreau, M.-C., & Robey, D. (2005). Enacting integrated information technology: A human agency perspective. *Organization Science, 16*(1), 3-18.

Boulton, R. E. S., Libert, B. D., & Samek, S. M. (1997). *Cracking the value code: How successful businesses are creating wealth in the new economy*. New York: Harper Collins Publishers.

Bourdieu, P. (1977). *Outline of a theory of practice*. Cambridge: Cambridge University Press.

Bourdieu, P. (1991). *Language and symbolic power*. Cambridge: Polity Press.

Bourdieu, P. (2004). *Distinction: A social critique of the judgement of taste*. London: Routledge.

Bourdieu, P., Passeron, J.-C., & Martin, M. (1994). *Academic discourse*. Cambridge: Polity.

Bourne, M. (Ed.). (2001). *Handbook of performance measurement*. London: GEE Publishing Ltd.

Boutellier, R., Gassmann, O., Macho, H., & Roux, M. (1998). Management of dispersed product development teams: The role of information technologies. *R&D Management*, *28*(1), 13-25.

Boynton, A. C., Zmud, R. W., & Jacobs, G. C. (1994, September). The influence of IT management practice on IT use in large organizations. *MIS Quarterly, 18*(3), 299.

Brazil, K., Serdella, A. (2005). *Next generation extended enterprise*. Juniper Networks, USA.

Brief, A. P., & Downey, H. K. (1983). Cognitive and organizational structures: A conceptual analysis of implicit organizing theories. *Human Relations*, *36*, 1065-1090.

Bright, J.R. (1979). Technology forecasting as an influence on technological innovation: Past examples and future expectations. In M.J. Baker (Ed.), *Industrial innovation* (pp. 228-255). Basingstoke, UK: The Macmillan Press Ltd.

Brondmo, H. P. (2000). *The engaged customer. The new rules of Internet direct narketing*. New York: Harper Business.

Brooking, A. (1996). *Intellectual capital: Core asset for the third millennium enterprise*. London: International Thomson Business Press.

Brown, J. S., & Duguid, P. (2000). *The social life of information*. Boston: Harvard Business School Press.

Brown, J. S., & Duguid, P. (2001). Knowledge and organization. *Organization Science, 12*(2), 198-213.

Browne, J., Sackett, P. J., & Wortmann, J. C. (1995). Future manufacturing systems—Towards the Extended Enterprise. *Computers in Industry*.

Brubaker, R. (2002). Ethnicity without groups. *European Journal of Sociology, XLIII*(2), 163-189.

Bruckman, A. (2002). The Future of e-learning communities. *Communications of the ACM, 45*(4), 60-63.

Bruno, S. F., & Osterloh, M. (2002). *Successful management by motivation: Balancing intrinsic and extrinsic incentives*. Berlin Herdelberg: Springer-Verlag

Bucklew, M., & Edvinsson, L. (1999). *Intellectual capital at Skandia*. Retrieved December, 30, 2007, from http://www.fpm.com/cases/el3.html

Buckley, P., Carter, J., Clegg, J., & Tan, H. (2005). Language and social knowledge in foreign-knowledge transfer to China. *International Studies of Management and Organization, 35*(1), 47-65.

Bueno-Campos, E. (1998). El capital intangible como clave estratégica en la competencia actual. *Boletín de Estudios Económicos*, *53*, 207-229.

Bukh, P. N. (2002). *Disclosure of intellectual capital – Indicators or models? A matter of accounting or strategy*. Working paper, Aarhus School of Business.

Bukh, P. N., & Johanson, U. (2003). Research and knowledge interaction: Guidelines for intellectual capital reporting. *Journal of Intellectual Capital*, *4*(4), 572-583.

Bukh, P. N., Larsen, H. T., & Mouritsen, J. (2001). Constructing intellectual capital statements. *Scandinavian Journal of Management*, *17*(1), 87-108.

Burgelman, R.A., Maidique, M.A., & Wheelwright, S.C. (1996). *Strategic management of technology and innovation* (2nd ed.). Boston: Irwin/McGraw-Hill.

Burke, W., & Litwin, G. (1992). A casual model of organizational performance and change. *Journal of Management*, *18*, 523-545.

Burns, T., & Stalker, G. (1961). *The management of innovation*. London: Tavistock.

Burt, R. S. (1992). *Structural holes: ThesSocial structure of competition*. Cambridge, MA: Harvard University Press.

Burt, R. S. (1992). The social structure of competition. In N. Nohria, & R. G. Eccles (Eds.), *Networks and organisation*. Boston: Harvard Business School Press.

Burton, T. T., & Shaw, T. E. (2005). *Building the lean extended enterprise through adaptive supply chain networks*. LAI (Lean Aeronautics Imitative).

Burton-Jones, A. (1999). *Knowledge capitalism*. London: Oxford University Press.

Busby, J. S., & Fan, I. S. (1993). The extended manufacturing enterprise: Its nature and its needs. *International Journal of Technology Management*, Special Issue on Manufacturing Technology: Diffusion, Implementation and Management.

Butler, T., & Grace, A. (2005). Beyond knowledge management: Introducing learning management systems. *Journal of Cases on Information Technology, 7*, 53-70.

Byrd, T. A., Cossick, K. L., & Zmud, R. W. (1992). A synthesis of research on requirements analysis and knowledge acquisition techniques. *MIS Quarterly, 16*(1), 117-138.

Cabrera, Á., & Cabrera, E. F. (2002). Knowledge-sharing dilemmas. *Organisation Studies, 23*(5), 687-710.

Camp, R. S. (1989). *Benchmarking: The search for industry best practices that lead to superior performance*. Milwaukee, WI: ASQC Quality Press.

Campos, A. R., da Silva, R., & Stokic, D. (2004). Integrated approach for innovation and problem solving in dynamic virtual enterprises. *Proceedings of the INDIN 04*, Berlin.

Cañibano, L., García-Ayuso, M., & Sánchez, M. P. (2000). Accounting for intangibles: A literature review. *Journal of Accounting Literature, 19*, 102-130.

Cantwell, J. (1995). The globalization of technology: What remains of the product cycle model? *Cambridge Journal of Economics, 19*, 155-174.

Capron, L, & Hulland, J. (1999). Redeployment of brands, sales forces, and general marketing management expertise following horizontal acquisitions: A resource-based view. *Journal of Marketing, 63*(2), 41–54.

Carlile, P. (2002). A pragmatic view of knowledge and boundaries: Boundary objects in new product development. *Organization Science, 13*(4), 442-455.

Carlile, P., & Rebentisch, E. (2003). Into the black box: The knowledge transformation cycle. *Management Science, 49*(9), 1180-1195.

Carlucci, D., & Schiuma, G. (2007). Exploring intellectual capital concept in strategic management research. In L. Joia (Ed.), *Strategies for Information Technology and Intellectual Capital: Challenges and Opportunities*. London: Idea Group Inc.

Carlucci, D., Marr, B., & Schiuma, G. (2004). The knowledge value chain – How intellectual capital impacts business performance. *International Journal of Technology Management, 27*(6-7), 575-590.

Carmeli, A., & Tishler, A. (2004). The relationships between intangible organizational elements and organizational performance. *Strategic Management Journal, 25*, 1257-1278.

Caskey, K. R. (1995). *Co-operative distributed simulation and optimization in extended enterprise*. IFIP WG5.7 Conference Proceedings.

Cassel, C., & Symon, G. (Eds.). (1994). *Qualitative methods in organisational research: A practical guide*. London: Sage.

Castells, M. (2001). Information technology and global capitalism. In W. Hutton, & A. Giddens (Eds.), *On the edge, living with global capitalism*. London: Vintage.

CEDEFOP & EURYDICE. (2001). *National actions to implement lifelong learning on Europe*. Brussels: EURYDICE.

Chan, D., & Schmitt, N. (2002). Situational judgment and job performance. *Human Performance, 15*(3), 233-254.

Chase, R. L. (1997). The knowledge-based organization: An international survey. *The Journal of Knowledge Management, 1*, 38-49.

Chatzkel, J. (2002). A conversation with Göran Roos. *Journal of Intellectual Capital, 3*(2), 96-117.

Chatzkel, J. (2007). Conference report: 2006 KMWorld Conference review. *Journal of Knowledge Management, 11*(4), 159-166.

Chen, E. K. Y. (1983). Multinational corporations and technology diffusion in hong kong manufacturing. *Applied Economics, 15*(3), 309-312.

Chesbrough H. (2003). The era of open innovation. *Sloan Management Review, 44*(3), 35-41.

Chesbrough, H. (2003). *Open innovation: The new imperative for creating and profiting from technology.* Harvard Business School Publishing Corporation.

Chesbrough, H. W., & Teece, D. (1996). When is virtual virtuous? Organising for innovation. *Harvard Business Review, January-February,* 65-73.

Chesbrough, H., & Schwartz, K. (2007). Innovating business models with co-development partnerships. *Research-Technology Management*, Jan-Feb.

Christensen, C. (1997). *The innovator's dilemma: When new technologies cause great firms to fail.* Boston: Harvard Business School Press.

Chua, A (2002). The influence of social interaction on knowledge creation. *Journal of Intellectual Capital, 3*(4), 375-392.

Churchill, Jr., G. A. (1979). A paradigm for developing better measures of marketing constructs. *Journal of Marketing Research, XVI*, February, 64-73.

Chute, A. G., Thompson, M. M., & Hancock, B. W. (1999). *The Mcgraw-Hill handbook of distance learning.* New York: McGraw-Hill.

Ciborra, C. U., & Lanzara, G. F. (1994). Formative contexts and information technology: Understanding the dynamics of innovation in organizations. *Accounting, Management and Information Technology 4*(2), 61-86.

CIC. (2003). *Modelo intellectus: Medición y gestión del capital intelectual* (Serie Documentos Intellectus No. 5). Madrid: Centro de Investigación sobre la Sociedad del Conocimiento (CIC).

Clariana, R. B. (1997). Considering learning style in computer-assisted learning. *British Journal of Education Technology, 28*(1), 66-68.

Clark, E., & Geppert, M. (2002). Management learning and knowledge transfer in transforming societies: Approaches, issues, and future directions. *Human Resource Development International, 5*(3), 263-277.

Clark, E., & Soulsby, A. (1999). *Organisational change in post-communist Europe: Management and transformation in the Czech Republic.* Routledge.

Clement, J. (1989). Learning via model construction and criticism: Protocol evidence on sources of creativity in science. In J. Glover, R. Ronning, & C. Reynolds (Eds.), *Handbook of creativity: Assessment, theory and research* (pp. 341 – 381). NY: Plenum.

Clifford, J., & Marcus, G. E. (1986). *Writing culture: The poetics and politics of ethnography.* Berkeley: University of California Press.

Coase, R. H. (1937). The nature of the firm. *Economica, 4*, 386-405.

Cohen, M. D., & Bacdayan, P. (1994). Organizational routines are stored as procedural memory: Evidence from a laboratory study. *Organization Science, 5*, 554-568.

Cohen, V. L. (1997). Learning styles in a technology-rich environment. *Journal of Research on Computing in Education, 29*(4), 339-350.

Cohen, W. M., & Levinthal, D. A. (1990). Absorptive capacity: A new perspective on learning and innovation. *Administrative Science Quarterly, 35*, 128-152.

Coleman, D. (1999). GroupWare: Collaboration and knowledge sharing. In J. Lebowitz (Ed.), *Knowledge management handbook.* Orlando: CRC pres LLC.

Collier, P. M. (2001). Valuing intellectual capital in the police. *Accounting, Auditing & Accountability Journal, 14*(4), 437-455.

Collis, J., & Hussey, R. (2003). *Business research: A practical guide for undergraduate and postgraduate students.* New York: Palgrave Macmillan.

Comaroff, J. N. (1996). Ethnicity, nationalism, and the politics of difference in an age of revolution. In E. N. Wilmsen & P. McAllister (Eds.), *The politics of differ-*

ence (pp. 162-184). Chicago: The University of Chicago Press.

Conner, K. R. (1991). A historical comparison of the resource-based theory and five schools of thought within industrial organization economics: Do we have a new theory of the firm? *Journal of Management, 17*(1), 121-154.

Cook, S. J. B. (1999). Bridging epistemologies: The generative dance between organizational knowledge and organizational knowing. *Organization Science, 10*(4), 381-400.

Cooper, R. B., & Zmud, R. W. (1990, February). Information technology implementation research: A technological diffusion approach. *Management Science, 36*(2), 123.

Cooren, F. (2006). The organizational world as a plenum of agencies. In F. Cooren, J. R. Taylor, & E. J. Van every (Eds.), *Communication as organizing* (pp. 81-101). London: LEA.

Corti, E., & lo Storto, C. (1997). Technical problem solving and learning processes during product innovation: Some empirical evidence for the development of a theoretical framework of knowledge creation in small firms. In *Proceedings of the PICMET'97*, Portland (Oregon).

Corti, E., & lo Storto, C. (2000). Knowledge creation in small firms during product innovation: An empirical analysis of cause-effect relationships among its determinants. *Enterprise & Innovation Management Studies, 1*, 245-263.

Corti, E., lo Storto, C., & Trombetta, A. (1996). Fattori critici nell'innovazione di prodotto all'interno delle piccole imprese nelle aree deboli: apprendimento, competenze, e risorse ambientali.In *Proceedings of the AiIG Workshop*, Potenza.

Cotas Computer Technology. (2000). *There is only one thing we want to show you….*

Council of the European Union. (1999). Council Regulation (EEC) No. 1784/1999 of the European Parliament and of the Council of 12 July 1999 on the European Social Fund. *Official Journal of the European Communities, L 213*, 13/08/1999, 0005–0008.

Covin, J. G., & Slevin, D. P. (1988). The influence of organization structure on the utility of an entrepreneurial top management style. *Journal of Management Studies, 25*, 3, 217-234.

Cox, T., & Blake, S. (1991). Managing cultural diversity: Implications for organizational competitiveness. *The Academy of Management Executive 5*, 92-100.

Crosby, B., & Bryson, J. (2005). A leadership framework for cross-sector collaboration. *Public Management Review, 7*(2), 177-201.

Crossen, M. M., Lane, H. W., & White, R. E. (1998). An organizational learning framework: From induction to institution. *Academy of Management Review, 24*, 522-539.

Crossroads. (2001). *A sector report: Consumer products.* Retrieved September 12, 2002, from http://www.xroadsllc.com/pdf/cp_report.pdfDay, G. S. (1999). *The market driven organization.* New York: The Free Press.

Cyert, R. M., & March, J. G. (1963). *A behavioral theory of the firm.* Englewood Cliffs, NJ: Prentice-Hall.

D'Aveni, R. A. (1994). *Hypercompetition: Managing the dynamics of strategic maneuvering.* New York: Free Press.

Daft, R. L. (1978). A dual-core model of organizational innovation. *Academy of Management Journal, 21*(2), 193-210.

Daft, R. L., & Lengel, R. H. (1986). Organizational information requirements, media richness, and structural design. *Management Science, 32*, 554-571.

Daft, R. L., & Macintosh, N. B. (1981). A tentative explanation into the amount and equivocality of information processing in organizational work units. *Administrative Science Quarterly, 26*, 207-224.

Daft, R. L., & Weick, K. E. (1984). Toward a model of organizations as interpretation systems. *Academy of Management Review, 9*, 284-295.

Damanpour, F. (1987). The adoption of technological, administrative, and ancillary innovations: Impact of organizational factors. *Journal of Management, 13*(4), 675.

Damanpour, F. (1991). Organizational innovation: A meta-analysis of effects of determinants and moderators. *Academy of Management Journal, 34*(3), 555-590.

Damanpour, F., & Gopalakrishnan, S. (1998). Theories of organizational structure and innovation adoption: The role of environmental change. *Journal of Engineering and Technology Management, 15*(1), 1-24.

Danish Agency for Development of Trade and Industry (DATI). (2003). *Intellectual capital statements—the new guideline.* Author.

Danish Agency for Trade and Industry (DATI). (1999). *Developing intellectual capital accounts. Experiences from 19 companies.* Ministry of Business and Industry, Copenhagen.

Daum, J. (2001). Interview with Leif Edvinsson: Intellectual capital: The new wealth of corporations. *The new New Economy Analyst Report.* Retrieved December, 30, 2007, from http://www.juergendaum.com/news/11_13_2001.htm

Davenport, T. (2001). How do they know their customers so well? *Sloan Management Review, 42*(2), 63-73.

Davenport, T. H. (1998). Putting the enterprise into the enterprise system. *Harvard Business Review, 76*(4), 121-131.

Davenport, T. H. (2001). *From data to knowledge.* San Jose, CA: Oracle Inc.

Davenport, T. H., & Prusak, L. (1998). *Working knowledge. How organizations manage what they know.* Boston: Harvard Business School Press.

Davenport, T. H., De long, D. W., & Beers, M. C.(1998). Successful knowledge management projects. *Sloan Management Review*, 443-57.

Davenport, T., de Long, D., & Beers, M. (1998). Successful knowledge management projects. *Sloan Management Review, 39*(2), 43-57.

Davis, E. W., & Spekman, R. E. (2003). The extended enterprise: Gaining competitive advantage through collaborative supply chains. *Financial Times Prentice Hall.*

Davis, F. D. (1989). Perceived usefulness, perceived ease of use, and user acceptance of information technology. *MIS Quarterly, 13*(3), 318-340.

Davis, F. D., Bagozzi, R. P., & Warshaw, P. R. (1992). Extrinsic and intrinsic motivation to use computers in the workplace. *Journal of Applied Social Psychology, 22*(14), 1111-1132.

Davis, G., Wilt, C., Dillon, P., & Fishbein, B. (1997). *Extended product responsibility: A new principle for product-oriented pollution prevention.* The University of Tennessee. The Gordon Institute, INFORM.

De Long, D. (1997). *Building the knowledge-based organization: How culture drives knowledge behaviors.* Unpublished manuscript.

De Long, D., & Fahey, L. (2000). Diagnosing cultural barriers to knowledge management. *The Academy of Management Executive, 14*(4), 113-127.

Deci, E. L., & Ryan, R. M. (1987). The support of autonomy and the control of behavior. *Journal of Personality and Social Psychology, 53*(6), 1024-1037.

Dei Otatti, G. (1994). Trust, interlinking transaction and credit in the industrial district. *Cambridge Journal of Economics, 18*, 529-546.

Deloitte Research. (2002). *From e-learning to enterprise learning, becoming a strategic organization.* Retrieved from www.dc.com/research

DeLurgio, S.A. (1998). *Forecasting principles and applications.* Boston: Irwin/McGraw-Hill.

Deng, Z., Lev, B., & Narin, F. (2003). Science and technology as predictors of stock performance. In J. Hand& B. Lev (Eds.), *Intangible assets: Measures, values and risks.* NY: Oxford University Press.

Dennis, A. R., & Vessey, I. (2005). Three knowledge management strategies: Knowledge hierarchies, knowledge markets and knowledge communities. *MIS Quarterly Executive, 4*(4), 399-412.

Desjardins, R., Murray, T., & Tuijnman, A. (Eds). (2005). *Learning a living: First results of the adult literacy and life skills survey.* Paris & Ottawa: OECD and Statistics Canada.

Desouza, K. C. (2003). Knowledge management barriers: Why technology imperatives seldom works. *Business Horizons, 46*(1), 25-29.

Dewalt, K. M., Dewalt, B. R., & Wayland, C. B. (1998). Participant observation. In H. R. Bernard (Ed.), *Handbook of methods in cultural anthropology* (pp. 259-300). Walnut Creek: AltaMira.

Dewar, R. D., & Dutton, J. E. (1986). The adoption of radical and incremental innovations: An empirical analysis. *Management Science, 32*(11), 1422-1433.

Dewey, J. (1933). *How ee think.* Boston: D.C. Heath & Company.

Dey, A.K., & Abowd, G.D. (2000). *Towards a better understanding of context and context-awareness.* Atlanta: Graphics, Visualization and Usability Center and College of Computing, Georgia Institute of Technology.

Dhir, K. S. (2005). The value of language: Concept, perspectives, and policies. *Corporate Communications: An International Journal, 10*(4), 358-382.

Dhir, K. S., & Góké-Paríolá, A. (2002). The case for language policies in multinational corporations. *Corporate Communications: An International Journal, 7*(4), 241-251.

Diakoulakis, I. E., Georgopoulos, N. B., Koulouriotis, D. E., & Emiris, D. M. (2004). Towards a holistic knowledge management model. *Journal of Knowledge Management, 8*, 32-46.

DiBella, A. J., & Nevis, E. C. (1998). *How organizations learn. An integreted strategy for building learning capability.* Jossey-Bass Publishers.

Dierickx, I., & Cool, K. (1989a). Assets stock accumulation and sustainability of competitive advantage. *Management Science, 35*(12), 1504-1511.

DiMattia, S., & Oder, N. (1997). Knowledge management: Hope, hype, or harbinger? *Library Journal, 122*, 33-35.

Dowling, G., & Uncles, M. (1997). Do customers loyalty programs really work? *Sloan Management Review, 38*(4), 71-82.

Dowling, P. J., & Welch, D. E. (2004). *International human resource management - Managing people in a multinational environment.* London: Thomson Learning.

Downs, G. W., & Mohr, L. B. (1976). Conceptual issues in the study of innovation. *Administrative Science Quarterly,* (21), 700-714.

Drucker, P. (1999). *Mangement challenge of the 21st century.* HarperCollins.

Drucker, P. F. (1993). *Post-capitalist society.* New York: Harper Collins.

Drucker, P.F. (1996). *Managing in a time of great change.* Boston: Butterwort-Heinemann.

du Plessis, M. (2007). The role of knowledge management in innovation. *Journal of Knowledge Management, 11*(4), 20-29.

Duffy, J., & Tod, M. (2004). *The extended enterprise: Eliminating the barriers.* CIO Magazine. Retrieved from http://www2.cio.com/analyst/report2118.html

Duggan, S., & Barich, S. (2001). *The knowledge economy and corporate e-learning.* CA: The Silicon Valley World Internet Centre.

Duncan, R. B. (1976). The ambidextrous organization: Designing dual structures for innovation. In R. H. Kilmann, L. R. Pondy & S. D. P. (Eds.), *The Management Of Organization: Strategy And Implementation* (Vol. 167-188). New York: North- Holland.

Dunning, J. H. (1993). *Multinational enterprises and the global economy.* New York: Addison-Wesley.

Dyer, J. H. (2000). *Collaborative advantage: Winning through extended enterprise supplier networks.* Oxford University Press.

Dynes, S., Breschbühl, H., & Johnson, M. (2005). *Information security in the extended enterprise.*

Easter-Smith, M., & Lyles, M. A. (2003b). Introduction: Watersheds of organizational learning and knowledge management. In M. Easter-Smith & M. A. Lyles (Eds.), *Handbook of organizational learning and knowledge management* (pp. 1-17). Oxford: Blackwell Publishing.

Easter-Smith, M., & Lyles, M. A. (Eds.). (2003a). *Handbook of organizational learning and knowledge management.* Oxford: Blackwell Publishing.

Eccles, R. G., Herz, R. H., Keegan, E. M., & Phillips, D. M. (2001). *The value reporting revolution: Moving beyond the earnings game.* New York: John Wiley & Sons.

Eccles, R., & Mavrinac, S. (1995). Improving the corporate disclosure process. *Sloan Management Review*, Summer, 11-25.

Edvinsson, L. (1997). Developing intellectual capital at Skandia. *Long Range Planning, 30*(3).

Edvinsson, L. (2000). Some perspectives on intangibles and intellectual capital 2000. *Journal of Intellectual Capital, 1*(1), 12-16.

Edvinsson, L., & Malone, M. (1997). *Intellectual capital: Realizing your company's true value by finding its hidden brainpower.* New York: Harper Collins Publishers, Inc.

Eierman, M. A., Niederman, F., & Adams, C. (1995). DSS theory: A model of constructs and relationships. *Decision Support Systems, 14*, 1-26.

Eisenhardt, K. M. (1989). Building theories from case study research. *Academy of Management Review, 14*, 532-550.

Eisenhardt, K. M., & Bourgeois, L. J. I. (1988, December). Politics of strategic decision making in high-velocity Envi. *Academy of Management Journal, 31*(4), 734-737.

e-learning industry. In (pp. 1-51.). San Francisco: Thomas Weisel Partners.

Elisa. (2006). *Annual report.* Retrieved 6/12/2007, from http://www.elisa.com/english/docimages/attachment/Elisa_vk2006_uk.pdf

Elisa. (2007). *Presentation.* Retrieved 6/12/2007, from http://www.elisa.com/english/docimages/attachment/Q2%202007%20English.pdf

Ellen, K. (1997). Know-how's not easy. *Computerworld, 31*(11), L1-L11.

Engeström, Y. (1998). Innovative learning in work teams: Analyzing cycles of knowledge creation. In Y.Engeström, R. Miettinen, & R-L. Punamäki (Eds.), *Perspectives in activity theory* (pp. 377-404). Cambridge University Press.

Erez, M., & Earley, P. C. (1993). *Culture, self-identity and work.* New York: Oxford University Press.

Eriksen, T. H. (2002). *Ethnicity and nationalism.* London: Pluto Press.

Eriksson, H. (1992). A survey of knowledge acquisition techniques and tools and their relationship to software engineering. *The Journal of Systems and Software, 19*, 97-107.

European Commission. (2000). *Towards a European research area.* Luxemburg: Office for Official Publications of the European Communities.

European Commission. (2000). *A memorandum on lifelong learning.* Luxembourg: Office for Official Publications of the European Communities.

European Commission. (2001). *Making a European area of lifelong learning a reality.* Luxembourg: Office for Official Publications of the European Communities.

European Commission. (2005). *Progress towards the Lisbon objectives in education and training, 2005 report.* Commission staff working paper, Luxemburg: Office for Official Publications of the European Communities.

Evans, P., Pucik,V., & Barsoux, J. (2002). *The global challenge: Frameworks for international human resource management.* Boston: McGraw-Hill.

Evans-Pritchard, E. E. (1951). *Social anthropology.* London: Cohen and West.

Farjoun, M. (1994). Beyond industry boundaries: Human expertise, diversification and resource-related industry groups. *Organization Science, 5*(2), 185–199.

Feeny, D. F., & Willcocks, L. P. (1998). Core IS capabilities for exploiting information technology. *Sloan Management Review, 39*(3), 9-21.

Feldman, M. S. (2000). Organizational routines as a source of continuous change. *Organization Science, 6*, 611-629.

Ferner, A. (1997). Country of origin effects and HRM in multinational companies. *Human Resource Management Journal, 7*(1), 19-37.

Festinger, L., Schachter, S., & Back, K. W. (1950). *Social pressures in informal groups: A study of human factors in housing.* New York: Harper Brothers.

Fichman, R. G. (2001). The role of aggregation in the measurement of it-related organizational innovation. *MIS Quarterly, 25*(4), 427-455.

Fichman, R. G. (2004). Going beyond the dominant paradigm for information technology innovation research: Emerging concepts and methods. *Journal of the Association for Information Systems, 5*(8), 314-355.

Fichman, R. G., & Kemerer, C. F. (1997, October). The assimilation of software process innovations: An organizational learning perspective. *Management Science, 43*(10), 1345-1363.

Field, J. (2000). *Lifelong learning and the new educational order.* Trent: Trentham Books.

Fincham, R., & Roslender, R. (2003). *The management of intellectual capital and its implications for business reporting.* The Institute of Chartered Accountants of Scotland.

Fiol, C. (1994). Consensus, diversity, and learning in organizations. *Organization Science, 5*, 403-420.

Fiol, C. M., & Lyles, M. A. (1985, October). Organizational learning. *Academy of Management Review,* 10, 803.

Fisher, W. A. (1980). Scientific and technical information and the performance of R&D groups. *TIMS Studies in the Management Sciences, 15*, 67-89.

Fleming, L. (2007). Breakthroughs and the "long tail" of innovation. *MIT Sloan Management Review, 49*(1), 69-74.

Fountain, J. E. (2001). *Building the virtual state.* Washington, DC: The Brookings Institution.

Fountain, J. E. (2001). Paradoxes of public sector customer service. *Governance: An International Journal of Policy and Administration, 14*(1), 55-73.

Foxall, G. R. (1988). The theory and practice of user-initiated innovation. *Journal of Marketing Management, 4*(2) 230-248.

Frappaolo, C. (1998).Defining knowledge management: Four basic functions. *Computerworld.* Retrieved from http://www.computerworld.com/home/featu

Frederickson, H. G. (2005). Transcending the community: Local leadership in a world of shared power. *Public Management, 87*(10), 8-15.

Freeman, C., & Soete. L. (1997). *The economics of industrial innovation* (3rd ed.). Pinter Publishers.

Freeman, L. (2000). Visualizing social networks. *Journal of Social Structure, 1*(1).

Frost, T. (2001). The geographic sources of foreign subsidiaries' innovations. *StrategicManagement Journal, 22*, 101-123.

Fulmer, R. M., & Keys, J. B. (1998). A conversation with Argyris: The father of organizational learning. *Organizational Dynamics, 27.* 21-33.

Gadde, L-E., & Håkansson, H. (2001). *Supply network strategies.* IMP group. John Wiley and Sons Ltd.

Gaines, B.R., & Shaw, M.L.G. (1986). A learning model for forecasting the future of information technology. *Future Computing Systems, 1*(1), 31-69.

Galbraith, J. K (1952). *American capitalism: The concept of countervailing power.* Boston: Houghton Mifflin.

Galbraith, J. R. (1973). *Designing complex organizations*, Reading. MA: Addison-Wesley.

Garner, W. R. (1962). *Uncertainty and structure as psychological concepts*. New York: John Wiley & Sons.

Garshol, L.M. (2002). What are topic maps? Retrieved May 22, 2007, from http://www.XML.com

Garvin, D. A. (1993). Building a learning organization. *Harvard Business Review*, July-August, 78-91.

Gascó, M. (2004). E-gobierno en Bolivia y Paraguay. In R. Araya Dujisin & M. A. Porrúa Vigon (Eds.), *América Latina puntogob: Casos y tendencias en gobierno electrónico* (pp. 125-150). Santiago, Chile: FLACSO-Chile/AICD-OEA.

Geertz, C. (1988). *Works and lives: The anthropologist as author.* Standford: Standford University Press.

Gelb, D. S. (2002). Intangible assets and firms' disclosures: An empirical investigation. *Journal of Business Finance & Accounting, 29*(3-4), 457-476.

Gerybadze, A., & Reger, G. (1999). Globalization of R and D: Recent changes in the management of innovation in transnational corporations. *Research Policy, 28*, 251-274.

Geschka, H. (1992). The strategic aspect in the process of innovation. In H. Geschka & H. Hubner (Eds.), *Innovation strategies: Theoretical approaches - experiences - improvements* (pp. 69-78). Amsterdam: Elsevier Science Publishers.

Getzels, F., & Csikszentmyhalyi, M. (1976). *The creative vision: A longitudinal study of problem solving in art.* New York: Wiley.

Gibbert, M., Leibold, M., & Voelpel, S. (2001). Rejuvenating corporate intellectual capital by co-opting customer competence. *Journal of Intellectual Capital, 2*(2), 109-126.

Giles, H., & Johnson, P. (1981). The role of language in ethnic group relations. In J. C. Turner & H. Giles (Eds.), *Intergroup behavior* (pp. 199-243). Oxford: Blackwell.

Gil-García, J. R., & Helbig, N. (2006). Exploring e-government benefits and success factors. In A.-V. Anttiroiko & M. Malkia (Eds.), *Encyclopedia of digital government* (pp. 803-811). Hershey, PA: Idea Group Reference.

Gill, J., & Johnson, P. (1991). *Research methods for managers*. London: Paul Chapman.

Glaser, B. G., & Strauss, A. L. (1967). *The discovery of grounded theory: Strategies for qualitative research.* New York: Aldine Publishing.

Glasser, P. (1998). The knowledge factor knowledge management. *CIO Magazine.* Retrieved from http:// www.cio.com/archive/010199_know_content.htm

Glesne, C., & Peshkin, A. (1992). *Becoming qualitative researchers.* New York: Longman.

Gloor, P. A., & Cooper, S. M. (2007). The new principles of a swarm business. *MIT Sloan Management Review, 48*(3), 81-84.

Gloor, P., Laubacher, R., Dynes, S., & Zhao, Y.(2003). Visualization of communication patterns in collaborative innovation networks: Analysis of some W3C working groups. In *Proc. ACM CIKM 2003*, New Orleans, November 5-6, 2003.

Glucksberg, S., & Weisberg, R. W. (1966). Verbal behavior and problem solving: Some effects of labeling in a functional fixedness problem. *Journal of Experimental Psychology, 71*, 659-664.

Goh, A. L. S. (2005). Harnessing knowledge for innovation: An integrated management framework. *Journal of Knowledge Management, 9*(4), 6-18.

Gooderham, P.N., & Nordhaug, O. (2003). *International management: Cross-boundary challenges.* Oxford: Blackwell.

Goodman, J. (1999). Basic facts on customer complaint behavior and the impact of service on the bottom line. *TARP - Technology Assistive Resource Program.*

Goodman, P. S., & Darr, E. D. (1998). Computer-aided systems and communities: Mechanisms for organizational learning in distributed environments. *MIS Quarterly, 22*(4), 417-440.

Gouldner, A. W. (1960). The norm of reciprocity: A preliminary statement. *American Sociological Review, 25*(2) 161-178.

Granger, C.W.J. (1989). *Forecasting in business and economics.* San Diego: Academic Press.

Granovetter, M. (1973). The strength of weak ties. *American Journal of Sociology,78*(6), 1360-1379.

Grant, R. M. (1991). The resource-based theory of competitive advantage: Implications for strategy formulation. *California Management Review, 33*(3), 14-35.

Grant, R. M. (1998). *Contemporary strategic analysis: Concepts, techniques, applications.* Oxford: Blackwell.

Gray, J. (1999). *False dawn: The delusion of global capitalism.* London: Granta.

Gray, P. (2001). A problem-solving perspective on knowledge management practices. *Decision Support Systems, 31*, 87-102.

Griffith, T. L., Mannix, E. A., & Neale, M. A. (2003). Conflict in virtual teams. In S. G. Cohen & C. B. Gibson (Eds.),*Virtual teams that work* (pp. 335-352). San Francisco: Jossey-Bass.

Gruninger, M., & Uschold (1996). Ontologies: Principles, methods, and applications. *Knowledge Engineering Review, 11*(2).

Gu, F., & Lev, B. (2001). *Intangible assets: Measurement, drivers.* Usefulness. working paper. Boston University.

Gudykunst, W. B. (2004). *Bridging differences: Effective intergroup communication.* London: Sage Publications.

Gunawardena, C. N., & Boverie, P. E. (1992). *Impact of learning styles on instructional design for distance education.* Paper presented at the World Conference of the International Council of Distance Education,, Bangkok Thailand.

Guthrie, J. (2001). The management, measurement and the reporting of intellectual capital. *Journal of Intellectual Capital, 2*(1), 27-41.

Guthrie, J., & Boedker, C. (2006). Perspectives on "new" models of business reporting: A reflective note. *Accounting, Auditing & Accountability Journal, 19*(6), 785-792.

Guthrie, J., & Petty, R. (2000). Intellectual capital: Australian annual reporting practices. *Journal of Intellectual Capital, 1*(3), 241-251.

Hage, J., & Aiken, M. (1967). Program change and organizational properties: A comparative analysis. *American Journal of Sociology, 72*, 503-519.

Hagel, J., & Singer, M. (1999). Unbundling the corporation. *Harvard Business Review, March-April 1999.*

Hair, J. F., Anderson, R. E., Tathan, R. L., & Black W. C. (1998). *Multivariate data analysis* (5th ed.). Upper Saddle River, NJ: Prentice Hall.

Håkansson, H., & Waluszewski, A. (2002). *Managing technological development. IKEA, the environment and technology. Routledge Advances in Management and Business Studies.* London: Routledge.

Hall, E., & Hall, R. (1990). *Hidden differences: Doing business with the Japanese.* New York: Double Day Anchor Books.

Hall, H. (2000). Online information sources: Tools of business intelligence? *Journal of Information Science, 26*(3), 139-143.

Hall, R. (1992). The strategic analysis of intangible resources. *Strategic Management Journal, 13,* 135-144.

Hall, R. (1993). A framework linking intangible resources and capabilities to sustainable competitive advantage. *Strategic Management Journal, 14*, 607-618.

Hambrick, D. C., Davison, S. C., Snell, S. A., & Snow, C. C. (1998). When groups consist of multiple nationalities. *Organization Studies, 19*(2), 181-206.

Hamel, G. (1990). Competition for competence and inter-partner learning within international strategic alliances. *Strategic Management Journal, 12*, 83-103.

Hamel, G. (2000). *Leading the revolution*. Boston: Harvard Business School Press.

Hamid, A. A. (2001). E-Learning-Is it the"E"or the learning that matters? *The Internet and Higher Education, 4*(3-4), 311-316.

Han, J., & Kamber, M. (2001). *Data mining: Concepts and techniques*. San Diego: Academic Press.

Hand, J. R. M. (2003). Profits, losses, and the nonlinear pricing of Internet stocks. In J. Hand, & B. Lev (Eds.), *Intangible assets: Measures, values and risks*. NY: Oxford University Press.

Hannabuss, S. (1987). Knowledge management. *Library Management, 8*(5), 1-50.

Hansen, M. T., Nohria, N., & Tierney, T. (1999). What is your strategy for managing knowledge? *Harvard Business Review, 77*(2), 106-107.

Hargadon, A. (2003). *How breakthroughs happen: The surprising truth about how companies innovate*. Boston: Harvard Business School Press.

Harreld, J. B. (1998). Building faster, smarter organizations. In D. Tapscott, A. Lowy & N. Klym (Eds.), *Blueprint the digital economy: Creating wealth in the era of e-business*. New York: McGraw Hill.

Harrington, L. (1995). Taking Integration to the next level, *Transportation and Distribution*.

Harris, H., & Kumra, S. (2000). International manager development. *Journal of Management Development, 19*(7), 607-620.

Harris, K., Fleming, M., Hunter, R., Rosser, B., & Cushman, A. (1999). *The knowledge management scenario: Trends and directions for 1998 –2003*. London: Gartner.

Harrison, J. S., Hitt, M. A., Hoskisson, R. E., & Ireland, R. D. (2001). Resource complementarity in business combinations: Extending the logic to organizational alliances. *Journal of Management, 27*, 679–690.

Hartley, J. F. (1994). Case studies in organisational research. In C. Cassel & G. Symon, (Eds.), *Qualitative methods in organisational research: A practical guide*. London: Sage.

Harvey M. G., & Lusch R. F. (1999). Balancing the intellectual capital books: Intangible liabilities. *European Management Journal, 17*(1), 85-92.

Harzing, A., & van Ruysseveldt, J. (Eds.). (2004). *International human resource management* (2nd ed.). London: Sage.

Hasan, A. (1996). Lifelong learning. In A. C. Tuijnman (Ed.), *The international encyclopedia of adult education and training* (2nd ed.) (pp. 33-41). Oxford: Pergamon Press.

Haskell, D. (2005). *What is extended product responsibility?* NZ2000 Plastics, Otaki, New Zealand.

Hatch, N. W., & Dyer, J. H. (2004). Human capital and learning as a source of sustainable competitive advantage. *Strategic Management Journal, 25*, 1155–1178.

Hauschild, S, Licht, T., & Stein, W. (2001). Creating a knowledge culture. *The McKinsey Quarterly, 1*, 74-81.

Hayek, A. (1945). The use of knowledge in society. *American Economic Review, 35*, 519-530.

Hayek, F. (1945). The use of knowledge in society. *The American Economic Review, 35*(4), September.

Hayes, J. R. (1978). *Cognitive psychology. Thinking and creating*. Homewood, IL: Dorsey Press.

Hedberg, B. (1981). How organizations learn and unlearn. In P. C. Nystrøm, & W. H. Starbuck (Eds.), *Handbook of organizational design*, volume I. Oxford University Press

Hedberg, B. L. T., Dahlgren, G., Hansson, J., & Olve, N. G. (1997). *Virtual organizations and beyond: Discover imaginary systems*. London: Wiley and Sons.

Hedman, J., & Kalling, T. (2001). *The business model: A mean to understand the business context of information and communication technology*. Working paper 2001/9, Institute of Economic Research, School of Economics and Management, Lund Universitet.

Heeks, R. (2006). *Implementing and managing egovernment: An international text*. London: Sage Publications.

Heene, A., & Sanchez, R. (Eds.). (1997). *Competence-based strategic management*. Chichester: John Wiley and Sons.

Heer, J., & Boyd, D. (2005). Vizster: Visualizing online social networks. In *InfoVis 2005, IEEE Symposium on Information Visualization*.

Heide, J .B., & John, G. (1995). Measurement issues in research on interfirm relations. In K. Håkansson, & I. Snehota (Eds.), *Developing relationships in business networks*. London: Routledge.

Hellström, T., Kemlin, P., & Malmquist, U. (2000). Knowledge and competence management at Ericsson: Decentralization and organizational fit. *Journal of Knowledge Management*, *4*, 99-110.

Hendriksen, E. S., & van Breda, M. F. (1992). *Accounting theory* (5th ed.). Burr Ridge: Irwin.

Hendry, C. (1996). Understanding and creating whole organizational change through learning theory. *Human Relations*, *49*, 621-641.

Hicks, W. D., & Klimoski, R. J. (1987). Entry into training programs and its effects on training outcomes: A field experiment. *Academy of Management Journal*, *30*, 542-552.

Hislop, D. (2003). Linking human resource management and knowledge management via commitment: A review and research agenda. *Employee Relations*, *25*, 182-202.

Hitt, M. A., & Ireland, R. D. (2002). The essence of strategic leadership: Managing human and social capital. *Journal of Leadership and Organizational Studies*, *9*, 3-12.

Hofstede, G. (1991). *Cultures and organizations: Intercultural cooperation and its importance to survival*. Glasgow: HarperCollins.

Hofstede, G. (1991). *Cultures and organizations: Software of the mind*. London: MCGraw publications.

Hofstede, G. (2001). *Culture's consequences: Comparing values, behaviours, institutions, and organizations across nations* (2nd ed.). London: Sage Publications.

Holland, C. P., & Light, B. (1999). A critical success factors model for ERP implementation. *IEEE Software*, May/June, 30-36.

Holsapple, C., & Whinston, A. (1983). Software tools for knowledge fusion. *Computerworld*, *17*(15),11-18.

Hölttä, P. (2000). *Piimäki 2000: Laajakaistaisen alueverkon uudet palvelut. tuotekehityshakemuksen liite 2*. Tutkimus- ja kehitysprojektisuunnitelma TEKESin 'Tietoliikenteellä maailmalle' teknologiaohjelmaan. HPY Tutkimuskeskus.

Hong, J., & Ståhle, P. (2005). The coevolution of knowledge and competence management. *Int. Journal of Management Concepts and Philosophy*, 1(2).

Huber, G. P. (1991). Organizational learning: The contributing processes and the literatures. *Organization Science*, *2*(1), 88-115.

Hull, F., & Hage, J. (1982). Organizing for innovation: beyond burns and stalker's organic. *Sociology*, *16*(4), 564-577.

Human, L. (1996). Managing workforce diversity: A critique and example from South Africa. *International Journal of Man Power*, *17*, (4 & 5), 46-64.

Hunt, D. P. (2003). The concept of knowledge and how to measure it. *Journal of Intellectual Capital*, *4*(1), 100-113.

Hunt, I., Pereira Klen, A., & Zhang, J. (1997). Cross border enterprises: Virtual or extended! *ISIP'97 OE/IFIP/IEEE International Conference on Integrated and Sustainable Industrial Production*, Lisboa, Portugal.

Hurst, D. K. (1986). Why strategic management is bankrupt. *Organizational Dynamics*, Spring, 5-27.

Hussi, T., & Ahonen, G. (2002). Managing intangible assets – A question of integration and delicate balance. *Journal of Intellectual Capital*, *3*(3), 277-286.

Huynh, M. Q., Umesh, U. N., & Valacich, J. S. (2003). E-Learning as an emerging entrepreneurial enterprise in universities and firms. *Communications of the Association for Information Systems, 12*, 48-68.

Hwang, Y., & Yi, M. Y. (2003). Predicting the use of web-based information systems: Self-efficacy, enjoyment, learning goal orientation, and the technology acceptance model. *International Journal of Human-Computer Studies, 59*(4), 431-449.

Ichijo, K. (2004). From managing to enabling knowledge. In H. Takeuchi & I. Nonaka (Eds.), *Hitosubashi on knowledge management* (pp. 125-153). Singapore: John Wiley and Sons.

Igbaria, M., A., & Livari, J. (1995). The effects of self-efficacy on computer usage. *OMEGA International Journal of Management Science., 23*(6), 587-605.

Ilinitch, A. Y., & Zeithaml, C. P. (1995). Operationalizing and testing Galbraith's center of gravity theory. *Strategic Management Journal, 16*(5), 401–410.

Imai, K, Nonaka I., & Takeuchi H. (1985). Managing the new product development process : How Japanese companies learn and unlearn. In K. B. Clark, R. H. Hayes, & C. Lorenz (Eds.), *The uneasy alliance: Manging the productivity-technology dilemma* (pp. 337–376). Boston, MA: Harvard Business Press.

Ingwersen, P. (1992). *Information retrieval interaction.* London: Taylor Graham Publishing.

Institute of Chartered Accountants in England and Wales (ICAEW). (2004). *Information for better markets: New reporting models for business.* Institute of Chartered Accountants in England and Wales, London.

interKnowledge Technologies. *Interview with Leif Edvinsson.* Retrieved December, 30, 2007, from http://www.interknowledgetech.com/brainovation.html

International Accounting Standards Board [IASB]. (2005). *Discussion paper: Management commentary.* London: IASCF Publications Department

Itami, H., & Roehl, T. (1987). *Mobilizing invisible assets.* Cambridge, MA: Harvard University Press.

Iwuagwu, O. (2007). Creativity and innovation in business success. *Business Day*, December 23, .8.

Jackson, T. (2004). *Management and change in Africa.* London: Routledge.

Jacoby, J. (1978). Consumer research: A state of the art review. *Journal of Marketing, 42*, April, 87-96.

Jaffe, D. T., Scott, C. D., & Tobe, G. R. (1994). *Rekindling commitment: How to revitalize yourself, your work, and your organization.* San Francisco: Jossey-Bass Publishers.

Janssens, M., Lambert, J., & Steyaert, C. (2004). Developing language strategies for international companies: The contribution of translation studies. *Journal of World Business, 39,* 414-430.

Janz, B. D., Colquitt, J. A., & Noe, R. A. (1997). Knowledge worker team effectiveness: The role of autonomy, interdependence, team development, and contextual support variables. *Personnel Psychology ,50*(4), 877-904.

Jasimuddin, S. M., Klein, J. H., & Connell, C. (2005). The paradox of using tacit and explicit knowledge: Strategies to face dilemmas,.*Management Decision, 43*, 102-112

Jefferson, T. (1813). *Thomas Jefferson to Isaac McPherson, 1813.* ME 13:333. Retrieved from http://etext.virginia.edu/jefferson/quotations/jeffcont.htm

Jenkins, R. (1996). *Social identity.* New York: Routledge.

Jenkins, R. (1997). *Categorization and power.* England: Sage Publication.

Jenkins, R. (1997). *Rethinking ethnicity - Arguments and explorations.* London: Sage Publications.

Joel, L. (1995). Leverage, exploitation, and intellectual capital. *The American Journal*

Johannessen, J., Olaisen, J., & Olsen, B. (2001). Management of tacit knowledge: The importance of tacit knowledge, the danger of information technology, and what to do about it. *International Journal of Information Management, 21*, 3-20.

Johanson M. *White Paper: Sharing Product Data Through Life in the Extended Enterprise –the share-A-space™ solution.* Eurostep Commercial Solutions AB, Sweden.

Johnson, H. T., & Kaplan, R. S. (1987). *Relevance lost: The rise and fall of management accounting.* Boston: Harvard Business School Press.

Johnson, W. H. A (1999). An integrative taxonomy of intellectual capital: Measuring the stock and flow of intellectual capital components in the firm. *International Journal of Technology Management, 18*(5/6/7/8), 562-575.

Johnson-Laird, P. N. (1983). *Mental modes.* Cambridge, MA: Harvard University Press.

Johnston, R., & Gibbons, M. (1975). Characteristics of information usage in technological innovation. *IEEE Transaction on Engineering Management, 22*, 27-34.

Joia, L. A (2000). Measuring intangible corporate assets: Linking business strategies with intellectual capital. *Journal of Intellectual Capital, 1*(1), 68-84.

Jones, A. M., & Hendry, C. (1992). *The learning organization: A review of literature and practice.* The HRD Partnership.

Jorgensen, D. L. (1989). *Participant observation: A methodology for human studies.* London: Sage.

Julien, P. A. (1993). Small businesses as a research subject: Some reflections on knowledge of small businesses and its effects on economic theory. *Small Business Economics, 5*, 157-166.

Juntunen, A. (2005). *The emergence of a new business through collaborative networks: A longitudinal study in the ICT sector.* Acta Universitatis Oeconomicae Helsingiensis. Printed in HSEPrint. A-series, no 256, ISSN 1237-556X. ISBN: 951-791-957-3/1.

Juntunen, A. (2007). Creating competitive advantage: The emergence of a new business through collaborative networks – An empirical case study in the ICT sector. In H. Rahman (Ed.), *Developing successful ICT strategies: Competitive advantages in a global knowledge-driven society.* Idea Group Publishing. Information Science Reference.

Juntunen, A. (2008). Data warehouse in the Finnish police - A case study. In J. Wang (Ed.), *Encyclopedia of data warehousing and mining* (2nd ed.). Idea Group Publishing. Forthcoming.

Kaasinen, K. (2001). *Describing business concept based on partnership network.* Thesis. Lappeenranta University of Technology.

Kalling, T., & Styhre, A. (2003). *Knowledge sharing in organizations.* Copenhagen: Copenhagen Business School Press.

Kannabiran, G., Xavier, M. J., & Anantharaaj, A. (2004). Enabling e-governance through citizen relationship management: Concept, model and applications. *Journal of Services Research, 4*(2), 223-240.

Kanter, R. M. (1983). *The change masters.* New York: Simon and Schuster.

Kaplan, R. S., & Norton, D. P. (1996). *The balanced scorecard - Translating strategy into action.* Boston: Harvard Business School Press.

Kaplan, R., & Norton, D. (1992). The balanced scorecard: Measures that drive performance. *Harvard Business Review, 70*, 71-79.

Kaplan, R., & Norton, D. (1997). *The balance scorecard.* Boston: Harvard Business School Press.

Kaplan, R.S., & Norton, D.P. (1993). Putting the balanced scorecard to work. *Harvard Business Review,* (September-October), 134-147.

Kaplan, R.S., & Norton, D.P. (1996). Using the balanced scorecard as a strategic management system. *Harvard Business Review,* (January-February), 76.

Kaufman, E. (2004). E-gobierno en Argentina: Crisis, burocracia y redes. In R. Araya Dujisin & M. A. Porrúa

Vigon (Eds.), *América Latina puntogob: Casos y tendencias en gobierno electrónico* (pp. 151-188). Santiago, Chile: FLACSO-Chile/AICD-OEA.

Keeley, L. (In press). *Taming the new: The emerging discipline of innovation*. Boston: Harvard Business School Press.

Keesing, R. (1972). Paradigm lost: The new ethnography and the new linguistics. *South-western Journal of Anthropology 28*(2), 299-332.

Kim, J., & Mueller, C. W. (1978). *Factor analysis. Statistical methods and practical issues*. Sage University Paper series on Quantitative Applications in the Social Sciences, 07-014. Beverly Hills and London: Sage Publications.

Kim, Y. Y. (2005). Inquiry in intercultural and development communication. *Journal of Communication, September*, 554-577.

Kirchhoff, U., Kuczynski, A., & Stokic, D. (2005). *Set-up and maintenance of ontologies for innovation support in extended enterprises*. Int J Adv Manuf Technol, Published online: 12 October 2005

Kirton, M. J. (1976). Adaptors and innovators: A description and measure. *Journal of Applied Psychology, 6*, 622-629.

Knoop, R. (1994). Work values and job satisfaction. *Journal of Psychology, 128*(6), 683.

Kochan, T. A., & Useem, M. (1992). *Transforming organizations*. Oxford University Press.

Kodama, M. (1999). Customer value creation through community-based information networks. *Journal of Information Management, 19*, 495-508.

Kogut, B. (2000). The network as knowledge: Generative rules and emergence of structure. *Strategic Management Journal, 21*, 405-425.

Kogut, B., & Zander, U. (1992). Knowledge of the firm, combinative capabilities, and the replication of rechnology. *Organization Science, 3*(3), 383-397.

Kogut, B., & Zander, U. (1996). What firms do? Coordination, identity, and learning. *Organization Science, 7*(5), 502-518.

Kogut, B., & Zander, U. (1997). Knowledge of the firm, combinative capabilities, and the replication of technology. In N. J. Foss (Ed.), *Resources, fims and strategies – A reader in the resource-based perspective*. Oxford: Oxford University Press.

Kohnhauser, V. (1999). Use of TRIZ in the Development Process. *Triz Journal, June 1999*.

Kolb, D. A. (1984). *Experiential learning: Experience as the source of learning*. Englewood Cliffs, NJ: Prentice-Hall.

Kolb, D. A., Rubin, I. M., & McIntyre, J. M. (1979). *Organizational Psychology:An Experiential Approach* (3rd ed.). Englewood Cliffs, NJ: Prentice-Hall.

Konopaske, R., & Ivancevich. (2004). *Global management and organizational behaviour*. New York: McGraw Hill.

Kostova, T. (1999). Transnational transfer of strategic organizational practices: A contextual perspective. *Academy of Management Review, 24*, 308-324.

Kotabe, M., & Swan, K. S. (1995). The role of strategic alliances in high-technology new product development. *Strategic Management Journal, 16*, 621-636.

Kotler, P. (1999). *Kotler on marketing: How to create, win, and dominate markets*. New York: Free Press.

KPMG. (1998). *Knowledge management: Research report*. London: KPMG Management Consulting.

KPMG. (2000). *Knowledge management: Research report*. Retrieved October 2002, from http://www.kpmg.nl/Docs/Knowledge_Advisory_Services/KPMG%20KM%20Research%20Report %202000.pdf

Kristensen, P. H. (1995). On the constitution of economic actors in Denmark: Interacting skill containers and project organizers. In P. H. Hull, & R. W. Whitley (Eds.), *The changing European firm: Limits to convergence*. London: Routledge.

Krizner, I. M. (1973). *Competition and entrepreneurship.* University of Chicago Press

Kuada, J. (2007). Cultural impacts on employee goals and behaviour in Africa. In J. Okpara (Ed.), *Management and economic development in sub-Saharan Africa: Theoretical and applied perspectives,* (pp. 28-43). London: Adonis and Abbey Publishers Ltd.

Kühule H, Wagenhaus G (2005) *Extended Enterprise Architectures (E2A)-Towards a powerful Mode of Production.* Otto-von-Guericke-University Magdeburg.

Kunda, G. (1992). *Engineering culture.* Philadelphia: The University Press.

Kusiak, A. (2007). Innovation: The living laboratory perspective. *Computer-Aided Design & Applications, 4*(6), 863-876.

Lagerström, K., & Andersson, M. (2003). Creating and sharing knowledge within a transnational team: The development of a global business system. *Journal of World Business, 38,* 84-95.

Lam, A. (2003). Organizational learning in multinationals: R and D networks of Japanese and US multinational enterprises in the UK. *Journal of Management Studies, 40,* (3), 673-703.

Larkin, J. H., & Simon H. A. (1987). Why a diagram is (sometimes) worth 10,000 words. *Cognitive Science, 11*, 65-100.

Larsen, R. E. (1992). Relationship of learning style to the effectiveness and acceptance of interactive video instruction. *Journal of Computer-based Instruction, 19*(1), 17-21.

Lave, J. (1993). The practice of learning. In S. Chaiklin & J. Lave (Eds.), *Understanding practice: Perspectives on activity and context* (pp. 3-32). Canada: Cambridge University Press.

Lazonick, W. (2000). *The theory of innovative enterprise: Organization of innovation in the learning economy, DRUID 2000 Summer Conference paper.*

Leader, G. (2003). Lifelong learning: Policy and practice in further education. *Education + Training, 45,* 361-370.

Leavitt, H. J. (1996). The old days, hot groups, and manager's lib. *Administrative Science Quarterly, 41*(2), 288-300.

Lee, S. M., Tan, X., & Trimi, S. (2005). Current practices of leading e-government countries. *Communications of the ACM, 49*(10), 99-104.

Leech, S. A., & Sutton, S. G. (2002). Editorial: Knowledge management issues in practice: Opportunities for research. *International Journal of Accounting Information Systems, 3*, 60-73.

Leidner, D. E., & Kayworth, T. (2006). A review of culture in information systems research: Toward a theory of information technology culture conflict. *MIS Quarterly, 30*(2), 357-399.

Lelic, S. (2003). The knowledge: Leif Edvinsson. *InsideKnowledge Magazine, 6*(6). Retrieved December, 30, 2007, from http://www.ikmagazine.com/xq/asp/sid.0/chapterid.9942D3E4-534F-44D4-B8A4-2207F95A8174/eTitle.The_knowledge_Leif_Edvinsson/qx/display.htm

Lenz, M., Bartsch-Spörl, B., Burkhardt, H., & Wess, S. (1998). *Case-based reasoning technology: From foundations to applications.* Berlin: Springer-Verlag.

Leonard, D., & Sensiper, S. (1998). The role of tacit knowledge in group innovation. *California Management Review, 40*(3), 112-132.

Lev B. (1999). Seeing is believing-A better approach to estimating knowledge capital. *CFO Magazine*, April.

Lev, B. (2001). *Intangibles – Management, measuring and reporting.* Brookings Institution Press.

Lev, B., & Sougiannis, T. (1996). The capitalization, amortization, and value relevance of R&D. *Journal of Accounting and Economics, 21*, 107-138.

Levina, N. (2005). Collaborating on multiparty information systems development projects: A collective reflection-in-action view. *Information Systems Research, 16*(2), 109-130.

Levina, N., & Vaast, E. (2005). Competence in practice: Implications for implementation and use of information systems. *MIS Quarterly, 29*(2), 335-363.

Levitt, B., & March, J. G. (1988). Organizational learning. *Annual Review of Sociology, 14*, 319-340.

Levy, A., Rajaraman, & Ordille, K. (1996). Querying heterogeneous information sources using source descriptions. *Proceedings of the 22nd VLDB Conference*.

Lewin, K. (1989). Changing as three steps: Unfreezing, moving, and freezing of group standards. In W. L. French, C. H. Bell Jr., & R. A. Zawacki (Eds.), *Organizational development. theory, practice, and research* (3rd ed.) (p. 87). Irwin.

Li, F. W. B., & Lau, R. W. H. (2006). On-demand e-learning content delivery over the internet. *International Journal of Distance Education Technologies, 4*(1), 46-55.

Liang, D. W., Moreland, R., & Argote, L. (1995). Group vs. individual training and gGroup performance: The mediating role of transactive memory. *Personality and Social Psychology Bulletin, 21*(4), 384-393.

Liebowitz, J. (Ed.). (1999). *Knowledge management handbook*. London: CRC Press.

Liebowitz, J., & Suen, C. Y. (2000). Developing knowledge management matrics for measuring intellectual capital. *Journal of Intellectual Capital, 1*(1), 54-67.

Lim, L. L. K., & Dallimore, P. (2002). To the public-listed companies, from the investment community. *Journal of Intellectual Capital, 3*(3), 262-276.

Limón, M. (2001). On the cognitive conflict as an instructional strategy for conceptual change: critical appraisal. *Learning and Instruction, 11*, 357-380.

Lind, M. R., & Zmud, R. W. (1991). The influence of a convergence in understanding between technology providers and users on information technology innovativenss. *Organization Science, 2*(2), 195-217.

Lippman, S., & Rumelt, R.P. (1982). Uncertain imitability: An analysis of interfirm differences in efficiency under competition. *Bell Journal of Economics, 13*, 418-438.

Liuhto, K. (1999). *The organisational and managerial transformation in turbulent business environments – Managers' views on the transition of their enterprise in some of the European former Soviet Republics in the 1990's*. Publications of the Turku School of Economics and Business Administration. Series A-9.

Livingstone, D. W. (2000). Researching expanded notions of learning and work and underemployment: Findings for the first Canadian Survey of informal learning practices. *International Review of Education, 46*, 491-514.

Low, J. (2000). The value creation index. *Journal of Intellectual Capital, 1*(3), 252-262.

Luchins, A. S., & Luchins, E. H. (1959). New experimental attempts in preventing mechanization in problem solving. *The Journal of General Psychology, 42*, 279-291.

Luna-Reyes, L. F., Gil-García, J. R., & Cruz, C. B. (2006, August). *Collaborative digital government in Mexico: Some lessons from federal Web-based inter-organizational information integration initiatives*. Paper presented at the 12th Americas Conference on Information Systems, Acapulco, Mexico.

Luna-Reyes, L. F., Zhang, J., Gil-García, J. R., & Cresswell, A. M. (2005). Information systems development as emergent socio-technical change: A practice approach. *European Journal of Information Systems, 14*(1), 93-105.

Lundval, B. A. (1988). Innovation as an interactive process: From user-producer interaction to the national systems of innovation. In G. Dosi, C. Freeman, R. Nelson, G. Silverberg, & L. Soete (Eds.), *Technical change and economic theory* (pp. 349 – 369). London: Pinter.

Lundvall, B. Å. (2000). Understanding the role of education in the learning economy: The contribution of economics. In OECD, *Knowledge management in the learning society* (pp. 11-35). Paris: OECD.

Lundvall, B-Å. (1985). *Product innovation and user-producer interaction.* Aalborg: Aalborg University Press.

Lundvall, B-Å. (1993). Explaining interfirm coorporation and innovation – limits of the transaction cost approach. In G. Graebher. (Ed.), *The embedded firm.* Routledge.

Lundvall, B-Å. (1995). *The learning economy – Challenges to economic theory and policy.* Working Paper no 9514, Bureau D'Economie Theorique et Appliquee, Universite Louis Pasteur, Strasbourg.

Lundvall, B-Å. (1997). Competition and industrial dynamics in a small, open economy. In *Proceedings from Druid Summer Seminar.*

Lusti, M. (2002). *Data warehousing und data mining: Eine Einführung in entscheidungs-unterstützende Systeme.* Berlin: Springer-Verlag.

Lynn, B. E. (2000). Intellectual capital. *Ivey Business Journal, 64,* 48- 51.

Lytras, M., & Pouloudi, N. (2006). Towards the development of a novel taxonomy of knowledge management systems from a learning perspective. *Journal of Knowledge Management, 10*(6), 64-80.

Lyytinen, K., & Robey, D. (1999). Learning failure in information systems development. *Information Systems Journal,* 9, 85-101.

Machlup, F., & Mansfield, U. (1983). *The study of information: Interdisciplinary messages.* New York: John Wiley & Sons.

Maglitta, J. (1996). Know-how, Inc.. *Computerworld,* 74-76.

Magretta, J. (2002). Why business models matter. *Harvard Business Review,* May, 3-8.

Mahler, J. (1997). Influences of organizational culture on learning in public agencies. *Journal of Public Administration Research & Theory,* 7(4), 519-541.

Mahoney, J.T. (1995). The management of resources and the resource management. *Journal of Business Research, 33,* 91-101.

Maidique, M. A., & Zirger, B. J. (1988). The new product learning cycle. In K. Gronhaug, & G. Kaufmann (Eds.), *Innovation: A cross-disciplinary perspective.* Norwegian University Press.

Majchrzak, A., Rice, R. E., King, N., Malhotra, A., & Ba, S. (2000). Computer-mediated interorganizational knowledge-sharing: Insights from a virtual team innovating using a collaborative rool. *Information Resources Management Journal, 13*(1), 44-53.

Malhotra, Y. (2000). Knowledge management for e-business performance: Advancing information strategy to "Internet time." *Information Strategy, The Executive's Journal, 16*(4), 5-16.

Malinowski, B. (1922). *Argonauts of the western Pacific.* London: Routledge.

Maltz, E., & Kohli, A. K. (1995). Market intelligence dessemination across functional boundaries. *Journal of Marketing Research, 33*(1), 47.

Mannix, E. A., & Griffith, T. L. (Eds.), (2000). Stamford, CT: JAI Press.

March, J. (1991). Exploration and exploitation in organizational learning. *Organization Science, 2,* 71-87.

March, J. G. (1988). *Decisions and organizations.* Oxford: Basil Blackwell.

March, J. G., & Olsen, J. P. (1975). The uncertainty of the past: Organizational learning under ambiguity. *European Journal of Political Research, 3,* 147-171.

March, J. G., & Simon, H. A. (1958). *Organizations.* New York: John Wiley and Sons.

Marr, B., & Schiuma, G. (2003). Intangible assets – Defining key performance indicators for organisational knowledge assets. *Business Process Management Journal, 10,* 4.

Marr, B., Grey, D., & Schiuma, G. (2004). Measuring and valuing intangible assets – What, why, and how. In M. Bourne (Ed.), *Handbook of performance measurement.* London: Gee.

Marschan, R., Welch, D., & Welch, L. (1997). Language: The forgotten factor in multinational management? *European Management Journal, 15*(5), 591-598.

Marschan-Piekkaria, R., Welch, D., & Welch, L. (1999). In the shadow: The impact of language on structure, power and communication in the multinational. *International Business Review, 8,* 421–440.

Mårtensson, M. (2000). A critical review of knowledge management as a management tool. *Journal of Knowledge Management, 14*, 204-216.

Martin, W. (1999). Approaches to the measurement of the impact of knowledge management programs. *Journal of Information Science, 26*(1), 21-27.

Martino, J.P. (1983). *Technological forecasting for decision making.* New York: Elsevier Science Publishers.

Martiny, M. (1998). Knowledge management at HP consulting. *Organizational Dynamics, 27*, 71-77.

Maskell, P., & Malmberg, A. (1997). Proximity, institutions, and learning Towards an explanation of industry agglomeration and regional specialization. In H. Eskelinen (Ed.), *Regional specialisation and local environment - Learning and competitiveness*, NordREFO Report 1997:3.

Matusik, S. F., & Hill, C. W. L. (1998). The utilization of contingent work, knowledge creation, and competitive advantage. *Academy of Management Review, 23*(1), 680–697.

Mavrinac, S., & Siesfield, G. A, (1997). *Measures that matter: An exploratory investigation of investors' information needs and value properties.* Cambridge, MA:

Mayor, T. (1999). What dreams may come. *CIO Magazine.* http://www.cio.com/archive/011599_wish_content_open.htm

McAdam, R. (2000). Knowledge management as a catalyst for innovation within organizations: A qualitative study. *Knowledge and Process Management, 7*(4), 233-241.

McCarthy, E. J. (1960). *Basic marketing: A managerial approach.* IL: R. D. Irwin.

McCrea, F., K. , Gay, R., & Bacon, R. (2000). Riding the big waves: A white paper on the B2B

McElroy, M. W. (2000). Integrating complexity theory, knowledge management and organizational learning. *Journal of Knowledge Management, 4*, 195-203.

McKenna, R. (1993) (reprint). *Relationship marketing: Successful strategies for the age of the customer.*. Cambridge: Perseus Publishing.

McPherson, P. K., & Pike, S. (2001). Accounting, empirical measurement, and intellectual capital. *Journal of Intellectual Capital, 2*(3), 246-260.

Merchant, S., Kreie, J., & Cronan, T. (2001). Training end users: Assessing the effectiveness of multimedia CBT. *Journal of Computer Information Systems, 41*(3), 20-25.

Meritum. (2002). Guidelines for managing and reporting on intangibles. L. Cañibano, Sanchez, M. Garcia-Ayuso, & C. Chaminade (Eds.), *Fundación Airtel Móvil.*

Merline, K. (1997). Leading lights. Interview with Leif Edvinsson. *Community Intelligence Labs.* Retrieved December, 30, 2007, from http://www.co-i-l.com/coil/knowledge-garden/ic/edvinsson.shtml

Metcalfe, J. S., & James, A. (2000). Knowledge and capabilities: A new view of the firm. In N. J. Foss & P. L. Robertson (Eds.), *Resources, technology, and strategy - Exploration in the resource-based perspective.* New York: Routledge.

Miles, M. B., & Huberman, A. M. (1994). *Qualitative data analysis: An expanded sourcebook* (2nd ed.). CA: SAGE Publications.

Miles, R. E., & Snow, C. S. (1992). Causes of failure in network organisations. *California Management Review, Summer*, 53-72.

Mintzberg, H., Ahlstrand, B., & Lampe, J. (1998). *Strategy safari. The complete guide through the wilds of strategic management.* London: Prentice Hall Financial Times.

Mintzberg, H., Duru, R., & Theoret, A. (1976). The structure of unstructured decision process. *Administrative Science Quarterly, 21*, 246-275.

Mohr, L. B. (1969). Determinants of innovation in organizations. *American Political Science Review, 63*, 111-126.

Möller, K., & Svahn, S. (2006). Role of knowledge in value creation in business nets. *Journal of Management Studies, 43*(5), 985-1007.

Moody, M., & Duff, A. (2000). Is that public knowledge? *Director, 53*, 21-24.

Moreland, R. L., Argote, L., & Krishnan, R. (1998). Training people to work in groups. In *Applications of Theory and Research on Groups to Social Issues,* (4), 37-60. New York: R. S. Plenum Press.

Mouritsen, J., & Larsen, H. T.. (2005). The 2nd wave of knowledge management: The management control of knowledge resources through intellectual capital information. *Management Accounting Research, 16*(4), 371-394.

Mouritsen, J., Bukh, P. N., Flagstad, K., Thorbjørnsen, S., Johansen, M. R., Kotnis, S., Larsen, H. T., Nielsen, C., Kjærgaard, I., Krag, L., Jeppesen, G., Haisler, J., & Stakemann, B. (2003). *Intellectual capital statements – The new guideline.* Copenhagen: Danish Ministry of Science, Technology and Innovation. Retrieved from http://www.vtu.dk/icaccounts

Mouritsen, J., Bukh, P. N., Larsen, H. T., & Johansen, M. R. (2002). Developing and managing knowledge through intellectual capital statements. *Journal of Intellectual Capital, 3*(1), 10-29.

Mouritsen, J., Larsen H. T., & Bukh, P.,N. (2001). Valuing the future: iltellectual capital supplements at Skandia. *Accounting, Auditing & Accountability Journal, 14*(4), 399-422.

Mouritsen, J., Larsen, H. T., & Bukh, P. N. (2001). Intellectual capital and the "capable firm": Narrating, visualising and numbering for managing knowledge. *Accounting, Organisations and Society, 26*(7), 735-762.

Mouritsen, J., Larsen, H. T., Bukh, P. N., & Johansen, M. R. (2001). Reading an intellectual capital statement: Describing and prescribing knowledge management strategies. *Journal of Intellectual Capital, 2*(4), 359-383.

Mumford, A. (1999). Individual and organizational learning: The pursuit of change. In C. Mabey, & P. Iles (Eds.), *Managing learning* (pp. 77-86). International Thompson Business Press.

Myers, P. S., & Swanborg, R. W., Jr. (1998). Packaging knowledge. *CIO Enterprise Magazine.,* Retrieved from http:/www.cio.com/archive/enterprise/041598_intellectual_content.htm

Nahapiet, J., & Earl, M. (2000). *Creating organizational capital through intellectual and social capital.* Working chapter for presentation at the Organization Science Winter Conference. Retrieved December, 30, 2007, from http://faculty.fuqua.duke.edu/oswc/2000/papers/wednesday/JanineNahapiet.doc

Nahapiet, J., & Ghoshal, S. (1998). Social capital, intellectual capital, and the organizational advantage. *Academy of Management Review, 23*, 242-266.

Nambisan, S., Agarwal, R., & Tanniru, M. (1999). Organizational mechanisms for enhancing user innovativeness in information technology. *MIS Quarterly, 23*(3), 365-395.

Nanonet. (2003). *Nanonet–Styria intellectual capital report.* Retrieved from *www.nanonet.at*

Nazari, J. A., & Herremans, I. M. (2007). Extended VAIC model: Measuring intellectual capital components. *Journal of Intellectual Capital, 8*(4), 595-609.

Neely, A. (1998). *Performance measurement - Why, what, and how.* London: The Economist Books.

Nelson, R. R., & Winter, S. G. (1982). *An evolutionary theory of economic change*. Cambridge, MA: Harvard University Press.

Nevis, E. C, DiBella, A. J., & Gould, J. M . (1995). Understanding organizations as learning system. *Sloan management review, 36*, 73-92.

Newell, A., Shaw, J. C., & Simon, H. A. (1979). The processes of creative thinking. In H. A. Simon (Ed.), *Models of thought*. New Haven: Yale University Press.

Newell, S., Scarborough, H., Swan, J., & Hislop, D. (2000). Intranets and knowledge management: De-centred technologies and the limits of technological discourse. In C. Pritchard, R. Hull, M. Chumer, & H. Willmott (Eds.), *Managing knowledge: Critical investigations of work and learning* (pp. 88-106). London: MacMillan.

Nielsen, C., & Dane-Nielsen, H. (2008). *The emergent properties of intellectual capital: A conceptual offering*. Working paper submitted to Accounting, Organizations and Society.

Nonaka, I. (1991). The knowledge creating company. *Harvard Business Review, 69*, 96-104.

Nonaka, I. (1994). A dynamic theory of organizational knowledge creation. *Organizational Science, 5*, 14-37.

Nonaka, I. (1996). The knowledge-creating company. In K. Starkey (Ed.), *How organizations learn* (pp. 18-31). London: International Thompson Business Press.

Nonaka, I., & Noboru, K. (1998). The concept of "Ba": Building a foundation for knowledge creation. *California Management Review*.

Nonaka, I., & Takeuchi, H. (1995). *The knowledge creating company: How Japanese companies create the dynamics of innovation*. Oxford: Oxford University Press

Nonaka, I., Toyama, R., & Konno, N. (2001). SECI, Ba and leadership: A unified model of dynamic knowledge creation. In I. Nonaka & D. J. Teece (Eds.), *Managing industrial knowledge. Creation, transfer, and utilization* (pp. 13-43). London: Sage.

Nooteboom, B. (1999). Innovation and interfirm linkages: New implications for policy. *Research Policy, 28*, 793-805.

Nord, W. R., & Tucker, S. (1987). *Implementing routine and radical innovation*. Lexington, MA: Lexington Books.

Norman, R., & Ramirez, R. (1993). From value chain to value constellation: Designing interactive strategy. *Harvard Business Review, 71*, 65-77.

Nunnally, J. C. (1967). *Psychometric theory*. New York: McGraw-Hill Book Company.

Nurmi, R. (1999). Knowledge-intensive firms. In J. W. Cortada & J. A. Woods (Eds.), *The knowledge management yearbook*. Boston: Butterworth-Heinemann.

Nutt, P. C., & Backoff, R. W. (1997). Crafting vision, *Journal of Management Inquiry, 6*(4), 308-329.

Nystrom, H. (1979). *Creativity and innovation*. Chichester: John Wiley & Sons.

O' Reilly, C., & Chatman, J. (1996). Culture as social control: Corporations, culture, and commitment. In B. Staw & L. Cummings (Eds.), *Research in organizational behaviour, 18*, (pp. 157-200). Greenwich, CT: JAI Press.

O'Hare, M. (1988). *Innovate! How to gain and sustain competitive advantage*. Oxford: Basil Blackwell Ltd.

O'Neill, H., & Sackett, P. J. (1994). *The extended manufacturing enterprise paradigm*. Management Decision.

OECD & Statistics Canada. (2000). *Literacy in the information age: Final report on the international adult literacy survey*. Paris: OECD.

OECD. (1997). *Sustainable flexibility. A prospective study on work, family and society in the information age*. Paris: OCDE.

OECD. (1998). *Human capital investment. An international comparison*. Paris: OECD.

OECD. (2000). Knowledge management in the learning society. In OECD, *Knowledge management in the learning society. Education and Skills* (pp. 11-104). Paris: OECD.

Okpara, J. (2007). Cultural influences on the work attitudes: A theoretical perspective. In J. Okpara (Ed.) *Management and economic development in sub-Saharan Africa: Theoretical and applied perspectives*, (pp. 209-223). London: Adonis and Abbey Publishers Ltd.

Ong, C.-S., Lai, J., & Yishun, W. (2004). Factors affecting engineers' acceptance of asynchronous e-learning systems in high-tech companies. *Information, 41*(6), 795-804.

Ordóñez de Pablos, P. (2001). Relevant experiences on measuring and reporting intellectual capital in European pioneering firms. In N. Bontis & C. Chong (Eds.), *Organizational intelligence: The cutting edge of intellectual capital and knowledge management.* Butterworth-Heinemann.

Ordonez de Pablos, P. (2002). Evidence of intellectual capital measurement from Asia, Europe, and the Middle East. *Journal of Intellectual Capital, 3*(3), 287-302.

Ordóñez de Pablos, P. (2004). Knowledge flow transfers in multinational corporations: Knowledge properties and implications for management. *Journal of Knowledge Management, 8*(4), 105-116.

Ordóñez de Pablos, P. (2004). A guideline for building the intellectual capital statement: The 3R model. *International Journal of Learning and Intellectual Capital, 1*(1), 3-18.

Ordonez de Pablos, P. (2005). Intellectual capital reports in India: Lessons from a case study. *Journal of Intellectual Capital, 6*(1), 141-149.

Ordóñez de Pablos, P. (2005). Intellectual capital accounts: What pioneering firms from Asia and Europe are doing now. *International Journal of Knowledge and Learning, 1*(3), 249-268.

Ordóñez de Pablos, P. (2006). Transnational corporations and strategic challenges: An analysis of knowledge flows and competitive advantage. *The Learning Organization.*

Ordóñez de Pablos, P., & Edvinsson, L. (2006). *The intellectual capital statements: Evolution and how to get started.* Working Paper.

Ordóñez de Pablos, P., & Peteraf, M. (2004). Managing and measuring knowledge-based resources. *International Journal of Learning and Intellectual Capital, 1*(4), 377-379.

Ordóñez de Pablos, P., & Peteraf, M. (2005). Organizational learning, innovation and knowledge: The creation of a sustained competitive advantage. *International Journal of Learning and Intellectual Capital, 2*(2), 111-113.

Orlikowski, W. J. (1992). The duality of technology - Rethinking the concept of technology in organizations. *Organization Science, 3*(3), 398-427.

Orlikowski, W. J. (1993). Case tools as organizational-change - Investigating incremental and radical changes in systems-development. *MIS Quarterly, 17*(3), 309-340.

Orlikowski, W., J. (2002). Knowing in practice: Enacting a collective capability in distributed organizing. *Organization Science, 13*(3), 249-273.

P. Karnøe, P. H. Kristensen, & P. H,. Andersen (Eds.), *Mobilising resources and generating competencies.* Copenhagen Business School Press.

Pablos P. O. (2002). Evidence of intellectual capital measurement form Asia, Europe, and Middle East. *Journal of Intellectual Capital, 3*(3), 287-302.

Park, H., Hwangt, S. D., & Harrison, J. K. (1996). Sources and consequences of communication problems in foreign subsidiaries: The case of United States firms in South Korea. *International Business Review, 5*(1), 79-98.

Parr, A., & Shanks, G. (2000, December). A model of ERP project implementation. *Journal of Information Technology, 15*(4), 289-303.

Patricia, L., Nemetz, C., & Sandra, L. (1996). The challenge of cultural diversity: Harnessing a diversity of views to understand multiculturalism. *Academy of Management Review,* April, 434-462.

Pearce, R., & Papanastassiou, M. (1999). Overseas R and D and the strategic evolution of multinational enterprises: Evidence from laboratories in the UK. *Research Policy, 28*, 23-41.

Pedler, M., Bourgoyne, J., & Boydell (1991). *The learning company: A strategy of sustainable development.* London: McGraw-Hill.

Pelz, D. C., & Andrews, F. M. (1976). *Productive climates for research and development*. Ann Arbor, MI: Institute for Social Research, University of Michigan.

Pennings, J. M., Barkema, H., & Douma, S. (1994). Organizational learning and diversification. *Academy of Management Journal, 37*, 608-640.

Penrose, E.T. (1959). The theory of the growth of the firm. New York: Wiley.

Pentland, B. T. (1995). Information systems and organizational learning: The social epistemology of organizational knowledge systems. *Accounting, Management, and Information Technologies, 5*(1), 1-21.

Pentland, B. T., & Rueter, H. H. (1994). Organizational routines as grammar of actions. *Administrative Science Quarterly, 39*, 484-510.

Peppard, J., & Rylander, A. (2001). Leveraging intellectual capital at APION. *Journal of Intellectual Capital, 2*(3), 225-235.

Peppers, D., & Rogers, M. (1993). *The one to one future: Building relationships one customer at a time*. New York: Doubleday.

Peppers, D., & Rogers, M. (1997). *Enterprise one to one: Tools for competing in the interactive age*. New York: Doubleday.

Perlmutter, H.V. (1969). The tortuous evolution of the multinational corporation. *Columbia Journal of World Business, 4*(1), 9-18.

Perlmutter, H.V., & Heenan, D.A. (1974). How multinational should your top managers be? *Harvard Business Review, 52*(6), 121-132.

Peteraf, M.A. (1993). The cornerstone of competitive advantage: A resource based-view. *Strategic Management Journal, 14*, 179-191.

Peters, T. J., & Waterman, R. H. (1982). *In search of excellence: Lessons from America's best run companies*. New York: Harper and Row.

Pettigrew, A. (1995). Longitudinal field research on change: Theory and practice. In G. P. Huber & A. H. Van de Ven (Eds.), *Longitudinal field research methods: Studying processes of organizational change* (p. 91). Thousand Oaks, CA: Sage.

Pettigrew, A. M. (1997). What is a processual analysis? *Scandinavian Journal of Management, 13*, 337-348.

Petty, R., & Guthrie, J. (2000). Intellectual capital literature review: Measuring, reporting and management. *Journal of Intellectual Capital, 1*(2), 155-176.

Pfeffer, J., & Sutton, R. (2000). *The knowing-doing gap* (1st ed.). Harvard Business School.

Phillips, J. J. (1997). *Handbook of training evaluation and measurement methods* (3rd ed.). Houston, TX: Gulf Publishing.

Piaget, J. (1975). *L'e'quilibration des structures cognitives. Proble'me central du de'velopment*. Paris: PUF (*The development of thought: equilibration of cognitive structures*. Eng. trans. New York: Viking Press).

Pierce, J. L., & Delbecq, A. (1977). Organization structure, individual attitudes and innovation. *Academy of Management Review, 2*(1), 27.

Polanyi, M. (1996). *The tacit dimension*. New York: Doubleday.

Porter, M. E. (1985). *Competitive advantage*. New York: Free Press.

Porter, M. E. (1996). What is strategy? *Harvard Business Review*, November-December, 61-78.

Porter, M. E. (1998). Clusters and the new economics of competition. *Harvard Business Review, November-December*, 77-90.

Postman, L. (1976). Methodology of human learning. In W. K. Estes (Ed.), *Handbook of learning and cognitive processes* (pp. 11 – 69), vol. 3. New York: John Wiley.

Postrel, S. (2002). Islands of shared knowledge: Specialization and mutual understanding in problem-solving teams. Organization Science, 13(3), 303-320.

Powell, W. W. (1998). Learning from collaboration: Knowledge and networks in the biotechnology and pharmaceutical industries. *California Management Review, 40*(3), 228-340.

Prahalad, C. K., & Bettis, R. A. (1986). The dominant logic: A new linkage between diversity and performance. *Strategic Management Journal, 7*(6), 485–501.

Prahalad, C., & Hamel, G. (1990). The core competence of the corporation. *Harvard Business Review, 90*, 79-91.

Pribram, K. I. (1983). The brain, cognitive commodities, and the enfolded order. In K. Boulding, & L. Senesch (Eds.), *The optimum utilization of knowledge*. Westview Press.

Purvis, R. L., Sambamurthy, V., & Zmud, R. W. (2001, March/April). The assimilation of knowledge platforms in organizations: An empirical investigation. *Organization Science, 12*(2), 117-135.

Quinn, R., & Spreitzer, G. (1997). The road to empowerment: Seven questions every leader should answer. *Organisational Dynamics, 26*(2), 37-50.

Quintas, P. (2003). Managing knowledge in practice. In OECD & Statistics Canada, *Measuring knowledge management in the business sector: First steps* (pp. 385-391). Paris: OECD.

Quintas, P. Lefrere, P., & Jones, G. (1997). Knowledge management: A strategic agenda. *Long RangePlanning, 30*, 385-391.

Rabelo, R., & Camarinha-Matos, L. (1996). Towards agile scheduling in extended enterprise. In L. M. Camarinha-Matos, H. & Afsarmanesh (Eds.), *Proceedings of BASYS'96: BalancedAutomationSystems II—Implementation Challenges for Anthropocentric Manufacturing*. Chapman & Hall.

Ramboll Management. (2005). Slututvärdering Växtkraft Mål 3: Final version. Stockholm: Ramboll management. (Ramboll Management (2005). *Final evaluation of the Objective 3*. Stockholm: Ramboll management.).

Ramirez, R. (1999). Value co-production: Intellectual origins and implications for practice and research. *Strategic Management Journal, 20*, 49–65.

Rao, M. (2005). The social life of KM tools. In M. Rao (Ed.), *Knowledge management tool and techniques: Practicioners and experts evaluate KM solutions* (pp. 1-77). London: Elsevier.

Rath, H.H., & Pepper, S. (1999). Topic maps: Introduction and Allegro. In *Proceedings of the Markup Technologies, 99*. Philadelphia, USA.

Rayport, J. B. J. (2001). *E-commerce* (1st ed.). New York: McGraw-Hill.

Reed, R., & DeFillippi, R. (1990). Causal ambiguity, barriers to imitation and sustainable competitive advantage. *Academy of Management Review, 15*(1), 88-102.

Reger, G. (2001). Technology foresight in companies: From an indicator to a network and process perspective. *Technology Analysis & Strategic Management, 13*(4), 533-553.

Reichheld, F. F., & Sasser, W. E., Jr. (1990). Zero defections: Quality comes to services. *Harvard Business Review*, September-October, 105-111.

Reichheld, F. F., & Teal, T. (1996). *The loyalty effect: The hidden force behind growth, profits, and lasting value*. Boston: Harvard Business School Press.

Reinartz, W., & Kumar, V. (2000). On the profitability of long-life customers in a noncontractual setting: An empirical investigation and implications for marketing. *Journal of Marketing, 64*, 17-35.

Reinartz, W., & Kumar, V. (2002). The mismanagement of customer loyalty. *Harvard Business Review*, July, 86-94.

Remenyi, D., Williams, B., Money, A., & Swartz, E. (1998). *Doing research in business and management: An introduction to process and method*. London: SAGE Publications.

Renée, E. D., Barbara, A. F., & Eduardo, S. (2005). E-Learning in organizations. *Journal of Management, 31*(6), 920-940.

Reuber, R. (1997). Management experience and management expertise. *Decision Support Systems, 21*(2), 51-60.

Richard, F., Robert, C., & Gary, G. (2002). When social capital stifles innovation. *Harvard Business Review, 80*, 20-26.

Rieber, L. R. (1991). Animation, incidental learning, and continuing motivation. *Journal of Educational Psychology, 83*(3), 318.

Riempp, G. (2004). *Integrierte wissensmanagement-systeme—Architektur und praktische anwendung*. Berlin: Springer.

Riesbeck, C.K., & Schank, R.C. (1989). *Inside case-based reasoning*. Hillsdale: Lawrence Erlbaum Associates.

Robey, D., & Markus, L. M. (1998). Beyond rigor and relevance: Producing consumable research about information systems. *Information Resources Management Journal, 11*(1), 7-15.

Robey, D., Ross, J. W., & Boudreau, M. C. (2002, Summer). Learning to implement enterprise systems: An exploratory study of the dialectics of change. *Journal of Management Information Systems, 19*(1), 17-46.

Robichaud, D. (2006). Steps toward a relational view of agency. In F. Cooren, J. R. Taylor, & E. J. Van every (Eds.), *Communication as organizing* (pp. 101-115). London: LEA.

Robins, J. A, & Wiersema, M. F. (1995). A resource-based approach to the multibusiness firm: Empirical analysis of portfolio interrelationships and corporate financial performance. *Strategic Management Journal, 16*(4), 277–299.

Robson, C. (2002). *Real world research: A resource for social scientists and practitioner-researchers*. Oxford: Blackwell.

Rocheleau, B. (2006). *Public management information systems*. Hershey, PA: Idea Group Publishing.

Rodov, I., & Leliaert, P. (2002). FiMIAM: Financial method of intangible assets measurement. *Journal of Intellectual Capital, 3*(3), 323-336.

Rogers, E. M. (1983). *The diffusion of innovations*. New York: The Free Press.

Romer, P. (1995). Beyond the knowledge worker. *World Link, January/February*, 56-60.

Roos G., Pike S., & Fernström L., (2005). Valuation and reporting of intangibles – State of the art in 2004. *International Journal of Learning and Intellectual Capital, 2*(1), 21-48.

Roos, G., & Roos, J. (1997). Measuring your company's intellectual performance. *Long Range Planning, 30*, 3.

Roos, J., Roos, G., Dragonetti, N. C., & Edvinsson, L. (1997). *Intellectual capital: Navigating the new business landscape*. London: Macmillan Press Ltd.

Roosens, E. E. (1989). *Creating ethnicity*. London: Sage.

Rosenberg, M., 2001. . (2001). *E-learning: Strategies for delivering knowledge in the digital age*. Toronto: McGraw-Hill.

Rosenstiel, L., & Koch, S. (2001). Change in socioeconomic values as a trigger of organisational learning. In M. Dierkes, A.B. Antal, J. Child, & I. Nonaka (Eds.), *Organisational learning and knowledge* (pp. 198-220). Oxford University Press.

Roslender, R., & Hart, S. J. (2002). Integrating management accounting and marketing in the pursuit of competitive advantage: The case for strategic management accounting. *Critical Perspectives on Accounting, 13*, 255-277.

Rothwell R., Freeman C., Horsley A., Jervis, V. T. P., Robertson A., & Townsend J. (1974). SAPPHO updated – Project SAPPHO phase II. *Research Policy, 3*, 259-291.

Rouse, M.J., & Daellenbach, U.S. (1999). Rethinking research methods for the resource-based perspective: Isolating sources of sustainable competitive advantage. *Strategic Management Journal, 20*, 487-494.

Rubenson, K. (2001). Lifelong learning for all: Challenges and limitations of public policies. In Ministry of Education and Science in Sweden (Ed.), *Adult lifelong learning in a Europe of knowledge* (pp. 29-39), Ekilstuna, Sweden,

21-23 March 2001. Stockholm: Ministry of Education and Science in Sweden,.

Rubenson, K. (2003). Adult education and cohesion. *Lifelong Learning in Europe*, *8*, 32-36.

Ruggles, R. (1997). *Using technology to manage knowledge better.* Unpublished manuscript.

Rumelt, R. P. (1984). Towards a strategic theory of the firm. In R. B. Lamp (Ed.) *Competitive strategic management.* NJ: Prentice Hall.

Saint-Onge, H. (1996). Tacit knowledge. The key to the strategic alignment of intellectual capital. *Strategy & Leadership*, *24*, 10-14.

Sakakibara, S., Hansson, B., & Yosano, T. (2005). *Japanese analysts' perception of intellectual capital information.* Working paper presented at the EIASM workshop on "Visualising, measuring and Managing Intangibles and Intellectual Capital" in Ferrara, Italy, October 2005.

Salton, G., & McGill, M.J. (1983). *Introduction to modern information retrieval.* New York: McGraw-Hill.

Sambamurthy, V., Bharadwah, A., & Grover, V. (2003). Shaping agility through digital options: Reconceptualizing the role of information technology in contemporary firms. *MIS Quarterly*, *27*(2), 237-263.

Sampson, D., Karagiannidis, C., & Cardinali, F. (2002). An architecture for Web-based e-learning promoting re-usable adaptive educational e-content. *Educational Technology and Society, 5*(4), 27-36.

SanAntonio, P. M. (1988). Social mobility and language use in an American company in Japan. In W. B. Gudykunst (Ed.), *Language and ethnic identity* (pp. 35-45). Clevedon: Clevedon, Multilingual Matters Ltd.

Sánchez, P., Chaminade, P., & Olea M. (2000). Management of intangibles: An attempt to build a theory. *Journal of Intellectual Capital*, *1*(4), 312-327.

Sandberg, K. D. (2002). Is it time to trade in your business model? *Harvard Management Update*, January, 3-5.

Santos, A. M., & Costa, C. S. (1997). Características Gerais do Varejo no Brasil. *BNDES – Banco Nacional de Desenvolvimento Econômico e Social,* Setorial nº 5, March.

Sarker, S., & Lee, A. S. (2003). Using a case study to test the role of three key social enablers in ERP implementation. *Information & Management, 40*(8), 813.

Saunders, M., Lewis, P., & Thornhill, A. (2000). *Research methods for business students.* Harlow: Pearson Education Limited.

Sawaguchi, M. (2001). Study of effective new product development activities through combination of patterns of evolution of technological systems and VE. *Triz Journal. March 2001.*

Sawhney, M., Wolcott, R. C., & Arroniz, I. (2006). The 12 different ways for companies to innovate. *MIT Sloan Management Review*, *47*(3), 75-81.

Saxenian, A. L. (1991). The origins and dynamics of production networks in Silicon Valley. *Research Policy*, *20*, 423-437.

Schatz, B. R. (1991). Building an electronic community system. *Journal of Management Information System*, *8*(3), 87-107.

Scheerer, M. (1963). Problem solving. *Scientific American*, *208*, 118-128.

Schein, E. H (1996). *Organizational learning as a cognitive redefinition: Coercive persuasion revisited.* Retrieved from http:/learning.mit.edu/res/wp/10010.html

Schein, E. H. (1992). *Organizational culture and leadership.* Jossey Bass Publishers.

Schein, E. H. (1993). How can organizations learn faster? The challenge of entering the green room. *Sloan Management Review, 34*(2), 85-92.

Schein, E. H. (1993). On dialogue, culture, and organizational learning. *Organizational Dynamics*, *22*, 40-51.

Schekkerman, J. (2004). *Another View at Extended Enterprise Architecture Viewpoints.* Institute For Enterprise Architecture Developemets.

Schoonhoven, C. B. (1981). Problems with contingency theory: Testing assumptions hidden within the language of contingency "theory." *Administrative Science Quarterly, 26*, 349-77.

Schultz, D., & Hayman, D. (1999). The two sides of loyalty. *Interactive marketing*, April.

Schultze, U. (2000). A confessional account of an ethnography about knowledge work. *MIS Quarterly, 24*(1), 3-41.

Schulz, M. (2001). The uncertain relevance of newness: Organizational learning and knowledge flows. *Academy of Management Journal, 44*(4), 661-681.

Schumpeter, J. (1934). *The theory of economic development*. Cambridge, MA: Harvard University Press.

Scott, J. E., & Vessey, I. (2000). Implementing enterprise resource planning systems: The role of learning from failure. *Information Systems Frontiers, 2*(2), 213-232.

Scott-Morton, M. S. (1991). IT-induced business reconfiguration. In M. S. Scott-Morton (Ed.), *The corporation of the 1990s: Information technology and organizational transformation* (pp. 3-23). Oxford: Oxford University Press.

Senge, P. (1990). *The fifth discipline: The art and science of the learning organization*. New York: Doubleday.

Senge, P. (1996). The leader's new work: Building learning organizations. In K. Starkey (Ed.), *How organizations learn* (pp. 288-315). London: International Thompson Business Press.

Senge, P. M. (1999). The leader's new work: Building learning organization. In C. Mabey, & P. Iles (Eds.), *Managing learning* (pp. 5-21). International Thompson Business Press.

Senge, P.M. (1990). The leader's new work: Building learning organizations. *Sloan Management Review, 3*(1), 15–26.

Servage, L. (2005). Strategizing for workplace e-learning: Some critical considerations. *The Journal of Workplace Learning, 17*(5-6), 304-317.

Sethi, V., & King, W. R. (1994). Development of measures to assess the extent to which an information technology application provides competitive advantage. *Management Science, 14*(2), 1601-1627.

Seybold, P. B. (1998). *Customers.com: How to create a profitable business strategy for the Internet and beyond*. Auckland: Random House Publishing.

Shafritz, J., & Ott, S. (Eds.). (1996). Classical organizational theory. In J. Shafritz, & S. Ott, *Classics of organizational theory*. FL: Harcourt Brace and Company.

Sharma, S., Durand, R. M., & Gur-Arie, O. (1981). Identification and analysis of moderator variables. *Journal of Marketing Research, 18*, 291-300.

Shepard, H. A. (1967). Innovation-resisting and innovation-producing organizations. *Journal of Business, 40*, 470-477.

Sheth, J. N., Sisodia, R. S., & Sharma, A. (2000). The antecedents and consequences of customer-centric marketing. *Journal of the Academy of Marketing Science*, 28, (2), Winter.

Short, J., & Venkatraman, N. (1992). *Beyond business process redesign: Redefining Baxter's business network*. Sloan Management Review, *34*(1), Fall 1992

Silver, C. (2000). Where technology and knowledge meet. *The Journal of Business Strategy, 21*(6), 28-33.

Simon, H. (1991). Bounded rationality and organizational learning. *Organization Science*, *2*(1), 125-134.

Simon, H. A. (1977). *The new science of management decision, Chapter2* . Englewood Cliffs, NJ: Prentice-Hall.

Skandia. (1994). *Visualizing intellectual capital at Skandia*. Supplement to Skandia's 1994 Annual Report.

Skandia. (1996). *Customer value*. Supplement to Skandia's 1996 Annual Report.

Slater, S. F., & Narver, J. C. (1995). Market orientation and the learning organization. *Journal of Marketing, 59*(3), 63.

Small, C. T., & Sage, A. P. (2005/2006). Knowledge management and knowledge sharing: A review. *Information Knowledge Systems Management, 5*, 153–169.

Smith, M. D., Bailey, J., & Brynjolfsson, E. (1999). Understanding digital markets: Review and assessment. Retrieved August 4, 2001, from http://ecommerce.mit.edu/papers/ude/ude.pdf Stevenson, W. J. (1978). *Business statistics: Concepts and applications.* Harper & Row Publishers, Inc.

Smith, S. J. (1984). Negotiating ethnicity in an uncertain environment. *Ethnic and Racial Studies, 7,* 360-372.

Smolnik, S., Kremer, S., & Kolbe, L. (2005). Continuum of context explication: Knowledge discovery through process-oriented portals. *International Journal of Knowledge Management, 1*(1), 27-46.

Snehota, I. (1990). *Notes on a theory of business enterprise.* Doctoral Dissertation, Uppsala University.

Snowden, D. (1999). Three metaphors, two stories and a picture. *Knowledge Management Review, 7*, 30-33.

Snyder, W. M., & de Souza Briggs, X. (2003). *Communities of practice: A new tool for government managers.* Retrieved March 20, 2007, from http://www.businessofgovernment.org/pdfs/Snyder_report.pdf

Snyder, W. M., Wenger, E., & de Souza Briggs, X. (2004). Communities of practice in government: The case for sponsorship. *The Public Manager, 32*(4), 17-21.

Sodexho. (2007). *Corporate diversity.* North America: Sodexho.

Sorensen, J. (2002). The strength of corporate culture and the reliability of firm performance. *Administrative Science Quarterly, 47*, (1), 70-91.

Sorli, M. (1999). Innovación en el Diseño de Productos. *Forum Calidad Journal.*

Sorli, M., Mendikoa, I., Barbero, J. I., & Carrillo, A. (2006). *Distributed product design and manufacturing based on KBE. Computer Supported Cooperative Work in Design II*; Lecture Notes in Computer Science 3865. Springer-Verlag Berlin Heidelberg, 2006, ISSN 0302-9743.

Sorli, M., Stokic, D., Gorostiza, A., & Campos, A. (2006). *Managing product/process knowledge in the concurrent/simultaneous enterprise environment.* Robotics and Computer Integrated Manufacturing. Elsevier (2006) p. 399–408. Volume 22, October-December 2006. ISSN 0736-5845.

Sorli, M., Stokic, D., Gorostiza, A., & Campos., A. (2006). Fostering innovation in practice through TRIZ-based CAI tool. *International Journal of Computer Applications in Technology (IJCAT),* special issue on Computer Aided Innovation (CAI).

Spencer, J. W. (2003). Firms' knowledge-sharing strategies in the global innovation system: Empirical evidence from the flat panel display industry. *Strategic Management Journal, 24,* 217-233.

Spender, J. C. (1996). Making knowledge the basis of a dynamic theory of the firm. *Strategic Management Journal, 17*(2), 45-62.

Spradley, J. P. (1980). *Participant observation.* New York: Holt Rinehart and Winston.

St. Leon, M. V. (2002). Strategic intellectual capital creation: Decontextualizing strategy process research. *Journal of Intellectual Capital, 3*(2), 149-166.

Stabell, C. B., & Fjeldstad, Ø. D. (1998). Configuring value for competitive advantage: On chains, shops, and networks. *Strategic Management Journal, 19*, 413–437.

Stalk, G., Evans, P., & Shulman, L. E. (1992). Competing on capabilities: The new rules of corporate strategy. *Harvard Business Review, 90*(2),.57–69.

Standing, G. (1997). Globalisation, labour flexibility, and insecurity: The era of market regulation. *European Journal of Industrial Relations, 3*(1), 7-37.

Stankosky, M. (Ed.). (2005). *Creating the discipline of knowledge management: The latest in university research.* London: Elsevier.

Stankosky, M. A. (2005). Advanced in knowledge management: University research toward an academic discipline. In M. A. Stankosky (Ed.), *Creating the discipline of knowledge management: The latest in university research* (pp. 1-15). Oxford: Elsevier.

Starbuck, W. H. (1992). Learning by knowledge-intensive firms. *Journal of Management Studies, 29*, 713-738.

Starovic, B. & Marr., D. (2003). *Understanding corporate value: Managing and reporting intellectual capital.* Cranfield School of Management, Chartered Institute of Management Accountants.

Stein, E. W., & Zwass, V. (1995). Actualizing organizational memory with information systems. *Information Systems Research, 6*(2), 85-117.

Steinmueller, W. E. (2000). *Knowledge and learning in the information age*. DRUID conference paper, Rebild 2000.

Stenhouse, L. (1982). The conduct, analysis, and reporting of case study in educational research and evaluation. In R. Murphy & H. Torrance (Eds.), (1987), *Evaluating education: Issues and methods* (pp. 74-80). London: Paul Chapman Publishing.

Stewart, T. (1991). Brainpower. *Fortune, 123*, 44-50.

Stewart, T.A. (1997). *Intellectual capital: The new wealth of organization.* Currency New York: Doubleday.

Stokic, D. (2006). *A New Collaborative Working Environment for Concurrent Engineering in Manufacturing Industry.* Proc. CE 2006, 13th ISPE International Conference on Concurrent Engineering, Juan-les-Pins, France.

Stone, B. (1984). *Successful direct marketing methods* (3rd ed.). Lincolnwood: NTC Publishing.

Storper, M., & Salais, R. (1997). *Worlds of production.* Harvard University Press.

Sullivan, Jr., P. H., & Sullivan, Sr., P. H. (2000). Valuing intangible companies: An intellectual capital approach. *Journal of Intellectual Capital, 1*(4), 328-340.

Sumner, M. (2000, December). Risk factors in enterprise-wide/ERP projects. *Journal of Information Technology, 15*(4), 317-327.

Sveiby, K. (1997). *The new organizational wealth.* San Francisco: Berrett-Koeheler Publishers, Inc.

Sveiby, K. E. & Simons, R. (2002). Collaborative climate and effectiveness of knowledge work – An empirical study. *Journal of Knowledge Management, 6*, 420-433.

Sveiby, K. E. (1997). *The new organizational wealth: Managing and measuring knowledge-based assets.* San Francisco: Berrett-Koehler Publishers.

Sveiby, K. E., Linard, K., & Dvorsky, L. (2002). *Building a knowledge-based strategy: A system dynamics model for allocating value-adding capacity.* Retrieved October 2004, from, *http://www.sveiby.com/Portals/0/articles/sdmodelkstrategy.pdf*

Swan, J., & Scarbrough, H. (2005). The politics of networked innovation. *Human Relations, 58*(7), 913-943.

Swartout, W. R., & Smoliar, S. (1987). On making expert systems more like experts. *Expert Systems, 4*(3), 196-207.

Swedish ESF Council. (2001). *Summary of the Swedish objective 3: Single program document (SPD)* 2000-2006. August 19th, 2002. Retrieved from http://europa.eu.int/comm/employment_social/esf2000/ms/s-obj-3-doc-en.pdf

Swedish Ministry of Finance and Ministry of Industry, Employment, and Communications. (1999). *Sweden's action plan for employment, 2000.* Stockholm: Government of Sweden. Retrieved November 2002, from *http://www.sweden.gov.se/sb/d/108/a/1859;jsessionid=aFVFi7RjXjp*_Swedish Ministry of Finance and Ministry of Industry, Employment and Communications. (2004). *Sweden's action plan for employment, 2004.* Stockholm: Government of Sweden. Retrieved November 2005, from *http://www.regeringen.se/sb/d/2530/a/36642*

Sweet, P. (2001). Strategic value configuration logics and the "new" economy: A service economy revolution? *International Journal of Service Industry Management, 12*(1), 70-83.

Szgeo, O., & Andersen, B. *Modeling the Extended Enterprise: A comparison of Different Modeling Approaches.*

Szulanski, G. (1999). The process of knowledge transfer: A diachronic analysis of stickiness. *OBHDP*.

Szulanski, G. (2003). *Sticky knowledge: Barriers to knowing in the firm*. London: Sage.

Szulanski, G.. (1996). Exploring internal stickiness: Impediments to the transfer of best practiceswithinthe firm. *Strategic Management Journal, 17*(10), 27-43.

Tajfel, H. (1982). Social psychology of intergroup relations. *Annual Review of Psychology, 33*, 1-39.

Tanriverdi, H., & Venkatraman, N. (2005). Knowledge relatedness and the performance of multibusiness firms. *Strategic Management Journal, 26*, 97–119.

Taylor, C.nW. (1972). Can organizations be creative too?. In C. W. Taylor (Ed.), *Climate for creativity* (pp. 1 – 15). New York: Pergamon Press.

Teece, D. (1998). Capturing value from knowledge assets: The new economy, markets for know-how, and intangible assets. *California Management Review, 40*, 55-79.

Teece, D. J. (1986). Profiting from technological innovation: Implication for integration, collaboration, licensing, and public policy. *Research Policy, 15*, 285-305.

Teece, D. J. (2000). *Managing intellectual capital*. Great Britain: Biddles Ltd., Guildford and King's Lynn.

Teece, D. J. (2003). Explicating dynamic capabilities: Asset selection, coordination, and entrepreneurship. *Strategic Management Theory* (August).

Teece, D. J., Pisano, G., & Shuen, A. (1997). Dynamic capabilities and strategic management. *Strategic Management Journal, 18*(7), 509-533.

Terninko J, Zlotin B. & Zusman A (1996). *Step by Step TRIZ. Creating Innovative Solution Concepts*. Responsible Management Inc.

Thomas, L. G. (1996). The two faces of competition: Dynamic resourcefulness and the hypercompetitive shift. *Organization Science, 7*(3), 221–242.

Thomas, R. G., & Litowitz, L. (1986). *Vocational education and higher-order thinking skills: An agenda for inquiry*. St: Paul, MN: Research and Development Center for Vocational Education.

Thompson, J. D. (1967). *Organizations in action*. New York: McGraw-Hill.

Thompson, V. A. (1965). Bureaucracy and innovation. *Administrative Science Quarterly, 10*, 1-20.

Thorton, E. (1993). Thailand: Japan vs. the U.S. *Fortune, 28*, 145-149.

Tidwell, L. C., & Walther, J. B. (2002). Computer-mediated communication effects on disclosure, impressions, and interpersonal evaluations. *Human Communication Research, 28*(3), 317-348.

Tippins, M. J., & Sohi, R. S. (2003). IT competency and firm performance: Is organizational learning a missing link? *Strategic Management Journal, 24*(8), 745.

Tongo, C. (2005). *Re-assessing the organizational and national culture interface*. Paper presented at the International Conference of Human Development, Covenant University, June 27-30, 2005.

Tongo, C. (Forthcoming). Building the intellectual capital of African enterprises in a knowledge economy: Impediments and requirements. *International Journal of Learning and Intellectual Capital*.

Torrance, E. P., & Myers, R. E. (1970). *Creative learning and teaching*. New York: Dodd.

Tsang, E. W. K. (1997). Organisational learning and the learning organisation: A dichotomy between descriptive and prescreptive research, *Human Relations, 50*, 73-89.

Tschan, F., & Von Cranach, M. (1996). Group structure, process, and outcome. In M. E. West (Ed.), *Handbook of Work Group Psychology* (95-121). New York: John Wiley & Sons.

Tuijnman, A. C. (1999). Research agenda for lifelong learning: A report by the task force of the International Academy of Education. In A. C. Tuijnman & T. Schuller (Eds.), *Lifelong Learning Policy & Research: Proceedings of an International Symposium* (pp. 1-22). London: Portland Press.

Tuomi, I. (1999). Hierarchy for knowledge management and organizational memory. *Journal of Management Information Systems, 16*, 103-117.

Tuomi, I. (2002). Towards the third generation of knowledge management. *Lifelong Learning in Europe, 7*, 69-80.

Tushman, M. L. (1979). Managing communication networks in R&D laboratories. *Sloan Management Review*, 37-49.

Ukens, L. (2001). *What smart trainers should know: The secrets of success from the world's foremost experts.* San Francisco: John Wiley & Sons, Inc.

Urdan, T. A., & Weggan, C. C. (2000). *Corporate e-learning: exploring a new frontier.* New York: Hambrecht & Co.

Usunier, J. (1998). *International and cross-cultural management research.* London: Sage Publications.

Utterback, J. M. (1971). The process of innovation: A study of the origination and development of ideas for new scientific instruments. *IEEE Transaction on Engineering Management, 18*, 124-131.

Valentin, F., Andersen, P. H., Dalum, B, Pedersen, T., & Villumsen, G. (1995). *Strategiske Virksomhedsrelationer (Strategic firm relationships)*, Velstand og Velfærd, bd. 5, Erhvervsministeriet.

Vallerand, R. J. (1997). Toward a hierarchical model of intrinsic and extrinsic motivation. *Advances in Experimental Social Psychology, 27*, 271-360.

Van de Ven, A. H., & Poole, M. S. (1990). Methods for studying innovation development in the Minnnesota innovation research program. *Organization Science, 1*(3), 313-335.

Van Kooji, E. H. (1990). *Technology transfer in the Japanese electronics industry, Economic Research Institute for Small and Medium Sized Business.* The Netherlands, Zoertmeer.

Van Winkelen, C., Birchall, D., & Smith, G. (2004). A framework for comparing knowledge management practices. In E. Truch (Ed.), *Levering corporate knowledge* (pp. 23-33). Aldershot, UK: Gower.

Vanston, J.H. (1996). Technology forecasting: A practical tool for rationalizing the R&D process. *The New Telecom Quarterly, 4*(1), 57-62. Technology Futures Inc.

Varey, R. J. (2006). Accounts in interactions: Implications of accounting practices for managing. In F. Cooren, J. R. Taylor, & E. J. Van every (Eds.), *Communication as organizing* (pp. 181-197).

Venkatesh, V. (1999). Creation of favorable user perceptions: Exploring the role of intrinsic motivation. *MIS Quarterly, 23*(2), 239-260.

Venkatraman, N. (1989). The concept of fit in strategy research: Toward verbal and statistical correspondence. *Academy of Management Review, 14*, 423-444.

Victoria, D., Gregory, M., Faye, G., & Thomas, N. (2001). Managing culturally diverse buyer-seller relationships: The role of intercultural disposition and adaptive selling in developing intercultural communication competence. *Academy of Marketing.Science, 29,* 391-404.

Villalba, E. (2006). *The uniqueness of knowledge management in small enterprises: Knowledge management as an employer strategy for lifelong learning.* Studies in International and Comparative Education, No. 70. Stockholm: Stockholm University.

Virkkunen, J., & Ahonen, H. (2000) *Knowledge management as creative dialogue about the future.* Paper presented in Knowledge Management Conference in Sao Paulo, Brazil, 7/2000.

von Hippel, E. (1987). Cooperation between rivals: Informal know-how trading. *Research Policy, 16*, 291-302.

von Hippel, E. (1994). «Sticky information» and the locus of problem solving: Implications for innovation. *Management Science, 40*, 429-439.

von Hippel, E., & Tyre, M. (1993). *How learning by doing is done: Problem identification in novel process equipment.* Massachusetts Institute of Technology, SSM Working Paper#BPS 3521-93.

von Krogh, G., Ichijo, K., & Nonaka, I. (2000). *Enabling knowledge creation: How to unlock the mystery of tacit knowledge and release the power of innovation*. Oxford: Oxford University Press.

Wagner, E. D., & Reddy, N. L. (1987). Design considerations in selecting teleconferencing for instruction. *The American Journal of Distance Education, 1*(3), 49-56.

Wall, A. (2005). The measurement and management of intellectual capital in public sector. *Public Management Review, 7*(2), 289-303.

Wall, T. D., & Lischeron, J. H. (1977). *Worker participation: A critique of the literature and some fresh evidence*. Maidenhead (England): McGraw-Hill.

Walsh, J. P., & Ungson, G. R. (1991). Organizational memory. *Academy of Management Review, 16*(1), 57-91.

Walsham, G. (2005). Knowledge management systems: Representation and communication in context. *Systems, Signs & Actions, 1*(1), 6-18.

Wasko, M. M., & Faray, S. (2000). It is what one does: Why people participate and help others in electronic communities of practice. *Journal of Strategic Information Systems, 9*(1), 155-173.

Wastell, D. (1999). Learning dysfunction in information systems development: Overcoming the social defenses with transitional objectives. *MIS Quarterly, 23*(4), 581-600.

Watson , S. (1998). Getting to "aha"! *Computerworld, 32*(4), S1-S2.

Watson, G. (1973). Resistance to change. In G. Zaltman (Ed.), *Processes and phenomena of social change* (pp. 117 – 131). New York: John Wiley & Sons.

Watson, R. T. (1990). Influences on the IS manager's perceptions of key issues: Information scanning and the relationship with the CEO. *MIS Quarterly, 14*(2), 217.

Watson, W. E., Michaelsen, L. K., & Sharp, W. (1991). Member competence, group interaction, and group decision making: A longitudinal study. *Journal of Applied Psychology, 76*(6), 803-809.

Watzlawick, P., Weakland, J. H., & Fisch, R. (1974). *Change: Principles of problem formulation and resolution*. New York: Norton.

Wegner, D. M. (1995). A computer network model of human transactive memory. *Social Cognition, 13*(3), 319-339.

Wei Choo, C., & Bontis, N. (Eds.). (2002). *The strategic management of intellectual capital and organizational knowledge*. Oxford: Oxford University Press.

Wei Choo, C.. & Bontis, N. (2002). Knowledge, intellectual capital, and strategy. In C. Wei Choo, & N. Bontis, (Eds.), *The strategic management of intellectual capital and organizational knowledge* (pp. 3-19). Oxford: Oxford University Press.

Weick, K. E. (1991). The nontraditional quality of organizational learning. *Organization Science, 2*(1), 116-123.

Weick, K. E. (1995). *Sensemaking in organizations*. SAGE Publications.

Weick, K. E., & Roberts, K. H. (1993). Collective mind in organizations: Heedful interrelating on flight decks. *Administrative Science Quarterly, 38*, 357-381.

Welch, D., Welch, L., & Marschan-Piekkari, R. (2001). The persistent impact of language on global operations. *Prometheus, 19*(3), 193-209.

Welch, D., Welch, L., & Piekkari, R. (2005). Speaking in tongues: The importance of language in international management processes. *International Studies of Management & Organization, 35*(1), 10-27.

Welsh, J., & White, J. (1981). A small business is not a little big business. *Harvard Business Review*, July-August, 18-32.

Wenger, E. (1999). *Communities of practice. Learning, meaning, and identity.* Cambridge: Cambridge university Press.

Wenger, E., & Snyder, W. (2000). Communities of practice: The organizational frontier. *Harvard Business Review, 78*(1), 139-145.

Wernerfelt B. (1984). A resource-based view of the firm. *Strategic Management Journal, 5*(2), 171–180.

Wernerfelt, B. (1995). The resource-based view of the firm: Ten years after. *Strategic Management Journal, 5*(2), 171-174.

West, M. A., & Farr, J. L. (1989). Innovation at work: Psychological perspectives. *Social Behaviour, 4*, 15-30.

Whelan-Berry, K. S., Gordon, J. R., & Hinings, C. R. (2003). The relative effect of change drivers in large-scale organizational change: An empirical study. In R. W. Woodman, & W. A. Pasmore, W. A. (Eds.), *Research in organizational change and development* (vol. 14, pp. 99-146). Greenwich: JAI Press.

Wherry, R. J., & South, J. C. (1977). A Worker Motivation Scale. *Personnel Psychology, 30*(4), 613-636.

Whipple, L. (2006). *Skandia Insurance Company Ltd.* Retrieved December, 30, 2007, from http://www.answers.com/topic/skandia-insurance-company-ltd?cat=biz-fin

Wiig, K. M. (1997). Knowledge management: An introduction and perspective. *The Journal of Knowledge Management, 1*(1), 6-14.

Wiig, K. M. (1997). Knowledge management: Where did it come from and where will it go? *Expert Systems with Applications, 13*, 1-14.

Wiig, K. M. (1997). Integrating intellectual capital and knowledge management. *Long Range Planning, 30*, 399-405.

Wiig, K. M. (1999). Introducing knowledge management into the enterprise. In J. Liebowitz (Ed.), *Knowledge management handbook* (pp. 3.1- 3.41). Boca Raton: CRC Press.

Wiig, K. M. (2000). Knowledge management: An emerging discipline rooted in long history. In C. Despres & D. Chauvel (Eds), *Knowledge horizons: The present and the promise of knowledge management* (pp.3-27). Woburn, MA: Butterworth-Heinemann.

Wilkinson, H. E., Orth, C. D., & Benfari, R. C. (1986). Motivation theories: An integrated operational model. *SAM Advanced Management Journal, 51*(4), 24.

William, B. (2000). Global work force: The new world labour market. In C. Mary. (Ed.) (1994), *Differences that work: Organizational excellence through diversity.* Cambridge, MA: Harvard Business Review.

Williamson, O. E. (1985). *The economic institutions of capitalism.* Free Press

Wittgenstein, L. (1969). *On certainty.* New York: Harper.

Wittgenstein, L. (1996). *Philosophical investigations.* Oxford: Basil Blackwell.

Wolfe, R. A. (1994). Organizational innovation: review, critique and suggested research. *Journal of Management Studies, 31*(3), 405-431.

Wong, K. Y., & Aspinwall, E. (2004). Characterizing knowledge management in the small business environment. *Journal of Knowledge Management, 8*, 44-61.

Wonnacott, T., & Wonnacott, R. (1972). *Introductory statistics for business and economics* (2nd ed.). NY: John Wiley & Sons, Inc.

Wren, D. (1994). *The evolution of management thought.* New York: John Wiley and Sons.

Wright, C., Kumagai, F., & Bonney, N. (2001). Language and power in a Japanese transplant in Scotland. *Sociological Review, 49*(2), 236-250.

Yeh, R. (1995). Downward influence styles in the cultural diversity settings. *International Journal of Human Resources Management, 6*, 625-641.

Yin, R. K. (1993). *Applications of case study research.* Applied social research methods series, volume 34. London: SAGE Publications.

Yin, R. K. (1994). *Case study research: Design and methods.* Thousand Oaks, CA: Sage Publications.

Yli-Renko, H., Autio, E., & Tontti, V. (2002). Social capital, knowledge, and the international growth of technology-based firms. *International Business Review, 11*, 279-304.

Zack, M. (1999). Developing a knowledge strategy. *California Management Review, 41*(3), 125-145.

Zack, M. H. (1999). Managing codified knowledge. *MIT Sloan Management Review, 40*(4), 45-58.

Zahra, S.A., & George, G. (2002). Absorptive capacity: A review, reconceptualization and extension. *Academy of Management Review, 27*(2), 185-203.

Zaltman, G., Duncan, R., & Holbeck, J. (1973). *Innovations and organizations*. Chichester: John Wiley & Sons.

Zanfei, A. (2000). Transnational firms and the changing organization of innovation activities. *Cambridge Journal of Economics, 24,* 515-542.

Zelewski, S. (2001). Ontologien—ein Überblick über betriebswirtschaftliche Anwendungsbereiche. In Workshop Forschung in schnellebiger Zeit", Beitrag 5, Appenzell.

Zhang, D. (2004). Virtual mentor and the lab system—Toward building an interactive, personalized, and intelligent e-learning environment. *Journal of Computer Information Systems, 44*(3), 35-43.

Zhang, D., & Nunamaker, J. F. (2003). Powering e-learning in the new millennium: An overview of e-learning and enabling technology. *Information Systems Frontiers, 5*(2), 207-218.

Zhang, J., Cresswell, A. M., & Thompson, F. (2005). Participants' expectations and the success of knowledge networking in the public sector. In W. Huang, K. Siau, & K. K. Wei (Eds.), *Digital government: Strategies and implementation from developing and developed countries* (pp. 260-281). Hershey, PA: Idea Group Inc.

Zlotin B. & Zusman A. (1999). Managing Innovation Knowledge. *Triz Journal.*

Zmud, R. W. (1982). Diffusion of modern software practices: Influence of centralization and formalization. *Management Science, 28*(12), 1421-1431.

Zollo, M., & Winter, S. G. (2002). Deliberate learning and the evolution of dynamic capabilities. *Organization Science, 13*(3), 339-351.

Zuboff, S. (1988). *In the age of the smart machine: The future of work and power.* New York: Basic Books.

About the Contributors

Miltiadis D. Lytras is an assistant professor in the Computer Engineering and Informatics Department-CEID (University of Patras). His research focuses on semantic Web, knowledge management and e-learning, with more than 100 publications in these areas. He has coedited / coedits, 25 special issues in international journals (e.g., *IEEE Transaction on Knowledge and Data Engineering, IEEE Internet Computing, IEEE Transactions on Education, Computers in Human Behaviour,* etc.) and has authored/[co]edited 12 books [e.g., *Open Source for Knowledge and Learning management, Ubiquitous and Pervasive Knowledge Management, Intelligent Learning Infrastructures for Knowledge Intensive Organizations, Semantic Based Information systems*]. He is the founder and officer of the Semantic Web and Information Systems Special Interest Group in the Association for Information Systems (http://www.sigsemis.org). He serves as the (co) editor in chief of 12 international journals [e.g., *International Journal of Knowledge and Learning, International Journal of Technology Enhanced Learning, International Journal on Social and Humanistic Computing, International Journal on Semantic Web and Information Systems, International Journal on Digital Culture and Electronic Tourism, International Journal of Electronic Democracy, International Journal of Electronic Banking, International Journal of Electronic Trade*] while he is associate editor or editorial board member in 7 more.

Patricia Ordóñez de Pablos is professor in the Department of Business Administration and Accountability, at the Faculty of Economics of The University of Oviedo (Spain). Her teaching and research interests focus on the areas of strategic management, knowledge management, intellectual capital measuring and reporting, organizational learning, and human resources management. She is *executive editor of the International Journal of Learning and Intellectual, the International Journal of Strategic Change Management* and coexecutive editor of *International Journal of Chinese Culture and Management.*

* * *

Ruth Alas is the vice-rector for Scientific Affairs and head of Management Department in Estonian Business School. She has written 21 management textbooks and more than 100 articles. She is teaching change management. Ruth Alas has given lectures about change management in China and South Africa Republic. Her research is focusing on employee attitudes, learning abilities, organisational culture, leadership, crises management, business ethics, and corporate social responsibility. She has organized several international conferences in Estonia, and is chair of EIASM workshops' series "Organizational development and change." Ruth Alas is on editorial boards of nine journals: *European Journal of International Management, Chinese Management Studies, International Business: Research, Teaching and Practice, Baltic Journal of Management, Problems & Perspectives in Management, Journal of Business Economics and Management, Journal for East European Management Studies, The Open Ethics Journal and EBS Review.*

Poul Houman Andersen is the ASB professor in international business with a particular emphasis on strategic organization and management of global market activities. He is heading the Centre for Global Business Designs at the Aarhus School of Business, University of Aarhus. Recently his research has focused on management and organization of global sourcing processes and globalization of industrial clusters. His has more than 100 scholarly publications. His work is published in *California Management Review, Journal of World Business, Research Policy, Strategic Organization and Industrial Marketing Management* among several other journal and book outlets.

Dimitris Bibikas is a research associate and PhD candidate at SEERC (South East European Research Centre), a Research Centre of The University of Sheffield and CITY College. He holds a BSc in mathematics of Aristotle University of Thessaloniki, a Masters in Information Systems and a Masters in Business Administration, both from the University of Macedonia, Greece. His research interests include the impact of information and communication technologies on knowledge and innovation management, social networks and organisational adaptive strategies. He has extensive experience in coordinating R&D projects awarded by the European Commission, the Greek General Secretariat for Research and Technology, and the Greek Information Society Programme.

Toke Bjerregaard conducts research within areas such as entrepreneurship and innovation, and has investigated knowledge exchange mechanisms between universities and industry. **Per Nikolaj Bukh** is professor at the Department of Business Studies at Aalborg University, Denmark (http://www.pnbukh.com/). He has published about 200 articles, book chapters, reports, and books on a number of subjects including knowledge management, intellectual capital reporting, benchmarking, and management accounting. In addition to his research activities, Per Nikolaj Bukh often contributes to postgraduate programs and conferences.

Huei-Chen Hsu is an associate professor in the Department of Management Information System, Transworld Institute of Technology, Taiwan. She received her PhD from the National Yunlin University of Science and Technology, Taiwan. Her research focuses on managerial and global information systems topics, including the exercise of influence by information technology professionals and the diffusion of IT innovations in developing countries. She has published in the *Journal of Strategic Information Systems and Journal of Advertising Research* as well as presented papers at conferences like the International Conference on Information Systems, the Academy of Management, and the Americas Conferences on Information Systems.

Tongo Constantine Imafidon is a lecturer at the Department of Business Studies at Covenant University in Nigeria. His teaching and research interests include management, industrial relations, and behavioural science. He has published and presented papers on organizational commitment, industrial relations, management, and human resource issues. His work has appeared in many international and local journals. He has a strong flair for tools in operations research

Luiz Antonio Joia is an associate professor and MBA head at the Brazilian School of Public and Business Administration of Getulio Vargas Foundation, and an adjunct professor at Rio de Janeiro State University, Brazil. He has published three books, several chapters, and more than 50 scientific papers in international journals and conferences. He holds a BSc in civil engineering from the Militar Institute of Engineering, Brazil, and an MSc in civil engineering and a DSc in production engineering from the Federal University of Rio de Janeiro, Brazil. He also holds an MSc in management studies from the Oxford University, UK.

Arla Juntunen is a PhD from the Marketing and Management Department of the Helsinki School of Economics (HSE) in Finland, and a Master's degree in Social Sciences/Administrative Information Systems at the University of Helsinki, is a post-doc researcher and senior advisor in Finland's Ministry of the Interior. Her research interests focus on strategic management, business networks, knowledge management, and managerial capabilities.

Jakob Lauring has generally conducted research in the area of cross-cultural interaction, especially with regard to the management of knowledge sharing and communication. Departing from this theoretical field, he has investigated the behaviour of international managers, expatriates, tourists, immigrants, and refugees. These studies of human interaction in cross-cultural settings are mainly based on anthropological approaches combined with organization and management theory. Special areas of interest are organisational ethnography, diversity management, innovation and social responsibility, knowledge management and organisation learning, expatriation, and cross-cultural interaction.

Corrado lo Storto received a Laurea in Aeronautical Engineering cum laude, an MBA and a PhD in Science of Industrial Innovation. Currently, he is an associate professor in Economic and Management Engineering at the Universita' di Napoli Federico II (Italy) where he teaches economics and business organisation. His research and professional interests include technology transfer, innovation management, knowledge management, project risk management, and program and project evaluation. He has published several papers in *International Journal of Technology Management*, *Technovation*, *International Journal of Knowledge Management Studies*, *Enterprise and Innovation Management Studies* and *International Journal of Information Systems and Change Management*. He is the chair of the Italian Technology Management-IEEE chapter and editor in chief of the *International Journal of Engineering Management and Economics*.

Christian Nielsen works as equity strategist at Danske Andelskassers Bank (http://www.dabank.dk/uk/) and is furthermore employed as associate professor at Department of Business Studies at Aalborg University, Denmark. His research interests focus on the interaction between companies and the capital market, and he has published several articles concerning companies reporting and communication related to business models, intellectual capital, and strategy.

Iraklis Paraskakis is a senior research officer, academic director of the Doctoral Programme at SEERC and senior lecturer at Computer Science Department of CITY College. His research interests are in the area of education and information technology, information systems, knowledge management, and semantic Web sServices. He is interested in exploring the impact and overlap of these areas into learning and organisations. He has published in various journals and conferences (ITS, CAL, PEG, EARLI, ESWC, BIS) and is a member of the Artificial Intelligence and Education Society (AIED), European Association for Research on Learning and Instruction (EARLI) and IEEE. He has been the principal investigator in a number, of successfully completed, EU projects, as well as current ones in the areas of e-learning, knowledge management, and semantic Web services.

Alexandros G. Psychogios is a lecturer and academic research coordinator of the Business Administration and Economics Department of CITY College, Affiliated Institution of The University of Sheffield. His research interests include knowledge management, organisational learning, organisational change and its impact on human resources, and total quality management. He has published in a variety of journals, such as the *International Journal of Human Resource Management, The TQM Magazine, The Qualitative Report*, and so forth.

Robin Roslender is a professor in accountancy and director of research in the School of Management and Languages at Heriot-Watt University. A trained sociologist and accountant, he divides his research effort between managerial accounting and critical accounting topics. Currently, Dr. Roslender is looking at the relationship between workforce health and well-being and intellectual capital. In early 2008, he was appointed editor of the *Journal of Human Resource Costing and Accounting.*

Paulo Sanz is a researcher and an adjunct professor at the Brazilian School of Public and Business Administration of Getulio Vargas Foundation, Brazil. He has published several scientific papers in international journals and conferences. He holds a BSc in systems analysis and an MBA from the Brazilian School of Public and Business Administration of Getulio Vargas Foundation.

Giovanni Schiuma is scientific director of the Centre for Value Management at the Università della Basilicata in Italy, and visiting research fellow at the Cranfield School of Management. He is also research director of the Institute of Knowledge Asset Management (IKAM) in Italy. Giovanni's research, teaching, and consulting focus on linking knowledge assets and organization behavior to performance management and organization value creation. Giovanni is also strongly involved in executive education, running seminars for public and private organisations, and regularly offers seminars in Europe and Middle East. He has authored or coauthored more than 100 publications, including books, articles, research reports, and white papers on a range of research topics particularly embracing knowledge asset and intellectual capital management, performance measurement and management, Italian industrial districts, and energetic organisation. He is recognized as a passionate and influential thinker on knowledge assets and intellectual capital management, and he is committed to developing theoretical and practical frameworks, approaches, and tools to drive both public and private organizations towards the improvement of their value creation dynamics by understanding, exploiting, measuring, and managing knowledge and intangible assets. Among others, his current research interest is focused on organisational behaviour, and particularly on how complex organisations can be transformed into intelligent organisations by leading and managing energy and emotions. He is a regular speaker at conferences, and has teaching and consultancy experience across Europe on knowledge and innovation management as well as on performance measurement and management. He is specialized particularly in the design, implementation, and review of knowledge asset management initiatives and performance measurement systems designed to drive innovative change and learning dynamics in organizations and to support company's performance improvement and value creation.

Ana C. Vasconcelos is a lecturer at the Information Studies Department of the University of Sheffield. Her research interests include the interface between information systems development and the management of knowledge and information, with a focus on discourse and identity, the role of discursive practices in IS adaptation, organisational and political arenas, communities of practice and virtual communities, professional discourses, and identity in information work.

Ernesto Villalba graduated in psychology at the Autonomous University of Madrid. He obtained his PhD in international and comparative education at the Institute of international Education at Stockholm University with a thesis on the relationship of knowledge management and training in Swedish companies. He is currently working at the Centre for Research on Lifelong Learning at the Joint Research Centre of the European Commission. His major areas of interest are knowledge management, lifelong learning, and education for innovation.

Index

K

L

M

N

O

P

R

S

T

W